Contemporary Creative Nonfiction

The Art of Truth

BILL ROORBACH
The Ohio State University

New York ∼ Oxford
OXFORD UNIVERSITY PRESS
2001

Oxford University Press

Oxford   New York
Athens   Auckland   Bangkok   Bogotá   Buenos Aires   Calcutta
Cape Town   Chennai   Dar es Salaam   Delhi   Florence   Hong Kong   Istanbul
Karachi   Kuala Lumpur   Madrid   Melbourne   Mexico City   Mumbai
Nairobi   Paris   São Paulo   Shanghai   Singapore   Taipei   Tokyo   Toronto   Warsaw

and associated companies in
Berlin   Ibadan

Copyright © 2001 by Bill Roorbach

Published by Oxford University Press, Inc.
198 Madison Avenue, New York, New York 10016
http://www.oup-usa.org

Oxford is a registered trademark of Oxford University Press

Library of Congress Cataloging-in-Publication Data

Contemporary creative nonfiction: the art of truth / edited by Bill Roorbach.
   p. cm.
   ISBN 978-0-19-513556-5
      1. College readers. 2. Creative writing—Problems, exercises, etc. 3. English
language—Rhetoric—Problems, exercises, etc. 4. Reportage literature—Authorship—Problems,
exercises, etc. 5. Journalism—Authorship—Problems, exercises, etc.   I. Roorbach, Bill.

   PE1417 .A765 2000
   808'.0427—dc21   00-037347

For Phillip Lopate, teacher and friend

Acknowledgments

This project owes much to many: my warm thanks go to all who have helped. Special thanks go to my spring 1999 graduate forms class at Ohio State, in which Jacki Bell, Lisa Farina, Theresa Kulbaga, Beth Lindsmith, Aimee Nezhukumatathil, David O'Connell, Deborah Sobeloff, Maureen Stanton, Laura Swenson, and Matt Zambito engaged the issues defined in this volume, suggested selections, and helped me form all my best ideas. Additional thanks to Aimee Nezhukumathathil, who was my graduate assistant, and to the English Department at The Ohio State University for making her help possible. Special thanks to Adrien Ardoin, who was my "Comix" consultant. And thanks to all my colleagues at Ohio State.

Thanks to friends who write nonfiction and know how to talk about it: David Bradley, Brenda Brueggemann, Stephen Dubner, Robert Kimber, Georgina Kleege, Liesel Litzenburger, Wesley McNair, Rick Moody, Jay Parini, Vince Passaro, Lore Segal.

Many thanks to the teachers who got me started thinking about creative nonfiction, not so many years ago: Joyce Johnson, Frank MacShane, Phillip Lopate.

Thanks to the Ohio Arts Council for 1999 grants in criticism and creative nonfiction, which bought me time.

Thanks to the College of Humanities at Ohio State for research support.

Many thanks to D. Anthony English, Christine D'Antonio, and Charmaine Lim, of the Oxford University Press, and to their colleagues there, and to Michael Pearson and all the other outside reviewers whose criticism helped shape this volume.

Finally, and as always, thanks to Juliet Karelsen.

Contents

Credits   x

Introduction   1

SECTION 1   Literary Diaries and Journals   9

John Cheever
FROM The Journals   11

May Sarton
FROM Journal of a Solitude   23

Gerald Early
"Digressions"   31

M. F. K. Fisher
"Paris Journal"   39

George Dennison
FROM Temple   42

Gretel Ehrlich
"From the Journals"   50

Edward Robb Ellis
FROM Diary of a Century   66

SECTION 2   Literary Memoir   79

James Thurber
"Snapshot of a Dog"   81

Mary McCarthy
FROM Memories of a Catholic Girlhood
"Yonder Peasant, Who Is He?"   83

Annie Dillard
FROM An American Childhood   95

Maxine Hong Kingston
FROM The Woman Warrior
"No Name Woman"   106

Hilton Als
"Notes on My Mother"   113

Andre Dubus III
"Tracks and Ties"   118

Kathryn Harrison
FROM The Kiss   122

Dorothy Allison
FROM Two or Three Things I Know for Sure   130

Andre Dubus
FROM Broken Vessels
"Lights of the Long Night"   135
"Husbands"   137

Fenton Johnson
FROM Geography of the Heart   141

Mary Karr
FROM The Liar's Club   143

Judy Ruiz
"Oranges and Sweet Sister Boy"   156

Spalding Gray
"Sex and Death to the Age 14"   161

Tobias Wolff
FROM In Pharaoh's Army
"A Federal Offense"   176

Harvey Pekar and R. Crumb
"The Harvey Pekar Name Story"   186

SECTION 3   The Personal Essay   191

E. B. White
"Once More to the Lake"   193

James Baldwin
FROM Notes of a Native Son
"Equal in Paris"   197

Ralph Ellison
"On Being the Target of Discrimination"   206

Shirley Abbott
FROM Womenfolks
"That Old-Time Religion"   211

Hayden Carruth
"Country Matters"   217

Phillip Lopate
"The Dead Father: A Rememberance of Donald Barthelme"   220

Vivian Gornick
"At the University: Little Murders of the Soul"   235

Jamaica Kincaid
"A Small Place"   250

Nancy Mairs
FROM Waist-High in the World
"Body in Trouble"   254

Henry Louis Gates, Jr.
FROM Colored People
"Current Events"   264

Thomas Lynch
"The Undertaking"   270

Jane Shapiro
"This Is What You Need for a Happy Life"   275

Joy Williams
"Save the Whales, Screw the Shrimp"   286

Ntozake Shange
"What Is It We Really Harvestin' Here?"   295

Stanton Michaels
"How to Write a Personal Essay"   299

SECTION 4   Literary Journalism   303

John Hersey
FROM Hiroshima
"The Fire"   305

Truman Capote
FROM In Cold Blood   317

Michael Herr
FROM Dispatches
"Illumination Rounds"   326

Norman Mailer
FROM The Executioner's Song
"The Turkey Shoot"   336

Mikal Gilmore
FROM Shot in the Heart
"Last Words"   351

Joyce Johnson
FROM What Lisa Knew
"November 1987"   364

Barbara Ehrenreich
"Nickel-and-Dimed: On (Not) Getting By in America"   370

Ann Hodgman
"No Wonder They Call Me a Bitch"   389

Joan Didion
FROM Salvador   392

Tom Wolfe
FROM The Right Stuff
"Yeager"   398

Jon Krakauer
FROM Into Thin Air
"Summit, 1:25 P.M., May 10, 1996, 29,028 Feet"   406

Sebastian Junger
FROM The Perfect Storm
"The Zero-Moment Point"   414

SECTION 5   The Art of the Particular: Creative
Nonfiction Classified by Subject   421

NATURE WRITING

Edward Abbey
Memoir: FROM Desert Solitaire
"Havasu"   424

Sue Hubbell
Personal Essay: FROM A Country Year
"Spring"   429

John McPhee
Literary Journalism: FROM Annals of the Former World   442

LITERARY TRAVEL

Gretel Ehrlich
Memoir: FROM Questions of Heaven
"Lijiang"   450

Naomi Shihab Nye
Personal Essay: "One Village"   465

Eddy L. Harris
Literary Journalism: FROM Mississippi Solo   476

THE SCIENCE ESSAY

Elizabeth Marshall Thomas
Memoir: FROM The Hidden Life of Dogs   491

Lewis Thomas
Personal Essay: "The Medusa and the Snail"   500

Atul Gawande
Literary Journalism: "When Doctors Make Mistakes"   502

CREATIVE CULTURAL CRITICISM

Meghan Daum
Memoir: "Music Is My Bag: Confessions of a Lapsed Oboist"   517

Janet Malcolm
Personal Essay: FROM The Silent Woman   525

David Foster Wallace
Literary Journalism: "Shipping Out: On the (Nearly Lethal)
Comforts of a Luxury Cruise"   534

CREDITS

Introduction

A very sweet and gentle friend of mine some years back was a food stylist. Not a chef, not a cook, not a sandwich maker. What she did was prepare food to be photographed—whole menus for food magazines, sample dishes for cookbooks, convincing chefs' creations for Hollywood. She was brilliant at her work and made a good living because she was indispensable. And the reason the likes of *Gourmet* magazine couldn't live without her was that even the most beautiful, most appetizing dishes photographed as they were, fresh out of the oven, no matter how renowned the chef, looked . . . plain. And sometimes ugly. Or even *sickening.* Roasted chickens—plump and gorgeous on sterling platters—looked gray and scrawny, the silver mere metal. Mashed potatoes—steaming, fresh, delicious—looked dull and sludgy. Salads, forget it. Salads looked like so many leaves raked into a pile. Ice cream just melted into pools under the photographer's lights.

The food stylist knows what the chef does not—that food for photos, aimed at the palate of the imagination, is not the same as food to be eaten.

So my friend in her special kitchen would baste turkeys in motor oil to get the exact golden brown that on film signaled perfection. She'd spray green beans with Lemon Pledge and buff each bean with a chamois—hours of work till the bean bowl was full. She made ice cream out of lard, with melt-proof chocolate chips made from broken Guinness Stout bottles. She mixed concoctions of rice and shaving cream in her blender to make convincing mashed potatoes, whipping up disgusting, odiferous white mounds that on film (with a dollop of molasses and a pat of yellow shoe polish) looked *delicious,* just perfect.

They weren't perfect, of course. They were actually poison, in many cases. But what my ingenious friend was up to was this: bringing the truth of those meals to a flat page, trying with every tool at her disposal to fool the eyes and thence the taste buds of tens of thousands of magazine readers and moviegoers into perceiving the delicious truth of an actual meal, when to simply photograph the actual meal would result in a kind of lie, rendering a magnificent creation as a limpish and ugly arrangement of soulless foods.

You've guessed where I'm going by now: food styling is "creative nonfiction."

1

Straight photography? Maybe that would be traditional journalism (even noting how often news photos are posed or staged). A painting in oils? Maybe a painting is more like fiction in this model. Of course it would be easy to push my little metaphor too far, though I'd like to say that poems are sculptures. And it *is* a little metaphor, terribly reductive: creative nonfiction is no mere advertising game, but the stuff of the greatest literary art.

When I've talked about food styling in my classes, some sensibly skeptical listener always says, "But wait! Wouldn't the writer of creative nonfiction do something interesting with the *actual* potatoes?"

Well, maybe eat them. But the *actual* potatoes can never, never, never get onto the page, except as a spill. What the writer of creative nonfiction gets onto the page is words, words alone, and not potatoes, no matter how hard he may try.

What the writer of nonfiction has is paper and a system of funny inked markings that somehow she is supposed to turn into a representation of reality that people will call true, a representation to which the taste buds of the soul will respond passionately. But the marks on the page are never the reality they evoke or attempt to evoke, and never can be. A page of words is not your father, no matter how carefully those words are arranged to approximate him. A column of words and numbers is not last night's baseball game. Only the game itself is the game, and the game is history, gone forever, irretrievably gone. A carefully built sentence, added to another sentence and another to make a carefully built paragraph, then added to more paragraphs to make an idea clear, or to set forth an argument, is a beautiful thing—but it is not the idea itself, nor the argument.

Words and numbers on paper, whether put there by a memoirist, journalist, or essayist (or historian, scientist, or philosopher, to move into wider realms) are always attempts to recover some form of experience, and are always a form of memory, as is knowledge itself. And memory is always faulty, no matter how well-meaning, honest, careful, factual-minded, and exact its owner. Even the best science books are repositories of fiction after a few decades pass. (The best books of old essays, by contrast, are still true, even hundreds of years past the writing—but that's another matter.)

All writers of nonfiction use every tool at their disposal—voice, language, drama, passion, characters, literary talent—and every scrap of learning, to make their marks on paper create something in their readers' minds that approximates experience, whether that experience be the writer's father, a baseball game, an idea, or a roasted free-range chicken stuffed with oranges for fragrance (and to keep the breast meat moist).

Some writers of nonfiction use their tools so magically well that their work can be generally regarded as art. And these are the writers of what we've come to call "creative nonfiction," a selection of whom and of which I will feature in this book.

❖　❖　❖

What a troublesome term *creative nonfiction* is, and yet we seem to be stuck with it. I mean, what could "creative nonfiction" possibly mean, when all writing is creative, and most writing is nonfiction? Some very smart people have proposed all kinds of other terms to name this old form (the idea that "creative nonfiction" is just emerging as a genre is ridiculous—"creative nonfiction" is only just emerging as a *label* for a kind of work—we'll define it shortly—that's been with us for ages at least, and that flourished throughout the twentieth century, and embarks on the twenty-first as a leading literary mode): "literary nonfiction," "the literature of reality," "the literature of fact," "the Fourth Genre" (with poetry, fiction, and drama being the first three), "memoir," "literary memoir," "the personal essay," "New

Journalism," "artful nonfiction," "narrative nonfiction," "art journalism"—the labeling suggestions go on and on. But none is any more accurate or inclusive than "creative nonfiction," and some are much less accurate, and too exclusive.

With this volume I vote for keeping the term "creative nonfiction" (it names most of the classes I teach, after all), and taking the quotation marks out from around it, and for letting it—creative nonfiction as generic label—be the widest sort of umbrella, with room underneath it for nonfiction writing across a spectrum of written work that has in common *humanity,* and just one thing more: all creative nonfiction, like all literature, aspires to art.

I vote thus because, before this, back in the contentious and monstrous twentieth century, no one could really agree on what kind of writing creative nonfiction should encompass. The solution, I think, now that we've held on to the term, is to accept what poets accept, and what fiction writers accept, too, and dramatists and the critics of all three: that under the large umbrella of the largest generic titles—fiction, poetry, drama (and now creative nonfiction)—many, many types and styles and attitudes and altitudes of writing flourish, some deeply opposed to one another in philosophy and approach, some repeatedly rejected, cast aside, made fun of by opposing camps. But opposing camps are just camps no matter what weapons they pull out and no matter what casualties they cause or take; when it comes to literary genres, most wars turn out to be civil wars.

Writers with a journalistic leaning will never be comfortable with memoirists (even when they themselves are the memoirist in question). Memoirists will never be comfortable with science writers (even when . . .). Essayists will always disdain mere reporters of experience. But they are all laboring in the same salt mine, their divisions no deeper than those between formal poets and writers of free verse, which are deep enough.

Another awful term, while we're at it, is *creative writing.* And its awfulness will continue to be debated, even while the term is freely used, until the end of English. Another is *literature,* and with it, *art.* Who decides what sorts of work fall under either category? It's convenient to say that time decides—and time, in a way, does, but the truth is that writers and readers and critics decide continually and contentiously what writing is good and what writing is bad (that is, what writing is art and what writing is not) and in this continuing debate lies the very life of the creature they cannot agree upon. Only dead things bear strict definition. And literature, to be literature, must be alive.

Life, of course, may be discussed in the abstract and in general, but what life always comes down to is an individual, a single being holding itself together and performing its self-preservative actions despite all odds and among other individual beings, no other exactly like the first. Similarly, what good, alive writing always comes down to is an individual—one person, writing in a way not quite like anyone else's, yet enough like everyone else's (grammar, structure, language, syntax, content, form) that other humans can make sense of it. And past mere sense comes emotion, from the rawest—anger, fear, joy—to the most refined: intellectual pleasure.

⚘ ⚘ ⚘

For the sake of continued definition, let us say that creative nonfiction is nonfiction that deserves (or in workshops among apprentice and journeyperson practitioners, that *aspires* to deserve) to be placed up there on the literature shelves along with the best fiction and poetry.

Just as there are arguments among poets about what kind of poetry belongs on the great shelf in the library of humankind marked *poetry,* there are continuing arguments among writers about what sort of nonfiction belongs on the great shelf in the library of humankind now marked *creative nonfiction*. Many teachers and students and anthologists of creative nonfiction (if not too many critics), would have the creative nonfiction shelf include *only* literary memoir (and other strictly autobiographical and true storytelling based primarily on memory). Others narrow the definition so that it might encompass *only* literary journalism (storytelling and character development and other artful techniques in the service of news, verifiable facts, and information). Still others see creative nonfiction as *only* the personal essay, or various refinements thereof (such as nature writing, lyrical essay, belles lettres, and so forth—ideas and analysis as expression). Others—probably a majority of writers in creative nonfiction—don't much worry about the label at all, but get to work making art.

The truth is that all three of the subgenres I've identified here—literary memoir, the personal essay, and literary journalism—belong on the creative nonfiction shelf. All three have talented artists under their sway. None need be slighted by practitioners of the others, since there is room on the big shelf for all.

◦ ◦ ◦

If literary memoir, literary journalism, and the personal essay are all creative nonfiction, then they must have some values in common. Of course they do, with the single most important being humanity, which is summed up in all the items following:

• *Language.* Nothing is more important in literature and therefore in creative nonfiction than language—it is language that makes all the other values possible. After humanity, particular talent with language is the one absolutely sure thing every writer represented in this book shares. And after language talent comes language skill—a matter of craft, of years of study and practice (and much reading). With skill comes precision and clarity. With talent and skill come freedom—and with this particular kind of freedom the individual writer (often laboring under conditions of no freedom) emerges on the page.

The traditional journalist, famously, must write for a public with a twelve-year-old's reading ability. His words must operate inside a formula. And inside the particular restrictions of his field, the journalist may be a genius, and his work of the highest quality. But he, and with him his language, is not aspiring to art, but to other purposes. The academic writer must operate inside a formula specific to her field, and most often must use the jargon specific to that field, jargon that will exclude most readers, even many who are extremely intelligent and well-read. And inside the particular restrictions of her field, the academic writer may be a genius, too, and a genuinely great writer—but without being or caring to be an artist.

But that's not to say some journalists and some academicians and some writers of all the other sorts of nonfiction (perhaps even some writers of lawn-mower operating manuals) don't make art at times or in specific instances.

• *The Person.* All creative nonfiction, to be called creative nonfiction, must have a discernable and subjective self at its center: the writer. The writer may reveal himself in different ways, depending on his approach, but he's always a presence, most often a direct presence, using the first person freely. But sometimes the human presence is more hidden, the writer never saying "I" but appearing nonetheless as a fully identifiable individual because of his language or technique, and because of a clearly apparent, living passion for the subject at hand.

The writer of creative nonfiction is simply herself, or a version of herself, never hiding behind a fiction writer's narrator, or a poet's speaker, or a traditional journalist's professional invisibility and sincerely attempted objectivity, or the traditional academic's formulized language and approach and proud and appropriate eschewal of the first person. And as we read we recognize individual writers the way we recognize friends in the distance (unmistakable gestures, tics, size and shape, manner of dress) or over the phone (accent, intonation, choice of words).

This self emerging from lines and pages of mere words is often called voice, and it is a presence as real as the art of the given writer can make it. Obviously enough, giving the name "voice" to what we hear in our heads as we read is a metaphorical gesture. We aren't actually hearing—but our minds create a kind of hearing that is absolutely one of the pleasures of reading.

Voice is that sense we have that we are listening to a writer talk as we silently read. This writerly voice emerges as the result of an individual writer's idiosyncratic way of mixing and matching words, of inserting punctuation, of vocabulary. Things we might call accent or inflection or tone or attitude in actual conversation appear in writing, too. A writer may seem confident to her reader, or unsure, or anything on a continuum between the two. A writer may seem (and actually, through many drafts, may *contrive* to seem) angry or resigned or sanguine or miserable or cheerful or restless or morose or insouciant or grumpy or amused—on and on, through the very range of human emotion. A writer may seem charming or off-putting or chilly or aggressive—again on and on, through the range of human interactions with one another. A writer's words may seem terse or musical or monotonic or explosive. A writer may seem old or young, fat or thin, British or American, male or female, and so forth—all on the basis of language cues. Quickly, in a piece of nonfiction that fits on the shelf of creative nonfiction, the reader knows who's talking.

• *Accuracy.* What makes nonfiction nonfiction is its attention to facts, of course. The "creative" in creative nonfiction does not refer to invention, not at all, but to the manner of delivery. But I think too many critics make a fetish of accuracy, putting too much emphasis on mere factuality as the basis for judgment of a given piece of nonfiction.

Listen: verifiable accuracy is not one of the *primary* values of creative nonfiction, as it must be for traditional journalism or science. Verifiable accuracy is an *important* value in creative nonfiction, but sometimes, especially in memoir and memory sections of personal essays, it must hold the door for the greater values of drama and character, and the peculiar artistic force of memory, and let them enter the ballroom first. And here we do run into ethics, which are as individual as voice. I believe an overinsistence (as opposed to a reasonable insistence) on verifiable accuracy has about the same deadening effect on art as an overinsistence on conformity in style or subject. What's verifiable isn't always what's true, and the writer of creative nonfiction will always err on the side of truth over facts. When verifiable accuracy takes over as the primary value in a piece of writing, we are moving away from creative nonfiction and back toward traditional journalism.

But the mores of writers of nonfiction are crucial to the trust of readers. A reader has a right to expect that what is represented as true and accurate is true and accurate. But then again, if an unethical writer fools an unwary reader, reading satisfaction may still result. Being fooled to whatever small degree is perhaps one of the pleasures of reading creative nonfiction. Remember that we are basting turkeys with motor oil here.

Trouble is, some of those turkeys may be characters who have a right to expect (and it is a legal right, in most cases) that their representation be true and accurate. Of course, not everyone likes the look of his photo, or his voice on tape, or even his image in a mirror, despite the obvious truth and accuracy in those cases (mirror images, being reversed, might be said to be *etarucca:* accurate, but backward).

And wait a minute—what are we really talking about when we use the word *accuracy* in discussing representations of the self? I present various selves to the world as I go about my day, and present various selves to myself, come to think of it. A writer adopts a persona that perforce is a simplification of the multiplicity of threads and contradictory impulses that make every human being *human*. Then what could a journalist possibly mean, when talking about accuracy in depictions of others? Allegiance to the public persona of a particular individual? Or is the reporter's so-called accuracy just a record of one fallible human's perceptions of another fallible human's mask on a particular day, that mask influenced by the presence of the reporter?

Memoirists, working with faulty memory, struggle perhaps more with the issue of accuracy than journalists or essayists. On a given page, it may be more dramatic—more like life, and thus more true—to provide some dialogue that is not so much remembered from thirty years past as re-created in good faith. And this re-creation is not the same as the work fiction writers do, which is often pure creation. And memoir is never fiction, even when the writer has to admit to conjecture and faulty memory: the intentions are too different, the products very different indeed, on what amounts to a cellular level. Between fiction and memoir, no genes are shared. Smart readers know that the risks are different for people making fiction from for those making nonfiction, even if in certain examples of creative nonfiction the techniques look similar to those of fiction, and even if in certain fictions shades of real life glimmer. The reason readers know this about writerly risks in nonfiction and fiction is that *reading* fiction is different from *reading* nonfiction. The spell of the real is *different* from the spell of fiction. Extraordinary coincidence, for example (man falls out of a commercial airliner at thirty thousand feet, lands on his own house), is a source of great fun and mystery and depth in nonfiction, but in fiction can go unbelieved and ruin the art utterly.

Smart readers don't expect memoirists to be journalists, won't ask for a tape of the conversation between the writer and her old great-grandma, dead these thirty years. Readers do expect the writer to be true to something—true to memory, true to remembered speaking styles (if not exact words), true to what I'll call *the encyclopedia of the self,* true, most of all, to great-grandma, and thus true to writer and reader alike.

Good faith is the key. And part of that faith is trust in a readerly understanding of the differing rules and traditions and emphases of the subgenres under the wide and inclusive and elegant rubric of creative nonfiction.

• *Urgency.*   In every selection in this anthology, and quickly, the writer establishes that the subject at hand is not only important, but crucial. The reader finds herself caring, and caring deeply, about the writer's story, or idea, or information. In good creative nonfiction, we know from the outset not only who is talking, but why he is talking, and we know it even when we are coming into an essay or article or even a book halfway.

• *Surprise.*   Good creative nonfiction confounds our expectations. A sentence in its excellence may move us unawares to emotional or intellectual territory we've never seen before. A character may say something that shocks us, something for certain that we'd never say, not in a million years, and that thus moves us, one way or the other, toward enlightenment or disgust. Or a writer might have an idea so simple that we must stop reading to consider the idea, and think about why we never thought it ourselves till just now, as the words go by. As in a good relationship, there are always new depths of character and thought and personality to be explored in the words of a fine writer.

• *Complexity*.   Nothing is easy in creative nonfiction—no smug acceptance of received wisdom, no satisfaction with surfaces, no argument without the careful inspection of counterargument, no naive acceptance of what a source has to say, or the results of an experiment.

And good creative nonfiction is layered deeply. A chronological narrative is never simply a string of events, but rings with metaphor and emotion and information and character. A personal essay is never only an idea, but an idea illustrated with experience, an idea juxtaposed to competing ideas, and exposed to emotion. And one of the complexities of good creative nonfiction is implicit acceptance of the simple awful truth that people aren't gods and can be sure of very little.

• *Ambition*.   The good stuff always wants to be better, and its writers are always reaching way above their heads, to create something even they weren't sure was possible at the outset, something that hasn't yet existed in the world. Formula work seeks only to fulfill the formula. Mediocre work seeks only adequacy. Commercial work seeks cash first. Art—real art—seeks the unknown.

• *Intelligence*.   Good creative nonfiction is smart. Sometimes, it's hard to believe how smart.

The selections herein reflect all of the values above, and, of course, at least one further value: my reading taste. I love every selection in this book, and have read every selection so many times that each is part of me now, in its own way. Early on, my editor and I made the decision to include only American work, both to add focus and to keep the book's weight under ten pounds. Many of the selections here are excerpts or chapters from book-length works, and I hope those selections will lead you to the works whole, and that all of the selections will lead you to the bodies of work of authors you already know, and of those you may not have encountered before. In building this volume I struggled, as you can imagine, with priorities of space and representation and diversity, and of course with the arbitrary limitation to American writers, and had to exclude literally hundreds of works of art (many by friends, mainly *because* they are friends) that are in no way inferior to those that eventually found inclusion here.

Section 1, "Literary Diaries and Journals," makes a good starting place for the study of our genre, for both writers and readers: here are the seeds of creative nonfiction, the most unalloyed expression of self and mind, in the most casual forms. The next three sections, "Literary Memoir," "The Personal Essay," and "Literary Journalism," give examples of work from the three main formal subcategories. Section 5, "The Art of the Particular: Creative Nonfiction Classified by Subject," switches the method of categorization from form to content, and examines four important content subgenres: nature writing, literary travel, the science essay, and creative cultural criticism. Each section includes an introduction in which you'll find further definition and at least a little history and other context for each division. Here's hoping there is plenty in these introductions to argue about, plenty to discuss, lots to question, both in class and by way of your own writing of creative nonfiction.

But let the writers I've assembled here provide the essential overview. Essay by essay and article by article and memoir by memoir, I know they will continue the work I've only started of defining a protean genre, and will stretch that definition as far as it can possibly go between the covers of a thick anthology so that you may stretch it further as you read and write past this book, and into the future.

1
Literary Diaries and Journals

Not all writers keep journals, of course, and not all of those who keep journals think of themselves as writers. But seldom is there a more living record of the person behind the words. Journals provide a sort of pure narrative in time (or at least seemingly pure—revision can never be discounted and probably shouldn't be disdained, especially for journals whose writers fully expected publication, either while alive or after death). The writer never has the benefit of hindsight as his chronology unfolds (here again, though, we must consider the problem of possible revision, which tends the journals we read ineluctably toward other forms: memoir, essays). Indeed, the writing unfolds as a life unfolded, with the earlier pages knowing nothing of the later.

I'm using the words *journal* and *diary* more or less interchangeably, and both come from root words having to do with the word *day,* though I do think of diaries as more private, and journals as less personal. But every interesting example of the form creates its own definitions, as with all good writing. I use the term *literary* to make it clear that it's not all journals and diaries we are interested in for this discussion.

The compulsive record-keeping of a literary diarist or journal keeper creates a character for readers to enjoy, of course, but in some very real ways the record-keeping creates the writer, too. His diary entries serve not only as memory aids, but actually give structure and meaning to his life, add up to a narrative of self that he can hone and perfect outside of experience.

The accuracy of a diary, rightly or wrongly, is taken for granted by readers. The implicit question is, Who could lie to his diary? The implicit answer is, Anyone could lie to his diary! And probably many do, most in the way we all lie to ourselves, especially when it comes to ourselves, but some, perhaps, in the way we lie to others, trying to make a more impressive self from the materials at hand, or just as often, to deprecate ourselves. Yet historians and biographers use diaries extensively as proof of the ways of disappeared worlds and people—there must be some truth in there, yes?

Accuracy aside, in a diary, consciousness lives on past its owner. As Ohio State graduate student Theresa Kulbaga once observed in a fine paper: "Reading someone's diary or journal is a bit like stepping into her consciousness: the categories of reader and writer collapse into each other as the reader thinks the writer's thoughts, experiences her life, and comes to know her innermost joys and fears."

The issue of art may seem superfluous in any discussion of diaries and journals—those private and necessarily artless repositories—and yet it's in these notebooks and on these scraps of paper (or in John Cheever's case, in these neatly typed and bound volumes . . .) that the artist very often begins her process of finding out what she thinks, of uncovering what's important, and of clarifying and ultimately discovering her vision.

I'm about to speak of memoirists and essayists and literary journalists as if they are distinct groups—but of course, quite a few writers are all three, and most writers are at least two, usually all at once, and shifting project by project. And some of the greatest journals we have were written by fiction writers and poets, men and women whose only nonfiction was private. But with your forbearance, and for the sake of discussion, I'll continue in my folly.

The memoirist (and of course the fiction writer and poet) may use her diaries as a bank of research materials, not only for accuracy (scraps of faithfully recorded dialogue, logs of dates and times, records of names and numbers and sizes and shapes), but to remember the exact feelings associated with events, the subtle tics of the people involved, the language of the moment, the mood in the air.

The essayist, of course, will use his diaries and journals in the same way, but may go further, trying out ideas, arguing with himself, recording quotations from his reading, passages from his music listening, facts and figures from his research, and whatever else comes either internally or externally to mind.

The journalist will use her diaries and journals in the same ways as the memoirist and essayist, but further takes the opportunity to show herself how she fits into the stories she reports, how her day intersected with the news, how impressed she was with herself for talking with President Reagan or Cher, how terrified (or not) she was running with guerrillas, how conflicted she felt covering a political dustup, the stuff that can't get into the traditional newspaper story, but that might eventually, in some unpredictable form, get into a work of literary journalism. The journalist's notebook—full of facts and figures and accurate quotations—is quite a different tool from her personal diary.

Travelers who write keep journals too, and some travel writing may take the form of dressed-up journals. Something as simple as a bird-watcher's journal may find itself material for nature essays. Any kind of daily (or nearly daily) record of events or experiments or observations or feelings can be eventually the basis for more polished work.

The diaries and journals selected here may have been written for private reasons and for an audience of one, but nearly all the writers probably knew their words would be published one day—perhaps some kind of greater audience was in their heads even as they wrote. The essayist M. F. K. Fisher provided her "Paris Journal" to the editors of the literary magazine *Witness*, for example. And John Cheever, in his voluminous journals, mentions his dream that they be published after his death. The poet and fiction writer and essayist May Sarton published her *Journal of a Solitude* (and other books of journal entries) while she was alive, and revised them continually and extensively in order to present a stable face to the world. In the pages reproduced here, journalist and essayist Gerald Early ponders not so much his soul as his attitudes, bringing his ideas to light before they fully find their development into essays: what's reproduced here is the private side of public issues. Journalist Edward Robb Ellis kept his journal so long—more than sixty years—that it filled scores of volumes and found a place in the *Guinness Book of Records*. He lived long enough to see the publication of representative excerpts from his enormous diary in 1995, and took delight in seeing it public. Nature writer Gretel Ehrlich's pages here are deeply personal, but were offered by her for publication in the elegant literary magazine (now sadly defunct) *Antaeus*. The selection she chose is an eclectic gathering of quotes and impressions and thoughts and feelings that reflects her essayist's well-stocked mind.

Perhaps only George Dennison, who died in his fifties of cancer, would be surprised to find his private notes and thumbnail character studies and many quotidian fears and worries published for us to read in a book called *Temple*, named after his tiny town in Maine. His family and subsequent editors thought, though, that what he'd written held many lessons and pleasures and *frissons* of recognition for the living. For you and me, that is.

John Cheever

from The Journals

1971

THE FIRST DAY OF THE NEW YEAR. NO TOOTHACHE, AND I WAKE FEELING VERY HAPPILY horny. I trust the year will end this way.

We walk to the F. s', where we are shown home movies of the Cairo bazaar and where much that is said seems to have been said before. My little camera is my memory, etc. Later, just before dark, I go to see S., a pleasant woman, with an open fire, who gives me whiskey. A drunken scene, for which I am heartily sorry.

I claim again that the Sunday *Times* derails me. Shovel snow, walk the dogs over the hill. Mary's sister calls and when I say she's in Chappaqua she says, "Oh, I'm terribly sorry. Did they let her come home for Christmas?" "Chappaqua," I say, "is the next village." "Oh," says she, "I thought it was a rest home."

◦-◦   ◦-◦   ◦-◦

Drinking with R. and S. and M., I seem to glimpse—no more—the fact that I can be difficult, ungainly, prone to flare up at trifling misunderstandings. I think of my brother, examine what I remember of his conduct and misconduct, since the end of his marriage resembled in some ways mine. He drank too much, and so do I, although I will not end up in a hospital. He seemed morbidly sensitive to any sort of discrimination. I remember his stamping off the playing field. When I asked him what was wrong he said that P. was cheating. We were playing touch football, bluff was half the game. Sorehead. I trust I don't do this. He would punish his wife by refusing to speak to her for a week or two. He merely punished himself, of course. We have the same blood, the same memories, and make, I suppose, the same mistakes. Who, after all, is that man who puts a dime in the lock of the public toilet and in this privacy drinks from a flask of vodka? It is I. When? Last month, last year, six years ago. I seem to have changed more than the airport. The imitation orange drink still geysers in a sort of glass showcase. The coffee is weak. The cock drawn on the toilet door seems a size smaller than it did last time. My hair is gray.

Are these the accents of contempt or is this my morbid sensibility? For example, I mix drinks and ask her to join me. "I have to wash the spinach," she says. The voice strikes me as unnatural, unwarm. I do not, of course, check on the truth of this. Once I said, "Let's fuck," and she said, "I have to find the baking potatoes." "I'll find the potatoes," I said, and I did, but when I returned to the bedroom she had dressed. Saturday night, I suggested again that she join me. I want someone to talk with, but I also feel that the sound of conversation might relax my son. Hours pass when the only voices one hears are electronic. To this invitation she says, "I have to go to the bathroom." "Well, won't you join me after you've been to the bathroom?" I say. She does, but she holds a book in front of her face. I talk about Lorca, whose poetry she is reading. "I will not be lectured about a book you have not read," says she, leaving the room. I did not intend to lecture her, but perhaps I mistook my tone of voice. Later—and I may now be as my brother was, moved in the stumbling and ungainly way of gin, half deaf, half blind, responding to some blow that was dealt so far in the past it can't be remembered—"I won't listen to your shit." The raised voice will be heard by my son, and my good intentions have come to nothing. I climb another flight of stairs and watch something asinine on TV.

She is, to say the least, laconic this afternoon. At dusk, she takes the dog for a walk, the first in months. She returns at dark. She is excited. "I saw Josephine, I saw Josephine for the first time since Christmas, and I didn't have an apple or some sugar for her." Josephine is a lonely and unridden horse, owned by the superintendent in the next place. Now it is dark and cold, and Josephine's corral is perhaps a mile away. Mary takes an apple and some sugar and goes off into the winter night. Can I, having dived into the pond in October to pick some water lilies, claim that she is eccentric? I am pleased to see that she is moved and excited, but there is an unpleasant trace of skepticism in my thinking. Later, on TV, a polar bear is murdered. "They've shot the mother polar bear!" she cries; and she cries, she sobs. "They've shot the mother polar bear!" And I think that perhaps I should go on TV, that if I approached her through the tube on the shelf above the sink I might win her interest and her affection, but I would have to be disguised as a mother polar bear, or some other wild, innocent, and wronged animal.

⚭ ⚭ ⚭

I think of my father, but nothing is accomplished. The image of him is an invention, not a memory, and an overly gentle invention. There was his full lower lip, wet with spit; his spit-wet cigarette; his hacking cough; the ash on his vest; and the shabby clothes he wore, left to him by dead friends. "Let's give Fred's suits to poor Mr. Cheever." I find in some old notes that my mother reported that he had, just before his death, written a long indictment of her—as a wife, a mother, a housekeeper, and a woman. I never saw the indictment. I suppose, uncharitably, that the effect on her would have been to fortify her self-righteousness. She had worked so hard to support a helpless old man, and her only reward was castigation. Sigh—how deep were her sighs. I have no idea of what their marriage was like, although I suspect that he worshipped her as my brother worshipped his choice and as perhaps I have worshipped mine. In my brother's case there was, I think, that rich blend of uxoriousness in which praise has a distinct aftertaste of bitterness, not to say loathing. I think that Mary was wounded years before I entered her life, and who is this ghost whose clothes I wear, whose voice I speak with; what were the cruelties of which I am accused? She may look for another lover; I certainly do. Are we, lying in our separate beds and our separate rooms, only two of millions or billions who wake a little before dawn each morning thinking hopefully that surely there is some man or woman who would be happy to lie at our sides? Happy for cheerful kissing, fucking, jokes, the day to come. I suppose we outnumber the felicitous by millions, and I must say that had I been given a loving and uncomplicated woman I might very well have run.

❦ ❦ ❦

The terrifying insularity of a married man and woman, standing figuratively toe to toe, throwing verbal blows at each other's eyes and genitals. Their environment is decorous, a part of their culture. The clothes they wear are suitable for this part of the world, this time of year, this income bracket. There are flowers (hothouse) on the table (inherited). Children sleep or lie awake in upstairs bedrooms. They seem as well rooted and native to this environment as the trees on the lawn, but at the height of their quarrel they seem to stand on some crater of the moon, some arid wilderness, some Sahara. Their insularity is incomprehensible. This is an abandoned place.

❦ ❦ ❦

I read the three stories and don't much like them. Phony modesty, perhaps. I've never much liked my work. The point is not to count my losses but to exploit what remains. I pick up "Crime and Punishment" and exclaim with pleasure over the opening sentence. Halfway down page 3 I close the book and watch TV. So the great books drop from our hands. Skating, I swing my arms, swing back happily into my youth, my childhood. The black ice on Braintree Dam, through which you could see the grasses. The instant the sun went down, the ice made a sound like cannon. And I think of the green valley of the Rorty and the hum of wild bees in the hall of the ruined castle. The sound was so loud you could hear it from the banks of the stream. I was thankful that I had heard nothing so romantic earlier in life. Mary swam in the stream, and the water seemed to magnify the size of her backside. My knees buckled.

❦ ❦ ❦

Palm Sunday. Federico and I go to church. During the years that I've said my prayers here the priest's hair has turned white and his eyeglass prescription has been strengthened. J. L. smells of hair oil and toothpaste, a clash of scents. S. seems not beautiful, not at all, but she seems this morning to remind one powerfully of how beautiful she must have been thirty years ago. I remember, years ago, that she cried during the service. Why? The priest, a pleasant fellow, embraces me. I put the palm frond behind the clock, and my house seems truly blessed. I think of the swan, the gorilla, and other monogamous species. It does seem possible on this splendid afternoon that a man and a woman can love each other passionately until death do them part. A lovely hour in bed. Thank God, thank God, thank God, is what I say on waking. Thank God.

❦ ❦ ❦

That voice in the dark that gives me so much advice says, "You will not be as great as Picasso, because you are an alcoholic."

I have a homosexual dream, which deals muchly with the spirit. I do not know in whose arms I lie; I know only that he will take care of me. He will pay the bills, the taxes, balance the checking account, and drive the car through the storm. "Were you lovers?" she asked him. "I wouldn't use that word," he said. "It was more like an improvised contact sport, scored or punctuated by ejaculations."

It was two or a little later. He was woken by his wife, who was crying in her sleep. A heavy rain was falling. She called a man's name three times: "Matthew, Matthew, Matthew." Was this in love or anger, and who was Matthew? He knew two Matthews, but neither of them seemed threatening. She went on sobbing, and he thought how puerile was his concept of a woman. He had reduced this continent of memory and longing into a pussywussy, a yummy snatch. The loudness of the rain woke her. "You were crying," he said. "Yes," she said, "I had a nightmare." She moved away from him and fell asleep again.

⌁ ⌁ ⌁

I drink gin and read some stories of mine. There is the danger of repetition. Walking in the woods, I heard a man shouting, "Love! Valor! Compassion!" I followed the voice until I saw him. He was standing on a rock shouting the names of virtues to no one. He must have been mad. The difficulty here is that I wrote that scene ten years ago. Oh-ho.

⌁ ⌁ ⌁

The hour between five and six is my best. It is dark. A few birds sing. I feel contented and loving. My discontents begin at seven, when light fills the room. I am unready for the day—unready to face it soberly, that is. Some days I would like to streak down to the pantry and pour a drink. I recite the incantations I recorded three years ago, and it was three years ago that I described the man who thought continuously of bottles. The situation is, among other things, repetitious. The hours between seven and ten, when I begin to drink, are the worst. I could take a Miltown, but I do not. Is this the sort of stupidity in which I used to catch my brother? I would like to pray, but to whom—some God of the Sunday school classroom, some provincial king whose prerogatives and rites remain unclear? I am afraid of cars, planes, boats, snakes, stray dogs, falling leaves, extension ladders, and the sound of the wind in the chimney; Dr. Gespaden, I am afraid of the wind in the chimney. I sleep off my hooch after lunch and very often wake feeling content once more, and loving, although I do not work. Swimming is the apex of the day, its heart, and after this—night is falling—I am stoned but serene. So I sleep and dream until five.

⌁ ⌁ ⌁

It seems to me extraordinary that Mary should have summered here every summer of her life; that here is a place, a hill, a dozen simple cottages, and a mountain view that she can return to and find, at least in spirit, unchanged. The famous gardens are dead and so is the gardener. A few roses bloom, choked with weeds, and the three greenhouses have lost some of their panes from the weight of snow, but who any longer wants catalogues of ruin, who any longer studies the sadness of fallen greenhouses? The mysterious spirit of the place—I think it mysterious—remains. There is here and there Charlie's violin music, Bertha's second year German Grammar, moldy copies of the *Vassarian,* and Grandpa's telescope. Things of the past outnumber the new toaster, the new coffee machine, and the new refrigerator. Walking up from the beach, we are unique as one can only be in the summer. Who are they? They are the W.s, and everybody else is less secure, intelligent, and interesting. The cottages are simple frame buildings. Planks are laid on the rafters, and the shingle nails stick through the ceiling. The electric lines are naked and black and are strung through the rafters with porcelain insulators. I wake at night and hear the rain on the shingles. I have not heard this for years. The roof not only receives the rain—there are leaks here and there—it seems to amplify the sound, and with some erotic or infantile thrill I hear the sound increase and louden. Now the storm passes over, the wind blows, and water showers onto the roof. I am three years old.

Thirty years ago, when we were courting, I used to leave the guesthouse, where everyone seemed asleep, and walk, naked, through the woods to this cottage, where we made love. Thirty years later, I still want to make love, but I am given no encouragement and my drive is not great enough to overwhelm the few bitter things that are said.

᳘   ᳘   ᳘

Is Halloween as a masquerade confined to this part of the world? I don't recall it in Massachusetts. A rainy night. Groups of children wander along the edge of the road, disguised as skeletons, animals, and there is even a fairy princess. A boy wears a cape, and a headdress of oak leaves. He must have an artistic mother. The children's only uniformity is that they all carry large shopping bags for the candy they will be given. At the station I give a ride to a stranded nun. "I will say a special prayer for you," says she. The train seems to be making its last journey.

I think, yesterday morning, that I can bring it off: I mean a book. Try, try.

᳘   ᳘   ᳘

New York, Moscow, Tbilisi, Leningrad, Moscow, New York. I have the jet blues as well as the booze fight. It is not that I have difficulty recalling the trip. It is that I cannot always give my recollection significance. A wicked man, asleep on a 707 halfway across the Atlantic, seems a figure of the purest innocence. The stale sandwiches in the London in-transit lounge. We go to the Bolshoi for one of those old-fashioned vaudeville performances—an orchestra, a recitation, a mezzo-soprano. I nearly fall asleep. Walking before dawn, I have the traveller's blues. If there is a knock on the door shall I jump out of the window? There are no exits, fire escapes, or stairs in the Ukraine, and in case of fire we will roast. I drink vodka for breakfast, and we fly to Tbilisi. The first feast is with a family, and all the toasts stress this. The oldest man is toasted first, then the youngest. I find this very moving. The next feast is in the mountains near the Turkish border. I see two women walking along the road with bunches of autumn leaves. Are they going to make medicinal tea or are they going to put the leaves in a vase on a table? Geese, pigs, cows, and sheep wander over the road. A bus collides with a bull. We come to the center of the province, a place of the most outstanding bleakness. This is what Russian literature and Russian song are about. In the distance are the mountains covered with snow. It is dusk in the corridors of the headquarters of the Central Committee. The clocks are broken. The toilet is smeared with shit and urine. In the main square there is a statue of Lenin and there is a cow. So we drive up into the mountains for our feast. The next feast is at the N.s', where Mrs. N. spills wine on the tablecloth. When we reach Leningrad it is 3 P.M., dusk. The city this time seems shabby and depressing. The Winter Palace badly needs a coat of paint. We have a quarrel on the banks of the Neva, the only quarrel during this trip. I love my son so intensely that it amounts to a capillary disturbance. I also loved his brother, but that was different. We rush around Leningrad, dine at the Europa, where I find the dances depressing. Why is this? I think the tall woman with the short man has on her face a look of implacable sexual discontent. He seems to be giving her a dry fuck. Is this because my bladder is inflamed with vodka? We go to the opera, and hook the midnight train. The Kremlin in the morning. The disinfected atmosphere of most offices, except for the shoeshine machine. Our guide seems thrown into life with a more desirable velocity than I enjoy. He is definitely very engaging; definitely engaged. There is a cast in his right eye that makes him seem irresistible. I think that I may faint. The table seems to swim.

The Winter Palace at six. A dark night on the Neva. Snow. Will I have vertigo on the grand staircase, as I once did in Washington? I want a drink, a cigarette, a friend, a more intimate source of light and heat. I think of myself sitting on the B.s' sofa with a second or third drink, chatting merrily with Mrs. X in French. Now I experience a terrifying sense of nothingness. Would such a life be tolerable? Would I not cut my throat? Is this what my friends in the prison experience? So we drive back through the snow to the hotel, where I drink half a glass of vodka and dress for the opera.

Why is it so difficult for me to bring into focus the image of a young man with thick eyelashes on the plane from Tbilisi? Is this a temperamental infirmity, a national trait, a sort of neurosis? Why, watching some kilted pipers crossing a bridge in Ireland, did I feel that my life was passing by? What is this unhappy mystery?

The flight back from Moscow is painful. A gray day. If I feel well enough tomorrow I must do the eight stories.

⌁ ⌁ ⌁

In town with D. His 65th birthday. The face is strong, his gray hair is long. We do not mention his remarkable wife, who choked to death during lunch a month ago. His mistress has called him in Australia and asked him to marry her, and I suppose he will. The barbershop at the Biltmore has been cut in half, and there are only three barbers on the job. Do people get their hair cut elsewhere or don't they get it cut at all? One used to have to wait, reading copies of *The Tatler*. What is the significance of a dying barbershop? The barbers are all old friends, and we talk in Italian. I spend a dollar in tips for being whisk-broomed and drink a Martini at the bar, where there is a new, and more attractive, painting of a nude. The face seems unusually sensitive. But as I walk up Madison Avenue the city escapes me. What has happened to this place where I used to happily to pound the sidewalks? Where has my city gone, where shall I look for it? In the Playboy Club, the Century Club, the Princeton Club, or the Links? In the steam room at the Biltmore, in L.'s panelled apartment, in the skating rink, in the Park, in the Plaza, on the walks where someone behind me makes tonguing noises with his or her mouth? I don't look. I know the city well, why does it not know me? A pair of well-filled boots, pretty legs, a tossed head. A restaurant where all the lights are pink, and so my hands are pink, and pink is the face of my friend. Everybody is pink. Fifteen or twenty men stand at the urinal in Grand Central. Their looks are solicitous, alert, sometimes wistful. They use the polished marble as a glass for pickups, and most of them are fondling or pulling their various-sized and -colored cocks. Why does the sight of fifteen or twenty men jerking off seem more significant than the string music in the Palm Court? One young and attractive man, the point of contact concealed by a raincoat, is making an accelerated jerking, as if he was approaching juice time. These are the darkest days of the year, and when the 3:40 pulls out of the tunnel into the Bronx it is nearly dark, although very few lights burn in the new housing developments. Perhaps everyone is still at work. By the time we reach the river, it is dark, and the only water traffic is barges and tugs. When I was younger I would wonder about the tug crews, wonder about what they would have for supper. I no longer much care. In the early dark the barges seem like mangrove islands—shoal water—you could wreck your boat. Three men behind me are talking loudly about the collapse of the government, the railroads, the U.N. Is this really the end of a world, as they seem to think it is? The men beside me seem so gored and emasculated by time that I look away. One has no gray in his hair, so I suppose he is rather young. His face is finely lined, rather like a woman's. He opens his briefcase busily, but it contains nothing but a printed brochure. Will such a weary face be welcomed anywhere? The face seems incapable of any sensual provocation or response. But when it is time for him to leave he jauntily slaps on a sealskin hat with a bright feather cockade and braces his shoulders in his raincoat. He's ready for the next round. I wanna go home, I wanna go home. I've lunched and had my hair cut, and now I am exhausted and I wanna go home.

◦ ◦ ◦

My daughter says that our dinner table is like a shark tank. I go into a spin. I am not a shark; I am a dolphin. Mary is the shark. Etc. But what we stumble into is the banality of family situations. As for Susie, she makes the error of daring not to have been invented by me, of laughing at the wrong times and of speaking lines I have not written. Does this prove I am incapable of love, or can love only myself?

◦ ◦ ◦

I read "Bullet Park," which is an extract of my most intimate feelings, and wonder why it should have antagonized Broyard. Is there some discernible falling off, some trace of my struggle with alcohol and age? It is a struggle, but I have come through before, and pray that I will bring if off again.

◦ ◦ ◦

In the middle of Sunday afternoon I think that perhaps my dishevelled and unpunctual muse will return. I seem to stand above the characters at hand as if they were pawns on a chessboard. Chess, however, is a game I never learned to play. My mind approaches some unsavory matters, and I put Serkin on the record player and seem to enter into some community of accomplished men, who are passionately concerned with their deepest intuitions about love and death. The music, especially the Schubert, sounds like a powerful narrative. I see the stream, the Roman bridge, the leaves on the trees, the flaxen-haired woman leaning from her casement window. The dialogues are much more forceful and moving than any dialogue in any of the books on my table. I would like the story to be called "Glad Tidings," but I'm not sure where I go from there.

◦ ◦ ◦

It seems today that all I can write is letters. I am too shaken to take the car to the garage. I think of P. inviting me drunkenly to take a nap in his room. What was intended, and are these fleeting hints at erotic tenderness between men natural? What men have I desired? A stranger in a shower in Guam twenty-five years ago, who seemed so comely and so natural that I felt disenfranchised. What did I desire? Is this some force of self-love?

1972

My incantation has changed. I am no longer sitting under an apple tree in clean chinos, reading. I am sitting naked in the yellow chair in the dining room. In my hand there is a large crystal glass filled to the brim with honey-colored whiskey. There are two ice cubes in the whiskey. I am smoking six or seven cigarettes and thinking contentedly about my interesting travels in Egypt and Russia. When the glass is empty I fill it again with ice and whiskey and light another cigarette, although several are burning in the ashtray. I am sitting naked in a yellow chair drinking whiskey and smoking six or seven cigarettes.

❧   ❧   ❧

An interview. A young woman. Her eyes are nice, and her figure is fine, but she was not quite the right flavor. I didn't make a pass; I didn't even kiss her. I nag myself with the usual questions and come up with the usual answers. Early and happily to bed. On with the blue skies.

❧   ❧   ❧

Good Friday. No mourning doves sing; no bells ring.

❧   ❧   ❧

I've put it down before, and I'll put it down again, but when I remember my family I always remember their backs. They were always indignantly leaving places, and I was always the last to go. They were always stamping out of concert halls, sports events, theatres, restaurants, and stores. "If Koussevitzky thinks I'll sit through that . . ."; "That umpire is a crook"; "This play is filthy"; "I didn't like the way that waiter looked at me"; etc. They saw almost nothing to its completion, and that's the way I remember them: heading for an exit. It has occurred to me that they may have suffered terribly from claustrophobia and disguised this madness with moral indignation.

In the summer my father used to play three or four holes of golf before breakfast, before he went to work. I sometimes went along with him. The links were only a short walk from the house. The course was set above the river, and from the first fairway he played you could see down to Travertine and the blue water of the bay. Early one morning, he noticed something hanging from a tree in the woods beside the fairway. He thought it was perhaps some clothing left there by the lovers who used the woods at night. As he walked down the grass, he saw it was the body of a man. The face was swollen and contorted, but he recognized his old friend Harry Dobson. He cut down the body with a pocketknife and called Dr. Henry from the nearest house, although he should have called the police. He gave away his clubs that afternoon and never played golf again.

❧   ❧   ❧

In my dreams or reveries—I'm not sure which—I walk along the carriage drive at Yaddo with a man about whom I know absolutely nothing beyond the fact that he wears a dark-blue cashmere suit. He bumps into me in a suggestive and amorous way, and I do not protest. He puts his arm around my shoulders and says how much he likes me, and I say that I like him. We disappear into the woods. I'm not quite sure what happens, but it's profoundly gratifying. We dine at different tables, keenly and happily aware of each other. There is nothing flamboyant. We observe the force of scandal. We approach his room by different stairways and spend the night together. I also imagine us holding hands in a movie. Since, as I see it, nothing of the sort could possibly take place in fact, what room has it in my sleep? There is no such man. With the exception of Endymion, the only homosexuals I've seen there aroused my vigorous uninterest. X was silly and narcissistic, Y had a dental plate that clacked, and Z spit when he spoke. Their sexual tastes seemed to be the product of vanity, stupidity, and bad luck. But dreaming gives me the license to invent this anonymous and manly spirit in a cashmere suit. Is this narcissism; is this some impediment of my nature, put there by my unhappiness with my father? How the light of day, the fire, bolsters and hones my ego. With my eyes closed in sleep I seem to be a very different man. The moral quality of light.

❖   ❖   ❖

The incantation this morning is that I can cure myself. The problem is, can I? Is this thing bigger than either of us, Mabel?

❖   ❖   ❖

Wake at three in the morning and seem to have in my mouth that single grain of sand, that hair, that means my life. Oh, I will have it all back, once more—the work, the girls, and money to burn. Things are less golden at seven.

❖   ❖   ❖

Sauced, I speculate on a homosexual romance in prison. Sober, it doesn't seem to amount to much. Who would it be? A much younger man. Why would he find him beautiful? That the dynamism between youth and age was as powerful as the dynamism between men and women. That he feels the man shaken with the paroxysm of an orgasm, so like pain. They were both men, and the drama of sexual difference was lost. Stacy was hirsute, Johnny was smooth. He would not mention his infatuation to the psychiatrist. Why should he? Under the circumstances, or perhaps under any circumstances, it seemed most natural. Why should he consider it distorted, and root through his childhood to discover the origins of this distortion? He had hated his father, because his father was cruel, stupid, and dishonest. He had not loved his mother, because she did not allow this. There is the set piece about having been merely furloughed from his adolescence and its disorders. That they developed no expertise. They never kissed each other. They simply embraced, caressed, and fondled one another's genitals. Sodomy and fellatio were impossible for both of them. Stacy wondered if this was inhibition, repression, some bow to the society that had imprisoned him. Why wonder? He was content with this rudimentary horseplay, and by "content" I mean that when he was holding and being held by Johnny, the absorption of his flesh, his memory, and his spirit was complete. And then there is the scene in the visiting room with his wife and perhaps his children.

❖   ❖   ❖

Very sticky. I am given such a harrowing glance at dinner that I am nauseated. Why can't I bring this distemper into focus? Once, as I bent down to kiss her good night, she gave me a look of such revulsion that I felt ill. But I seem unable to bring to my feelings and my conduct as clear and strong a light as I would choose. With a disposition made up of suppurating wounds and miraculous cures, I seem unable to distinguish the force the past plays in my reactions. Am I nauseated because of something Mother did or is my nausea the reaction of a healthy man to a situation dominated by sickness? There is, of course, also the problem of drink. I clip the hedges and feel better. I watch with great interest a vulgar TV show. Waking, I ask if she would like me to meet her at the garage. Tears and hysteria.

I sit on the terrace, watching the clouds pass over, watching the night fall. What is the charm of these vaporous forms, why do they remind me of love and serenity? But look, look. There is no glass in his hand. Is it under the chair? Nope. Is it hidden in the flower bed? No, no. There is, for the moment, no glass within his reach.

◆ ◆ ◆

My cruel addiction begins sometimes at five, sometimes later. Sometimes before daybreak. On waking, I want a drink. I imagine that the water glass on the table beside my bed is filled with whiskey. Sometimes there is ice, sometimes none. To entertain myself, I then take one of my imaginary girls for a trip through some city. These excursions are highly educational. In Tokyo we go both to the National Museum and the Museum of Asiatic Art. We spend several days in Luxor. I've not seen H. in two years, and I find her hard to summon. I've not seen S. for two weeks, but she is usually with me these days. We are lovers; we joke; she bakes corn bread for breakfast. All through this tourism I am aware of the glass beside my bed, filled with imaginary whiskey. Things worsen at around seven. Now I can think of nothing but the taste of whiskey. Orange juice and coffee help a little, and I sit at the table sighing as my mother used to sigh. Also my brother. I can't remember my father sighing. I sigh and sigh. At about half past nine my hands begin to shake so that I can't hold a paper or type correctly. At around ten I am in the pantry making my fix. Then my shaken carcass and my one-track mind are miraculously joined, and another day begins.

◆ ◆ ◆

Yesterday my hands shook so that I could not type. In the morning I drank half a bottle of Courvoisier, there being nothing else in the house. In the afternoon I drank more than half a bottle of Bushmills. Early to bed without another drink, but there wasn't much left. This morning—a brilliant day for the first time in weeks—things are better, but I suffer from a slight psychological double vision: a melancholy at the edge of my consciousness that has no discernible imagery. It is rather like a taste. I claim there is some connection between my need for drink and my need for love of some sort, and I'm determined to put it down, however clumsily.

This may be a neurotic condition, some injury done in my childhood. The situation has gone on for many years. Mary responds periodically, but then, in the twinkling of an eye, and for no discernible reason, we enter the galls and barrens and stay there for months. I am not allowed a kiss; I am barely granted a "good morning." This is acutely painful and is not, I think, the lot of every married man. There is the love I bear my children, but this, of course, has its limitations. The need for love is a discernible form of nausea, an intestinal pain. I cure it by imagining that I am with S., although I have not seen her for six weeks. There are three reasons here—I am older than her father, shaken with drink, and afraid of trains. Perhaps I can see her in the fall. S. is too young and Y. is too old these days. I embrace strangers until their bones crack. Thus I embraced T. in the corridor in Moscow. There is more despair than ardor in these demonstrations. I have gone away, hoping that this would improve when I returned. It sometimes does, but seldom. I have thought of taking a mistress, but they are not easy to come by, and I am timid. I claim that my timidity is exacerbated by the situation. After a particularly bitter quarrel twenty years ago I stood in the garage, sobbing for love. We have no garage here, but otherwise the situation is the same. I don't divorce, because I am afraid to—afraid of aloneness, alcoholism, and suicide. These rooms, these lawns, and the company of my son help to keep me alive. I cannot discuss these matters without provoking a venomous attack on my memory, my intellect, my sexual organs, and my bank account. I mean, I suppose, by all of this to justify my having humped the wrong people, but in some lights—the lights of day—I seem to have had little choice.

⊷   ⊷   ⊷

S. has, I know, a farm in Vermont and so I summon this. There is snow on the ground, but the paths are shovelled. It is dark. I am leaving. This is a heartbreaking separation. She is crying. But since I'm making the whole thing up, why don't I invent an arrival instead of a departure? I do. There is still snow on the ground; it is still dark. I come up the walk, carrying a suitcase. She greets me passionately. A fire is burning. It is I who cut the wood. We go directly upstairs, undress, and bound into bed. Then we dress and go back to the fire and have—this I've been waiting for—several drinks. Whiskey, I think. The conversation is about the progress I've made in my work. My depressions are over. I've come into a new way of life, a new cadence, a new enthusiasm. We go into the kitchen, and I talk about my work while she cooks calves' liver and bacon. What do I look like? My hair is white, my abdomen is flat, my back is straight. I am sixty-five, she is twenty-eight. After dinner we drink a little more whiskey and go to bed. It is snowing. I don't screw again, because once is all I'm up to these days. "Once is enough, darling," says she. In the morning, of course, she makes corn bread. I go to an outbuilding, where I work serenely until past noon. When I return, I find a note saying that she has gone to the village for groceries. I have a drink, a large Martini. When she returns I help bring in the groceries. After lunch we take a loving nap. Then I drive to the village and get the mail. Checks, love letters, honors, and invitations. I shovel the walks until dark, when we have the cocktail hour. Roast beef for dinner.

⊷   ⊷   ⊷

My daughter throws up her job and follows her husband to San Francisco. This pleases me intensely. Mary is in a loving spirit, and all is meadows and groves. B_{12} seems to help, although, as they say, one has to help oneself. After the shot I feel that the craving has diminished, and I run upstairs with the gin bottle to show her how little I have drunk. I seem to have forgotten that there was another bottle. For at least half a day I am convinced that all my problems can be traced back to a vitamin deficiency. Now with B_{12} I will be able to board trains, cross bridges, drive across the country. Mary is tender and loving these days, and why speculate on the fact that this might not go on forever? I do not drink after dinner for two nights and have two mornings of feeling like a man. I do not seek it for long, but how wonderful it is to see at least a vision of wholeness, including some mountains.

⊷   ⊷   ⊷

After planning to visit A.A. for twenty years, I finally make it. The meeting is in the parish house of the Congregational church. This is a new building—by that I mean that the architecture is mildly unconventional. The main room is very high-peaked, with rafters, and globe lights are suspended from long rods—a little like the traffic lights at a busy intersection. The table where we sit, however, is lighted by candles. We are fifteen or twenty, come to confess the vice of drinking. One by one we give our first names and confess to being alcoholic. But the essence of the meeting, and there must be one, escapes me. It seems neither sad nor heartening. One woman describes the neglect her children endured when she was drinking. One describes a five-day binge in which she locked herself into a room and did nothing but drink. This was after her husband, a mischief at the local parties, blew off most of his head. The man beside her describes his binge—six months. He came to in the county mental hospital. Three of the confessors have been in mental hospitals, and one of them is still a patient. I suppose he's furloughed for the night. The long speech I have prepared seems out of order and I simply say that I am sometimes presented with situations for which I am so poorly prepared that I have to drink. I don't mention my visit to the Kremlin, but this is what I mean. We stand and recite the Lord's Prayer. I am introduced to the chairman, who responds by saying that we do not use last names. Perhaps I am imperceptive from having drunk too much, or perhaps the meeting is as dreary as I find it.

I'm not cured but I'm definitely better. At ten o'clock I still know where the bottles in the pantry are, and what they contain.

⋄ ⋄ ⋄

Another morning when I seem to see the mountains, seem at least prepared to see them. I don't know if this is blessedness, luck, or B$_{12}$. Yesterday's fine morning was countered by an equally squalid afternoon. I don't know why. Bad Scotch, the humidity, some chemical instability in my lights and vitals that makes the lows equal the highs.

⋄ ⋄ ⋄

I want to sleep. I seem to make the remark with some serenity. I am tired of worrying about constipation, homosexuality, alcoholism, and brooding on what a gay bar must be like. Are they filled with scented hobgoblins, girlish youths, stern beauties? I will never know. I desire women and sometimes men, but shouldn't I exploit my sensuality rather than lash myself until I bleed? I will never, of course, be at peace with myself, but some of these border skirmishes seem uncalled-for.

⋄ ⋄ ⋄

Vodka for breakfast. Mary mentions her mother for the third time in thirty-five years. "I wanted a Teddy bear for Christmas, and she said I was too old. She pronounced 'doll' with the same terribly Massachusetts accent you have." So we are people we have never met.

I read "Moll Flanders" with diminishing interest. Mary makes and addresses cards. "I shall now take a little rest," says she, wearily. "After that, I will decide what work to do for the rest of the afternoon." She sacks out for two hours. The afternoon is gone. She walks the dog, feeds the horse, and cooks a good dinner, but the atmosphere, so far as I'm concerned, is lethal. Now and then I lie down with what seems like an emotional fatigue, ready for the next round. I watch TV with Federico to distract myself, to enjoy his company, to stay away from the bottle, and to allay the peculiar stillness of this place.

1973

I think of the ruses and maneuvers I have used to stay away from the bottle. I have painted the kitchen. I have painted the porch. I have painted a bedroom. I have raked leaves on a windy day, scythed a field, sat in the balconies of movie theatres watching bad pictures, watched TV, walked, cut grass, cut and split wood, made telephone calls, taken massive shots of vitamins and three kinds of tranquillizers, but the singing of the bottles in the pantry is still seductive.

⋄ ⋄ ⋄

I wake with a bleeding nose and think that the Godhead is continence, common sense, and work. I wish I could harness, channel, and exploit the love I feel for my son into industriousness and temperance. I remember walking the road in Saratoga on a winter night, thrilled by my conviction in the Divinity.

◦ ◦ ◦

The gin bottle, the gin bottle. This is painful to record. The gin bottle is empty. I go to the post office and stay away from the gin shop. "If you drink you'll kill yourself," says my son. His eyes are filled with tears. "Listen," say I. "If I thought it would benefit you I'd jump off a ten-story building." He doesn't want that, and there isn't a ten-story building in the village. I drive up the hill to get the mail and make a detour to the gin store. I hide the bottle under the car seat. We swim, and I wonder how I will get the bottle from the car to the house. I read while brooding on this problem. When I think that my beloved son has gone upstairs, I hide the bottle by the side of the house and lace my iced tea. He practices his driving in a neighborhood I've never seen before. These are the hills above the river. The houses are, without exception, small, and close together, and are, without exception, neatly painted and maintained with conspicuous love. Even the wax tulips in the window boxes, the parched lawns, seem produced, tended, and enjoyed with a deep sense of love. Children play games in the street. There is a shrillness to their voices, which seems to heighten as it grows dark. People sit on their porches watching the end of the day—a much more civilizing performance than the double feature at the drive-in, which costs two dollars anyhow. They call on one another wearing yesterday's clothes, torn slippers—the recognizable costumes for this time of day. "From the way the children scream," says Federico, "you'd think I'd run them down." So we drive back in time to turn on the car lights. I watch a Greta Garbo movie with wonderful dramatic situations, confrontations of greed and lust, and in the end this woman, whose beauty has been cataclysmic, is a streetwalker, her brain addled with Pernod. All this because of a broken heart. Indeed, she sees the man for love of whom she has been destroyed cheered by crowds. He offers to help her but she seems not to recognize him, and when he has left she mistakes a bum in the café for Jesus Christ and gives him her last souvenir of love, a ruby ring. This is the color of blood, the caption reads. You died for love. There is no walkaway shot, no rain at all. We go out on the bum discovering that the ruby is genuine. Here is a grand passion—romantic and erotic love shaping a life—and am I wrong in thinking that such passions are no longer among us?

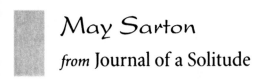

May Sarton

from Journal of a Solitude

March 20th

THE FIRST DAY OF SPRING AND WE ARE IN THE MIDST OF A WILD SNOWSTORM! WHEN IT began yesterday swarms of birds came to the feeders—first a flock of goldfinches; then I glimpsed the bright pink head of a purple finch. Now there are redwing blackbirds and, alas, starlings. When they have gone the evening grosbeaks and jays will have their turn. Two pairs of downy woodpeckers and one of hairies come and go all day long for suet. How empty the white world outdoors would look without all these wings!

I have had two visits from painters these last days, the Vogel-Knotts and Anne Woodson, and I have been thinking that painters are enriching friends for a poet, and vice versa. Because the medium is different there is not the slightest shadow of competition, which I fear is always there between writers. The criticism we give each other, the way we look at each other's work, is pure and full of joy, a spontaneous response. I envy painters because they can set their work up and look at it whole in a way that a writer cannot, even with a single page of prose or a poem. But how hard it must be to give up a painting! When a book appears it goes out into the world, but the writer still keeps it and can go on giving it to friends over and over again. The painting is gone forever.

I suppose I envy painters because they can meditate on form and structure, on color and light, and not concern themselves with human torment and chaos. It is restful even to imagine expression without words.

April 6th

After another week away lecturing, home at last to melting snow! There are tiny bunches of snowdrops out by the granite front steps, and a few crocuses blooming between the spruce boughs . . . too soon, I fear, to take them off, for we shall surely have more cold. Only red-wing blackbirds and starlings at the feeder these days. The raccoon climbs up on the wood-pile on the back porch and steals the seed cake. I saw a huge woodchuck out by the barn. Has he already eaten the first tender shoots of hollyhock? Last year he devoured them all. Finally I planted tomato plants there against the warm, weathered wood. They did well, but I missed the hollyhocks.

The brooks are unlocked at last. That rush of water, foaming over rocks, dark brown, alive, bursting into small water falls over boulders, that is what says "spring."

But we are promised a cold northeaster and heavy snow tomorrow, so I was wise not to have the snow tires taken off.

April 7th

A tremendous white northeaster has come roaring in as predicted. Even Punch is silent this morning and sits hunched in his cage. But for me it is exhilarating—a whole empty day to try to use well, to get out of the clutter of these last "catching-up" days and what feels like thickets of undigested experience. It is hard not to be thrown by the re-entry into solitude after a week away, for I am at once attacked by many needs; many different kinds of response are required, when all I long for is to have twenty-four hours in which to sort out what has happened to me. I feel like a river when the tide changes and for a while the waters flow in crosscurrent, with no direction, only a pulling from all sides.

It was disturbing, for instance, to find a note asking me to send my letters from Louise Bogan to her literary executor, who wants to bring out selected letters. What I have to do is open that big folder and dive down into a relationship that had great meaning for me long ago.

I shall not ever forget walking into the apartment at 137 East 168th Street for the first time, after an all-night drive from Washington. I felt a sharp pang of nostalgia as I walked into that civilized human room, filled with the light of a sensitized, bitter, lucid mind. The impact was so great because not since I walked into Jean Dominique's two rooms above the school in Brussels had I felt so much at home in my inner self. In each instance the habitation reflected in a very special way the tone, the hidden music, as it were, of a woman, and a woman living alone, the sense of a deep loam of experience and taste expressed in the surroundings, the room a shell that reverberated with oceans and tides and waves of the owner's past, the essence of a human life as it had lived itself into certain colors, *objets d'art*, and especially into many books. The nostalgia comes from the longing to be taken into that world by what the French call an *amitié amoureuse*, recognized from the start as an attraction that will never be "realized" as a love affair, but where there is a strong echo of feeling on each side, whether uttered or not—perfume on the air of sadness, renunciation even, or the light bitter taste of a persimmon. Louise's word for this atmosphere was "life-enhancing."

The substance of such relationships lies in certain affinities close to the soul—affinities that will keep the relationship nonpassionate, tender, and full of revelation.

Those rooms were inhabited by women older than I, for whom I felt homage as well as love. I have felt at home in the same way occasionally in a house or room where a marriage has flowered or where two friends (Bill and Paul's apartment in San Francisco comes to mind) live in communion. But then one is inevitably shut out from the essence. Not enough has been said of the value of a life lived alone in that it is lived in a house with an open door, with room for the stranger, for the new friend to be taken in and cherished. For Louise, Jean-Do, and for me availability had and has to be handled with delicacy or one could be swamped. Detachment must be cultivated against the longing to be perfectly open and receptive. It all comes back to poise, the poise of the soul when it is in true balance. The human mistakes I make often come from rushing in fast in order to be "done" with something, to have answered, to get it off the desk . . . and this forced response may go too far, give away too much, or not selectively enough.

Whatever people I take into my life I take in because they challenge me and I challenge them at the deepest level. Such relationships are rarely serene, but they are nourishing. As I wrote the above, Kot* came vividly to mind. He would have agreed perfectly with this statement, and as I opened an old journal, I came upon parts of his letters, copied out after his death. These two showed me again what a friend he was:

> You see, I am very fond of you and I should like you to possess all virtues, without a spot or stain. You have millions of virtues, but you postpone their practice. Hence my preaching at you. But as you are not only a darling but a terribly wise being, you must listen to me seriously, although you are allowed to smile. (See what an inconsistent person I am, for the sake of your smile, I spoil my whole case.) . . . I want you to be aware of what you call your "steel," and what I call your wisdom, all the time. I mean, that whatever mad or chaotic things you do, never forget that there is your ultimate wisdom that must keep you safe and whole. . . .
>
> Of course I shall be scolding you and be terribly severe, and even beat you on occasion. And all of this out of very good and so tender love for you.

April 12th

Quite preposterous that there is still snow on the ground! I always forget how maddening mud season can be. A raccoon climbs up and steals the seed cake every night if I don't remember to take it in, and I then have to search about in the snow and mud for the empty basket. At the regular feeder there are now only starlings, redwing blackbirds, and cow birds. Too stupid! And the apparition of that enormous, probably pregnant woodchuck is no help at all!

* S. S. Koteliansky.

But today there is a feel of spring in the air at last, and it will be seventy by noon. In front of the house, where it is warmest, a row of crocuses have survived the big snow and are now wide open to the sun—lots of white ones, lavender striped with purple, and yellow ones. But in the storm a while back, when the grader was used to plough, massive blocks of packed snow were piled on top of the big pink Rugosa rose that I planted ten years ago, and this time I'm afraid it is done for. Last year it was decimated, but did recover.

It is an exciting day because a critic is coming to talk with me. It makes me laugh to think that it is the first time this has happened. I have waited a long time for the professors to take notice. It is a time of suspense and stirring up in every way. Change of a radical kind is in the air. Doors open. the guardian angel has made an appearance; my days in Nelson may be numbered, and I feel relief. It has been a long solitary pull here and time now for a fresh start. If I go, in a year or so, it will be to the sea . . . strange how those lines of Millay's have haunted me lately!

April 13th

Now that the snow has melted, I can see awful mole tunnels crisscrossing the front lawn in the most appalling way. But yesterday was the real first day of spring, such balmy air, such a lift! I even went out and started brushing pebbles off the lawn with an old broom (the snow ploughs shower the flower beds and grass with gravel from the drive). But with the spring languor came also a feeling of exhaustion before the work to be done outdoors, and of grief that this spring will pass and I shall hardly see X. I have done little, it sometimes seems to me, in this house but wait for people who do not or cannot come.

It did not cheer me that Carol Heilbrun, up here from Columbia yesterday, feels that what I have done best—and what she thinks altogether new in my work—is to talk about solitude. I cried bitterly last night, as if a prison door were closing. But this is a mood, of course. Solitude here is my life. I have chosen it and had better go on making as great riches as possible out of despair.

In the *Times* yesterday this by Valéry from the translation of *History and Politics:*

> Under our very eyes a new society is taking shape, a wider Christendom, a *civitas mundi* less theological than medieval Christendom, less sentimental and abstract than the "humanity" of our ancestors. It is not based on the beyond but on the here and now; it draws its strength not from sentiment and opinion but from facts and necessities. Its domain is nothing but the earth; its constituents are men, races, and nations; its creative moral force is culture; its creative natural forces are place and climate; its guide is reason; its faith is the intuition of order—which is to say, the relatively modest dogma that God is not crazy.

In the spring air I decided to take Carol up to the Warners' "Farm of Contented Animals." It has been ages since I have been able to go because I am afraid of getting stuck during mud season and it is possible only rarely in winter. But for me it is always a kind of homecoming because Grace Warner, the matriarch of this great clan, has been one of my best friends in Nelson, and also because Esmeralda, the donkey I borrowed for a summer, is there and must be hugged, her soft long ears and velvety nose caressed and lumps of sugar presented to be crunched, one by one.

After the winter, the farm looked a little more frail and sunken into the earth than ever, standing in the crest of a hill, with the children's houses spread out below it near the pond, and the cow barn towering behind it. There used to be a magnificent elm beside it, but that had to be cut down last year. One looks up, wondering what is missing, what should be there in that empty space in the air.

There are always four or five cars parked around and about and I came to a stop behind them. A dog barked and barked, a cat was dozing under a wagon. For a moment we stood there getting our bearings, and then Gracie, Grace Warner's granddaughter who has kept my garden going since Perley Cole left, ran out, and Grace herself, looking a little more stooped and wan than usual, came to greet us and to be introduced to Carol.

I have brought many friends here over the years, bringing them as if to a secret treasure lost up in the hills, for there are not many such farms to be seen anywhere any longer. Gracie looks about seventeen but must be in her twenties now, a slim trim figure, her long hair loose over her shoulders, her eyes the blue eyes of her granny. Everyone in this family is crazy about animals and children, but it is Gracie who somehow finds time among all the farm chores to bring up innumerable pets and to take care of them. It was she who took us on the tour of one small shed or outbuilding after another, each like a magic box to be opened to show some dear creature.

First we went into the cow barn, the domain of Bud, Grace Warner's eldest son, who farms with his sister Helen and brings his great horses to mow my field every fall. The cows were out, but we smelled the sweet smell of ammonia and scratched the foreheads of three blunt-nosed black-and-white calves, tethered to posts. No animal at this farm is ever afraid; all are used to being handled with gentle loving care.

Then on to more magic boxes, the first a tiny shed where Carol had to go in alone as there was not room for two humans at a time . . . on the right a very old sheep and two wild-eyed goats munching on bits of hay . . . back to a row of guinea-pig cages. The next stop was at a small stable, where we pushed our way around the fat rumps of two ponies to darling Esmeralda. I had forgotten the sugar, but luckily found some large hard peppermints in the car, and these were quietly enjoyed. Esmeralda turned her great head toward me and again I was moved by those Greta Garbo eyes, the very long lashes, happy to see my old friend looking so well. Gracie told me Esmeralda's arthritis is really better and she kicks up her heels when she is let out. She is part of my private mythology of Nelson. I borrowed her as an adventure to pull me out of a bad time. She was so crippled she could hardly walk and I wanted to see whether I could cure her. It turned out to be a great success on all counts. With the help of cortisone injections and a man to clip her hoofs (donkeys are not shod; their hoofs grow like fingernails and must be cut periodically), we got her not only walking but running away in what became a ritual caper every afternoon at four when I came to lead her out of the field to the barn for the night. By the end of the summer both Esmeralda and I had become cheerful animals again.

Grace and I talked over the winter's news while Gracie and Carol paid the silvery guinea hens and the white ducks a visit. (I heard Gracie saying that a mink had got in and killed half her ducks.) We caught up at the rabbits' winter quarters, where Carol was holding a large white rabbit in her arms. Isn't it true that long-eared animals—rabbits, donkeys—have a special charm? At any rate, Gracie's big rabbits, some with black noses and black-tipped ears, one all-black one, are beautiful creatures. We proceeded on to the bantam hens and the glorious little cock, to the muscovy ducks, and finally to the pig way down the field in his private domain. And then we came back up the hill to the horse barn, dark, piled up with hay, where at first one can just barely discern the towering rumps of the two great work-horses, Bud's pride. Gracie has two ponies in that barn now, but it is the horses that make one catch one's breath. They are huge, looming there in the dark. I never see them without marveling that man ever tamed them to his own use, for they seem like gods.

I felt that my friendship with Carol had been cemented there at the farm, something shared and enjoyed without words. And on the way home I told her more about the Warners—how hard they work, how much we all depend on them. Gracie's mother, Doris, drives one of the school buses, cleans for and takes care of three of the old ladies who are permanent residents, lifts everyone on her energy and caring, turns up if a car won't start in winter, says, "Call me at any time of the day or night if you need help." And Gracie is the hardest, swiftest worker I ever saw. It would take me a week to do what she accomplishes in a day in my garden, working with a fierce concentrated joy. She keeps in touch with my friends, those who have lived in the house when I have been away, and so, from the farm up on the hill, reaches out to Holland and San Francisco, to Wellesley and Lynnfield, pushes the boundaries of her life outward.

April 14th

Just a bit too much life pouring in lately, so I feel agitated and up in the air. Let me quiet down by copying a letter from Basil de Selincourt, dated December 19th, 1954, about women as poets. I looked it up as I was thinking over some things Carol said the other day.

> You ask me for a personal pronouncement on women's poetry (if there is such a thing!). For several years I wanted to make an anthology of them, which several poets have now done. My hunch is that if anything is needed it is that women should quietly realize that theirs is creatively the primary role; man and his mind are an offshoot like sparks thrown out; woman is at the centre to "be still and know." One must no doubt allow that poetry and the other arts use derivative material on which the mind has worked analytically and separatively and in that degree are masculine efforts; but the whole and original and continual creative process is from within outwards, and it is the woman's prerogative to possess that place and power—a fact which she cannot fail, if she has confidence and patience, to use to effect even when handling language and other artificial modes of expression which are man-made. If women's poetry has so far shown signs of eccentricity or overemphasis, it must have been because of a feeling of strain and of a handicap to be made good. All this disappears for the woman who realizes that she is spiritually at the center. The thought and words springing from that realization and the vision natural to it are bound to have a quality which will go straight home.

Carol feels that I have willed the women in my novels to be or to fit in with Freudian views, that (like others of my generation) I have unconsciously tried to fit women into the required ethos. Even in Mélanie's case (she felt), in *The Bridge of Years,* too little was said about the business and she "gives in" to her husband, and Carol also felt that his philosophical speculations were more "real" than Mélanie's work as seen in the novel. This amazed me! Is what Carol is asking the portrait of a woman (like herself?) who has managed to bring up three children, keep her marriage very much alive and happy, and do distinguished work as a professor? Yet she told me that *three* of her married friends, women with children, have committed suicide because each felt her life was at a dead end, because she did not feel used or needed. This is a staggering figure, and gave me to think.

Later on in our conversation I asked her how she had managed. Apparently students often ask her what the price of such a life is, and she always answers, "The price is everything." But in our effete American civilization few people are willing to pay the price of any-thing—a garden, children, a good marriage, a work of art. And they resent the small price they manage to pay. Carol gives me the sense that she is exceptionally well-balanced, cool, discriminating, humorous, but never unfeeling. She appears to be a great exception!

Part of my agitation has been that after Carol had left I found fifty pages of manuscript I had promised to read, by a woman in her forties who is trying for a fellowship. She also paints, writes poems and short stories. She has not begun to understand what the price of excellence is. I say this with humility because I am still dashed by Carol's pointing out that certain trite phrases in my work should have been vetted. Certainly Eleanor Blair's sensitive editing eye has helped enormously in my last books. Carol admitted that *Plant Dreaming Deep* was free of these lapses.

I read the manuscript and telephoned my reactions; that at least saved writing a letter. But what I had needed was to sit down and think over the rich and fruitful day of dialogue with Carol instead of, once more, "taking in" and responding to someone else's experience. I fear that this insoluble problem of my life is becoming the leitmotif of this journal. *Basta!*

Carol would react violently against Basil's dicta, especially to the phrase that insists on a passive role for the woman, "be still and know." Where I agree with her, and was refreshed by insights I have laid aside lately, is that every artist is androgynous, that it is the masculine in a woman and the feminine in a man that proves creative. This I have always believed. But where she brought me a fresh image was to suggest that we should place all human lives in a spectrum with the very masculine man at one end and the very feminine woman at the other, and then every gradation toward the middle. I would agree also that the ultrafeminine may be as off the beam as the ultramasculine and that people of the greatest creativity and force, as well as the greatest understanding, come near the middle of the spectrum. If we could lay aside worrying about these percentages, and each of us come to a sense of moving from his *own* center (wherever it may be on the spectrum) we would obviously be a great deal freer and happier.

April 21st

Life comes in clusters, clusters of solitude, then a cluster when there is hardly time to breathe. Gracie Warner is here raking pebbles off sodden grass to try to get the lawn into shape. It is a great comfort to have her here, always cheerful and the most efficient worker I ever saw; watching her out there makes me resolve to work harder now that spring is at last in the air, or rather, "on the ground." It has been in the air for some time. Almost all the snow has gone from the flower beds, and I am gradually taking the spruce branches off. One daffodil is in bloom in front of the house, but I felt *outrage* when I left to go southward for the weekend in a thick white blizzard! And this morning it is only forty.

There is a great pelting in of life just now, but under it all runs a seam or fault that keeps me thinking. It is because of the big question Carol raised as to whether the time for passionate involvement in my life should not be past. I held back all love poems from *A Grain of Mustard Seed,* and for that reason it feels like a truncated book to me. Always before, I have wanted all facets to be included, the poems of a whole person—the conflicts, the loves, the rages, the political angst too. (I have always been beaten down for the latter, long ago by Conrad Aiken, more lately by Louise Bogan. Rhetorical poetry—and political poetry is bound to be that—is out of fashion.) But since *Plant Dreaming Deep* I feel that a false image of me is being built up, the image of a wise old party who is "above it all." I believe Carol was somewhat disappointed *not* to find that mythical person, but to find, instead, a far more vulnerable, involved, and unfinished person than she had imagined. In a letter she quoted back to me parts of the final sonnets in the "Divorce of Lovers" sequence, and the implication was that not to have given up personal life was a regression. But I think this is absurd, and shows rather *her* need of such a person than *my* need to be it. She ends, "Human beings were not meant for moderation. Yet if one needs the extremes to know the middle, as I believe with Blake and all others, perhaps moderation is the final reward of a *lived* life where we choose the center not through fear, but wisdom."

I do not think it is the business of a poet to become a guru. It is his business to write poetry, and to do that he must remain open and vulnerable. We grow through relationships of every kind, but most of all through a relationship that takes the whole person. And it would be pompous and artificial to make an arbitrary decision to "shut the door."

The problem is to keep a balance, not to fall to pieces. In keeping her balance in her last years Louise Bogan stopped writing poems, or nearly. It was partly, I feel sure, that the detachment demanded of the critic (and especially his absorption in analyzing the work of others) is diametrically opposed to the kind of detachment demanded of the poet in relation to his own work. We are permitted to become detached only after the *shock* of an experience has been taken in, allowed to "happen" in the deepest sense. Detachment comes with examining the experience by means of writing the poem. But this is critical perception at white heat, and has nothing whatever to do with Carol's "moderation."

If I should wear the mask of that mythical person *Plant Dreaming Deep* has created in readers' minds, I would be perpetuating a myth, not growing, not casting off that skin in order to make a new one. All this is much in my mind because for the last ten days I have been contemplating a radical change in my life, one that will alarm and even rouse panic in some people who want to think of me as "the man on the hill," settled into this solitude for life.

Some days ago two friends came here, one of them Beverly Hallam, the painter, and I learned that there will be a house available for rent on an estate they have bought in Maine—a stretch of wild woodland, rocky coast, meadows running down to the sea as in Cornwall (what a dream!)—an amazing "find" along that highly populated shore line of Maine. They will build a modern house on the rocks and would rent me the "old house." I saw it yesterday, and am imagining myself into it, feeling a little clumsy. It is far grander than Nelson, but without Nelson's distinction . . . built in the 1920's, is my guess, solid and comfortable, with a superb outlook right down a golden meadow to the ocean itself. I roved about it trying to find a nest where I could work, and it is just that that I wonder about. But I have an idea that a rather sheltering paneled room on the third floor might work. And oh, the sea—"*La mer, la mer, toujours recommencée!*"

It is time for a change. My spirits are lifted by the very idea of it—living by the sea, the rhythm of the tides, the long-held dream come true. For when I was looking for a house and finally came to Nelson, I looked first at the sea. I shall have two years before the move can be made—time to feel and think my way into it. There is an already "made" garden, a lot easier to handle and better designed than mine at Nelson, the possibility of a small "greenhouse" window, a plot for a picking garden dug and ready, lots of climbing roses along a fence and clematis (even a white one), low terraces for bulbs and perennials, and an old wisteria climbing the front of the house. So the place combines a certain order and formality with the open stretch of field down to the sea.

The whole tract is almost unbelievably diverse, even to a marsh (for wild birds), a shingle beach, and big rocks. It is like a specimen tract of Maine . . . beauty and wildness.

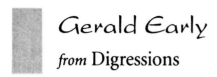

Gerald Early

from Digressions

> Everything's allowed inside oneself.
> —*Louis-Ferdinand Céline*

March 28, 1988

AND SO JESSE JACKSON HAS WON THE MICHIGAN PRIMARY AND ALL THE POLITICAL PUNDITS and pollsters are left aghast, faced with a horror they cannot comprehend and which they did not believe possible: a black man may receive the Democratic nomination for the presidency, a black man has to be taken seriously as a national political figure. It is a sign, this failure of the pundits to assess Jackson correctly, of how expertise and professionalism in this country is nothing more than a mask for an ignorant or, worse yet, a half-ignorant opinion stated with the glib guile of authority. The gestalt of knowledge in our society is a white man sitting in a plush book-lined office, computer terminal on his desk, holding forth for reporters from television and the newspapers, the uniquely contrived hybrid of scholar and mountebank. How can we now predict that Jesse Jackson cannot be nominated and that he cannot become president? We have never had a black mount a serious campaign of such magnitude before. What is the precedent to guide the experts here? The fact that it is virtually impossible for a black to become a third base coach in baseball or a head coach in professional football? But politics is not a game of skill, despite the wins and losses, but the virtuosi rendition of a set of overly familiar images. If the pundits and pollsters, if the party officials had been more knowledgeable of American social and cultural history, Jackson's success would not have come as a surprise, indeed, it would and should have been foreseen and confidently predicted. It should be realized that Jackson's force is his enactment of the myth of the American Joseph, prince in an alien land.

It was to be expected after 1984 that blacks, for two reasons, would back Jackson more heavily in 1988. First, blacks felt that they gained nothing for their loyalty at the 1984 Democratic convention, a loyalty that does indeed date back as far as FDR. When the massacres of the McGovern candidacy in 1972, the Carter candidacy of 1980, and the Mondale candidacy of 1984 occurred and the traditional white Democratic coalitions left the party to vote Republican, blacks stood by the losers. Whites could be romanced away by an appealing conservative Republican, so blacks argued, but we have remained through thick and thin; a steadfastness which has been a two-edged sword for the white Democratic leaders, for they fear that it has been loyalty from black voters which has driven whites away. If that has been the case, it is not the fault of black voters, nor is it their burden to assuage whites that they will vote as a dependable bloc but not act as a special interest. Second, Jackson was much more appealing to blacks than any white who might decide to run with the possible exception of Ted Kennedy, as black attachment to that name rivals their attachment to the names Lincoln and King. The groundswell message was clear to black politicians and ward leaders well before the primary season: blacks generally wished to empower their vote and voice by voting for Jackson. And there were to be no more sellouts as there were in 1984. (Many blacks I talked to thought Jackson should not have capitulated in 1984 to Mondale which, in hindsight, would appear to anyone to have been an horrendous move guaranteed to shut him out of the party forever and to set back the possibility of a black seriously running for president for maybe another twenty years.) The sudden death of Chicago's black mayor,

31

Harold Washington, which resulted in an entire issue of *Jet* magazine being devoted to him, (although no comparable honor was given James Baldwin, a much more important historical and cultural figure; but one has to expect that kind of Philistinism from Johnson Publications), simply galvanized the national black masses to Jackson even more. The bourgeois sensibility, symbolized by Bill Cosby and *Ebony* magazine, was solidly behind Jackson. There was no split this time in the black community over the issue of whether he could be elected. So, we have the nationalist dream of blacks being realized in Jackson's run: all classes of blacks united on the Black Star Line to the White House; for blacks have always wished for some strong leader to unite them. Of course, such unity means that ethnicity, at last, becomes the political and social, psychological and metaphysical refuge that blacks desperately wish it to be. And it is so hard to have ethnicity mean anything anymore in this country which absorbs the novelty of difference like a sponge. No serious criticism was ever presented about a Jackson candidacy, for to criticize him was tantamount to being an enemy of the race or, put in a bourgeois way, an enemy to the advancement of the race. And Jackson is, above all else, a preacher, and black Americans are among those people in this country who still believe that ministers have something to say that is actually worth listening to. It is their historical and cultural legacy: the church and ministers have led them to freedom and to an uneasy, often tragic, if profound, citizenship.

But what of Jackson's ability to attract whites? He could not do so in 1984 because he seemed too much a black candidate, hanging around Louis Farrakan and all that. Now he runs as a liberal and a Populist. And that change accounts for a good deal. It is obvious that what the experts and party bigwigs really fear is not that Jackson is "unelectable"; they do not fear him losing. How could they as a loss gets him out of the way. They fear the possibility that he may win in November and that he could attract whites' votes, that a black politician may be able to speak to and for whites. But there is, undeniably, a decidedly distasteful aspect to this. The liberals and blue-collar workers who voted for Jackson and who will deny that race is the reason are actually supporting him for no other reason than race. Suppose Jackson were white with the same credentials, the same ministerial garb, the same message of, as *The New Republic,* which is now not too far removed for *The National Review* and can be taken just as seriously which means not seriously at all, labeled it, "negative Populism." To be sure, by this point of the springtime in Michigan, this candidate would certainly not be around. Such a candidate would have been hooted out, really, distrusted because of his being a minister, because he smacked too much of being a true demagogue. In other words, the only type of politician who can seriously espouse liberalism in this country is now black. Everyone can believe the sincerity of his message because he is, after all, black and the burden of blackness in this country has been that it is tied to the liberalization of the franchise, to the growth and enlargement of our understanding of the citizen, to the expansion of our conception of humanity. Jackson has this cultural weight which he can use to his advantage. Moreover, he is a civil rights leader, which more deeply authenticates his liberalism than anything else: liberalism and civil rights having become synonymous. So the white who votes for Jackson wishes to express freedom from race consciousness while actually acting inevitably and predictably from the cultural compulsions of race consciousness. We have had eight years of a president whom we would not criticize for fear of facing a truth about why he was elected that we could not bear. Can we afford another such president whom we are reluctant to criticize even as a candidate? Or worse, can we afford a president whom we would wish to destroy for fear of facing a truth about why he was elected that we could not bear? Moreover, how much more of this simplistic Populism can we stand? Are Jackson's facile answers any more serviceable than Reagan's, or do liberals condemn sense-less political chatter only from dumb white conservatives? In 1972 George Wallace won the Michigan democratic primary and I wouldn't be surprised if some of the whites who voted for him then voted for Jackson this time around. I suspect at times that Populism is a blind behind which the oligarchy can operate as well as any other.

Jackson reminds one so much of the narrator in Ellison's *Invisible Man,* the southern kid who wanted only to be a black leader and to make rousing speeches which he did, much, ultimately, to his regret. And it is that truculent opportunism and obsessive self-mythmaking that makes Jackson so typically the American confidence man, so seductive as a politician, and so intriguingly ambiguous, if somewhat fraudulent, as a true leader. And so blacks respond that the whites who are running for the Democratic nomination have noth-ing better to offer and so it is the case. But mediocrity in a black man is not excused simply because we have been for years drowning in white mediocrity passing itself off as merit. But one has to admire Jackson endlessly, the striking mixture of delirium and endurance which mark his tireless campaigning, the brazen egotism and courage to run for such an office and know that he will be the target of more right-wing racist nuts than all the white candidates in history put together; the wiliness that can give credence to such a slogan as "economic vi-olence"—and politics in America has come down to nothing but a series of slogans and ges-tures of leadership and abilities, not rhetoric, which would be acceptable, but the utter nega-tion of discourse, an admission, a deep confession of futility on the part of those running: they have no answers to problems. They are all like the Invisible Man: they simply wish to give speeches and become leaders, give orders, act important, boss some underlings around. Economic violence is a completely meaningless phrase: what could it truly mean? and one can scrutinize: more jobs, more social programs, more legislation to protect the public from the onslaught of corporations, the redistribution of wealth in America. Who can say? But it sounds so much more forceful than anything anyone else is saying. And it does sound hu-mane, a freshness which is compelling, since we have heard nothing humane from Reagan for eight years. In the end, Jackson's candidacy and our response to it is a signal that Amer-ica is at the crossroads. The old regime, the old value system based on white male supremacy is breaking up and now, what will be the new cultural consensus? That is the hope, the only real attraction, of a Jackson presidency: that he can help us achieve a new consensus simply on the strength of who he is and not for what he says because Populism as a political mes-sage is dead. (Populism is just another form of the strange death of a romanticized Amer-ica: the family farm died in 1900 or thereabouts; there has never been a chicken in every pot.) And the choice will be clear if he is nominated: more of the old way of the grotesque with the Republicans or something new, possibly a politics freed from the grotesque, with Jackson. Jackson symbolizes our ambivalence. Whites would love to see a black president, the symbolic leader, to end the old race bit once and for all. (And if a black is president it would seem to solve the race problem from a distance; one would still not have to have a black in one's home, one can still hate busing. Indeed, one can still hate blacks with an even greater justification because one can point to the black man in the White House and say, "I voted for him.") But whites are also afraid of what that united symbolism means: the black, symbolic of everything the white has wished to suppress while being everything that he has wished to reach, the paradoxical emblem of both his humanity and inhumanity; and the presidency, that seat of power from which the image of all other power extends. It is easy to say that a white who does not vote for Jackson on racial grounds is simply mirroring the confusion and terror that has become his cultural legacy, but those who wish to flee that heart of darkness by voting for him may, in the end, be spellbound by a greater confusion, entangled in a greater terror, spun by an even more wild frenzy.

March 25, 1988

> There's a small hotel with a wishing well.
>
> —*Rodgers and Hart*

We have passed still another piece of Civil Rights legislation and one wonders how long this ritual will continue. It seems as if we have adopted the position that if we cannot give the dispossessed money or something really useful, then we will shower them with rights that cannot possibly make a real difference in their lives. We ought to be disturbed by the fact that in our attempt to transcend categorizing human beings, we allow our government for humane purposes to categorize them so that in the effort to escape it all one is trapped, Kafkaesque, forever in a perfect labyrinth of nonsense that will not stop people from discriminating but only force them fill out more forms to justify it in their reportage to the government. And the madness of categorizing eventually hypnotizes those who have been victims of it. The deaf students at Gallaudet College rightly demand a deaf president at the cost of wrongly condemning a woman who had been chosen for the job simply because she was not. Is this the only way the oppressed can free themselves in the end, by expanding themselves in symbolic, token oppression? Moreover, ought we to understand human beings in some way other than as part of a category? Could we not make proper use of discrimination, approaching people because we know they are different, instead of insisting that they are the same? Or am I more sinning than sinned against because I can hear Beethoven and a deaf person cannot? It is a loss that cannot be taken lightly and my pity surely will not help but pretending it is not a loss does not help either. I personally am sick of being a "minority," sick of seeing meaningless statistics lumping me with Asians, Native Americans, Hispanics, and other folk on the idiotic basis of not being white (why not lump us together on the basis of not being birds or reptiles?), sick of seeing ads in *The Chronicle of Higher Education* where colleges request vita for their minority vita banks when they have no intention of hiring any blacks—the minority we're really talking about here—at all, which is why they want your vita instead of you; thus I hereby sign off and break off all pledges that I have in that line. I cannot even recall God naming me man. If He or She did, I have forgotten because it happened so long ago. In returning to the subject of expansion, what about the terrific expansion of government powers under the new Civil Rights bill? Are liberals no longer wary of that? I, like Thoreau and Jefferson, have a tremendous distrust of giving the government more powers when it has yet to prove it can handle the ones that it has. Do we really want to expand government intrusion in the field of education, which this bill does, when the government has made such a mess of public and private education that one can only dream of the day when it will get out once and for all? It is a bad business to expand government powers even with the best and most humane intentions unless the government is going to protect us from excessive and unfair taxes, from having to pay for our own health care, from saddling our young with staggering student loans while attempting to get an education that by right ought to be free, from the savage disregard and contempt of corporations. Of course, this new bill will do none of these things; therefore, I cannot possibly see what good it is. It must be admitted that all this Civil Rights business is pure mystification, failing to get at the heart of the problem which is not the attempt to reshape the humanity of people, to get some people to be less racist, sexist, etc.; it is to reshape economic and political realities in this society so that racism and sexism and all the rest become impossible. But it is alas easier to shower people with rights than with money. To continue to pass bills is to admit that not only do these social ills exist but they are practically thriving out of control. In that sense, to pass the bills is to confess the uselessness of them. To get a government to do good is an enormous and largely wasted undertaking, but to try to make the leap from that to making a government be good is impossible. And that is what all this Civil Rights legislation is all about.

January 23, 1988

The talk in Stimage's barbershop this morning was the Mike Tyson–Larry Holmes fight of the night before which everyone in these crowded quarters either saw or heard.

"Holmes was just a shot fighter. Shouldn'ta fought that young boy. That boy just too strong to be messing with."

"Holmes shoulda been sticking and moving like he did them first three rounds. Holmes coulda beat that boy. You just gotta be slick to beat somebody like Tyson."

"Hell, that why Holmes got beat. You can't box Tyson. Holmes just shoulda traded with him from jump street. Just go on out there and say, 'Ok, mother jumper, you think you bad? Well, I'm bad too. Can't be two bad dudes here, so let see who gonna to the hospital'"

"Man, Holmes just woulda got his butt kicked sooner is all."

"Hey, all I know is Tyson ain't gonna beat on Mike Spinks the way he beat on Holmes."

"Yeah, I'm for that. I'm all for the homeboy. Spinks gonna do better than a lot of folk think."

"You got that right. Especially a lot of white folk. Cause you know it's them white folk that's playing up Tyson big. All that old 'Iron Mike' stuff."

"He's the white folk's fighter. And you hear that sucker's voice?! Sound like Michael Jackson or somebody."

"Emile Griffith used to sound like that, real high. That's why Benny Paret called him a faggot and got killed in the ring."

"Voice sound higher than his old lady's, Robin Givens."

"What you think she marry that cat for, ugly as he is?"

"What you think? She marry him for that money. Cause now she is Mrs. Heavyweight Champion."

"All I know is that Mike Spinks gonna do a number on Tyson. He gonna whip old Iron Mike. Have to call him scrap iron when it's over."

When my barber said that, blowing cigarette smoke whose menthol fragrance reminded me of the comforts of home, a sweetness and longing, because my mother smokes, and that odor of her cigarettes when I was a boy was the pleasure of her company, I thought of an old fighter named Scrap Iron Johnson who once fought Joe Frazier. Indeed, I began to think about my days watching fights in Philadelphia at places called the Blue Horizon and the Arena. Whatever happened to Stanley "Kitten" Hayward who once beat Emile Griffith and gave the welterweight champ two tough fights? He was my favorite local fighter when I was making the transitions from boyhood to puberty to young manhood. I had heard that after his boxing career ended he spent some time in New York and Europe making pornographic films. That was just a rumor. Perhaps he is back in Philly. I always promise myself on my infrequent returns there that I will look him up. But it is never really good to see boyhood heroes in their afterlife. I remember what a favorite he was in Philadelphia, a town which could boast a number of good fighters during the Kitten's heyday, and how often he fought there. I would read every column in the papers about him by sportswriter Stan Hochman. He was never a very good fighter, only competent, sometimes good but never consistently so. He had some good nights and some bad ones. One of his best was when he fought Griffith at the Arena in Philadelphia on October 29, 1968. Gil Clancy, Griffith's manager, screamed that referee Zack Clayton did everything but hold Griffith's hands. As a loyal Kitten fan, I didn't see it that way and agreed wholeheartedly with the judges giving Kitten the win. He did not fare so well the following spring when he lost to Griffith in New York where, I suppose (I don't remember), the referee was not Zack Clayton. The Kitten had other good nights such as when he beat Bad Bad Bennie Briscoe, another popular local fighter, in 1965 by decision. (Briscoe in 1966 put the finishing touches on middleweight George Benton's career by knocking him out in ten. The loss for us Philadelphia fight fans seemed like the end of one love affair and the beginning of another.) But Hayward had his bad nights as well: he lost to popular, one-eyed local favorite Gypsy Joe Harris in seven in 1966, to welterweight champ Curtis Cokes of Dallas in four in 1964 and he ended his career by being kayoed in one round by Eugene "Cyclone" Hart, a hot local prospect at the time, in 1971. He was not in condition for that fight, as I remember. He was, in fact, completely shot as a fighter by then. Of course, all the fellows in the shop preferred Spinks over Tyson because Spinks was the local fighter, although he no longer lives in St. Louis. Some began to recall the Spinks brothers' local amateur fights and the brutish, sad, absurd professional life of the older Leon. (Alas poor Leon, who brings to mind no one as much as Tommy "Hurricane" Jackson, whose one moment in the sun was the merciless beating he took at the hands of Floyd Patterson during a heavyweight title fight in 1957. He was knocked out in the tenth round. After his fight career, he wound up driving a gypsy cab. In January 1982, Jackson was hit by a car while trying to get into the cab. He seemed on the road to recovery in the hospital but suddenly in February took a turn for the worse and died after developing a blood clot on the brain. Patterson visited him while Jackson was in the hospital. I remember the papers getting a bit of mileage out of that. I keep thinking that Leon will wind up like that, bloody and bowed.) Naturally, for black locals, the "other" fighter, the "enemy" fighter is always white or someone who represents white interests. It is the only way they can symbolize the psychological stakes of the prizefight, capture the design of its adversity. Besides, Tyson is a fighter who always makes his opponents look very bad; they never fight their best fights against him. Muhammad Ali, on the other hand, to make a noteworthy comparison, was someone who brought out the best in his opponents, who seemed gracious and egotistical enough to say: I can beat you even if you fight your best fight. Fighters who bring out the worst in their opponents are not liked so well. Alas, one always waxes sentimental over the local fighter no matter how far from home he is or you are. It is the way of establishing a sense of place and time. And, inevitably, it is a way of saying goodbye to that same place, to that same time over and over again in a kind of homesick craze of wishing always that, as the line goes, you were here.

August 12, 1987

> What a lovely world this world will be
> With a world of love in store.
>
> —*The Gershwin Brothers*

My father-in-law owns one of those big-screen televisions, the sort that looks like a small movie screen, and he owns one of those satellite dishes that were quite the vogue a few years for people who wanted to beat the high cost of cable until the cable stations fought back by scrambling their signals. The picture on the big television is kind of soft and blurry, not as sharp as a smaller television, and the color is not as true. In other words, my father-in-law now has a virtually useless dish and a television that has mediocre focus. Not a good deal, take it all around. One of the few unscrambled channels still available is the Playboy channel and I once spent the better part of a late night watching some of the programs. I can only recall something entitled *Electric Blue,* which seemed to consist of nothing more than the less outrageous portions of pornographic movies, thrown together in a messy, certainly plotless montage. But I suppose the original movies were plotless enough since one goes to see those sorts of things for the genitals in action and nothing else. And so it was here: pederasty, cunnilingus, group sex, huge breasts that wanted nothing more than to be free of clothing, thighs that wanted nothing more than to be open and receptive to other thighs or to someone's mouth. Of course, now and then, while watching, one wishes one too could be making love to the willing women on the screen or to any woman. But ultimately there seems a huge loneliness that surrounds pornography, the gestures, the bad acting, the dexterity of sex in these films where people are always maddeningly aroused and so easily fulfilled by an act which is paradoxical because it seems so fulfilling and we are so maddeningly aroused yet it does not fulfill and arousal is simply the inveterate flight from the abyss of boredom. Sometimes one is aroused because one is bored. Pornography reminds us that we live in a culture of seduction which, like the film that is misadvertised in Toni Cade Bambara's short story, "Gorilla, My Love," is simply the corruption of genuine allurement, or which finally denigrates our fantasies by making them boring, or, worse still, the obsessively fearful and self-conscious alternative to boredom. What makes pornography bad is not that it graphically shows sexual gyrating. How can someone truly be offended by that? What harm is there in people making love with abandon? Is it bad because they are male fantasies being rendered? But would the actual acts of lovemaking, would the pederasty, group sex and all the rest be any different if they were women's fantasies, would the men be any less objectified than they are in their own fantasies? No, what makes pornography bad is that gyrations are all it *can* render, all it wishes to render and so we have reduced the greatest intimacy, the power of that intimacy, to simply the seduction of taboo-breaking. To watch pornography in the end is simply to watch bad filmmaking and to be made to feel like the little girl in Bambara's story: that you have been cheated, that you are watching the wrong movie.

November 24, 1987

> . . . and the blues has got my heart.
>
> —*Louis Armstrong*

Few activities can be as boring as attending academic conferences, listening to papers that you cannot understand, that are not worth the effort of trying to understand, that seem dutiful and unimaginative and filled with the current "hip" lingo of the business, terms like "megafiction" and "postmodern" and such. (As an uneducated friend once said to me, "Folks never know when they talking shit until somebody honest get an urge to wanna open some windows.") For in this too as in everything else in our culture one must be "current," even in the expressions of one's nostalgia. It is too much to listen to papers from people like yourself, unknowns who wish to be known, who are writing for job promotions, or to listen to the pomposity of the bigwigs, the stars, who have nothing to say that you did not already know and who do nothing but repeat the ideas of their latest book, which would not be so bad except the book has nothing much to offer. I know one thing: hardly any of these people would be here if they did not have to be; few would be writing if they could find another job which would pay them as poorly, give them as much fake prestige and free time, and that did not require "publications." It is unfortunate that people in this business are forced to talk endlessly when they have nothing to say and no way to say it, to borrow an old black saying.

I skipped most of the afternoon sessions to go to Harlem, just as I had skipped most of the morning sessions to walk in Central Park. I had been at the conference two days and had only heard one-half of one paper. I went to Harlem to do a spot of reading at the Schomburg, a place I had never set foot in before, despite being an Easterner, despite having gone to New York several times before, despite having been to Harlem.

Harlem looked worse than ever. I thought I was on a street somewhere in Bombay. So many unemployed people milling around, so many junkies milling around. A black woman, Jackie, who I believe is from Oregon, also attending the conference, accompanied me or rather I accompanied her as she approached me about the idea of going there. We were both well-dressed and this made us the target of panhandlers and beggars. One man was particularly insistent: "Aren't you a Christian?" he asked, but it was too late in the day to make an appeal based on religious guilt or the pious fake duty of doing good for people who, if truth were told, you really would not care were dead or alive. "You are black people too, you know," he shouted at us finally. And so he was right. But race guilt was not enough anymore either. At that moment my race was not enough, not nearly enough to make me one of these. I was torn between feeling: who are these black people? They are none of mine, not my black people, not my poor. Begone from me! But I felt as well the utter squalor, despair, dirt, lonesomeness, loathesomeness of the place was what I could bear because I had grown up black and I had grown up poor. But I could not bear it, not this much, not to this extreme. I only wished to turn my head in shame: To stop feeling a pounding dishonor that hammered in my head like a migraine because I had money, because I was well-dressed, because I was staying down-town at an expensive hotel that was really so close to this as to seem just outside my room window. I wanted to shout: "But I cannot afford to stay in such a hotel; someone else supports me here." I knew it would have made no difference for I had patrons who were willing to support me and they had none; I had access to money and they had none. Finally, I did not have to be there, in bright sunlight, watching in a kind of dreadful fascination, the voyeurism of the removed bourgeoisie, as a line of the dirtiest, most bedraggled people I have ever seen snaked its way through the street and into a store front building on Lennox Avenue. What was it? Why were they lined up there? At last, I discovered that someone, some agency, was giving away food. So this is autumn in New York; it *is* good to *live* it again.

I thought of Warner Sombart's *Why There Is No Socialism in the United States* and Oscar Wilde's "The Soul of Man Under Socialism" and thought that in a crude way the poor here do live under a kind of socialism. They deal with the state and only the state through its numerous agencies which are designed solely to keep the poor alive and to keep them miserable and contained. And they are, the poor, certainly all equal in the measurement of dispossession that has been allotted them. To look about the streets of Harlem is to see the soul of man under America's socialism, is to know that there is too much of a type of socialism in the United States. It is the socialism of the bourgeoisie who refuse to leave the poor alone and whose meddling does the poor little good. And it is all self-serving in the end. Give them food, give them drugs so they won't organize and turn the country upside down. Here we have people with so much leisure that they could cultivate themselves by using museums, libraries, and the parks; but we have so corrupted them with nonsense, made the parks, the libraries, and the museums the provinces of the bourgeoisie to use to cultivate their "precious" children, the playgrounds of the educated, that we scarcely permit the poor to enter these hallowed grounds of culture. That is the double tragedy: that we waste the poor by not putting them to useful work or useful leisure.

I stayed at the Schomberg for a few hours and then left to find a cab back to the hotel which soon became a matter of desperation as few cabs rumble up this way, I discovered, either by day or by night. I was not desperate to leave Harlem from fear. I felt no fear during the entire time I was there and indeed I have never felt fear strolling in any poor black neighborhood and I have walked in more than my share. I had to return to the hotel on time to deliver my paper. I was on. It was showtime in academe.

M. F. K. Fisher
Paris Journal

I WANT TO KEEP A NOT-TOO-SKETCHY LIST OF MEALS, FOR FUN. ON THE PLANE, THERE WAS the usual drawn-out procedure: two martinis, with olives and mixed nuts in a generous dish between my neighbor and me; a spoonful of mediocre caviar which tasted very good; turbot with mushrooms and little peas, which I nibbled; a few bites of Gruyere. I drank a poor white wine and a glass of good champagne and a very small brandy, over some three artfully prolonged hours. About two hours before we landed, I drank two more martinis in the long Northern dawn (it was dark only an hour or so on that flight), and then ate part of a very good crêpe filled with creamed chicken and drank another glass of the white wine— still not good, but I enjoyed it.

About 6:30 yesterday, after settling into my delightful little room, and a deep bath, and a long fine sleep, I roamed this way and that, sniffing out old paths like a hound dog, and of course ended at le Café de la Paix. It was Sunday, and June, and bright. *Tout le monde et son petit fils!* I spent an hour or so on a brandy and soda. I asked the waiter if one could eat at that hour, and when he pointed into the new snack bar Pacific, I asked him if it was all right for a single woman, which amazed him. He was nice. (*Everybody* is nice to me. It is my fat gentle face!)

I'm just about cured of that preoccupation with being alone. For this alone the

Time/Life job is worth every hazard. I was not really morbid, nor even apprehensive. But it is true that *I do not enjoy* eating alone in American restaurants. In Fowler's and lower-class places the countless other single people depress me physically. In places where I pay for attention and better food I am suspect: all single women are either lushes or on the prowl, good waiters and restaurateurs have assured me. So . . . I am put near the bar if I look like a quick pickup (which I don't), and behind an aspidistra or a service table if I look like a troublesome drinker (which I *may*, judging by the aspidistras and service tables I have peeked through and over). In even "good" places I am served in a cursory way, something to be got through.

Well, all this seemed especially dismal when I thought of it in terms of *French* meals, to be eaten alone too. Where would I go? Should I ask the concierge? Would he send me to Smith's Tearoom? Was I doomed to replace the Clift French Room (where I go to be quiet) with the Continental—Paris and London dowagers instead of San Franciscan?

Le Pacific, where I sat once more watching the sidewalk, was quiet, rather busy, with harried waiters. I had a small carafe of a rather acrid but pleasant "Beaujolais," a good but oniony beef tartare, a silver of almost infamous Brie. It was fun. I needed to eat. It was right for then.

This morning I awoke very early. Across the empty rue de Rivoli the birds sang wildly in the lush trees. I waited as long as I could, but was almost surely the first one to ring for breakfast (I am reading a good Simenon-non-Maigret: l'homme du petit chien).

I drank half the coffee and milk *hot*. Delicious. Then I ate most of a croissant and a roll, all the butter, most of the strawberry jam. Then I finished the coffee and milk—almost too cool, but bitter and good. (The bread, like that at la Paix, was disappointing. Of course yesterday was Sunday.) The butter was sweet and pale, in a little foil thing, as was the jam. Ho hum for the old sticky messy unsanitary *pots* . . . I felt fine.

This morning I made motions toward my employers. Nobody was there. Finally Mme. Dupont was. She sounds nice—quite efficient for a change. I was to call at 2:30ish.

I went out and walked great distances—really not more than about two miles probably, but getting used to traffic, and going in little shops, and crawling over street repairs . . . I bought some bath oil, eau de cologne and soap!!! Worth's *Je reviens*. I would *never* do such a self-indulgent thing if I weren't alone. I bought six oeillets, yellow and red, and two bunches of a clear light yellow flower that looks like a little thistle blossom. They are lovely in the room. I got this cahier, air paper, pencils and so on.

When I came back, Janet Flanner had called. She called again. I went up to her room, above mine. She has just moved here permanently. It is exactly like mine but perhaps four feet more shallow, being higher in the mansard. It made me dream again of coming here when I am old.

She is effusive, amusing, kind and cold. I like her very much, and am attracted to her sureness of power.

I roamed off again, to find a small charcuterie-restaurant the room waiter told me about last night and JF verified as good, and amusing. It was both—La Quetsch, on the rue des Capucines. Downstairs stools (high—JF is afraid of falling off one) and a wild business at the sausage counter, for things to take out; upstairs on a good balcony on two sides, the restaurant. The prices are high, the food is *much* better than at le Pacific, the portions are very big.

I was fascinated by the delicatessen and snack bar below me. I had a good waiter. I ordered a vin blanc—Cassis, which he surprised me by calling a Kir, which I thought was strictly Dijonnais. It did not interest me—tepid, watery, sweet. Then I ate viande crue de

Grisons, the first time I ever saw it in France. It was *very* good. Then asparagus. It was good, but I really did not want it—I had eaten all the v.c., most of a really good roll (the first truly fresh good bread so far), and some sweet butter. (This was served instead of the olive oil of the ticino, I suppose—a good idea, to cut the salt.) I drank most of a half bottle of an Alsatian rosé, which I did not know existed, a specialité de la maison. It was good. It had more character than most Provencal rosés. Rather like Heitz' Grignolino . . .

This afternoon I planned to go to the Orangerie to see an exhibit of a big collection given to the nation—four great Cézannes. Instead I *slept*. It is very nice to be removed enough from Duty to remain unabashed (which I do) . . .

I put some order in my papers, and after the apparently routine rain storm between six and seven went out for a walk. I went to the Rond Point and then the whole length of the Tuileries, straight down the middle except for a few wanderings to locate the Punch & Judy, with no luck. This is one of the longest days of the year, with the sun almost directly due west, shining straight through the Arc de Triomphe. The children and old people had gone home, but lovers still tangled, and people walked briskly.

I am in favor, as always, of the knowing tender slow embraces in public of the French. I find them sane. The surly furtive lovemaking in movies and parks of American teenagers is sad and ugly in comparison.

In the same way I really enjoy being noticed here as a human female being. At home men are supposed to look openly only at toothsome young girls. Here men of all ages look at me and in an instant *place* me, not with shy lust but with instinct and logic: I am "of a certain age," sure of myself, not interested in dalliance, experienced in living, clean, well-dressed but not modish, etc., etc. This flash of appraisal pleases me. It makes me enjoy things more, perhaps, than the cautious limited looks on Geary or Park can ever do. There is complete lack of interest, past the one appreciative recognition. Unless I myself would ask for it, of course . . .

That reminds me that last night I was "bothered," except that it did not bother me at all, by one of those men who fall into step to one side of a single woman and a little behind her, and mutter feeble obscenities. I did not even look at this one. I strode along, wondering if I should give him a straight va-t-en, and stayed toward the curb, and dropped him in six or seven blocks. I wonder if those men ever really go with women, or get their kicks from the possible fright they may induce, or even the things they mutter. I admit I was a little surprised—the first time was in Paris too, 1929! Then I felt more actively bothered, or menaced, or smirched perhaps, being more innocent.

Well—I prowled like a wary beast through the traffic after I left the Tuileries this afternoon, and stopped at a small bar on the Ave. de l'Opera, after looking for some time at the Comédie, very rosy now in its clean face. I ordered a vermouth-gin-sans-glacé. It was delicious. Next to me two sisters dressed alike in pale pink linen and white gloves and so on, about twelve and fourteen, sat with their parents drinking hot chocolate. The younger was pretty and coquettish, and the parents were enslaved. The older was intense and gawky, quite homely. So she tipped all her chocolate into her pink lap. The mother led her dripping down to the lavabo, and the younger sister flirted wildly with her father. Guiltily he turned stern, and confiscated a little book on Dufy she had bought.

I got back here about nine, and ordered a vegetable soup and a salad, with a half bottle of 1962 Pouilly-Fuissé. Very good. Just right. I ate three bowls of soup, all the salad, and am now three swallows from the end of the little bottle.

I feel very well. I am glad I am here, and alone here.

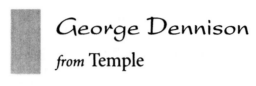

George Dennison

from Temple

April 1

THE WINTER BEGAN EARLY—FROZEN GROUND BEFORE THE SNOW (WHICH IS BAD FOR wells—rainwater can't get to them—and is bad in the spring run-off, because the ground can't absorb the melting snow and so everything goes into the streams, and they flood), and there were long spells, three to four weeks at a time, during which the temperature never got much above zero. But it was a good winter for skiing—no rain or ice (little thawing and refreezing) and I had six or seven good cross-country outings, the best being over the old Avon Road (continues the Day Mountain Road) with the Kimbers and others. Susie came once. I had been afraid it would tire her, but she came in fresh and lively where most of us were tired. This old farm road gives you an inkling of what it must have been like in the days before motors. Orchards, grape vines (on old stone walls)—pear, apple, crab apple—fields, wood lots, here and there a cellar hole, huge trees by the road, not killed by salt. But the orchards are mostly dead or dying etc.

⊸   ⊸   ⊸

Spring began early. It was warming up seriously by the first week in March. Bob Leso, the forest ranger, came with his assistant March 9. I went out with them on snowshoes, toured part of the woodlot. Both young, pleased with their work, self-justifying work. At the end of the trek (four hours) Leso put on a burst of speed, left us far behind, covering a section by himself—it was a way of saying, "You see what I can do? You see how considerate I've been?" and to his assistant, "You see what experience can do?"

A week later we all went out again, Mabel with us this time, and toured another section of the 500-plus acres. Still good snow, but getting heavy. A week later (by then I was with dad in Florida) the snow was too rotten even for snowshoes, so the remaining tours have been deferred.

⊸   ⊸   ⊸

Ten days in Miami visiting dad at the hospital. Everyone had feared he was dying, but he rallied. And our loving sympathy somewhat abated as he got his strength back, since one must defend oneself against him—a tough old buffalo. Yet he and I get on well these days—I suppose since the time we spent together with mother. (He referred to it—"I could never have made it without you"—and wanted me to stay longer. We have more in common than either with any of the others.)

Flew back to Boston (straight from Jai Alai—losses; looked terribly fixed that night. My only wins were number hunches—a *quinella*, as the previous night a *perfecta*). Stayed with Ruth and Curtis, Chinese food, talk with Alan Berger. Drove to Portland in warm, deep-spring weather. And Portland was warm, though a couple of weeks behind Boston. Two days there, working, catching my breath. Then to Temple, April 1, in the evening. Here it is early spring, bare ground in the fields, but patches of snow too, and much snow in the woods and hollows and the north-facing hills. Still some flooding on our road, and a couple of huge holes. We had to leave my Saab and transfer things to the four-wheel drive Toyota.

Presents for everyone, lively scene and pleasant for me.

They were cut off six days by the flooding while I was away.

Temple Stream floods almost every year, often during the winter thaws (and then the flooded road freezes and is hellish for the rest of the winter) but almost always in spring. It drains a system of hills with more run-off than it can handle. The stream bed is piled with boulders and full of sharp twists at several places. Ice jams here, and uprooted trees, form dams. And then there are beaver dams that clog the flow and cause trouble. These I haven't seen, have been told of. I can't imagine how they lie; they don't block the stream itself; must be across some of the little arms and pools between here and the village.

Our road gets it from both sides: on one the stream, which parallels the road for a stretch and is never very far below road level; and on the other the pond and the outlet from the pond.

Beaver work has been extensive in the pond for the last few years. The level of the pond has gone up eighteen inches. The dam across the outlet has been dynamited several times, but the beavers restore it quickly. Often at night in the summer I've seen the glint of moonlight on the back of a beaver swimming in the outlet. This probably means the traffic is fairly heavy there. They dig under the bank so that the stream becomes a little wider but is hidden at the edge by the overhanging bank, and they swim under the overhang. I've seen them too in the pond in the afternoon in summer.

The level of the pond is so high now that an arm of it has come right up to the road. Even a moderate rain will bring it creeping onto the road. And so for the first time in years the pond was opened to trappers. Tammy's husband, Steve, who lives by trapping now, took out thirty-four, many quite large. (I remember the first time I saw him in the woods, years ago—he was wearing his snowshoes upside down, so that the curved part bit the snow. These were shoes from the same man who outfitted Byrd to North Pole.) Another trapper took out five or six.

Our lower road was apparently under four to six feet of water (the stretch that lies between the pond and the stream). When this happens, the outlet reverses and carries water from the stream into the pond.

After the flood has receded the mud is sometimes too soft and deep even for the four-wheel drive. Long ago this was a corduroy road. Some of the logs still lie across it about a foot down. When the car wheels sink that low, you hit them with a thump.

April 2

The whole area, the houses, roads, fields, woods—everything looks bleak and mangled, as it always does this time of year—punched, scraped, flattened, torn apart, bleached . . . and then mud-covered and in danger of being washed away. Only the streams are thriving, roaring day and night, at their mightiest. The fields behind the houses near the stream—from the old red schoolhouse to the church—are sopping wet and muddy from having recently been under water. Yet this staggering, hung-over condition only lasts a couple of weeks, and green spring pushes through.

The road to my cabin still has a foot of snow on it, though there are many bare places a few feet away in the woods. The tree trunks—dark, for the most part—attract heat and radiate it. The snow melts first around the bases of the trunks, and then melts between the trees, while the nearby road—even the parts that weren't travelled by snowmobiles—still lies under snow. The longest lasting snow is, of course, the compacted "boilerplate" of the snowmobile tracks. This is why they are damaging the fields and gardens: the soil stays frozen underneath them and can't be worked up for planting as soon as the rest. Late in the summer you can still see the snowmobile paths across the fields where the grass is stunted.

These patches of soiled snow on the dead sandy-brown meadow grass, with reddish-brown spikes of meadow-sweet, dark brown weed stalks and little sprouts two feet high that will be saplings—all this with the myriad trunks of trees behind it, almost black if they're wet. There's something in these colors and textures that excites me—days in early spring when I'd tramp around the woods and fields at home, in the outlying suburbs of Pittsburgh, or look at the long hill, the woods, and fields out the windows of the grade school (Kelton). These colors and scratchy textures are handled with great genius by Bruegel, who must have loved them. They are certainly northern. I've seen similar colors in portrait sketches—mixed media (and apparently there aren't many of these) by Holbein. Perhaps coincidence, except that I've never seen these combinations in Italian paintings. The combinations I mean are: soiled snow, tree trunks, dried grass.

The woods this time of year have the simplicity and luridness of certain Expressionist painting—Munch, especially, and our own free-booter, Ryder. The snow lies in great "organic" patches—undulating edges, curved and sinuous (these patches may be bounded, more or less and here and there, e.g. in low places, by contour lines). They are very stark against the murky black or dark-brown forest floor (leaves, muck) just freed of its snow and very wet. And then the tree trunks, especially if wet, are stark against the snow, branches still stark against the sky. Some of the skies now retain a wintry cast, but by and large are brightening as the sun brightens, are often quite blue and cheerful.

❦ ❦ ❦

It rained heavily at night. Susie was staying at the Harrises', whose little trailer house was flooded (eight inches) last week. I began to worry—foolishly actually—about the stream flooding, thinking of the nightmare horror in my sister's life, when they were evacuated by rowboat from their home in West Virginia after flash floods had put the whole valley under water. She was carrying her infant daughter in her arms. The boat tipped and she fell into the water. Her husband jumped in to save the baby, but was struck by floating ice and almost drowned. The baby's body never was found. I walked down to the house. It was three in the morning. The rain had been fairly heavy for several hours. Poor Mabel had to wake up and tell me not to worry—it had taken several days of rain to lift the stream over its banks, all the way to the Harrises' house. And there had been heavy run-off from the snow.

April 3

There are fat buds on all the trees (they began as little swellings in the depths of the winter), and the poplars, some of them, already have tiny leaves.

Ferocious wind today. The dogs were afraid to go out. Full moon. Power failure—trees down across lines. Read "Tin-Tin" to the kids by kerosene lamp. Sweet for me to feel this closeness again, after being away for almost three weeks.

April 4

Power on. A calm day. The wind helped dry the ground—which is still wet, however. Yard around the house pocked by the ponies' hooves.

The snow is off the garden. The cat sits in the garden motionlessly. And Sashka digs for mice in the snowbanks downhill—listens, digs, listens, digs. The ponies wander in the wet field that was seeded last year.

We'll test our parsnips today or tomorrow.

Mabel has started tomatoes, okra, peppers, etc. on shelves in the windows.

On the poplars and red maples, the buds are almost leaves; same for the elms. There are great huge catkins on the basswood. The white birches seem ready to open, the buds are long. The sugar maples are not so far along yet.

Saw first robin on the way to the cabin. The dogs' prints in the oozy mud are splayed and large, as in the snow. One would think the dogs were huge.

The forest floor dried out a good bit by the day of fierce wind—shades of light brown, with here and there a rotten stump, and moss, a dim green, and gray rocks. The darkest shape is the wide, sinuous, temporary stream that carries run-off along the road, then under it and downhill to the swale where it becomes quite wide and swampy. There are tree limbs strewn across the road—such a pruning these winds give the woods—and the usual torn flags of birch bark.

The huge old sugar maple on the road by the tumbling house, just where the road turns to my cabin—this tree that looks so dead in the winter and does in fact have many peeled dead limbs—has sent out a great crown of buds, like the great oak that Prince Andrew sees in *War and Peace*.

April 5

Rain last night, corn snow today, almost hail, soft hail. About an inch. Gray and wintry, but not cold. The twigs with their new buds, and the needles on the pine trees, are all sheathed in ice.

April 6

Susie has been going to the public school for several weeks now, by choice. But there's terrible waste of hours every day—three hours—just getting there and back. The children were not consulted when this centralization took place. She gets up at 5:30 or 6:00, reads in bed a while, leaves the house at 7:30, walks a mile down our muddy dirt road, gets on the school bus, and arrives at school shortly before 9:00. A generation ago that first mile of walking would have brought her to the little red school house.

A blue sky today with lots of white clouds, sun shining low in the east—and the ice-sheathed twigs of the trees are sparkling unbelievably.

I helped Susie with her homework last night. There were some mimeographed sheets written by her school teacher, or principal, or someone, little squibs about Maine and famous people of Maine—abominably written, dead, journalistic clichés with here and there mistakes of grammar. And then the usual phony question: *Which of these stories did you like best?* I hadn't criticized the stories—I don't want to queer things for her, and she hears good writing here at home—but she said, "I didn't like any of them." She'll make a mark by the least lumpy, and that will do. This awakened some long-gone memories of *coping with the culture*. We live so out of it now! All the dodges and tricky accommodations of city life, and my early youth.

April 8

First sight in the morning: snow in the air, and three inches of snow everywhere—piled on the railings of the little bedroom balcony, and on the dilapidated picnic table out back, and on the cars.

Snow all day, coming down straight and slow, the large soft flakes of spring. They stick to the pine needles and pile up on the limbs of trees, and stick to the cabin roof and the house roof. The skylight at the cabin usually sheds the snow right away because it's so steep, but this snow clings to it, and is spread over it evenly—and the light inside is subdued, with an almost amber richness.

In early afternoon the quiet is disturbed by gentle puffs of wind. These are not strong enough to sweep the snow from the roof tops or the limbs of the hardwoods, but they agitate the springy boughs of the pines all around the cabin, and I hear a soft thumping everywhere as falling gobs of snow strike the snow on the ground.

Within an hour the wind has increased enormously. The pines are shrouded in a haze of snow as the wind stirs up all the snow left on them. This snow and the falling snowflakes are driven sharply in the wind coming from the west. Abruptly the quantity, the density of flying snowflakes, triples and everything is obscured in this flickering, agitated streaming whiteness. The wind has shifted and is blowing now from the SSW. The snowflakes are flying in long horizontal lines, broken by the complicated wind patterns of this little field in the woods that is part hillside and part level. Here and there in the swift horizontal flow there are columns of swirling snowflakes, and there are even pockets of stillness in which the big flakes are falling slowly straight down.

Twenty minutes later the quantity of snowflakes diminishes, but the wind is even stronger, and the flakes are streaming long long distances flat out, and the pine boughs that catch the wind are lifted and bent like bows and the clusters of needles bounce and stream in the wind.

An hour later the wind is still high, but there is no snow in it now. The sky is brighter, though it is still overcast and cloudy. The pines are dark green now, no snow left, but the hardwoods are all outlined in white. The wet snow survived the wind; it seems, actually, that the wind compressed it, glued it tighter to the trees.

The fields that yesterday had been bare brown grass are now white, five inches deep in wet snow. All the stalky weeds—the meadowsweet and Queen Anne's lace—that had been covered by the deep snow of the winter show starkly against this background of new white.

There is an alternate brightening and darkening as the sun finds openings and then is covered again. Forty-five minutes later the wind is coming in powerful gusts, the clouds have been pulled apart, there are great patches of blue sky, and the sun is bright.

At night the wind is still strong, perhaps even stronger. The dogs don't want to go out.

⚬ ⚬ ⚬

Sights of the storm: out the kitchen window we see the black Shetland pony standing patiently in the streaming flakes and the downpouring flakes. She stands motionless, her head drooping and one hind foot slightly cocked. The long black strands of her mane, fringe—a spectacle of dumb endurance, some calamity of the old west, though she isn't suffering at all. The snow blankets her rear and back, almost an inch of it.

I remember the granular snow, or rather ice pellets, that covered the ground several days ago to the depth of an inch—and the peculiar sound of walking in it. Each stride kicked up pellets ahead and they scattered audibly, like spilled bird shot, especially when I was going downhill and they rolled noisily for two or three feet. All that melted the following day, and it seemed that spring was coming right on. But this now is a reversion to winter.

Tommy and his girl friend are here (their VW is stuck on the road). Both are living in the Yale Psychiatric Institute halfway house. I talked for several hours with Tom at breakfast. My own schizy make-up gives me great access to his experience; we share certain problems and certain joys, perhaps in different degrees. The schizy child-presence is there, and it's this that I find sympathetic and can talk with.

April 9

Bright, windy. Last night the temperature was no better than fifteen degrees, but now (afternoon) the snow is melting.

I stayed up late baking bread (eight loaves) by the laborious method I hit on and that gives such good results—building up the loaves of rolled-out layers, almost as thin as pie crust, and painting each layer with water.

Tomorrow is Easter and Mabel's birthday. Tommy and his girl will leave after breakfast, which we'll make do as a birthday breakfast, if I can figure a way to cook the turkey in time. The kids are downstairs with Tommy and the girl. Mabel is at a meeting devoted to the upcoming anti-nuclear-power demonstration in New Hampshire.

When Susie and I last went to town we bought a couple of potted plants for Mabel's birthday. And I have a canvas shoulder bag for her.

April 10—Easter

Mabel's birthday. The kids were up at 5:30, and came in to get me, came clambering on the bed, looking all lit-up and wonderful. Michael strides back and forth in the bed, right on me and over me. One effect of the great patience Mabel raises them with—the combination they've had of great liberty plus lots of attention, lots of mothering—is that their excitement never makes them clumsy, is never more than they can handle, but looks wonderful. This comes from the harmonious development of mind/hand, hand/eye, appetite/desire, etc. etc—which isn't possible if they aren't free to experiment and make mistakes. (Play with food, break cups, etc.—which I probably couldn't endure if I were alone with them.)

Mabel and I had stayed up late the night before fixing the Easter baskets and hiding jelly beans. The baskets were placed by the kids' heads as they slept. (I tied Susie's to the hanging plants by her bed in her richly cluttered—an orderly clutter, actually—corner by the dormer.) They had already found the baskets, were waking me to watch the jelly bean hunt. I had placed a lot of easy ones for Michael and mentioned it to the girls, who were wonderful about helping him. They do this kind of thing without greediness or harsh competitiveness. For the difficult hiding places we did "hot/cold."

Pleasant breakfast while Tom and his girlfriend Ruth slept. The turkey was in the oven and Mabel was baking a cake. I had done the cooking for the past three days or so, now she was baking her own birthday cake.

Tommy like an exposed nerve, but much improved. His girlfriend more disturbed than he. He seems to be taking care of her.

April 11

A little butterfly, about the size of a guitar pick (and if the pick were of horn, the same color) beating this way and that over the patches of snow near the.cabin.

Gorgeous blue sky. Mild.

April 12

Beautiful spring day. I came down from the cabin early—preparation to leave for Vermont. Mabel greeted me brusquely: "Nell just called. Your father died last night. She wants you to call Adele."

This was not unexpected. Nell had called several days ago to tell me that his heart was fibrillating, he was getting oxygen, the doctor had told her to notify the family. I called Adele. Dick called from Minneapolis, not knowing that Nell had already told me. He said, "I hope I go as easily. He had everything taken care of, right down to the last detail. Of course it helps to know where you're going"—a strange tone, part conceited, part didactic—and pious. "Well, I'm conducting a successful career . . . etc."

I told the children. It rolled off Becky, who is too young to let such things register. Susie looked shocked and dismayed. "He died?" That reaction touched something in me; I went out of the room crying.

April 23

Rain last night, overcast today with occasional blue and sun breaking through.

The peepers in the swampy flats have begun their night-time chirping that sounds like masses of crickets—not yet the incredible, pulsating screaming of May, but getting louder.

There is still ice in some of the ponds, and clumps of snow in the woods. The road to the cabin is wet, running still and still spongy with the oozy, utterly bodiless mud of thaw. Wherever one goes in these hilly woods this time of year, one hears the sound of running water. The pulsing sound that in a large stream can sound like a babble of voices, and that in a small one can sound (though muted) like a tree full of little birds at evening.

Upset and sad because of the failure of our family life—which for me means the failure of life here—I walked through the woods to Porter Hill, stopping at the cabin to drop off some books. I could hear a partridge drumming in the woods—hard to tell how far away, the sound is so hollow and so carrying. It begins with stately, emphatic, slow *thumps*—as if calling for attention and making a great display of *presence*; and then very rapidly the thumping accelerates to a flutter that loses loudness as it gains speed.

The newly-seeded (last year) southerly field has a lot of fresh green in it; and there was a haze of green in all the fields along the Sandy River between here and New Sharon (I took Mabel's Aunt Frances to the airport yesterday), and a pervasive, pungent odor—both sharp and musky—of newly-spread manure. The early fields have all been plowed.

Flickers, nut hatches, starlings, swifts. I saw a partridge in a tree at the edge of the Porter Hill fields.

Sashka ran up out of god-knows-where and joined me in my walk.

Elms and basswoods, and the poplars on the high fields are all in leaf—a bright chartreuse. The brown fields on Porter Hill are covered by this lovely spring green in the tops of the poplars, very bright against milk-blue sky. Long catkins on white birches; and some of the birches (not yet in leaf) seem to have sprouted new twigs, look feathery against the sky—drawn in black lines.

Sashka hears a noise in the woods and dashes off. The woods are alluring this time of year—full of animal activity.

The old house at the end of the cabin field crumbles more every year, sagging in on itself, filling its rooms with fallen roof, fallen walls. Sky through the windows and half of the roof, sky and trees through the piecemeal walls. What's left of the roof has a sweeping of moss over it, and the moss has the same delicate bright green I see everywhere.

A huge wasp or bumble bee, gigantic and noisy, comes hurtling by as I walk. It follows me into the woods, but soon goes its own way.

The woods are a mess—strewn with fallen trees, fallen limbs, great tatters of white birch bark, debris of winter and the windstorms of spring.

The dead leaves on the little beeches—bleached looking, translucent, pale sand color, three and four inches long—look like little fish skewered through the gills and arranged in rows to dry in the sun.

I heard Sashka barking in the woods after we got back to the cabin. Ten minutes later she came in the open door with porcupine quills in her snout. There weren't many. I pulled them out with pliers. There was one in her mouth that was hard to get, and one broken one at the point of her nose that was harder still, as she kept flinching, dodging, squirming. It took twenty minutes to get those two. Later I discovered a broken quill in the side of her paw. I watched her eat, to see if she favored any part of her mouth.

April 25

Three days of rain, that changed to snow last night and left a thin snow cover over everything—but then more rain melted it off. Now the rain has stopped, but it's cold, gray, and listless, like November, except that the brooks are roaring and there's a bright green haze over many of the trees.

April 26

Warmer. Heard a loon down on the pond. The starlings are back, and some of the big roadside trees are filled with rooks, several hundred in a single tree, black and glossy along the branches, very decorative and sprightly.

Farmers tilling the big fields by the Sandy River, odor of manure—a dense, pungent odor with piercing elements (ammonia, probably) so that it combines the broad, pungent quality of tobacco with the sharp quality of vinegar. The odor is so strong and carries so far that one hesitates to say that it's pleasant—but it is not unpleasant. It is one of the country odors that one respects, perhaps is fond of without knowing it. It's an odor that is deeply reassuring, like the odors of sex and of good food. One inhales it and knows that life is right.

May 2

The trout stream—from Day Mountain Road down to Ted's mountain house (and I couldn't continue on down to Temple Stream as it was too dark to keep clambering over boulders, and I couldn't see to bait the hook). I walked home from there—seven hours all told, and exhausted.

The stream: at first alders and scrub growth, patches of blackberry canes, some slash. This entire area heavily cut maybe ten years ago. Many places hard to push through. Where the stream bed became deeper, the debris of the winter and of the spring floods was striking: bleached wood scattered this way and that, matted bark, grass, leaves lying in tangles here and there like gobs of hair—this establishes the high water mark. Also, on tree trunks near the stream bright orange wounds in the trees where ice barked them.

Then to a stretch where the stream bed was sandy and the banks level (this nearer the first big beaver dam). Then the large, almost circular basin of debris and muck, thousands of small sticks—say seven feet by two inches—a clutter, a basin of muck, and the remnants of the semi-circular dam broken by ice. A mile or so downstream they had built another. (But no fish in either, and none between them—maybe too new.) Then handsome stretches of stream, big trees. Caught three trout and spitted them on a small fire on a rock over the stream.

May 14

After the gathering at Nancy and David's (Jack's talk of Seabrook interesting—but the gathering dull, dull in a way I detest—them holding hands sitting in circle on floor singing and swaying), I dreamt that night of a marvelous party, crowded and with Scots and Britishers present, and maybe Irishers—all these, I think, because they're great talkers, and this co-counselling mob seems to hate talk. And my dream party was lively, inspired, dancing, talking, cavorting. Marty Washburn was there, elated, comic. A small Scots lad, very handsome, laid eyes on a diminutive Scots lass, very pretty and feisty, and they fell madly in love and she shouted a gay announcement of their troth: "Look what Fate has sent me! What a fine lad to wrap my shawl around! Which I will! I'm his forever, and may he use me heavily and reductively."

That phrase *heavily and reductively* delighted me in the dream. Later I wondered where it had come from.

Gretel Ehrlich
From the Journals

Spring, 1985

ALL THESE PENT-UP LUSTS, PASSIONS, SORROWS, RAGES AT POLITICAL CORRUPTION, CORROsion of the spirit, unnecessary deaths, discriminations, impossible loves . . . what are these? Why do I collapse across my writing table, the sun full on me, the day spectacular, and cry? Why do I feel, not bored, but unused (in the best sense) by a society enslaved? Against mediocrity, against a society that refuses to find solutions to real problems, but only tinkers, whose ingenuity is restricted to the perpetuation of the frivolous . . . against this and against the living dead, the brain-dead, the dead-beats, the heartbeats that make no noise— what sharpness and number of swords could prick holes into the dogmas of greed?

March 31

Dream of the long, twisted branch of a eucalyptus tree with a huge bowl-like nest at the very end and a scarlet tananger flying to and from the nest with a single piece of straw in its beak which she had brought all the way from another part of California.

From Ionesco: "Nothing is true except what happens in dreams within the imaginary world. Realism is an odious fraud. Someone who is a realist is someone who only sees part of reality, who uses this to prop up dogma, an ideology that will pass. . . ."

Then the day really does go, sallow light washes the room like something spit out. Motionless I watch the windows go black and the hayfields bend away in green silence.

April 1

What Flaubert refers to as the "*mélancholies du voyage*" is like the sadness I feel as one season departs and another arrives.

The only restaurant and bar in Shell, the only place for us to gather, was burned down last night, the result of a feud.

June 19

Watched Ray Hunt work with young colts today. He says: "You have to find the life in the body of the horse. It's a force that either tries to escape or gets redirected in circular shapes. Everything goes in a circle, the world ain't flat, and a wheel moves smoothly. When the horse is smooth you can feel the life going through from the hind end, through the feet, into the mind. When the horse's mind gets congested, when his thoughts get wadded up, when he's acting out of control with no thought for the person—there can be a lot of anguish in this. Watch him. When he begins letting his energy go all the way through, when he begins doing the right thing, the easy thing, then he's at peace with the world and with himself."

June 26

Irrigating the lower place, I smell something sweet and look up to see irises blooming. Planted fifty years ago by the homesteader, they still bloom, untended, with no house or gardener nearby. Amazing, in this harsh place where almost nothing grows, where flowers are stunted by deer, elk, cattle, horses, or by miserable heat or cold. Dream that the lights in a tall Manhattan building going on and off all night are really flowers.

July 1

A wild wind comes up. Rain begins and stops. Now it's just blowing and no rain comes out of it; it's blowing the dryness around, mocking our desert needs, blowing the water out of the creeks, blowing the cows down. My colt bucks in place as if the wind had lifted his hind quarters. The sudden lightness we feel is gravity bucking in a wild wind.

July 2

Flaubert: "What a heavy oar the pen is and what a strong current ideas are to row in."

July 4

Cowcamp. Go to bed in the back of my pickup because the bunkhouses were full. The stars above a lone pine tree look like a Ukiyoe print. A string of clouds passes, shaped like carpenter's tools shaken out across the sky. I feel happy and forlorn.

July 15

> Then the days stretch out like single rods
> the color of rust, nicked and scored by the various
> sexual heats, limbic vines twist and travel, bunching
> out in grapes, their green antennae vining my arms,
> and all that we know, which, twisted against who
> we are, climbs the trellis of the day.

July 17

98° in the shade. A whirling leaf catching the light falls like a cinder.

August 2

"Phillips looked away, as he sometimes looked away from the great pictures where visible forms suddenly become inadequate for the things they have shown to us."—E. M. Forster.

August 5

Rain finally. And then, still unbound, the clatter of cicadas clacking high up in every tree, over the wide square of the lake. The mind dappled by sound. Everything resembles the mind, big and small, or, the mind resembles everything in nature, the diffident, resounding chaos. Feel sick, then hungry, then a fast trip to the outhouse. Lie naked in the sun, then sit up with shirt on. Shoes on, then off, all the while, the green that came as suddenly as a blaze because of the rains, loses its tint as if drought blanched and bleached everything it touched, blades of grass are brown fingers of death pointing. A conference of sedimentologists crawls up and down the dry hills on this once-upon-a-time ocean: David Love, Mary Kraus, David Uhlir all say: each rock, each stratum of soil tells such a deep, unfolding story of how the continent was made. Sitting on the lawn outside the banker's house, Tom Brown says, "Knowledge is an upside-down pyramid, starting at a narrow point and forever expanding . . ." Go home and watch the moon rise through binoculars. It is more spectacular for its not being quite full, for its imperfection, and Jupiter's tiny moons are like earrings. From this night on, there will be geologists in my life.

Morning. I walk. I don't cry *about* my life, but cry because of its fullness. The road is dry, kiln-dried with the glaze cracked or is it porcelain without a sheen? The birds' flight grows effortless as the drought continues, pulls the drawstring of moisture. In the colorless sky—what is there?—the geologists visit again and I turn groundward from shifting shadows and heats, changing breezes, wafting sounds of another drainage; choke-cherries ripening and the grass dying and the squash growing obscenely large in soil that cradled shallow seas and submitted to ash that fell continuously for ten thousand years. . . .

August 14

Why is my heart racing? I open the window. Have I been holding my breath all my life? Rocks dance. Their jetés are violent upthrusts, unlimbed blunt percussions. I skitter on subduction faults, detachment faults—like Heart Mountain, which moved twice; and down its rock face, red streaks—like the Buddhist's red threads of passion. Night. The back legs of running horses emit sparks; the moonless sky gathers them.

I lie in bed. The day is motionless, or so I think. But the tectonic plates are at odds. In my California home, they crash against each other, the continent moving west and the Pacific plates moving east. Here, granite pushes against sedimentary rock, producing undulations—synclines and anticlines result and rock, big as a mountain, is thrust up, upended.

August 27

Imagined poverty, real asceticism, the need, always to feel the rockiness of life, and in places where there are berries, the thorns. In ordinary life, in sex, in writing, I laugh at how stiffness and softness trade places. After lovemaking, a softness pervades all parts of the body. One surrenders further, gives up the idea of surrendering, the pretense of acceptance, real fear and self-delusion. Gradually, you harden again and I laugh because it's not just desire but the flip side of what has just come before: it is a gesture of protection, self-defense, an instinct to move against death.

At every moment, we're fractured this way, going toward death, then life, so there is, everywhere, a constant movement, a swelling and deflating, an urge to accommodate opposites. Life magnetizes death and death magnetizes life; we grapple at the edge of things, save ourselves though we don't know it, thrash in the current, hold out compasses that do not give us true north, and leave behind only the beautiful, dunelike, evanescent ripples of each foray, fossilized in rock.

August 28

Dream. I entered a bookstore that became a foodstore. There were booths, as at a county fair. I stopped at one where two naked men with long ponytails were making vinegar. They asked me to taste some and I did. "It's Chinese," I said and they laughed, retorting, "But we're Italian." The vinegar tasted like bean paste mixed with something acrid. I said I'd buy a bottle. Before capping it, they cut off the tentacles of an octopus and dropped them in.

September 1

Woke up cold. Slept with a shotgun on my bed because there's a horse rustler loose, the sheriff said. He made me put the phone by my bed with his home phone number emblazoned on the receiver—"Call if you hear or see anything strange in the night," he said. But there was nothing. Stayed in bed and reread the opening portions of *A Farewell to Arms*. It's like jumping into a symphony. I was swept up at once, then it was music all the way through.

"A holy man named Shinkai was so aware of the impermanence of the world that he never even sat down and relaxed, but always remained crouching."—The Tsurezuregusa of Kenko.

September 17

Annie Dillard talks about how the narrative line has been devalued by modern physics. The narrative line to me is like a Mexican mural: flattened in perspective so all is present; cramped by detail, erotic, various, the flat depth held up in the imagination, its transience, and impermanence nakedly apparent. The narrative does not lead from one place to another, from the past to the future, but more deeply into the present, always the present and its sense of time is in tune with the human heart rather than the chessman's calculating mind; present moves are a means to the future. The narrative line, then, is at rest and jostling at the same time. Like a sonogram of a pregnant woman's belly: the fetus' tiny heartbeat jostled by gas.

September 19

Rain tonight, a slow steady drizzle. I cook a pork roast and drink wine. How delightful after a summer of garden vegetables. Wang Fan-Chih writes:

> All of us receive an empty body
> All of us take the universe's breath
> We die and still must live again
> come back to earth all recollection lost.
> Ai! no more than this?
> Think hard about it
> All things turn stale and flat on the tongue
> It comforts people? No
> Better now and again
> to get blind drunk on the floor
> alone.

September 21

Now when I look out across the Basin I see not just ocean (mirage) but shallow seas, geological twists of fate, ancient depositions like thoughts stacked up, rotting ash, and overhead, the tail of a comet. Recently, they sent a satellite through its tail, its "plasma," which is the primal matter of the universe, its particulars. How delighted W. C. Williams would have been. I think about newness, about primacies of all sorts, about the earth's crust and mantle, how water that is new—"juvenile water"—comes up through the ocean floor and mixes with water that has received the earth's salts. . . . During an intense earthquake, the earth liquifies.

   I drink and drink to sleep so I won't dream of emeralds or be dropped in cactus or watch the elk, carved by anazazi into rock, jump into the universe where they will be shot down by men. Is this fall storm a form of sadness that originates in comet tails, a sadness that has been here from the moment of the big bang?

   Italo Calvino died Thursday of a stroke in Siena.

October 7

Get up at 3:30 A.M. drive to the mountain for first day of roundup and, holding my saddle on my arm, am sent home by Stan because of my bad cold. "You've already had pneumonia this year and you ain't gettin' it again on my outfit," he said. Vitality zapped. Laundry hanging on the line goes stiff with ice. I've been working on my novel for five months and am still rewriting the first twenty-five pages. I'm suffering from seasonal violence: no fall this year. We went from heat and drought to winter with only one brief interlude of rain. I want to sit quietly and be warm.

October 11

I want to feel snow come down in me; to know its precise quality; to give it words.
   "Ontological neurosis—an hysteria of being."

October 19

I go east. At a friend's house I'm fed, loved, kept warm. We listen to opera in the middle of the night and I find myself sobbing. The scars of last winter's serious illness dissolve. I relax for the first time in two years.

October 22

At a party, someone talks about adolescent sex: "The first time I beat off, I did it on a rock. The rock was covered with lichen. I can't remember what color it was. The forest was wet and dark."

October 25

Dinner in Chinatown with Dan Halpern, Carolyn Forché, Harry Mattison, Grace Schulman, Bill Matthews, Russell Banks, etc. In the middle of dinner, Harry gets up and rubs Dan's shoulders. "You look tired," he says. He has to have his hands on things always and I love the intense way he looks at each of us. "When I went to visit Carolyn's writing class at Columbia, I told the students they were underprivileged. 'You haven't had the privilege of poverty, of war, or suffering . . .'" That, because they've just returned from years in Central America, the Middle East, and next, South Africa. But I wonder—to keep ourselves honed, must we always sit in the charnel ground, must we always go to the battlefields of the world, isn't all of that here and everywhere, if we'd only see it, sense it, extend our sympathies sufficiently to know the sorrows of plants, earth, watersheds, animals, ourselves?

October 26

Dinner at Carla Maxwell's. It's her fortieth birthday. Among the guests are Pina Bausch's company from Germany. While they converse in German, Carla and I drink champagne from martini glasses, shove our chairs back, and dance to the music of Sophie Tucker singing, "Life Begins at Forty."

October 28

In Vermont, I see a weeping willow whose soft branches, blowing in the wind, look like shoulders heaving—breathlessness or tears?

Halloween

I walk in the Village Halloween parade with Ted Hoagland. He's dressed like a fox and we stop midavenue and howl. The streets are packed, blocked completely from traffic and everywhere I look I see smiling faces—a glorious moment for New York. The parade is made up of undulating dragons, twenty-foot-high puppets, dancing skeletons, African drummers, a single Puerto Rican dandy, coyote-women and wolf-men, all of us carrying tall corn stalks, our flags, our pledge of allegiance to maize. After the parade breaks up at Washington Square, we drift west, through carless streets. One 6'8" transvestite dressed in a girl's cheerleading suit twirls a baton and, holding a ghetto blaster under the other arm, strides to a Sousa march. On Bleecker Street, a man with a raincoat leans back against stairs. As we pass, he flashes: a huge fabric penis springs out toward us—ten feet long, to much laughter.

Thanksgiving

In Jackson's Hole. Give Mardy Murie "Solace." The next day she said she stayed up half the night reading it, then hugs me, and speaks in a gentle voice about it. We talk wolves, mountain lions, and about why coyotes howl.

November 30

Six below zero. What is beyond Desire, but Desire?

December 3

Saw Steve Canady in the post office. Asked him how he liked my book. He said, "Well, hell, I haven't finished it yet . . . where'd you get all them eight-cylinder words?"

December 10

Dream: I was leading horses across a dam bank to a pasture in the trees. Halfway across, the horses became "horse-men"—human faces, animal bodies. They had gathered at a monastery in the trees. A long white carpet had been laid down as an aisle through the middle of these "disciples." A priest or lama held a huge silver chalice filled with red wine. As everyone turned toward him, he hurled the chalice and the wine spilled across the white rug. I led the horse-men away.

December 18

My friend, my pal, the one most like a younger brother, the one his father wanted me to marry, the best cowboy I've ridden with, the most moral, dignified, wild of them all, the wisest, the oldest for his age as if he were his father—an exact replica in a young man's body, died today. This place, this Wyoming, these days of cowboying will never be the same without him. Can I even write his name? Joel, Joey, Little Smoke . . .

January 4, 1986

Robert Graves died last week. I read his poem aloud to Joel's friends:

Take delight in
momentariness,
Walk between dark and dark—
A shining space
With the grave's narrowness
though not its peace.

January 5

Desolation after desolation rolls through me. When Joel's father—Smokey—was rolled into the church in a wheelchair (he'd taken ill after Joel's death), he shook the coffin and cried out, "Why have you done this to me? Everything I did in my life was for you."

As for the verity of rural constancy, of sameness, there is no such thing. I know that of course. If I know anything, it is to expect impermanence . . . and yet . . .

January 14

Last night, saw Comet Halley, gauzy-tailed, moving from left to right, from southwest to northeast, with a beautiful, constrained sense of falling, as if flung against a resistent cloth, but coming anyway, the way people newly in love sometimes do. It was a movement so large, so cosmically grandiose, that its course could not be perceived, yet the overpowering feeling on sighting it in amongst the other glass eyes, was precisely that—of a surging descent, an elegant, unstoppable fall as if the comet were very heavy and the air dense.

Because it's warm, the dogs lie out in the snow.

February

Snow on snow on snow and bright hot cobalt days. After eight hours at the typewriter, the dogs get me, and I ski off the veranda until dark.

March

"A poet's morality is the morality of the right sensation."—Wallace Stevens.

Meanwhile, a tongue-shaped cloud dominates the entire sky. Dantean hell—an historical darkness as well as a momentary one; visionary signs, not just descriptions; the residue of phenomenal shimmerings, of lost heats, natural irridescence; erotic intensities without any specific mention of it.

◦ ◦ ◦

"Matter gets its 'moving orders' directly from space itself, so that rather than regarding gravity as a force, it should be viewed as a geometry."—John Wheeler.

June 14

Eyes itch, grass going to seed, the strange cry of a bird by the lake we can't see or identify. Shot a rattlesnake with my .410 yesterday. It was coiled only six inches from my leg.

At the rodeo Chrissy Fitch came into the grandstands holding a bird's nest. She walked through the stands yelling at everyone to look at it!

Thinking of the word "crush"—denoting St. Augustine's "weight of love." What if love (infatuation, a crush on somebody) were viewed like matter, not as a force, but as a geometry . . .

June 16

Talked with someone I've loved this morning, in person. His physical presence—and the charged air between our two bodies—heavy, saturated, Mahleresque, a complex music with rocking, emotional swells, a flashflood of red creekwater drenching us suddenly, then gone dry, to bone.

June 18

To make a book of essays, a book of questions.

June 19

My colt ran away with me two days ago and I baled off on my ass. No injuries, just bruises.

June 26

> The balm of the body—
> What of that?
> Against consciousness' hurling and the
> clock's eventful diatribe. Sweat
> links us uncoupled. Mind
> hurts like a fist
> through glass. White brain, knob
> of indecency.

July 17

Bucked off on my head. Hung in there, checked the cows, though I have no idea what I was looking at, rode home, helped Press trailer a horse to the neighbors, as he's leaving today. Face cut and swollen.

July 18

I'm having trouble seeing. Blotches of black behind my eyes. I feel dizzy, nauseous, disoriented. My eyes don't move in my head. Press gone. I feel like a blind person, troubling surfaces with tentative hands because my—head doesn't work. Drive to Shell—so hard to see, have to stop and look for the road, then continue slowly on. A friend takes me to the hospital. The doctor tells me he hates horses. Nice bedside manner. I'm having a little hemorrhage, that's all, and they may have to med-vac me to Billings to drill holes in my skull. How will I find Press, get him out of the mountains?

Cat scan. They tape my head and chin down, then I have to pee. Strapped down a second time, I move backward. This is like a tunnel of love, I think, only a tunnel of light and eerie, spacey silence, the kind of white noise a distant waterfall makes, hushed . . .

I'm sent home with my hulk of a nurse. He carries me from the pickup and lays me on the couch where I will stay for the rest of the summer, unable to read, think, laugh, feel the gaiety of anything. I feel betrayed by my colt; or else, out of stupidity, I betrayed him. After he got me off his back, he ran up a hill and back to me again, then turned and kicked me. The more afraid I am of him, the more afraid he is of me, but I'm down for the count now and know I must get rid of him.

July 24

The black behind my eyes has gone and I can see but don't want to. Head pressure, as if the brain tissue were jellyfish, not muscle with nerves; I have no nerve; nothing connects. People come and go. I can't see, truly, who they are. No memory loss, but eyes water, and it's sometimes hard to talk. Then there are glitches, or is that just age? Ursula comes and goes. She looks like a moon, a mermaid—big, graceful, quiet, bright—lovely. A letter: Dear Puffy, I was so afraid I would die and join David and Joel in a limbo that looked like intestines and smelled of human gas. Anyway, because of the face cuts and swelling, my smile isn't right.

July 25

I remember one moment—airborne—hunched over the colt's withers and right shoulder, but I don't remember how I must have rolled to my right, legs splayed, stomach skidding the ground.

Birds. That's all I look at. Today a scarlet tanager makes me happy, then a belted kingfisher during a forbidden drive to the mailbox, and at home, two baby swallows learning to fly.

July 26

Rain. Wake with the same headache, the same lack of desire, the same deadness inside. Nothing stirs me. The twenty-five roosters we raised from chicks spar under the parked pickup truck as if the shaded space between the four wheels was a ring.

July 28

Despair that rambles. This injury is a form of psychic isolation. It plucks my head out of the stream and holds it dry and dark and motionless on a rock where no one can see me. No one who comes around can feel the bruise-heat or the coolness of no desire. My head feels as if it might topple from a frail stem.

August 10

And after the piquant verdancy, all the grasses are rolled up, and the wind funnels them and they drop as something black behind my eyes. Some days to touch you would be everything, would be a single lifetime smoking under a magnifying glass, a single flame. All the clichéd words of ardor make sense to me: flame, crush, sweetheart. Last night, the crescent moon fell down west of my body. A thin cloud pierced it, making a black stitch. Hips jut up from cool sheets—architectural, continental—I opened my eyes and saw where the Milky Way ended, where its white heat tapered off in indigo and in the north, where it began again.

August 25

Tenderness, self-mockery, depression, carefree jocularity, sadness, isolation.

September

A correspondence between the body and the natural world. An equality—between everything and everything. Oceanic cadences.

As he/she drives away, the loins, then the heart actually cramp.

October

Hunting Camp (thankfully, without hunters). The top of Little Baldy—bright silver—pink sky, then steam rising from snow. Air is mist and clouds are snowfalls going elsewhere.

October 10

Hot sun on snow. A howling wind before I woke made me dream about surf—the correlations between water movement, midsea currents, and currents of air. The winds are tides; tides are moons; moons are drops of water. . . . The horses lie down in midday sun.

October 22

"I remember at the Albany airport how you called me sweetie by mistake and how you held me and it made me miss the way you would have been if you had loved me years before. I'm out of my mind here, the wind howls, the green leeches into a white sky. I don't know, maybe it's the time of year or the time of life. I've loved you for twenty years—first, with a childish, shut-mouthed, suicidal passion, and now, with a voluble longing that does not have as its end, any thought of possession . . ."

October 25

Soseki's (the Japanese novelist) wife was so suicidal, he tied himself to her at night so she couldn't get out of bed while he was asleep.

October 27

Hunting in full swing here. Gunshots volley at Hudson Falls—as if bullets were being fired into a woman's vagina. That's how hunting makes me feel. Every sacred place here sullied. These men gun down bulls and bucks who are in rut, as if abridging sexuality, subsuming virility, making the animals' power their own. And only the ornament of big horns and antlers will satisfy them—not the palatability of the meat. To hunt for meat is one thing, to kill for sport is unconscionable.

November

Miami Book Fair. Hot nights, hot days, swinging palms, jet-powered speedboats, a draw-bridge that opens at my feet, Richard Ford's sweet volubility—where his stories are hard and spare, his presence is tender and talkative.

Key West

I go straight to Hemingway's house and where I thought it would be on a high hill with a winding driveway and coral walls and a grand, breezy view of the sea, it is on the same flat that all of Key West is on, shrouded by trees, cheaply furnished, and all the rooms stink with catpiss. Fly north across the Keys at dawn.

I meet, by chance, a childhood friend who's been a close aide to Reagan in the White House. Despite moral and political differences so huge as to be ridiculous, the old closeness, the childhood affinity built on horseback and beaches remains innocently there. How is this possible?

Richard Ford's pale, ice eyes, the sadness in his hands as he reads from his work, and afterward, his amiable chatter.

I find Stephen Spender wandering around the lobby looking for the door. It's a confusing place. I guide him to the exit. The next night, come in from dinner to find the lobby and three of the floors filled with black families there for a reunion of a black sorority. A wonderful liveliness fills the place—laughter, talking, drinking, singing everywhere. We get out of the elevator, all heads turn to us. Are we on the right floor? C. asks, and everyone laughs. Drinks are offered.

Dialogue:

> Why are we doing this?
> Because we're getting old. We want to find out what we missed as children.
> My dear. May I call you that? You won't be mad?
> Stop teasing.
> I'm not. (Then he teases.)
> But you are.
> No, that's different.
> I can never tell if you're serious.

> (Their legs float out behind them like bait for the past that lies submerged
> under hot, green water.)

Sunday

Dreamed that I was in small room with a huge north window and one of the characters from my novel, Carol Lyman, took a picture of me.

November 19

Home. A gray day and colder than it looks, than it could possibly be. Winter is a betrayal. I ski on it, imperially, but I am the one who is conquered.

A child's prescience—for which he/she gets no credit—i.e., the way we pick people to love who, years after, are still loved by us. But in between, a Dantean journey—hellish years swaying between childhood and maturity. We know everything about who we are, what we need to survive, to be human; then it's forgotten, confused with other things and, like misguided missiles fired from Vandeberg at dawn, we shoot out over the horizonless sea . . . and only if we're lucky, do we ever come back. By age six, I knew everything I know now. By age twelve, I had loved seriously, two men whom I still love now.

December 18

The anniversary of Joel's death. Get up at 3:00 A.M. A glowing, red and yellow star falls, exploding across the sky. At dawn, go for a walk. A coyote runs across lake ice up Grouse Hill. At lunch I cut an artery with a knife by mistake and think of the priest on the Reservation whose throat was cut. He bled to death because no one had the sense to pinch the bleeding artery closed. I stop the flow of my own blood with a butterfly bandage. Touching it is like touching my pumping heart, like putting my hand deep inside my own body.

December 20

Seeing way back into his eyes: the jolt of the handshake—lightning.

December 21

Winter Solstice.

> A grasping buffeting wind brings clouds
> back—the blue above us
> shrunken as if soured. Up steep
> stairs your ghost-hands
> tremble me
> against blue horseblankets. We strike down
> where the lightning is woven through
> and the cloudbank, the
> white deep, stretches. Treebark slips
> and drops all-of-a-piece
> and you gather my breasts to your hunger.

June 3, 1987

Rain stopped. Now the sky was stretch marks: clouds thin as scar tissue. High water scours out a hidden room in rock and rolls its silt into our pastures, mounding them with red sand. When Chernobyl burned, one of the radioactive clouds blew over Wyoming. It rained that day and as I was irrigating, pulling and setting dams, the diamonds of water in new grass looked poisoned and I hated the green that came. Everything conspires to do the planet in— perhaps it hurts more to see it happen in this pristine-seeming landscape where water mixes with farmer's chemicals, where birds and coyotes are poisoned, where the air has, for the first time, taken on a dull, smokey look, so that each tiny affront to life, even the killing of a fly, is torture to me. I look away.

June 9

Driving home from Cody, an antelope runs with her two tiny twins behind her. They're so small—but perfectly shaped and colored. They run with their mouths open, drinking air . . . beautiful miniatures.

Dream: he and I were in a Japanese shopping arcade, like the ones in Kyoto, buying silk kimonos and bamboo fishing rods. We were sent to a waiting room, but it was a train platform. We stood, as at the edge of a planet, no sound of a train, only wind. I said, "This is the kind of wind that brings black rain. They have that here." The way we stood, our bodies touched, so bonded and linked, he said, "Listen. Our bodies read our minds."

More rain. Flash floods. Summer tries to come but fails.

June 13

Bluebird is dead. My horse who has been with me since I came to Wyoming, who has herded sheep, followed me from town to town, tracked cattle . . . who, clownishly, shared pans of dogfood with Rusty, clambered up stairs to the veranda and looked in the house, who often stuck his head in the kitchen door on summer days to beg for cookies, who would not be caught the first six months I owned him just to show who had the upper hand, who never bucked, who hated most men, who was so ugly, big-headed, hairy-legged that some ranchers refused to haul him in their trailers, who was the butt of many jokes, who laughed silently at all of us, who knew things but wouldn't tell me except when I wasn't asking, who gave me a look one day that told me something about the pain of not having language, of the longing to have a communication that was not muddled (on my part), that said, "Animals know things and want things too," who comforted me because we shared hard winters and harrowing lonely years.

Press found him, standing in the corner of the pasture, eating, with his back leg broken in three places, hanging off. To think of that moment of betrayal, of aiming a gun at him and he knew what it was for and why but a betrayal is a betrayal . . . that is and always will be unimaginable. It stops me. It is untouchable.

June 24

Alone in the house, husbandless, horseless, for the first time since November. Now I have the longed-for solitude but I have to wonder which is the greater vanity—solitude in the midst of physical beauty, or the agitated effect of people who stir my heart. The clean pages of this notebook console me. A new beginning after the mire of a long work. Though I know better than to think there are ever new beginnings. Like the walk I took this afternoon—I followed the creek downhill through a field of lilies, blooming cactus. I stared hard at a small waterfall. Ravens tumbled in the dark blue air. But the stench of my dead horse's decaying body permeated the valley. It is the last thing I will know about him.

I pick up a rock. It breaks open in my hand. Inside, its red and blue-gray agate looks like a legbone surrounded by flesh. Like Blue's back leg, broken, dangling. Later, one lazuli bunting comes again and again to the birdfeeder to eat seed, its neck feathers irridescent, turquoise.

July

He sleeps with his mouth open, head back, legs wobbling from side to side, the animal beard stiff in sunlight. He sleeps on his back, one leg hiked up, arms out, wrists loose, fingers spread, like a crane landing. "I feel like a lizard crawling over you, over the sun of you, over the smooth, sweet beauty of your body."

Tesuque, N.M. Arrived at Charlie and Michele's to find them bent over the radio. Three convicts are loose and believed to be in their area. We go out for dinner. The house is at the bottom of a narrow dirt road that winds through arroyos and barrancas and there are no locks on the doors or screens on the windows. "Let them hide here," Charlie says. Coming home, we see the light of a helicopter swinging over piñon trees and bare ground. There are roadblocks on every highway. Cops come and go. "Who are you?" they ask, shining a light into my face. I feel like saying, "I don't know." Three days later, the escapees are discovered in California.

Home and I'm reeling. The sky is black with swallows. It snowed on Bastille Day; a baby bird fell out of its nest and broke its neck; a rabbit is eating its way out of my garden. During my absence, the lake filled so much my blue canoe came unmoored and floats empty. I like talking to you; I'm reeling from that also, my brainstem-bodystem—carbonated. I feel giddy thinking of having you in my life in the human "forever," or in your Franciscan heaven, or if not in the after-life, then now, no?

God, it's beautiful here . . . lazuli buntings follow the cattle flying up creekbeds and the stiff purple heads of timothy grass teetering on the windy brink of fruition. But there's no one to talk to—no one of like mind, though now I feel as if we were talking all the time, even when you have other women in your arms and you're not listening and I'm laughing at you.

Today I cowboyed. Someone opened the gates on the lower pasture and the cows scattered. I gathered them and trailed them to the pasture by the house. Later, I drank late enough with friends that the Milky Way was hard over our heads like the rib of a whale and your voice came into the noise of my sleep waking me to laughter.

August

Desire. In the midst of people—relatives, children, spouses, he took my hand and said, Let's go to Lake Tahoe (where I've never been). I said yes. We went to a whorehouse built out over the water. The view of the lake was astonishing—black water like lacquer and a huge silhouette of a heron looming close. X told the madame that we wanted a room for a few hours. She laughed at us, our desperation and innocence, and showed us to a tiny space: a mattress fit into a glass cube cantelevered way out over the water—fifty feet or so. When she left we crawled under the comforters and made love over and over and over. There was no stopping it. But once I looked down at the water and asked why it was so black.

❧ ❧ ❧

Albuquerque again. At the airport, rented a car. When they saw that I was working for *Time* magazine they said, "Oh, are you covering the Harmonic Convergence?" I laughed and said no. Airport chock full of all sorts—latter-day hippies, women with painted fingernails clutching crystals, long-hairs with guitars and bedrolls, a group of garrulous girls from New Jersey. Drove to Tesuque. Charlie and I make drinks and sit on the patio. We can see Los Alamos from there—a direct shot west from his house. The air smells of mineral. We laugh about the "Convergence," we two childhood friends whose lives converge and reconverge in odd, persistent ways. His beeper goes off. He's the medic and fire chief and is always on call. There's a woman at the Bingo Parlor hyperventilating. "She probably lost all her money," Charlie says, as we take off, siren on, red light flashing on top of his car. Bingo parlors are big on Indian Reservations. We run into a tiny room off the enormous, cavernous "parlor"—as big as a K-mart with rows and rows of tables and metal folding chairs, neon lights, and a fish-faced man on a perch in front of a transparent globe bursting with numbered Ping-Pong balls, and women, often siting in pairs, smoking and drinking RC Cola and cherry Coke, bent over their cards.

The woman in question is middle-aged, obese, and hysterical. We put a paper bag over her nose and mouth—high tech, no? and tell her to breathe calmly. She doesn't know "calm." She pants distractedly. Charlie takes her pulse, and tries to soothe her. Nothing works. He listens to her heart and gives her oxygen. She keeps taking the little mask away to talk and he puts it back over her nose. "I'm dying, I'm dying . . ." she keeps crying in a loud voice. "No you're not," he says. Finally, the ambulance comes and we go to dinner. Later, we lie out on the lawn. Are we converging? I ask. A weather satellite draws a straight line through erupting meteor showers and I feel what I can only call a molecular lushness close to my face: the deep powder of friendship. I breathe in. We sleep and roam the hills at dawn.

August 21

I walk along the high road by the lake, muttering to myself. Dreamed I lay across a topographical map of California. The wrinkled top sheet on my feet was a mountain range and a valley. I moved my toes across it, feeling each feature of the landscape. He lay diagonally across the central part of the state. He stared at me and, finally, smiled. "Welcome home," he said, extending his arms, and flying across a vast distance, I let him embrace me. Now, walking, I feel as if my ankles are tied and I'm stretched over the edge of a dark universe. Yet I see things. But what are they to me or I to them? What is my geographical destiny?

November 16

Nothing matters but this. It demolishes the days and happily turns them into passageways. All has become a gangplank to you. I walk the turnabouts, the hesitancies and all goes like smoke, twisting into air. We meet in the eye of our own storm and grope over the rich debris of impossible love. The calm is the false calm of loss and union commingling, of simultaneous hopelessness and fruition. (novel notes)

January 21, 1988

After a morning snowfall—hours of melting quiet—a wind, high in the timbered mountains, issues a steady, hushed roar. If the bicameral mind is two very different things, then the heart is also—like the towering split rock through which a creek patiently drives. The waterfall of my imagination and the real one whose cataracts I climb like a vine, lifts out of my life and goes into my novel, then comes free again. Walking there today, on my birthday, I see that a huge chunk of ice has dropped out of the middle of the frozen cascade, leaving black, wet rock exposed. And so it is with me . . .

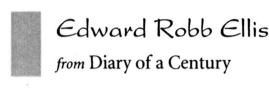

Edward Robb Ellis

from Diary of a Century

1974

THURSDAY, AUGUST 8, 1974

JANET STEINBERG CALLED FROM HER OFFICE TO SAY THERE ARE RUMORS THAT NIXON WILL resign today. And he did!

At 6 P.M. I turned on my TV set and continued to watch it until 1 A.M., for the networks gave massive coverage to this historic event.

I suppose I was like many other Americans in feeling that this was not happening, that it was some surrealistic experience, for never in the history of this nation had any President resigned from office. For a fleeting moment I wondered whether Nixon would end his resignation speech on TV and then pull out a revolver and shoot himself in the head. The other day this was done by a young woman who worked as a newscaster for some TV station. However, I've always felt Nixon never will take his life. Instead, to quote one commentator tonight, he has committed "psychic suicide." I agree.

Why did Nixon let that tape recorder run when he and his aides were discussing criminal acts? Why did he fail to destroy the tapes after their existence became known? Down through all the years I have seen Nixon on TV—and once shook hands with him—I felt he was a man who did not know himself. He never behaved naturally. His every gesture was calculated, not casual. He is awkward, not graceful. For a long time I have paid attention to his rapid eye blink, which I consider a sign that a man is trying to hide something. Having hidden himself from himself, he worked hard at hiding his true self from the public. The total political animal, he nonetheless managed to protect an image of himself that was accepted as reality by the 47 million Americans who voted for him the last time.

Born in humble circumstances, clawing his way to the top, all his life he may have been plagued with the queasy feeling that at bottom he did not amount to much. Yet, by god, he would show everyone what he could do! But when at last he won the highest honor in the land he may have felt he did not deserve the honor, and so set out on a course ending in self-destruction. At least he may have the satisfaction of having been brought down by his own behavior, rather than by some outside agency. I realize I am indulging in amateur analysis about a very complex man—but why not? His actions practically beg for it.

All his life Nixon has behaved as though he were alone in this world, and to feel all alone is to be mad. Nixon's conscious mind is brilliant, as was Hitler's, and on this level he functioned very well. He sometimes raged that the enemy was the public, but in fact the enemy was his unconscious. Since he seldom glimpsed his soul he lived his life split down the middle—a schizophrenic. As is well known, many schizophrenics are brilliant.

Suddenly I am struck with a strange thought: In some dim and uncomprehending way, Nixon may have regarded those tapes as his unconscious, the part of him seldom seen by himself or others, and maybe he preserved them because he was trying to preserve his sanity, his very life. Although full disclosure of the tapes would destroy him, he clung to them in a compulsion beyond his rational will.

I recalled that famous poster with a leering Nixon and the caption: "Would you buy a used car from this man?" The person who prepared that poster was a close student of human nature. What the American public almost bought from Nixon was fascism. Except for the Joe McCarthy era, never had this nation come so close to totalitarianism as in the last two years of the Nixon administration. This evening some TV commentators declared that today's event proved that our political system works, that the checks and balances among the three branches of government proved adequate to the crisis, but I wonder why we let ourselves get this close to a dictatorship.

As I lay in bed watching the final act in the fall of the most powerful person on earth, I recalled the times when Ruthie and I watched crises together, such as the assassination and burial of President Kennedy.

At 9 P.M. Nixon appeared on TV, speaking from the White House. I wrote notes on a clipboard as I watched: . . . Nixon's face was a ruins . . . his cheeks sagged . . . his voice quavered at times . . . he was close to tears . . . he looked very old . . . a few times he smiled a weak smile . . . he was barely holding himself together . . . never natural, he now looked more artificial than ever . . . he has ugly hands, and with his right hand he made little, chopping motions on the top of the desk . . . he said he had made errors of judgment, confessed to no crime, extolled his record as President, especially in foreign affairs . . . trying to the very end to sound like a statesman, he sounded instead like a madman in a mental hospital insisting that he is Napoleon . . . once the idol of millions of people, Nixon now is so powerless that he finished talking to himself.

He spoke for 16 minutes and at the end his lower lip quavered. I would not be surprised to learn that the next moment he burst into tears.

Then came the comments on television. Some of the TV reporters who covered Nixon tried so hard not to gloat over his fall that they went to the other extreme and called his speech "majestic." Majestic? It was cheap. Nixon said: "I have never been a quitter!" No? He quit today.

1975
SUNDAY, FEBRUARY 2, 1975

As I do every Sunday morning, I drank coffee while reading the *Times* and then came into this study to write my diary. To my surprise, my fingers stumbled over the keys. My mind was dull. I felt so dizzy I thought I might faint—something that never happened to me in my life. I was disoriented. I was not hung-over. I'd never felt like this before. Aware I would be unable to work on my book, I just loafed all afternoon and evening.

At midnight I was awake when I got a call from Eugene, Oregon. No, it was not my daughter calling, but a friend of hers named Barbara Smith, whom I'd never met. In a hesitant voice she said Sandy had been in a terrible auto accident, a three-car crash, and is badly injured. Even as Barbara spoke, Sandy was in a hospital undergoing emergency surgery. I felt as though a sledgehammer had hit my heart. My voice trembling, I asked Barbara whether Sandy might die. Barbara replied that she will live, but I detected a note of uncertainty in her voice. I began weeping. This alarmed Barbara, who urged me to get someone to stay with me.

I went into shock. Nine years ago my wife died. Now my daughter may be taken from me. Sitting like a lump on the edge of the bed I wailed aloud . . . confusion . . . mind blank . . . fear . . . I started to feel cold . . . losing control . . . slipping into hysteria. To be a writer is a curious thing because a part of me stands back to watch the other part. My mind collapsed like a heap of strings.

Shaking all over, I called relatives and friends. Time passed—I don't know how much. Then, beginning to get ahold of myself, I called the hospital in Eugene and spoke to the surgeon who had attended Sandy. She had been in the operating room two and a half hours.

EUGENE, OREGON, JUNE 10—JUNE 25, 1975

Sandy's doctors decided that she should recuperate awhile before undergoing reconstructive surgery. When I learned that this operation was sheduled for June 11, my sister Kay and I flew to Oregon to be with Sandy for the operation. The two weeks I've been away from home I've been unable to keep my diary, so what I now write is only impressionistic.

I was shocked when I saw my daughter. She has a hole in her forehead. At the back of the hole a thin membrane can be seen throbbing with the pulsations of her brain. To my horror she said her surgeons warned her that when she emerged from the operation she might be paralyzed from the neck down.

The day before the operation Kay and I sat with Sandy in her hospital room. Two surgeons and an anesthetist came into the room, one after the other. Sandy asked a series of intelligent questions. Each said that while the threat of paralysis was slight, none could guarantee that she might not wind up totally paralyzed.

No soldier entering battle was more courageous than my daughter. In mounting admiration, I watched as she held herself together, never giving in to hysteria, only a couple of tears trickling down her gashed cheeks. I felt I would explode. As the third doctor left the room, Kay started to say something, but I waved her away and when my daughter and I were alone I took her into my arms to try to comfort her.

Her operation was set for 7:45 A.M., June 11. Since none of us would be allowed to see her that morning, I did not reach the hospital until 11:30. I was driven there by Sandy's friend, Barbara Smith. Kay was waiting in a room set aside for relatives and friends of patients undergoing surgery. Soon we were joined by Sandy's husband, Victor Emelio.

We sat . . . waited . . . sweated. At a desk sat a kind white-haired Red Cross lady who kept telephoning to check on the condition of Mrs. Emelio. Sandy was still in surgery. . . . Noon . . . One o'clock . . . two o'clock . . . two-fifteen. Barbara's eyes were wet. She and Victor drank coffee from plastic cups that shook in their hands. The operation was supposed to last only three hours. Had something gone wrong?

At 2:25 P.M. the Red Cross lady reported Sandy was out of surgery and okay. We sighed in relief.

A couple of hours later they let us go to Sandy's room. Her head and eyes were covered with a bandage as thick as a turban worn by a sultan. She lay on her back, taking glucose intravenously in her left arm. Her cheeks were stained with what looked like iodine. *And she was not paralyzed!*

She lay very still. She wafted in and out of consciousness. Dehydrated, when awake she wanted water. To her face I held a glass of water with a bent plastic straw in it. Confused and stubborn. Sandy insisted upon holding the glass. She tilted it so far to one side that she almost spilled the water. Then she wanted a cigaret. I walked into the hall to check with a nurse, who said it would be all right. I lit a cigaret and held it to her lips. She insisted upon holding it herself. She was unable to see because her eyes were bandaged and because she was groggy from the anesthetic. When I gave her the cigaret she pulled it to her chin, rather than her lips. Leaning forward, I guided it to her mouth. Then she passed out.

When she returned to consciousness, she murmured; "I feel like a Buddhist flower-pusher."

I didn't know what she meant and doubted whether she did. But because she was out of surgery and free of paralysis, my heart soared.

Days later we took her home.

One evening when Sandy and I were alone I told her something: I said that had she been left paralyzed, and had she wanted me to do so, I would have killed her with a revolver. If she had been unable to speak, we could have worked out a series of eye-blinks. One blink of her eyes would mean *yes*. Two blinks would mean *no*. Three blinks would mean *let me think it over*. Now, what did Sandy think about that? She agreed that she would have wanted me to kill her. She certainly would not care to live paralyzed from the neck down.

Staring into her eyes I said: "Honey, you know of course that had you wanted me to shoot you, and had I done so, the next instant I would have turned the gun on myself." My daughter said: "I know."

After the death of my wife I saw a lot of our mutual friend, Selma Seskin Pezaro. I had met Selma through her brother Steve, whose bookstore near the World-Telegram was a favorite haunt of mine. In many ways she was like Ruthie because she was mature and sweet-tempered, reliable and hard-working, and she also happened to be a non-religious Jew.

Selma had been matured by tragedy. When she was 21 she married, soon discovered her husband had cancer, and at night she tied her ankle to him so if he stirred she would awaken and take care of him. They had been married only a year and a half when he died. At first she cowered alone in her apartment, as I had done, but a husband and wife persuaded her to join a family-oriented nudist colony in New Jersey. There, among people ranging from babies to grandparents, she began to recover her emotional balance.

Irrationally, she felt she had not done enough to save her husband when, in fact, she had done everything possible. Now the widow resolved to save the new widower—me. She tolerated my black moods, made sure I ate well, typed notes for the books I wrote, was totally generous of her time and money. She even coped with me when I felt suicidal. One day in her apartment I picked up a sharp letter-opener and held it in my hand while staring melodramatically at my belly. Selma just sat and stared at me. Over the years I came to love her — not in the way I loved Ruth, of course, and Selma understood. Our favorite recreation was sitting behind her apartment building to watch children at play.

At times Selma could be witty. At one party I started to tell a joke, forgot the punchline, shrugged and said: "Well, I guess I'm just no raconteur."

Selma added, "Not only that, Eddie! You don't tell jokes very well."

WEDNESDAY, JULY 2, 1975

After publication of a story about my diary in our neighborhood paper, the *Chelsea Clinton News*, I got a letter from a man who lives in a housing project a few blocks south of my home. After saying he is impressed by my journal, he offered to give me some books. I wanted to call, but there is no number listing him in the Manhattan telephone directory. I walked to the project and met James F. McShea.

What an original! A retired elevator operator, he now does almost nothing but sit alone in his home reading the 2,000 books in his private library. His hobby is educating himself.

He was born in Hell's Kitchen on the west side of mid-Manhattan, an area known for producing gangsters, not scholars. Both his parents were born in Ireland. There his father walked to school in winter in bare feet, getting an education so scant that even as an adult he had trouble writing letters.

After emigrating to New York City, the father worked in a slaughterhouse and the family was so poor that little Jimmy had to go to work after only six years of schooling. One teacher was so impressed by his yearning for learning that she lent him a children's book called *Teddy and Carrots*. He read it 15 times. To this day he remembers its plot and characters.

When he was 14 and working as an office boy he attended a high school graduation ceremony because his best friend was valedictorian. Jimmy McShea wept. He felt ashamed of his ignorance. He vowed that, despite everything, he would educate himself.

He opened the doors of carriages stopping at stores on 5th Avenue, did menial work on a ship sailing around the world, served in the army 14 months, became an elevator operator.

When he retired more than a decade ago he took a small apartment in Chelsea and settled down to his books. Divorced, he lives alone. A small man with the map of Ireland on his face, he has thinning gray hair, grizzly eyebrows, blue-gray eyes and so much energy he almost hums like a dynamo.

He built his own bookshelves and the swinging book-rest attached to the left side of his deep chair. Nailed to this book-rest is an empty can of Campbell's chicken rice soup, to hold his pencils and pens, for he underlines as he writes. He has a 100-watt bulb in an overhead lamp, wears glasses and has his eyes checked once a year. There are dark patches under both eyes.

Existing on Social Security, he cooks his meals to save money. With his time his own, free of interruptions because he refuses to own either a telephone or television set, he reads all day long, seven days a week. He gets through three to five books each week.

He told me that thinking is almost as important to him as breathing. His favorite subjects are history, politics, international affairs, business and finance. He is fond of the works of the late John Maynard Keynes, the British economist, and also dotes on books by the American economist, Eliot Janeway. Sir Winston Churchill's style fascinates him because, he says, Churchill wrote majestically but simply. He has read every word of Karl Marx's monumental *Capital* but had trouble finishing *The Wealth of Nations* by Adam Smith.

Politically, McShea says, he is neither a reactionary nor a radical, but something in between. Like Harry Truman and some other self-educated people, McShea sometimes mispronounces some of the words he uses correctly. He has an extensive vocabulary.

I asked whether he would agree with my wife's definition of an intellectual as someone excited by ideas. His eyes lit up and he cried that yes he agrees, but quickly added that he is too modest to apply this definition to himself. He confessed that his voracious reading and his dislike of small talk have left him rather isolated. He scorns non-readers or those who read trash. He declared he never is lonely. Why? He said he can't explain this even to himself.

He gave me as many books as I could carry, telling me to return to pick up more. Before he dies he wants to give his books only to someone who appreciates them. That's me, me, me!

As I began to run out of money I knew I had to find a part-time job. I got in touch with Dr. Louis M. Starr, director of the Oral History Collection at Columbia University. He remembered me because when I worked for the World-Telegram *I wrote a long article about this worthy project.*

It was started in 1948 by Allan Nevins, a great historian. He reasoned that people of the present write fewer letters than the people of the past, so to preserve the memories of famous men and women it would be helpful to tape-record interviews with them. The interviews are conducted by historians and journalists. The words then are transcribed and made available to scholars and authors writing biographies and histories.

I asked Dr. Starr to let me interview Alger Hiss, and he agreed. Years ago I met Hiss at a cocktail party, but that night we did not discuss his celebrated case. Instead, we talked about publishing, for he was completing a book telling his side of the story. Dr. Starr made an appointment with Hiss for me. To prepare myself, I spent days rereading the dozen books I own about the Hiss-Chambers case.

For folks too young to remember, let me sketch the background of this case: In 1948 Whittaker Chambers, a senior editor of *Time* magazine and a self-confessed former spy for the Soviet Union, publicly accused Alger Hiss of belonging to an underground communist cell in Washington, D.C., and of stealing federal documents. That was when Hiss was a high official in the State Department. By the time Chambers made this accusation Hiss was president of the Carnegie Endowment for International Peace.

In 1948 Hiss denied these charges before a federal grand jury in New York. Then he was indicted on two counts of perjury. The first count said he lied when he denied giving federal documents to Chambers. The second count said he also lied when he denied having conversed with Chambers in, or about, February and March of 1938.

In 1949 Hiss stood trial and got a hung jury. In 1949–50 he stood trial a second time and was convicted of perjury. He was sentenced to five years in prison. He insisted he was innocent and, like millions of other Americans who followed this celebrated case, I believed him.

Now Hiss agreed to Dr. Starr's request that I interview him. I must point out that since I was working for the Oral History Collection, I cannot reveal in this book what Hiss told me on tape. Everyone who is interviewed may stipulate the date when his revelations may be made public. Trust in the integrity of those connected with the project is paramount to its existence. However, there is nothing unethical about reporting my impressions of Hiss the man.

WEDNESDAY, JULY 9, 1975

Alger Hiss walked into the restaurant. I was waiting for him in the Chelsea Steak House at 248 Eighth Avenue near West 23rd Street. Glancing up, I saw the lean six-footer peering around, so I stood up and snatched off my glasses to gesture with them toward Hiss. He saw me and smiled and walked over and sat down.

His face was quite unlined for a man of 70. He was carrying a *New York Times* and a big envelope and after we shook hands he put them on the floor. When a waiter asked whether we cared to order a drink we both declined. Since I always begin an interview with small questions, I asked Hiss whether he had used the subway to come uptown this sweltering day and he said he had, adding that he likes heat so he did not feel bothered. Then he picked up the menu, which has a map of my neighborhood on its cover.

Hiss, born in Maryland, said he would like the soft shell crabs if they were fresh, not frozen. Fresh, said the waiter. Hiss also ordered ice tea. The waiter kept forgetting his tea and every time he asked Hiss what he wanted to drink, Hiss repeated his order with no trace of annoyance.

He asked what college I attended. When I said the University of Missouri, he said his friend Edgar Snow had taken his journalism degree there. Snow went to China and became friendly with Mao tsetung. Hiss said that on the radio he had heard Mao quoted as saying nice things about Richard Nixon. I said I was surprised. Hiss said he was only mildly surprised, since American leaders and Red China have entered into detente. Aware that Nixon had been instrumental in ruining the life of Hiss, I asked what he thinks about Nixon's mental health. Hiss replied that he dislikes dealing in personalities.

I was sensitive to the fact that I was with a man who figured in one of the most celebrated trials in American history. Hiss asked what form my interview would take when we reached my apartment. I said that of course I would go into his case in great detail, I also would ask his opinion of the great men with whom he had worked in the federal government.

We finished eating. The waiter brought the check, and I took it. His put out his hand and said we must go Dutch, for this has been his habit since his days as a young New Dealer, because he never wanted to feel obligated to anyone. I said that during my career as a reporter I had been offered several bribes, the first one for $5 and the last one for $35,000. Hiss chuckled. When I said that not for one second did I feel tempted, he nodded understandingly. Each of us left $7 on the table and walked out.

We were in my neighborhood. On the northwest corner of West 21st Street and 9th Avenue there is a small old-fashioned grocery owned by Louis P. Chavell. Since it is only a half block from my home I have come to know Lou well. Hiss surprised me by saying he knows Lou and wanted to step in to say hello. Lou saw Hiss, held out his hand and said: "Alger! How are you?"

"Fine Lou. And you?"

The two men exchanged pleasantries. Hiss behaved with Lou just as he had with me—courteously and pleasantly. As we left to walk to my place, Hiss pointed to a brownstone four doors east of mine and explained that he lived there a couple of months after he quit his job with the State Department in Washington and come to New York to take up his position as president of the Carnegie Endowment for International Peace.

We reached my brownstone and climbed the winding stairway to my apartment on the third floor. Hiss walked up slowly, sighing that his son lives in a five-story walk-up. Then he added that his stepson, with whom he is close, is a surgeon, lives in California and owns a private airplane. I said I have a brother who owns a plane, but I've been poor most of my life. Smiling, Hiss said, "I've been poor, too."

Although my apartment is air-conditioned, I suggested that he remove his jacket, which he did, also stripping off his tie. I put the tape recorder on a piano stool in front of the sofa, where I had asked him to sit. The microphone itself I placed on a nearby coffee table. When I asked him to say a few words so that I might test his voice level, I found that his voice was so soft that I wondered how I could get the mike closer to his lips. He offered to hold it. This I resisted, but he insisted. Gently.

Before I began asking questions, I said he knew from our brief telephone conversation that I always have believed in his innocence. However, to do a proper job of interviewing him, I felt I must ask blunt questions and even behave as though I were a prosecuting attorney. Hiss, a graduate of Harvard Law School, agreed.

Alger Hiss has thinning brown hair, a high forehead and a lean face, ears with edges as thin as the rims of shells, few wrinkles in his forehead, a long neck and long slim fingers. When we were in the restaurant I had mentioned that whenever I saw Nixon on TV I had noted his rapid eye blink, which I considered proof that he was trying to hide his feelings.

Surprised, Hiss said that only yesterday a friend of his, a psychiatrist, had said the same thing.

From time to time Hiss reached for his tobacco pouch to fill his pipe, although he played with the pipe more than he smoked it. He was so kind and gentle and considerate that I wondered whether I was being taken in by him. No, I decided, I didn't think so. Sitting only a few feet apart, we looked into one another's eyes and he kept his gaze fixed on me with such candor that he almost seemed transparent. I was reminded of the day when one of my friends said I am so frank I seemed to be transparent, that he seemed to be able to see through me. I considered that a compliment. I encourage others to see through me and now believe Hiss does the same thing.

Although I have met Chief Justice Earl Warren and Judge Learned Hand, I doubt whether I ever encountered any judge or attorney with a mind as legalistic as that of Alger Hiss. This, in fact, is what is wrong with the book he wrote in his defense, *In the Court of Public Opinion*. His book was devoid of all emotion.

Now, as he answered my questions, Hiss was emotionless, for the most part. Over-controlled? I don't think so. When he spoke of a woman friend, his voice became warmer. Earlier, when I mentioned my daughter's auto accident, compassion showed in his face as he asked about her present condition. Nonetheless, Hiss remains an enigma to me—a comment, so I've read, made by many of his friends. Courteous in an old-world way, he has a cool personality.

I once saw Whittaker Chambers, the man who wrecked his life. That was in 1951, when Chambers spoke at a *Herald Tribune* forum I attended. Sitting in the front row that day, I drew a sketch of Chambers. This accuser of Hiss had what I regarded as a furtive air about him, even in the presence of an audience in sympathy with him. Today, for more than three hours, I stared into the eyes of Alger Hiss, and if he actually was a Soviet spy, then I know nothing about human nature.

I wonder whether Chambers, a man fragmented and perhaps even demented by the many tragedies in his life, saw in Hiss the kind of man he wanted to be. If this were so, then perhaps the only way he could absorb Hiss into himself was by denigrating and then destroying him.

This noon at lunch I told Hiss I had met Huey Long a few times, studied his life, and now know that a demagogue is one who says out loud what others think but dare not speak. Hiss agreed—but with one qualification. He said my definition of a demagogue also could be applied to sincere and truly great leaders. Thinking of Franklin D. Roosevelt, I agreed. So the difference between the demagogue and the statesman is the difference between evil intentions and good ones.

At the end of the interview this afternoon, Hiss asked how much more time I wanted from him. I said I'd like to see him a couple of more times. He said he has had two heart attacks that have left him unsteady on his feet—something I had noticed as we walked here— and now he must hoard his energy. With a smile he agreed to meet me for two more sessions. He said he dislikes being interviewed, but had liked my voice on the phone, liked the letter I wrote to him, and so he will join me a couple of more times.

"I'm doing this just for you," he said.

I hope he didn't see me wince. Was he sincere? If he was, I'd feel pleased, but I had hoped he would consent to further sessions for his own sake and that of the Oral History Collection—and therefore posterity. As regards these interviews, I am nothing but an instrument.

WEDNESDAY, JULY 30, 1975

For a second time I met Alger Hiss in the Chelsea Steak House. When I asked whether his work as a salesman for a stationery firm takes him out of the office much, he said he is outside half the time and inside the other half.

A few days ago about 5 P.M. he went to a 21-story building on 42nd Street to call on a client. He was the only passenger in the elevator. As it rose it suddenly shot to the top of the elevator shaft and stuck there. Finding the squawk-box in the elevator, he called the guard in the lobby, who said he would send for help. Thanking him, Hiss asked that he call his customer to report his predicament and say he would be late. Aware he had to spend time in the hot elevator, Hiss sat down on the floor, opened his *New York Times* and began reading.

Afterwards, some friends said they would have panicked. Hiss said he knew he would be rescued, and besides he does not suffer from claustrophobia. An elevator repair man— "a nice young man from Brooklyn," as he put it—arrived and released him within an hour. I asked whether that experience reminded him of the years he spent in jail. He did time in the federal penitentiary at Lewisburg, Pennsylvania.

He told me that when he entered prison he resigned himself to reality. In fact, he appreciated the silence, since by nature he is a rather solitary person. Over the prison's radio network he heard symphonic music an hour a day. Since few other prisoners liked this kind of music, one hour of it was all he could hear.

In his cell he studied the Babylonian Talmud. I had not known that the Talmud was a part of Babylonian culture. When I expressed surprise that such a book was in prison, Hiss said it probably was there because of some Jewish organization, since the people of ancient Israel were taken into exile by the Babylonians.

Other prisoners, aware he is an attorney, asked him to become their "jailhouse lawyer," so he helped then with their appeals.

"How could I not," he asked rhetorically, "help men whose only hope lay in winning freedom?"

I said I enjoy solitude, but if I were ever imprisoned, I might kill myself. While behind bars, had he ever thought of suicide?

"Oh, never!"

Hiss's reply was so intense it almost was passionate—a surprise because usually his voice is soft, his manner cool. He said he used his time in prison to peer deeply within himself in the hope of discovering his motives for his general behavior. This reminded me of a profound remark by the German mystic, Meister Eckhart: "The eye with which I see God is the eye with which God sees me."

Hiss smiled and said he did not understand. He asked me to explain. I said I consider this remark so deep it cannot be explained; it can only be felt after one has studied mysticism.

Hiss said my next book should not be about history but philosophy. I said that if I live long enough I will write a book about the history of mysticism. Then I added that the more I study history the better I realize that all history begins and ends in psychology and philosophy. Agreeing, Hiss said every great historian works from philosophical premises.

Since Hiss had told me he suffered two heart attacks, I asked about his present health. "It's not good."

His reply was so casual I wanted to be sure I had heard him correctly, so I asked him to repeat what he had said.

"It's not good."

He said that since his condition is irreversible, he accepts it. I said I hope he lives long enough to clear his name. His face lighting up, Hiss said that tomorrow, for the first time, he and his lawyers will see three of the microfilms that Whittaker Chambers hid in a pumpkin on his farm.

When we got to my home, Hiss took off his jacket and tie and sat on the sofa while I perched in a big chair in front of him. Before leaving to meet him, I had set up the tape recorder, but now when I pressed the button it would not run. Then I realized I had forgotten to plug in the machine, and I laughed at my usual ineptitude.

After my first session with Hiss I had played back a part of the recording we made that first day; it contained burbling sounds. After some reflection I remembered he had toyed with his pipe as he talked, and sometimes he also shifted the microphone he held in his hands. This taught me a lesson; put the mike on a table where it will remain immobile. Explaining this, I took the mike from his hand.

By the light from a window I saw again that his face is not very lined for a man his age. His blue-gray eyes are sunk even more deeply within his skull than I had remembered. Again as we talked he kept his eyes on mine with such intensity that at last my eyes tired and I wanted to shift them to ease them, but did not wish to violate our rapport.

Perhaps because he now knows me a little better, Hiss seemed more relaxed and his face became more animated. Previously I had wondered whether he is over-controlled. He is not. Always he simply is *controlled*.

"A sentimentalist," he said, "is unable to feel genuine affection."

The truth of his remark hit me so hard that instantly I thought of an old woman I know who is sentimental and cruel.

Hiss then said something to the effect that he is an intellectual—adding, with a smile, that he cannot be sure he is one. I said my wife defined an intellectual as one who is excited by ideas.

At lunch today Hiss had told me he once lectured in a city in upstate New York where there were many members of the John Birch Society, which I regard as a loony bin of mindless wild-eyed anti-communists. When the session was opened to questions, some Birchers grabbed the microphone on the floor of the auditorium and peppered him with loaded questions. At the end of the evening a few Birchers remained and his friend asked whether he would like to meet them "Sure!" Hiss replied, but when he approached them they turned and fled. His friend laughed and said: "Look, you have to realize that to them you are the devil incarnate!"

Today, for a second time, Hiss and I discussed the nature of demagogues. He said he was reminded of the late Senator Robert R. Reynolds of North Carolina, whom he called a demagogue, but one who did not advocate violence. I remembered having read that during one campaign Reynolds told an audience of farmers that his opponent "had a sister who went to New York and became a *thespian!*"

Hiss laughed, "That's the man!"

Now, alone with me in my apartment, Hiss told me exactly how he hopes to clear his name. In surprise I realized he was revealing his entire legal strategy. I said I was astonished at his frankness. He said: "Well, I hope you won't use any of this information for a year or so—until after the case is decided."

At last we reached the crucial question of whether Hiss lost his second trial because of alleged "forgery by typewriter." He went into a long complex explanation. As an interviewer, I had to do five things at the same time:

- make sure the tape recorder was working properly
- maintain rapport with Hiss by keeping my eyes on his
- truly listen to everything he said
- write more questions on the paper on my clipboard
- find certain passages in the many books about the Hiss case that lay open near me

Hiss said he had tried without success to find a copy of *A Nation in Torment,* my narrative history of the Great Depression. Saying I wanted to show my appreciation for all the time he has given me, I found a copy, autographed it and gave it to Hiss. Thanking me, he said he will use it when he writes his history of the New Deal.

WEDNESDAY, AUGUST 6, 1975

The *New York Times* said today that Alger Hiss has been reinstated as a lawyer in Massachusetts by order of that state's highest court. I wrote him a note of congratulations.

WEDNESDAY, SEPTEMBER 17, 1975

For the third and final time, Hiss came here and again I interviewed him for three hours. In total, I was alone with him for nine hours. Today I got him talking about all the famous people he knew: Justices Holmes, Brandeis and Cardozo; Franklin and Eleanor Roosevelt; Adlai E. Stevenson, John Foster Dulles, James F. Byrnes, Harry Hopkins, Arthur Vandenberg, Tom Connolly, Dean Acheson, et al.

On April 20, 1994, the New York Times *published a picture of Hiss and a four-paragraph piece about a birthday party given for him by some 70 friends. He was born in Baltimore on November 11, 1904, but his 90th birthday was celebrated in advance. Almost every big dictionary and encyclopedia includes an article about Alger Hiss.*

FRIDAY, DECEMBER 19, 1975

The other night at a cocktail party I met a man from New Jersey named Arnold Tversky. He is assistant superintendent of the Dover High School, which has 1,100 students. We chatted together a long time. I liked him and he said he found me so interesting that he invited me to speak to his students. Surprised and flattered, I agreed. This morning he came in his car to drive Selma and me to New Jersey.

In his office he introduced me to Ray Schwartz, a young man with brown eyes and a bubbling personality, who teaches English. In the first of three appearances today, I was supposed to talk to his English class. Ray warned me that his students would look at me as though I were a TV set. This remark disturbed me.

Selma and I were led into the library. Wire cables snaked over the floor because my talk was to be broadcast on closed-circuit television. About 40 boys and girls sat in silence. Holding up a copy of *A Nation in Torment,* Ray identified me as its author, said he had read my book and liked it, then gave me a long and flattering introduction. When he finished I arose and said I'd like to meet the man who sounded so important. Not a snicker.

Two boys and two girls had been chosen to ask me questions. All looked scared—perhaps because of me, perhaps because they knew they were on television. None asked any sharp, significant, provocative question. For 35 minutes I talked, ending with the story of how some Jewish boys being taught to read by their elders are told to lick a drop of honey off the cover of a book so that they would associate sweetness and learning. No response from the kids.

At the end of this first session we went to the cafeteria where Ray said he flipped when I told this story because he came from an orthodox family and this very thing happened to him. Arnold Tversky, I learned, liked to be called "Mr. T." He, Ray, Selma and I wondered why these days children are so non-verbal. Why don't they read? Why are they emotionally flat? I told these educators that they are competing with the deadening influence of an ignorant society lying just outside the school doors. They agreed.

Then I was led before two more classes, and both times I was met with an aloofness that was palpable. Straining for rapport with the children, I drifted away from the subject of writing and began talking about life itself. Nothing I said evoked any reaction from the kids. I felt as though I were slogging through a swamp, my boots mired in ignorance and indifference.

In desperation I told the students I wanted to give them a demonstration of curiosity. Then, without pausing for breath, I rattled off perhaps 30 questions about the dimensions of the room, the kind of wood in their chairs, the material used to make the handbags the girls carried, etc. I did hear a murmur of amazement—but that was all.

During my third appearance of the day I asked a girl in the front row to come sit with me so that I might show her how reporters interview people. Shyly, she stepped forward. I asked questions about her life. When she said she wants to design women's clothes, I cried that already she must sew well.

"No, not really," she said hesitantly.

"I won't let you get away with that," I told her. "You said you want to design women's clothes and I know you sew, so surely you must sew well. There's nothing wrong with admitting it. You do sew well, don't you?"

A little startled, the girl said: "Well, yes, I do."

In the second row I saw an Hispanic girl. I asked what she likes to do best.

"Read poetry." she replied.

Taking heart, I praised her. Perhaps because of her Spanish heritage, I remembered that my daughter had spoken to me about a Spanish poet named Lorca, and asked the girl whether she had read him. Her black eyes blazing with joy, she said yes she has read him. I told her she was ahead of me because I never have read Lorca.

But those were the only sparks I lit in the eyes staring at me. I thought, to these kids I *am* only a substitute for a television set. Day after day they sit and watch TV. There is neither the opportunity nor necessity for them to communicate with the images they see on the screen. I was bombing and knew it. Taking a deep breath, I said:

"Hey, tell you what, all of you who find me boring, please hold up your hands. I promise I won't get angry, and I'll ask your teacher not to rebuke you. Now, how many of you think I'm boring? Let me see your hands!"

Not a hand went up. I thought: Oh, my god! I can't even elicit a negative response from these kids.

Heavy-hearted, I left the room. Ray said I got to his students. I scoffed that I didn't believe him. He said that although none asked any questions, at least they gave me their full attention—which is more, he added, than he gets from them. This made me feel even worse. Television is turning our children into zombies.

2
Literary Memoir

All literary memoirs are reports from exotic territory, territory the reader would never otherwise be able to visit. When Mary McCarthy tells us about the Seattle of her youth it is a Seattle that is lost forever. When she tells us about her life with a neglectful and selfish uncle (after the death of her fun-loving and affectionate parents in the flu epidemic of 1918), it is life with a particular man, he and no other, a country unto himself. When she tells about her protective grandfather, she tells about a man long dead, a man particular. When she uses the first person, it is a first person only she knows the depths of.

Is Kathryn Harrison's father like your father? Is Hilton Als's mother like your mother? Well, no, of course not. And then again, yes. In that *yes* lies our connection to every writer of memoir. In that *no*—that exotic *no*—lies our curiosity, one expression of our human need for fresh knowledge.

So why do memoirists and their works stir up so much controversy? Memoir seems to threaten everyone, at times even its own practitioners and its legions of readers. Certain journalists and historians, whose collective illusion is that facts alone inform their writing, and never their opinions or world views, and certainly never their faulty memories (though the memories of sources are used rather confidently, I've come to notice), turn purple with apoplexy at my very mention of the word *memoir*—if they're not already dead on the library floor from my mention of a much-misunderstood genre called creative nonfiction.

Lovers of fact may scoff at novelistic re-creations of life, knowing how faulty their own memories are, and allowing for no re-creation, but our very lives are acts of re-creation, of assembling narratives around events to build selves.

Even the critic James Wolcott, who devoted several *Vanity Fair* pages in October 1997 to trashing and thrashing the concept of creative nonfiction, admits to liking certain memoirists' work: "I eat literary memoirs like candy, if there's a crunchy Mary McCarthy anecdote inside." He just doesn't like *bad* memoir (and uses the word *literary* to help him make the distinction, as I think I had better do), a discrimination many lesser critics following his lead have failed to note.

The method of memoir-bashing in the popular press these days is to pick a terrible gushy memoir, compare it to an episode of artless soul-baring on *Oprah* (which, as I hope at least one reader out there doesn't know, is a television "talk" show), or to an abject confession in an Alcoholics Anonymous meeting, and finish with a smug but flawed denouncement, a faulty inductive leap from too little evidence: memoir is inferior, beneath contempt, and should be disdained. Of course, we could make similar arguments against fiction and poetry based on bad samples, too, and arguments against anything in the world.

Lovers of decorum, like their Victorian forebears, would prefer that we not talk about certain things. There's never been so much name-calling and viciously self-righteous accusation over a book as over Kathryn Harrison's *The Kiss*, yet reading it we find a tender and terrifying and self-aware account of an extraordinary situation, the author's sexual affair with her hypermanipulative natural father when she was twenty. Much of the outcry about that book seems to be over the fact that she would *tell*, that she wouldn't simply hide in shame. But a lot of good memoir is about beating shame, giving voice to the formerly silent, which in turn teaches us about ourselves when we are not the saints we'd prefer to be. And, despite the outcry, *The Kiss* is no messy, impulsive confession; indeed, it is a carefully built book, arranged in three classical acts of uniform length, with all the rising action and character development and narrative movement of a great play.

Memoirists are often accused of being self-indulgent, but it's also possible to see them as *generous*, as Philip Lopate has pointed out: they let us look behind the veils of polite denial to see and learn from and enjoy life as it is actually lived. The first person, after all, is something every human shares.

Lovers of fiction may feel that working from given material instead of from invention is cheating, somehow. But literary memoir does not threaten fiction. James Atlas is dead wrong when he says in *The New York Times Magazine*, "Fiction isn't delivering the news. Memoir is." What's right is that in the hands of good writers, *both* are delivering the news, and have always done, and will. Fiction and memoir are two very different art forms. They don't meet, not really, even when the fiction is autobiographical, and the memoir is fictionalized. The intention is too different, the expectations of the reader too important. Readers apprehend a true story differently from one known or believed to have been made up.

The argument goes on. These days—the beginning of a new century—agents and editors talk about a memoir glut. Hundreds of articles have been published, defending or decrying the form. Meanwhile, Frank McCourt lives on the bestseller lists. His *Angela's Ashes* is a revelation and a history lesson and fine entertainment, as well, deserves its success for the powerful and funny and poignant voice McCourt musters to tell his comic and tragic tale. And, if you are interested in further reading in literary memoir, it's the first book I'd recommend. Reading *Angela's Ashes*, I couldn't figure out how to apply all I've heard about how awful memoir is. Where was the huge failure of form we read about? Why did I so enjoy my laughter and my tears? Is there a reason I should not?

Of course, there is enormous evidence that memoir isn't awful at all, but a genre in which literary artists of the first rank have produced masterpieces. Mary McCarthy, James Thurber, Annie Dillard, Maxine Hong Kingston, Andre Dubus, Tobias Wolff: these are among our best writers, and in all their works of memoir put together is not a teaspoonful of self-pity, though horrors, as you shall see, visited all of them. Their work shares grace of language, form, and vision, and moves us. Newer writers, too, are making fine works of memoir, and it is the best writers—those who make memoir literary—we must reckon with in making generalizations about the form.

For readers interested in literary memoir, a good place to continue investigation would be the anthology *Modern American Memoirs,* edited by Annie Dillard and Cort Conley, or *The Granta Book of the Family,* edited by Bill Buford, or *The Norton Book of Autobiography,* edited by Jay Parini.

For now, though, let's just say this: in memoir we get the whole truth, and not only the verifiable facts. In memoir, we get how it feels to be at the center of an exotic kingdom—the kingdom of the self, and from this we learn what it is to have a self. In memoir we get memory whole, and memory, even when faulty, is what people are made of.

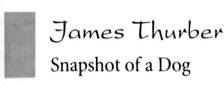

James Thurber
Snapshot of a Dog

I RAN ACROSS A DIM PHOTOGRAPH OF HIM THE OTHER DAY, GOING THROUGH SOME OLD things. He's been dead twenty-five years. His name was Rex (my two brothers and I named him when we were in our early teens) and he was a bull terrier. "An American bull terrier," we used to say, proudly; none of your English bulls. He had one brindle eye that sometimes made him look like a clown and sometimes reminded you of a politician with derby hat and cigar. The rest of him was white except for a brindle saddle that always seemed to be slipping off and a brindle stocking on a hind leg. Nevertheless, there was a nobility about him. He was big and muscular and beautifully made. He never lost his dignity even when trying to accomplish the extravagant tasks my brothers and myself used to set for him. One of these was the bringing of a ten-foot wooden rail into the yard through the back gate. We would throw it out into the alley and tell him to go get it. Rex was as powerful as a wrestler, and there were not many things that he couldn't manage somehow to get hold of with his great jaws and lift or drag to wherever he wanted to put them, or wherever we wanted them put. He could catch the rail at the balance and lift it clear of the ground and trot with great confidence toward the gate. Of course, since the gate was only four feet wide or so, he couldn't bring the rail in broadside. He found that out when he got a few terrific jolts, but he wouldn't give up. He finally figured out how to do it, by dragging the rail, holding onto one end, growling. He got a great, wagging satisfaction out of his work. We used to bet kids who had never seen Rex in action that he could catch a baseball thrown as high as they could throw it. He almost never let us down. Rex could hold a baseball with ease in his mouth, in one cheek, as if it were a chew of tobacco.

He was a tremendous fighter, but he never started fights. I don't believe he liked to get into them, despite the fact that he came from a line of fighters. He never went for another dog's throat but for one of its ears (that teaches a dog a lesson), and he would get his grip, close his eyes, and hold on. He could hold on for hours. His longest fight lasted from dusk until almost pitch-dark, one Sunday. It was fought in East Main Street in Columbus with a large, snarly nondescript that belonged to a big colored man. When Rex finally got his ear grip, the brief whirlwind of snarling turned to screeching. It was frightening to listen to and to watch. The Negro boldly picked the dogs up somehow and began swinging them around his head, and finally let them fly like a hammer in a hammer throw, but although they landed ten feet away with a great plump, Rex still held on.

The two dogs eventually worked their way to the middle of the car tracks, and after a while two or three streetcars were held up by the fight. A motorman tried to pry Rex's jaws open with a switch rod; somebody lighted a fire and made a torch of a stick and held that to Rex's tail, but he paid no attention. In the end, all the residents and storekeepers in the neighborhood were on hand, shouting this, suggesting that. Rex's joy of battle, when battle was joined, was almost tranquil. He had a kind of pleasant expression during fights, not a vicious one, his eyes closed in what would have seemed to be sleep had it not been for the turmoil of the struggle. The Oak Street Fire Department finally had to be sent for—I don't know why nobody thought of it sooner. Five or six pieces of apparatus arrived, followed by a battalion chief. A hose was attached and a powerful stream of water was turned on the dogs. Rex held on for several moments more while the torrent buffeted him about like a log in a freshet. He was a hundred yards away from where the fight started when he finally let go.

⋄ ⋄ ⋄

The story of that Homeric fight got all around town, and some of our relatives looked upon the incident as a blot on the family name. They insisted that we get rid of Rex, but we were very happy with him, and nobody could have made us give him up. We would have left town with him first, along any road there was to go. It would have been different, perhaps, if he'd ever started fights, or looked for trouble. But he had a gentle disposition. He never bit a person in the ten strenuous years that he lived, nor ever growled at anyone except prowlers. He killed cats, that is true, but quickly and neatly and without especial malice, the way men kill certain animals. It was the only thing he did that we could never cure him of doing. He never killed, or even chased, a squirrel. I don't know why. He had his own philosophy about such things. He never ran barking after wagons or automobiles. He didn't seem to see the idea in pursuing something you couldn't catch, or something you couldn't do anything with, even if you did catch it. A wagon was one of the things he couldn't tug along with his mighty jaws, and he knew it. Wagons, therefore, were not a part of his world.

Swimming was his favorite recreation. The first time he ever saw a body of water (Alum Creek), he trotted nervously along the steep bank for a while, fell to barking wildly, and finally plunged in from a height of eight feet or more. I shall always remember that shining, virgin dive. Then he swam upstream and back just for the pleasure of it, like a man. It was fun to see him battle upstream against a stiff current, struggling and growling every foot of the way. He had as much fun in the water as any person I have known. You didn't have to throw a stick in the water to get him to go in. Of course, he would bring back a stick to you if you did throw one in. He would even have brought back a piano if you had thrown one in.

That reminds me of the night, way after midnight, when he went a-roving in the light of the moon and brought back a small chest of drawers that he found somewhere—how far from the house nobody ever knew; since it was Rex, it could easily have been half a mile. There were no drawers in the chest when he got it home, and it wasn't a good one—he hadn't taken it out of anybody's house; it was just an old cheap piece that somebody had abandoned on a trash heap. Still, it was something he wanted, probably because it presented a nice problem in transportation. It tested his mettle. We first knew about his achievement when, deep in the night, we heard him trying to get the chest up onto the porch. It sounded as if two or three people were trying to tear the house down. We came downstairs and turned on the porch light. Rex was on the top step trying to pull the thing up, but it had caught somehow and he was just holding his own. I suppose he would have held his own till dawn if we hadn't helped him. The next day we carted the chest miles away and threw it out. If we had thrown it out in a nearby alley, he would have brought it home again, as a small token of his integrity in such matters. After all, he had been taught to carry heavy wooden objects about, and he was proud of his prowess.

I am glad Rex never saw a trained police dog jump. He was just an amateur jumper himself, but the most daring and tenacious I have ever seen. He would take on any fence we pointed out to him. Six feet was easy for him, and he could do eight by making a tremendous leap and hauling himself over finally by his paws, grunting and straining; but he lived and died without knowing that twelve- and sixteen-foot walls were too much for him. Frequently, after letting him try to go over one for a while, we would have to carry him home. He would never have given up trying.

There was in his world no such thing as the impossible. Even death couldn't beat him down. He died, it is true, but only, as one of his admirers said, after "straight-arming the death angel" for more than an hour. Late one afternoon he wandered home, too slowly and too uncertainly to be the Rex that had trotted briskly homeward up our avenue for ten years. I think we all knew when he came through the gate that he was dying. He had apparently taken a terrible beating, probably from the owner of some dog that he had got into a fight with. His head and body were scarred. His heavy collar with the teeth marks of many a battle on it was awry; some of the big brass studs in it were sprung loose from the leather. He licked at our hands and, staggering, fell, but got up again. We could see that he was looking for someone. One of his three masters was not home. He did not get home for an hour. During that hour the bull terrier fought against death as he had fought against the cold, strong current of Alum Creek, as he had fought to climb twelve-foot walls. When the person he was waiting for did come through the gate, whistling, ceasing to whistle, Rex walked a few wabbly paces toward him, touched his hand with his muzzle, and fell down again. This time he didn't get up.

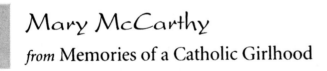

Mary McCarthy
from Memories of a Catholic Girlhood

YONDER PEASANT, WHO IS HE?

WHENEVER WE CHILDREN CAME TO STAY AT MY GRANDMOTHER'S HOUSE, WE WERE PUT TO sleep in the sewing room, a bleak, shabby, utilitarian rectangle, more office than bedroom, more attic than office, that played to the hierarchy of chambers the role of a poor relation. It was a room seldom entered by the other members of the family, seldom swept by the maid, a room without pride; the old sewing machine, some cast-off chairs, a shadeless lamp, rolls of wrapping paper, piles of cardboard boxes that might someday come in handy, papers of pins, and remnants of material united with the iron folding cots put out for our use and the bare floor boards to give an impression of intense and ruthless temporality. Thin white spreads, of the kind used in hospitals and charity institutions, and naked blinds at the windows reminded us of our orphaned condition and of the ephemeral character of our visit; there was nothing here to encourage us to consider this our home.

Poor Roy's children, as commiseration damply styled us, could not afford illusions, in the family opinion. Our father had put us beyond the pale by dying suddenly of influenza and taking our young mother with him, a defection that was remarked on with horror and grief commingled, as though our mother had been a pretty secretary with whom he had wantonly absconded into the irresponsible paradise of the hereafter. Our reputation was clouded by this misfortune. There was a prevailing sense, not only in the family but among storekeepers, servants, streetcar conductors, and other satellites of our circle, that my grandfather, a rich man, had behaved with extraordinary munificence in allotting a sum of money for our support and installing us with some disagreeable middle-aged relations in a dingy house two blocks distant from his own. What alternative he had was not mentioned; presumably he could have sent us to an orphan asylum and no one would have thought the worse of him. At any rate, it was felt, even by those who sympathized with us, that we led a privileged existence, privileged because we had no rights, and the very fact that at the yearly Halloween or Christmas party given at the home of an uncle we appeared so dismal, ill clad, and unhealthy, in contrast to our rosy, exquisite cousins, confirmed the judgment that had been made on us—clearly, it was a generous impulse that kept us in the family at all. Thus, the meaner our circumstances, the greater seemed our grandfather's condescension, a view in which we ourselves shared, looking softly and shyly on this old man—with his rheumatism, his pink face and white hair, set off by the rosebuds in his Pierce-Arrow and in his buttonhole—as the font of goodness and philanthropy, and the nickel he occasionally gave us to drop into the collection plate on Sunday (two cents was our ordinary contribution) filled us not with envy but with simple admiration for his potency; this indeed was princely, *this* was the way to give. It did not occur to us to judge him for the disparity of our styles of living. Whatever bitterness we felt was kept for our actual guardians, who, we believed, must be embezzling the money set aside for us, since the standard of comfort achieved in our grandparents' house—the electric heaters, the gas logs, the lap robes, the shawls wrapped tenderly about the old knees, the white meat of chicken and red meat of beef, the silver, the white tablecloths, the maids, and the solicitous chauffeur—persuaded us that prunes and rice pudding, peeling paint and patched clothes were *hors concours* with these persons and therefore could not have been willed by them. Wealth, in our minds was equivalent to bounty, and poverty but a sign of penuriousness of spirit.

Yet even if we had been convinced of the honesty of our guardians, we would still have clung to that beneficent image of our grandfather that the family myth proposed to us. We were too poor, spiritually speaking, to question his generosity, to ask why he allowed us to live in oppressed chill and deprivation at a long arm's length from himself and hooded his genial blue eye with a bluff, millionairish grey eyebrow whenever the evidence of our suffering presented itself at his knee. The official answer we knew: our benefactors were too old to put up with four wild young children; our grandfather was preoccupied with business matters and with his rheumatism, to which he devoted himself as though to a pious duty, taking it with him on pilgrimages to Ste. Anne de Beaupré and Miami, offering it with impartial reverence to the miracle of the Northern Mother and the Southern sun. This rheumatism hallowed my grandfather with the mark of a special vocation; he lived with it in the manner of an artist or a grizzled Galahad; it set him apart from all of us and even from my grandmother, who, lacking such an affliction, led a relatively unjustified existence and showed, in relation to us children, a sharper and more bellicose spirit. She felt, in spite of everything, that she was open to criticism, and, transposing this feeling with a practiced old hand, kept peering into our characters for symptoms of ingratitude.

We, as a matter of fact, were grateful to the point of servility. We made no demands, we had no hopes. We were content if we were permitted to enjoy the refracted rays of that solar prosperity and come sometimes in the summer afternoons to sit on the shady porch or idle through a winter morning on the wicker furniture of the sun parlor, to stare at the player piano in the music room and smell the odor of whisky in the mahogany cabinet in the library, or to climb about the dark living room examining the glassed-in paintings in their huge gilt frames, the fruits of European travel: dusky Italian devotional groupings, heavy and lustrous as grapes, Neapolitan women carrying baskets to market, views of Venetian canals, and Tuscan harvest scenes—secular themes that, to the Irish-American mind, had become tinged with Catholic feeling by a regional infusion from the Pope. We asked no more from this house than the pride of being connected with it, and this was fortunate for us, since my grandmother, a great adherent of the give-them-an-inch-and-they'll-take-a-yard theory of hospitality, never, so far as I can remember, offered any caller the slightest refreshment, regarding her own conversation as sufficiently wholesome and sustaining. An ugly, severe old woman with a monstrous balcony of a bosom, she officiated over certain set topics in a colorless singsong, like a priest intoning a Mass, topics to which repetition had lent a senseless solemnity: her audience with the Holy Father; how my own father had broken with family tradition and voted the Democratic ticket; a visit to Lourdes; the Sacred Stairs in Rome, bloodstained since the first Good Friday, which she had climbed on her knees; my crooked little fingers and how they meant I was a liar; a miracle-working bone; the importance of regular bowel movements; the wickedness of Protestants; the conversion of my mother to Catholicism; and the assertion that my other grandmother must certainly dye her hair. The most trivial reminiscences (my aunt's having hysterics in a haystack) received from her delivery and from the piety of the context a strongly monitory flavor; they inspired fear and guilt, and one searched uncomfortably for the moral in them, as in a dark and ridding fable.

⊷　⊷　⊷

Luckily, I am writing a memoir and not a work of fiction, and therefore I do not have to account for my grandmother's unpleasing character and look for the Oedipal fixation or the traumatic experience which would give her that clinical authenticity that is nowadays so desirable in portraiture. I do not know how my grandmother got the way she was; I assume, from family photographs and from the inflexibility of her habits, that she was always the same, and it seems as idle to inquire into her childhood as to ask what was ailing Iago or look for the error in toilet-training that was responsible for Lady Macbeth. My grandmother's sexual history, bristling with infant mortality in the usual style of her period, was robust and decisive: three tall, handsome sons grew up, and one attentive daughter. Her husband treated her kindly. She had money, many grandchildren, and religion to sustain her. White hair, glasses, soft skin, wrinkles, needlework—all the paraphernalia of motherliness were hers; yet it was a cold, grudging, disputatious old woman who sat all day in her sunroom making tapestries from a pattern, scanning religious periodicals, and setting her iron jaw against any infraction of her ways.

Combativeness was, I suppose, the dominant trait in my grandmother's nature. An aggressive churchgoer, she was quite without Christian feeling; the mercy of the Lord Jesus had never entered her heart. Her piety was an act of war against the Protestant ascendancy. The religious magazines on her table furnished her not with food for meditation but with fresh pretexts for anger; articles attacking birth control, divorce, mixed marriages, Darwin, and secular education were her favorite reading. The teachings of the Church did not interest her, except as they were a rebuke to others; "Honor thy father and thy mother," a commandment she was no longer called upon to practice, was the one most frequently on her lips. The extermination of Protestantism, rather than spiritual perfection, was the boon she prayed for. Her mind was preoccupied with conversion; the capture of a soul for God much diverted her fancy—it made one less Protestant in the world. Foreign missions, with their overtones of good will and social service, appealed to her less strongly; it was not a *harvest* of souls that my grandmother had in mind.

This pugnacity of my grandmother's did not confine itself to sectarian enthusiasm. There was the defense of her furniture and her house against the imagined encroachments of visitors. With her, this was not the gentle and tremulous protectiveness endemic in old ladies, who fear for the safety of their possessions with a truly touching anxiety, inferring the fragility of all things from the brittleness of their old bones and hearing the crash of mortality in the perilous tinkling of a tea cup. My grandmother's sentiment was more autocratic: she hated having her chairs sat in or her lawns stepped on or the water turned on in her basins, for no reason at all except pure officiousness; she even grudged the mailman his daily promenade up her sidewalk. Her home was a center of power, and she would not allow it to be derogated by easy or democratic usage. Under her jealous eye, its social properties had atrophied, and it functioned in the family structure simply as a political headquarters. Family conferences were held there, consultations with the doctor and the clergy; refractory children were brought there for a lecture or an interval of thought-taking; wills were read and loans negotiated and emissaries from the Protestant faction on state occasions received. The family had no friends, and entertaining was held to be a foolish and unnecessary courtesy as between blood relations. Holiday dinners fell, as a duty, on the lesser members of the organization: the daughters and daughters-in-law (converts from the false religion) offered up Baked Alaska on a platter, like the head of John the Baptist, while the old people sat enthroned at the table, and only their digestive processes acknowledged, with rumbling, enigmatic salvos, the festal day.

Yet on one terrible occasion my grandmother had kept open house. She had accommodated us all during those fatal weeks of the influenza epidemic, when no hospital beds were to be had and people went about with masks or stayed shut up in their houses, and the awful fear of contagion paralyzed all services and made each man an enemy to his neighbor. One by one, we had been carried off the train which had brought us from distant Puget Sound to make a new home in Minneapolis. Waving good-by in the Seattle depot, we had not known that we had carried the flu with us into our drawing rooms, along with the presents and the flowers, but, one after another, we had been struck down as the train proceeded eastward. We children did not understand whether the chattering of our teeth and Mama's lying torpid in the berth were not somehow a part of the trip (until then, serious illness, in our minds, had been associated with innovations—it had always brought home a new baby), and we began to be sure that it was all an adventure when we saw our father draw a revolver on the conductor who was trying to put us off the train at a small wooden station in the middle of the North Dakota prairie. On the platform at Minneapolis, there were stretchers, a wheel chair, redcaps, distraught officials, and, beyond them, in the crowd, my grandfather's rosy face, cigar, and cane, my grandmother's feathered hat, imparting an air of festivity to this strange and confused picture, making us children certain that our illness was the beginning of a delightful holiday.

◆ ◆ ◆

We awoke to reality in the sewing room several weeks later, to an atmosphere of castor oil, rectal thermometers, cross nurses, and efficiency, and though we were shut out from the knowledge of what had happened so close to us, just out of our hearing—a scandal of the gravest character, a coming and going of priests and undertakers and coffins (Mama and Daddy, they assured us, had gone to get well in the hospital)—we became aware, even as we woke from our fevers, that everything, including ourselves, was different. We had shrunk, as it were, and faded, like the flannel pajamas we wore, which during these few weeks had grown, doubtless from the disinfectant they were washed in, wretchedly thin and shabby. The behavior of the people around us, abrupt, careless, and preoccupied, apprised us without any ceremony of our diminished importance. Our value had paled, and a new image of ourselves—the image, if we had guessed it, of the orphan—was already forming in our minds. We had not known we were spoiled, but now this word, entering our vocabulary for the first time, served to define the change for us and to herald the new order. Before we got sick, we were spoiled; that was what was the matter now, and everything we could not understand, everything unfamiliar and displeasing, took on a certain plausibility when related to this fresh concept. We had not known what it was to have trays dumped summarily on our beds and no sugar and cream for our cereal, to take medicine in a gulp because someone could not be bothered to wait for us, to have our arms jerked into our sleeves and a comb ripped through our hair, to be bathed impatiently, to be told to sit up or lie down quick and no nonsense about it, to find our questions unanswered and our requests unheeded, to lie for hours alone and wait for the doctor's visit, but this, so it seemed, was an oversight in our training, and my grandmother and her household applied themselves with a will to remedying the deficiency.

Their motives were, no doubt, good; it was time indeed that we learned that the world was no longer our oyster. The happy life we had had—the May baskets and the valentines, the picnics in the yard, and the elaborate snowman—was a poor preparation, in truth, for the future that now opened up to us. Our new instructors could hardly be blamed for a certain impatience with our parents, who had been so lacking in foresight. It was to everyone's interest, decidedly, that we should forget the past—the quicker, the better—and a steady disparagement of our habits ("Tea and chocolate, can you imagine, and all those frosted cakes—no wonder poor Tess was always after the doctor") and praise that was rigorously comparative ("You have absolutely no idea of the improvement in those children") flattered the feelings of the speakers and prepared us to accept a loss that was, in any case, irreparable. Like all children, we wished to conform, and the notion that our former ways had been somehow ridiculous and unsuitable made the memory of them falter a little, like a child's recitation to strangers. We no longer demanded our due, and the wish to see our parents insensibly weakened. Soon we ceased to speak of it, and thus, without tears or tantrums, we came to know they were dead.

Why no one, least of all our grandmother, to whose repertory the subject seems so congenial, took the trouble to tell us, it is impossible now to know. It is easy to imagine her "breaking" the news to those of us who were old enough to listen in one of those official interviews in which her nature periodically tumefied, becoming heavy and turgid, like her portentous bosom, like peonies, her favorite flower, or like the dressmaker's dummy, that bombastic image of herself that, half swathed in a sheet for decorum's sake, lent a museumlike solemnity to the sewing room and aroused our first sexual curiosity. The mind's ear frames her sentences, but in reality she did not speak, whether from a hygienic motive (keep the mind ignorant and the bowels open), or from a mistaken kindness, it is difficult to guess. Perhaps really she feared our tears, which might rain on her like reproaches, since the family policy at the time was predicated on the axiom of our virtual insentience, an assumption that allowed them to proceed with us as if with pieces of furniture. Without explanations or coddling, as soon as they could safely get up, my three brothers were dispatched to the other house; they were much too young to "feel" it, I heard the grownups murmur, and would never know the difference "if Myers and Margaret were careful." In my case, however, a doubt must have been experienced. I was six—old enought to "remember"—and this entitled me, in the family's eyes, to greater consideration, as if this memory of mine were a lawyer who represented me in court. In deference, therefore, to my age and my supposed powers of criticism and comparison, I was kept on for a time, to roam palely about my grandmother's living rooms, a dangling, transitional creature, a frog becoming a tadpole, while my brothers, poor little polyps, were already well embedded in the structure of the new life. I did not wonder what had become of them. I believe I thought they were dead, but their fate did not greatly concern me; my heart had grown numb. I considered myself clever to have guessed the truth about my parents, like a child who proudly discovers that there is no Santa Claus, but I would not speak of that knowledge or even react to it privately, for I wished to have nothing to do with it; I would not co-operate in this loss. Those weeks in my grandmother's house come back to me very obscurely, surrounded by blackness, like a mourning card: the dark well of the staircase, where I seem to have been endlessly loitering, waiting to see Mama when she would come home from the hospital, and then simply loitering with no purpose whatever; the winter-dim first-grade classroom of the strange academy I was sent to; the drab treatment room of the doctor's office, where every Saturday I screamed and begged on a table while electric shocks were sent through me, for what purpose I cannot conjecture. But this preferential treatment could not be accorded me forever; it was time that I found my niche. "There is someone here to see you"—the maid met me one afternoon with this announcement and a half-curious, half-knowledgeable smile. My heart bounded; I felt almost sick (who else, after all, could it be?), and she had to push me forward. But the man and woman surveying me in the sun parlor with my grandmother were strangers, two unprepossessing middle-aged people—a great-aunt and her husband, so it seemed—to whom I was now commanded to give a hand and a smile, for, as my grandmother remarked, Myers and Margaret had come to take me home that very afternoon to live with them, and I must not make a bad impression.

◦ ◦ ◦

Once the new household was runnig, our parents' death was officially conceded and sentiment given its due. Concrete references to the lost ones, to their beauty, gaiety, and good manners, were naturally not welcomed by our guardians, who possessed none of these qualities themselves, but the veneration of our parents' *memory* was considered an admirable exercise. Our evening prayers were lengthened to include one for our parents' souls, and we were thought to make a pretty picture, all four of us in our pajamas with feet in them, kneeling in a neat line, our hands clasped before us, reciting the prayer for the dead. "Eternal rest grant unto them, oh Lord, and let the perpetual light shine upon them," our thin little voices cried, but this remembrancing, so pleasurable to our guardians, was only a chore to us. We connected it with lights out, washing, all the bedtime coercions, and particularly with the adhesive tape that, to prevent mouth-breathing, was clapped upon our lips the moment the prayer was finished, sealing us up for the night, and that was removed, very painfully, with the help of the ether, in the morning. It embarrassed us to be reminded of our parents by these persons who had superseded them and who seemed to evoke their wraiths in an almost proprietary manner, as though death, the great leveler, had brought them within their province. In the same spirit, we were taken to the cemetery to view our parents' graves; this, in fact, being free of charge, was a regular Sunday pastime with us, which we grew to hate as we did all recreation enforced by our guardians—department-store demonstrations, band concerts, parades, trips to the Old Soldiers' Home, to the Botanical Gardens, to Minnehaha Park, where we watched other children ride on the ponies, to the Zoo, to the water tower—diversions that cost nothing, involved long streetcar trips or endless walking or waiting, and that had the peculiarly fatigued, dusty, proletarianized character of American municipal entertainment. The two mounds that now were our parents associated themselves in our minds with Civil War cannon balls and monuments to the doughboy dead; we contemplated them stolidly, waiting for a sensation, but these twin grass beds, with their junior-executive headstones, elicited nothing whatever; tired of this interminable staring, we would beg to be allowed to go play in some collateral mausoleum, where the dead at least were buried in drawers and offered some stimulus to fancy.

For my grandmother, the recollection of the dead became a mode of civility that she thought proper to exercise toward us whenever, for any reason, one of us came to stay at her house. The reason was almost always the same. We (that is, my brother Kevin or I) had run away from home. Independently of each other, this oldest of my brothers and I had evolved an identical project—to get ourselves placed in an orphan asylum. We had noticed the heightening of interest that mention of our parentless condition seemed always to produce in strangers, and this led us to interpret the word "asylum" in the old Greek sense and to look on a certain red brick building, seen once from a streetcar near the Mississippi River, as a haven of security. So, from time to time, when our lives became too painful, one of us would set forth, determined to find the red brick building and to press what we imagined was our legal claim to its protection. But sometimes we lost our way, and sometimes our courage, and after spending a day hanging about the streets peering into strange yards, trying to assess the kindheartedness of the owner (for we also thought of adoption), or a cold night hiding in a church confessional box or behind some statuary in the Art Institute, we would be brought by the police, by some well-meaning householder, or simply by fear and hunger, to my grandmother's door. There we would be silently received, and a family conclave would be summoned. We would be put to sleep in the sewing room for a night, or sometimes more, until our feelings had subsided and we could be sent back, grateful, at any rate, for the promise that no reprisals would be taken and that the life we had run away from would go on "as if nothing had happened."

Since we were usually running away to escape some anticipated punishment, these flights at least gained us something, but in spite of the taunts of our guardians, who congratulated us bitterly on our "cleverness," we ourselves could not feel that we came home in triumph as long as we came home at all. The cramps and dreads of those long nights made a harrowing impression on us. Our failure to run away successfully put us, so we thought, at the absolute mercy of our guardians; our last weapon was gone, for it was plain to be seen that they could always bring us back and we never understood why they did not take advantage of this situation to thrash us, as they used to put it, within an inch of our lives. What intervened to save us, we could not guess—a miracle, perhaps; we were not acquainted with any *human* motive that would prompt Omnipotence to desist. We did not suspect that these escapes brought consternation to the family circle, which had acted, so it conceived, only in our best interests, and now saw itself in danger of unmerited obloquy. What would be the Protestant reaction if something still more dreadful were to happen? Child suicides were not unknown, and quiet, asthmatic little Kevin had been caught with matches under the house. The family would not acknowledge error, but it conceded a certain mismanagement on

Myers' and Margaret's part. Clearly, we might become altogether intractable if our home-coming on these occasions were not mitigated with leniency. Consequently, my grand-mother kept us in a kind of neutral detention. She declined to be aware of our grievance and offered no words of comfort, but the comforts of her household acted upon us soothingly, like an automatic mother's hand. We ate and drank contentedly; with all her harsh views, my grandmother was a practical woman and would not have thought it worthwhile to un-settle her whole schedule, teach her cook to make a lumpy mush and watery boiled pota-toes, and market for turnips and parsnips and all the other vegetables we hated, in order to approximate the conditions she considered suitable for our characters. Humble pie could be costly, especially when cooked to order.

Doubtless she did not guess how delightful these visits seemed to us once the fear of punishment had abated. Her knowledge of our own way of living was luxuriously remote. She did not visit our ménage or inquire into its practices, and though hypersensitive to a squint or a dental irregularity (for she was liberal indeed with glasses and braces for the teeth, disfiguring appliances that remained the sole token of our bourgeois origin and set us off from our parochial-school mates like the caste marks of some primitive tribe), she appeared not to notice the darns and patches of our clothing, our raw hands and scare-crow arms, our silence and our elderly faces. She imagined us as surrounded by certain play-things she had once bestowed on us—a sandbox, a wooden swing, a wagon, an ambulance, a toy fire engine. In my grandmother's consciousness, these objects remained always in pris-tine condition; years after the sand had spilled out of it and the roof had rotted away, she continued to ask tenderly after our lovely sand pile and to manifest displeasure if we de-clined to join in its praises. Like many egoistic people (I have noticed this trait in myself), she was capable of making a handsome outlay, but the act affected her so powerfully that her generosity was still lively in her memory when its practical effects had long vanished. In the case of a brown beaver hat, which she watched me wear for four years, she was clearly blinded to its matted nap, its shapeless brim, and ragged ribbon by the vision of the price tag it had worn when new. Yet, however her mind embroidered the bare tapestry of our lives, she could not fail to perceive that we felt, during these short stays with her, *some* difference between the two establishments, and to take our wonder and pleasure as a compliment to herself.

She smiled on us quite kindly when we exclaimed over the food and the nice, warm bathrooms, with their rugs and electric heaters. What funny little creatures to be so im-pressed by things that were, after all, only the ordinary amenities of life! Seeing us content in her house, her emulative spirit warmed slowly to our admiration: she compared herself to our guardians, and though for expedient reasons she could not afford to deprecate them ("You children have been very ungrateful for all Myers and Margaret have done for you"), a sense of her own finer magnanimity disposed her subtly in our favor. In the flush of these emotions, a tenderness sprang up between us. She seemed half reluctant to part with whichever of us she had in her custody, almost as if she were experiencing a genuine pang of conscience. "Try and be good," she would advise us when the moment for leave-taking came, "and don't provoke your aunt and uncle. We might have made different arrangements if there had been only one of you to consider." These manifestations of concern, these tacit admissions of our true situation, did not make us, as one might have thought, bitter against our grandparents, for whom ignorance of the facts might have served as a justification, but, on the contrary, filled us with love for them and even a kind of sympathy—our sufferings were less terrible if someone acknowledged their existence, if someone were suffering for us, for whom we, in our turn, could suffer, and thereby absolve of guilt.

◦ ◦ ◦

During these respites, the recollection of our parents formed a bond between us and our grandmother that deepened our mutual regard. Unlike our guardians or the whispering ladies who sometimes came to call on us, inspired, it seemed, by a pornographic curiosity as to the exact details of our feelings ("Do you suppose they remember their parents?" "Do they ever *say* anything?"), our grandmother was quite uninterested in arousing an emotion of grief in us. "She doesn't feel it at all," I used to hear her confide, of me, to visitors, but contentedly, without censure, as if I had been a spayed cat that, in her superior foresight, she had had "attended to." For my grandmother, the death of my parents had become, in retrospect, an eventful occasion upon which she looked back with pleasure and a certain self-satisfaction. Whenever we stayed with her, we were allowed, as a special treat, to look into the rooms they had died in, for the fact that, as she phrased it, "they died in separate rooms" had for her a significance both romantic and somehow self-gratulatory, as though the separation in death of two who had loved each other in life were beautiful in itself and also reflected credit on the chatelaine of the house, who had been able to furnish two master bedrooms for the emergency. The housekeeping details of the tragedy, in fact, were to her of paramount interest. "I turned my house into a hospital," she used to say, particularly when visitors were present. "Nurses were as scarce as hen's teeth, and *high*—you can hardly imagine what those girls were charging an hour." The trays and the special cooking, the laundry and the disinfectants recalled themselves fondly to her thoughts, like items on the menu of some long-ago ball-supper, the memory of which recurred to her with a strong, possessive nostalgia.

My parents had, it seemed, by dying on her premises, become in a lively sense her property, and she dispensed them to us now, little by little, with a genuine sense of bounty, just as, later on, when I returned to her a grown-up young lady, she conceded me a diamond lavaliere of my mother's as if the trinket were an inheritance to which she had the prior claim. But her generosity with her memories appeared to us, as children, an act of the greatest indulgence. We begged her for more of these mortuary reminiscences as we might have begged for candy, and since ordinarily we not only had no candy but were permitted no friendships, no movies, and little reading beyond what our teachers prescribed for us, and were kept in quarantine, like carriers of social contagion, among the rhubarb plants of our neglected yard, these memories doled out by our grandmother became our secret treasures; we never spoke of them to each other but hoarded them, each against the rest, in the miserly fastnesses of our hearts. We returned, therefore, from our grandparents' house replenished in all our faculties; these crumbs from the rich man's table were a banquet indeed to us. We did not even mind going back to our guardians, for we now felt superior to them, and besides, as we well knew, we had no choice. It was only by accepting our situation as a just and unalterable arrangement that we could be allowed to transcend it and feel ourselves united to our grandparents in a love that was the more miraculous for breeding no practical results.

In this manner, our household was kept together, and my grandparents were spared the necessity of arriving at a fresh decision about it. Naturally, from time to time a new scandal would break out (for our guardians did not grow kinder in response to being run away from), yet we had come, at bottom, to despair of making any real change in our circumstances, and ran away hopelessly, merely to postpone punishment. And when, after five years, our Protestant grandfather, informed at last of the facts, intervened to save us, his indignation at the family surprised us nearly as much as his action. We thought it only natural that grandparents should know and do nothing, for did not God in the mansions of Heaven look down upon human suffering and allow it to take its course?

~ *THERE ARE SEVERAL DUBIOUS POINTS IN THIS MEMOIR.*

". . . *we had not known that we had carried the flu with us into our drawing rooms.*" *Just when we got the flu seems to be arguable. According to the newspaper accounts, we contracted it on the trip. This conflicts with the story that Uncle Harry and Aunt Zula had brought it with them. My present memory supports the idea that someone was sick before we left. But perhaps we did not "know" it was the flu.*

". . . *we saw our father draw a revolver.*" *If Uncle Harry is right, this is wrong. In any case, we did not "see" it, I heard the story, as I have said, from my other grandmother. When she told me, I had the feeling that I almost remembered it. That is, my mind promptly supplied me with a picture of it, just as it supplied me with a picture of my father standing in the dining room with his arms full of red roses. Actually, I do dimly recall some dispute with the conductor, who wanted to put us off the train.*

"*We awoke to reality in the sewing room several weeks later.*" *We cannot have been sick that long. The newspaper accounts of my parents' death state that "the children are recovering." We must have arrived in Minneapolis on the second or third of November. My parents probably died on the sixth and seventh of November, I say "probably" because the two newspaper stories contradict each other and neither my brothers nor I feel sure. I know I was still sick on the day of the false armistice, for I remember bells ringing and horns and whistles blowing and a nurse standing over my bed and saying that this meant the war was over. I was in a strange room and did not understand how I had got there, I only knew that outside, where the noise was coming from, was Minneapolis. Looking back, putting two and two together, it suddenly strikes me that this must have been the day of my parents' funeral. My brother Kevin agrees. Now that I have established this, or nearly established it, I have the feeling of "remembering," as though I had always known it. In any case, I was in bed for some days after this, having had flu and pneumonia. Kevin says we were still in our grandmother's house at Christmas. He is sure because he was "bad" that day: he punched out the cloth grill on the library phonograph with a drumstick.*

"'*There is someone here to see you*'—*the maid met me one afternoon with this announcement.*" *I believe this is pure fiction. In reality, I had already seen the people who were going to be my guardians sometime before this, while we were convalescent. We were brought down, in our pajamas, one afternoon to my grandmother's sun parlor, to meet two strangers, a man and a woman, who were sitting there with the rest of the family, like a reception committee. I remember sensing that the occasion had some importance; possibly someone had told us that these people were going to look after us while Mama and Daddy were away, or perhaps stress had merely been laid on "good behavior." Or could it have been just that they were all dressed in black? The man evinced a great deal of paternal good humor, taking my brothers, one by one, on his lap and fondling them while he talked with my grandparents. He paid me no attention at all, and I remember the queer ebb of feeling inside me when I saw I was going to be left out. He did not like me, I noticed this with profound surprise and sorrow. I was not so much jealous as perplexed. After he had played with each of my brothers, we were carried back upstairs to bed. So far as I remember, I did not see him or his wife, following this, for weeks, even months. I cannot recall the circumstances of being moved to the new house at all. But one day I was there, and the next thing I knew, Aunt Margaret was punishing me for having spoiled the wallpaper in my room.*

⚬ ⚬ ⚬

The reader will wonder what made me change this story to something decidedly inferior, even from a literary point of view—far too sentimental, it even sounds improbable. I forget now, but

I think the reason must have been that I did not want to "go into" my guardians as individuals here, that was another story, which was to be told in the next chapter. "Yonder Peasant," unlike the chapters that follow, is not really concerned with individuals. It is, primarily, an angry indictment of privilege for its treatment of the underprivileged, a single, breathless, voluble speech on the subject of human indifference. We orphan children were not responsible for being orphans, but we were treated as if we were and as if being orphans were a crime we had committed. Read poor for orphan throughout and you get a kind of allegory or broad social satire on the theme of wealth and poverty. The anger was a generalized anger, which held up my grandparents as specimens of unfeeling behavior.

My uncle Harry argues that I do not give his mother sufficient credit: if she had lifted her little finger, he says, she could have had me cut out of his father's will. He wants me to understand this and be grateful. (I was fourteen or fifteen when my grandfather died.) This is typical McCarthy reasoning, as the reader will recognize: ". . . clearly, it was a generous impulse that kept us in the family at all."

Nevertheless, in one sense, I have been unfair here to my grandmother: I show her, as it were, in retrospect, looking back at her and judging her as an adult. But as a child, I liked my grandmother, I thought her a tremendous figure. Many of her faults—her blood-curdling Catholicism, for example—were not apparent to me as faults. It gave me a thrill to hear her go on about "the Protestants" and the outrages of the Ku Klux Klan, I even liked to hear her tell about my parents' death. In her way, "Aunt Lizzie," as my second cousins used to call her, was a spellbinder. She spent her winters in Florida, but in the summer she would let me come in the afternoon, quite often, and sit on her shaded front porch, watching her sew and listening to her. Afterward, I was allowed to go out and give myself a ride on the turntable in her big garage— a sort of merry-go-round on which the chauffeur turned her cars, so that they never had to be backed in or out. Besides her Pierce-Arrow, for winter use, she had a Locomobile, canvas-topped, for summer, which she sometimes took me driving in, out to Minnetonka or Great Bear Lake or Winona. Once we visited an Ursuline convent, and once we went up to St. Joseph to look at St. Benedict's Academy. On these occasions, in her motoring costume, veils, and high-crowned straw hat, she was an imposing great lady.

You felt she could be "big" when she wanted to. "My mother was square," says Uncle Harry. She also had a worldly side, fancying herself as a woman of fashion and broad social horizons. One summer, she and my grandfather took me with them to a snappy resort in northern Minnesota called Breezy Point. It was run by a man named Billy Fawcett, the editor of Captain Billy's Whiz Bang; there I first saw a woman smoke. On the way back, we stopped to visit my grandfather's brother, my uncle John, just outside Duluth, where the grain-elevator company had its main offices. He had a large country house, with formal gardens and walks, set in a deep forest. They showed me phosphorescent wood and fireflies, there were fairies in the garden, they said. Before going to bed, I left a note for the fairies in a rose, fully expecting an answer. But the next morning there was only dew in the rose, and I felt very troubled, for this proved to me that fairies didn't exist.

There was a spaciousness in my grandmother's personality that made her comfortable to be with, even though you were in awe of her. Marshall Field's, she often related, had offered her a thousand dollars for a tapestried chair she had sewn, but she had promised the chair to Uncle Louis, so, naturally, she had had to turn down the offer. This impressed me mightily, though I wondered why she did not just make another one if she had wanted to sell it to Marshall Field's. Whenever I went shopping with her, I felt that she was about to give me a present, though there was nothing, except her manner, to encourage this notion. On my way east to Vassar, she did propose buying me an electric doughnut-maker for my room. Fortunately, I refused; I later discovered that she was in the habit of deducting the presents she gave my brothers from the trust fund that had been left them. Thus her ample character was strangely touched with meanness.

◦ ◦ ◦

I have stressed the family's stinginess where we were concerned, the rigid double standard maintained between the two houses. Yet my grandfather, according to Uncle Harry, spent $41,700 for our support between the years 1918 and 1923. During this time, the Preston family contributed $300. This peculiar discrepancy I shall have to deal with later. What interests me now is the question of where the money went. Approximately $8,200 a year was not a small sum, for those days, considering, too, that it was tax free and that nothing had to be put aside for savings or life insurance. Could some of the money really have been embezzled, as we children used to think?

With that figure before my eyes, I understand a little more than I did of my grandparents' feelings. In view of his check stubs, my grandfather would have had every reason to assume that we children were being decently taken care of in the house he had bought for us. I do remember his surprise when he found that we were being given only those two pennies to put in the collection plate on Sundays. But he did not see us very often, and when he did, we did not complain. This seems odd, but it is true. I do not think we ever brought our woes to our grandparents. When we finally spoke, it was to our other grandfather, the one we hardly knew. We were afraid of punishment, I suppose. The only form of complaint, from us, that was visible to the family was that silent running away. It was I who spent the night in a confessional and a day hiding behind the statue of Laocoön in the Art Institute. That was as far as I got, for I did not have the carfare that was needed to get me to that red brick orphan asylum. Kevin was hardier. Traveling on a transfer he had somehow acquired, he reached a yellow brick orphan asylum called "The Sheltering Arms" that was run by the Shriners. He did not like it as well, in spite of its name, as the red brick one, and though he peered over the wall for a long time, in the end he was afraid to go in. A householder found him crying, fed him, and eventually the Pierce-Arrow came with Uncle Louis to get him; this made the householder think Kevin a terrible fraud.

The family, I think now, must have been greatly perturbed by our running away. It meant either that we were unhappy or that we were incorrigibly bad. I had stolen a ring from the five-and-ten, and my aunt had had to march me back with it into the manager's office. Kevin had altered his report card when the prize of a dime (no, a nickel) had been offered to the one with the highest marks, and one month I had torn and defaced mine because I was afraid to show a low mark at home. At home, threats of reform school hung over us, yet at school, paradoxically, we, or at least I (I cannot remember about Kevin), stood high in conduct. And when I went to my weekly confession, I seldom got anything but the very lightest penance—those little Our Fathers and Hail Marys were almost a disappointment to me. As my grandmother must have known, I was a favorite with the parish priests.

My present impression is that my grandparents slowly came to realize the true situation in our household and that they themselves were on the point of acting when my other grandfather intervened. Looking back, I believe my grandmother was planning to enter me in the Ursuline convent we visited; certainly, that was the hope her behavior on the trip gave rise to. No doubt, they blinded themselves as long as possible, for to admit the truth was to face up to the problem of separating us children and either putting us in schools to board (for which we were really too young) or distributing us among the family (which my aunts and uncles would probably have resisted) or letting the Protestants get some of us.

Annie Dillard

from An American Childhood

WE LIVED IN A CLEAN CITY WHOSE CENTER WAS NEW; AFTER THE WAR, A FEW BUSINESS leaders and Democratic Mayor David L. Lawrence had begun cleaning it up. Beneath the new city, and tucked up its hilly alleys, lay the old Pittsburgh, and the old foothill land beneath it. It was all old if you dug far enough. Our Pittsburgh was like Rome, or Jericho, a palimpsest, a sliding pile of cities built ever nearer the sky, and rising ever higher over the rivers. If you dug, you found things.

Oma's chauffeur, Henry Watson, dug a hole in our yard on Edgerton Avenue to plant a maple tree when I was born, and again when Amy was born three years later. When he dug the hole for Amy's maple, he found an arrowhead—smaller than a dime and sharp. Our mother continually remodeled each of the houses we lived in: the workmen knocked out walls and found brick walls under the plaster and oak planks under the brick. City workers continually paved the streets: they poured asphalt over the streetcar tracks, streetcar tracks their fathers had wormed between the old riverworn cobblestones, cobblestones laid smack into the notorious nineteenth-century mud. Long stretches of that mud were the same pioneer roads that General John Forbes's troops had hacked over the mountains from Carlisle, or General Braddock's troops had hacked from the Chesapeake and the Susquehanna, widening with their axes the woodland paths the Indians had worn on deer trails.

Many old stone houses had slate-shingle roofs. I used to find blown shingles cracked open on the sidewalk; some of them bore—inside, where no one had been able to look until now—fine fossil prints of flat leaves. I heard there were dinosaur bones under buildings. The largest coal-bearing rock sequence in the world ran under Pittsburgh and popped out at Coal Hill, just across the Monongahela. (Then it ducked far underground and ran up into Nova Scotia, dove into the water and crossed under the Atlantic, and rolled up again thick with coal in Wales.) There were layers of natural gas beneath Pittsburgh, and pools of petroleum the pioneers called Seneca oil, because only Indians would fool with it.

◦ ◦ ◦

We children lived and breathed our history—our Pittsburgh history, so crucial to the country's story and so typical of it as well—without knowing or believing any of it. For how can anyone know or believe stories she dreamed in her sleep, information for which and to which she feels herself to be in no way responsible? A child is asleep. Her private life unwinds inside her skin and skull; only as she sheds childhood, first one decade and then another, can she locate the actual, historical stream, see the setting of her dreaming private life—the nation, the city, the neighborhood, the house where the family lives—as an actual project under way, a project living people willed, and made well or failed, and are still making, herself among them. I breathed the air of history all unaware, and walked oblivious through its littered layers.

◦ ◦ ◦

Outside in the neighborhoods, learning our way around the streets, we played among the enormous stone monuments of the millionaires—both those tireless Pittsburgh founders of the heavy industries from which the nation's wealth derived (they told us at school) and the industrialists' couldn't-lose bankers and backers, all of whom began as canny boys, the stories of whose rises to riches adults still considered inspirational to children.

95

We were unthinkingly familiar with the moguls' immense rough works as so much weird scenery on long drives. We saw the long, low-slung stripes of steel factories by the rivers; we saw pyramidal heaps of yellow sand at glassworks by the shining railroad tracks; we saw rusty slag heaps on the outlying hilltops, and coal barges tied up at the docks. We recognized, on infrequent trips downtown, the industries' smooth corporate headquarters, each to its own soaring building—Gulf Oil, Alcoa, U.S. Steel, Koppers Company, Pittsburgh Plate Glass, Mellon Bank. Our classmates' fathers worked in these buildings, or at nearby corporate headquarters for Westinghouse Electric, Jones & Laughlin Steel, Rockwell Manufacturing, American Standard, Allegheny Ludlum, Westinghouse Air Brake, and H. J. Heinz.

The nineteenth-century industrialists' institutions—galleries, universities, hospitals, churches, Carnegie libraries, the Carnegie Museum, Frick Park, Mellon Park—were, many of them, my stomping grounds. These absolute artifacts of philanthropy littered the neighborhoods with marble. Millionaires' encrusted mansions, now obsolete and turned into parks or art centers, weighed on every block. They lent their expansive, hushed moods to the Point Breeze neighborhoods where we children lived and where those fabulous men had lived also, or rather had visited at night in order to sleep. Everywhere I looked, it was the Valley of the Kings, their dynasty just ended, and their monuments intact but already out of fashion.

All these immensities wholly dominated the life of the city. So did their several peculiar social legacies: their powerful Calvinist mix of piety and acquisitiveness, which characterized the old and new Scotch-Irish families and the nation they helped found; the walled-up hush of what was, by my day, old money—amazing how fast it ages if you let it alone—and the clang and roar of making that money; the owners' Presbyterian churches, their anti-Catholicism, anti-Semitism, Republicanism, and love of continuous work; their dogmatic practicality, their easy friendliness, their Pittsburgh-centered innocence, and, paradoxically, their egalitarianism.

For all the insularity of the old guard, Pittsburgh was always an open and democratic town. "Best-natured people I ever went among," a Boston visitor noted two centuries earlier. In colonial days, everybody went to balls, regardless of rank. No one had any truck with aristocratic pretensions—hadn't they hated the British lords in Ulster? People who cared to rave about their bloodlines, Mother told us, had stayed in Europe, which deserved them. We were vaguely proud of living in a city so full of distinctive immigrant groups, among which we never thought to number ourselves. We had no occasion to visit the steep hillside neighborhoods—Polish, Hungarian, Rumanian, Italian, Slav—of the turn-of-the-century immigrants who poured the steel and stirred the glass and shoveled the coal.

We children played around the moguls' enormous pale stone houses, restful as tombs, houses set back just so on their shaded grounds. Henry Clay Frick's daughter, unthinkably old, lived alone in her proud, sinking mansion; she had lived alone all her life. No one saw her. Men mowed the wide lawns and seeded them, and pushed rollers over them, over the new grass seed and musket balls and arrowheads, over the big trees' roots, bones, shale, coal.

⋆ ⋆ ⋆

We knew bits of this story, and we knew none of it. Odd facts stuck in the mind: On the Pennsylvania frontier in the eighteenth century, people pressed hummingbirds as if they were poppies, between pages of heavy books, and mailed them back to Ulster and Scotland as curiosities. Money was so scarce in the western Pennsylvania mountains that, as late as the mid-nineteenth century, people substituted odds and ends like road contracts, feathers, and elderberries.

We knew that before big industry there had been small industry here—H. J. Heinz setting up a roadside stand to sell horseradish roots from his garden. There were the makers of cannonballs for the Civil War. There were the braggart and rowdy flatboat men and keelboat men, and the honored steamboat builders and pilots. There were local men getting rich in iron and glass manufacturing and trade downriver. There was a whole continentful of people passing through, native-born and immigrant men and women who funneled down Pittsburgh, where two rivers converged to make a third river. It was the gateway to the West; they piled onto flatboats and launched out into the Ohio River singing, to head for new country. There had been a Revolutionary War, and before that the French and Indian War. And before that, and first of all, had been those first settlers come walking bright-eyed in, into nowhere from out of nowhere, the people who, as they said, "broke wilderness," the pioneers. This was the history.

◦ ◦ ◦

I treasured some bits; they provided doll-like figures for imagination's travels and wars. There in private imagination were the vivid figures of history in costume, tricked out as if for amateur outdoor drama: a moving, clumsy, insignificant spectacle like everything else the imagination proposes to itself for pure pleasure only—nothing real, nobody gets hurt, it's only ketchup.

WHILE FATHER WAS MOTORING DOWN THE RIVER, MY READING WAS GIVING ME A TURN.

broken up almost like chapters?

At a neighbor boy's house, I ran into Kimon Nicolaides' *The Natural Way to Draw*. This was a manual for students who couldn't get to Nicolaides' own classes at New York's Art Students League. I was amazed that there were books about things one actually did. I had been drawing in earnest, but at random, for two years. Like all children, when I drew I tried to reproduce schema. The idea of drawing from life had astounded me two years previously, but I had gradually let it slip, and my drawing, such as it was, had sunk back into facile sloth. Now this book would ignite my fervor for conscious drawing, and bind my attention to both the vigor and the detail of the actual world.

For the rest of August, and all fall, this urgent, hortatory book ran my life. I tried to follow its schedules: every day, sixty-five gesture drawings, fifteen memory drawings, an hour-long contour drawing, and "The Sustained Study in Crayon, Clothed" or "The Sustained Study in Crayon, Nude."

While Father was gone, I outfitted an attic bedroom as a studio, and moved in. Every summer or weekend morning at eight o'clock I taped that day's drawing schedule to a wall. Since there was no model, nude or clothed, I drew my baseball mitt.

I drew my baseball mitt's gesture—its tense repose, its expectancy, which ran up its hollows like a hand. I drew its contours—its flat fingertips strung on square rawhide thongs. I drew its billion grades of light and dark in detail, so the glove weighed vivid and complex on the page, and the trapezoids small as dust motes in the leather fingers cast shadows, and the pale palm leather was smooth as a belly and thick. "Draw anything," said the book. "Learning to draw is really a matter of learning to see," said the book. "Imagine that your pencil point is touching the model instead of the paper." "All the student need concern himself with is reality."

With my pencil point I crawled over the mitt's topology. I slithered over each dip and rise; I checked my bearings, admired the enormous view, and recorded it like Meriwether Lewis mapping the Rockies.

One thing struck me as odd and interesting. A gesture drawing took forty-five seconds;

a Sustained Study took all morning. From any still-life arrangement or model's pose, the artist could produce either a short study or a long one. Evidently, a given object took no particular amount of time to draw; instead the artist took the time, or didn't take it, at pleasure. And, similarly, things themselves possessed no fixed and intrinsic amount of interest; instead things were interesting as long as you had attention to give them. How long does it take to draw a baseball mitt? As much time as you care to give it. Not an infinite amount of time, but more time than you first imagined. For many days, so long as you want to keep drawing that mitt, and studying that mitt, there will always be a new and finer layer of distinctions to draw out and lay in. Your attention discovers—seems thereby to produce—an array of interesting features in any object, like a lamp.

By noon, all this drawing would have gone to my head. I slipped into the mitt, quit the attic, quit the house, and headed up the street, looking for a ball game.

⌁   ⌁   ⌁

My friend had sought permission from his father for me to borrow *The Natural Way to Draw*; it was his book. Grown men and growing children rarely mingled then. I had lived two doors away from this family for several years, and had never clapped eyes on my good friend's father; still, I now regarded him as a man after my own heart. Had he another book about drawing? He had; he owned a book about pencil drawing. This book began well enough, with the drawing of trees. Then it devoted a chapter to the schematic representation of shrubbery. At last it dwindled into its true subject, the drawing of buildings.

My friend's father was an architect. All his other books were about buildings. He had been a boy who liked to draw, according to my friend, so he became an architect. Children who drew, I learned, became architects; I had thought they became painters. My friend explained that it was not proper to become a painter; it couldn't be done. I resigned myself to architecture school and a long life of drawing buildings. It was a pity, for I disliked buildings, considering them only a stiffer and more ample form of clothing, and no more important.

⌁   ⌁   ⌁

I began reading books, reading books to delirium. I began by vanishing from the known world into the passive abyss of reading, but soon found myself engaged with surprising vigor because the things in the books, or even the things surrounding the books, roused me from my stupor. From the nearest library I learned every sort of surprising thing—some of it, though not much of it, from the books themselves.

The Homewood branch of Pittsburgh's Carnegie Library system was in a Negro section of town—Homewood. This branch was our nearest library; Mother drove me to it every two weeks for many years, until I could drive myself. I only very rarely saw other white people there.

I understood that our maid, Margaret Butler, had friends in Homewood. I never saw her there, but I did see Henry Watson.

I was getting out of Mother's car in front of the library when Henry appeared on the sidewalk; he was walking with some other old men. I had never before seen him at large; it must have been his day off. He had gold-rimmed glasses, a gold front tooth, and a frank, open expression. It would embarrass him, I thought, if I said hello to him in front of his friends. I was wrong. He spied me, picked me up—books and all—swung me as he always did, and introduced Mother and me to his friends. Later, as we were climbing the long stone steps to the library's door, Mother said, "That's what I mean by good manners."

⤶ ⤶ ⤶

The Homewood Library had graven across its enormous stone facade: FREE TO THE PEOPLE. In the evenings, neighborhood people—the men and women of Homewood—browsed in the library, and brought their children. By day, the two vaulted rooms, the adults' and children's sections, were almost empty. The kind Homewood librarians, after a trial period, had given me a card to the adult section. This was an enormous silent room with marble floors. Nonfiction was on the left.

Beside the farthest wall, and under leaded windows set ten feet from the floor, so that no human being could ever see anything from them—next to the wall, and at the farthest remove from the idle librarians at their curved wooden counter, and from the oak bench where my mother waited in her camel's-hair coat chatting with the librarians or reading—stood the last and darkest and most obscure of the tall nonfiction stacks: NEGRO HISTORY and NATURAL HISTORY. It was in Natural History, in the cool darkness of a bottom shelf, that I found *The Field Book of Ponds and Streams*.

The Field Book of Ponds and Streams was a small, blue-bound book printed in fine type on thin paper, like *The Book of Common Prayer*. Its third chapter explained how to make sweep nets, plankton nets, glass-bottomed buckets, and killing jars. It specified how to mount slides, how to label insects on their pins, and how to set up a freshwater aquarium.

One was to go into "the field" wearing hip boots and perhaps a head net for mosquitoes. One carried in a "rucksack" half a dozen corked test tubes, a smattering of screw-top baby-food jars, a white enamel tray, assorted pipettes and eyedroppers, an artillery of cheesecloth nets, a notebook, a hand lens, perhaps a map, and *The Field Book of Ponds and Streams*. This field—unlike the fields I had seen, such as the field where Walter Milligan played football—was evidently very well watered, for there one could find, and distinguish among, daphniae, planaria, water pennies, stonefly larvae, dragonfly nymphs, salamander larvae, tadpoles, snakes, and turtles, all of which one could carry home.

That anyone had lived the fine life described in Chapter 3 astonished me. Although the title page indicated quite plainly that one Ann Haven Morgan had written *The Field Book of Ponds and Streams*, I nevertheless imagined, perhaps from the authority and freedom of it, that its author was a man. It would be good to write him and assure him that someone had found his book, in the dark near the marble floor at the Homewood Library. I would, in the same letter or in a subsequent one, ask him a question outside the scope of his book, which was where I personally might find a pond, or a stream. But I did not know how to address such a letter, of course, or how to learn if he was still alive.

I was afraid, too, that my letter would disappoint him by betraying my ignorance, which was just beginning to attract my own notice. What, for example, was this noisome-sounding substance called cheesecloth, and what do scientists do with it? What, when you really got down to it, was enamel? If candy could, notoriously, "eat through enamel," why would anyone make trays out of it? Where—short of robbing a museum—might a fifth-grade student at the Ellis School on Fifth Avenue obtain such a legendary item as a wooden bucket?

The Field Book of Ponds and Streams was a shocker from beginning to end. The greatest shock came at the end.

When you checked out a book from the Homewood Library, the librarian wrote your number on the book's card and stamped the due date on a sheet glued to the book's last page. When I checked out *The Field Book of Ponds and Streams* for the second time, I noticed the book's card. It was almost full. There were numbers on both sides. My hearty author and

I were not alone in the world, after all. With us, and sharing our enthusiasm for dragonfly larvae and single-celled plants, were, apparently, many Negro adults.

Who were these people? Had they, in Pittsburgh's Homewood section, found ponds? Had they found streams? At home, I read the book again; I studied the drawings; I reread Chapter 3; then I settled in to study the due-date slip. People read this book in every season. Seven or eight people were reading this book every year, even during the war.

Every year, I read again *The Field Book of Ponds and Streams*. Often, when I was in the library, I simply visited it. I sat on the marble floor and studied the book's card. There we all were. There was my number. There was the number of someone else who had checked it out more than once. Might I contact this person and cheer him up? For I assumed that, like me, he had found pickings pretty slim in Pittsburgh.

The people of Homewood, some of whom lived in visible poverty, on crowded streets among burned-out houses—they dreamed of ponds and streams. They were saving to buy microscopes. In their bedrooms they fashioned plankton nets. But their hopes were even more vain than mine, for I was a child, and anything might happen; they were adults, living in Homewood. There was neither pond nor stream on the streetcar routes. The Homewood residents whom I knew had little money and little free time. The marble floor was beginning to chill me. It was not fair.

❧   ❧   ❧

I had been driven into nonfiction against my wishes. I wanted to read fiction, but I had learned to be cautious about it.

"When you open a book," the sentimental library posters said, "anything can happen." This was so. A book of fiction was a bomb. It was a land mine you wanted to go off. You wanted it to blow your whole day. Unfortunately, hundreds of thousands of books were duds. They had been rusting out of everyone's way for so long that they no longer worked. There was no way to distinguish the duds from the live mines except to throw yourself at them headlong, one by one.

The suggestions of adults were uncertain and incoherent. They gave you Nancy Drew with one hand and *Little Women* with the other. They mixed good and bad books together because they could not distinguish between them. Any book which contained children, or short adults, or animals, was felt to be a children's book. So also was any book about the sea—as though danger or even fresh air were a child's prerogative—or any book by Charles Dickens or Mark Twain. Virtually all British books, actually, were children's books; no one understood children like the British. Suited to female children were love stories set in any century but this one. Consequently one had read, exasperated often to fury, *Pickwick Papers*, *Désirée*, *Wuthering Heights*, *Lad, a Dog*, *Gulliver's Travels*, *Gone With the Wind*, *Robinson Crusoe*, Nordhoff and Hall's *Bounty* trilogy, *Moby-Dick*, *The Five Little Peppers*, *Innocents Abroad*, *Lord Jim*, *Old Yeller*.

The fiction stacks at the Homewood Library, their volumes alphabetized by author, baffled me. How could I learn to choose a novel? That I could not easily reach the top two shelves helped limit choices a little. Still, on the lower shelves I saw too many books: Mary Johnson, *Sweet Rocket*; Samuel Johnson, *Rasselas*; James Jones, *From Here to Eternity*. I checked out the last because I had heard of it; it was good. I decided to check out books I had heard of. I had heard of *The Mill on the Floss*. I read it, and it was good. On its binding was printed a figure, a man dancing or running; I had noticed this figure before. Like so many children before and after me, I learned to seek out this logo, the Modern Library colophon.

The going was always rocky. I couldn't count on Modern Library the way I could count on, say, *Mad* magazine, which never failed to slay me. *Native Son* was good, *Walden* was pretty good, *The Interpretation of Dreams* was okay, and *The Education of Henry Adams* was awful. *Ulysses,* a very famous book, was also awful. *Confessions* by Augustine, whose title promised so much, was a bust. *Confessions* by Jean-Jacques Rousseau was much better, though it fell apart halfway through.

In fact, it was a plain truth that most books fell apart halfway through. They fell apart as their protagonists quit, without any apparent reluctance, like idiots diving voluntarily into buckets, the most interesting part of their lives, and entered upon decades of unrelieved tedium. I was forewarned, and would not so bobble my adult life; when things got dull, I would go to sea.

Jude the Obscure was the type case. It started out so well. Halfway through, its author forgot how to write. After Jude got married, his life was over, but the book went on for hundreds of pages while he stewed in his own juices. The same thing happened in *The Little Shepherd of Kingdom Come,* which Mother brought me from a fair. It was simply a hazard of reading. Only a heartsick loyalty to the protagonists of the early chapters, to the eager children they had been, kept me reading chronological narratives to their bitter ends. Perhaps later, when I had become an architect, I would enjoy the latter halves of books more.

◦ ◦ ◦

This was the most private and obscure part of life, this Homewood Library: a vaulted marble edifice in a mostly decent Negro neighborhood, the silent stacks of which I plundered in deep concentration for many years. There seemed then, happily, to be an infinitude of books.

I no more expected anyone else on earth to have read a book I had read than I expected someone else to have twirled the same blade of grass. I would never meet those Homewood people who were borrowing *The Field Book of Ponds and Streams;* the people who read my favorite books were invisible or in hiding, underground. Father occasionally raised his big eyebrows at the title of some volume I was hurrying off with, quite as if he knew what it contained—but I thought he must know of it by hearsay, for none of it seemed to make much difference to him. Books swept me away, one after the other, this way and that; I made endless vows according to their lights, for I believed them.

The interior life expands and fills; it approaches the edge of skin; it thickens with its own vivid story; it even begins to hear rumors, from beyond the horizon skin's rim, of nations and wars. You wake one day and discover your grandmother; you wake another day and notice, like any curious naturalist, the boys.

◦ ◦ ◦

There were already boys then: not tough boys—much as I missed their inventiveness and easy democracy—but the polite boys of Richland Lane. The polite boys of Richland Lane aspired to the Presbyterian ministry. Their fathers were surgeons, lawyers, architects, and businessmen, who sat on the boards of churches and hospitals. Early on warm weekday evenings, we children played rough in the calm yards and cultivated woods, grabbing and bruising each other often enough in the course of our magnificently organized games. On Saturday afternoons, these same neighborhood boys appeared wet-combed and white-shirted at the front door, to take me gently to the movies on the bus. And there were the dancing-school boys, who materialized at the front door on Valentine's Day, holding heart-shaped boxes of chocolates.

I was ten when I met the dancing-school boys; it was that same autumn, 1955. Father was motoring down the river. The new sandstone wall was up in the living room.

Outside the city, the mountainside maples were turning; the oaks were green. Everywhere in the spreading Mississippi watershed, from the Allegheny and the Ohio here in Pittsburgh to the Missouri and the Cheyenne and the Bighorn draining the Rocky Mountains, yellow and red leaves, silver-maple and black-oak leaves, or pale cottonwood leaves and aspen, slipped down to the tight surface of the moving water. A few leaves fell on the decks of Father's boat when he tied up at an Ohio island for lunch; he raked them off with his fingers, probably, and thought it damned strange to be raking leaves at all.

Molly, the new baby, had grown less mysterious; she smiled and crawled over the grass or the rug. The family had begun spending summers around a country-club pool. Amy and I had started at a girls' day school, the Ellis School; I belted on the green jumper I would wear, in one size or another, for the next eight years, until I left Pittsburgh altogether. I was taking piano lessons, art classes. And I started dancing school.

❖   ❖   ❖

The dancing-school boys, it turned out, were our boys, the boys, who ascended through the boys' private school as we ascended through the girls'. I was surprised to see them that first Friday afternoon in dancing school. I was surprised, that is, to see that I already knew them, that I already knew almost everyone in the room; I was surprised that dancing school, as an institution, was eerily more significant than all my other lessons and classes, and that it was not peripheral at all, but central.

For here we all were. I'd seen the boys in, of all places, church—one of the requisite Presbyterian churches of Pittsburgh. I'd seen them at the country club, too. I knew the girls from church, the country club, and school. Here we all were at dancing school; here we all were, dressed to the teeth and sitting on rows of peculiar painted and gilded chairs. Here we all were, boys and girls, plunged by our conspiring elders into the bewildering social truth that we were meant to make each other's acquaintance. Dancing school.

There in that obscure part of town, there in that muffled enormous old stone building, among those bizarre and mismatched adults who seemed grimly to dance their lives away in that dry and claustrophobic ballroom—there, it proved, was the unlikely arena where we were foreordained to assemble, Friday after Friday, for many years until the distant and seemingly unrelated country clubs took over the great work of providing music for us later and later into the night until the time came when we should all have married each other up, at last.

❖   ❖   ❖

"Isn't he cute?" Bebe would whisper to me as we sat in the girls' row on the edge of the ballroom floor. I had never before seen a painted chair; my mother favored wood for its own sake. The lugubrious instructors were demonstrating one of several fox-trots.

Which?

"Ronny," she whispered one week, and "Danny," the next. I would find that one in the boys' row. He'd fastened his fists to his seat and was rocking back and forth from his hips all unconsciously, open-mouthed.

Sure.

"Isn't he cute?" Mimsie would ask at school, and I would think of this Ricky or Dick, recall some stray bit of bubbling laughter in which he had been caught helpless, pawing at his bangs with his bent wrist, his saliva whitening his braces' rubber bands and occasionally forming a glassy pane at the corner of his mouth; I would remember the way his head bobbed, and imagine those two parallel rods at the back of his neck, which made a thin valley where a short tip of hair lay tapered and curled; the way he scratched his ear by wincing, raising a shoulder, and rubbing the side of his head on his jacket's sleeve seam. Cute?

You bet he was cute. They all were.

-o-   -o-   -o-

Onstage the lonely pianist played "Mountain Greenery." Sometimes he played "Night and Day." It was Friday afternoon; we could have been sled riding. On Fridays, our unrelated private schools, boys' and girls', released us early. On Fridays, dancing school met, an hour later each year, until at last we met in the dark, disrupting our families' dinners, and at last certain boys began to hold our hands, carefully looking away, after a given dance, to secure us for the next one.

We all wore white cotton gloves. Only with the greatest of effort could I sometimes feel, or fancy I felt, the warmth of a boy's hand—through his glove and my glove—on my right palm. My gloved left hand lay lightly, always lightly, on his jacket shoulder. His gloved right hand lay, forgotten by both of us, across the clumsy back of my dress, across its lumpy velvet bow or its long cold zipper concealed by brocade.

Between dances when we held hands, we commonly interleaved our fingers, as if for the sheer challenge of it, for our thick cotton gloves permitted almost no movement, and we quickly cut off the circulation in each other's fingers. If for some reason we had released each other's hands quickly, without thinking, our gloves would have come off and dropped to the ballroom floor together still entwined, while our numbed bare fingers slowly regained sensation and warmth.

We were all on some list. We were to be on that list for life, it turned out, unless we left. I had no inkling of this crucial fact, although the others, I believe, did. I was mystified to see that whoever devised the list misunderstood things so. The best-liked girl in our class, my friend Ellin Hahn, was conspicuously excluded. Because she was precisely fifty percent Jewish, she had to go to Jewish dancing school. The boys courted her anyway, one after the other, and only made do with the rest of us at dancing school. From other grades at our school, all sorts of plain, unintelligent, lifeless girls were included. These were quiet or silly girls, who seemed at school to recognize their rather low places, but who were unreasonably exuberant at dancing school, and who were gradually revealed to have known all along that in the larger arena they occupied very high places indeed. And these same lumpish, plain, very rich girls wound up marrying, to my unending stupefaction, the very liveliest and handsomest of the boys.

The boys. There were, essentially, a dozen or so of them and a dozen or so of us, so it was theoretically possible, as it were, to run through all of them by the time you finished school. We saw our dancing-school boys everywhere we went. Yet they were by no means less extraordinary for being familiar. They were familiar only visually: their eyebrows we could study in quick glimpses as we danced, eyebrows that met like spliced ropes over their noses; the winsome whorls of their hair we could stare at openly in church, hair that radiated spirally from the backs of their quite individual skulls; the smooth skin on their pliant torsos at the country-club pool, all so fascinating, each so different; and their weird little graceful bathing suits: the boys. Richard, Rich, Richie, Ricky, Ronny, Donny, Dan.

⌖ ⌖ ⌖

They called each other witty names, like Jag-Off. They could dribble. They walked clumsily but assuredly through the world, kicking things for the hell of it. By way of conversation, they slugged each other on their interesting shoulders.

They moved in violent jerks from which we hung back, impressed and appalled, as if from horses slamming the slats of their stalls. This and, as we would have put it, their messy eyelashes. In our heartless, condescending, ignorant way we loved their eyelashes, the fascinating and dreadful way the black hairs curled and tangled. That's the kind of vitality they had, the boys, that's the kind of novelty and attraction: their very eyelashes came out amok, and unthinkably original. That we loved, that and their cloddishness, their broad, vaudevillian reactions. They were always doing slow takes. Their breathtaking lack of subtlety in every particular, we thought—and then sometimes a gleam of consciousness in their eyes, as surprising as if you'd caught a complicit wink from a brick.

⌖ ⌖ ⌖

Ah, the boys. How little I understood them! How little I even glimpsed who they were. How little any of us did, if I may extrapolate. How completely I condescended to them when we were ten and they were in many ways my betters. And when we were fifteen, how little I understood them still, or again. I still thought they were all alike, for all practical purposes, no longer comical beasts now but walking gods who conferred divine power with their least glances. In fact, they were neither beasts nor gods, as I should have guessed. If they were alike it was in this, that all along the boys had been in the process of becoming responsible members of an actual and moral world we small-minded and fast-talking girls had never heard of.

They had been learning self-control. We had failed to develop any selves worth controlling. We were enforcers of a code we never questioned; we were vigilantes of the trivial. They had been accumulating information about the world outside our private schools and clubs. We had failed to notice that there was such a thing. The life of Pittsburgh, say, or the United States, or assorted foreign continents, concerned us no more than Jupiter did, or its moons.

The boys must have shared our view that we were, as girls, in the long run, negligible— not any sort of factor in anybody's day, or life, no sort of creatures to be reckoned with, or even reckoned in, at all. For they could perhaps see that we possessed neither self-control nor information, so the world could not be ours.

There was something ahead of the boys, we all felt, but we didn't know what it was. To a lesser extent and vicariously, it was ahead of us, too. From the quality of attention our elders gave to various aspects of our lives, we could have inferred that we were being prepared for a life of ballroom dancing. But we knew that wasn't it. Only children practiced ballroom dancing, for which they were patently unsuited. It was something, however, that ballroom dancing obliquely prepared us for, just as, we were told, the study of Latin would obliquely prepare us for something else, also unspecified.

Whatever we needed in order to meet the future, it was located at the unthinkable juncture of Latin class and dancing school. With the declension of Latin nouns and the conjugation of Latin verbs, it had to do with our minds' functioning; presumably this held true for the five steps of the fox-trot as well. Learning these things would permanently alter the structure of our brains, whether we wanted it to or not.

So the boys, with the actual world before them, had when they were small a bewildered air, and an endearing and bravura show of manliness. On the golden-oak ballroom floor, every darkening Friday afternoon while we girls rustled in our pastel dresses and felt at our hair ineffectually with our cotton gloves, the boys in their gloves, standing right in plain view between dances, exploded firecrackers. I would be waltzing with some arm-pumping tyke of a boy when he whispered excitedly in my ear, "Guess what I have in my pocket?" I knew. It was a cherry bomb. He slammed the thing onto the oak floor when no one was looking but a knot of his friends. The instructors flinched at the bang and stiffened; the knot of boys scattered as if shot; we could taste the sharp gunpowder in the air, and see a dab of gray ash on the floor. And when he laughed, his face reddened and gave off a vaporous heat. He seemed tickled inside his jiggling bones; he flapped his arms and slapped himself and tears fell on his tie.

They must have known, those little boys, that they would inherit corporate Pittsburgh, as indeed they have. They must have known that it was theirs by rights as boys, a real world, about which they had best start becoming informed. And they must have known, too, as Pittsburgh Presbyterian boys, that they could only just barely steal a few hours now, a few years now, to kid around, to dribble basketballs and explode firecrackers, before they were due to make a down payment on a suitable house.

Soon they would enter investment banking and take their places in the management of Fortune 500 corporations. Soon in their scant spare time they would be serving on the boards of schools, hospitals, country clubs, and churches. No wonder they laughed so hard. These were boys who wore ties from the moment their mothers could locate their necks.

⋄ ⋄ ⋄

I assumed that like me the boys dreamed of running away to sea, of curing cancer, of playing for the Pirates, of painting in Paris, of tramping through the Himalayas, for we were all children together. And they may well have dreamed these things, and more, then and later. I don't know.

Those boys who confided in me later, however, when we were all older, dreamed nothing of the kind. One wanted to be top man at Gulf Oil. One wanted to accumulate a million dollars before he turned thirty. And one wanted to be majority leader in the U.S. Senate.

But these, the boys who confided in me, were the ones I would love when we were in our teens, and they were, according to my predilection, not the dancing-school boys at all, but other, oddball boys. I would give my heart to one oddball boy after another—to older boys, to prep-school boys no one knew, to him who refused to go to college, to him who was a hood, and all of them wonderfully skinny. I loved two such boys deeply, one after the other and for years on end, and forsook everything else in life, and rightly so, to begin learning with them that unplumbed intimacy that is life's chief joy. I loved them deeply, one after the other, for years on end, I say, and hoped to change their worldly ambitions and save them from the noose. But they stood firm.

And it could be, I think, that only those oddball boys, none of whom has inherited Pittsburgh at all, longed to star in the world of money and urban power; and it could be that the central boys, our boys, who are now running Pittsburgh responsibly, longed to escape. I don't know. I never knew them well enough to tell.

Maxine Hong Kingston

from The Woman Warrior

NO NAME WOMAN

"You must not tell anyone," my mother said, "what I am about to tell you. In China your father had a sister who killed herself. She jumped into the family well. We say that your father has all brothers because it is as if she had never been born.

"In 1924 just a few days after our village celebrated seventeen hurry-up weddings—to make sure that every young man who went 'out on the road' would responsibly come home—your father and his brothers and your grandfather and his brothers and your aunt's new husband sailed for America, the Gold Mountain. It was your grandfather's last trip. Those lucky enough to get contracts waved good-bye from the decks. They fed and guarded the stowaways and helped them off in Cuba, New York, Bali, Hawaii. 'We'll meet in California next year,' they said. All of them sent money home.

"I remember looking at your aunt one day when she and I were dressing; I had not noticed before that she had such a protruding melon of a stomach. But I did not think, 'She's pregnant,' until she began to look like other pregnant women, her shirt pulling and the white tops of her black pants showing. She could not have been pregnant, you see, because her husband had been gone for years. No one said anything. We did not discuss it. In early summer she was ready to have the child, long after the time when it could have been possible.

"The village had also been counting. On the night the baby was to be born the villagers raided our house. Some were crying. Like a great saw, teeth strung with lights, files of people walked zigzag across our land, tearing the rice. Their lanterns doubled in the disturbed black water, which drained away through the broken bunds. As the villagers closed in, we could see that some of them, probably men and women we knew well, wore white masks. The people with long hair hung it over their faces. Women with short hair made it stand up on end. Some had tied white bands around their foreheads, arms, and legs.

"At first they threw mud and rocks at the house. Then they threw eggs and began slaughtering our stock. We could hear the animals scream their deaths—the roosters, the pigs, a last great roar from the ox. Familiar wild heads flared in our night windows; the villagers encircled us. Some of the faces stopped to peer at us, their eyes rushing like searchlights. The hands flattened against the panes, framed heads, and left red prints.

"The villagers broke in the front and the back doors at the same time, even though we had not locked the doors against them. Their knives dripped with the blood of our animals. They smeared blood on the doors and walls. One woman swung a chicken, whose throat she had slit, splattering blood in red arcs about her. We stood together in the middle of our house, in the family hall with the pictures and tables of the ancestors around us, and looked straight ahead.

"At that time the house had only two wings. When the men came back, we would build two more to enclose our courtyard and a third one to begin a second courtyard. The villagers pushed through both wings, even your grandparents' rooms, to find your aunt's, which was also mine until the men returned. From this room a new wing for one of the younger families would grow. They ripped up her clothes and shoes and broke her combs, grinding them underfoot. They tore her work from the loom. They scattered the cooking fire and rolled the new weaving in it. We could hear them in the kitchen breaking our bowls and banging the pots. They overturned the great waist-high earthenware jugs; duck eggs, pickled fruits, vegetables burst out and mixed in acrid torrents. The old woman from the next field swept a broom through the air and loosed the spirits-of-the-broom over our heads. 'Pig.' 'Ghost.' 'Pig,' they sobbed and scolded while they ruined our house.

"When they left, they took sugar and oranges to bless themselves. They cut pieces from the dead animals. Some of them took bowls that were not broken and clothes that were not torn. Afterward we swept up the rice and sewed it back up into sacks. But the smells from the spilled preserves lasted. Your aunt gave birth in the pigsty that night. The next morning when I went for the water, I found her and the baby plugging up the family well.

"Don't let your father know that I told you. He denies her. Now that you have started to menstruate, what happened to her could happen to you. Don't humiliate us. You wouldn't like to be forgotten as if you had never been born. The villagers are watchful."

Whenever she had to warn us about life, my mother told stories that ran like this one, a story to grow up on. She tested our strength to establish realities. Those in the emigrant generations who could not reassert brute survival died young and far from home. Those of us in the first American generations have had to figure out how the invisible world the emigrants built around our childhoods fits in solid America.

The emigrants confused the gods by diverting their curses, misleading them with crooked streets and false names. They must try to confuse their offspring as well, who, I suppose, threaten them in similar ways—always trying to get things straight, always trying to name the unspeakable. The Chinese I know hide their names; sojourners take new names when their lives change and guard their real names with silence.

Chinese-Americans, when you try to understand what things in you are Chinese, how do you separate what is peculiar to childhood, to poverty, insanities, one family, your mother who marked your growing with stories, from what is Chinese? What is Chinese tradition and what is the movies?

If I want to learn what clothes my aunt wore, whether flashy or ordinary, I would have to begin, "Remember Father's drowned-in-the-well sister?" I cannot ask that. My mother has told me once and for all the useful parts. She will add nothing unless powered by Necessity, a riverbank that guides her life. She plants vegetable gardens rather than lawns; she carries the odd-shaped tomatoes home from the fields and eats food left for the gods.

Whenever we did frivolous things, we used up energy; we flew high kites. We children came up off the ground over the melting cones our parents brought home from work and the American movie on New Year's Day—*Oh, You Beautiful Doll* with Betty Grable one year, and *She Wore a Yellow Ribbon* with John Wayne another year. After the one carnival ride each, we paid in guilt; our tired father counted his change on the dark walk home.

Adultery is extravagance. Could people who hatch their own chicks and eat the embryos and the heads for delicacies and boil the feet in vinegar for party food, leaving only the gravel, eating even the gizzard lining—could such people engender a prodigal aunt? To be a woman, to have a daughter in starvation time was a waste enough. My aunt could not have been the lone romantic who gave up everything for sex. Women in the old China did not choose. Some man had commanded her to lie with him and be his secret evil. I wonder whether he masked himself when he joined the raid on her family.

Perhaps she had encountered him in the fields or on the mountain where the daughters-in-law collected fuel. Or perhaps he first noticed her in the marketplace. He was not a stranger because the village housed no strangers. She had to have dealings with him other than sex. Perhaps he worked an adjoining field, or he sold her the cloth for the dress she sewed and wore. His demand must have surprised, then terrified her. She obeyed him; she always did as she was told.

When the family found a young man in the next village to be her husband, she had stood tractably beside the best rooster, his proxy, and promised before they met that she would be his forever. She was lucky that he was her age and she would be the first wife, an advantage secure now. The night she first saw him, he had sex with her. Then he left for America. She had almost forgotten what he looked like. When she tried to envision him, she only saw the black and white face in the group photograph the men had taken before leaving.

The other man was not, after all, much different from her husband. They both gave orders: she followed. "If you tell your family, I'll beat you. I'll kill you. Be here again next week." No one talked sex, ever. And she might have separated the rapes from the rest of living if only she did not have to buy her oil from him or gather wood in the same forest. I want her fear to have lasted just as long as rape lasted so that the fear could have been contained. No drawn-out fear. But women at sex hazarded birth and hence lifetimes. The fear did not stop but permeated everywhere. She told the man, "I think I'm pregnant." He organized the raid against her.

On nights when my mother and father talked about their life back home, sometimes they mentioned an "outcast table" whose business they still seemed to be settling, their voices tight. In a commensal tradition, where food is precious, the powerful older people made wrongdoers eat alone. Instead of letting them start separate new lives like the Japanese, who could become samurais and geishas, the Chinese family, faces averted but eyes glowering sideways, hung on to the offenders and fed them leftovers. My aunt must have lived in the same house as my parents and eaten at an outcast table. My mother spoke about the raid as if she had seen it, when she and my aunt, a daughter-in-law to a different household, should not have been living together at all. Daughters-in-law lived with their husbands' parents, not their own; a synonym for marriage in Chinese is "taking a daughter-in-law." Her husband's parents could have sold her, mortgaged her, stoned her. But they had sent her back to her own mother and father, a mysterious act hinting at disgraces not told me. Perhaps they had thrown her out to deflect the avengers.

She was the only daughter; her four brothers went with her father, husband, and uncles "out on the road" and for some years became western men. When the goods were divided among the family, three of the brothers took land, and the youngest, my father, chose an education. After my grandparents gave their daughter away to her husband's family, they had dispensed all the adventure and all the property. They expected her alone to keep the traditional ways, which her brothers, now among the barbarians, could fumble without detection. The heavy, deep-rooted women were to maintain the past against the flood, safe for returning. But the rare urge west had fixed upon our family, and so my aunt crossed boundaries not delineated in space.

The work of preservation demands that the feelings playing about in one's guts not be turned into action. Just watch their passing like cherry blossoms. But perhaps my aunt, my forerunner, caught in a slow life, let dreams grow and fade and after some months or years went toward what persisted. Fear at the enormities of the forbidden kept her desires delicate, wire and bone. She looked at a man because she liked the way the hair was tucked behind his ears, or she liked the question-mark line of a long torso curving at the shoulder and straight at the hip. For warm eyes or a soft voice or a slow walk—that's all—a few hairs, a line, a brightness, a sound, a pace, she gave up family. She offered us up for a charm that vanished with tiredness, a pigtail that didn't toss when the wind died. Why, the wrong lighting could erase the dearest thing about him.

It could very well have been, however, that my aunt did not take subtle enjoyment of her friend, but, a wild woman, kept rollicking company. Imagining her free with sex doesn't fit, though. I don't know any women like that, or men either. Unless I see her life branching into mine, she gives me no ancestral help.

To sustain her being in love, she often worked at herself in the mirror, guessing at the colors and shapes that would interest him, changing them frequently in order to hit on the right combination. She wanted him to look back.

On a farm near the sea, a woman who tended her appearance reaped a reputation for eccentricity. All the married women blunt-cut their hair in flaps about their ears or pulled it back in tight buns. No nonsense. Neither style blew easily into heart-catching tangles. And at their weddings they displayed themselves in their long hair for the last time. "It brushed the backs of my knees," my mother tells me. "It was braided, and even so, it brushed the backs of my knees."

At the mirror my aunt combed individuality into her bob. A bun could have been contrived to escape into black streamers blowing in the wind or in quiet wisps about her face, but only the older women in our picture album wear buns. She brushed her hair back from her forehead, tucking the flaps behind her ears. She looped a piece of thread, knotted into a circle between her index fingers and thumbs, and ran the double strand across her forehead. When she closed her fingers as if she were making a pair of shadow geese bite, the string twisted together catching the little hairs. Then she pulled the thread away from her skin, ripping the hairs out neatly, her eyes watering from the needles of pain. Opening her fingers, she cleaned the thread, then rolled it along her hairline and the tops of her eyebrows. My mother did the same to me and my sisters and herself. I used to believe that the expression "caught by the short hairs" meant a captive held with a depilatory string. It especially hurt at the temples, but my mother said we were lucky we didn't have to have our feet bound when we were seven. Sisters used to sit on their beds and cry together, she said, as their mothers or their slaves removed the bandages for a few minutes each night and let the blood gush back into their veins. I hope that the man my aunt loved appreciated a smooth brow, that he wasn't just a tits-and-ass man.

Once my aunt found a freckle on her chin, at a spot that the almanac said predestined her for unhappiness. She dug it out with a hot needle and washed the wound with peroxide.

More attention to her looks than these pullings of hairs and pickings at spots would have caused gossip among the villagers. They owned work clothes and good clothes, and they wore good clothes for feasting the new seasons. But since a woman combing her hair hexes beginnings, my aunt rarely found an occasion to look her best. Women looked like great sea snails—the corded wood, babies, and laundry they carried were the whorls on their backs. The Chinese did not admire a bent back; goddesses and warriors stood straight. Still there must have been a marvelous freeing of beauty when a worker laid down her burden and stretched and arched.

Such commonplace loveliness, however, was not enough for my aunt. She dreamed of a lover for the fifteen days of New Year's, the time for families to exchange visits, money, and food. She plied her secret comb. And sure enough she cursed the year, the family, the village, and herself.

Even as her hair lured her imminent lover, many other men looked at her. Uncles, cousins, nephews, brothers would have looked, too, had they been home between journeys.

Perhaps they had already been restraining their curiosity, and they left, fearful that their glances, like a field of nesting birds, might be startled and caught. Poverty hurt, and that was their first reason for leaving. But another, final reason for leaving the crowded house was the never-said.

She may have been unusually beloved, the precious only daughter, spoiled and mirror gazing because of the affection the family lavished on her. When her husband left, they welcomed the chance to take her back from the in-laws; she could live like the little daughter for just a while longer. There are stories that my grandfather was different from other people, "crazy ever since the little Jap bayoneted him in the head." He used to put his naked penis on the dinner table, laughing. And one day he brought home a baby girl, wrapped up inside his brown western-style greatcoat. He had traded one of his sons, probably my father, the youngest, for her. My grandmother made him trade back. When he finally got a daughter of his own, he doted on her. They must have all loved her, except perhaps my father, the only brother who never went back to China, having once been traded for a girl.

Brothers and sisters, newly men and women, had to efface their sexual color and present plain miens. Disturbing hair and eyes, a smile like no other, threatened the ideal of five generations living under one roof. To focus blurs, people shouted face to face and yelled from room to room. The immigrants I know have loud voices, unmodulated to American tones even after years away from the village where they called their friendships out across the fields. I have not been able to stop my mother's screams in public libraries or over telephones. Walking erect (knees straight, toes pointed forward, not pigeon-toed, which is Chinese-feminine) and speaking in an inaudible voice, I have tried to turn myself American-feminine. Chinese communication was loud, public. Only sick people had to whisper. But at the dinner table, where the family members came nearest one another, no one could talk, not the outcasts nor any eaters. Every word that falls from the mouth is a coin lost. Silently they gave and accepted food with both hands. A preoccupied child who took his bowl with one hand got a sideways glare. A complete moment of total attention is due everyone alike. Children and lovers have no singularity here, but my aunt used a secret voice, a separate attentiveness.

She kept the man's name to herself throughout her labor and dying; she did not accuse him that he be punished with her. To save her inseminator's name she gave silent birth.

He may have been somebody in her own household, but intercourse with a man outside the family would have been no less abhorrent. All the village were kinsmen, and the titles shouted in loud country voices never let kinship be forgotten. Any man within visiting distance would have been neutralized as a lover—"brother," "younger brother," "older brother"—one hundred and fifteen relationship titles. Parents researched birth charts probably not so much to assure good fortune as to circumvent incest in a population that has but one hundred surnames. Everybody has eight million relatives. How useless then sexual mannerisms, how dangerous.

As if it came from an atavism deeper than fear, I used to add "brother" silently to boys' names. It hexed the boys, who would or would not ask me to dance, and made them less scary and as familiar and deserving of benevolence as girls.

But, of course, I hexed myself also—no dates. I should have stood up, both arms waving, and shouted out across libraries, "Hey, you! Love me back." I had no idea, though, how to make attraction selective, how to control its direction and magnitude. If I made myself American-pretty so that the five or six Chinese boys in the class fell in love with me, everyone else—the Caucasian, Negro, and Japanese boys—would too. Sisterliness, dignified and honorable, made much more sense.

Attraction eludes control so stubbornly that whole societies designed to organize relationships among people cannot keep order, not even when they bind people to one another from childhood and raise them together. Among the very poor and the wealthy, brothers married their adopted sisters, like doves. Our family allowed some romance, paying adult brides' prices and providing dowries so that their sons and daughters could marry strangers. Marriage promises to turn strangers into friendly relatives—a nation of siblings.

In the village structure, spirits shimmered among the live creatures, balanced and held in equilibrium by time and land. But one human being flaring up into violence could open up a black hole, a maelstrom that pulled in the sky. The frightened villagers, who depended on one another to maintain the real, went to my aunt to show her a personal, physical representation of the break she had made in the "roundness." Misallying couples snapped off the future, which was to be embodied in true offspring. The villagers punished her for acting as if she could have a private life, secret and apart from them.

If my aunt had betrayed the family at a time of large grain yields and peace, when many boys were born, and wings were being built on many houses, perhaps she might have escaped such severe punishment. But the men—hungry, greedy, tired of planting in dry soil—had been forced to leave the village in order to send food-money home. There were ghost plagues, bandit plagues, wars with the Japanese, floods. My Chinese brother and sister had died of an unknown sickness. Adultery, perhaps only a mistake during good times, became a crime when the village needed food.

The round moon cakes and round doorways, the round tables of graduated sizes that fit one roundness inside another, round windows and rice bowls—these talismans had lost their power to warn this family of the law: a family must be whole, faithfully keeping the descent line by having sons to feed the old and the dead, who in turn look after the family. The villagers came to show my aunt and her lover-in-hiding a broken house. The villagers were speeding up the circling of events because she was too shortsighted to see that her infidelity had already harmed the village, that waves of consequences would return unpredictably, sometimes in disguise, as now, to hurt her. This roundness had to be made coin-sized so that she would see its circumference: punish her at the birth of her baby. Awaken her to the inexorable. People who refused fatalism because they could invent small resources insisted on culpability. Deny accidents and wrest fault from the stars.

After the villagers left, their lanterns now scattering in various directions toward home, the family broke their silence and cursed her. "Aiaa, we're going to die. Death is coming. Death is coming. Look what you've done. You've killed us. Ghost! Dead ghost! Ghost! You've never been born." She ran out into the fields, far enough from the house so that she could no longer hear their voices, and pressed herself against the earth, her own land no more. When she felt the birth coming, she thought that she had been hurt. Her body seized together. "They've hurt me too much," she thought. "This is gall, and it will kill me." With forehead and knees against the earth, her body convulsed and then relaxed. She turned on her back, lay on the ground. The black well of sky and stars went out and out and out forever; her body and her complexity seemed to disappear. She was one of the stars, a bright dot in blackness, without home, without a companion, in eternal cold and silence. An agoraphobia rose in her, speeding higher and higher, bigger and bigger; she would not be able to contain it; there would no end to fear.

Flayed, unprotected against space, she felt pain return, focusing her body. This pain chilled her—a cold, steady kind of surface pain. Inside, spasmodically, the other pain, the pain of the child, heated her. For hours she lay on the ground, alternately body and space. Sometimes a vision of normal comfort obliterated reality: she saw the family in the evening gambling at the dinner table, the young people massaging their elders' backs. She saw them congratulating one another, high joy on the mornings the rice shoots came up. When these pictures burst, the stars drew yet further apart. Black space opened.

She got to her feet to fight better and remembered that old-fashioned women gave birth in their pigsties to fool the jealous, pain-dealing gods, who do not snatch piglets. Before the next spasms could stop her, she ran to the pigsty, each step a rushing out into emptiness. She climbed over the fence and knelt in the dirt. It was good to have a fence enclosing her, a tribal person alone.

Laboring, this woman who had carried her child as a foreign growth that sickened her every day, expelled it at last. She reached down to touch the hot, wet, moving mass, surely smaller than anything human, and could feel that it was human after all—fingers, toes, nails, nose. She pulled it up on to her belly, and it lay curled there, butt in the air, feet precisely tucked one under the other. She opened her loose shirt and buttoned the child inside. After resting, it squirmed and thrashed and she pushed it up to her breast. It turned its head this way and that until it found her nipple. There, it made little snuffling noises. She clenched her teeth at its preciousness, lovely as a young calf, a piglet, a little dog.

She may have gone to the pigsty as a last act of responsibility: she would protect this child as she had protected its father. It would look after her soul, leaving supplies on her grave. But how would this tiny child without family find her grave when there would be no marker for her anywhere, neither in the earth nor the family hall? No one would give her a family hall name. She had taken the child with her into the wastes. At its birth the two of them had felt the same raw pain of separation, a wound that only the family pressing tight could close. A child with no descent line would not soften her life but only trail after her, ghost-like, begging her to give it purpose. At dawn the villagers on their way to the fields would stand around the fence and look.

Full of milk, the little ghost slept. When it awoke, she hardened her breasts against the milk that crying loosens. Toward morning she picked up the baby and walked to the well.

Carrying the baby to the well shows loving. Otherwise abandon it. Turn its face into the mud. Mothers who love their children take them along. It was probably a girl; there is some hope of forgiveness for boys.

⋄   ⋄   ⋄

"Don't tell anyone you had an aunt. Your father does not want to hear her name. She has never been born." I have believed that sex was unspeakable and words so strong and fathers so frail that "aunt" would do my father mysterious harm. I have thought that my family, having settled among immigrants who had also been their neighbors in the ancestral land, needed to clean their name, and a wrong word would incite the kinspeople even here. But there is more to this silence: they want me to participate in her punishment. And I have.

In the twenty years since I heard this story I have not asked for details nor said my aunt's name; I do not know it. People who can comfort the dead can also chase after them to hurt them further—a reverse ancestor worship. The real punishment was not the raid swiftly inflicted by the villagers, but the family's deliberately forgetting her. Her betrayal so maddened them, they saw to it that she would suffer forever, even after death. Always hungry, always needing, she would have to beg food from other ghosts, snatch and steal it from those whose living descendants give them gifts. She would have to fight the ghosts massed at crossroads for the buns a few thoughtful citizens leave to decoy her away from village and home so that the ancestral spirits could feast unharassed. At peace, they could act like gods, not ghosts, their descent lines providing them with paper suits and dresses, spirit money, paper houses, paper automobiles, chicken, meat, and rice into eternity—essences delivered up in smoke and flames, steam and incense rising from each rice bowl. In an attempt to make the Chinese care for people outside the family, Chairman Mao encourages us now to give our paper replicas to the spirits of outstanding soldiers and workers, no matter whose ancestors they may be. My aunt remains forever hungry. Goods are not distributed evenly among the dead.

My aunt haunts me—her ghost drawn to me because now, after fifty years of neglect, I alone devote pages of paper to her, though not origamied into houses and clothes. I do not think she always means me well. I am telling on her, and she was a spite suicide, drowning herself in the drinking water. The Chinese are always very frightened of the drowned one, whose weeping ghost, wet hair hanging and skin bloated, waits silently by the water to pull down a substitute.

Hilton Als

Notes on My Mother

UNTIL THE END, MY MOTHER NEVER DISCUSSED HER WAY OF BEING. SHE AVOIDED EXPLAINing the impetus behind her emigration from Barbados to New York. She avoided explaining that she had not been motivated by the same desire for opportunity that drove most female immigrants but instead had followed a man whom she had known in Barbados as her first and only husband's closest friend—a man who eventually became my father. She was silent about the fact that she had left her husband, by whom she had two daughters, after he returned to Barbados from the Second World War addicted to morphine, and that, having been married once, she refused to marry again. She was also silent about the fact that my father, who had grown up relatively rich in Barbados, had emigrated to America with his two sisters and his mother—women with whom he continued to live, throughout my childhood, in a brownstone in Brooklyn. My mother never discussed how she would visit my father in his room there, at night, and afterward sneak back to her own home and her six children, four of them produced by her union with my father: two girls and two boys. She never explained the bond that they shared, a bond so deep and mysterious that we children felt forever excluded from their love, and forever diminished by it.

My mother also never told me whether she recognized or understood where my fascination with her would take me, a boy of seven, and eight, and ten: to a dark crawl space behind her closet, where I put on her hosiery one leg at a time, my heart racing, and, over the hose, my jeans and sneakers, so that I could have her, what I so admired and coveted, near me, always. As a Negress—for that was what she called herself—my mother was powerful in her silence, and for years she silently watched me, her first son, try to emulate her forbearance. She avoided discussing what that forbearance was worth.

·◇·   ·◇·   ·◇·

For years before and after her death, I tried to absorb my mother by referring to myself as a Negress, and by living the prescribed life of an auntie man, which is what Barbadians call a faggot. I socialized myself as an auntie man long before I committed my first act as one. I had four older sisters, and I also wore their clothes when they were not home; the clothes relieved some of the pressure I felt at being different from them. My mother responded to the Negress inside me with pride and anger: pride because I identified with women like herself; anger because I identified with women at all. When I was five or six years old, we were sitting on a bench in the subway station near our building, and seated not far from us was a woman my mother knew from the neighborhood with her teenage son. My mother did not speak to this woman, because she did not approve of the woman's son, who, like me, was a Negress. Unlike me, he dressed the part. He was wearing black shoes with princess heels, flesh-colored hose through which dark hairs sprouted, a lemon-yellow shift with grease stains on it, a purple head scarf, and bangles. He carried a strapless purse, from which he removed a compact and lipstick, so that he could dress his face, too. As my mother looked at that boy, she brushed my eyes closed with the back of her hand, and she hissed the words "auntie man." I've never known whether she was referring to both of us.

Did my mother call herself a Negress as a way of wryly reconciling herself to that most hated of English colonial words, which fixed her as a servant in the eyes of Britain and of God? I don't think so; she was not especially interested in Britain or in history. My mother was capricious in her views about most things, including race. As a West Indian who lived among other West Indians, she did not feel "difference"; in her community, she was in the majority. She dropped her West Indian accent a few years after she became a United States citizen, in the early 1950s. She didn't like people who capitalized on being exotic. She didn't like accents in general. She lived in America and wanted to sound like an American, which she did, unless she was angry. She was capable of giving a nod toward the history of "injustice," but only if it suited her mood. I think my mother took some pleasure in the embarrassment that white and black Americans alike felt when she called herself a Negress, since their image of her, she thought, was largely sentimental, heavy with suffering. When my mother laughed in the face of their deeply presumptuous view of her, one of her front teeth flashed gold.

❧ ❧ ❧

My mother's lack of interest in politics freed her mind for other things, like her endless ill health, which she treated as though it were a protracted form of suicide. She first became sick when my father fell in love with someone else and her thirty-year love affair with him ended. The difference between my mother and my father's new girlfriend was this: the new woman consented to live with my father while my mother had not. (After my mother refused to marry him, in the early fifties, my father never asked her again.) When my mother became ill with one thing and another, I was eight; by the time she died, I was twenty-eight. I was so lonely knowing her; she was so busy dying.

My mother was always polite, even at the end. For a long time, she imposed her will by not telling anyone what was really wrong; this kept everyone poised and at her service. She would not speak of the facts that contributed to her dying. She was quietly determined, functional, and content in her depression; she would not have forfeited her sickness for anything, since it had taken her so many years to admit to her need for attention, and being ill was one way of getting it. When diabetes cost her one of her legs, she said politely, "Oh, I'm dying now." When they removed a lymph node in her neck as a test for something, she said politely, "Oh, I'm really dying now." When her kidneys failed and a machine functioned in their place, she was still polite. She said, "Well, I'm dying." When she lost the vision in one eye, when, eventually, she could not breathe without effort, when her blood pressure was abnormally high and her teeth were bad and she could not urinate or take sugar in her tea or eat pork or remember a conversation, she remembered these two things: that she was polite and that she was dying.

One of my aunts told me that my mother encountered my father's girlfriend once, on the street, and took a good look at her. She saw a certain resemblance between herself and this woman: they were both homely but spirited, like Doris Day. It was clear to my mother that, like her, this woman would be capable of withstanding my father's tantrums, his compulsive childishness, and his compulsive lying. I think the resemblance my mother saw between herself and my father's new girlfriend shattered any claim to originality that she had. In the end, I think my mother's long and public illness was the only thing she experienced as an accomplishment, as something separate from her roles as mother, lover, Negress. And it was.

⋄   ⋄   ⋄

Certain facts about my mother's religious, cultural, culinary, sexual, and literary interests: She attended Sunday services at St. George's Episcopal Church, a Gothic structure in the Bedford-Stuyvesant section of Brooklyn, surrounded by brownstones, vacant lots, and children. The congregation was largely West Indian, and was judgmental of my mother because she had chosen not to marry my father, while she did choose to have his children. Many of the women in that congregation had had children out of wedlock as well, but they judged my mother just the same, because she wasn't bitter about not being married. At St. George's, my mother sometimes sang, in her sweet, reedy voice, "I Surrender All," her favorite hymn.

My mother wanted to be different from her own mother, who had always been a bitter woman, but she avoided contradicting my grandmother when she said things like "Don't play in the sun. You are black enough"—which is what my grandmother said to me once. My mother attempted to separate herself from her parents and siblings by being "nice," which they weren't. An early memory of this: my mother's family sitting in a chartered bus as it rained outside during a family picnic; my mother, alone, in the rain, cleaning up the mess as my great-aunt said, "Marie is one of God's own," and my heart breaking as the bus rocked with derisive laughter.

She loved the foods of her country: *sous*, blood pudding, coconut bread, *cou-cou*. She enjoyed her own mother most when her mother prepared those foods for her on special occasions: birthdays, Christmas, wakes. She herself was a mediocre cook who pretended to be better at it than she was by preparing elaborate meals from French cookbooks. I learned to cook in reaction to the meals she prepared.

She was in love with my father until she died; they spoke every day on the telephone. They amused and angered each other. She called him Cyp, which was short for Cyprian, his given name. When he said her name, Marie, he said it in a thick Bajan accent, so that the *a* was very flat. In his mouth, her name sounded like this: *Ma-ree*.

My mother was bright and had a high school education, but she saw clearly that her passport to the world was restricted. Over the years, in Brooklyn, she worked as a housekeeper, as a hairdresser in a beauty salon, and as a teacher's assistant in a nursery school. My mother told one story about being a servant among the Jews when she was a young woman and new to America. With other women her age, she would go to the Flatbush section of Brooklyn and wait on a particular street corner for people—mostly Jews—to drive by in their big cars, from which they would look out to see which of the women seemed healthy and clean enough to do day work in their homes. "We called ourselves Daily Woikers," my mother said in a Yiddish-American accent, laughing. She called the hair salon where she worked "the shop." It was frequented by Negresses. I went there after school. At the shop, my mother wore a white smock. She straightened hair and rubbed bergamot into women's scalps. She listened to women talk all day. After a while, their problems became pretty general to her. People complained, no matter what; she learned that for some people complaining was a way of being. After a while, she didn't respond to her customers' problems; she knew that they didn't really want a solution. The more my mother heard, the more impersonal she became in her support and encouragement of everyone. She addressed most of those women as "honey," because, after a while, she couldn't remember their names.

❧   ❧   ❧

We lived for many years in a two-story brownstone with a narrow stairway in Flatbush. The Schwartzes, the elderly Jewish couple who owned the building, lived below us. Sometimes my brother and I would watch television with the Schwartzes. I marveled at the orderliness of Mr. and Mrs. Schwartz's home, the strange smells, and the candles that they burned on Friday nights. I loved them. I wanted to be a Jew. I told Mrs. Schwartz that I wanted to be a Jew, but how? One day when I was with my mother, Mrs. Schwartz stopped her on that narrow stairway to tell her that I wanted to be a Jew. I was ten. My mother looked at me. She told Mrs. Schwartz that I wanted to be a *writer.* Shortly afterward, Mrs. Schwartz gave me a gift. It was a typewriter that had belonged to her son, the Doctor.

My mother was not ambitious for her children, but she was supportive of their ambitions. After I decided to be a writer, my mother gave me writing tablets at Christmas; she also gave me books to read that she bought at the Liberation Bookshop, on Nostrand Avenue in Bedford-Stuyvesant. The books were almost always novels or collections of poems, and were almost always written by women. She gave me Alice Childress's *A Hero Ain't Nothin' But a Sandwich* and *Maud Martha* by Gwendolyn Brooks and *A Tree Grows in Brooklyn* by Betty Smith. I felt just like the heroine, Francie, who dreams of being a writer and longs to see the world but can't imagine how she's ever going to get out of Brooklyn to do so.

My mother spent many hours alone with me, in the dark, in her bedroom, listening to me lie. Somehow, she knew that most writers became writers after having spent their childhood lying. Or perhaps she didn't know that at all. But she was extremely tolerant of my lies. And she was not impatient with my pretensions. When, at thirteen or fourteen, I began wearing a silk ascot to school, and took to writing by the light of a kerosene lamp like my then hero, Horace Greeley, the famous nineteenth-century journalist, she didn't say a word.

My mother loved *Crime and Punishment.* She read it over and over again while locked in the bathroom. Her second-favorite novel was Paule Marshall's *Brown Girl, Brownstones,* the story, in part, of a Brooklyn girl named Selina who is of Bajan descent. My mother passed this book on to me, and I read it eleven times. I was eleven years old. I read the author's biography on the book flap and looked her name up in the Manhattan telephone directory. When Paule Marshall answered the telephone, I told her, in a rush, how much my mother loved her novel, and that we did not live very far from where Selina had grown up. Paule Marshall was surprised and pleased; she made her son pick up the extension and listen in. Later, when I told my mother what I had done, she looked at me in amazement. She knew that I had telephoned Paule Marshall for both of us.

My brother and I didn't like Barbados. In the summers we were sent there, with packages of clothes and food as gifts, but we preferred to imagine the island through my mother's memories of it. In 1979, when I was seventeen, I read a story by a writer from the West Indies. In the story, "Wingless" by Jamaica Kincaid, I read this description of the Caribbean Sea and its surroundings: "The sea, the shimmering pink-colored sand, the swimmers with hats, two people walking arm in arm, talking in each other's faces, dots of water landing on noses, the sea spray on ankles, on overdeveloped calves, the blue, the green, the black, so deep, so smooth, a great and swift undercurrent, glassy, the white wavelets." This story changed everything for me. After reading it, I read it aloud to my mother, and when I finished she said, "Exactly."

        ❧   ❧   ❧

As a pubescent Negress, I spent a great deal of time in thrall to the sister who was eleven years older than I was; she continued to live at home for years after our other sisters had left. She was the only college student I knew. She created a world in her bedroom that resonated with style and intellectual possibility. She was beautiful: she had long legs and a long neck and shoulder-length black hair that she wore in a chignon. She wore straight skirts and cardigans and flats. She had many lovers, which later prompted one of our other sisters to say, "She's so nasty. Like a dog." In her room, we danced to Dionne Warwick singing "Don't Make Me Over" as my sister began getting dressed for the evening. When she asked for my advice on what to wear, I knew she was pleased with me. Sometimes, in a sudden fit of pique, she would demand to know what I was anyway, hanging around a girl's bedroom.

As I grew up, it became increasingly clear that one of the reasons for my sister's occasional sharp annoyance with me was this: she wanted to be able to see herself in contrast to me. All the women in my family wanted me to become a black male for the same reason: they wanted to define themselves against me. I tried to please them, because I adored them. I thought that being an auntie man was a fair compromise, but it wasn't.

When I was thirteen, I went to a party given by one of my mother's relatives. I didn't know why my mother did not attend the party until I returned home and told her about it. We were standing in the kitchen, and I told her how I had met a man there who had asked after her. I described him: bald head, a square figure, deep dark skin. I met him on the stoop of the house where the party was. I remembered everything about the meeting, and spoke of it excitedly. I didn't tell my mother about the man's charm, and my attraction to his charm. Nor did I describe the orange sun setting behind his large brown head; rubbing my moist hands against the stoop's bumpy concrete; admiring his graceful saunter as he walked away. My mother's face became hard when I mentioned his first name, Eldred. She would not look at me when she said, "That was the man I was married to. That was my husband." The air was still between us; it became a wall. I knew I was a Negress because of the jealousy I felt at her having rejected someone I wanted. I glanced at my mother; her face, her body, told me that she had been where I wanted to be long before I began imagining it. We stood in the kitchen for quite some time. I saw myself in my mother's eyes: a teenage girl, insecure, jealous, and vengeful.

Like my sister, I grew up to lie with first one man and then another, or, more accurately, to bend over one man and then another in parked cars that lined the piers on the West Side Highway. Until the end, I avoided recounting these facts to my mother. I avoided explaining the impetus that propelled me to leave her home in Brooklyn for the piers on the West Side Highway. I avoided explaining that I had been motivated by the same desire and romantic greed that had propelled her to move from Barbados to New York. I avoided explaining that when I sat in parked cars with one man and then another, I felt closer to her experience of the world than I ever did in her actual presence. I avoided mentioning that the men I seduced were almost always white, and that, with my mouth tentatively poised over another man's mouth, I sometimes thought, I am not my mother; this is *my* story. I sometimes fantasized, If she knew I was performing this act, this gesture, she would perhaps die, releasing me to live fully in the moment. I never told her how I met other Negresses like myself, the boy children of women who had emigrated to New York from islands like Jamaica, Cuba, Antigua, Anguilla, Barbados, Barbuda. And we never mentioned to one another how, when we left those cars and bars in our soiled bluejeans, and after the long subway ride home to Brooklyn or Queens or the Bronx, we were met at the kitchen door by our mirror image—Mom, a Negress, who rarely recounted anything at all about her life.

⊸   ⊸   ⊸

My mother died in Barbados, our ancestral home. Before she left New York for the last time, I did not visit her; this was only one of many leave-takings, and we could not bear to say goodbye. Neither did she say goodbye to her sister, who was to return to Barbados later, after my mother's death. "I knew she wouldn't come back to New York. I knew she would die here," my aunt told me when I went there to see where my mother had died. My visit meant nothing to my aunt. She is unsentimental—a family trait. She said several things when I went to visit her in her ugly house surrounded by coconut trees on a pitiful plot of land. She said, "Your mother was so angry at the end." She asked, "When did you know you were going to be an auntie man?" She asked, "When will you write a story about me?" And I did not ask myself, "Am I not a Negress, too? Will I ever be capable of writing a story about any of us?" In that ugly house in Barbados as the trade winds blew, my aunt was telling me that I would.

Andre Dubus III
Tracks and Ties

YEARS LATER, WHEN I WAS TWENTY-SIX, SHE SAID IN THE *NEW YORK TIMES* YOU WOULD TIE her naked and spread-eagled on the bed, that you would take a bat to her. She said you'd hit her for any reason. But in Haverhill, Massachusetts, you were my best friend, my brother's too. I was fifteen and you two were fourteen and in 1974 we walked the avenues on cold gray days picking through dumpsters for something to beat off to. We'd beat off to anything, though I was shy about it and couldn't do it just anywhere.

One February morning we skipped school and went downtown. It was ten or eleven degrees and the dirty snow piled along both sides of River Street had become ice; the air made my lungs hurt and our noses, ears, and fingers felt burned, but you wore your faded blue jean jacket with the green magic marker peace signs drawn all over it. You wore sneakers and thin fake denim pants that looked more purple than blue. It was so cold I pulled the rubber band from my ponytail and let my hair down around my neck and leather-jacketed shoulders. Your hair was long too, brown and stringy. My brother, barely fourteen, needed a shave.

We had a dollar between us so we sat in a booth at Vahally's Diner and drank coffee with so much milk and sugar in it you couldn't call it coffee anymore. The Greek man behind the counter hated us; he folded his black hairy forearms across his chest and watched us take our free refills until we were giddy with caffeine. You went for your seventh cup and he yelled something at you in Greek. On the way out you stole two dollars someone had left on their check under a sugar shaker.

You paid our way on the city bus that was heated and made a loop all the way through town, along the river, up to the Westgate shopping center, then back again. We stayed on it for two hours, taking the loop six times. In the far rear, away from the driver, you took out your black-handled Buck knife and carved a peace sign into the aluminum-backed seat in front of you. For a while I looked out the window at all the red brick factory building, the store-fronts with their dusty windows, bright neon price deals taped to the bottom and top. Barrooms on every block. I probably thought of the high school algebra I was flunking, the gym class I hated, the brown mescaline and crystal meth and THC my sister was selling. The bus was warm, too warm, and more crowded than before. A woman our mothers' age sat in her overcoat and scarf in the seat in front of you both. Her back was to you and I'm sure she heard you laughing but she didn't see my brother hunched forward in his seat, jerking back and forth on his penis and coming in no time, catching it all in his hand. I think I looked away and I don't remember what he did with it.

After the bus, we made our way through the narrow factory streets, most of the build-ings' windows covered with gray plywood, though your mother still worked at Schwartz's Shoe, on the fifth floor, when she wasn't drinking. We walked along the railroad tracks, its silver rails flush with the packed snow, the wooden ties gone under. And we laughed about the summer before when we three built a barricade for the train, a wall of broken creosote ties, an upside-down shopping cart, cinder blocks, and a rusted oil drum. We covered it with brush, then you siphoned gas from a Duster behind Schwartz's and poured it on. My brother and I lit it, air sucked by us in a whoosh, and we ran down the bank across the parking lot into the abandoned brewery to the second floor to watch our fire, to wait for the Boston & Maine, to hear the screaming brakes as it rounded the blind curve just off the trestle over the river. But a fat man in a good shirt and tie showed up at the tracks, then a cop, and we ran laughing to the first floor where we turned on the keg conveyor belt, lay on it belly-first, and rode it up through its trap door over and over.

As we made our way through town it began to snow. My brother and I were hungry, but you were never hungry; you were hawny, you said. One morning, as we sat in the basement of your house and passed a homemade pipe between us, your mother upstairs drunk on Kappy's vodka and Pepsi, singing to herself, you said: "I'm always hawny in the mawnin'."

My brother and I laughed and you didn't know why, then you inhaled resin on your next hit and said, "Shit man, the screem's broken."

"The *what?*"

"The screem. You know, the *screem*. Like a screem door?"

By the time we reached the avenues the snow had blanketed the streets. There were two sisters on Seventh who lived in the projects that always had motorcycles in front of them, and trash, and bright-colored babies' toys. Trish and Terry were older, sixteen and seventeen and so skinny their breasts looked like prunes beneath their shirts, but they had dark skin and long hair and sometimes, if they were high, they'd suck you. But there was a day party on the first floor of their building, and it had only been two weeks since Harry Wright and Kevin McConigle, rent collectors for Fat Billy, both twenty-three or -four, beat us up, you and me, just walked us out of a pot party we were both quiet at, walked us off the front porch into the mud then kicked and punched us until they were through. So we kept walking, heading for a street close to the highway where we knew three girls who would fuck if you had wine and rubbers, though after the wine they didn't mention the rubbers.

On Cedar Street, cars spun out snow as they drove from the curb or the corner store.

You let out a yelp and a holler and went running after a Chevy that had just pulled away, skidding slightly as it went. You ran low, bent over so the driver wouldn't see you, and when you reached the back bumper you grabbed it and squatted on your sneakers, your butt an inch or two from the road. And you skied away, just like that, the snow shooting out from under the wheels of the car, out from under your Zayre Department Store sneakers, blue exhaust coughing out its pipe beside you.

In the spring and summer we hopped trucks. A mile from the highway was a crosswalk on Main with a push-button traffic signal pole that we three leaned against until a truck came along and one of us pressed the button to turn red. I was the decoy that day, for a white refrigerator truck from Shoe City Beef. It stopped at the line, and I crossed the street jerking my head like a chicken to keep his attention from the mirrors while you two ran around to the back and climbed up on the foot-wide iron ledge at the bottom of its rear doors. As soon as I got to the sidewalk I heard the driver shift from neutral to first, heard him give it the gas. I waited for a car to drive by from the opposite direction, then I ran out into the street behind the truck, which was only shifting up to second. You and my brother stood on the ledge waiting, smiling, nodding your heads for me to hurry. I reached the ledge just as the truck moved into higher gear and I grabbed the bolt lock on its back doors and pulled myself up, the truck going faster now, shifting again, dipping and rattling through a low spot in the road. You both held an iron handle on opposite sides of the door so I stayed down, gripping the bolt lock with both hands, sitting on the ledge.

A car horn behind us honked and the driver, some man who combed his hair to the side like a teacher, shook his head and honked his horn again. You gave him the finger and we laughed but it was a scared laugh because the truck wasn't slowing down as it got to the gas stations and Kappy's Liquor near the highway, it was speeding up. Before, we'd jumped off into the grass of the highway ramp, but now we couldn't; he took the turn without leaving third gear and you yelled: "He *knows!* He friggin' *knows!*" My brother wasn't smiling anymore, and he stuck his head around the corner and let the growing wind hit him in the face, run through the hair on his cheeks as he squeezed the handle with both hands and I wanted to stand, to get my feet on something solid, but there was no room and now the driver was in fourth gear, heading north on 495, going fifty, then sixty, then sixty-five. He moved to the middle lane and I tried not to look down at the zip of the asphalt a foot beneath my dangling boots, but it was worse looking out at the cars, at the drivers looking at us like we might be a circus act they should catch sometime. Some honked as they passed so I looked up at you, at the side of your face as you looked around the corner, the June wind snapping your hair back past your forehead and ears, your mouth open in a scream I could barely hear. You smiled and shook your head at my brother then down at me, your brown eyes wet from the wind, your cheeks flushed in a satisfaction so deep I had to look back at the cars behind us, at the six or seven I was convinced would run me over one after the other, after my fingers failed. Miles later, at the tollbooths of the New Hampshire line, the truck slowed to a stop and we jumped off exhausted, our fingers stiff, and thumbed home.

That fall you went to the trade school, my brother joined me at the high school, and I saw you six years later in an all-night store in Monument Square. I was buying cigarettes for my college girl-friend. She waited in the car. It was winter. The floor was dirty with people's slush and mud tracks, the overhead light was fluorescent and too bright, and I was waiting my turn at the register when I saw you, watching me, smiling as you walked up. You carried a carton of ice cream and a quart of Coke. I had on a sweater and a jacket but you wore only a T-shirt, green Dickie work pants, and sneakers. You were taller than me, lean, and your young black mustache and goatee made you look sinister until you started talking in that high voice that hadn't changed since you'd told us you were hawny in the mawnin'. You said you were living down on the avenues, that you were getting married soon. I said congratulations, then I was at the counter asking for a pack of Parliaments and you touched me on the shoulder, said to say hi to my brother. I said I would. At the door I glanced back at you and watched you dig into your front pocket for crumpled bills. You nodded and smiled at me, winked even, and as I left the store, the cold tightening the skin on my face, I remembered the time your mother went to visit her sister in Nebraska for a whole month. I could never understand why she went alone, why she'd leave her family like that to go off for a visit. Then my mother told me it was detox she went to, some twenty-eight-day program in Boston. When I told you I knew, you laughed and said, "Nah," but you swallowed twice and walked away to do nothing in particular.

Six months after I saw you in the store my brother and I got invitations to your wedding. We didn't go.

Four more years and you were dead.

I heard about it after you were buried. They said your wife stabbed you in the back. That was it; she stabbed you. But a year later I was behind the bar at McMino's Lounge and Fat Billy's son, Bill Jr., told me what really happened, that you were cooked, always thinking your wife was cheating on you, always beating her up. That night you ran outside off the porch to go kill the guy you thought she was fucking. This was down on one of the avenues, behind the projects, and you took the trail in back of your house. But your wife opened your black-handled Buck knife and chased after you, screaming. She was short and small, barely five feet, and just as you reached the weeds she got to you and drove it in low, sinking the blade into your liver, snipping something called the portal artery. You went down without a sound. You curled up in a heap. But your wife spent four hours at a neighbor's house crying before they called anyone, and then it was the cops, and you were gone.

I served Bill Jr. another White Russian and for a second I felt sure it was him she went to that night, and I thought about hitting him for not making a faster call, but I felt no heat in my hands, no pull inside me. And I've always hated woman beaters. Part of me thought you got what you deserved. I left Bill Jr. to finish his too-sweet drink.

The following winter I was living in New York City, in a one-room studio with my girlfriend. It was late on a Sunday morning and we both sat with our feet up on the couch reading the *New York Times*. Outside our barred window snow fell on parked cars, on the sidewalk and street. I got tired of the movie section and picked up a story about three women in prison, all there for the same reason, for killing the husbands who beat them. And your wife was one of them; they gave her full name, *your* name. They wrote how she chased you outside and stabbed you. They described the town you both lived in as economically depressed, once a thriving textile town but no more. I lowered the paper and started to tell my girlfriend all about you, but she and I weren't doing so well, both past wanting to hear anything extra about each other, so I pulled on my boots and jacket and went walking. I crossed Third Avenue and Second and First. A car alarm went off in front of some Chinese laundry. I stuck my hands in my pockets and wished I'd worn a hat. I passed an empty basketball court, then I waited for the traffic on FDR Drive and walked the last block to the East River. To my right and left were bridges over to Queens. Though from where I stood I could see only the backs of warehouses, dry weeds five feet tall, then the gray river, swirling by fast.

The snow had stopped and I started walking along the cobblestone walk. One morning I skipped school and cut through back yards to your house. I didn't know your mother was home from Nebraska and I almost stepped back when she answered the door. She'd dyed her brown hair black, she wore sweatpants and a sweater, she had a cold sore on her bottom lip, and she'd gained weight, but she smiled and kissed me on the cheek and invited me in. The small kitchen was clean and warm. It smelled like coffee and cinnamon rolls. She put one on a napkin and handed it to me. I thanked her, and while I chewed the sweet buttery bread, she lit up a cigarette and asked about my mother. Then you came downstairs in just your jeans, no shirt, your chest pale and thin, your nipples pink, and your mother rushed over and kissed and hugged you like you'd been gone and just gotten home. And you didn't pull away, you hugged her back, and when your eyes caught mine, you lowered your face into the hair at her shoulder, and kept hugging.

Kathryn Harrison

from The Kiss

HIGHWAY REPAIRS AND A DETOUR MAKE THE DRIVE HOME FROM COLLEGE EVEN LONGER than usual, and I arrive at my mother's barely in time to sit down for dinner, something French and ambitious to which she must have devoted an afternoon of labor. Even so, we leave the television on during the meal, and taste rather than eat what she prepared.

"You get it," my mother says whenever the phone rings. I find this odd—she's usually so secretive about her social life—but when it rings at nine-thirty, I understand. It's him, my father, calling to give us his flight number. His voice, which I have not heard for ten years, surprises me with its high pitch. I'll learn, in time, that it doesn't always sound this way, but rises and falls in concert with his emotions. On this night, however, we speak only as long as it takes to confirm the necessary details.

"I'll be wearing a brown suit," he says.

"Okay," I say.

"See you soon," he says, ordinary words made extraordinary by the fact that I have never heard them from him, a man I would have seen under other circumstances every day for all the years of my life.

"Okay," I say. "Yes." He's due to arrive at two the next afternoon.

❖ ❖ ❖

Everything is disrupted for this visit. My mother's companion of many years is banished; I'm not sure where he goes. Perhaps to stay with his estranged wife, the one he can't bring himself to divorce. My grandparents, disapproving, will share one dinner with us at my mother's, one tea at their house. The rest of the week's plans do not include them. I am not sure whether to regard this as a slight, a mercy, or merely a pragmatic consideration of what we all think we might be able to handle together.

My mother and I go to our beds, where we spend our separate, sleepless nights. As only a narrow hallway divides our rooms, we can hear each other sigh and shift beneath the blankets. At one point she gets up. I hear her open and close a drawer in her bathroom.

❖ ❖ ❖

My bedroom at my mother's is the first she's ever had for me. She furnished it the summer after I graduated from high school, when, as I was moving from my grandparents' house to college, I would no longer need it. It's a modern room, with a futon whose brightly colored bedding strikes a garish note among the other rooms' understated fugues of beige. The comforter bears a floral pattern of restless, itchy pinks that are echoed in the window blinds. Through them the morning sun streaks in and falls in warm patches on the cream carpet, the pink and cream blending together into a color I associate with inflamed eyelids, epic weeping.

On the wall is a print, a watercolor by Jean-Michel Folon, a painting of a single chair that stands on a hill amidst a grove of leafless trees. The chair is as large as the trees and is in metamorphosis; branches and twigs project from its wooden back. Either it is becoming fully a chair, or it is reverting back to tree. I chose this print with my mother, undoubtedly because it expresses my sense of always striving to become what I am not and because the longing I find expressed in the chair—mute, paralyzed—is also so familiar. Still, despite its beauty, I don't enjoy looking at it. The pink glow coming from behind the hill is too faint to suggest hope: there's no way to know if it's sunrise, sunset, or the light of an approaching fire.

The print is reflected twice, in full-length mirrors on closet doors, and the whole room shines with an optimism neither of us has ever felt about the other. Because most of my school holidays are spent with my grandparents, it's place of brief visits.

~o~ ~o~ ~o~

We agree that we have to leave for the airport by one o'clock, but I'm dressed to go long before noon. It's not unusual for me to be ready this early. I'm always too early. I arrive at restaurants whole hours before dinner dates and have to walk around neighboring blocks or wait in nearby stores until I'm merely painfully punctual. I'm helpless against it, this response to my mother's chronic lateness, to having always been the last child to be picked up from school, camp, church, birthday parties, dental appointments, dance lessons.

Always in tears, always sure that this time she wouldn't come at all but would leave me forever with the dentist or the Russian ballet mistress who slapped the backs of my knees with her yardstick. Even after my mother moved out, the arrangement between her and my grandmother was that she would provide at least half of whatever transportation I required; and so in hallways and foyers, on dank stone benches or the vinyl-upholstered couches of waiting rooms, I silently rehearsed my grandparents' phone number and their address, to which the police should return me.

My mother's lateness is so extreme it transcends hostile insult. The reason for lost jobs and lost loves, for useless sessions of behavior therapy, it implies she exists in another temporal frame. In being late, if in little else, my mother is so predictable that my grandmother routinely gives her the wrong time for family gatherings, adjusting it as much as two whole hours forward, and still my mother nearly misses them. But I am not as pragmatic as my grandmother; and I never get used to it.

~o~ ~o~ ~o~

At 12:45 I knock on the bedroom door. She's out of the bath, she's set her hair, but she has not put on her makeup. She's not wearing anything but a bra and a slip. Discarded blouses and skirts and trousers cover every surface of her usually immaculate bedroom. Shoes tumble from the closet as if arrested in the attempt to escape. I sit in the rocker and watch her. "That looks nice," I encourage with each change of clothes, but she looks in the mirror and tears whatever it is off.

"Please," I say. "It's one." And then, after a few more outfits, "It's one-fifteen."

"You go," she says. "I can't. I'm not ready." She sits on the bed, still undressed. She puts her face in her hands.

"Alone?" I say. "I can't."

"You'll have to. Or you'll be late."

"Just put something on," I beg. "Please. I'll drive, and you can do your makeup in the car."

"No. You go."

At one-thirty I leave, transfixed with dread, whether of the solitary meeting or of being late, I can't say. I speed on the highway, flooded with adrenaline, nervous enough that my back aches, a cold clench.

I park the car and run all the way from the lot and through the terminal to the gate. I arrive breathing hard. A man wearing a tan suit, not a brown one, straightens slowly from the drinking fountain, and turns to look at me. We recognize one another immediately. We've exchanged recent photographs, but it's more than that: we look like each other.

As my father walks toward me, he wipes his wet mouth with the back of his free hand. The other carries a heavy-looking black case—his camera, he explains. "You're late," he says. Even though the plane was delayed, it has been on the ground for some minutes.

"I know," I say. "I'm sorry. The traffic . . ."

I lie to protect my mother, so naked in her bra and curlers. I could give her away, let him know how much this visit means to her, enough to warrant a frenzied morning before the mirror, but I don't. I protect her, as I've learned to do from her own example, from the mask, the secret phone number. I cannot remember a time that I was not aware of my mother's fragility. It's part of what has convinced me of her surpassing worth, the way only the best teacups break easily.

⬦ ⬦ ⬦

In the terminal, my father leads me out of the flow of passengers and the friends and family who have come to meet them. He finds an empty spot by one of the big plate-glass windows that look out onto the airfields. "Don't move," he says. "Just let me look at you."

My father looks at me, then, as no one has ever looked at me before. His hot eyes consume me—eyes that I will discover are always just this bloodshot. I almost feel their touch. He takes my hands, one in each of his, and turns them over, stares at my palms. He does not actually kiss them, but his look is one that ravishes.

"Oh!" he says. "Turn around!" I feel his gaze as it moves over my neck, my back, and down to my feet.

"God," he says when I face him again. "Oh God." His eyes, now fixed on mine, are bright with tears. "Your hair," he says. "It's . . . it's longer than I imagined. Than I could have. It was behind your shoulders in the picture you sent."

I nod. I don't speak. His eyes rob me of words, they seem to draw the air from my mouth so that I can barely breathe.

The girl my father sees has blond hair that falls past her waist, past her hips; it falls to the point at which her fingertips would brush her thighs if her arms were not crossed before her chest. I'm no longer very thin—away at school I've learned to eat—but, as if embarrassed to be caught with a body, I hide whatever I can of it.

We walk to the baggage claim in silence and wait where the metal plates of the luggage conveyor slide one under the other as the stream of suitcases turns the corner. My father picks up his bag and we walk, still without talking, out of the terminal.

Once outside, he takes one of my hands in his. I feel his fingers tremble. "Do you mind?" he says. "Could I?" I don't take my hand away.

"It isn't brown," I say of his suit as we get in the car.

"Yes it is," he says.

"Isn't it more of a tan or a khaki?"

"It's brown."

The trip home from the airport is mostly silent. I can't think of anything to say, and I don't dare do what I want, escape into music on the stereo. Turned sideways in his seat, my father watches me, and his look doesn't allow my hand to reach for the knob. As I drive I make mistakes I rarely make. My hands, wet from nerves, slip on the steering wheel. As we cross an intersection, my foot loses the clutch and I stall the car in traffic.

At home, my mother is wearing the clothes she set out the previous night: black trousers and a cream-colored cashmere sweater that sets off her dark shining hair. She's in high spirits, a little too high perhaps—her laughter sounds shrill to me. On her breast is a small gold miraculous medal, rays of light bursting from the Virgin's open palms. My parents embrace quickly, almost shyly. They kiss each other's closed mouths with their lips thrust forward in prissy, monkey-like puckers.

-ი-   -ი-   -ი-

We try hard to make it work, the three of us together. We sit in the living room and drink iced tea. "At last," one of us says, "a family." Calling ourselves this, saying the words—Who says them? My mother? My father? Do I?—it's meant ironically, but the pain the words bring, the admission of failure, is so intense that afterward no one speaks. My mother breaks away and goes into the kitchen. She returns with a platter of cheeses and vegetables and little sandwiches, her comments arranged with as much care as the food.

We all stare at one another, fascinated, years of observation collapsed into minutes. We catalog similarities, differences. Whose am I? From the neck down I'm a replica of my mother, but my head resembles his. The line of his jaw is echoed in mine, as are his cheekbones, his ears, his brow. And how mysterious it is that my father and I do the same things with our hands as we talk. I've never had the chance to see his gestures and learn to mimic them.

I watch and listen as my parents begin to argue. They can't reconstruct a year, a season, or even a week from the past without disagreeing. Whatever they talk about—their wedding day, my birth—it's as if my mother and father experienced two separate, unconnected realities, a disjuncture that allows no compromise, no middle ground. The picture that I form of their courtship is one that I have to piece together; no matter how hard I try to make things fit, it will always have the look of an incomplete collage—some details too large, others too small, many missing.

-ი-   -ი-   -ი-

My father takes pictures of my mother and me. An accomplished amateur photographer, he owns a number of large-format cameras and develops his work himself in a darkroom he's set up in his parsonage. I watch as he poses and records images of her, and she watches as he poses me. Though no one counts aloud, I sense that he is careful to make an equal number of exposures of both of us, and that we all keep track of this quantifiable measure of his attention. Then, "How about the two of you together?" he asks, and my mother and I sit next to each other on the hearth.

These pictures of my mother and me are the last I have of us together. As it turns out, they are overexposed; my father never makes individual prints of them, so I have only the proof sheets showing the two of us, our heads inclined, our bodies not touching. Behind my mother and me, visible between our shoulders, are tongues of flame from the gas log. In certain of the poses the fire looks as if it comes from our clothes themselves, as if the anguished expression we each wear is not the smile we intended but the first rictus of pain. As if what my father caught with his camera was the moment when suddenly we knew we'd begun to burn.

⟳ THE THREE OF US SPEND MUCH OF OUR WEEK TOGETHER AT ART MUSEUMS AND botanic gardens and other tourist attractions. We are drawn to these places of silent staring and confused, enervated wandering because they make us seem and feel less like freaks as we stare in speechless shock at one another. Rather than increasing the strain, the time we spend with my grandparents is a relief in that it diffuses and refracts our attention, filling a few hours with polite, careful conversation about politics and gardening and books we've all read.

⊸ ⊸ ⊸

Each night at my mother's house we stay up as late as we can, trying to drain sensation from every minute. Whatever I do—peel an orange, tie my shoe, pour water from a pitcher into the dry soil of a house-plant—enthralls my father. I get up to brush my teeth, and he follows me into the bathroom. He leans against the doorjamb to watch as I squeeze the paste from the tube. His scrutiny both excites and exhausts me. How can it be that anyone finds me so interesting?

"Is that the brand you always use?" he says. "Crest?"

I nod. My teeth, as we've observed aloud, match his in shape and color.

"Did you ever wear braces?" he asks.

"No," I say. He nods.

I'm as captivated by him. I've never really known who my father was, and revelation is inherently seductive. There is, too, the fascination of our likeness, that we resemble each other in ways that transcend physical similarities.

"You walk like your father," my mother used to say to me when I was younger. "As soon as you stood up and put one foot in front of the other, I could see it."

"What do you mean?" I'd say. "How?"

"I can't explain it," she'd say. And she wouldn't try. What she said was spoken wistfully sometimes, but mostly it wasn't a compliment. So much of what my mother and her mother seem to regard in me as alien—my bookishness, for example, or my killjoy disinterest in fashion and in what they consider the fun of manicures and facials and going out for high tea in a tea shop—has always been blamed on the other, rogue half of my genes. What a surprise to find that this judgment, which previously struck me as facile, turns out to be correct. In my father I meet someone not only familial but familiar: like myself. Now, my stubborn streak, my willful, marching walk, and the way I frown when I'm thinking—all such traits are not evidence of my separateness but of my belonging.

⊸ ⊸ ⊸

"Pretty is as pretty does." My grandfather has said these words to me all my life, and since I'm always doing something wrong I know just how ugly I must be.

My grandfather was seventy-one when I was born, and he often took care of me when I was a small child. A tall, remarkably vigorous man, he gardened, he swam, he drove me to school and helped me with my homework.

It was my grandfather who taught me how to ride a bicycle, and in his shirt pocket he kept a small pad of paper on which he wrote pretend traffic tickets when I went too fast on the long driveway or ran into one of his flower beds. The penalties he doled out were usually tasks that I had to perform in order to insinuate myself back into his good graces. This game of make-believe crimes and punishments was one of which I never tired.

I was a tomboy; I tagged after my grandfather, underfoot so often that my first nickname was Shadow, as in "Me and My——." He whistled the old music-hall tune whenever he heard me coming. Because his patience was greater than theirs, my mother and grandmother turned me over to him at bedtime, and sometimes he had to sing for hours until I fell asleep.

Our companionship gave both of us great pleasure—"Oh, you keep him young! You keep him young!" his wrinkled friends said, tweaking my ear or cheek—but everything changed abruptly when I went through puberty.

"You're too big for that now," my grandfather would say, and he'd push me out of his lap. When he hugged me, he didn't let our bodies touch, he made sure that my breasts and hips didn't press against him. I suppose the same thing must have happened to my mother when she turned twelve or thirteen, her flesh announcing to him that she had become sexual and therefore untouchable, and that his rejection as she slipped from childhood into womanhood must have wounded her as it did me.

Born in 1890, my mother's father is a true Victorian. He was raised in houses in which even a table's curved leg was draped, and he has remained squeamish about what he would call our animal nature. My grandmother can be derisive about his prudishness, Victorian mores being to her like a language she can speak but mostly chooses not to. She alludes disparagingly to my grandfather's willful innocence, and when he turns the television off because an ad for a feminine-hygiene product has interrupted the news broadcast, she throws her magazine down in disgust. "Good God!" she cries. "Are you going to leave the world still thinking the stork brought you into it!"

Whatever it is about my father that so draws me to him must have to do in part with the very different ways he and my grandfather respond to my femaleness. As a child of five or of ten, happiest at my grandfather's elbow while he grafted a branch onto a fruit tree or nailed perches to a bird feeder, I couldn't keep my father's attention. During his two brief visits, his eyes passed quickly over me on their way to my mother. But now that I am grown up, my fingernails no longer rough and black with earth from the garden, my once-bobbed hair long, and my flat chest filled out, my father's eyes are fixed on me; he tears his gaze away with reluctance. This kind of besotted focus is intoxicating, especially for a girl schooled in self-effacement and taught that virtue believes more in its ugliness than in its beauty.

⚬ ⚬ ⚬

One afternoon, when we've returned from a gallery, I fall asleep sitting next to my father on the couch. When I wake up, whole hours later, my head is in the crook of his elbow, like a baby's. I startle, arms jerking in alarm. "I'm sorry!" I say. "I was so tired."

"Oh, no!" my father says. "Please don't apologize! I'm not sorry at all." He looks at me with his hungry eyes. "My arm went to sleep," he says. "I had to go to the bathroom, but I didn't dare move. If it was up to me, I would have sat holding you forever, I would never have woken you.

"They didn't let me hold you," he says. "Not at all. I don't remember that they ever let me. They had you on a schedule. It was sacrosanct, it was absolute. They tolerated no exceptions. They fed you, they changed you, they put you down. If you cried, no one was allowed to pick you up."

By *they* he means the baby nurse, my mother and grandmother. "They didn't even let me say good-bye," he says. He puts his hand under my chin and turns my face toward his.

My mother is watching him. At one point she opens her mouth as if to say something, but then closes it. As my father talks, tears seep into the crow's feet at the corners of his eyes. They don't fall so much as spread into a glittering web over his face, following the fine lines made by the sun, by laughter, by sorrow. I've never seen a man cry before.

⋅❧   ❧   ❧⋅

My father's eyes: what is it about them? Their color is utterly familiar—the same as mine, the same as my mother's—but they burn like no other eyes I've ever seen before or since. burn like a prophet's, a madman's, a lover's. Always shining, always bloodshot, always turned on me with absolute attention. Intelligent eyes, enraptured eyes, luminous, stricken, brilliant, spellbound, spellbinding eyes.

I don't know it yet, not consciously, but I feel it: my father, holding himself so still and staring at me, has somehow begun to *see* me into being. His look gives me to myself, his gaze reflects the life my mother's willfully shut eyes denied. Looking at him looking at me, I cannot help but fall painfully, precipitously in love. And my loving him is inseparable from a piercing sense of loss. Whenever I am alone—in my bedroom, the bathroom—I find myself crying, sometimes even sinking to my knees. How am I to endure this new despair? How can it be that I am twenty years old, that I've had to grow up without a father, only to meet him now when it's too late, when childhood is over, lost?

⋅❧   ❧   ❧⋅

On the last night my father spends with us, I wake after only two hours of sleep. I sit up in bed and find my wristwatch on the nightstand. It's ten minutes before three. My throat is sore as if I'm catching a cold, and I go downstairs for a glass of orange juice. I move quietly so as not to disturb my father sleeping in the den. The thick carpet on the stair treads absorbs my footfalls. As I pass the den's open door, I see that the convertible sofa is empty, my father is not on it. I turn on the lights in the living room just to make sure he's not sleeping on that couch, but already I know where he is: in my mother's bed.

I sit on the carpeted stairs to consider this, their cheating on his current wife and my mother's banished, trusting partner. Do my parents perhaps consider their bond so primary that it is absolute, ungovernable by the dictates that guide more pedestrian relationships? Maybe they believe that they are being faithful only when they're sleeping together, and that other loves are the betrayal. Alone, outside my mother's closed bedroom door, I feel jealous. And, like all children, I discover that I'm squeamish at the thought of my mother and father having intercourse. I'm both fascinated and repelled.

When I turn on the light in the kitchen, I find a cockroach on the counter; rather than kill it, I gingerly and at arm's length place a water glass upside down over the insect—leaving the problem for my mother to resolve in the morning. I dislike insects, and cockroaches in particular have always frightened me.

As I drink the juice, I see the roach circle inside the glass, rising occasionally on its hind legs to touch the clear, smooth, obstructing surface with its forefeet and sensitive antennae.

I watch how it must relentlessly search for the seam, the tiny ridge or rill in the glass that might offer some hope of climbing, penetrating, escaping. But there is nothing about the glass that it understands.

The next day, while my mother is taking a shower, my father talks about what happened the previous night. "I heard you," he says. "I heard you go downstairs." He leans forward over the breakfast table. "I did it because I had to," he says. "She asked me." I say nothing, but we both know that I know what he's talking about.

He describes their making love not as sacred, the way I've imagined it, but as an act of charitable reassurance. He answers a question I never voice. "I didn't do it because I wanted to," he says. Humiliated on behalf of my mother, and shocked that he would betray her this way, I look not at him but at my plate.

⌁   ⌁   ⌁

When it's time to take my father to the airport, again my mother says she cannot go. She has a headache. She is flattened by discouragement. This visit, like all his others, has convinced her that she's wasted years on the wrong men, the wrong life. "You drive him," she says. "He seems more interested in your company than in mine, anyway."

As during our previous conversation about getting to the airport on time, I'm sitting in the rocking chair in her bedroom and she is on her bed, her face in her hands. Looking at her, I can't think of any words that might reach across the divide between us. "All right," I say at last, and I kiss her cheek under her closed eyes. "I'll go. You stay."

When I tell my father she's not coming, he smiles. "Oh good," he says. "I'm glad to have you to myself for a little while." He picks up his bags.

"Maybe you should go up and say good-bye," I say, surprised by his callousness, the way he doesn't seem to consider her feelings when she is slain by as little as a glance from him.

⌁   ⌁   ⌁

In the terminal, he puts down the camera case to embrace me with both arms. "I love you," he says. "God, I love you. I lost you, but now I have you back, and I'll never let you go again." He says the words and he holds me tightly, so tightly. How solid he is, how real. Father. My father. The word made flesh.

"You don't know how I suffered when they sent me away," he says. "You can't imagine the pain of losing you."

He takes my face in his hands and kisses my forehead, my eyes. "How can a daughter of mine be this beautiful?" he murmurs. "When I look at you, I wonder if I, too, must not be handsome."

My father knows he is a good-looking man. He's overweight, and I have to stretch to get my arms around him, but his features—a strong jaw, high cheekbones, and long nose—are good enough to excuse the excess. I smile, but I don't return to him the compliment I suspect he's trying to prompt.

We look at each other. We search each other's faces. "What happens now?" I say, and we make promises that we'll be together again soon.

"In the summer, maybe," I say.

"No," he says. "Sooner. Sooner."

With his hand under my chin, my father draws my face toward his own. He touches his lips to mine. I stiffen.

I've seen it before: fathers kissing their daughters on the mouth. A friend of mine's father has kissed her this way for years, and I've watched them, unable to look away, disquieted by what I see. In my family, lip-to-lip kisses between parent and child are considered as vulgar as spitting in public or not washing your hands after using the toilet, all of which failures my grandmother would judge as evidence of poor upbringing. She might excuse such kisses from a person raised in an exotic, backward culture, but never from a decent American.

A voice over the public-address system announces the final boarding call for my father's flight. As I pull away, feeling the resistance of his hand behind my head, how tightly he holds me to him, the kiss changes. It is no longer a chaste, closed-lipped kiss.

My father pushes his tongue deep into my mouth: wet, insistent, exploring, then withdrawn. He picks up his camera case, and, smiling brightly, he joins the end of the line of passengers disappearing into the airplane.

How long do I stand there, my hand to my mouth, people washing around me? The plane has taxied away from the gate before I move. Through the terminal's thick wall of glass, I watch it take off, the thrust that lifts its heavy, shining belly into the clouds.

I am frightened by the kiss. I know it is wrong, and its wrongness is what lets me know, too, that it is a secret.

Dorothy Allison

from Two or Three Things I Know for Sure

I HAD THIS GIRLFRIEND ONCE SCARED ALL MY OTHER GIRLFRIENDS OFF. BIG, BLOND, SHY, and butch, just out of the army, drove a two-door Chevy with a reinforced trunk and wouldn't say why.

"What you carry in that thing, girl? You moving contraband state to state?" I was joking, teasing, putting my hand on her butt, grinning at her scowl, touching her in places she couldn't quite admit she liked.

"I an't moving nothing," she told me.

"Uh-huh. Right. So how come I feel so moved?"

She blushed. I love it when women blush, especially those big butch girls who know you want them. And I wanted her. I did. I wanted her. But she was a difficult woman, wouldn't let me give her a backrub, read her palm, or sew up the tear in her jeans—all those ritual techniques Southern femmes have employed in the seduction of innocent butch girls. A basic error, this one was not from the South. Born in Chicago, she was a Yankee runaway raised in Barbados by a daddy who worked as a Mafia bagman and was never really sure if he was bringing up a boy or a girl. He'd bought her her first three-piece suit, then cursed at how good it looked on her and signed the permission form that let her join the army at seventeen.

"My daddy loves me, he just don't understand me. Don't know how to talk to me when I go back." She told me that after I'd helped her move furniture for two hours and we were relaxing over a shared can of beer and stories of how she'd gotten to Tallahassee. I just nodded, pretty sure her daddy understood her as much as he could stand.

I seduced her in the shower. It was all that furniture-moving, I told her, and insisted I couldn't go out in the condition I was in. Simple courtesy. I sent her in the shower first, came in after, and then soaped her back in businesslike fashion so she'd relax a little more. I kept chatting—about the women's center, books I'd read, music, and oh! how long and thick her toenails were. I got down on my knees to examine her toenails.

"Woman," I said, "you have the most beautiful feet."

I let the water pour down over both of us. It was a silly thing, to talk that way in that situation, but sex is like that. There I was, kneeling for her, naked, my hands on her legs, my mouth just where I wanted it to be. I smiled before I leaned forward. She clenched her fists in my hair, moaned when my tongue touched her. The muscles in her thighs began to jump. We nearly drowned in that shower.

"Don't laugh at me," she said later when we were lying limp on wet sheets, and I promised. No.

"Whiskey and cigarettes," she mumbled. "I move whiskey and cigarettes without tax stamps, for the money, that's what I move."

I smiled and raked my teeth across her throat. "Uh-huh."

"And . . ." She paused. I put one leg between her thighs and slid myself up and down until we fit tight, the bone of my hip resting against the arch of her public mound, the tangle of her blond curls wiry on my belly. I pushed up off her throat and waited. She looked up at me. Her cheeks were bright red, her eyes almost closed, pearly tears showing at the corners.

"Shaklee! Shaklee products. Oh God! I sell cleaning supplies door to door."

I bit her shoulder, didn't laugh. I rocked her on my leg until she relaxed and laughed herself. I rocked her until she could forgive me for asking. Then she took hold of me and rolled me over and showed me that she wanted me as much as I had wanted her.

"You're quite a story," I whispered to her after.

"Don't tell," she begged.

"Who would I tell?"

Who needs to know?

❧ ❧ ❧

Not until I was thirty-four did my sister Anne and I sit down together to talk about our lives. She came out on the porch, put a six-pack on my lap, and gave me a wary careful grin.

"All right," Anne said. "You drink half the six-pack and then we'll talk."

"I can't drink," I said.

"I know." She grinned at me.

I frowned. Then, very deliberately, I pulled one of the cans free from the plastic loop, popped it open, and drank deeply. The beer wasn't as cold as it should have been, but the taste was sweet and familiar.

"Not bad," I complimented Anne.

"Yeah, I gave up on those fifty-nine-cent bargains. These days I spend three dollars or I don't buy."

"I'm impressed."

"Oh, don't start. You've never been impressed with anything I've done or said or thought of doing. You were so stuck up you never noticed me at all."

"I noticed." I looked at her, remembering her at thirteen—the first time she had accused me of being weird, making fun of me for not wearing makeup or even knowing what kind of clothes I should have been begging Mama to buy me. "You don't do nothing but read, do you?" Her words put her in the hated camp of my stepfather, who was always snatching books out of my hands and running me out of the house.

"We didn't like each other much," Anne said.

"We didn't know each other."

"Yeah? Well, Mama always thought you peed rose water."

"But you were beautiful. Hell, you didn't even have to pee, you were so pretty. People probably offered to pee for you."

"Oh, they offered to do something, right enough." She gave me a bitter smile.

"You made me feel so ugly."

"You made me feel so stupid."

I couldn't make a joke out of that. Instead, I tried to get her to look at me. I reached over and put my hand on her arm.

When we were girls, my little sister Anne had light shiny hair, fine skin, and guileless eyes. She was a girl whose walk at twelve made men stop to watch her pass, a woman at thirteen who made grown men murderous and teenage boys sweaty with hunger. My mother watched her with the fear of a woman who had been a beautiful girl. I watched her with painful jealousy. Why was she so pretty when I was so plain? When strangers in the grocery store smiled at her and complimented Mama on "that lovely child," I glared and turned away. I wanted to be what my little sister was. I wanted all the things that appeared to be possible for her.

It took me years to learn the truth behind that lie. It took my sister two decades to tell me what it was really like being beautiful, about the hatred that trailed over her skin like honey melting on warm bread.

My beautiful sister had been dogged by contempt just like her less beautiful sisters—more, for she dared to be different yet again, to hope when she was supposed to have given up hope, to dream when she was not the one they saved dreams for. Her days were full of boys sneaking over to pinch her breasts and whisper threats into her ears, of girls who warned her away from their brothers, of thin-lipped adults who lost no opportunity to tell her she really didn't know how to dress.

"You think you pretty, girl? Ha! You an't nothing but another piece of dirt masquerading as better."

"You think you something? What you thinking, you silly bitch?"

I think she was beautiful. I think she still is.

My little sister learned the worth of beauty. She dropped out of high school and fell in love with a boy who got a bunch of his friends to swear that the baby she was carrying could just as easily have been theirs as his. By eighteen she was no longer beautiful, she was ashamed: staying up nights with her bastard son, living in my stepfather's house, a dispatcher for a rug company, unable to afford her own place, desperate to give her life to the first man who would treat her gently.

"Sex ruined that girl," I heard a neighbor tell my mama. "Shoulda kept her legs closed, shoulda known what would happen to her."

"You weren't stupid," I said, my hand on Anne's arm, my words just slightly slurred.

"Uh-huh. Well, you weren't ugly."

We popped open more cans and sat back in our chairs. She talked about her babies. I told her about my lovers. She cursed the men who had hurt her. I told her terrible stories about all the mean women who had lured me into their beds when it wasn't me they really wanted. She told me she had always hated the sight of her husband's cock. I told her that sometimes, all these years later, I still wake up crying, not sure what I have dreamed about, but remembering something bad and crying like a child in great pain. She got a funny look on her face.

"I made sure you were the one," she said. "The one who had to take him his glasses of tea, anything at all he wanted. And I hated myself for it. I knew every time, when you didn't come right back—I knew he was keeping you in there, next to him, where you didn't want to be any more than I did."

She looked at me, then away. "But I never really knew what he was doing," she whispered. "I thought you were so strong. Not like me. I knew I wasn't strong at all. I thought you were like Mama, that you could handle him. I thought you could handle anything. Every time he'd grab hold of me and hang on too long, he'd make me feel so bad and frightened and unable to imagine what he wanted, but afraid, so afraid. I didn't think you felt like that. I didn't think it was the same for you."

We were quiet for a while, and then my sister leaned over and pressed her forehead to my cheek.

"It wasn't fair, was it?" she whispered.

"None of it was," I whispered back, and put my arms around her.

"Goddamn!" she cursed. "Goddamn!" And started to cry. Just that fast, I was crying with her.

"But Mama really loved you, you know," Anne said.

"But you were beautiful."

She put her hands up to her cheeks, to the fine webs of wrinkles under her eyes, the bruised shadows beneath the lines. The skin of her upper arms hung loose and pale. Her makeup ended in a ragged line at her neck, and below it, the skin was puckered, freckled, and sallow.

I put my hand on her head, on the full blond mane that had been her glory when she was twelve. Now she was thirty-two, and the black roots showing at her scalp were sprinkled with gray. I pulled her to me, hugged her, and kissed her neck. Slowly we quieted our crying, holding on to each other. Past my sister's shoulder, I saw her girl coming toward us, a chubby dark child with nervous eyes.

"Mama. Mama, y'all all right?"

My sister turned to her daughter. For a moment I thought she was going to start crying again, but instead she sighed. "Baby," she called, and she put her hands out to touch those little-girl porcelain cheeks. "Oh baby, you know how your mama gets."

"You know how your mama gets." The words echoed in me. If I closed my eyes, I could see again the yellow kitchens of our childhood, where Mama hung her flowered curtains every time we moved, as if they were not cotton but spirit. It was as if every move were another chance to begin again, to claim some safe and clean space for herself and her girls. Every time, we watched her, thinking this time maybe it would be different. And when different did not come, when, every time, the same nightmarish scenes unfolded—shouting and crying and Mama sitting hopelessly at her kitchen table—she spoke those words.

"Oh, girls, you know how your mama gets."

I clenched my hands on my thighs, seeing my niece's mouth go hard. She clamped her teeth as I remembered clamping mine, looked away as I would have done, not wanting to see two tired, half-drunk women looking back at her with her own features. I shook my head once and caught her glance, the wise and sullen look of a not quite adolescent girl who knew too much.

"Pretty girl," I said. "Don't look so hard."

Her mouth softened slightly. She liked being told she was pretty. At eleven so had I. I waved her to my hip, and when she came, I pushed her hair back off her face, using the gestures my mama had used on me. "Oh, you're going to be something special," I told her. Something special.

"My baby's so pretty," Anne said. "Look at her. My baby's just the most beautiful thing in the whole wide world." She grinned, and shook her head. "Just like her mama, huh?" Her voice was only a little bitter, only a little cruel. Just like her mama.

I looked into my niece's sunburned frightened face. Like her mama, like her grandmama, like her aunts—she had that hungry desperate look that trusts nothing and wants everything. She didn't think she was pretty. She didn't think she was worth anything at all.

"Let me tell you a story," I whispered. "Let me tell you a story you haven't heard yet." Oh, I wanted to take her, steal her, run with her a thousand miles away from the daddy who barely noticed her, the men who had tried to do to her what my stepfather had done to me. I wanted to pick her up and cradle her. I wanted to save her.

My niece turned her face to me, open and trusting, waiting to be taken away, to be persuaded, or healed, or simply distracted.

All right, I thought. That will do. For one moment, this moment leading to the next, the act of storytelling connecting to the life that might be possible, I held her attention and began.

"Let me tell you about your mama."

My niece looked from me to my sister, and my sister stared at me uncertainly, wondering if I was going to hurt her, her and her girl.

"Sit down, baby. I got a story to tell you. Look at your mama. You know how she is? Well, let me tell you about the day death was calling your mama's name, death was singing her song and luring her away. She was alone, as alone as only a woman waiting to birth a baby can be. All she saw was darkness. All she heard was her blood singing death. But in the deepest part of that night she heard something else. She heard the baby in her belly crying soft, too weak to make a big noise, too small to know it was alive at all. That's when your mama saved her own life—by choosing it, by claiming it, alone and scared as she was. By pulling you into the world and loving you with her whole heart."

I watched my sister's eyes go wide, watched her mouth work. "Now you telling stories about me?"

I just smiled. "Oh, I got one or two."

That night I sat with my niece and watched my sister going in and out her back door, picking up and sweeping, scolding her dogs for jumping up on her clean work clothes. My niece was sleepy, my sister exhausted. Their features were puffy, pale, and too much alike. I surprised myself then, turning my niece's face to mine and starting another story.

"When your mama was a girl," I told her, "she was so beautiful people said the sun shone brighter when she walked out in the day. They said the moon took on glitter when she went out in the night. But, strangest of all, people said the June bugs catching sight of her would begin to light and try to sing an almost human song. It got to the point she had to stay home and hide to keep the sun from getting too hot, the moon from burning up, the June bugs from going hoarse and dying out."

"Ahhh." The two of them looked at me, almost smiling, almost laughing, waiting. I put my hand out, not quite touching my sister's face, and drew my fingers along the line of her neck from just below her ear to the softness of her chin. With my other hand I made the same gesture along my niece's face.

"See here?" I whispered. "This is where you can see it. That's the mark of the beautiful Gibson women, both of you have it."

My niece touched her cheek, mouth open.

"Here?" she asked.

Yes.

⋄ ⋄ ⋄

Two or three things I know, two or three things I know for sure, and one of them is that if we are not beautiful to each other, we cannot know beauty in any form.

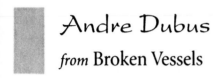

Andre Dubus

from Broken Vessels

LIGHTS OF THE LONG NIGHT

I REMEMBER THE HEADLIGHTS, BUT I DO NOT REMEMBER THE CAR HITTING LUIS SANTIAGO and me, and I do not remember the sounds our bodies made. Luis died, either in the ambulance, or later that night in the hospital. He was twenty-three years old. I do not remember leaving the ground my two legs stood on for the last instant in my life, then moving through the air, over the car's hood and windshield and roof, and falling on its trunk. I remember lying on my back on that trunk and asking someone: *What happened?*

I did not lose consciousness. The car did not injure my head or my neck or my spine. It broke my right hand and scraped both arms near my wrists, so my wife believes I covered my face with my arms as I fell. I lay for a while on the trunk, talking to a young man, then to a woman who is a state trooper, then I was in an ambulance, stopped on the highway, talking to a state trooper, a man, while he cut my trousers and my right western boot. That morning my wife saw the left boot on the side of the highway, while she was driving home from the hospital in Boston. The car had knocked it off my foot. The state troopers got the boot for my wife, but I did not leave the hospital with a left foot or, below the middle of my knee, a left leg.

While the state trooper was cutting and we were talking, I saw Luis Santiago on a stretcher. People were putting him into an ambulance. Lying in the ambulance and watching Luis I knew something terrible had happened and I said to the trooper: *Did that guy die?* I do not remember what the trooper said, but I knew then that Luis was either dead or soon would be. Then I went by ambulance to a clinic in Wilmington where Dr. Wayne Sharaf saved my life, and my wife Peggy and my son Jeb were there, then an ambulance took me to Massachusetts General Hospital in Boston, where they operated on me for twelve hours.

Luis Santiago said what were probably his last words on earth to me: *Por favor, señor, please help, no hablo Ingles.* This was around one o'clock in the morning of 23 July 1986. I was driving north on Route 93, going from Boston to my home in Haverhill, Massachusetts. The highway has four lanes and I was driving in the third. That stretch of road is straight and the visibility on 23 July was very good, so when I saw the Santiagos' car I did not have to apply the brakes or make any other sudden motions. It was ahead of me, stopped in the third lane, its tail lights darkened. I slowed my car. To the right of the Santiagos' car, in the breakdown lane, a car was parked and, behind it, a woman stood talking into the emergency call box. Her back was to me. I was driving a standard shift Subaru, and I shifted down to third, then second, and drove to the left, into the speed lane, so I could pass the left side of the Santiagos' car and look into it for a driver, and see whether or not the driver was hurt. There were no cars behind me. Luz Santiago stood beside the car, at the door to the driver's side, and her forehead was bleeding and she was crying. I drove to the left side of the road and parked near the guard rail and turned on my emergency blinker lights. Because of the guard rail, part of my car was still in the speed lane. I left the car and walked back to Luz Santiago. She was still crying and bleeding and she asked me to help her. She said: *There's a motorcycle under my car.*

I looked down. Dark liquid flowed from under her engine and formed a pool on the highway, and I imagined a motorcycle under there and a man dead and crushed between the motorcycle and the engine and I knew I would have to look at him. Then, for the first time, I saw Luis Santiago. He came from the passenger's side, circling the rear of the car, and walked up to me and Luz, standing beside the driver's door and the pool of what I believed was blood on the pavement. Later I learned that it was oil from the crankcase and the abandoned motorcycle Luz had run over was no longer under her car. Luis was Luz's brother and he was young and I believe his chest and shoulders were broad. He stopped short of Luz, so that she stood between us. That is when he spoke to me, mostly in his native tongue, learned in Puerto Rico.

I do not remember what I said to him, or to Luz. But I know what I was feeling, thinking: first I had to get Luz off the highway and lie her down and raise her legs and cover her with my jacket, for I believed she was in danger of shock. Then I would leave Luis with Luz and return to her car and look under its engine at the crushed man. We left her car and walked across the speed lane to the left side of the highway. We did not have to hurry. No cars were coming. We walked in column: I was in front, Luz was behind me, and Luis was in the rear. At the side of the road we stopped. I saw headlights coming north, toward us. We were not in danger then. If we had known the car was going to swerve toward us, we could have stepped over the guard rail. I waved at the headlights, the driver, my raised arms crossing in front of my face. I wanted the driver to stop and help us. I wanted the driver to be with me when I looked under Luz's car. We were standing abreast, looking at the car. I was on the right, near the guard rail; Luz was in the middle, and Luis stood on her left. I was still waving at the car when it came too fast to Luz's car and the driver swerved left, into the speed lane, toward my Subaru's blinking emergency lights, and toward us. Then I was lying on the car's trunk and asking someone: *What happened?*

Only Luis Santiago knows. While I was in Massachusetts General Hospital my wife told me that Luz Santiago told our lawyer I had pushed her away from the car. I knew it was true. Maybe because my left thigh was the only part of my two legs that did not break, and because the car broke my right hip. When the car hit us, Luis was facing its passenger side, Luz was between its headlights, and I was facing the driver. In the hospital I assumed that I had grabbed Luz with my left hand and jerked and threw her behind me and to my right, onto the side of the highway. That motion would have turned my body enough to the left to protect my left thigh, and expose my right hip to the car. But I do not think the patterns of my wounds told me I had pushed Luz. I knew, from the first moments in the stationary ambulance, that a car struck me because I was standing where I should have been; and, some time later, in the hospital, I knew I had chosen to stand there, rather than leap toward the guard rail.

On 17 September 1986 I left the hospital and came home. In December, Dr. Wayne Sharaf talked to me on the phone. He is young, and he told me I was the first person whose life he had saved, when he worked on me at the clinic in Wilmington. Then he said that, after working on me, he worked on Luz Santiago, and she told him I had pushed her away from the car. I thanked him for saving my life and telling me what Luz had told him. I said: *Now I can never be angry at myself for stopping that night.* He said: *Don't ever be. You saved that woman's life.* Perhaps not. She may have survived, as I have. I am forever a cripple, but I am alive, and I am a father and a husband, and in 1987 I am sitting in the sunlight of June and writing this.

HUSBANDS

On a sunlit December afternoon a UPS man carrying a long, wide package came up the steep hill of my driveway. The width of the package was from his armpit to his hand. I saw him through the glass door in front of my desk, and wheeled to the kitchen door and opened it, and waited for him to come up the series of six connected ramps, four of them long and parallel to each other. One ramp would be too steep; you need one inch of grade for every twelve inches you climb or descend. Turning onto the last ramp he saw me and smiled and asked how I was doing. I see a lot of UPS men. It is a simple way to shop. He had blond hair and a face reddened by the winter sun and wind, and perhaps from climbing the hill. I told him I was fine.

"That's an exercise machine," I said. "How do you feel about putting it in the bedroom?"

Whenever I ask someone to do something for me, I am saying aloud that I cannot do it, or cannot do it well, or simply, or easily. So I very often ask with odd sentences. In the first year after my injury, with one leg gone above the knee and the other in a cast and usually hurting, I said things like *I wonder if there's any cheese* or *Does anyone want hot chocolate?* I still do.

"Sure," the UPS man said. "Where is it?"

"Down at the end of the hall."

I wheeled backward out of the kitchen to get out of his way, made a backward turn in the dining room to let him by, then followed him in the hall, and said: "All this time you've been waiting for a young wife to ask you to put it in the bedroom, and you get an old buck in a wheelchair."

Still in the hall, he said over his shoulder: "I wish my wife would do that."

"Do what?"

He was in the bedroom, and I was rolling through the door.

"Tell me to put it in the bedroom," he said.

⚬ ⚬ ⚬

The summer before that, I had a lap pool built in my front yard, so I could have motion out of my chair. A lap pool is three feet deep. Beside mine is a concrete slab level with my chair; from the slab, steps with aluminum railings go to the pool, and by lifting myself on the railings, I can go down and up on my butt. Most of all, the pool is to replace the beach. I love the beach, and probably will always miss it, but I cannot go there anymore without someone to pull my chair backward and tilted, so the small front wheels are above the sand. They are the ones that sink. So now, when my little girls are with me in summer, we play in the pool. My two grown sons and two friends, on payroll, built the ramp to the pool, and, at the top of my driveway, to a built-up rectangle of asphalt with railroad ties as a curb. My driveway is all steep slope, and this flat asphalt allows me to get in and out of my car.

On a beautiful early summer afternoon my son Jeb and the two friends and I were sitting on the ramp, our shirts off, when the man who delivers for the pharmacy drove up the driveway. He is a short pleasant man, retired from the gas company. He wears thick glasses, always a visored cap, and has grey hair. Reading gas meters taught him to carry dog biscuits; he says they worked better than the spray designed to fend off dogs. Always he brought biscuits for my dog, Luke, a golden retriever. Luke was lying in the shade that day, and went to the man and sat at his feet to be fed. Someone brought the bag of vitamins and medicine inside and fetched my checkbook and I paid. I see this delivery man at least every other week, yet I had forgotten his wedding anniversary. But Bill remembered, and said: "How was the fiftieth wedding anniversary?"

"Oh, it was something. They picked us up at the house in a limousine, took us to the function room. There was a hundred people there. We had cocktails, prime rib, cake, champagne, the works. I says to the wife, when you've had a car this long, it's time to trade in on a new model. She says I was thinking the same thing. I says I was thinking of trading in for two twenty-five-year-olds. She says they'd kill you."

"Fifty years," Jack said. "That's something to celebrate. Any marriage is hard."

"Oh, sure, it was hard. That first year, back in 1939, I couldn't get regular work at the shoe factory. For about six months, I couldn't get a forty-hour week. But after that it was all right."

Jeb and Jack and Bill and I looked at each other; only Bill had a girlfriend, his fiancee. We looked back at the delivery man, reaching in his pocket for a dog biscuit.

"After the dinner and the toasts and everything, they put us in the limousine and took us home. We go upstairs and get into the bed and I says to the wife: You think we ought to try what we tried fifty years ago? She says it'll cost you money just to touch it. So next morning I go downstairs and I put a dollar bill under her orange juice glass, and I put another one under her cereal bowl, and one under her coffee cup. I put one under the sugar bowl and the salt shaker and the pepper shaker. Then I put one under my glass and bowl and cup, and one under her napkin so she'd get the message. Then I sat down and waited for her."

He stood facing us, smiling, petting Luke, putting another bone-shaped biscuit in Luke's mouth. I said: "Aren't you going to tell us the end of that story?"

"That is the end," he said, smiling, and lifted his hand in a wave, and walked away from us to his car.

❧ ❧ ❧

On a warm blue September afternoon I went to see my paraplegic friend. A few years ago he fell off a ladder. I will call him Joe. He works for disabled people, out of an office in a nearby town on the Merrimack River. He taught me to drive with hand controls, but that is not part of his job. He did it one Sunday afternoon, at my house, saving me eight hours of lessons at ten dollars an hour.

In the parking lot outside his office, Joe was waiting in his chair. He wanted to see my new two-thousand-dollar rig: a steel box on the roof of my car that, with two chains like a bicycle's and an elongated hook, folds and lifts my chair into it, and lowers it to the ground beside my door. A button inside the car controls it. I parked beside him and opened my door and watched his face as I lowered the chair. He is a lean man with a drooping but trimmed black moustache. As the chair descended, he smiled and shook his head.

"It's too easy, Andre. It's too easy."

I had learned to drive in his Cadillac. To remove the wheels from the chair and place them and the seat cushion then the folded chair behind the driver's seat, you must sit sideways in the car, with your legs outside, so you can pull the seat as far as possible toward the steering wheel. My right knee does not bend enough for me to swing my leg in and out of a car, but in Joe's Cadillac, I could shift backward to the passenger seat and get my leg inside. In my Toyota Celica the console and handbrake are in my way, and the car's lack of depth makes this movement difficult. I said: "Nothing is too easy."

But he liked the machine. People who like machines admire its simple efficiency. People in parking lots stop to watch it work. Joe wheeled closer to the car to see the cellular phone I had bought the day before. Without a MacArthur Fellowship I would have none of this; and I would not have the car or the two-thousand-dollar wheelchair that is so much more comfortable and mobile and durable than those nine-hundred-dollar blue chairs you see in hospitals. You can go through two of them in a year, if you are active. I got the phone in case of car trouble. Joe wanted to know how the phone worked, and I showed him, and he called his office. Then we went inside and met the people working there. All but one was disabled. There was a blind man, and Joe grinned and asked him if he had read my books. The blind man laughed.

On our way out Joe introduced me to a quadriplegic, perhaps in his early forties. With him was a pretty blonde woman. Then we went through wide doors that open and close by buttons on the wall beside them, so that if you are in a chair you do not have to pull the door toward you or hold it open while you wheel across its threshold. Outside was a concrete porch and a long L-shaped ramp to the parking lot. We faced the sun and I took off my shirt and watched a black man drive a van into the parking space in front of the porch. He and Joe waved. Joe said he was from Nigeria and had a wife before his accident, a car wreck, but now she was gone. The man put his key ring between his teeth, transferred to his wheelchair on the passenger side, worked a switch there, and behind him a lift came out of the van. He wheeled onto it, worked the switch again, and came down to the asphalt. At the side of the van, he took the keys from his mouth, turned one of them in a switch, and the lift went up and back into the van, whose door closed behind it. Then he put his keys in a bag attached to the back of his chair. He wheeled to our left, to the ramp and up the first leg of it. As he turned up the last leg, facing us now, I said: "Are you having fun?"

"Oh yes; I am pumping iron."

He had a strong torso and his face was broad and young and handsome. Joe introduced us. The Nigerian was lightly sweating, and had a good handshake. I said: "I'm just starting my fourth year. How about you?"

"Six now," he said, smiling. "I love it."

"That's right," Joe said. "The crying days are over."

"And who is listening?"

He is a paraplegic. For a few minutes he and Joe talked about burning themselves, carrying hot coffee and spilling it and not knowing they were being scalded. I said: "So when my leg hurts I should think about you guys, right?"

"That's right," Joe said.

"I don't carry coffee anymore," the Nigerian said.

Then he went inside. I looked at Joe.

"You can't feel anything? From the waist down?"

"It's funny. I can feel my left nut. And look: I can move my left leg from side to side." He moved it a few times. "I can't feel it but, see, it moves. Everybody's different. One guy may be able to feel his toe. Just one of them. You know anything about the spine?"

"No."

He clenched a fist, leaving an opening in it.

"Your spine is like the fucking phone company. There's all these wires." He stuck his forefinger into the hole. "It depends on what gets cut."

"Did you see *Coming Home?*"

"That's a good movie."

"He couldn't feel her, right?"

"No."

"But you get erections."

"Voluntary, and involuntary."

"Then what?"

"It's better. Look, before you get hurt, what do you do? You get on the wife and pump away, then it's over. Now I take my time. That's why it's better. It's in the brain, Andre. Why do you want to get laid? For your brain, right?"

"I guess so. Can you have an orgasm?"

"No. It takes muscles. So what?"

"I had a problem, my first year. Making love made me think about my legs, and I couldn't come. Sometimes, but not all the time."

"So?"

"I know. But it got to me. Then in the third year, that lady you met at my house, remember her?"

"She was nice."

"She surely was. She made me feel whole again."

Behind us the door opened and the quadriplegic came out in his mechanical chair, the blonde woman behind him. They told me Nice to meet you, we all said goodbye, and Joe and I watched them go down the ramp and across the lot to his van, watched him go up a lift behind the passenger's seat, then move his chair to the steering wheel. He is able to drive with his hands. She climbed in beside him.

"Look at him," Joe said. "A quad. She's been with him for seven years, *after* he got fucked up. What do you think *he's* got, a seven-inch tongue?"

They drove out to the street and she waved at us. We waved and I watched her smile and hair. Then I looked at Joe.

"What," he said.

"You're telling me that you go to bed with your wife, you take your time, you get hard, your wife gets on top and does what she wants to do till she's finished, and you don't feel anything."

"That's right. And, let me tell you, there's a lot more to our marriage than sex."

⚬ ⚬ ⚬

That night Jack and I went to dinner at a restaurant in Haverhill with Gene and Jean Harbilas. Gene is my doctor. He and I drank vodka martinis, then we had a good bordeaux with dinner. The dinner was very good, but I had been sitting, either in the car or my chair, since leaving home early that afternoon to visit Joe, and for the last hour or so my lower back muscles ached enough to make me sweat. After dinner the young black chef came out to meet us. He was from the Gold Coast and spoke English with a French accent. He told us he had studied in Paris, and met his wife there. Someone asked what brought him to Haverhill.

"It is my wife's home," he said.

I thought how strange it was, to meet two men from Africa on the same day in the Merrimack Valley.

Fenton Johnson

from Geography of the Heart

XX

THE LAST DAY, THE FIRST DAY.

No sleep. In the middle of the night I phoned and reached Larry's doctor in his San Francisco office, just as he was leaving for the day. His first question: "How could you let him get this sick?"

The next morning I carried Larry to the car. At the bottom of the stairs the hotel manager and her daughter watched. Arms folded. No help.

In the car: accelerator to the floor. Five hours to Paris. Larry slept. At a stop for gas he tried to use the bathroom. I helped him across the gas station apron but he was too weak to stand at a urinal. Stares, glares, this time from the station attendants.

In Paris: lost, then boxed in a blocked one-way street. Sidewalk driving. Bad directions, then good directions misunderstood.

At the American Hospital: I couldn't locate the emergency entrance. I parked at the main entrance, left Larry in the car, and dashed up the stairs. Three women at the reception desk (volunteers?). "*Mon copain est gravement malade avec le SIDA.*" ("My friend is gravely ill with AIDS.") My words echoed in the small waiting area, or was this my imagination? The low hum of reception-room chatter fell silent. Two of the three receptionists rose and walked quickly into the rear offices. The third rose to follow. "*S'il vous plaît, madame, je vous en prie.*" I was begging now. The silent watching waiting room. The receptionist sat and called for emergency staff. Attendants came with a wheelchair and got Larry from the car.

Across the frantic drive from Tours he had been all but comatose, but now we were at the hospital and the hope of help and the need to put on a good show revitalized him and he walked, leaning on my arm, through the doors and to the desk. The receptionist pushed forms at us. Larry tendered his credit card and signed his name, forming each letter with care and precision on a slip of paper whose carbon sits before me now, years later—even in this, his last signature, the letters might be copied directly from the idealized cursive script posted, white lettering on green background, above elementary school blackboards. In that cramped, perfectly formed hand I read the story of one perhaps too devoted to being the man others wanted him to be; loved, maybe, too much (is this possible?) by parents who had survived the worst where others had not.

The doctors: "*Tout va bien.*" ("Everything is fine.") IVs, private room, then the move to intensive care, waiting. Late in the evening I returned the car to the rental lot at de Gaulle Airport, then spent the night at Larry's friend's apartment.

No sleep.

Next day: I phoned early and reached the intensive care unit's head nurse. "*Monsieur Rose se repose. Tout va bien.*" ("Monsieur Rose is resting. Everything is fine.") Visiting hours would begin at 2:15 P.M. No one would be allowed to see or speak to a patient before then. (Weeks later, back in America, reviewing the computerized, detailed billings, I would discover that he'd had a heart attack in the middle of the night—that he'd died and been revived [*réanimé*] with CPR and electric shock to the heart.)

I paced the apartment—might as well be at the hospital. I arrived there late in the morning and climbed the stairs to the intensive care ward.

Entrée interdite (Entry forbidden).

An American angel hovered at my ear. "Go on in," she said. "To hell with the rules. What can they do but throw you out?"

His bed was straight across from the ICU door. He saw me and struggled to sit up. He tried to say something about the night before. I made him lie down, put my finger to my lips. "They'll throw me out if they see me in here."

They saw me in there. They asked me to leave. I nodded politely and made an appearance of standing. Once they were gone, I sat back down and took his hand.

"*Ne pleure pas,*" he said. ("Don't cry.")

They came back. The head nurse this time, the busty Scotswoman with whom I'd spoken earlier in the day ("*Tout va bien*"). In forceful English she ordered me to leave or she would call hospital security to have me bodily thrown out. I left.

I walked around an hour, two hours. *Je pleure.* At exactly 2:15 I opened the ICU door.

He was in the midst of his second heart attack. I saw the cardiac monitor rise, then fall, 70, 60, 45, 20. The monitor alarm sounded. No one came. I stood frozen, watching, unbelieving, afraid to move for fear of being seen and thrown out. The monitor went dead, a flat line. No one came.

At my ear my American angel spoke. "Keep quiet. Let him die. The man has earned his death."

I waited. I waited. The monitor cried, a harsh flat plaintive hum zero zero zero. No one came.

I moved to embrace him, and in my crossing to his bed I was spotted by the nurses' station. A nurse moved toward me, then noticed the monitor's blaring hum. "*Appelez 84!*" she cried. Several nurses pushed me aside and rushed to his bed. They began the violent dance of CPR. I backed from the room. I had no need to witness this.

Five minutes, ten minutes, fifteen minutes. The doctor emerged. "*Il vit encore?*" I asked, unable to speak in either language any form of the evil word.

"*Non. Il est mort. Je suis désolé.*"

The walls fell away, the floor fell from under my feet, the doctor was no longer there. I was alone, as alone as it was possible to be, falling into a well so deep I didn't know how deep, falling. In this single moment my youth fell away, I was no longer innocent, I was no longer young. I embraced all that I had been given and my arms closed on nothing. Now I was falling free, free-falling, and as I fell, I thought of all those candles lit, all those wishes made—a painless death, a speedy death, a death with me at hand.

⚬ ⚬ ⚬

At the American Hospital the nurses would not allow me to watch or help as they cleaned Larry after his death. I would not want to see him, they told me, in this state. And I acceded—did I have a choice? They had his body, on which I had no legal claim. While I waited I thought, *I who have bathed his sores, wiped sweat from his forehead, embraced him in passion and in need; I who have in some small way risked my life to shepherd him to this death— I know his body as none of them know it; I want to know it once more, in the time of his death, but I'm denied this. I am, after all, only his friend.*

Mary Karr

from The Liar's Club

CHAPTER 13

MAYBE IF MOTHER HADN'T TAKEN IT IN HER HEAD TO SHOOT HECTOR, WE'D NEVER HAVE got back to Texas. But the sight of Mother green-eyed drunk on the other side of a nickel-plated pistol with a pearl handle—a weapon like something a saloon girl might pull out of her velvet drawstring bag to waggle at some mouthy, card-playing cowpoke in a bad Western—proved too much for Lecia. She got us the hell out of there. However, had she been polled in advance, Lecia might well have come down on the side of shooting Hector. So would I have. In some basic way, it was as good an idea as any that bobbed up that whole dark time.

They'd been staying at the bar a lot, Mother and Hector, leaving us home. I kept a late watch for them every night. The bar sat only a few blocks away, but Mother seemed a prime candidate for plowing drunk into something with more molecular density than herself—a slab of concrete or brick wall, maybe. After last call, I stood in my stripy Sears PJs at the upstairs window waiting for the Impala to surge up the snowy drive. I rubbed a fist-sized clear spot in the glass frost so I could better study the garage, its square black mouth like some toothless set of jaws. The driveway could lie unmarred by headlights and tire treads for what seemed a zillion heartbeats while I watched.

Lecia and I stopped hanging out at the Longhorn when guns showed up there in the palsied, uncertain, and sometimes liver-spotted hands of the Longhorn patrons and help. A robbery at the steakhouse up the block led Deeter to get fitted with a small shoulder holster. He wore it under his barkeep's apron. A few days later, Hector set out for the pawnshop to pick up a .22 pistol for his cousin to keep her husband at bay. Then he got his own Colt .45. All one afternoon he sat at a cocktail table fiddling with it. He'd sight down the barrel at a pedestrian trotting down Main Street. This was troubling. In Texas any four-year-old knew you didn't point a firearm at a live creature unless you wanted it dead. Even a busted, empty gun got handled like a snake.

Mother's pearl-handled job struck me as silly at first. I'd seen a cigarette lighter shaped much like it at a roadside joke shop once. It hung in a plastic bag from a spinning rack of other gags, including a small pink puddle of plastic dog vomit I spent my last nickel on.

Mother swore to keep the pistol tucked safe in her Coach bag. She just wanted it, she said, in case anybody ever tried to bother her. *Who*—my eight-year-old head wondered—*would ever dare mess with Mother?* I knew for a fact that she would have smacked the dogshit out of any yahoo who even approximated getting ready to bother her. The gun was—in a word I pinched off Lecia's sixth-grade spelling list—superfluous.

Guns per se didn't worry me. Every pickup in Leechfield sported a National Rifle Association sticker and rifle rack in the back window. I'd fired my first pistol way before kindergarten. Two-handed on New Year's Eve, I'd leveled Daddy's .22 over the garage roof and straight at the pie-faced moon. At the stroke of midnight, I squeezed the trigger. My hand flew up a good half yard, but I barely flinched at the blast. When the moon itself didn't go hissing across the black sky like a plugged balloon, I busted out crying. Later, my BB gun took down all manner of sparrows and blackbirds. By second grade, if Daddy braced himself behind me, I could shoulder and shoot a four-ten shotgun without the recoil knocking my arm out of socket. That meant I waded into the black marshes during duck season in winter, and spring found me trotting behind while the men bagged brown morning doves for gumbo.

Still, the sudden appearance of those guns in that bar set a shimmer of anxiety going in some watery place in my middle. They rested in the hands of people who'd never held firearms before. Fools, to a one. Like Hector, Gordon would draw his Magnum like Wyatt Earp for a joke, then shoo me off, saying the safety was on, or the chamber hollow.

One night Joey fell into a crying jag at the bar. His poor poppa had died in the mines at forty, and he pressed Mother's pistol to his temple, that shallow place where his hairline was starting to back up. After that, we'd stopped going to the bar, Lecia and I. But Mother hung on to her joke pistol. The night she decided to shoot Hector, it appeared in her hand fast.

Lecia had been playing the piano when Hector two-stepped out of the bedroom sloshing scotch. He stood behind the bench all misty-eyed. After a few bouncing renditions of "Alley Cat," he asked her to play the national anthem. She said she didn't feel like it. Hector even dug down in his trouser pocket and hauled out a wadded-up ten-dollar bill. He smoothed it flat on the keyboard. He said that money was all hers if she'd only play "America the Beautiful." I pointed out that "America the Beautiful" wasn't the national anthem, which insight caused Hector to smile blurrily at me while Lecia wadded up his ten-spot and pitched it onto the strings. She banged down the keyboard cover and stood up. She wasn't playing diddly-squat, she said.

Usually, that would have sent old Hector sulking off to bed. But for some reason, he took offense. Maybe because at dinner he'd been talking about the brother he'd lost in World War II. Hearing the national anthem got all balled up in his mind with that brother's funeral—the flag folded neat in a navy-blue triangle some officer handed over to his mother, the fistful of dirt Hector himself had tossed down the oblong hole onto the polished box they lowered by hand on straps.

Anyway, Lecia stood, and Hector's face worked itself into a twist we'd never seen. He wound up calling Lecia a spoiled little bitch. Now, nobody would dispute we were spoiled. But the "bitch" part hit some string in Mother, and the next thing we knew she held that pistol.

Night had blacked out the bay windows behind her. She had on a silk slip the color of mayonnaise. Underneath that slip was her long-line conical bra, which turned breasts into something not unlike artillery. Hector slumped in the rose chintz armchair. His head bobbed down, so folds of neck skin gathered around his chin like a basset hound's. He said go on and shoot, his life wasn't worth a nickel anyway.

I got the idea to fling myself across his body. I was betting Mother wouldn't plug me to get at him. And the move did draw her up short. She squinted at me as if I were a long ways off. When she waved the gun sideways to motion me out of the way, her arm looked boneless and wiggly as an eel. *Scoot over,* she said.

Lecia begged her not to pull the trigger, while I draped the length of my body down his front like a lobster bib. He smelled of Burma-Shave and scotch. His belly was wishy under all the knobs and angles of me. I sank into that softness a notch, then craned my head back to see what effect I was having on Mother.

A mist from somewhere inside her skull seemed to skitter behind her green eyes. She was considering. Her hand even dropped a few degrees from its straight-on angle. *My poor, poor babies,* she said. Then the lines of her face drew up and hardened into something like resolve. *Get offa him, Mary Marlene,* she said. Hector's breath was wicked sour when he pleaded back to her, *Honey . . .* to which she said shut up.

Lecia took her place at Mother's elbow. She stared up with an expression that struck me as lawyerly, like Perry Mason's at the jury box. At any second she might've drawn out a pointer and clicked on an overhead projector, the better to list her arguments, which, by the way, struck me as real obvious. If you shoot him, you'll go to jail, maybe forever—that sort of thing. This didn't trouble Mother one whit. She tossed her head and squared her shoulders. *At least I'd have done something worthwhile,* she said. *Killing that low-life sonofabitch.* She studied Hector like he was some worn-out farm mule she was fixing to plug. She waxed lyrical about what a worthless sack of shit he was.

Her talk ground Hector down worse. He sighed a lot, sour air whooshing out of him. I practically scanned his neck for the nozzle that had come unplugged, for with every sigh his whole body sagged a level flatter. So I sank deeper into him, the softness of him. Had this progression gone on forever, he might well have melted to nothing but a puddle under me. I stared at his ear, long and leathery with a few stiff white whiskers tufting out of it.

Hector stopped not caring whether Mother shot him or not and started to lobby actively for it. Like getting shot was some kind of solution. Big alligator tears rivered down the folds in his face. *She's right,* he said. His voice had a crimp in it. *I ain't never been worth a damn.*

I turned from where I lay on him to Lecia, who'd dropped her lawyer pose entirely. She was off on another tack. The look in her brown eyes under the shiny blond shelf of bangs was no longer set. It was weary. And the accent she used next was pure Texan, straight from what you might call The Ringworm Belt. *He's not worth the bullet it'd take to kill him,* she said. She wasn't talking to Mother like some Yankee newscaster anymore. She was buddying up, appealing to Mother's fury, which she'd apparently adjudged immovable. *Jesus, lookit him,* Lecia said. She rolled her eyes. She might have been Mother's cocktail waitress, offhandedly doling out comfort while picking through change on her drink tray. *If Hector was on fire,* Lecia said, *nobody'd so much as piss on him to put him out.* Mother said that was dead straight, and under me Hector seconded the idea.

Then Lecia grabbed my foot and tugged. She wanted to lay across Hector too, she said. That seemed a sisterly gesture, helping out with a chore, as if she knew how gross it felt breathing in his whooshed-out scotchy fumes. She heaved herself up beside me as onto some squishy raft bobbing under us in the Gulf.

I saw she'd transformed again. The tired frown she'd carved with her mouth was unbent. Her forehead had given up its furrow. Her round face was the only accurate barometer for the subtle atmospheric shifts in the room. And that face had gone blank and white as dough. Lecia had slap given up. I glanced back at Mother, who was sighting the short length of that nickel barrel as if to draw a very fine bead around us at Hector.

Somehow I'd buried any real fear till then. The whole scene had struck me as goofy. Sure I was anxious, but a low thrum of worry ran through me more or less constantly like current. Anxiety made me a nail-biter, a restaurant fidgeter, the kind of kid liable, in a given day, to spill at least one glass of liquid. But the deep fear that draws all air from your lungs and sends the world into slow motion hadn't pulled on me for weeks. I'd submerged it till that very instant when Lecia took her place beside me looking wholly empty of herself.

She was telling me to run. But in her pass-the-butter voice. Run across the street to the Janisches' house. Mother was fixing to shoot Hector right that second unless I could fetch some grown-up to stop it.

Sure enough, Mother had shifted into her ghost self, holding that very real gun with a hand so pale you could practically see through it. She didn't hear Lecia tell me to go fetch somebody, for she was past hearing. Her lips moved in a whispery way, as if she was praying. But her gun arm stayed straight. Her hair was spiky wild, and her jaw set.

She didn't move to stop me dashing by. I might have been a cockroach that scuttled past for all the notice she paid. And I didn't look back. I couldn't have seen my sister laying so deep in her ten-year-old body, stared at by that silver pistol's round and careless black eye, and still been able to run off.

Or so I tell myself outside, where time starts to shift. The night itself seems heavy. It drags against my shoulders and keeps me from running as fast as I'm able.

The fresh snow on the street I step into is blue as pool water. I don't even feel my bare feet go cold in that snow. Nor do I note under my white gown the constellation of gooseflesh that must break out down my stick legs. Even the fact that my legs are pumping doesn't fully register. I can only see the still street bob, which phenomenon reassures me that I'm running. The Janisches' mahogany front door with its wreath of holly jerks closer to me one stride at a time, in stop-action.

Their porch light is gold, their doorbell lit like a bright period at the end of some long dark sentence I've crossed. The finger pressing that doorbell must be mine, for there are my nails, square, with slivers of dirt underneath. A shape moves across the window lace. Then, where the door was, there's a rectangle of light holding Mrs. Janisch in her blue duster.

What I tell her is a mystery, though I can feel my jaw working. It's sharp cold, I think, for my very words to get eaten soon as they leave my mouth, before I can even hear them myself. Then Mr. Janisch appears wiping a clear path through the shaving cream on his jaw with a gym towel. He's wearing a T-shirt and dress slacks. And dangling around his neck is a tin medal of St. Jude, the patron saint of lost causes. If you can't sell your house, you buy a statue of Jude, get the priest to dab holy water on it, then bury it upside down in your yard before dawn. And by suppertime, you'll be knocking your for-sale sign over with a hammer.

That's the fact that must for a while occupy all my available brain space, for next thing I know, I'm not at the Janisches' anymore at all, but back across the street on my own porch, at my own front door with a breathing presence behind me that must be Mr. Janisch. The padded arms of his parka make a *whipe, whipe* noise when he moves. I can still smell his mint shaving foam.

I feel dumb knocking instead of just walking in yelling hey. But he insists. After nobody comes, though, I watch my raw-looking little hand start slapping flat on that door over and over.

Mr. Janisch grabs my wrist with his leather-gloved hand to stop me, but I twist loose and bang again with both fists. I've neglected to listen back on Mother's house. I was across the street, sunk deep in my own task. So my house has gone grinding through time minus my vigilance.

If, for instance, a gun went off, I'd have missed hearing it. Two or three shots might have been fired. This thought causes me to kick the door with my numb bare foot, so hard that later the big toenail will go black.

Suddenly there sails through my head a hand-lettered banner that used to hang in front of Central Baptist Church back home: *Prayer changes things*, it said. So if I can eke out the right prayer before that door opens on everybody sprawled around dead like deer you'd line up for a Polaroid before strapping them over the truck hood, maybe I can change the scene we'll find. I have to pray fast and get it right the first time. God'll want a convincing trade, not just that weary promise to be good I always back up on.

Then in a flash, the idea comes. How Abraham was ready to cut his own son's throat solely because God said to. Thinking that, I let one bullet have its way. I give God that bullet killing Hector the way you'd spot points in football when you got only the puny kids on your team.

But God's counteroffer comes in a backwash. I halfway wanted Hector dead from the git-go anyways. So that bullet may not count as offering enough. In church back home, Deacon Sharp always says—while he slips the offering envelope from his shirt pocket to drop in the prayer basket that's swooping up the pew on a long stick—he always says to give till it hurts. The real choice is between Mother and Lecia. Mother lying sprawled on the floor in that creamy slip. Or Lecia in a hump across Hector in the chintz armchair.

I would like to claim that I worried the bone of this choice a long time, but I did not. In an eyeblink's time, I killed the very sister who'd taken my place in the bullet's path. No sooner did the choice present itself than I chose. I just begged *please God.* Then I pictured Mother standing upright, the gun having fallen from her hand.

And God must have heard, for Mother did answer the door, and not even wild-eyed like a TV murderess in her slip. She had on her black turtleneck and stretch pants, and a little beret like a black pancake over her weird hair. She told old Janisch we were just having a family argument. You know how kids exaggerate. Guns, for God's sake? Her husband didn't even hunt. She shook her head at me. *Mary Marlene,* she said, wearing her TV housewife smile. I'd never seen Mother's face so completely free of irony. *Mary Marlene has such an imagination,* she said. Then you won't mind, Mr. Janisch said, if I come in. Mother stepped aside.

There Hector sat in the same parlor chair, Lecia wedged in by him. She had a Nancy Drew mystery on her lap. Mr. Janisch shook Hector's trembling hand, then looked down at me and said he'd be seeing me at school.

From the doorway, Mother and I watched him stride across the street. She drew me under one arm, to warm me in my eyelet gown. It was then I felt the pistol, sticking out from where she'd jammed it in the waistband of her pants.

That was the night Lecia called Daddy collect. She waited till Hector was passed out and Mother was making popcorn in the kitchen. I could hear the pot bang against the stove burner and the explosions inside it like firecrackers on a string.

What Lecia said to Daddy stays with me, for she was suddenly issuing orders again, first for the operator to put us through, then to the daddy absent so long I faltered on conjuring his face. Here's exactly what Lecia said: "Daddy, you need to get us two airplane tickets back down there from Denver." She didn't ask. There was no *maybe* threaded through her voice, no sliver of doubt. Had I been making the call, I would've told about Mother's pistol and laying across Hector and fetching the principal. The whole story would have rolled out. Daddy would've wanted whys and where-fores. Watching Lecia, I knew no further wangling would take place. She doled out a few cursory yessirs and nossirs. But Mother wouldn't get summoned to the phone to check was this okay. In short, it was a done deal.

That hits me funny, now. Here you had a fifty-year-old veteran of one major war and innumerable bar fights taking orders from a girl whose age had only recently nudged into the realm of double digits. Daddy didn't go along with Lecia's plan because it made sense. It didn't much. Maybe he'd been missing us so bad that he was set to grab us any way he could. But even that doesn't explain it. No, what moved him was Lecia, her sudden solidity and power, the sheer force of her will.

I was coiling the phone cord around my index finger when this knowledge settled on me. Lecia's eyes were the same calm brown as always, her blond bangs were still lacquered straight above dark brows. But her voice held less waver. By the time she handed me the phone, the small space between us had stretched into some uncrossable prairie. She'd moved forever away from me. For my part, I was still skidding around in the slippery, internal districts of childhood. I still half-wondered whether Mother might shoot us as we slept. But Lecia had stopped wondering about such things, had let go wonder altogether. She was set on enduring, no matter what. She'd harden into whatever shape survival required. From that second forward, she had to figure what-all she'd have to lose for that survival, what-all and who.

The receiver was warm on my ear. Daddy wanted to know one thing: "You 'bout ready to come on home, Pokey?" I told him I'd *been* ready. To which he said him too.

Early the next morning, we washed our faces. I brushed each tooth with the neat circle stroke Captain Kangaroo had instructed me to; then we buttoned ourselves into church dresses. By dawn, we stood side by side in the full-length mirror. Lecia had tied the hood of my car coat too tight under my chin, so I felt like a sausage in oversmall casing. Her face floating next to mine in the mirror would never again be the face of a child.

Mother must have squawked about our leaving. She would have yelled or wept or folded up drunk and sulking. I recall no such scene. Nor can I picture Lecia announcing our leaving, as she must done first thing that morning. Mother would have been smoothing Ben-Gay on her shoulder. The Sunday *Times* crossword, each box with a penciled capital letter, would have lain between Mother's body and Hector's. (She tended to come up with some kind of answer for each square fast, then erase mistakes later, so the puzzle always looked done but seldom was.)

But I'm making this up. The French door on that scene never swung open. Any talk with Mother after Lecia's call was siphoned clean from my head. Mother herself was clipped from my memory, though some days went by before we actually left, and I must have said goodbye to her. We must have wept, being a family of inveterate weepers, the makers-of-scenes in airport terminals. She did promise vaguely to come for us soon, but I can't exactly hear her saying that, nor does even a ghost of her Shalimar hang in the car that ferried us to the airport.

Joey was hired to fly along, to squire us through plane changes. He right off got wasted on scotch in the bar while Lecia and I wolfed peanuts and sipped Shirley Temples. Our square-bottomed stools were covered in black Naugahyde. They swiveled, bumping into each other like big padded metronomes marking off the morning. On the bar before us, our twin Barbies sat, backs ramrod straight. They had on matching prom dresses in baby-blue crinoline with silver sashes. But we'd lost their white plastic sandals in transit, so their arched feet stuck out bare.

Joey's first act on the plane, after he'd buckled Lecia and me into our seats across the aisle, was to barf volubly into his airsick bag. Lecia and I then dug down in our seat pockets, so our Barbies could do their own make-believe barfing, which troubled the old woman cat-a-corner from me. She sighed disapproval. She shook her head so hard at me her cheek wattles shook above the triple strands of blue-tinted pearls. We moved from Barbie barfing to Barbie fart-jokes and kept those up at top volume clear to Albuquerque, where I announced that my Barbie batched her prom dress with diarrhea squirts. She'd be forced to wear a TWA napkin to the prom, with a rubber-band belt, and minus any underpants.

In Albuquerque, we boarded the wrong plane. Airlines discourage that sort of thing, naturally. They post a fellow at the gate to read your ticket before you even step on a runway. It says right on the front where you paid to fly to. But somehow, against odds I can't fathom, we all wound up in Mexico City, illegally, of course. Maybe Joey even booked us there on purpose. Mother had planted in his noggin her romantic notion of disappearing to Mexico. He may have fancied living cheap in some beach shack flapped over by palm trees, with an Aztec princess bringing him rock lobsters and tortillas patted out with her own small hands.

The *federales* who met us at the customs gate had other ideas, especially when it turned out that Joey had dropped his wallet—with all evidence of U.S. citizenship—in the airplane toilet. He claimed he'd been rising from the toilet and suddenly bent over sick. His bowels had just seized up. He didn't know what fell in the blue toilet water till after he'd zipped up. Then he patted around and found his back pocket light. All his ID had flushed away with an eardrum-sucking pop somewhere over the Sonora desert. He patted his pockets to show the small, official-looking crowd how it happened. Joey had that drunk man's myopic sense of how interesting this all was for everybody.

Meanwhile, the *capitán* shifted his weight from one shiny black boot to the other. He whispered to the customs officials. When he lifted one sinewy hand, two men with rifles at the baggage rack trotted over. Our luggage was called for and disemboweled—dresses, jeans, nylon pajamas. My torn-legged panties got waved a second like some tattered flag of surrender. Joey looked like a smuggler, or like some Mexican national crossing the border without papers. But his bigger crime—or so I guessed from where Lecia and I stood by the coffee machine with three stewardesses who'd taken hold of us—was his lack of seriousness. He just couldn't stop giggling.

They kept him, of course, the customs officials. They had to. The miracle was that Lecia and I were let go. The airline folks even took it on themselves to phone Daddy, telling him they'd tote us back to Texas.

Anyway, I never got to ask Joey if he was kidnapping us, or himself running off, or what. My last sight of him was in that customs holding area, where his face under fluorescent lights resembled the washed-out green of a martini olive. For some reason, they'd made him take off his shoes and one sock. He stood on one leg like a stork, arms held out. Periodically, he exploded with laughs so his big toe dipped down to touch the dirty linoleum.

In the airport employees' lounge, a waiter delivered us an oval platter of huevos rancheros while Lecia told the wide-eyed stews how Joey planned to sell us to some men he knew down there, the extremity of which tale caused me to kick her under the table. Those ladies were paying the check, and I didn't aim to piss them off before it came.

But Lecia knew the furthest limits of credibility. She always had. The women hung on her every word. Their perfectly manicured hands patted our uncombed heads and squeezed our skinny shoulders through our dress plaid. Eventually, they waved us onto a night plane heading for Harlingen, Texas.

I woke to clouds. A whole Arctic wasteland of them bubbled up in the round plane window where Lecia's sleeping head was tipped. The clouds seemed to have seized up in violent motion, like some cauldron that got frozen mid-boil. A full moon shone across them. It cut a wide white path straight to us, the beauty of which flooded me with some ancient sense of possibility. Maybe there was hope for me yet, even from the vantage point of being a kid, hurtling across the black sky with my sister, whom I would never know the heart of again. (When mystics talk about states of grace, surely that's the feeling they mean—hope rising out of some Dust Bowl farmer's heart when he's surveying the field of chewed stems that locusts left.) This hope lacked detail. From it came neither idea nor impetus. I only felt there was something important I had to do, held by the clear light of that unlikely, low-slung moon.

Then it was gone. The man in front of me clicked off his overhead light. He tilted his seat back so deep his bald head seemed to plop in my lap. He can't have been that close, but that's how it felt. I stared at his head, which was white as a worm. He reached up to unscrew his wind-vent.

The stale air that blasted across his scalp and into my face somehow carried the familiar backdraft of doubt. Surely hope was for boneheads. Surely any goodwill God held for my future was spent. Hell, I'd wished my own sister dead a few days back. I glanced over at her glossy blond head tipped in sleep. The rough red blanket was pulled clear to her chin. *Just like a kid*, I thought. I wanted to shake her shoulder and tell her how much I loved her, but she would have said to pipe down.

I glared hate rays at the bald man's head. The monk's fringe of black hair circled his pate like some greasy halo. Earlier, I'd wedged my bare-assed Barbie between the seat cushion and the arm-rest. Now I grabbed her legs like a club and drew back. No thought for consequence, I brought her down on that guy's bare scalp with every ounce of force I had, popping her head off.

The fellow jerked up and let out a whoop. He held his skull with both hands, twisting around to see what had whacked him. I slipped the headless doll under Lecia's red blanket and quick faked sleep on the arm-rest. When he started dinging the stewardess bell, though, Lecia startled up. She blinked and rubbed her eyes, so I blinked and rubbed mine. Meanwhile, the stewardess tripped over that blond and pony-tailed Barbie head. It skittered up the aisle, then swerved under a seat, never to be recovered.

Lecia and I meandered back to Daddy through an underworld of airport personnel. Pilots, baggage handlers, stews and off-duty janitors washed us and fed us. We traveled gratis, without corporate okay. And not only were we never menaced or pinched, beaten or buggered, we never stared with longing at a deck of cards or chocolate doughnut that some stranger didn't ante up for it. Their particular faces have been worn featureless as stones, but those uniforms I walked next to at waist-level prove that hope may not be so foolish. (Sure the world breeds monsters, but kindness grows just as wild, elsewise every raped baby would grow up to rape.)

On each leg of the trip, the planes got littler and more ragged. In Houston, we reached a green camouflage plane with shark's teeth painted on its nose and a big X of gray electrician's tape on the cargo bay. It was parked outside a tin hangar beyond view of commercial aircraft. The pilot wore bifocals. The cubby that he wedged Lecia and me into behind the cockpit was built for flight plans, maybe, or a thermos. We doubled our knees up under our chins. We must have looked, when the pilot turned around to say hold on tight, like a pair of groundhogs poking up from some hole.

The plane cut a tight circle, its headlight just brushing over thick fog. The pilot flipped some ceiling switches and talked back to radio static. We bumped around a lot taxiing. The wings shimmied against bracings thin enough for a backyard swingset. Still, Lecia's profile was calm studying the plane's dials, though the engine racket when we surged was like a vacuum cleaner we had to sit in. The pilot reached down at knee level and pulled back with effort, as if his very strength were hefting the plane's nose off the runway. After considerable bucking around, we pulled into a cloud.

And that was the cloud that held us—with only an occasional deep drop to tease my stomach—all the way to Jefferson County. The pilot used pink Kleenex to scrub at the window steam. But the fog pressed against the windshield was a thick membrane the headlights couldn't puncture. Even I could see we were flying blind.

Nor did visibility get better with landing. We stood on the wet runway with our Barbie cases. No terminal building or parking lot presented itself. Only a tower beam swept over our heads—a fuzzy cone of yellow light wheeling.

Then from an unmeasured distance, headlights flipped on. A car was parked right on the tarmac. I set down my Barbie case. Through the mist, I made out two shapes walking toward us, each in the riverbed of those twin lights. One was small and slight with a cowboy hat. The other had big hands dangling off a long frame. This second shape broke and ran for us, heavy work boots scuffing on the concrete.

There was no clear boundary Daddy ever crossed over, no second he assembled fully before us out of fog. He just gradually got brighter and denser till he was heaving us both up in his arms. He'd been drinking black coffee during his shift, the coffee that poured like tar from the foreman's beat-up percolator. That coffee brought my whole former Daddy back. I knew the solvent he used to strip grease from his hands, and the Lava soap applied with a fingernail brush. His chin bristles scraped my neck. And he must have been sweating from damp or work or worry, for the Tennessee whiskey he'd stood on the tarmac sipping was like fresh-cut oak coming off him. I could feel Lecia's arms on the other side of him hugging, and for once, she didn't swat me away, like my hug was messing hers up. For once, our arms reached around the tall rawboned bulk of him to make a cage he fit right into.

His partner was a small, birdlike man named Blue, which was appropriate for he was all over the color of flint. Blue was soundless, odorless, and completely without opinion. He was one of those clean, featureless men who can move for decades on the periphery of a pool game buying his fair share of beers without ever uttering a full sentence.

Blue had bought Lecia and me each a doll, curly-headed, near as tall as ourselves. Lecia's was blond, mine black-headed. Under the sedan's dome light, mine stared from its box on the wide back seat with an indifference bold enough to edge over into insult. A copper wire garroted her head in place. Her wrists and feet were likewise strapped down. Highway lights started streaking over the cellophane mask above her perfect features. She gazed out sullen. Her cold blue eyes announced that she wanted some other girl, not me. Well, I wanted my very own mother, and I'd have told her so, too, if the thought didn't put a lump in my throat. Instead I told her—out loud, I guess—"People in hell want ice water." Daddy said, "Say what?" And I told him I'd kill for a glass of ice water.

Surely Daddy said more to me in the car. But any other words were wiped clean from my head. He sounded real country talking to Blue while we drove. "Now you take old Raymond there . . ." he was saying to Blue. But it came out, "Nah yew tike ol Ryemon thar . . ." And slow, like he was addressing a deaf man.

In the house, Daddy slipped his jean jacket over a kitchen stool. We were fixing to eat, he said. Lecia unstacked the white melamine picnic plates on the plywood bar. They looked crude as Flintstone plates after our Colorado china. Each had three plastic compartments so you could keep your butter beans out of your greens, and the greens' pot liquor from sogging up your cornbread.

Daddy stood at the stove working with a long wooden spoon inside a pot of something muddy. He dribbled water from the silver kettle into the pot, and I heard it loosen up. In a few minutes you could smell garlic and pork back, and then came the steamy idea of sheer celery slices in a mess of red beans and rice. "This here'll be even better tomorrow," he said.

He'd also made a wheel of cornbread in an iron skillet, the bottom-crust burnt first in hot lard on the stovetop the way I liked. Lecia cut hers off and flipped it across the butter dish at me. There was a dish of raw green onions we ate between bites. And I nearly finished the whole cereal bowl of collards, spoon after slotted spoonful. "Pokey, you know what I'd do to them greens?" Daddy said. He didn't even wait for me to say what, just doctored them with vinegary sprinkles from a jar of yellow Tabasco peppers. He kept looking up to tell Lecia he loved her with all his heart, but mine was the plate he fussed over.

We didn't even have to beg to sleep with him, just bounce twice and say please once before he said okay. First, he lit the gas stove in the bedroom with a *whump*, then smoothed my socks over the top, so they'd be warm come morning. Lecia buttoned our dresses up on hangers while he stripped off his khakis. His legs were white and skinny poking out of blue-patterned boxers. The pinched fingernails he ran all along his pants crease, to sharpen it, made a stuttery noise in the cloth, *rrrrr.* After, he draped them over a chair back and hit the light.

Lecia and I lay down in the vast bed with Daddy in the middle. He slept on top of the covers because he couldn't stand anything binding his feet. And from the second Lecia and I slid our legs under the sheet on either side of him, he was crying.

It's a fine trait of Texas working men that they cry. My daddy cried at parades and weddings. Watching the American flag slide up the pole before a Little League game could send tears down his leathery face. That night, I stoppered my ears against it. Still, I could make it out under the seashell noise of my own skull. Sniff and sniff and a deep-chested moan of grief rising from him. Through the window, the refinery towers burned, sending out black strands of smoke against the acid-green sky, so many threads weaving around each other. I finally unplugged my ears and the sobs rushed in with gale force. I squeezed his broad hand in both my smaller ones till I thought the finger bones would snap like twigs. I only let go when he needed to reach under his pillow for a red bandana to wipe his nose on.

Long after I thought he'd drifted off, his cracked voice rose up to ask if we'd say a prayer that Mother would come on home.

He had to say it, of course, for such a request struck us wordless. I'd never heard Daddy pray. He'd only gone to church for funerals, when he was toting somebody in a box. "Lord," Daddy started, "please bring these babies' momma back—" Then he broke down crying some more. We patted on either side of him till he quieted and Lecia threw in a big hearty amen.

I lay awake a long time listening, Daddy with his arm over my shoulder, Lecia behind him. We warped together like planed lumber. At least, that's the thought I had. We were just like the three curved boards for the hull bottom of some boat that only needed gluing and caulking together.

When Mother did come back, she arrived unannounced in a rented yellow Karmann Ghia sports car with Hector behind the wheel. She unfolded from the car's low-slung seat. Her alligator heels sank in the spongy ground, leaving holes like a crawfish makes. For weeks, I'd practiced the cool indifference I'd greet her with if she ever came back. But when I saw that beaver coat hem swirl around her calves like so much sea foam, all my resolve washed away. I slammed out the door and bounded toward her. I would have reached her first, too, had not Lecia shoved me down in the flower bed crowded with English ivy.

They'd come to pick up some clothes, Mother told Daddy. No more was said in the way of plan or explanation. If he knew she was coming before, he hadn't let on. He leaned on the far porch while she stooped down to hug me, that coat soft as any bunny and exuding Shalimar. "I miss you, baby," she said. She eyed Daddy over my shoulder the way you'd check the chain length of a tethered hound before you stepped in his yard. He didn't flinch under the gaze. He stayed rock still, but gave her wide berth. Eventually, she and Hector set about dragging dresses by armloads to the car, trailing hangers all down the yard and walk.

If the pope had advanced on us, outfitted in embroidered robes with acolytes behind wagging gold incense burners, the neighbors would have been held in less thrall. No sooner had that low yellow car halted in its tracks than every family on the block started from their various houses, prepared to stay a while, wearing wind-breakers and winter jackets and rain slickers in case the fat clouds overhead broke open. They pulled their lawn chairs out of garage storage, aimed them to face us, and sat watching like we were some drive-in movie projected across the soft gray horizon. The misty rain that speckled the air didn't stop them. Mrs. Dillard just unfolded her clear plastic rain bonnet from its tuckaway pocket and tied it right under her chin, so her hairdo wouldn't get sticky. Mrs. Sharp wielded the massive black umbrella they toted to football games.

The men who weren't working stood together under the eaves of the Carters' garage, smoking, the red coals of their cigarettes visible when drawn on. They were watching too. Don't think they weren't. The kids scampered behind their front-yard ditches like nothing special was happening, all but Carol Sharp, who crossed the street to stand right at the edge of our yard. I gave her the finger in full view of everybody. That set her loping back to tattle, her Keds slapping against the wet asphalt.

I walked back and forth along the ditch's slope till it struck me that I'd once seen a cow dog patrol its territory with the exact same level of concentration I was bringing to bear. Mother and Hector toted some more dresses out the house. They were made of silk, colors of whipped cream and beige and palest tangerine shimmering in the gauzy air. I could just imagine the neighbor ladies reckoning their worth—"Why, one a them alone's worth Pete's whole paycheck . . ." I hated them at that instant, hated their broad heavy bottoms slung low in those stripy garden chairs. I hated their church suppers, their lumpy tuna casseroles, their Jell-O molds with perfect cubes of pear and peach hanging suspended. I hated their crocheted baby booties and sofa shawls, the toilet-paper covers shaped like poodles everybody worked on one summer.

For the first time, I felt the power my family's strangeness gave us over the neighbors. Those other grown-ups were scared. Not only of my parents but of me. My wildness scared them. Plus they guessed that I'd moved through houses darker than theirs. All my life I'd wanted to belong in their families, to draw my lunch bag from the simple light and order of their defrosted refrigerators. The stories that got whispered behind our supermarket cart, or the silence that fell over the credit union when Daddy shoved open the glass door—these things always set my face burning. That afternoon, for the first time, I believed that Death itself lived in the neighboring houses. Death cheered for the Dallas Cowboys, and wrapped canned biscuit dough around Vienna sausages for the half-time snack.

I picked up one of the coat hangers that had dropped on the ground, cocked my arm, and hurled it across the street at the Carters' house. It sailed like a boomerang, that hanger, but didn't even cross the street. Daddy called out to me then. "Pokey, come on in here." He'd moved just inside the screen, his profile sharp through the fine mesh.

Hector slammed down the Kharmann Ghia's hatch. Mother kept looking back at us, at Lecia and Daddy and me, behind the screen. I could feel us pulling on her like magnets. Her face went soft. On either side of her lipsticked mouth were deep parentheses of fret. I didn't hear what Hector said to her. I was too busy in my head pulling on Mother to stay with us, using a prayer full of thee's and thou's. Lecia later told me that Hector had told Mother to get her ass in gear, or some such.

What happened next points to Hector having said at least something that bad, for Daddy fast closed the space between himself and the yellow car. He reached inside and dragged Hector out by the shoulders, though Hector tried hanging on real hard to the wheel to prevent that happening. My stepfather was standing, though, before Daddy threw the first punch. I keep a very distinct image of Hector's thin-lipped mouth drawing itself into an "o" of surprise as it dawned on him that he was fixing to be hit. Hard, and more than once if necessary.

I would like to say the film clip I've shot for myself stops there, for I have seen men fight in the parking lots of certain bars. And always after the first collision of fist with face, or the first spots of blood down a shirtfront, I turned away, thinking myself too tenderhearted to watch. On that day I watched steady, for Daddy's pounding on Hector made me truly glad.

After he'd knocked Hector down once, he pulled him up to stand again, only to knock him down again. He practically dusted off Hector's shirt and adjusted his collar before clocking him the second time. Hector went down again easy, his legs swiveling under him like rope. He lay stretched there in the grass. Then Daddy did something I'd never seen him do before, which was to keep beating a fallen man. He sat down on Hector's chest and started swinging on him steady, pounding hard in the face without reason, for Hector had long since ceased to pose a threat to anybody. I watched Daddy's back muscles get very specific through his thin blue workshirt the way a boxer's would on a heavy-bag drill. He kept it up till I heard what must have been nose cartilage crunch.

That noise seemed to stop him. His shoulders dropped. He sat there on Hector's chest winded a second. Then he stood, staring down at his own bloody hands. He turned them over like objects of great curiosity, as if they belonged to another man and had been sent to Daddy solely for repair or inspection.

At that point I became aware Mother had been screaming. Her words—stored somewhere in my head all the while—came racing back like a tape I'd rewound. "Get offa him, Pete, you're killing him, Baby. Oh God. Lecia, Mary—somebody stop him—" She shut up as soon as Daddy stood. She didn't want to rouse him any worse. He looked at her across that yellow car roof and sighed. "I'm sorry," he said, and seemed to mean it, though when he glanced down at Hector again, the fury must have rushed back through him again, for he raised his boot and stomped down on my stepfather's rib cage. I heard ribs crack with a noise like icy branches going down in wind.

Hector rolled on his side, and I feared he was curling up like a tumblebug would if you'd squashed him too hard playing. But after a while, I saw his mouth suck for air.

Still, all the pity that surged through me that day was for Daddy, for the world of ugly he'd kept inside that came pouring out on my stepfather. In fact, seeing Hector's face like a slab of veal just pounded with one of those wooden kitchen mallets pleased me no end. Lecia and I moved outside to study him better. It amazed me that he wasn't dead. His breath was light and rattly. When he rolled over to spit out gouts of blood, you could hear tooth chips hit the sidewalk.

The few times I'd seen Daddy heave up a coffin with other men, he always toted more than his share of weight, doing so with that slow-paced, sweating dignity a funeral requires. That was the bearing Daddy brought to handling my stepfather that day. He helped Mother fold him into the seat with utmost gentleness.

When he turned to climb up on the porch, his face was blank and sweaty. There was a fan-shaped pattern of blood sprayed across his chambray shirt. "Y'all get on in the house," he said, but his voice lacked any edge. He brushed past me.

I watched the Karmann Ghia head down the street—a streak of canary yellow against the gray tract houses that acted as backdrop. Then I heard the pipes groan in the kitchen when Daddy cranked on the faucet to wash up.

Mother never said that she was coming back to us that evening. Per usual, nobody said spit. But I sensed that she would come back, eventually at least. She had a soft spot for Daddy whipping up on a man who'd spoken to her in disrespect. And back then, heat still passed between my parents. You could practically warm your hands on it.

That evening she dumped Hector at the nearest emergency room, checked out of the room they'd just checked into, and headed straight back to us on Garfield Road. She'd spent or been cheated out of every cent of her inheritance. So she came back not just broke but deep in debt. And she stayed. She stayed with Daddy till his death, stayed well into her own dotage.

The neighbors were folding up their lawn chairs, closing their umbrellas to head back indoors. I shoved into my own house, into the cool dark of its wax-papered windows, feeling something like peace. Daddy's public ass-whipping of Hector proved to me that my stepfather was a bad man. Our time with him had been a bad time. That was over now, Daddy had ended it. He'd drawn a big line in our lives between that bad time and our future. He was shirtless when Mother came back, and they slow-danced into the bedroom laughing.

When the sheriff stopped by after dark, Mother went to the door naked under her black silk kimono. Daddy wasn't home just then, she told him. Anyways, there'd just been a domestic disruption—that was the phrase she'd used. She was a terrible flirt, and her eyes while she talked to the sheriff were amused. He took his Stetson off and stood there on the porch while june bugs pelleted the screen and neighbors behind their windows drew back their Priscilla curtains.

Lecia and I hung over the sofa back, still gleeful from the triumph of Hector's exile and Mother's coming back. I'd never seen her eyes so green, deep green, green as the sea past the farthest sandbar where the waves start to head out away from the beach to all the unnamed archipelagoes. Her arms were long and white coming out of the vast black sleeves of that kimono. She clutched it closed at her sternum, the black heavy silk bunching up like an orchid. The sheriff was already backing down the porch when Mother's last words on the subject were spoken. Here's what she said before the door closed on that rectangle of night, closed on the red silent siren light whirling across our window, closed like a tomb door sealed over the subject of Hector entirely, for she never mentioned him again: *silliest thing,* she said, *no big deal,* she said, then, *nothing we couldn't handle.*

Judy Ruiz

Oranges and Sweet Sister Boy

I AM SLEEPING, HARD, WHEN THE TELEPHONE RINGS. IT'S MY BROTHER, AND HE'S CALLING to say he is now my sister. I feel something fry a little, deep behind my eyes. Knowing how sometimes dreams get mixed up with not-dreams, I decide to do a reality test at once. "Let me get a cigarette," I say, knowing that if I reach for a Marlboro and it turns into a trombone or a snake or anything else on the way to my lips that I'm still out in the large world of dreams. The cigarette stays a cigarette. I light it. I ask my brother to run that stuff by me again.

It is the Texas Zephyr at midnight—the woman in a white suit, the man in a blue uniform; she carries flowers—I know they are flowers. The petals spill and spill into the aisle, and a child goes past this couple who have just come from their own wedding—goes past them and past them, going always to the toilet but really just going past them; and the child could be a horse or she could be the police and they'd not notice her any more than they do, which is not at all—the man's hands high up on the woman's legs, her skirt up, her stockings and garters, the petals and finally all the flowers spilling out into the aisle and his mouth open on her. My mother. My father. I am conceived near Dallas in the dark while a child passes, a young girl who knows and doesn't know, who witnesses, in glimpses, the creation of the universe, who feels an odd hurt as her own mother, fat and empty, snores with her mouth open, her false teeth slipping down, snores and snores just two seats behind the Creators.

News can make a person stupid. It can make you think you can do something. So I ask The Blade question, thinking that if he hasn't had the operation yet that I can fly to him, rent a cabin out on Puget Sound. That we can talk. That I can get him to touch base with reality. "Begin with an orange," I would tell him. "Because oranges are mildly intrusive by nature, put the orange somewhere so that it will not bother you—in the cupboard, in a drawer, even a pocket or a handbag will do. The orange, being a patient fruit, will wait for you much longer than say a banana or a peach."

I would hold an orange out to him. I would say, "This is the one that will save your life." And I would tell him about the woman I saw in a bus station who bit right into her orange like it was an apple. She was wild looking, as if she'd been outside for too long in a wind that blew the same way all the time. One of the dregs of humanity, our mother would have called her, the same mother who never brought fruit into the house except in cans. My children used to ask me to "start" their oranges for them. That meant to make a hole in the orange so they could peel the rind away, and their small hands weren't equipped with fingernails that were long enough or strong enough to do the job. Sometimes they would suck the juice out of the hole my thumbnail had made, leaving the orange flat and sad.

The earrings are as big as dessert plates, filigree gold-plated with thin dangles hanging down that touch her bare shoulders. She stands in front of the Alamo while a bald man takes her picture. The sun is absorbed by the earrings so quickly that by the time she feels the heat, it is too late. The hanging dangles make small blisters on her shoulders, as if a centipede had traveled there. She takes the famous river walk in spiked heels, rides in a boat, eats some Italian noodles, returns to the motel room, soaks her feet, and applies small band-aids to her toes. She is briefly concerned about the gun on the nightstand. The toilet flushes. She pretends to be sleeping. The gun is just large and heavy. A

156

.45? A .357 magnum? She's never been good with names. She hopes he doesn't try to. Or that if he does, that it's not loaded. But he'll say it's loaded just for fun. Or he'll pull the trigger and the bullet will lodge in her medulla oblongata, ripping through her womb first, taking everything else vital on the way.

In the magazine articles, you don't see this: "Well, yes. The testicles have to come out. And yes. The penis is cut off." What you get is tonsils. So-and-so has had a "sex change" operation. A sex change operation. How precious. How benign. Doctor, just what do you people do with those penises?

News can make a person a little crazy also. News like, "We regret to inform you that you have failed your sanity hearing."

❖　❖　❖

The bracelet on my wrist bears the necessary information about me, but there is one small error. The receptionist typing the information asked me my religious preference. I said, "None." She typed, "Neon."

Pearl doesn't have any teeth and her tongue looks weird. She says, "Pumpkin pie." That's all she says. Sometimes she runs her hands over my bed sheets and says pumpkin pie. Sometimes I am under the sheets. Marsha got stabbed in the chest, but she tells everyone she fell on a knife. Elizabeth—she's the one who thinks her shoe is a baby—hit me in the back with a tray right after one of the cooks gave me extra toast. There's a note on the bulletin board about a class for the nurses: "How Putting A Towel On Sometime's Face Makes Them Stop Banging Their Spoon/OR Reduction of Disruptive Mealtime Behavior By Facial Screening—7 P.M.—Conference Room." Another note announces the topic for remotivation class: "COWS." All the paranoid schizophrenics will be there.

Here, in the place for the permanently bewildered, I fit right in. Not because I stood at the window that first night and listened to the trains. Not because I imagined those trains were bracelets, the jewelry of earth. Not even because I imagined that one of those bracelets was on my own arm and was the Texas Zephyr where a young couple made love and conceived me. I am eighteen and beautiful and committed to the state hospital by a district court judge for a period of one day to life. Because I am a paranoid schizophrenic.

I will learn about cows.

So I'm being very quiet in the back of the classroom, and I'm peeling an orange. It's the smell that makes the others begin to turn around, that mildly intrusive nature. The course is called "Women and Modern Literature," and the diaries of Virginia Woolf are up for discussion except nobody has anything to say. I, of course, am making a mess with the orange; and I'm wanting to say that my brother is now my sister.

Later, with my hands still orangey, I wander in to leave something on a desk in a professor's office, and he's reading so I'm being very quiet, and then he says, sort of out of nowhere, "Emily Dickinson up there in her room making poems while her brother was making love to her best friend right downstairs on the dining room table. A regular thing. Think of it. And Walt Whitman out sniffing around the boys. Our two great American poets." And I want to grab this professor's arm and say, "Listen. My brother called me and now he's my sister, and I'm having trouble making sense out of my life right now, so would you mind not telling me any more stuff about sex." And I want my knuckles to turn white while the pressure of my fingers leaves imprints right through his jacket, little indentations he can interpret as urgent. But I don't say anything. And I don't grab his arm. I go read a magazine. I find this:

> "I've never found an explanation for why the human race has so many languages. When the brain became a language brain, it obviously needed to develop an intense degree of plasticity. Such plasticity allows languages to be logical, coherent systems and yet be extremely variable. The same brain that thinks in words and symbols is also a brain that has to be freed up with regard to sexual turn-on and partnering. God knows why sex attitudes have been subject to the corresponding degrees of modification and variety as language. I suspect there's a close parallel between the two. The brain doesn't seem incredibly efficient with regard to sex."

John Money said that. The same John Money who, with surgeon Howard W. Jones, performed the first sex change operation in the United States in 1965 at Johns Hopkins University and Hospital in Baltimore.

Money also tells us about the *hijra* of India who disgrace their families because they are too effeminate: "The ultimate stage of the *hijra* is to get up the courage to go through the amputation of penis and testicles. They had no anesthetic." Money also answers anyone who might think that "heartless members of the medical profession are forcing these poor darlings to go and get themselves cut up and mutilated," or who think the medical profession should leave them alone. "You'd have lots of patients willing to get a gun and blow off their own genitals if you don't do it. I've had several who got knives and cut themselves trying to get rid of their sex organs. That's their obsession!"

Perhaps better than all else, I understand obsession. It is of the mind. And it is language-bound. Sex is of the body. It has no words. I am stunned to learn that someone with an obsession of the mind can have parts of the body surgically removed. This is my brother I speak of. This is not some lunatic named Carl who becomes Carlene. This is my brother.

◦ ◦ ◦

So while we're out in that cabin on Puget Sound, I'll tell him about LuAnn. She is the sort of woman who orders the inseason fruit and a little cottage cheese. I am the sort of woman who orders a double cheeseburger and fries. LuAnn and I are sitting in her car. She has a huge orange, and she peels it so the peel falls off in one neat strip. I have a sack of oranges, the small ones. The peel of my orange comes off in hunks about the size of a baby's nail. "Oh, you bought the *juice* oranges," LuAnn says to me. Her emphasis on the word "juice" makes me want to die or something. I lack the courage to admit my ignorance, so I smile and breathe "yes," as if I know some secret, when I'm wanting to scream at her about how my mother didn't teach me about fruit and my own blood pounds in my head wanting out, out.

> There is a pattern to this thought as there is a pattern for a jumpsuit. Sew the sleeve to the leg, sew the leg to the collar. Put the garment on. Sew the mouth shut. This is how I tell about being quiet because I am bad, and because I cannot stand it when he beats me or my brother.

"The first time I got caught in your clothes was when I was four years old and you were over at Sarah what's-her-name's babysitting. Dad beat me so hard I thought I was going to die. I really thought I was going to die. That was the day I made up my mind I would *never* get caught again. And I never got caught again." My brother goes on to say he continued to go through my things until I was hospitalized. A mystery is solved.

He wore my clothes. He played in my makeup. I kept saying, back then, that someone was going through my stuff. I kept saying it and saying it. I told the counselor at school. "Someone goes in my room when I'm not there, and I *know* it—goes in there and wears my clothes and goes through my stuff." I was assured by the counselor that this was not so. I was assured by my mother that this was not so. I thought my mother was doing it, snooping around for clues like mothers do. It made me a little crazy, so I started deliberately leaving things in a certain order so that I would be able to prove to myself that someone, indeed, was going through my belongings. No one, not one person, ever believed that my room was being ransacked; I was accused of just making it up. A paranoid fixation.

And all the time it was old Goldilocks.

⋅๑⋅ ⋅๑⋅ ⋅๑⋅

So I tell my brother to promise me he'll see someone who counsels adult children from dysfunctional families. I tell him he needs to deal with the fact that he was physically abused on a daily basis. He tells me he doesn't remember being beaten except on three occasions. He wants me to get into a support group for families of people who are having a sex change. Support groups are people who are in the same boat. Except no one has any oars in the water.

I tell him I know how it feels to think you are in the wrong body. I tell him how I wanted my boyfriend to put a gun up inside me and blow the woman out, how I thought wearing spiked heels and low-cut dresses would somehow help my crisis, that putting on an ultra-feminine outside would mask the maleness I felt needed hiding. I tell him it's the rule, rather than the exception, that people from families like ours have very spooky sexual identity problems. He tells me that his sexuality is a birth defect. I recognize the lingo. It's support-group-for-transsexuals lingo. He tells me he sits down to pee. He told his therapist that he used to wet all over the floor. His therapist said, "You can't aim the bullets if you don't touch the gun." Lingo. My brother is hell-bent for castration, the castration that started before he had language; the castration of abuse. He will simply finish what was set in motion long ago.

⋅๑⋅ ⋅๑⋅ ⋅๑⋅

I will tell my brother about the time I took ten sacks of oranges into a school so that I could teach metaphor. The school was for special students—those who were socially or intellectually impaired. I had planned to have them peel the oranges as I spoke about how much the world is like the orange. I handed out the oranges. The students refused to peel them, not because they wanted to make life difficult for me—they were enchanted with the gift. One child asked if he could have an orange to take home to his little brother. Another said he would bring me ten dollars the next day if I would give him a sack of oranges. And I knew I was at home, that these children and I shared something that *makes* the leap of mind the metaphor attempts. And something in me healed.

⋅๑⋅ ⋅๑⋅ ⋅๑⋅

A neighbor of mine takes pantyhose and cuts them up and sews them up after stuffing them. Then she puts these things into Mason jars and sells them, you know, to put out on the mantel for conversation. They are little penises and little scrotums, complete with hair. She calls them "Pickled Peters."

A friend of mine had a sister who had a sex change operation. This young woman had her breasts removed and ran around the house with no shirt on before the stitches were taken out. She answered the door one evening. A young man had come to call on my friend. The sex-changed sister invited him in and offered him some black bean soup as if she were perfectly normal with her red surgical wounds and her black stitches. The young man left and never went back. A couple years later, my friend's sister/brother died when s/he ran a car into a concrete bridge railing. I hope for a happier ending. For my brother, for myself, for all of us.

❧ ❧ ❧

My brother calls. He's done his toenails: Shimmering Cinnamon. And he's left his wife and children and purchased some nightgowns at a yard sale. His hair is getting longer. He wears a special bra. Most of the people he works with know about the changes in his life. His voice is not the same voice I've heard for years; he sounds happy.

My brother calls. He's always envied me, my woman's body. The same body I live in and have cursed for its softness. He asks me how I feel about myself. He says, "You know, you are really our father's first-born son." He tells me he used to want to be me because I was the only person our father almost loved.

The drama of life. After I saw that woman in the bus station eat an orange as if it were an apple, I went out into the street and smoked a joint with some guy I'd met on the bus. Then I hailed a cab and went to a tattoo parlor. The tattoo artist tried to talk me into getting a nice bird or butterfly design; I had chosen a design on his wall that appealed to me— a symbol I didn't know the meaning of. It is the Yin-Yang, and it's tattooed above my right ankle bone. I suppose my drugged, crazed consciousness knew more than I knew: that yin combines with yang to produce all that comes to be. I am drawn to androgyny.

Of course there is the nagging possibility that my brother's dilemma is genetic. Our father used to dress in drag on Halloween, and he made a beautiful woman. One year, the year my mother cut my brother's blond curls off, my father taped those curls to his own head and tied a silk scarf over the tape. Even his close friends didn't know it was him. And my youngest daughter was a body builder for a while, her lean body as muscular as a man's. And my sons are beautiful, not handsome: they look androgynous.

❧ ❧ ❧

Then there's my grandson. I saw him when he was less than an hour old. He was naked and had hiccups. I watched as he had his first bath, and I heard him cry. He had not been named yet, but his little crib had a blue card affixed to it with tape. And on the card were the words "Baby Boy." There was no doubt in me that the words were true.

When my brother was born, my father was off flying jets in Korea. I went to the hospital with my grandfather to get my mother and this new brother. I remember how I wanted a sister, and I remember looking at him as my mother held him in the front seat of the car. I was certain he was a sister, certain that my mother was joking. She removed his diaper to show me that he was a boy. I still didn't believe her. Considering what has happened lately, I wonder if my child-skewed consciousness knew more than the anatomical proof suggested.

❧ ❧ ❧

I try to make peace with myself. I try to understand his decision to alter himself. I try to think of him as her. I write his woman name, and I feel like I'm betraying myself. I try to be open-minded, but something in me shuts down. I think we humans are in big trouble, that many of us don't really have a clue as to what acceptable human behavior is. Something in me says no to all this, that this surgery business is the ultimate betrayal of the self. And yet, I want my brother to be happy.

◆ ◆ ◆

I was in the city of San Antonio that my father had his surgery. I rode the bus from Kansas to Texas, and arrived at the hospital two days after the operation to find my father sitting in the solarium playing solitaire. He had a type of cancer that particularly thrived on testosterone. And so he was castrated in order to ease his pain and to stop the growth of tumors. He died six months later.

Back in the sleep of the large world of dreams, I have done surgeries under water in which I float my father's testicles back into him, and he—the brutal man he was—emerges from the pool a tan and smiling man, parting the surface of the water with his perfect head. He loves all the grief away.

◆ ◆ ◆

I will tell my brother all I know of oranges, that if you squeeze the orange peel into a flame, small fires happen because of the volatile oil in the peel. Also, if you squeeze the peel and it gets into your cat's eyes, the cat will blink and blink. I will tell him there is no perfect rhyme for the word "orange," and that if we can just make up a good word we can be immortal. We will become obsessed with finding the right word, and I will be joyous at our legitimate pursuit.

◆ ◆ ◆

I have purchased a black camisole with lace to send to my new sister. And a card. On the outside of the card there's a drawing of a woman sitting by a pond and a zebra is off to the left. Inside are these words; "The past is ended. Be happy." And I have asked my companions to hold me and I have cried. My self is wet and small. But it is not dark. Sometimes, if no one touches me, I will die.

Sister, you are the best craziness of the family. Brother, love what you love.

Spalding Gray
Sex and Death to the Age 14

I CAN REMEMBER RIDING BESIDE THE BARRINGTON RIVER ON THE BACK OF MY MOTHER'S BI-cycle and she was shouting out and celebrating because we had just dropped the bomb on the Japs in Hiroshima, and that meant that her two brothers were coming home. A lot of people died in World War II. I didn't know any.

The first death which occurred in *our* family was a cocker spaniel. Jill. Jealous Jill. We called her that because she was very jealous when my little brother was born. Jill died of distemper, which I thought meant bad temper because she was always jealous. But before she died, she bit me. Not *just* before she died, but some time before. I was harassing her with a rubber submarine, as I often did in the pantry of our house in Barrington, Rhode Island, and she turned on me and took a chunk out of my wrist; it looked like a bite out of an apple from my point of view. I guess it wasn't because I don't have a scar. I ran to my mother and she said, "You had it coming to you, dear, for harassing the dog with a rubber submarine."

When we were 14, a group of us used to try to knock ourselves out. Organically. By taking 20 deep breaths, head held between our legs, and then coming up real fast and blowing on our thumbs without letting out any air. Then all the blood would rush up or down, I don't know which, but it would rush somewhere, fast. And we would hope to pass out, but it never worked. Then we'd spin in circles until we all got so dizzy that we fell down. Then we went home.

So one day I was in the bathtub taking a very hot bath. It was a cold day and the radiator was going full blast. I got out of the tub and thought, well, this is a good time to knock myself out, I'm so dizzy, I'm halfway there. So I took 20 deep breaths and went right out, and on my way out I hit my head on the sink, which was kind of a double knockout. When I landed my arm fell against the radiator. I must have been out quite a long time because when I came to, I lifted my arm up and it was like this dripping-rare-red roast beef, third-degree burn. Actually it didn't hurt at all because I was in shock, a steam burn on my finger would have hurt more. I ran downstairs and showed it to my mother and she said, "Put some soap in it, dear, and wrap it in gauze." She was a Christian Scientist, so she had a distance on those things.

The next day when I got to school, the burn began to drip through the gauze. I went down to the infirmary, and when the nurse saw it she screamed, "What, you haven't been to a doctor with this? That's a third-degree burn. You've got to get to a doctor right away." So I went back home and told my mother what the nurse had said, and my mother said, "Well, it's your choice, dear. It's your choice."

◦ ◦ ◦

Anyway, Jill died of distemper and I can remember I was wearing a tee shirt with a little red heart on it, and after the dog died I remember seeing the heart—my heart, the dog's heart, a heart—float up against a very clear blue sky. There was no pollution then in Barrington, Rhode Island. My mother told me that I stopped talking for a long time after that. She said they were thinking of taking me to a psychiatrist, but I don't know where they were going to find a psychiatrist in Barrington, Rhode Island, in 1946. Maybe they were thinking of Providence.

◦ ◦ ◦

After Jill died, we got another dog, a beagle. We named the beagle Bugle because he made a sound like a bugle when he followed a scent. And Bugle would often get a scent in the fields behind our house where we used to play. We had a particular little grassy area we called "Hitler's hideout," inspired by World War II, where we would play Korean war games on weekends. My mother forbade them on Sundays and discouraged them on weekdays, so Saturdays were usually pretty intense.

We had toy rifles and used a galvanized metal garden bug sprayer for a flame thrower, which one of us would wear on his back. It was attached to a long hose which led to a little pump handle, and instead of DDT we would shoot water out of it. Also, Ralston Russell's father had brought back a German luger from the war, as well as a German helmet, complete with swastikas. The luger had had its firing pin removed, but it was very real. The helmet seemed even more real. You could almost smell the dead German's sweat on the leather band inside. I assumed someone had taken this helmet right off a dead soldier, but I couldn't imagine Mr. Russell doing that. He was a Christian Science practitioner during the war and I didn't think he'd seen much combat. I had always thought of him as a gray flannel mystic in his little office off their basement rec room where he went every day, dressed in a three-piece suit, to pray for sick people. They didn't even have to be there. He just sat and concentrated real hard on knowing "the truth" and sent out all his thoughts to wherever his patients were lying, waiting to get better. But maybe Mr. Russell did see action. Maybe he was in the field trying to bring dead GIs back to life. But the gun and helmet were very real. I was sure I could smell the enemy on them.

Judy Griggs was the only girl in the neighborhood and she lived next door to us. Her father was my father's boss at the screw-machine plant, and I remember that they had a very big yard with an apple orchard at the end of it. Judy played a game with us in her yard called "Ice Lady." The Griggses had a clothesline shaped like the Pentagon, and Mrs. Griggs would hang her sheets out to dry on it. Judy, who was the Ice Lady, would chase us through the rows of clean sheets until she touched one of us, and we had to freeze and stand still like a statue. Judy was queen of her backyard, but she wanted more. She wanted to be a member of our gang, which had only four of us in it, all boys. Judy tried to prove to us that she was a boy by putting a garden hose between her legs while her sister, Bethany, turned on the water. Once she used a turkey baster, but that still wasn't enough to convince us. We forced her to go into the fields with us and pull down her pants to show us that she really was a boy. Instead of a tinkler we saw her, well, I don't think we had a name for it actually, but I remember it as this very small, fleshy slit where her tinkler might have been if she had one. Then we took her into our chicken coop and tortured her mildly by tying her to a post and stirring up all the dust from the dirt floor with a broom. We'd leave her there until the dust settled, and she seemed to like it. At least she gave every sign of liking it.

The Griggses had hired an Italian yard man named Tony Pazzulo. Tony was lots of fun—he used to pick us up and swing us around and bury us under piles of raked leaves. The most fun was being thrown around by him. Our fathers, Dad and Mr. Griggs, never touched us in that rough, playful way, and we all loved it. One day Tony took the cover off the cesspool for some reason and we all looked down into it. It was a great dark pool of "grunts" and "doots" (we called the big ones "grunts" and the small ones "doots"), and suddenly the Griggses' yard took on a new dimension, even after Tony put the cesspool cover back on.

Shortly after Tony uncovered the cesspool, Mr. Griggs bought a whole bunch of chickens. One Saturday he cut off all their heads while we watched. He used the stump of a big tree for a chopping block and held the chickens' heads down on it while he cut them off with an ax. Then the chickens ran headless around the yard with blood spurting from their necks until they flopped down on the ground and died.

Soon after Judy Griggs pulled her pants down, houses began to grow in the back fields. We played in the foundations and among the electrical wires and saw wallboards go on and the houses get finished and the new neighbors move in. I can remember once being up on some scaffolding and seeing some boards lying against a house, and I just decided to push them down on my friend Tim Morton. I didn't think about it. I just pushed and they fell and crushed him. I thought I had killed him, not only because of the way he was lying down there, but also because of the way his father ran, jumping over the hedge, to pick up Tim's limp body in his arms. I was terrified. I ducked back in through the window of the unfinished house to hide, and my older brother, Rocky, who stayed out on the scaffolding, had to take the blame. Tony Morton just stood there with his son's broken body in his arms, yelling up at Rocky, "I'll be back to deal with you, my friend." I felt scared for Rocky. I felt scared for all of us.

Not long after that, Tim died of lung cancer. He was very young and no one seemed able to diagnose it. They thought it was what they called a lung fungus that had been brought back by American soldiers from the Korean War. Tim's death was a strange kind of relief because we'd always heard that one in four would have to die of something—cancer, tuberculosis, polio, whatever—so I always wondered who would be the *one* of the four of us who hung out together. That was often on my mind.

⋄   ⋄   ⋄

We lost Bugle the beagle in the back fields during hunting season. My mother told me not to worry about it, this was something that happened. Hunters often stole dogs during the hunting season, so probably some nice, loving hunter had given Bugle a good warm home.

Shortly after Bugle disappeared we got a cocker spaniel that chased cars. I don't remember its name, but I do remember it chased cars and Harvey Flynt said we could cure this if we filled a squirt gun with vinegar and shot the spaniel in the eye with it every time it chased our car. But before we could try this, the dog was run over by a truck bringing cement to one of the new houses in the back fields.

Then we got another dog which we called Roughy because it was so rough with us. Soon after we got it, Dad said, "I'm sorry boys, but we're going to have to give Roughy away because he's too rough." By then my brother Rocky had become very attached to Roughy and didn't want to see him go. He wanted to save some memory of the dog, so he took one of Roughy's fresh "doots" and put it in a jelly jar with a tight cap and kept it by his bed next to the little radio that had a Bob Hope decal on it and a white plastic dial that looked like a poached egg when it was lit.

Some time after that my mother took us out into the yard. It was summer and we sat in the shade of a big elm while she read to us from a book about the reproduction of cows.

⋄   ⋄   ⋄

We gave up at last on dogs and switched to cats. Our first cat's name was Kitzel. All I remember about Kitzel was that she was a calico who lived a long time and liked to eat corn-on-the-cob. After Kitzel grew up, I wanted a kitten, so I got a kitten from the Griggses that I called Mittens. I named her Mittens because she had little white markings on her front paws. And I had this relationship with Mittens: I would make a sound, kind of a half-blow, half-whistle (we called it a *wumple*), and Mittens would come running. Then one weekend she didn't come and I looked everywhere for her. The only place I did not look was the cellar of our barn. My brother Rocky told me that he had seen footprints of the Blain brothers down there. The Blain brothers were ten-foot-tall hairy men who roamed the Rhode Island countryside and were known to jump over eight-foot-high hurricane fences with a deer under each arm, or a child, because they were running out of deer in Rhode Island. Rocky told me the brothers had last been seen at the Boy Scout camp, Camp Yiago, not too far from where we lived.

At the end of the weekend, my mother said that she had seen the trash truck pick up Mittens's little body on Friday by the side of Rumstick Road, and she hadn't had the heart to tell me. Mom cheered me up by telling me that I could get another kitten.

And I did. I got another kitten and I named it Mittens, Mittens the Second. That Mittens was killed on Rumstick Road by Mrs. Jessup driving a large black Chrysler at dusk. I saw it happen and began to run away, and Mrs. Jessup ran after me to try to apologize and comfort me, but I ran ahead of her because I didn't want to see her. I ran into my house and up to my bedroom. I couldn't catch my breath and felt like I was suffocating.

This reminded me of the time when I woke up in the middle of the night and saw my brother Rocky standing on his bed, blue in the face and gasping for air, crying out that he was dying. My mother and father were standing beside the bed trying to quiet him, and Mom said, "Calm down, dear, it's all in your mind." And after he calmed down, my father went back to bed, and my mother turned out the light and sat on the edge of Rocky's bed in the dark. The only illumination in the room was a cluster of fluorescent decals on the ceiling, of the Big Dipper, the Little Dipper, Saturn, and the Moon. We were all there very quiet, in the dark, and then Rocky would start in, "Mom, when I die, is it forever?" and Mom said, "Yes." And then Rocky said, "Mom, when I die is it forever and ever?" And she said, "Yes, dear." And then he said, "Mom, when I die is it forever and ever and ever?" And she said, "Uh-huh, dear." And he said, "Mom, when I die is it forever and ever and ever and ever. . . ." I just went right off to this.

⋅❂⋅ ⋅❂⋅ ⋅❂⋅

Rocky used to take me into the bottom of his bed—he called it Noss Hall, a foreign land under the blankets—and tell me that he loved me over and over again. I can remember the smell of his feet and how his sweat made a yellow ring around his collar—*yellow sweat.* Shortly after that, he left me for my Gram Gray, who lived with us. On Sundays I was allowed to go into their room and get into bed with my gramma, just to listen to Jack Benny and "Allen's Alley." I can remember the smell of my gramma—the smell of her flesh and the way it hung so soft and old—and the feel of her silk nightgown. I can remember that better than any contact with my mother.

My mother and I had two physical rituals that I clearly recall. One was the cleaning of my tinkler. We called it a tinkler then. Since I'm not circumcised, she would clean it every Saturday with cotton and baby oil and she would turn me quite firmly over her knee and go at it like a cleaning woman with a Chore Girl. She would do it very hard and it would hurt and I'd squirm in her arms.

The other ritual was "making a path"—she'd sit at the edge of my bed and I'd stick out my arm and she'd make a path with her finger up the inside of my arm. She'd do this until I was almost hypnotized and went right out. Sometimes, my friend Ralston Russell would stay overnight, and my mother would sit in between our twin beds and we'd both stick out our arms and she'd make double paths.

⋅❂⋅ ⋅❂⋅ ⋅❂⋅

After Mittens the Second died I got a third kitten that I named Mittens, which I think might have been a mistake. I found this Mittens's body one cold February day during double sessions. In the seventh grade we had double sessions because there weren't enough teachers to go around, so I went to school in the afternoons and got the mornings off to play. I'd go out and play and leave my math homework for my gramma to do, and then I'd come in and copy it over. I never learned how to add as a result. Gram smoked Viceroys and blew the smoke in my face. It went in blue and came out gray, and I liked the smell.

I would play outside with Patrick Scully and Scott Tarbox. Patrick Scully's father had a very good collection of pornographic pictures. He was in real estate and often had reason to go to Tijuana on business, and he would send back these picture postcards of matadors and bulls to his wife saying, "Hi, having a lovely time at the bullfights in Tijuana." And we thought, bullfights, yeah I bet. His entire bureau drawer was overflowing with these pornographic pictures, which he made no attempt to hide. Patrick and I would take out our favorite pictures, roll them up, put them in a jar, and bury them in Patrick's backyard. Then when we wanted to look at them again we'd just go dig them up. They were old and kind of yellowed, like tintypes. I used to imagine that the naked people in the pictures were very old or dead by the time I was looking at them, and somehow that added some spice to it.

Our favorite picture was an odd one, and that's why it was our favorite, I'm sure. We couldn't figure out what was going on in it. It was a picture of a man standing naked with this huge semi-erection (anything was huge to us, at 11 years old), and this semierection was just sort of lobbing down into a glass of water, which made it look even bigger because the glass magnified it. Then there was this naked woman kneeling in front of the glass, who was either about to drink out of it or had just finished drinking, I don't know which, but we found this photo fascinating because we couldn't imagine our parents doing this to have us. (Was that what sex was all about?) So we'd just look at it and then roll it up again, put it back in the jar, and bury it.

We didn't talk about this because we didn't have much of a vocabulary then. A penis was a tinkler, a dick, or a boner if it was hard, and my mother's breasts we called pontoons. That was about it, at 11 years old. Then one day Mrs. Tarbox caught us changing into our bathing suits to go for a swim. We were all naked, Patrick, Scott, and me, and we clutched our suits over our tinklers and Mrs. Tarbox said, "What, are you modest?" And we didn't know what *that* meant and we weren't the kind to go look it up. But all of us were stamp collectors, and we each had something called "The Modern Stamp Album." So we equated the word *modest* with *modern*. It became the key sexy phrase—kind of a catchall—that we used whenever we wanted to talk about something dirty. We'd giggle and ask, "Is that a Modern Stamp Album picture?" "Is that a Modern Stamp Album house?" "Is that a Modern Stamp Album movie?" Then we'd burst into hysterics and laugh until we fell down.

◦ ◦ ◦

So it was during double sessions that I found Mittens the Third frozen in the backyard, just frozen solid like a package of green beans. My mother said the cat must have gotten into some rat poison. She had an explanation for every death. It was never mysterious.

I never knew what happened to the bodies. Someone took care of them. I don't remember any funerals; in the Christian Science Church there are no funerals at all. But, come to think of it, we did have a little graveyard with popsicle-stick crosses out behind the outhouse. That was the graveyard where we buried the little wild animals like mice and sparrows. Once I found a mouse near our back steps and it was *alive* with maggots, so many maggots that its whole body was moving as though it were alive. We didn't bury that one. It was gone in three days.

As for domestic animals, most of them were buried out by the currant bushes in the apple orchard behind the house.

◦ ◦ ◦

Shortly after we made the popsicle-stick graveyard, the polio epidemic came to town. I was terrified of ending up in an iron lung. We'd see pictures of them on TV. Paul Winchell and

Jerry Mahoney were always trying to raise money for the March of Dimes, and we'd see them standing by an iron lung with huge rearview mirrors, and I'd think, God, how hideous. It would be like being buried alive.

Mrs. Brinch, our fifth-grade science teacher, didn't help. She was obsessed with polio. At the end of the year she showed us pictures of polio victims she was taking care of and said, "Now get plenty of rest this summer, drink a lot of water, be careful where you swim, don't go into any crowded movie theaters and remember, you can contact polio at any time."

⋅∘⋅ ⋅∘⋅ ⋅∘⋅

In the Christian Science Church you had to go to Sunday School until you were 20. There were a number of Sunday School teachers but the one I remember best is Chad Oswald. He always had a number of wonderful healings to tell about.

Each week we were asked to bring in a healing story of our own. This meant that each week something bad had to happen to us so we could be healed. For instance, I would say, "I came down our back steps, tripped and fell and hit my head on the cement, and I knew the Truth and I was healed." Then Ralston Russell, who was also in that class, would say, "Oh, *that* cement, that's cheap cement. It's not hard—it's like rubber." And I knew that was a class thing because the Russells had more money and could afford a firmer cement.

When I stayed over at Ralston's, we talked to each other in the dark from the twin beds. We pulled down our pajama bottoms and talked about how it felt to be naked against the cotton sheets. One time, Mrs. Russell, who was listening at the door, burst in and said, "You both pull up your pants right now!"

Once I had this little piece of flesh growing off my nose. It was like a little stalactite, and it wouldn't go away. It was very embarrassing because it looked like a piece of snot and all my friends kept telling me to wipe my nose. My mother asked the Christian Science practitioner to pray for the stalactite to drop off. I got impatient and wanted to have a doctor burn it off, but Mom said, "Please give it one more day, dear," so I agreed. On that last day I was being tutored in math (since my gramma had done all my math homework for me, I couldn't add without doing it on my fingers), my tutor said, "It looks like you need to wipe your nose. Let me get you some Kleenex." And I thought, oh, no, here we go again. So I pretended to be wiping my nose and the little stalactite just dropped right off.

Being Christian Scientists we had to work very hard in order to keep a hot line to God. If we let this hot line down, there was a chance that the polio germs might get in, so I was working overtime. When we got tired of working we could call the practitioner who would take over and pray for us while we rested up. We thought the polio germs were everywhere. Once Chan, my little brother, came home from kindergarten with his rest blanket, and on it were some little red threads. He said, "Look, these are polio germs; they're so big you can see them," and I believed him. Ralston Russell told me that he knew someone who stuck out his tongue and got polio instantly—the tongue just stayed out there, paralyzed. So I was getting fearful. I was washing my hands with rubbing alcohol and staying out of crowded movie theaters in August and swimming with my head very high above water. And I made it through the polio epidemic.

⋅∘⋅ ⋅∘⋅ ⋅∘⋅

After I found the third Mittens dead, I sort of gave up on cats and started to get involved with birds. Eddie Potter and I both bought ducks for Easter. He named his Carl Duck, after our seventh-grade teacher Carl Caputo. I don't remember what I named mine. Eddie and I were close friends. Eddie was the kind of guy who would laugh at anything. He would buy an orange popsicle, eat half of it, and then instead of offering it to me or another friend, he'd throw the other half in the sand and stamp on it and laugh. Another thing he laughed at was cars that got stuck in the sand, particularly those old double-ended Studebakers. He would stand there, screaming with laughter, pointing at the back tires spinning in the sand.

Eddie and I used to play strip poker together; I would usually win, so Eddie would end up naked. The rule was that the loser would have to go through some mild ordeal, some little punishment, nothing very big. One of my punishments was to make Eddie crawl down between his twin beds. Most of Barrington, Rhode Island, was made up of twin beds. I don't think I was a double bed until I got to Boston. My parents had twin beds that were very close together. When I was feeling anxious and no one was home I would go into my mother's walk-in closet, look at all her dresses, look at the line of shoes, and look at myself in her full-length mirror on the door. I liked that very much. Then, dressed only in my underwear, I would crawl between my parents' beds and hang there, just hang there until I felt all right.

My mother's parents, who lived down the street, had twin beds also, but theirs were wider apart because they had a larger bedroom. They fell in love at Hope High School and got married right after graduation. They had a good marriage and three children. My gramma's two sisters were not so lucky in love. There was Aunt Tud, who was jilted early on by a coffee plantation owner and never got involved with men after that. She became very plump. She'd always cook the meal bread and mince pies at Christmas and Thanksgiving. And then there was my Aunt Belle, who married Bob Budlong. They never had any children, but Bob made up for that because he was kind of like a half-child, half-man who ran a little grocery store in Scituate, Rhode Island. He could never stand collecting money from his customers, the poor people of Scituate, so he finally gave the whole store away and they ended up living in a trailer. It was very cold in that trailer, so when my grandparents went down to Florida for the winter, they'd invite Bob and Belle to stay in their home. This house was immaculate, like a joyful funeral parlor, with wall-to-wall carpeting.

At Christmas and Thanksgiving, Bob would blow up great long balloons that he brought from his store. He'd let them loose in my gramma's house and we'd all laugh as they sputtered around the room spraying juice over my grampa's bald head until at last they withered and dove into the after-dinner mints. Then Bob would fall asleep with his hands clasped over his belly and his stubby cigar stuck between his lips.

Bob would often take me for driving lessons. We'd drive all around Barrington waving at friends. I could barely see over the wheel or reach the clutch, never mind the brakes, and I loved it. After my driving lesson we'd come back to the house to watch "Queen for a Day." I don't know where Aunt Belle was all this time, maybe upstairs reading *Science and Health*. "Queen for a Day" was Uncle Bob's favorite TV show. We'd watch it together and he would weep and clap to try to make the applause meter go up for his favorite contestant. Then, exhausted from all his clapping, he would fall asleep, leaving his cigar balanced on my gramma's coffee table, flaking ashes on her rug. Next "The Mickey Mouse Club" would come on, and I'd stay very awake because I had a crush on Annette Funicello at the time. Sometime during the final song, Bob would wake up and say, "When is 'Queen for a Day' going to be on?" And I'd say, "Uh, Bob. We just saw 'Queen for a Day.'" And he'd say, "Well, tell me all about it, tell me who won." Then we'd go down to the Barrington shopping center, and he'd stick little hard candies down the backs of children. But I don't remember whether Bob and Belle had twin beds or a double bed in their trailer.

⊷ ⊷ ⊷

So Eddie's little punishment for losing at strip poker was to slip down between the twin beds and crawl naked over the little dust-balls, fuzzies we called them. Then he'd come up the other side of the bed smiling, covered with fuzzies and looking for more. I couldn't think of any more punishments, it wasn't my specialty, so he'd begin making up his own. I would be the witness. He'd take a little cocktail dish, the kind you'd use for pigs-in-the-blanket or smoked clams, and he would put his dick on it—still connected of course. Then he'd go downstairs and display it to Rita Darezzo, the cleaning woman, as though it were a rare hors d'oeuvre, calling, "Rita, it's cocktail time!"

⊷ ⊷ ⊷

Anyway, the ducks were growing up; they were reaching puberty and my duck's quack was getting deeper. Winter was coming, and I was keeping the duck in the playroom so that it wouldn't mess up the house and would go on the linoleum. I put a little game board, a Karom board, in the doorway of the playroom to keep it in there. One Sunday I went up to get ready for Sunday School. I had to wear this woolen suit, which I hated, and to keep it from itching I'd put on my pajamas first. I was very thick. When I came downstairs, the board had fallen down and the duck was gone. I searched the house, but I couldn't find it anywhere. Then I walked over and lifted up the board and there it was, flat, like pressed duck, like Daffy Duck after the steamroller has run over him. It didn't look real. It didn't look like any duck I'd known. I couldn't figure out how a board that thin could have done something like that. I thought my father must have stepped on it, by accident. I thought he must have come into the playroom and stepped on the board, but I didn't want to think that. I don't know who took care of the little body, but I went off to Sunday School.

After the duck, I continued with the birds and got a parakeet that I called Budgy. This parakeet was one of the blue ones—there were two kinds, blue and green—and it cost $7.50. I had a wonderful relationship with Budgy for about a year. I would whistle from my room and he would whistle back from downstairs. Then I would run down, feed him, change his water and clean the bottom of his cage. About a year went by and one day I whistled and whistled and . . . you know the rest. I went downstairs and there he was, on his back of the bottom of the cage with his little claws curled up. I thought he must have died of a heart attack or pneumonia because I was told these little tropical birds were not used to the New England climate.

⊷ ⊷ ⊷

After a short break with no pets, or maybe just a random turtle or two in between, a next-door neighbor offered me an empty 50-gallon fish tank. I thought, why not, they're 90 percent water and I won't give them names. I bought every kind of tropical fish. I had the black mollies, the zebra fish, the neons, the swordtails, the guppies, the catfish, the angel fish and the Siamese fighters, who bit the tails off the angel fish. And they died. They died often. The proliferation of death made me more indifferent to it, I think. I would take the little white net and scoop them up and ride them down on my bike to one of the lots in the neighborhood that hadn't been developed yet. I'd give them an outdoor burial by flicking them out of the net and into the grass.

About a mile down the road from that vacant lot lived the Lillows, who had the first television in the neighborhood, and we would go there to watch "Howdy Doody." One day a group of us were coming out of the house and we looked up and saw Stokes Lillow hanging from a pine tree, showing us his asshole. We were standing there looking up and he was just hanging there like a little koala bear, spreading his cheeks. I had never seen anything like that before. I don't think I had even seen my own.

❧   ❧   ❧

Shortly after Stokes Lillow showed us his asshole, that vacant lot was developed and a German family with a strange name moved in—the Lindbergers. Now this seemed odd to us, like they were from some other side of some other tracks. We hadn't seen any Germans, we hadn't seen any blacks, we hadn't seen any Jews, we hadn't seen anything but Rhode Island WASPs. So in came the Lindbergers, and they were a strange family. First of all, there were more than three children in the family, that was the first odd thing. The second odd thing was that Mr. Lindberger was having an affair with his secretary. Mrs. Lindberger told my mother this, and my mother told me. (My mother and I were very close—actually we dated all the way through college—and so she'd tell me these intimate things.) I didn't know anything about affairs. I thought they only happened in New Hampshire because my grandmother had lent me her copy of *Peyton Place*. It was the first real novel I ever read, and it got me started. After that I went on to Jack Kerouac and Thomas Wolfe. My mother said to me, "Mr. Lindberger is having an affair with his secretary because every time Mr. Lindberger touches Mrs. Lindberger she gets an electric shock." So they were having these electric shock treatments, but they weren't having any kind of love life. But he was a good provider. He would always come home late at night in his Lincoln Continental, a big black Lincoln Continental with the spare tire built into the trunk. He took very good care of his children—he had five of them—and he was a good father. He'd see his secretary at night and come home late.

I made friends with Larry Lindberger, who was a couple of years older and had a parakeet. But he had a completely different relationship with his parakeet than I did. He would let it out of the cage, let it fly around the dining room, then take a wet towel, twist it up and snap the bird right out of the air. And the bird would go like a feather bullet, ricochet off the window, and then flutter around with its tail dragging like an overloaded B-49 trying to take off. He'd snap it maybe one more time and then he'd put it back in its cage so it could rest up for the next day. When I saw this, I knew Larry and I had a different aesthetic. But I didn't stop him from hitting the bird, I just watched and took it in.

❧   ❧   ❧

So the fish died out and the tank got emptied and I gave up on animals and started to get interested in people. I had been putting this off as long as possible. But before I got involved with people I went on what you might call a shooting spree. I got a pellet pistol, went outside and started shooting everything in sight. All the songbirds on telephone wires, frogs, and one squirrel, which we ate—it tasted like a rat. The frog legs we ate too. They were very skinny, not what like you'd get in a French restaurant, but tasty.

I wanted to buy a shotgun so I could go duck hunting, but my father said no. And I knew by then that when my father said no it meant yes, so I kept at him. At last I got a single-barrel Winchester 20 gauge and began to hunt for black ducks. I wasn't a very good shot and would often only wound them and have to finish them off with my switchblade. I'd hold them down and slit their throats. It was awful.

Then one day when I was out on my paper route down near Potter's Cove I heard mallard ducks quacking and got very excited because I'd never shot a mallard before. So I got up real early the next morning and went down to Potter's Cove. Just when I got there a huge flock of mallards took off in this spectacular V-formation, and I just stood there and watched. I don't know why I didn't pull the trigger. I wanted to think it was against the law to shoot ducks before dawn.

Shortly after that I sold my gun to my father and he put it away in a closet.

⋄ ⋄ ⋄

Then I started going to dancing school on Friday nights. That meant Friday-night baths, after which I put on my pajamas and my blue wool suit over them, and my white gloves— then I went downstairs to wait for the car pool to pick me up. While I was waiting I would look for sexy pictures in any magazine I could find. We didn't have any *National Geographics*. The only sexy pictures in our house besides the underwear ads in the Sears Roebuck catalog were to be found in *Life* magazine, which arrived every Friday, just in time.

I found two erotic pictures in *Life* magazine that I kept going back to. One was of Prince Charles jumping over hurdles as a young boy, which I kept under the bed and used to look at every time I was anxious. The other was of the collapse of Rome, with everyone crawling around in the streets half naked. Maybe they had the plague. I thought, this is really sexy: Anything goes now because there are no more rules. Everyone can just do what they want sexually.

I'd be looking at this picture when the car pool would come and take me away to dancing school and I'd have to snap into the box step. I would dance with Sue Wheelock, my partner, and they would play "Sweet Sue" on the piano. I had a recording of "Sweet Sue" on a Paul Whiteman record. It was one of those painted records with a picture of the whole Paul Whiteman band that spun into a blur of color when I turned the record player on. I loved that song; it went, "Every star above, reminds me of the one I love, Sweet Sue, it's you" in one of those high, 1920s crooner voices. And I would say to Sue Wheelock, "Isn't it a coincidence that they're playing 'Sweet Sue'?" as though it implied that we were meant for each other. That chance and destiny had smiled down from above. But she thought I was just trying to put the make on her at an early age, so that didn't get me very far.

I had a relationship on another dancefloor with Sally Funk. We were in every jitterbug contest in the canteen in seventh grade. We were real good jitterbuggers, but it never went beyond the dancefloor. Then I fell in love with Julie Brooks, and Julie Brooks I can only describe as an angel—very full lips, olive skin, long brown hair. Julie and I and a bunch of us who were hanging out together would have kissing contests. We would all get together and see how long two people could hold a kiss. Someone would time it while the rest of us stood around watching, smoking Lucky Strike Regulars. Julie and I used to kiss for about 20 minutes, just holding our lips pressed tight with no movement at all. I was very uncomfortable because it was hard to breathe. The other thing we'd do is have make-out sessions in Julie's house when her mother wasn't there, playing "Sha-Boom, Sha-Boom" on her little automatic 45-record player. Then we got into dry humping in the field behind Julie's house in September in the sun. I always liked it in the sun. Six of us would go out there, three boys and three girls, and we'd make different spots in the grass and make out. Julie was always wearing those madras Bermuda shorts that were so popular in the late fifties, and I would get my hand up on her right thigh, and that was enough. I'd never go any further, in my mind the rest was a jungle. Once I did touch the jungle, briefly, and I told my friend Ryan Ryder about it. He said, "What, you touched the place she pees out of?" That brought me down and fast. I think he was jealous, but I didn't know about jealousy then. I didn't know about jealousy until two weeks later. So I went back to keeping my hand on her thigh, dry humping until I would come. I would come in my jeans and then we'd go have vanilla Cokes. I was happy and I thought she was happy, too; things were going fine until one of the girls, Linda Chipperfield, asked her mother if she could get pregnant through her clothes, and we never saw Linda again. I think her mother kept her in forever. So that broke up our club.

❧   ❧   ❧

Around that time I told Julie that I was going to fuck her; we had just gotten up the courage to say "fuck" in public. It was probably more exciting than the actual act, although none of us in the neighborhood had even done it yet. Ryan always warned us to be careful about saying it on the streets. He said that we could be brought up on a morals charge and we'd get our driver's licenses revoked. But none of us had our driver's licenses yet.

Telling Julie I was going to fuck her was kind of like a threat and a promise, a threat to me and a promise to her. I thought it was time. I gave her two weeks, I don't know why it was two, but it was going to be the second Saturday in October. I didn't know how I was going to do it.

The Saturday before the Saturday that I was going after Julie my father said that we should go play golf. This was odd to me, we had never played golf before. Later I found out from my gramma that my father's father, Grampa Gray, told him the facts of life out on a golf course. But we didn't even belong to a country club. In Barrington, Rhode Island, there were two classes of people, those who belonged to the Rhode Island Country Club and those who didn't. We didn't. So my father and I had to play golf at the Wampanaug public course, just over the border in Seekonk, Massachusetts. It was a little nine-hole course that we called Swampanaug because when it rained it was mostly under water. When we got to about the fourth hole, my father said, "You know, there was a gal at our plant . . ." he meant his factory—he worked at a very conservative factory that made screw machines and they didn't even allow Coca-Cola until the old boss retired) " . . . there was this gal at our office who had a turkey in the oven, and she wouldn't admit it because she wasn't married. Everyone knew she had a turkey in the oven, it was as plain as the nose on her face. Everyone was looking at it. It was disgusting. She stayed around until she had this turkey, and then she left."

After a long silence, he said, "You know, there are diseases that make you blind." Now I knew that sex and blindness somehow went together because Ray Strite told me that if you got sperm in your eyes, you could go temporarily blind and that men on Devil's Island would rub sperm in their eyes in the morning to get out of a particularly difficult work shift. So I did have that equation in my head.

Then I began to get paranoid. I suspected that there might be a plot afoot, that Mrs. Brooks had called my father and said, "You know, your son is going to fuck my daughter and you better take him out on a golf course and tell him he's going to go blind if he does that." Also Reverend Quigley's wife had seen Julie and me wrestling in the backyard and had come out and slapped a part of Julie's anatomy and said that people our age do not wrestle, boys and girls do not wrestle together, this was a rule in our neighborhood. I thought that maybe Mrs. Quigley had told Mrs. Brooks. I saw that my father was as nervous as I was, or more so, so I tried to relieve him by saying, "I won't do it, I won't do whatever it is that you're talking about. I won't do it."

That Saturday I went to see Julie. And I found out that Julie had played Spin the Bottle with Billy Patterson the night before, and that they had ended up exchanging shirts. That meant that he had seen Julie in her bra and she had seen his skinny bare chest. So that was it with Julie. That was pretty much it until I was 25, it was a heavy rejection. I went off with Ryan, the one who told me not to touch the place she pees out of, to see *Heaven Knows, Mr. Allison* in Providence.

Some weeks later I tried to get Julie back. I began to force myself on her. I would hold her down and try to kiss her, and she would push me away. And no one was around to tell me that this was not the way to win someone back. No one was giving me any information. They were telling me about turkeys and going blind, but they were not telling me how to get Julie Brooks back, which was the advice I was looking for.

❧ ❧ ❧

Shortly after that masturbation took hand. I'm not saying that it was Julie's fault—actually I had discovered it while I was going out with her. Thurston Beckingham had told me that if you took a piece of animal fur and rubbed your dick real fast it would feel good. That's all, just rub it and it would feel good. I didn't have any animal fur around the house and I wasn't the type of kid to go out and buy some just to do that. But there were a lot of Davy Crockett hats in the neighborhood. Then one night I just began doing it with my right hand (we called it Madam Palm and her five lovely daughters), just instinctively, like a monkey. I didn't expect anything to come of it, but after about half an hour I had an ejaculation. That was a surprise, no one had told me that I could do it on my own. I think I kept at it just because it felt good. Then it became a kind of . . . I wouldn't call it a habit exactly, but it was something that I practiced often at night. I would read *Sexology* magazine to try to find out if I was going to grow hair on my palms or go crazy.

Eventually, the masturbation became more elaborate, the way those things do. There was a big mansion across the street from our house that the president of Blackstone Valley Gas and Electric owned, and I would run around in his backyard, naked under a full moon, swinging from pine trees like a monkey, over marble statues of women in the nude. That was one of the excitements. The other was mirrors.

I began to like to masturbate in front of mirrors. The mirror was very important because, being a Christian Scientist, I kind of lost track of my body; for many years it was denied me. So it became important for me to look at what was there, to get a good sense of it. Also, my father had a deck of playing cards with naked women on them, airbrush jobs, like the photo of Marilyn Monroe naked on that red velvet spread. When my parents weren't home I would go into their room and take these cards out of his bureau drawer and look at them. Just look at them. This would get me excited and then I would cross the room to my mother's full-length mirror. On the way I would have to pass her bureau, on top of which were pictures of all my relatives: my grampa in his business suit, my aunt in her wedding dress, and my two uncles in their navy uniforms. They all had incredibly serious looks and their eyes seemed to follow me as I passed. I was young enough to maintain an erection past that, get to the mirror, and masturbate in front of it, catching glimpses over my shoulder of my uncles, my grampa, and my aunt.

There were no real private places to masturbate in the neighborhood, and no one had locks on their bedroom doors. Friends would sometimes report getting caught by their mothers, which I could not imagine. There was a bathhouse at the yacht club with private stalls, but my father would always rush me, calling out, "Hurry up! What's taking you so long to change?" There was a hole in the wall where you could look through to the girls' side, which I did only once and no one was there. Then we'd have group masturbation, in Gill Leach's attic. It wasn't exactly a circle jerk, it was just to see who would come first. I don't think we kept score.

⊸ ⊸ ⊸

But once again something happened to make me paranoid. My parents decided to send me away to a religious camp for the summer, Camp Genesis on Cape Cod. I don't know why. The camp had nothing to do with Christian Science, it was more of a Holy-Roller-type fire-and-brimstone camp. It was coeducational. The boys and girls were divided by a cold, cold lake: the boys on the north shore, the girls on the south. It was there at Camp Genesis that I fell in love with Timmy Cox. Timmy was as pretty as Julie Brooks, only he was a boy, which was very confusing. I decided to keep a safe distance. I just looked at Timmy, endlessly. Then one day he hit me in the head with his shoe. He must have sensed something, he just threw the shoe across the tent and hit me, knocked me out. They took me to the infirmary, and I guess they gave me some sort of sleeping pill to make me relax. I started to go out, but never having had sleeping pills before I thought the and sat down. Then Spike turned to me and said, "Hey, you see that guy who just went into the living room? I saw him here last night, he had his schlong out on the table and it was *huge*. It was like a piece of Polish sausage." And I said, "Oh, really?"

So we all went into the living room to wait to get our tubes cleaned in the tube-cleaning room, or whatever it was, the guest bedroom. And Dirty Dick kept coming out to take us in one at a time. At that point I'd given up on the idea of having my tubes cleaned, in fact, I didn't even feel like I had any tubes to be cleaned. I just sat there looking across at the Sunday School teacher, when suddenly a fight broke out. Spike Claxton hit Tony De Luca. Over went a chair. Over went a lamp. And the Sunday School teacher raced for the front door and we ran for the back. Spike and I jumped into his car, spun rubber, spun clamshells, got out of there, got home. I didn't tell anyone about it. I decided to keep it a secret.

The next day Spike called up and said, "Hey, Dirty Dick called me this morning and told me never to bring that Gray boy over again. What's the problem? What did you say to him? What's up?" I just said, "I don't know, Spike, I don't know." Then a week later my mother said to me, "Oh, I saw Chad Oswald at a concert with his mother. He'd make some gal a real good husband. Why do you think he doesn't get married?" And I just said, "I don't know, Mom, I don't know."

⊸ ⊸ ⊸

At the time I was getting straight E's in school. E was for failure, and they wrote it in red. So I was failing everything. I really wanted to transfer into the automobile mechanics course, but they only let Italians take that. I ended up in the business course, but I didn't do very well there either, since my gramma had always done all my math homework. So instead of adding and subtracting I began to systematically destroy the school.

I would get rotten eggs from in back of the supermarket. I'd bring them to school with me in the morning, and when the halls were crowded, I'd lob them into the Latin teacher's room. Other times I'd break off the lead from a pencil in the lock of Mrs. Brumage's door so we wouldn't have to go into her all-boys English class to stand and recite Portia's speech, "The quality of mercy is not strained. . . ."

At last I began building bombs. I'd take a birthday candle and stick it in a wad of clay, lay a big cherry bomb firecracker at the bottom of the candle, and put it behind a toilet in the boys' room. It's not as though I never thought someone might sit on that toilet—I did think about it, I did think that would be bad. Then I'd light the candle and head for English class from where, exactly 15 minutes later, I'd hear this enormous explosion and all the teachers would run out to try to catch the mad bomber. They'd round up all the boys, whose ears were still ringing from the blast, and take them down to be interrogated in the principal's office, but no one ever knew anything. Finally, Mr. Balducci, the science teacher, offered a $5 reward for any information leading to the identity of this mad bomber. No one turned me in.

My older brother, Rocky, also tried to wreck the high school. At last, he was suspended for jumping up and down on the roof during a band concert. He really wanted to be a Maine guide, and once he tried to run away to Maine. But he did it the hard way, by crawling out his bedroom window, inching along the gutter, and climbing down a pine tree. He only got as far as Pawtucket. When he got back, he couldn't stand living in the big house anymore, so he stole some lumber and built a shack in our backyard.

Rocky used to have this problem. When he was out on his paper route, he would see trucks dumping dirt into the new foundations of the big houses and he'd hallucinate a child being covered over by the dirt. He would come home and tell my mother, "I just saw someone being buried alive." My mother would say, "It's only your imagination, dear. Sit down." Then she'd read to him from the Bible or from *Science and Health* to ground his imagination. In the winter when he was out on his paper route riding alongside the Barrington River, he'd see a hole in the ice and imagine that a child was falling through it. He'd come back and tell my mother, "I saw a child falling through the ice, it's drowning! We've got to call the police." And she'd say, "Sit down, dear, let me read to you from the Bible." Finally, my parents thought Rocky should go away to school to straighten out and buckle down. They sent him to Fitchton Academy in New Hampshire, and he hated it there. He would call my father up and say, "You've got to get me out of this school, I'm very unhappy." Then my father would go up and get him and when they'd get as far as the Howard Johnson's at the Portsmouth rotary my father would say, "Let's stop here and get a clam roll." But Rocky was paralyzed. He couldn't go in. He was convinced that he was going to kill someone in the restaurant. They drove all the way back to Barrington on empty stomachs.

So my father said to me, "We're thinking of sending you to Fitchton Academy. It's time to buckle down or you'll end up in the navy. It's shape up or ship out for you, my friend."

Fitchton was run by a rabble-rouser, Colton W. Cartwright. He would have "squirm sessions" on Sundays with the students, at which he made these Cotton Mather speeches. He would start by holding up a water glass saying, "Eighty percent of the Coca-Cola glasses in America have active syphilis germs on the edge." That was just the opener. He'd go on from there for an hour. He'd say, "Today it is the jungles of Laos. Tomorrow it will be the cornfields of Fitchton!" This was the school that they were thinking of sending me to, and I had to go up there for an interview.

My mother drove. It was about a four-, five-hour trip up to Fitchton, New Hampshire. I might have been thinking about Susan Tice, the first girl in our neighborhood to get a two-piece, leopard-skin bathing suit. I was constantly dreaming of being on a desert island with Susan, just the two of us. I would dream of her in school, and I'd get an erection. Then I'd have to go up to the board to do some math, and I'd have to kind of force it down and then walk bent over like a cripple. So, I guess I was thinking of Susan Tice all the way up to Fitchton.

We got up there, walked in, and C. W. Cartwright in his three-piece suit looked at us from under his bushy eyebrows and said, "Well, my friend, what's going on with you? Look at this report card. Straight E's. Why aren't you buckling down? What's the problem?" Now, no one had asked me anything like this before, just straight out. He just took me aside, a stranger. It was kind of sobering. I wasn't ready for it.

Out of nowhere, I said, "Well, since *they* have invented the hydrogen bomb, there is no future. Not only does it negate my consciousness, it negates that of Beethoven's." There was a long pause. He looked back at me and said, "That's what *they* said when *they* invented the crossbow." Now I knew there was a difference between the hydrogen bomb and the crossbow, but I didn't know how to tell him because I was too intimidated by his three-piece suit and his bushy eyebrows. I just looked back at him, and Mom and I drove back in a kind of funk.

Later we got a letter from Fitchton Academy, and my father said, "This is awful. They are not going to accept you because of your attitude. You're going to end up in the navy." Which frightened me. I believed him this time. So my father said, "I'm going to write C. W. Cartwright a letter and request that he give you a second interview. Do you think you can promise me that you'll cooperate with him this time?" So I said, "All right, yes, I'll give it a try." And my mother drove me all the way up again. I walked into C. W. Cartwright's office, and he said, "Well, my friend, can you promise us that you'll buckle down?" And I said, "Yes, yes. I'll buckle down. I'll buckle down. I'll do it, I'll buckle down."

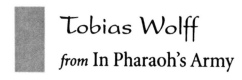

Tobias Wolff
from In Pharaoh's Army

A FEDERAL OFFENSE

JUST BEFORE TET MY FATHER SENT ME A BELATED CHRISTMAS CARD IN WHICH HE SAID HE watched the Vietnam news every day and was "damned proud" of me. I knew he meant well, but I couldn't help wondering what he had in mind. What did he think I was doing over here? What would he *like* me to be doing? Something "hush-hush," maybe, something understatedly brave and important as in the stories he used to tell, or imply, about flying with the RAF and serving with partisans just about everywhere. But maybe not. In fact I didn't know what he expected from me, or what to expect from him.

He had gotten out of prison a couple of years back while I was in Officer Candidate School. A friend of his from the old days found him an apartment in Manhattan Beach, and my father wrote me from there to send news of his release and simply to wish me well. There was no humbug in the letter, no talk of impending deals or bum raps. He said Geoffrey was helping him out every month and that was how he'd gotten my address. Years had passed since I'd heard from him or made any effort of my own to get in touch, and I was astounded to see his broad, outsized scrawl, the letters almost like ideograms, on the envelope. I sent back my own good wishes and thereafter we exchanged notes every six months or so.

When I was in language school my father wrote to propose that he come to Washington for a grand reunion. He could catch up with his boys, meet Priscilla and Vera, and pay his respects to our mother (he had either forgotten, or didn't care, that she had married again). He saw no reason, if he found Washington to his liking, why something couldn't be worked out with his parole board that would allow him to move there.

Geoffrey and I had a talk about it. His sense of humor was not on display. To him, the idea of the old man in Washington was a pit filled with man-eating possibilities. I could see his point. For once in his life he was solvent and in place, even, as book editor of the Washington *Post,* something of a personage in town, a favored ambassador from the trivial but charming realm of literature. Priscilla was expecting their first child in a few months.

Enter the old man. It was obvious to both of us how the play would go, we knew the script by heart: exotic cars paid for with rubber checks, stereos and Dunhill lighters charged to "my boy over at the *Post.*" Landlords, grocers, clothiers, purveyors of wine and spirits, loan sharks, all clamoring for justice—to Geoffrey. The whole thing would fall on him. It was unthinkable. But Geoffrey had thought about it; that was what made it hard for him. He had a lingering dream of somehow bringing the old man back into the family, and would have done just about anything to pull it off except let him destroy his life.

We declined our father's offer to join us, and he took it like a sport—nothing ventured, nothing gained—and said no more about it. But I'd gotten interested in seeing him again, and after my orders for Vietnam came in I arranged to take a quick detour to Manhattan Beach.

It started badly. When I got to LAX I couldn't find the envelope with his address. He was not allowed to have a phone—Ma Bell couldn't afford him. I tried calling Geoffrey, and got no answer. Then I remembered that a few months back there'd been a flap over some slippers and a tobacco pouch my father had charged at a Scandinavian imports store and neglected to pay for. He'd almost gone back to prison on account of it, but Geoffrey made good for him and the owner dropped charges. The name of the store had stayed with me. I looked it up in the phone book and found my way there.

My luck turned. The owner was on the premises and eager to be of help. A tall man with a mild, cultivated air and a faint accent, he immediately produced my father's address and insisted on driving me there. As soon as we got in his car he began to apologize. He never should have gotten the police involved, and he wouldn't have if he'd known Arthur was on parole. Never! Not for a moment! He was deeply sorry for the trouble he'd caused. "Such an extraordinary man, your father. Such things he has done. The airplanes, the dam in Turkey."

"It wasn't your fault," I told him.

"Such interesting conversations we had."

He went on this way until we reached the apartment, a converted garage on the ground floor of a stucco house. I could see the ocean between two apartment buildings at the end of the street; when the store owner turned the engine off I heard the crash and surge of waves. He came around to open the trunk for me and this was when my father stepped outside. He must have seen us pull up. He looked wary, and no wonder. I had omitted to tell him I was coming, because up to the last minute I wasn't sure I'd go through with it. He hadn't seen me for six years, since I was fifteen; I did not look like that boy anymore, especially in the uniform I'd worn so I could fly military standby. At first glance I was just a stranger with badges and shiny boots, the embodiment of civic compulsion in the company of a man he had defrauded. I wouldn't have recognized him either. He wore ugly black glasses. His face had thickened, his nose gone puffy as a cauliflower. He needed a shave.

"Hello, Arthur," the store owner said. "Here is your son."

He looked at me. "Toby?"

I put my hand out. He stood there, then took it, then bent toward me and kissed me clumsily on the lips.

The store owner put my duffel bag on the sidewalk. "Let me know if you need anything," he said to me. Then, sadly, "How are you, Arthur?"

"Tops, Peter. Hunky-dory." As we watched the car pull away my father asked me how I happened to arrive with "the melancholy Dane." I began a narration, but once I came to the matter of the unpaid bill he shook his head to let me know he'd heard enough.

It was a bad beginning, and we had trouble getting past it. My father went back and forth between cuffing my arm, calling me Buster and Chum and the pet names of my childhood, and standing back with a puzzled, watchful expression. He didn't know what to do with me. Of course I'd been a jackass to surprise him, but it went beyond that. It had to do with the whole of our history. He must have wondered where we stood in all this, what I'd forgiven, what I held against him, what I held against myself. I had questions of my own. The air between us was heavy with them.

After I'd changed clothes and had a sandwich we escaped the apartment and followed the walkway above the beach. The afternoon light glared on the water. My father noticed that I was squinting and pulled a pair of sunglasses out of his pocket. "Go on," he said, when I tried to refuse.

"What about you?"

"I'm used to it."

They were aviator glasses, the real thing, much better than the shades I'd left in the apartment. He had me put them on, take them off so he could make adjustments, put them on again. "Perfect," he said. "M-made for you. Keep 'em."

"I can't."

"They're yours. End of discussion."

I had the sense to stop arguing and after that he seemed happier to be with me. We walked and talked until he got winded and sat on a bench with his hands on his knees, looking for all the world like the old Jewish guys I used to see on the benches in Sarasota when I was a kid. Fleshy, bald, sorrow-eyed, hair bristling from their ears. That shouldn't have come as any surprise—he *was* an old Jewish guy, whether he admitted it or not—but I hadn't been prepared to see him in just this light. Not my father, whose physical presence could crowd a room, whose deep voice and imperial bearing had served as collateral for the most fabulous promises and claims. I never saw him do a moment's exercise, but the one time he ever really hit me—I'd asked for it—my head snapped back so hard that it shocked him even more than me, and he burst into tears. Even when I loved him, even when I despised him, there had always been a certain fear. No more. His weakening put me at ease. I waited as he collected himself, and let him set the pace on the walk home.

We had a couple of drinks when we got back. The apartment was small but he'd managed to furnish it comfortably and even with some style. I couldn't help but notice the color television, as I had earlier noticed the watch he was wearing—a Heuer chronograph that must have been worth several hundred dollars. There were other objects of value, more than could be strictly accounted for by welfare and Geoffrey's checks, but I kept my questions to myself. We washed a heap of dishes and listened to Art Tatum and got pretty loose, whereupon I suggested we go out for dinner, on me. He knew just the place. We duded ourselves up and drove there in his '53 Cadillac, which, he hurried to tell me, he'd picked up for a song.

❖   ❖   ❖

The restaurant bar was cool and dark. We made a stop there, then proceeded to our table with fresh glasses in hand. By the time our meat arrived, thick bloody steaks served on slabs of wood, we were pretty well oiled, but that didn't stop me, with my father's judicious concurrence—"I suppose I could manage a glass"—from ordering a bottle of red.

He did indeed manage a glass. So did I. We were flush, not so much with the wine itself as with the long tangled journey we'd made to share it. My father began to preen a little. He bantered with the waiter, sent tribute to the kitchen. He exchanged greetings with our neighbors ("My boy here's in for the day, making sure the old man's keeping his nose clean . . ."). His voice grew deeper as the night went on, his phrasing and inflections more urbane. He sat up straighter, squared his great shoulders, laughed from deep in his chest as he recalled the old stories, the old names. Nothing was said about the final destination of my trip. I noticed the perfect drape of his linen jacket, the way his gold signet ring flashed in the candlelight. I could see how pleasure lightened him and restored his patrician authority. This was when I chose to ask if it was true that his family was Jewish.

He went still, the light died out of his eyes. "No," he said. "Of course not. Why?"

"I'm just curious. They were my family too, and I don't know anything about them."

"Episcopalians."

"Really? Both sides?"

"Both sides."

"What about your mother? Her maiden name was Krotoshiner, right? Isn't that a Jewish name?"

"German."

"And Wolff?"

"German. East Prussian, if you want to be particular." He looked around as if to call for the bill.

"But—correct me if I'm wrong—wasn't your mother in Hadassah?"

"Hell's bells, son, I don't know. She belonged to every g-goddamned charity in Hartford, maybe she was in that one too. Sure! Why not."

I kept after him in this falsely innocent way, as if I were just trying to clear up some minor confusions of my own, until he lost patience.

"For Christ's sake," he said, "what do you want?"

I couldn't answer him. I didn't know what I wanted. He got up and went outside while I paid the check. I thought he might very well leave me there, but he was waiting in the car, staring dead ahead. We spoke only once on the drive home, when he ran a stop sign. I pointed this out to him. Without looking at me he said, "I stopped at the last one."

The couch was a pull-out. We made up the bed in silence, then he asked if I needed anything.

"Could we have a nightcap?"

He was stiff about it but he poured a couple of drinks and put on a record.

"Hey, that's great," I said. "Who is it?"

He told me, and then told me who the sidemen were, and when it was recorded, and why it was such a hard record to find nowadays. This led him to play me several more of his treasures. He listened exactly the way Geoffrey listened, making rhythm noises, leaning forward suddenly with narrowed eyes when one of the players commenced a star solo, compelling me to listen with him. When he saw that I was fighting sleep he collected our glasses and turned off the stereo. I stood up, weaving with drink and fatigue. "Good night," I said.

"You sure you have to leave tomorrow?"

"Afraid so."

"Well, kiddo . . ." He put his arms around me and I let myself lean against him. It was a relief not to have to look into his face anymore, into his terrible sadness. We didn't say a word. I don't know how long we stood like that, but it began to seem a long time. Then I straightened up, and he let go of me.

◆ ◆ ◆

At the replacement depot in Oakland I met up with an acquaintance from Fort Bragg, a young lieutenant with the 82nd Airborne. His name was Stu Hoffman. He was freckle-faced and skinny and excessively thoughtful. No command presence. An even more unlikely officer than I was. We weren't friends, but we used to run into each other at the officers club and talk about writing. He also had ambitions in that direction. I didn't take them very seriously because he was nuts about Thomas Wolfe, and I looked down on both Wolfe and his admirers, though I had recently admired him myself. Stu for his part didn't understand my reverence for Hemingway. Hemingway, he said, did not love words, and to be a writer you had to love words.

We were scheduled for the same flight to Vietnam. They'd given us two entire days in Oakland for out-processing but there really wasn't that much to do, and we were free by the afternoon of the first day. We changed into civvies and caught a cab into San Francisco, to the Haight-Ashbury, to see if we could find some hippies having LSD trips. Maybe there would be a Happening or a Be-In. That was the way we proposed the excursion, gee-whizzing it up, cartooning the expectations of a pair of rubes who got their picture of the world from the Des Moines *Register*.

In fact we did find a Happening in progress, right on Haight Street, and there were hippies, and some of them gave signs of being in touch with pretty far-off places. Stu and I were issued batik headbands and embraced by each of a party of soulful wanderers who identified themselves as "the Hug Patrol." We did not laugh at them, nor at the earnest demonstrations of candlemaking and tie-dyeing, nor at the bearded, bare-chested man in harem pants who sat on a blanket with his eyes closed, playing a sitar. Their goodwill was too naked and guileless for that. They were like children playing, but more touching because they weren't children. I was embarrassed by all this determined innocence yet somehow protective of it. Made wistful. Chastened.

We tied the headbands around our cropped skulls and moseyed along the street, returning smile for smile, walking tenderly in our spit-shined low quarters as if afraid of breaking something.

Afterward we went to a bar near the Panhandle where we drank pitchers and told our stories. I talked, but Stu talked more. He'd been raised in Chicago by his father's parents, because his mother had died when he was young and his father was out of the country for weeks and even months at a time. He was a petroleum engineer. A living legend, Stu said. Mention the name Bill Hoffman to anybody in the oil game and they'd buy you a drink on the spot. The man was amazing. He'd found oil in places there wasn't supposed to be any, time and time again. And before that, before he went to college and all, he'd been a champion motorcycle racer. And a war hero, one of the original paratroopers. Jumped with General Gavin over Normandy and all the rest of it. Two Purple Hearts, a Silver Star, and a whole shitload of other medals, including some from France. DeGaulle personally pinned one on him and kissed his cheeks. Stu had a picture of it in his room at home—Charles de Gaulle putting a lip-lock on his father.

His father was one in a million, just a little hard to talk to. He wouldn't tell you what he was thinking. You were supposed to know. When Stu decided to drop out of the Colorado School of Mines his father didn't say a word against it, though it was his own alma mater.

Stu would've stuck it out to keep him happy, but he was flunking most of his courses; the only thing he ever wanted to do was read and that didn't get you very far at CSM. Anyway his father didn't say much when he quit, just, "It's your life, live it any damn way you want." When Stu enlisted in the army the most he'd say about it was, "Don't let the bastards con you into anything," and to this day he hadn't managed to congratulate him on making it through Officer Candidate School and airborne training. Stu figured he must be happy to see him keeping up the family tradition, but it just wasn't his way to show it.

Terrific guy, though. Solid as a rock.

Stu said his father was flying in the next day to see him off. He asked if I'd join them for dinner, and took it as a big favor when I said yes.

"He's great," Stu said. "Really. Just a little hard to talk to sometimes."

Later that night we tried to get into the Top of the Mark and were turned away for not wearing ties. We stood outside the Mark Hopkins and howled, "O lost, and by the wind grieved, ghost, come back again!" The doormen were our only audience, and they ignored us. They stood at parade rest in their frogged overcoats and acted as if we weren't there. They made us look like imbeciles. We moved off down the street, staggering to show how drunk we were.

-◦- -◦- -◦-

I took a bus into town the next day and walked around North Beach, searching for Kerouac's old hangouts. Later I went back to the Haight. The Happening was over but I kept seeing the same credulous faces, or maybe they were different faces with the same look. Again I felt that wistfulness of the day before. Without talking to anyone except a girl who tried to sell me a belt, unconscious of my purpose in returning, I wandered the neighborhood until it was time for dinner.

We met up in a seafood restaurant down by Fishermen's Wharf. Stu had worn his uniform and looked completely implausible in the big jump boots and starched khakis covered with insignia, awkward and self-conscious, like a Boy Scout with all his merit badges on.

The first thing Mr. Hoffman said to me was, "So you're the other one about to get his ass shot off."

Stu laughed miserably.

"I hope not," I said.

"Well, that'll do you no end of good," Mr. Hoffman said. He didn't smile. He had freckles like Stu's and thin white lips—also freckled—and curly red hair. His skin looked taut over his high cheekbones. He ordered drinks and watched me impatiently while I answered Stu's questions about my day. I didn't mention going back to the Haight.

Mr. Hoffman wanted to know what I thought of General William Childs Westmoreland.

Stu slumped in his chair. He looked tired.

"I've never met him," I said.

"You must have an opinion." Mr. Hoffman broke off a piece of bread with a sharp twisting motion, the way you'd tighten a coupling. The backs of his freckled hands were covered with wiry hair. "Starting tomorrow he holds the papers on you, right? So what do you think?"

I didn't know how to answer—what he hoped to hear.

"You think he cares about you?"

I considered this. "Yes, given the exigencies of command."

"Exigencies!" He looked at Stu. "No wonder you two hit it off."

"We've been all through this, Dad."

"I'm asking your friend a simple question. You mind?" he said to me.

I looked over at Stu. He picked up the menu and started to read it.

"Stu wants to be a teacher," Mr. Hoffman said.

"Maybe even write some books. What do you think of that?"

"I think it's great."

"So do I. Nobody in our family has ever written a book, far as I know. He can do it too, Stu can. Stu is not your general-issue human being. But I guess you know that."

The waiter came over to take our orders. After he left, Mr. Hoffman said, "Did you know that General William Childs Westmoreland ordered a parachute jump in high winds that got a whole bunch of boys killed? Broke their necks and every other damned thing. This was Fort Campbell, understand—not Vietnam. No military necessity."

"I've heard mention of it."

"And what does that tell you about General William Childs Westmoreland?"

"I don't know. It was a training jump. I guess you could say training is a military necessity."

"Would you swallow that horseshit if one of those boys was your son?"

I took a drink and set my glass down carefully.

Mr. Hoffman said, "Every single one of those boys was somebody's son."

"Dad."

"He didn't lose a wink. Came out clean as a whistle. What do you owe those bastards anyway?" he said to Stu. "You think you owe them something?"

Stu closed his eyes.

"I'll tell you what he cares about, him and that sorry dickhead from Texas. *How he looks.* That's it. That is the be-all and end-all of his miserable existence."

Mr. Hoffman worked this vein until our dinners came. He shoved his food around for a while and then stood and said, "Excuse us." He waited while Stu got up, and the two of them left the dining room. They were gone long enough for me to finish my dinner. Neither of them said anything when they came back. Stu didn't look at me. He sat down and began eating, stiffly, the way they made us eat in OCS, shoulders squared, eyes glazed, chewing like a machine.

Mr. Hoffman took a few bites and pushed the plate away. "What does your father think?" he asked me.

"About what?"

"About you getting your ass shot off for the greater glory of Lyndon Baines Johnson and William Childs Westmoreland."

"I'm not sure. We haven't been in very close touch."

"Stu and I, we haven't been in close touch either. But that's damn well going to change. Right, Stu?" Mr. Hoffman touched his arm. Stu nodded. Mr. Hoffman took his hand away and Stu went on eating.

"You ought to talk to your father," Mr. Hoffman said. "He might have a thing or two to say about this."

"It doesn't look like we're going to have a chance."

"Well, that's a shame."

Mr. Hoffman insisted on going upstairs to the piano bar for a drink. Three customers were sitting together at the piano, a TWA pilot and two women. When the pianist finished the song he was playing, the TWA pilot asked for "Theme from *The Apartment.*" The woman to his right bumped him with her shoulder and said, "Ronnnn!" She rolled her eyes at us, miming exasperation with him for hinting at their secrets. She had a round face full of physical good nature. The pilot murmured something and she bumped him again. "You big goof," she said.

The other one looked at me just long enough to reveal how bored she was with the sight before her, then turned away. She was drooped over a cigarette, a bony blonde with a long pale neck and pouty lips.

The pianist doodled prettily around the keyboard, then entered the song. He played it with his eyes half closed. At the end he ducked his head at the applause and took a drink from a glass of milk.

The woman with the pilot leaned forward and, staring at Stu's jump wings, asked if he was in the air force. Her brother was in the air force, she said, in Guam.

"Army," Stu said. Then, with helpless pride, "Paratroops." He bent his head toward me. "Both of us."

"Been over yet?" the pilot asked.

"Tomorrow morning."

"Give 'em hell," the pilot said.

"Christ almighty," Mr. Hoffman said. "I need a cigar." He slid off his stool and left the room.

The pianist started playing "It Was a Very Good Year."

I looked at Stu. "I thought he wouldn't tell you what was on his mind."

He was picking at his cocktail napkin. "It's been like this all day. Bam bam bam. Bam bam bam. He just won't let up."

"What's he so worked up about?"

"He doesn't want me to go," Stu said.

"So I gather. It's not like you have a choice."

"He doesn't see it that way."

"Come on. What're you supposed to do—desert?" Stu didn't answer.

"What, he wants you to desert?"

Stu looked at me. He still didn't say anything.

"It's a federal offense," I said.

He grinned.

"Well, it is."

"A federal offense," Stu said. "That's great. I haven't heard that since I was a kid."

Mr. Hoffman was followed back into the bar by two women in rustling evening dresses and two men wearing fancy-stitched Western suits with bolo ties, pointy boots, and bronc-buster belt buckles. Their entry had the quality of a stampede. They came in and milled around, the women rubbing their arms in the chill of the air-conditioning, the men bellowing at each other and rocking back on their heels to fire bursts of laughter toward the ceiling. They found their way to the piano and set up a trading post—purses, piles of coins, wallets, cigarettes, lighters in silver-and-turquoise cases. The women wore a lot of brilliant jewelry. All four of them ordered margaritas and smiled around at the rest of us to show we had nothing to fear.

When the pianist played "The Yellow Rose of Texas," one of the women whooped. "Listen to him! You're in the wrong state, mister." She finally let on they were from Arizona.

Stu leaned over to me. "We're gonna split. You coming?"

I looked across the piano at the snooty blonde. She was staring into her drink.

"You go on," I said. "Catch you in the morning."

Mr. Hoffman gave my shoulder a squeeze, and they were gone.

The Arizonans had the pianist play "Hello, Dolly," and made the rest of us join in. One of the men draped his arm around the blonde and swayed back and forth with her. She didn't pull away but she didn't sing, either. She smiled in a tight-lipped way like someone with bad teeth.

We sang a few show tunes, then the Wild Bunch rolled up their sleeves: "Don't Fence Me In," "Cool Water," "Tumbling Tumbleweeds." It was their party now. They kept our glasses full and made sure we were loud enough. The blonde left. She didn't say good-bye to anyone, just got up and left. I wanted to sneak out after her but I couldn't find the right moment. We drank to the approaching nuptials of the pilot and his girlfriend. We drank to the piano player. We drank to the Cactus State, and to the States United. We sang some patriotic songs and everybody got choked up.

Then the pilot told the Arizonans I was shipping out the next morning. One of the women took this as an occasion to shed tears. Her husband patted her on the back a few times, then he and his friend took seats beside me and settled down to the business of giving me advice.

Jovial men get serious with a vengeance. It lurks there always behind their crinkled eyes, the eagerness to show you that even if they do know how to have a good time they can by God get down to cases too. These weren't the worst of the breed. They professed no gospel, no dietary plan, no road to riches. But all the same I could see how happy they were to close the party down, to pull long faces and speak of arms and war.

Both were vets and had plenty to say, though I couldn't follow much of it. "This country can mobilize!" one of them kept shouting. Finally the wives took pity on me and made them stop. Then we were all out on the street in glistening fog, shaking hands and embracing, promising to meet again, next year in Phoenix. The men guided me into a cab. As the driver counted the money they'd given him, one of them leaned inside and regarded me solemnly. "Son," he said. I could see he wanted to say something, something momentous. I bent toward him. He said, "Keep your head down, son."

◦ ◦ ◦

I lay awake in my room until the orderly called me. It was still dark when we boarded the buses. A sergeant got on and read our names out. Stu didn't answer. Neither did two other men. When the sergeant came to the end of his list he called their names again, then asked if anyone knew why they weren't present. Silence. He made a notation on his clipboard and got off the bus.

They kept the inside lights off on the way to the airport. Cigarettes burned in the gloom. Hardly anyone spoke, and then just a few words, quietly. There was no grab-ass, no swagger. Later, on the plane, we'd find our tongues and talk ourselves into a grotesquely festive state, but at this moment we were numbed by the grip of the current that was carrying us away. I was, anyway. Until now nothing had seemed irrevocable. I had persisted in the unconscious faith that no matter what I did, no matter how many steps I took, I would be excused from taking this last step. Something would happen—I didn't know what. The VC would surrender. My orders would get changed. The President would decide to pull out. Something. Up to now men had been going over in one long unbroken line, but I hadn't been one of them. My position in the line guaranteed that something would happen to make it stop. I hadn't really thought these things but I must have felt them, because I was in shock to find myself on the bus that morning, and I don't believe it was just my imagination that the others were in shock too.

We weren't meant to be here, every one of us knew that, but here we were.

An odd question came to me, one I've never forgotten. What would this bus look like if you could see us all exactly as we would be a year from now?

Nothing could stop it. Except . . . what? A breakdown? We'd just have to get on another bus. My pals from the Haight—the Hug Patrol in a human chain across the road? Nah, bunch of softies, they'd never get up this early. Hijackers. A gang of hijackers in front of a barricade, wielding shotguns and pitchforks and clubs, shining bright lights into the driver's eyes. The driver stops. The hijackers pound on the door until he opens it. They come up the steps and down the aisle, flashing their beams from face to face until they find the ones they're after. They call our names, and then we know who it is behind the blinding lights. It's our fathers. Our fathers, come to take us home.

Crazy.

But not as crazy as what they actually did, which was let us go.

Harvey Pekar and R. Crumb

The Harvey Pekar Name Story

3
The Personal Essay

People are so complex—so many layers of experience, of knowledge, of skills, of talents, of emotions, of enthusiams, of distastes, all juxtaposed in endless contradictions of meaning and form and intention. Our minds wander, moving from point to point in orderly trains only at the most focused of times, but more usually in unplanned linkages and interlinkings and unlinkings, and even in random bursts. Good conversation works like a good mind, the interlocutors following unforeseen threads and whole garments down unexplored passages without regret, erupting in laughter at times, or squirting with tears, or wincing with disagreement, or simply nodding with interest and pleasure. Meaning arrives unannounced, followed by understanding or argument, either way a meeting of human minds.

Like thinking itself, the personal essay makes use of whatever is available among all those layers of mind. And like conversation, a good personal essay needs at least two minds to function most fully. As in good people, the one common feature we can count on in all good personal essays is humanity.

The word *personal* in our phrase doesn't quite mean private, as in personal life, doesn't quite mean embarrassing, as in personal products, doesn't quite imply individual use or ownership, as in personal computer or personal property. So what does the word *personal* refer to here? I'd say: the person, the individual soul at the center of the writing, that soul that is the beating heart of all creative pursuit, of course, and of everything human.

❖   ❖   ❖

The difference between memoir and the personal essay isn't as strong as the difference between fiction and memoir because between memoir and the personal essay there is considerable overlap and interweaving, whereas (because one is offered as made up, the other offered as true) there is really none between fiction and memoir. The difference between the personal essay and memoir begins to emerge as the writer departs from storytelling to begin thinking (on the page, of course, and figuratively) about the meanings of the story told, using scenes and images and events from the writer's life—the stuff of memoir—as evidence for a kind of argument. So E. B. White, James Baldwin, Ralph Ellison, Shirley Abbott, and other writers in the selections that follow tell us stories, then go a step further and analyze those stories, tell us what they mean.

The difference between personal essay and memoir increases as the personal essayist moves across the essay continuum, using more and more exposition and less and less narrative, working more and more with ideas and less and less with images, more and more with explicit theses and overt logical and rhetorical strategies, less and less with chronologies. The movement across the continuum (I always picture this movement going from left to right on a blackboard, from right brain to left brain in the head, from traditionally feminine to traditionally masculine, from heart to mind, from emotion to logic, from yin to yang) is toward the formal essay, where again, the personal essay finds useful overlap with a neighbor, this one far to the ride side of the blackboard and well away from memoir (which is back on the left, overlapping but not touching fiction). The personal essay rides nicely on the wide area (color it gray, if you must, but rainbows will emerge) between the informal and the formal.

So, Phillip Lopate tells us about Donald Barthelme, happily operating without offering much dialogue or many scenes, but giving a great deal of reflection, and Vivian Gornick in "At the University: Little Murders of the Soul," moves toward a thesis summed up in her subtitle. She disguises the people she worked with and the places she worked, but her analysis of those places and the relationships they engender is devastating, and moves past her own experience toward something more universal.

The personal essay got its first name in opposition to the formal essay, though the formal essay took the family name later in history, having gotten started in ancient times as the art of oration, with all its classical rules and carefully delineated moves. Form is more important than speaker in the formal essay. The writer stays focused and sticks to his point, he's confident in its suppositions, never contradicts himself, slays the opposition, eschews the first person, takes on the persona of knowledge itself, speaking incontrovertible truths. The formal essay *is* its ideas, and its arguments, and lives for these things, aspires to these things. There is beauty in the formal essay, and excellence, but the formal essay does not particularly aspire to art.

The personal essayist is more comfortable with contradiction (a certain great poet called this negative capability), she likes to wander, to sidle up to a point, is even willing at times to forget the point altogether in favor of a felicitous phrase or observation. Most of all, she embraces the first person, loves the first person, sings in the first person fearlessly. The personal essay, in a way, *is* its writer. And the personal essay is human, striving more for passion than for logic (but loving logic too), more for emotion than exactitude (but loving accuracy), more for questions than answers. And it's not that the personal essay isn't formal enough at times, just that it allows and even requires the quirky touch of an individual human being. What an odd approach to the story of her love life Jane Shapiro takes in "This Is What You Need for a Happy Life"! How angry Joy Williams is in "Save the Whales, Screw the Shrimp"! How calm and even-tempered and matter-of-fact in the face of death is Thomas Lynch in "The Undertaking"!

The word *essay* comes from the French verb *essayer*, which means "to try." The French writer and minor noble Michel de Montaigne (1533–92) coined the term that has lasted so long and spread its use over so many cultures, by naming his rambling, roving, contradictory, prickly, warm, self-examining, doubting, and always smart prose inquiries "tries." He was just trying to get what he thought down on paper, letting each "try," or essay, find its own shape.

That's not to say there's no form in the personal essay. But the successful personal essay is always an experiment in form, finds its own best structure, never quite exactly like any other. Compare the classic "Once More to the Lake" by E. B. White, with Jane Shapiro's "This Is What You Need for a Happy Life" and you'll find that they are as different as alike. "Body in Trouble" by Nancy Mairs and "Country Matters" by Hayden Carruth are both about disabilities, and both use personal experience of disability to make their points—but the approaches to the subject as different as the two authors, that is to say: very different indeed.

⋆〇 ⋆〇 ⋆〇

Most of the selections in this section are complete essays, but some are chapters from book-length works—still essays, I would say, but too long to offer whole here. Readers who'd like to delve deeper into the form might look into the books of the writers at hand. And do read Phillip Lopate's *The Art of the Personal Essay* for historical and international and further contemporary examples, and for the introductory essay by Mr. Lopate, in which he defines the form once and for all. Another helpful book, coming at the issue from a slightly more academic angle, is *Essays on the Essay,* edited by Alexander J. Butrym.

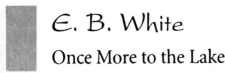

E. B. White
Once More to the Lake

August 1941

ONE SUMMER, ALONG ABOUT 1904, MY FATHER RENTED A CAMP ON A LAKE IN MAINE AND took us all there for the month of August. We all got ringworm from some kittens and had to rub Pond's Extract on our arms and legs night and morning, and my father rolled over in a canoe with all his clothes on; but outside of that the vacation was a success and from then on none of us ever thought there was any place in the world like that lake in Maine. We returned summer after summer—always on August 1 for one month. I have since become a salt-water man, but sometimes in summer there are days when the restlessness of the tides and the fearful cold of the sea water and the incessant wind that blows across the afternoon and into the evening make me wish for the placidity of a lake in the woods. A few weeks ago this feeling got so strong I bought myself a couple of bass hooks and a spinner and returned to the lake where we used to go, for a week's fishing and to revisit old haunts.

I took along my son, who had never had any fresh water up his nose and who had seen lily pads only from train windows. On the journey over to the lake I began to wonder what it would be like. I wondered how time would have marred this unique, this holy spot—the coves and streams, the hills that the sun set behind, the camps and the paths behind the camps. I was sure that the tarred road would have found it out, and I wondered in what other ways it would be desolated. It is strange how much you can remember about places like that once you allow your mind to return into the grooves that lead back. You remember one thing, and that suddenly reminds you of another thing. I guess I remembered clearest of all the early mornings, when the lake was cool and motionless, remembered how the bedroom smelled of the lumber it was made of and of the wet woods whose scent entered through the screen. The partitions in the camp were thin and did not extend clear to the top of the rooms, and as I was always the first up I would dress softly so as not to wake the others, and sneak out into the sweet outdoors and start out in the canoe, keeping close along the shore in the long shadows of the pines. I remembered being very careful never to rub my paddle against the gunwale for fear of disturbing the stillness of the cathedral.

The lake had never been what you would call a wild lake. There were cottages sprinkled around the shores, and it was in farming country although the shores of the lake were quite heavily wooded. Some of the cottages were owned by nearby farmers, and you would live at the shore and eat your meals at the farmhouse. That's what our family did. But although it wasn't wild, it was a fairly large and undisturbed lake and there were places in it that, to a child at least, seemed infinitely remote and primeval.

I was right about the tar: it led to within half a mile of the shore. But when I got back there, with my boy, and we settled into a camp near a farmhouse and into the kind of summertime I had known, I could tell that it was going to be pretty much the same as it had been before—I knew it, lying in bed the first morning, smelling the bedroom and hearing the boy sneak quietly out and go off along the shore in a boat. I began to sustain the illusion that he was I, and therefore, by simple transposition, that I was my father. This sensation persisted, kept cropping up all the time we were there. It was not an entirely new feeling, but in this setting it grew much stronger. I seemed to be living a dual existence. I would be in the middle of some simple act, I would be picking up a bait box or laying down a table fork, or I would be saying something, and suddenly it would be not I but my father who was saying the words or making the gesture. It gave me a creepy sensation.

We went fishing the first morning. I felt the same damp moss covering the worms in the bait can, and saw the dragonfly alight on the tip of my rod as it hovered a few inches from the surface of the water. It was the arrival of this fly that convinced me beyond any doubt that everything was as it always had been, that the years were a mirage and that there had been no years. The small waves were the same, chucking the rowboat under the chin as we fished at anchor, and the boat was the same boat, the same color green and the ribs broken in the same places, and under the floorboards the same fresh-water leavings and débris— the dead helgramite, the wisps of moss, the rusty discarded fishhook, the dried blood from yesterday's catch. We stared silently at the tips of our rods, at the dragonflies that came and went. I lowered the tip of mine into the water, tentatively, pensively dislodging the fly, which darted two feet away, poised, darted two feet back, and came to rest again a little farther up the rod. There had been no years between the ducking of this dragonfly and the other one— the one that was part of memory. I looked at the boy, who was silently watching his fly, and it was my hands that held his rod, my eyes watching. I felt dizzy and didn't know which rod I was at the end of.

We caught two bass, hauling them in briskly as though they were mackerel, pulling them over the side of the boat in a businesslike manner without any landing net, and stunning them with a blow on the back of the head. When we got back for a swim before lunch, the lake was exactly where we had left it, the same number of inches from the dock, and there was only the merest suggestion of a breeze. This seemed an utterly enchanted sea, this lake you could leave to its own devices for a few hours and come back to, and find that it had not stirred, this constant and trustworthy body of water. In the shallows, the dark, water-soaked sticks and twigs, smooth and old, were undulating in clusters on the bottom against the clean ribbed sand, and the track of the mussel was plain. A school of minnows swam by, each minnow with its small individual shadow, doubling the attendance, so clear and sharp in the sunlight. Some of the other campers were in swimming, along the shore, one of them with a cake of soap, and the water felt thin and clear and unsubstantial. Over the years there had been this person with the cake of soap, this cultist, and here he was. There had been no years.

Up to the farmhouse to dinner through the teeming, dusty field, the road under our sneakers was only a two-track road. The middle track was missing, the one with the marks of the hooves and the splotches of dried, flaky manure. There had always been three tracks to choose from in choosing which track to walk in; now the choice was narrowed down to two. For a moment I missed terribly the middle alternative. But the way led past the tennis court, and something about the way it lay there in the sun reassured me; the tape had loosened along the backline, the alleys were green with plantains and other weeds, and the net (installed in June and removed in September) sagged in the dry noon, and the whole place steamed with midday heat and hunger and emptiness. There was a choice of pie for dessert, and one was blueberry and one was apple, and the waitresses were the same country girls, there having been no passage of time, only the illusion of it as in a dropped curtain—the waitresses were still fifteen; their hair had been washed, that was the only difference—they had been to the movies and seen the pretty girls with the clean hair.

Summertime, oh, summertime, pattern of life indelible, the fade-proof lake, the woods unshatterable, the pasture with the sweetfern and the juniper forever and ever, summer without end; this was the background, and the life along the shore was the design, the cottagers with their innocent and tranquil design, their tiny docks with the flagpole and the American flag floating against the white clouds in the blue sky, the little paths over the roots of the trees leading from camp to camp and the paths leading back to the outhouses and the can of lime for sprinkling, and at the souvenir counters at the store the miniature birch-bark canoes and the postcards that showed things looking a little better than they looked. This was the American family at play, escaping the city heat, wondering whether the newcomers in the camp at the head of the cove were "common" or "nice," wondering whether it was true that the people who drove up for Sunday dinner at the farmhouse were turned away because there wasn't enough chicken.

It seemed to me, as I kept remembering all this, that those times and those summers had been infinitely precious and worth saving. There had been jollity and peace and goodness. The arriving (at the beginning of August) had been so big a business in itself, at the railway station the farm wagon drawn up, the first smell of the pine-laden air, the first glimpse of the smiling farmer, and the great importance of the trunks and your father's enormous authority in such matters, and the feel of the wagon under you for the long ten-mile haul, and at the top of the last long hill catching the first view of the lake after eleven months of not seeing this cherished body of water. The shouts and cries of the other campers when they saw you, and the trunks to be unpacked, to give up their rich burden. (Arriving was less exciting nowadays, when you sneaked up in your car and parked it under a tree near the camp and took out the bags and in five minutes it was all over, no fuss, no loud wonderful fuss about trunks.)

Peace and goodness and jollity. The only thing that was wrong now, really, was the sound of the place, an unfamiliar nervous sound of the outboard motors. This was the note that jarred, the one thing that would sometimes break the illusion and set the years moving. In those other summertimes all motors were inboard; and when they were at a little distance, the noise they made was a sedative, an ingredient of summer sleep. They were one-cylinder and two-cylinder engines, and some were make-and-break and some were jump-spark, but they all made a sleepy sound across the lake. The one-lungers throbbed and fluttered, and the twin-cylinder ones purred and purred, and that was a quiet sound, too. But now the campers all had outboards. In the day-time, in the hot mornings, these motors made a petulant, irritable sound; at night, in the still evening when the afterglow lit the water, they whined about one's ears like mosquitoes. My boy loved our rented outboard, and his great desire was to achieve single-handed mastery over it, and authority, and he soon learned the trick of choking it a little (but not too much), and the adjustment of the needle valve. Watching him I would remember the things you could do with the old one-cylinder engine with the heavy flywheel, how you could have it eating out of your hand if you got really close to it spiritually. Motor-boats in those days didn't have clutches, and you would make a landing by shutting off the motor at the proper time and coasting in with a dead rudder. But there was a way of reversing them, if you learned the trick, by cutting the switch and putting it on again exactly on the final dying revolution of the flywheel, so that it would kick back against compression and begin reversing. Approaching a dock in a strong following breeze, it was difficult to slow up sufficiently by the ordinary coasting method, and if a boy felt he had complete mastery over his motor, he was tempted to keep it running beyond its time and then reverse it a few feet from the dock. It took a cool nerve, because if you threw the switch a twentieth of a second too soon you would catch the flywheel when it still had speed enough to go up past center, and the boat would leap ahead, charging bull-fashion at the dock.

We had a good week at the camp. The bass were biting well and the sun shone endlessly, day after day. We would be tired at night and lie down in the accumulated heat of the little bedrooms after the long hot day and the breeze would stir almost imperceptibly outside and the smell of the swamp drift in through the rusty screens. Sleep would come easily and in the morning the red squirrel would be on the roof, tapping out his gay routine. I kept remembering everything, lying in bed in the mornings—the small steamboat that had a long rounded stern like the lip of a Ubangi, and how quietly she ran on the moonlight sails, when the older boys played their mandolins and the girls sang and we ate doughnuts dipped in a sugar, and how sweet the music was on the water in the shining night, and what it had felt like to think about girls then. After breakfast we would go up to the store and the things were in the same place—the minnows in a bottle, the plugs and spinners disarranged and pawed over by the youngsters from the boys' camp, the Fig Newtons and the Beeman's gum. Outside, the road was tarred and cars stood in front of the store. Inside, all was just as it had always been, except there was more Coca-Cola and not so much Moxie and root beer and birch beer and sarsaparilla. We would walk out with the bottle of pop apiece and sometimes the pop would back-fire up our noses and hurt. We explored the streams, quietly, where the turtles slid off the sunny logs and dug their way into the soft bottom; and we lay on the town wharf and fed worms to the tame bass. Everywhere we went I had trouble making out which was I, the one walking at my side, the one walking in my pants.

One afternoon while we were there at that lake a thunderstorm came up. It was like the revival of an old melodrama that I had seen long ago with childish awe. The second-act climax of the drama of the electrical disturbance over a lake in America had not changed in any important respect. This was the big scene, still the big scene. The whole thing was so familiar, the first feeling of oppression and heat and a general air around camp of not wanting to go very far away. In mid-afternoon (it was all the same) a curious darkening of the sky, and a lull in everything that had made life tick; and then the way the boats suddenly swung the other way at their moorings with the coming of a breeze out of the new quarter, and the premonitory rumble. Then the kettle drum, then the snare, then the bass drum and cymbals, then crackling light against the dark, and the gods grinning and licking their chops in the hills. Afterward the calm, the rain steadily rustling in the calm lake, the return of light and hope and spirits, and the campers running out in joy and relief to go swimming in the rain, their bright cries perpetuating the deathless joke about how they were getting simply drenched, and the children screaming with delight at the new sensation of bathing in the rain, and the joke about getting drenched linking the generations in a strong indestructible chain. And the comedian who waded in carrying an umbrella.

When the others went swimming, my son said he was going in, too. He pulled his dripping trunks from the line where they had hung all through the shower and wrung them out. Languidly, and with no thought of going in, I watched him, his hard little body, skinny and bare, saw him wince slightly as he pulled up around his vitals the small soggy, icy garment. As he buckled the swollen belt, suddenly my groin felt the chill of death.

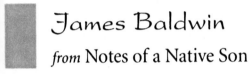

James Baldwin
from Notes of a Native Son

EQUAL IN PARIS

On the 19th of December, in 1949, when I had been living in Paris for a little over a year, I was arrested as a receiver of stolen goods and spent eight days in prison. My arrest came about through an American tourist whom I had met twice in New York, who had been given my name and address and told to look me up. I was then living on the top floor of a ludicrously grim hotel on the rue du Bac, one of those enormous dark, cold, and hideous establishments in which Paris abounds that seem to breathe forth, in their airless, humid, stone-cold halls, the weak light, scurrying chambermaids, and creaking stairs, an odor of gentility long long dead. The place was run by an ancient Frenchman dressed in an elegant black suit which was green with age, who cannot properly be described as bewildered or even as being in a state of shock, since he had really stopped breathing around 1910. There he sat at his desk in the weirdly lit, fantastically furnished lobby, day in and day out, greeting each one of his extremely impoverished and *louche* lodgers with a stately inclination of the head that he had no doubt been taught in some impossibly remote time was the proper way for a *propriétaire* to greet his guests. If it had not been for his daughter, an extremely hardheaded *tricoteuse*—the inclination of *her* head was chilling and abrupt, like the downbeat of an ax—the hotel would certainly have gone bankrupt long before. It was said that this old man had not gone farther than the door of his hotel for thirty years, which was not at all difficult to believe. He looked as though the daylight would have killed him.

I did not, of course, spend much of my time in this palace. The moment I began living in French hotels I understood the necessity of French cafés. This made it rather difficult to look me up, for as soon as I was out of bed I hopefully took notebook and fountain pen off to the upstairs room of the Flore, where I consumed rather a lot of coffee and, as evening approached, rather a lot of alcohol, but did not get much writing done. But one night, in one of the cafés of St. Germain des Près, I was discovered by this New Yorker and only because we found ourselves in Paris we immediately established the illusion that we had been fast friends back in the good old U.S.A. This illusion proved itself too thin to support an evening's drinking, but by that time it was too late. I had committed myself to getting him a room in my hotel the next day, for he was living in one of the nest of hotels near the Gare St. Lazare, where, he said, the *propriétaire* was a thief, his wife a repressed nymphomaniac, the chambermaids "pigs," and the rent a crime. Americans are always talking this way about the French and so it did not occur to me that he meant what he said or that he would take into his own hands the means of avenging himself on the French Republic. It did not occur to me, either, that the means which he *did* take could possibly have brought about such dire results, results which were not less dire for being also comic-opera.

It came as the last of a series of disasters which had perhaps been made inevitable by the fact that I had come to Paris originally with a little over forty dollars in my pockets, nothing in the bank, and no grasp whatever of the French language. It developed, shortly, that I had no grasp of the French character either. I considered the French an ancient, intelligent, and cultured race, which indeed they are. I did not know, however, that ancient glories imply, at least in the middle of the present century, present fatigue and, quite probably, paranoia; that there is a limit to the role of the intelligence in human affairs; and that no people come into possession of a culture without having paid a heavy price for it. This price they cannot, of course, assess, but it is revealed in their personalities and in their institutions. The very word "institutions," from my side of the ocean, where, it seemed to me, we suffered so cruelly from the lack of them, had a pleasant ring, as of safety and order and common sense; one had to come into contact with these institutions in order to understand that they were also outmoded, exasperating, completely impersonal, and very often cruel. Similarly, the personality which had seemed from a distance to be so large and free had to be dealt with before one could see that, if it was large, it was also inflexible and, for the foreigner, full of strange, high, dusty rooms which could not be inhabited. One had, in short, to come into contact with an alien culture in order to understand that a culture was not a community basket-weaving project, nor yet an act of God; was something neither desirable nor undesirable in itself, being inevitable, being nothing more or less than the recorded and visible effects on a body of people of the vicissitudes with which they had been forced to deal. And their great men are revealed as simply another of these vicissitudes, even if, quite against their will, the brief battle of their great men with them has left them richer.

When my American friend left his hotel to move to mine, he took with him, out of pique, a bedsheet belonging to the hotel and put it in his suitcase. When he arrived at my hotel I borrowed the sheet, since my own were filthy and the chambermaid showed no sign of bringing me any clean ones, and put it on my bed. The sheets belonging to *my* hotel I put out in the hall, congratulating myself on having thus forced on the attention of the Grand Hôtel du Bac the unpleasant state of its linen. Thereafter, since, as it turned out, we kept very different hours—I got up at noon, when, as I gathered by meeting him on the stairs one day, he was only just getting in—my new-found friend and I saw very little of each other.

On the evening of the 19th I was sitting thinking melancholy thoughts about Christmas and staring at the walls of my room. I imagine that I had sold something or that someone had sent me a Christmas present, for I remember that I had a little money. In those days in Paris, though I floated, so to speak, on a sea of acquaintances, I knew almost no one. Many people were eliminated from my orbit by virtue of the fact that they had more money than I did, which placed me, in my own eyes, in the humiliating role of a free-loader; and other people were eliminated by virtue of the fact that they enjoyed their poverty, shrilly insisting that this wretched round of hotel rooms, bad food, humiliating concierges, and unpaid bills was the Great Adventure. It couldn't, however, for me, end soon enough, this Great Adventure; there was a real question in my mind as to which would end soonest, the Great Adventure or me. This meant, however, that there were many evenings when I sat in my room, knowing that I couldn't work there, and not knowing what to do, or whom to see. On this particular evening I went down and knocked on the American's door.

There were two Frenchmen standing in the room, who immediately introduced themselves to me as policemen; which did not worry me. I had got used to policemen in Paris bobbing up at the most improbable times and places, asking to see one's *carte d'identité*. These policemen, however, showed very little interest in my papers. They were looking for something else. I could not imagine what this would be and, since I knew I certainly didn't have it, I scarcely followed the conversation they were having with my friend. I gathered that they were looking for some kind of gangster and since I wasn't a gangster and knew that gangsterism was not, insofar as he had one, my friend's style, I was sure that the two policemen would presently bow and say *Merci, messieurs,* and leave. For by this time, I remember very clearly, I was dying to have a drink and go to dinner.

I did not have a drink or go to dinner for many days after this, and when I did my outraged stomach promptly heaved everything up again. For now one of the policemen began to exhibit the most vivid interest in me and asked, very politely, if he might see my room. To which we mounted, making, I remember, the most civilized small talk on the way and even continuing it for some moments after we were in the room in which there was certainly nothing to be seen but the familiar poverty and disorder of that precarious group of people of whatever age, race, country, calling, or intention which Paris recognizes as *les étudiants* and sometimes, more ironically and precisely, as *les nonconformistes.* Then he moved to my bed, and in a terrible flash, not quite an instant before he lifted the bedspread, I understood what he was looking for. We looked at the sheet, on which I read, for the first time, lettered in the most brilliant scarlet I have ever seen, the name of the hotel from which it had been stolen. It was the first time the word *stolen* entered my mind. I had certainly seen the hotel monogram the day I put the sheet on the bed. It had simply meant nothing to me. In New York I had seen hotel monograms on everything from silver to soap and towels. Taking things from New York hotels was practically a custom, though, I suddenly realized, I had never known anyone to take a *sheet.* Sadly, and without a word to me, the inspector took the sheet from the bed, folded it under his arm, and we started back downstairs. I understood that I was under arrest.

And so we passed through the lobby, four of us, two of us very clearly criminal, under the eyes of the old man and his daughter, neither of whom said a word, into the streets where a light rain was falling. And I asked, in French, "But is this very serious?"

For I was thinking, it is, after all, only a sheet, not even new.

"No," said one of them. "It's not serious."

"It's nothing at all," said the other.

I took this to mean that we would receive a reprimand at the police station and be allowed to go to dinner. Later on I concluded that they were not being hypocritical or even trying to comfort us. They meant exactly what they said. It was only that they spoke another language.

In Paris everything is very slow. Also, when dealing with the bureaucracy, the man you are talking to is never the man you have to see. The man you have to see has just gone off to Belgium, or is busy with his family, or has just discovered that he is a cuckold; he will be in next Tuesday at three o'clock, or sometime in the course of the afternoon, or possibly tomorrow, or, possibly, in the next five minutes. But if he is coming in the next five minutes he will be far too busy to be able to see you today. So that I suppose I was not really astonished to learn at the commissariat that nothing could possibly be done about us before The Man arrived in the morning. But no, we could not go off and have dinner and come back in the morning. Of course he knew that we *would* come back—that was not the question. Indeed, there was no question: we would simply have to stay there for the night.

We were placed in a cell which rather resembled a chicken coop. It was now about seven in the evening and I relinquished the thought of dinner and began to think of lunch.

I discouraged the chatter of my New York friend and this left me alone with my thoughts. I was beginning to be frightened and I bent all my energies, therefore, to keeping my panic under control. I began to realize that I was in a country I knew nothing about, in the hands of a people I did not understand at all. In a similar situation in New York I would have had some idea of what to do because I would have had some idea of what to expect. I am not speaking now of legality which, like most of the poor, I had never for an instant trusted, but of the temperament of the people with whom I had to deal. I had become very accomplished in New York at guessing and, therefore, to a limited extent manipulating to my advantage the reactions of the white world. But this was not New York. None of my old weapons could serve me here. I did not know what they saw when they looked at me. I knew very well what Americans saw when they looked at me and this allowed me to play endless and sinister variations on the role which they had assigned me; since I knew that it was, for them, of the utmost importance that they never be confronted with what, in their own personalities, made this role so necessary and gratifying to them, I knew that they could never call my hand or, indeed, afford to know what I was doing; so that I moved into every crucial situation with the deadly and rather desperate advantages of bitterly accumulated perception, of pride and contempt. This is an awful sword and shield to carry through the world, and the discovery that, in the game I was playing, I did myself a violence of which the world, at its most ferocious, would scarcely have been capable, was what had driven me out of New York. It was a strange feeling, in this situation, after a year in Paris, to discover that my weapons would never again serve me as they had.

It was quite clear to me that the Frenchmen in whose hands I found myself were no better or worse than their American counterparts. Certainly their uniforms frightened me quite as much, and their impersonality, and the threat, always very keenly felt by the poor, of violence, was as present in that commissariat as it had ever been for me in any police station. And I had seen, for example, what Paris policemen could do to Arab peanut vendors. The only difference here was that I did not understand these people, did not know what techniques their cruelty took, did not know enough about their personalities to see danger coming, to ward it off, did not know on what ground to meet it. That evening in the commissariat I was not a despised black man. They would simply have laughed at me if I had behaved like one. For them, I was an American. And here it was they who had the advantage, for that word, *Américain*, gave them some idea, far from inaccurate, of what to expect from me. In order to corroborate none of their ironical expectations I said nothing and did nothing—which was not the way any Frenchman, white or black, would have reacted. The question thrusting up from the bottom of my mind was not *what* I was, but *who*. And this question, since a *what* can get by with skill but a *who* demands resources, was my first real intimation of what humility must mean.

In the morning it was still raining. Between nine and ten o'clock a black Citroën took us off to the Ile de la Cité, to the great, gray Préfecture. I realize now that the questions I put to the various policemen who escorted us were always answered in such a way as to corroborate what I wished to hear. This was not out of politeness, but simply out of indifference—or, possibly, an ironical pity—since each of the policemen knew very well that nothing would speed or halt the machine in which I had become entangled. They knew I did not know this and there was certainly no point in their telling me. In one way or another I would certainly come out at the other side—for they also knew that being found with a stolen bedsheet in one's possession was not a crime punishable by the guillotine. (They had the advantage over me there, too, for there were certainly moments later on when I was not so sure.) If I did *not* come out at the other side—well, that was just too bad. So, to my question, put while we were in the Citroën—"Will it be over today?"—I received a "*Oui, bien sûr.*" He was not lying. As it turned out, the *procès-verbal* was over that day. Trying to be realistic, I dismissed, in the Citroën, all thoughts of lunch and pushed my mind ahead to dinner.

At the Préfecture we were first placed in a tiny cell, in which it was almost impossible either to sit or to lie down. After a couple of hours of this we were taken down to an office, where, for the first time, I encountered the owner of the bedsheet and where the *procès-verbal* took place. This was simply an interrogation, quite chillingly clipped and efficient (so that there was, shortly, no doubt in one's own mind that one *should* be treated as a criminal), which was recorded by a secretary. When it was over, this report was given to us to sign. One had, of course, no choice but to sign it, even though my mastery of written French was very far from certain. We were being held, according to the law in France, incommunicado, and all my angry demands to be allowed to speak to my embassy or to see a lawyer met with a stony "*Oui, oui. Plus tard.*" The *procès-verbal* over, we were taken back to the cell, before which, shortly, passed the owner of the bedsheet. He said he hoped we had slept well, gave a vindictive wink, and disappeared.

By this time there was only one thing clear: that we had no way of controlling the sequence of events and could not possibly guess what this sequence would be. It seemed to me, since what I regarded as the high point—the *procès-verbal*—had been passed and since the hotel-keeper was once again in possession of his sheet, that we might reasonably expect to be released from police custody in a matter of hours. We had been detained now for what would soon be twenty-four hours, during which time I had learned only that the official charge against me was *receleur*. My mental shifting, between lunch and dinner, to say nothing of the physical lack of either of these delights, was beginning to make me dizzy. The steady chatter of my friend from New York, who was determined to keep my spirits up, made me feel murderous; I was praying that some power would release us from this freezing pile of stone before the impulse became the act. And I was beginning to wonder what was happening in that beautiful city, Paris, which lived outside these walls. I wondered how long it would take before anyone casually asked, "But where's Jimmy? He hasn't been around"—and realized, knowing the people I knew, that it would take several days.

Quite late in the afternoon we were taken from our cells; handcuffed, each to a separate officer; led through a maze of steps and corridors to the top of the building; fingerprinted; photographed. As in movies I had seen, I was placed against a wall, facing an old-fashioned camera, behind which stood one of the most completely cruel and indifferent faces I had ever seen, while someone next to me and, therefore, just outside my line of vision, read off in a voice from which all human feeling, even feeling of the most base description, had long since fled, what must be called my public characteristics—which, at that time and in that place, seemed anything but that. He might have been roaring to the hostile world secrets which I could barely, in the privacy of midnight, utter to myself. But he was only reading off my height, my features, my approximate weight, my color—that color which, in the United States, had often, odd as it may sound, been my salvation—the color of my hair, my age, my nationality. A light then flashed, the photographer and I staring at each other as though there was murder in our hearts, and then it was over. Handcuffed again, I was led downstairs to the bottom of the building, into a great enclosed shed in which had been gathered the very scrapings off the Paris streets. Old, old men, so ruined and old that life in them seemed really to prove the miracle of the quickening power of the Holy Ghost—for clearly their life was no longer their affair, it was no longer even their burden, they were simply the clay which had once been touched. And men not so old, with faces the color of lead and the consistency of oatmeal, eyes that made me think of stale *café-au-lait* spiked with arsenic, bodies which could take in food and water—any food and water—and pass it out, but which could not do anything more, except possibly, at midnight, along the riverbank where rats scurried, rape. And young men, harder and crueler than the Paris stones, older by far than I, their chronological senior by some five to seven years. And North Africans, old and young, who seemed the only living people in this place because they yet retained the grace to be bewildered. But they were not bewildered by being in this shed: they were simply bewildered because they were no longer in North Africa. There was a great hole in the center of this shed, which was the common toilet. Near it, though it was impossible to get very far from it, stood an old man with white hair, eating a piece of camembert. It was at this point, probably, that thought, for me, stopped, that physiology, if one may say so, took over. I found myself incapable of saying a word, not because I was afraid I would cry but because I was afraid I would vomit. And I did not think any longer of the city of Paris but my mind flew back to that home from which I had fled. I was sure that I would never see it any more. And it must have seemed to me that my flight from home was the cruelest trick I had ever played on myself, since it had led me here, down to a lower point than any I could ever in my life have imagined—lower, far, than anything I had seen in that Harlem which I had so hated and so loved, the escape from which had soon become the greatest direction of my life. After we had been here an hour or so a functionary came and opened the door and called out our names. And I was sure that *this* was my release. But I was handcuffed again and led out of the Préfecture into the streets—it was dark now, it was still raining—and before the steps of the Préfecture stood the great police wagon, doors facing me, wide open. The handcuffs were taken off, I entered the wagon, which was peculiarly constructed. It was divided by a narrow aisle, and on each side of the aisle was a series of narrow doors. These doors opened on a narrow cubicle, beyond which was a door which opened onto another narrow cubicle: three or four cubicles, each private, with a locking door. I was placed in one of them; I remember there was a small vent just above my head which let in a little light. The door of my cubicle was locked from the outside. I had no idea where this wagon was taking me and, as it began to move, I began to cry. I suppose I cried all the way to prison, the prison called Fresnes, which is twelve kilometers outside of Paris.

For reasons I have no way at all of understanding, prisoners whose last initial is A, B, or C are always sent to Fresnes; everybody else is sent to a prison called, rather cynically it seems to me, La Santé. I will, obviously, never be allowed to enter La Santé, but I was told by people who certainly seemed to know that it was infinitely more unbearable than Fresnes. This arouses in me, until today, a positive storm of curiosity concerning what I promptly began to think of as The Other Prison. My colleague in crime, occurring lower in the alphabet, had been sent there and I confess that the minute he was gone I missed him. I missed him because he was not French and because he was the only person in the world who knew that the story I told was true.

For, once locked in, divested of shoelaces, belt, watch, money, papers, nailfile, in a freezing cell in which both the window and the toilet were broken, with six other adventurers, the story I told of *l'affaire du drap de lit* elicited only the wildest amusement or the most suspicious disbelief. Among the people who shared my cell the first three days no one, it is true, had been arrested for anything much more serious—or, at least, not serious in my eyes. I remember that there was a boy who had stolen a knitted sweater from a *monoprix*, who would probably, it was agreed, receive a six-month sentence. There was an older man there who had been arrested for some kind of petty larceny. There were two North Africans, vivid, brutish, and beautiful, who alternated between gaiety and fury, not at the fact of their arrest but at the state of the cell. None poured as much emotional energy into the fact of their arrest as I did; they took it, as I would have liked to take it, as simply another unlucky happening in a very dirty world. For, though I had grown accustomed to thinking of myself as looking upon the world with a hard, penetrating eye, the truth was that they were far more realistic about the world than I, and more nearly right about it. The gap between us, which only a gesture I made could have bridged, grew steadily, during thirty-six hours, wider. I could not make any gesture simply because they frightened me. I was unable to accept my imprisonment as a fact, even as a temporary fact. I could not, even for a moment, accept my present companions as *my* companions. And they, of course, felt this and put it down, with perfect justice, to the fact that I was an American.

There was nothing to do all day long. It appeared that we would one day come to trial but no one knew when. We were awakened at seven-thirty by a rapping on what I believe is called the Judas, that small opening in the door of the cell which allows the guards to survey the prisoners. At this rapping we rose from the floor—we slept on straw pallets and each of us was covered with one thin blanket—and moved to the door of the cell. We peered through the opening into the center of the prison, which was, as I remember, three tiers high, all gray stone and gunmetal steel, precisely that prison I had seen in movies, except that, in the movies, I had not known that it was cold in prison. I had not known that when one's shoelaces and belt have been removed one is, in the strangest way, demoralized. The necessity of shuffling and the necessity of holding up one's trousers with one hand turn one into a rag doll. And the movies fail, of course, to give one any idea of what prison food is like. Along the corridor, at seven-thirty, came three men, each pushing before him a great garbage can, mounted on wheels. In the garbage can of the first was the bread—this was passed to one through the small opening in the door. In the can of the second was the coffee. In the can of the third was what was always called *la soupe*, a pallid paste of potatoes which had certainly been bubbling on the back of the prison stove long before that first, so momentous revolution. Naturally, it was cold by this time and, starving as I was, I could not eat it. I drank the coffee—which was not coffee—because it was hot, and spent the rest of the day, huddled in my blanket, munching on the bread. It was not the French bread one bought in bakeries. In the evening the same procession returned. At ten-thirty the lights went out. I had a recurring dream, each night, a nightmare which always involved my mother's fried chicken. At the moment I was about to eat it came the rapping at the door. Silence is really all I remember of those first three days, silence and the color gray.

I am not sure now whether it was on the third or the fourth day that I was taken to trial for the first time. The days had nothing, obviously, to distinguish them from one another. I remember that I was very much aware that Christmas Day was approaching and I wondered if I was really going to spend Christmas Day in prison. And I remember that the first trial came the day before Christmas Eve.

On the morning of the first trial I was awakened by hearing my name called. I was told, hanging in a kind of void between my mother's fried chicken and the cold prison floor, "*Vous préparez. Vous êtes extrait*"—which simply terrified me, since I did not know what interpretation to put on the word "*extrait*," and since my cellmates had been amusing themselves with me by telling terrible stories about the inefficiency of French prisons, an inefficiency so extreme that it had often happened that someone who was supposed to be taken out and tried found himself on the wrong line and was guillotined instead. The best way of putting my reaction to this is to say that, though I knew they were teasing me, it was simply not possible for me to totally *dis*believe them. As far as I was concerned, once in the hands of the law in France, anything could happen. I shuffled along with the others who were *extrait* to the center of the prison, trying, rather, to linger in the office, which seemed the only warm spot in the whole world, and found myself again in that dreadful wagon, and was carried again to the Ile de la Cité, this time to the Palais de Justice. The entire day, except for ten minutes, was spent in one of the cells, first waiting to be tried, then waiting to be taken back to prison.

For I was *not* tried that day. By and by I was handcuffed and led through the halls, upstairs to the courtroom where I found my New York friend. We were placed together, both stage-whisperingly certain that this was the end of our ordeal. Nevertheless, while I waited for our case to be called, my eyes searched the courtroom, looking for a face I knew, hoping, anyway, that there was someone there who knew *me*, who would carry to someone outside the news that I was in trouble. But there was no one I knew there and I had had time to realize that there was probably only one man in Paris who could help me, an American patent attorney for whom I had worked as an office boy. He could have helped me because he had a quite solid position and some prestige and would have testified that, while working for him, I had handled large sums of money regularly, which made it rather unlikely that I would stoop to trafficking in bedsheets. However, he was somewhere in Paris, probably at this very moment enjoying a snack and a glass of wine and as far as the possibility of reaching him was concerned, he might as well have been on Mars. I tried to watch the proceedings and to make my mind a blank. But the proceedings were not reassuring. The boy, for example, who had stolen the sweater *did* receive a six-month sentence. It seemed to me that all the sentences meted out that day were excessive; though, again, it seemed that all the people who were sentenced that day had made, or clearly were going to make, crime their career. This seemed to be the opinion of the judge, who scarcely looked at the prisoners or listened to them; it seemed to be the opinion of the prisoners, who scarcely bothered to speak in their own behalf; it seemed to be the opinion of the lawyers, state lawyers for the most part, who were defending them. The great impulse of the courtroom seemed to be to put these people where they could not be seen—and not because they were offended at the crimes, unless, indeed, they were offended that the crimes were so petty, but because they did not wish to know that their society could be counted on to produce, probably in greater and greater numbers, a whole body of people for whom crime was the only possible career. Any society inevitably produces its criminals, but a society at once rigid and unstable can do nothing whatever to alleviate the poverty of its lowest members, cannot present to the hypothetical young man at the crucial moment that so-well-advertised right path. And the fact, perhaps, that the French are the earth's least sentimental people and must also be numbered among the most proud aggravates the plight of their lowest, youngest, and unluckiest members, for it means that the idea of rehabilitation is scarcely real to them. I confess that this attitude on their part raises in me sentiments of exasperation, admiration, and despair, revealing as it does, in both the best and the worst sense, their renowned and spectacular hard-headedness.

Finally our case was called and we rose. We gave our names. At the point that it developed that we were American the proceedings ceased, a hurried consultation took place between the judge and what I took to be several lawyers. Someone called out for an interpreter. The arresting officer had forgotten to mention our nationalities and there was, therefore, no interpreter in the court. Even if our French had been better than it was we would not have been allowed to stand trial without an interpreter. Before I clearly understood what was happening, I was handcuffed again and led out of the courtroom. The trial had been set back for the 27th of December.

I have sometimes wondered if I would *ever* have got out of prison if it had not been for the older man who had been arrested for the mysterious petty larceny. He was acquitted that day and when he returned to the cell—for he could not be released until morning—he found me sitting numbly on the floor, having just been prevented, by the sight of a man, all blood, being carried back to *his* cell on a stretcher, from seizing the bars and screaming until they let me out. The sight of the man on the stretcher proved, however, that screaming would not do much for me. The petty-larceny man went around asking if he could do anything in the world outside for those he was leaving behind. When he came to me I, at first, responded, "No, nothing"—for I suppose I had by now retreated into the attitude, the earliest I remember, that of my father, which was simply (since I had lost his God) that nothing could help me. And I suppose I will remember with gratitude until I die the fact that the man now insisted: "*Mais, êtes-vous sûr?*" Then it swept over me that he was going *outside* and he instantly became my first contact since the Lord alone knew how long with the outside world. At the same time, I remember, I did not really believe that he would help me. There was no reason why he should. But I gave him the phone number of my attorney friend and my own name.

So, in the middle of the next day, Christmas Eve, I shuffled downstairs again, to meet my visitor. He looked extremely well fed and sane and clean. He told me I had nothing to worry about any more. Only not even he could do anything to make the mill of justice grind any faster. He would, however, send me a lawyer of his acquaintance who would defend me on the 27th, and he would himself, along with several other people, appear as a character witness. He gave me a package of Lucky Strikes (which the turnkey took from me on the way upstairs) and said that, though it was doubtful that there would be any celebration in the prison, he would see to it that I got a fine Christmas dinner when I got out. And this, somehow, seemed very funny. I remember being astonished at the discovery that I was actually laughing. I was, too, I imagine, also rather disappointed that my hair had not turned white, that my face was clearly not going to bear any marks of tragedy, disappointed at bottom, no doubt, to realize, facing him in that room, that far worse things had happened to most people and that, indeed, to paraphrase my mother, if this was the worst thing that ever happened to me I could consider myself among the luckiest people ever to be born. He injected—my visitor—into my solitary nightmare common sense, the world, and the hint of blacker things to come.

The next day, Christmas, unable to endure my cell, and feeling that, after all, the day demanded a gesture, I asked to be allowed to go to Mass, hoping to hear some music. But I found myself, for a freezing hour and a half, locked in exactly the same kind of cubicle as in the wagon which had first brought me to prison, peering through a slot placed at the level of the eye at an old Frenchman, hatted, overcoated, muffled, and gloved, preaching in this language which I did not understand, to this row of wooden boxes, the story of Jesus Christ's love for men.

The next day, the 26th, I spent learning a peculiar kind of game, played with matchsticks, with my cell-mates. For, since I no longer felt that I would stay in this cell forever, I was beginning to be able to make peace with it for a time. On the 27th I went again to trial and, as had been predicted, the case against us was dismissed. The story of the *drap de lit*, finally told, caused great merriment in the courtroom, whereupon my friend decided that the French were "great." I was chilled by their merriment, even though it was meant to warm me. It could only remind me of the laughter I had often heard at home, laughter which I had sometimes deliberately elicited. This laughter is the laughter of those who consider themselves to be at a safe remove from all the wretched, for whom the pain of the living is not real. I had heard it so often in my native land that I had resolved to find a place where I would never hear it any more. In some deep, black, stony, and liberating way, my life, in my own eyes, began during that first year in Paris, when it was borne in on me that this laughter is universal and never can be stilled.

Ralph Ellison

On Being the Target of Discrimination

IT ISN'T NECESSARILY THROUGH ACTS OF PHYSICAL VIOLENCE—LYNCHING, MOB ATTACKS, or slaps in the face, whether experienced first-hand or by word of mouth—that a child is initiated into the contradictions of segregated democracy. Rather, it is through brief impersonal encounters, stares, vocal inflections, hostile laughter, or public reversals of private expectations that occur at the age when children are most receptive to the world and all its wonders. It is then begins the process of conscious questioning of self, family, and the social order which determines a child's attitudes, hopeful or cynical, as a citizen of this freewheeling, self-improvised society. Thus for its victims segregation is far more than a negative social condition; it is also a perspective that fosters an endless exercise of irony, and often inspires a redeeming laughter.

It got to you first at the age of six, and through your own curiosity. With kindergarten completed and the first grade ahead, you were eagerly anticipating your first day of public school. For months you had been imagining your new experience and the children, known and unknown, with whom you would study and play. But the physical framework of your imagining, an elementary school in the process of construction, lay close at hand on the block-square site across the street from your home. For over a year you had watched it rise and spread in the air to become a handsome structure of brick and stone, then seen its broad encircling grounds arrayed with seesaws, swings, and baseball diamonds. You had imagined this picture-book setting as the scene of your new experience, and when enrollment day arrived, with its grounds astir with bright colors and voices of kids like yourself, it did indeed become the site of your very first lesson in public schooling—though not within its classrooms, as you had imagined, but well outside its walls. For while located within a fairly mixed neighborhood, this new public school was exclusively for whites.

It was then you learned that you would attend a school located far to the south of your neighborhood, and that reaching it involved a journey which took you over, either directly or by way of a viaduct which arched head-spinning high above, a broad expanse of railroad tracks along which a constant traffic of freight cars, switch engines, and passenger trains made it dangerous for a child to cross. And that once the tracks were safely negotiated you continued past warehouses, factories, and loading docks, and then through a notorious red-light district where black prostitutes in brightly colored housecoats and Mary Jane shoes supplied the fantasies and needs of a white clientele. Considering the fact that you couldn't attend school with white kids, this made for a confusion that was further confounded by the giggling jokes which older boys whispered about the district's peculiar form of integration. For you it was a grown-up's mystery, but streets being no less schools than routes to schools, the district would soon add a few forbidden words to your vocabulary.

It took a bit of time to forget the sense of incongruity aroused by your having to walk *past* a school to get *to* a school, but soon you came to like your school, your teachers and most of your schoolmates. Indeed, you soon enjoyed the long walks and anticipated the sights you might see, the adventures you might encounter, and the many things not taught in school that could be learned along the way. Your school was not nearly so fine as that which faced your home, but it had its attractions. Among them its nearness to a park, now abandoned by whites, in which you picnicked and played. And there were the two tall cylindrical fire escapes on either wing of its main building down which it was a joy to lie full-length and slide, spiraling down and around three stories to the ground—providing no outraged teacher was waiting to strap your legs once you sailed out of its chute like a shot off a fireman's shovel. Besides, in your childish way you were learning that it was better to take self-selected risks and pay the price than be denied the joy or pain of risk-taking by those who begrudged your existence.

Beginning when you were four or five you had known the joy of trips to the city's zoo, but one day you would ask your mother to take you there and have her sigh and explain that it was now against the law for Negro kids to view the animals. Had someone done something bad to the animals? No. Had someone tried to steal them or feed them poison? No. Could white kids still go? Yes. So why? Quit asking questions; it's the law, and only because some white folks are out to turn this state into a part of the South.

This sudden and puzzling denial of a Saturday's pleasure was disappointing, and so angered your mother that later, after the zoo was moved north of the city, she decided to do something about it. Thus one warm Saturday afternoon with you and your baby brother dressed in your best she took you on a long streetcar ride which ended at a strange lakeside park, in which you found a crowd of noisy white people. Having assumed that you were on your way to the integrated cemetery where at the age of three you had been horrified beyond all tears or forgetting when you saw your father's coffin placed in the ground, you were bewildered. But now as your mother herded you and your brother into the park you discovered that you'd come to the zoo, and were so delighted that soon you were laughing and babbling as excitedly as the kids around you.

Your mother was pleased, and as you moved through the crowd of white parents and children she held your brother's hand and allowed as much time for staring at the cages of rare animals as either of you desired. But once your brother began to tire she herded you out of the park and toward the streetcar line. And then it happened.

Just as you reached the gate through which crowds of whites were coming and going, you had a memorable lesson in the strange ways of segregated democracy as instructed by a guard in civilian clothes. He was a white man dressed in a black suit and a white straw hat, and when he looked at the fashion in which your mother was dressed, then down to you and your brother, he stiffened, turned red in the face, and stared as though at something dangerous.

"Girl," he shouted, "where are your *white* folks!"

"*White* folks," your mother said. "What white folks? I don't *have* any white folks. I'm a Negro!"

"Now, don't you get smart with me, colored gal," the white man said. "I mean where are the white folks you come *out* here with!"

"But I just told you that I didn't come here with any white people," your mother said. "I came here with my boys . . ."

"Then what are you doing in this park," the white man said.

And now when your mother answered you could hear the familiar sound of anger in her voice.

"I'm here," she said, "because I'm a *tax-payer*, and I thought it was about time that my boys have a look at those animals. And for that I didn't *need* any *white* folks to show me the way!"

"Well," the white man said, "*I'm* here to tell you that you're breaking the law! So now you'll have to leave. Both you and your chillun too. The rule says no niggers is allowed in the zoo. That's the law and I'm enforcing it!"

"Very well," your mother said, "we've seen the animals anyway and were on our way to the streetcar line when you stopped us."

"That's fine," the white man said, "and when that car comes you be sure that you get on it, you hear? You and your chillun too!"

So it was quite a day. You had enjoyed the animals with your baby brother and had another lesson in the sudden ways good times could be turned into bad when white people looked at your color instead of *you*. But better still, you had learned something of your mother's courage and were proud that she had broken an unfair law and stood up for her right to do so. For while the white man kept staring until the streetcar arrived she ignored him and answered your brother's questions about the various animals. Then the car came with its crowd of white parents and children, and when you were entrained and rumbling home past the fine lawns and houses, your mother gave way to a gale of laughter; in which, hesitantly at first, and then with assurance and pride, you joined. And from that day the incident became the source of a family joke that was sparked by accidents, faux pas, or obvious lies. Then one of you was sure to frown and say, "Well, I think you'll have to go now, both you and your chillun too!" And the family would laugh hilariously. Discrimination teaches one to discriminate between discriminators while countering absurdity with black (Negro? Afro-American? African-American?) comedy.

When you were eight you would move to one of the white sections through which you often passed on the way to your father's grave and your truly last trip to the zoo. For now your mother was the custodian of several apartments located in a building which housed on its street floor a drug store, a tailor shop, a Piggly Wiggly market, and a branch post office. Built on a downward slope, the building had at its rear a long driveway which led from the side street past an empty lot to a group of garages in which the apartments' tenants stored their cars. Built at an angle with wings facing north and east, the structure supported a servant's quarters which sat above its angle like a mock watchtower atop a battlement, and it was there that you now lived.

Reached by a flight of outside stairs, it consisted of four small rooms, a bath, and a kitchen. Windows on three of its sides provided a view across the empty frontage to the street, of the backyards behind it, and of the back wall and windows of the building in which your mother worked. It was quite comfortable but you secretly disliked the idea of your mother living in service and missed your friends who now lived far away. Nevertheless, the neighborhood was pleasant, served by a substation of the streetcar line, and marked by a variety of activities which challenged your curiosity. Even its affluent alleys were more exciting to explore than those of your old neighborhood, and the one white friend you were to acquire in the area lived nearby.

This friend was a brilliant but sickly boy who was tutored at home, and with him you shared your new interest in building radios, a hobby at which he was quite skilled. Your friendship eased your loneliness and helped dispel some of the mystery and resentment imposed by segregation. Through access to his family, headed by an important Episcopalian minister, you learned more about whites and thus about yourself. With him you could make comparisons that were not so distorted by the racial myths which obstructed your thrust toward self-perception; compare their differences in taste, discipline, and manners with those of Negro families of comparable status and income; observe variations between your friend's boyish lore and your own, and measure his intelligence, knowledge, and ambitions against your own. For you this was a most important experience and a rare privilege, because up to now the prevailing separation of the races had made it impossible to learn how you and your Negro friends compared with boys who lived on the white side of the color line. It was said by word of mouth, proclaimed in newsprint, and dramatized by acts of discriminatory law that you were inferior. You were barred from vying with them in sports games, competing in the classroom or the world of art. Yet what you saw, heard, and smelled of them left irrepressible doubts, so you ached for objective proof, for a fair field of testing.

Even your school's proud marching band was denied participation in the statewide music contests, so popular at the time, as though so airy and earth-transcending an art as music would be contaminated if performed by musicians of different races.

Which was especially disturbing because after the father of a friend who lived next door in your old neighborhood had taught you the beginner's techniques required to play valved instruments, you had decided to become a musician. Then shortly before moving among whites your mother had given you a brass cornet, which in the isolation of the servant's quarters you practiced hours on end. But you yearned to play with other musicians and found none available. Now you lived less than a block from a white school with a famous band, but there was no one in the neighborhood with whom to explore the mysteries of the horn. You could hear the school band's music and watch their marching, but joining in making the thrilling sounds was impossible. Nor did it help that you owned the scores to a few of their marches and could play with a certain facility and fairly good tone. So there, surrounded by sounds but unable to share a sound, you went it alone. You turned yourself into a one-man band.

You played along as best you could with the phonograph, read the score to *The Carnival of Venice* while listening to Del Steigers executing triple-tongue variations on its themes; played the trumpet parts of your bandbook's marches while humming in your head the supporting voices of horns and reeds. And since your city was a seedbed of Southwestern jazz you played Kansas City riffs, bugle calls, and wha-wha-muted imitations of blues singers' pleas. But none of this made up for your lack of fellow musicians. Then, late one Saturday afternoon when your mother and brother were away, and when you had dozed off while reading, you awoke to the nearby sound of live music. At first you thought you were dreaming, and then that you were listening to the high school band, but that couldn't be the source because instead of floating over building tops and bouncing off wall and windowpane, the sounds you heard rose up, somewhat muffled, from below.

With that you ran to a window which faced the driveway, and looking down through the high windowpane of the lighted post office you could see the metal glint of instruments. Then you were on your feet and down the stairs, keeping to the shadows as you drew close and peeped below. There you looked down upon a room full of men and women postal workers who were playing away at a familiar march. It was like the answer to a silent prayer because you could tell by the sound that they were beginners like yourself, and the covers of the thicket of bandbooks revealed that they were of the same set as yours. For a while you listened and hummed along, unseen but shaking with excitement in the dimming twilight. Then, hardly before the idea formed in your head, you were skipping up the stairs to grab your cornet, lyre, and bandbook and hurtling down again to the drive.

For a while you listened, hearing the music come to a pause and the sound of the conductor's voice. Then came a rap on a music stand and once again the music. Now turning to the march by the light from the window, you snapped score to lyre, raised horn to lip, and began to play, at first silently tonguing the notes through the mouthpiece and then, carried away with the thrill of stealing a part of the music, you tensed your diaphragm and blew. As you played, keeping time with your foot on the concrete drive, you realized that you were a better cornetist than some in the band, and grew bold in the pride of your sound. Now in your mind you were marching along a downtown street to the flying of flags, the tramping of feet, and the cheering of excited crowds. At last by an isolated act of brassy cunning you had become a member of the band.

Yes, but unfortunately you then let yourself become so carried away that you forgot to listen for the conductor's instructions which you were too high and hidden to see. Suddenly the music faded and you opened your ears to the fact that you were now rendering a lonely solo in the startled quietness. Before you could fully return to reality there came the sound of table legs across a floor and a rustle of movement, ending in the appearance of a white startled face in the opened window. Then you heard a man's voice exclaim, "I'll be damn, it's a little nigger!" Whereupon you took off like quail at the sound of sudden shotgun fire.

Next thing you knew, you were up the stairs and on your bed, crying away in the dark your guilt and embarrassment. You cried and cried, asking yourself how you could have been so lacking in pride as to shame yourself and your entire race by butting in where you weren't wanted. And this just to make some amateur music. To this you had no answers, but then and there you made a vow that it would never happen again. Then, slowly, slowly, as you lay in the dark, your earlier lessons in the absurd nature of racial relations came to your aid, and suddenly you found yourself laughing, both at the way you'd run away and the shock you'd caused by joining unasked in the music.

Then you could hear yourself intoning in your eight-year-old's imitation of a white Southern accent. "Well, boy, you broke the law, so you have to go, and that means you and your chillun too!"

Shirley Abbott

from Womenfolks

THAT OLD-TIME RELIGION

Anybody who grows up in the South may have to reckon, some time or another, with being born again. When I was a child, the religious fervor of my mother's family had faded to a phantom of its old self. They did not testify about the love of Jesus or shout in unknown tongues on Sunday mornings or even read the Bible at night and say grace at table. Yet they had not quite shaken off all ties with the hard-shell faith of the backwoods.

Most people I knew went to church, even if they omitted standing up and hollering. Occasionally they would go to a revival meeting and allow themselves to be shaken by it. And if you asked them, they'd tell you it was a sin to dance and smoke and drink, even though they did all these things once in a while. They still believed in heaven and hell and in the stark truths of the Bible, though they had quit reading it. Least of all had any of them questioned the foundation of all fundamentalist doctrine: that getting to heaven was a matter of one lone, orgasmic confrontation between the soul and Jesus. After that, even if the fleshly self insisted on visiting honky-tonks or breaking half the Ten Commandments, the soul within would one day return to righteousness, for it could never be lost.

My father, transplanted Yankee that he was, held the Baptists and their ilk in contempt. With his selective affinity for Southern culture, he slung the Baptists into some nether category of ignoramuses, along with people who put cow-dung poultices on broken bones and believed in hoop snakes. His inclination, when it came to my religious training, was to school me in Methodism. He didn't mean some walleyed, floor-stomping Methodism that had moved to town from the mountains. He meant something entirely un-Southern, with no taint of emotionalism. Something urban. A church that christened babies and sprinkled the forelocks of new members and had a minister with a tangle of DD's and LL's after his name who quoted Sir Walter Scott and Wordsworth and Browning and in any case, at the end of the sermon, did not launch into an unseemly tantrum about walking on down the aisle to get saved.

But my father's desire to turn me into a respectable Christian was much too slight to energize him, let alone me. How could he expect me to take Sunday school seriously when most often on Sunday afternoons, after we had gorged ourselves on fried chicken and cream gravy, Daddy read aloud to me from Gibbon? On the Lord's day he was almost deliberate about picking passages on the early Christians and how they had made a nuisance of themselves to the Romans. Edward Gibbon perceives the saintly band as a burden borne with commendable patience by the Roman upper classes, much as in his day the upper crust had to put up with Wesleyans and Luddites. This was the one time my father chose not to take the side of the underdog. He did not construe Christians as underdogs. They were, he knew very well, constantly trying to deprive him of his livelihood. To the Hot Springs Protestant Church Council, open gambling was the the work of the anti-Christ, and they would have liked to see all bookies in jail. Daddy could deposit me all brushed and ruffled on the front steps of the First Methodist Church as many Sundays as he cared to, but I never forgot which side he was on when it came to lions versus Christians.

Still, I was too young to join him in agnosticism, and when I slipped out of the Methodist net (my absence unfeelingly ignored by them), I fell heavily into the Baptist one. This was not because my mother had pushed me toward her ancestral faith, but because the

Baptists in a small Southern town make it their business to pick up stragglers. My mother, at least while I lived under her roof, never went to church regularly. Yet she had come out of the raw old tradition. I had snapshots of her on baptizing day—forty youngsters in white sheets, up to their waists in the North Fork River and scared to death, about to be dunked by a preacher who looked seven feet tall and had hands the size of shovels. When I was a child, however, something about religion embarrassed her. Most other mothers I knew went dutifully from Sunday school to prayer meeting to Circle (where they talked about foreign missions) to choir practice to Sunday vespers, and they hauled their daughters along with them. I suspect that the women went for one another's company more than Jesus' sake, but in any case, they went.

And I began to go, too, about the time I turned thirteen—the classic moment for the fundamentalist God to bring in the sheaves. Of course, my attraction to religion had something sexual in it. The preacher at the Baptist Church, ambivalently named Vergil Luther Radley, was a massive, good-looking man of about thirty-five, swarthy, brown-eyed, broad-faced, thin-mouthed, and powerfully muscled. The effect was Laurence Olivier as Othello. Brother Radley's suits were white, his Bible black. (Surely he switched to black broadcloth in the winter, but I recall only the white.) Even if he had not been young and handsome, he was a man. Not just a man, but an actor, a dancer, a performer. To young virgins such as I, he projected an almost lurid masculinity, which I loved—not knowing why or what—but knew I oughtn't to be sensing. Most Baptist ministers kept their masculinity tucked so far back that one would have sworn they were neuters. Not Brother Radley—he flaunted it, at least from the safety of the pulpit. And under his pastorate, the church flourished.

Working with the intelligence of a *premier danseur* or a quarterback running a complicated play, he could in three quarters of an hour work himself up to the classic Baptist frenzy. To the unpracticed eye, it might look uncontrolled, but one quickly learned what to expect. I relished the performance. First, with exaggerated calm, he read the Scriptures and prayed—maybe it was Saul on the road to Damascus. Before long he'd be crouching behind the lectern, the fiery black eyes staring just over the top of it as he gripped the front edge in his right hand. "Saul, Saul," he would cry out, as though the heavens had parted, "Why persecutest thou Me?" Then he'd thrust his long fingers into his breast pocket, rip out a white handkerchief, flourish it, tamp his agonized forehead with it, and wad it up, while at the end of his other arm the Bible flapped as if he meant to lob it into the top balcony. The baritone voice, rich as chocolate, sometimes bubbled with a sob. All this gesture he enhanced by darting to and fro, leaping up, slapping the Book. And as if a gale were blowing across the altar, the thick swatch of his coal-dark hair swept across his countenance and fell into his eyes.

Finally, stepping out from behind the lectern, planting his feet on the high ground and showing himself full length to the congregation, he would raise his hands skyward and cry out, "Don't remain in the darkness of sin denying Jesus. Come, come to your savior. Get up and come on down to Him and be saved." Then Brother Radley would open his arms to receive us, while the piano began to strum, and the choir murmured, "Just as I am, O Lamb of God, I come," or "There is a fountain filled with blood, drawn from Immanuel's veins." Many would be weeping aloud, and I always trembled in my pew. I had no idea what feelings—apart from the spiritual—he was playing upon in me, and neither, I believe, did he. It was all part of the preaching art, and he was good at it. I am certain that he was a rigorously faithful husband with never a roving thought.

On Sunday morning, weak-kneed and sobbing, I did go down that aisle for him. Yes, and he folded me in those white-clad arms, briefly pressed my cheek against his heaving hest, cupped my chin in his hand, and looked into my eyes. At his gentle command, I bowed my head and listened to him pray for me, thank God for me, thank Jesus that this fine young girl had come to accept Him as her Savior and Lord.

The trouble was that I was faking. Oh, I signed the card. I asked to be immersed. I sat down on the front pew and prayed with all my strength, waiting for the proper psychic jolt. Hanging on. Tensing my muscles. Even, I recall, uttering a groan or two. But it didn't happen. Apart from my now subsiding stage fright, I didn't feel any different than I had before. Soon after my baptism in the comfortably warm font, I was elected president of my Sunday school class. Lent my enthusiastic voice to the choir. Resolved to remain a nonsmoker and a pure teetotaler. Was outspoken in my disapproval of dancing—another adult skill I hadn't quite acquired. But even as I stood in the baptismal tank with a white sheet over my swimsuit, even as Brother Radley put one hand behind my shoulders, squeezed my nose shut with the other, and laid me back in the water, I knew I was a fraud.

I didn't give up hope. Maybe I could get right with God. All it took, they said, was "conviction of sin"; that is, I had to believe I deserved to go to hell, and I did believe it. And then I had to believe Jesus could save me. And I believed that, too. But for all that, it was like memorizing the rules of golf and then, out on the green, discovering that it couldn't be done.

My profoundest struggle to be born again came a couple of years later when I decided, to my father's disgust, to spend two weeks at the Baptist church camp at Siloam Springs, in the northwestern, almost primeval, corner of Arkansas. Over the two-lane roads of the day, it was at least a five-hour drive from home. Twelve or thirteen girls and three or four boys were going to church camp, the lot of us meticulously chaperoned by a pair of young marrieds who had temporarily foresworn the privileges of matrimony in order to shepherd us to Siloam. We set off from the church parking lot early one June morning in an ancient gray Sunday school bus with "Second Baptist" in big black letters on the side. The seats had no springs, and the hot wind cut scathingly through the open windows. We sang all the way— hymn books had been provided—which kept us occupied and drowned out the ominous knocks in the engine and the horrid screechings of the transmission when, on the slightest upgrade, the driver had to downshift.

Siloam, in the New Testament, is the spring outside Jerusalem where Jesus works a miracle: he sends a blind man there to wash his eyes and recover his sight. My eyes, as I approached Siloam, were blind in some sense, too. The camp site was a leafy mountain glade traversed by a brook. In the center, green and well-tended, was a kind of campus with a large tent pitched over a wooden amphitheater built on the slope of a hill. On the other side of this lawn was a white-washed dining hall. The dormitories teetered at a distance on the surrounding hills, on stilts. Boys were well separated from the girls. Instead of toilets, there were latrines, and water gushed (sometimes) from the end of a handpump. Swimming was not allowed since one needed a bathing suit to swim, and flesh was ipso facto immoral. Shorts and slacks were also forbidden, at least for the girls. Even sundresses were classed as not nice. We slept in cots in the screened-in dormitories and had no semblance of privacy—no possibility of reading or writing letters in bed. No books. No telephones. Not even some small crossroads Jerusalem to walk to and spend a quarter at the country store. Siloam was all there was.

At six we arose, dressed beside our cots, washed our faces at the pump, and heard an hour of preaching before breakfast. Afterward there were Bible classes, followed by more preaching. Lunch was at noon, and then we had a free hour before crafts classes. We made earbobs out of shells. Supper began at five. The dining room was far too small, and we languished, starving, in long lines, relieving the tedium with a lot of nervous adolescent flirting and raucous choruses of hymns. The meals consisted of canned vegetables, along with fried potatoes, hot dogs (limp), hamburgers (fried thin and crisp), huge stacks of white bread, and gluey fruit pies. Fortunately food was irrelevant to most of us.

Preaching began again just after supper and usually lasted until ten. This was the real service. At morning and noon the preachers and song leaders were most often students from some local Bible college, but at night we had the full professional complement, including what must have been the highest-stepping, loudest revival preacher in Arkansas. He frightened me. Brother Radley was always terrifying enough, with his hoarse invocations of hellfire and his implicit contempt for most human activities conducted outside sanctuary walls. But at least he was a D.D., and he had those dark eyes. This red-faced evangelist made Radley look like an Episcopalian rector. In my inmost heart, he aroused no feeling of tenderness.

He shouted, strutted, and stamped, described all the torments of hell, including pincers and demons jamming the redhot picks right into you, under your fingernails. He claimed that right here in this fine camp half the young people who thought they were saved *weren't*. If we were really saved, we'd be down here on our hands and knees at the altar, dedicating our lives to Christian service. We'd be pledging ourselves to become music directors, especially all us talented girls, or looking to marry ministers and be good helpmeets to them, or we'd be thinking about foreign missions. We'd be searching our souls for a vocation and praying to God. Instead, what were we doing? Unmindful of our immortal souls, according to him, we were strolling off into the darkness together in mixed couples, sitting down, boy next to girl, on benches at nightfall, not even bothering to come into the tent for the service. It turned his stomach to have to say it. (I had myself somewhat wistfully observed a pair of bench sitters: a crew-cut youth holding the hand of a girl whose blond perfection clearly paralyzed him. But they said he was a future preacher, and she was his betrothed.) Everybody else squirmed when he said this, as though guilty of multiple fornication. The counsellors looked stricken. I was relieved. This was the only charge of his that failed to nail me to the wall.

As the days went on, and the preaching got hotter, my soul festered. I was overwhelmed by my unholy state. I pleaded with the Lord to flood my soul with the right feelings. How could anybody want so desperately to be born again and not be able to slip through? The preacher said nobody had ever been turned away. But in addition to all this angst, I loathed standing in lines for meals. I yearned for a real bath. It stayed mercilessly hot, and it never rained. The mosquitoes finally died of the drought. I missed my mother, my books, my own bed. And in the middle of my deepest prayers my eyes would fill with pictures of strolling couples, and I would yearn to be led off into the twilight by one of those bad, backsliding boys.

Alas, there were no brief encounters. Life in the gulag went on—but only for its term. On the last evening, supper turned out to be ham, green beans, and potato salad—truly a banquet after what had gone before. I ate big helpings of everything, in spite of a faint metallic edge in the meat. I wondered why the milk was warm, and drank water instead. Then I went cheerfully off to the meeting. I knew they had cranked up for a coda, and if Jesus didn't claim me tonight, He never would. Tonight I meant to get religion, or else I'd bow out.

We sang more hymns than usual, and the preachers, as expected, painted hell as hotter than usual. When at last we stood for the invitation, I discovered I was so giddy I had to hang on to the back of the folding chair in front of me. "Amazing grace, how sweet the sound, that saved a wretch like me. I once was lost but now am found, was blind but now I see." Blind but now I see. The words scorched me, seared me, as though I had not previously understood the English language and now miraculously did. I felt faint, but someone caught my arm, and I didn't fall. Instead, my transfiguration began. The tears ran, the light under the tent turned a vivid yellow, and sobbing loudly, I battled my way down the rows and joined the throng that by now was pressing toward the altar. This was it. I had done it. *We* had done it. I felt a surge of joy that could only be the certifiable, genuine thing. I quaked and sweated. When at last some toiler in the vineyards finally led me to a chair, I signed two cards, one professing my faith in the Lord and testifying to my salvation and another stating my intention to become a missionary in Africa.

That night I twitched upon my cot—one cannot thrash on a couch so hard and narrow—trying to control my sense of elated dislocation, wishing I could sleep but disturbed by technicolor dreams whenever I did drop off. At dawn I got up and read the Bible—as the preacher had admonished us newborns to do. I drank the pump water with a drunkard's thirst and settled down to Revelations. But the words uncoupled themselves from one another on the page, and I could extract no meaning from them.

Bewildered and exhausted, I dressed and packed, then went down to wait for breakfast. Today the morning service was omitted. Bus time was eight. I had to sit down on the ground while waiting in line, and then found I could not eat. Was this rebirth? I wept waiting for the gray bus to roll up. I thought about the Africans. I figured they'd be standing in a line waiting for me, and what would I tell them? I'd be real nice. I'd hold the babies and not make a fuss if the women didn't wear blouses. Everybody would love me. Where would the mission board send me? The Congo? Nigeria? I'd go wherever they said.

The bus ride down from Siloam was as jolting and hot as the trip up, but this time nobody felt like singing. I stretched out on the long padded bench in the back of the bus and slept. I woke, occasionally, and remembered what my father had told me one time about certain tropical parasites that build their homes in people's muscles, just below the skin. I thought about leeches and tsetse flies. Kraits. Bugs that burrowed into your eyeballs and made you blind. Was blind but now I see. They liked us to come back from camp rejoicing, so our counsellors woke us up in time for a weak chorus of "That Old Time Religion" as we rounded the corner and stopped in front of the church. Brother Radley, his dark face set into a smile, was waiting to receive us. I descended from the bus, shook his hand, and wobbled into the arms of my father and mother.

I had food poisoning, of course. It set in explosively just as my anxious mother led me inside the back door. The retching was over in a few hours, but the fever lasted several days. I couldn't remember ever being so sick. I slept as if drugged for forty-eight hours. When I revived and recalled that I was now among the elect, I began to read brief passages of Charles Sheldon's *In His Steps*, which somebody gave me the night of the cataclysm. The notion of the book, which I later learned is one of the all-time best-sellers, is that before doing or saying anything, one must ask oneself whether Jesus would have done or said it, and how.

Would Jesus have drunk the glass of ginger ale my mother had just given me? Was there a Baptist position on soda pop? Mother was reading aloud from the *Arkansas Gazette*. An item on an inside page reported an epidemic of food poisoning among teen-agers around the state, which had been traced to a failure of refrigeration at Siloam Springs Baptist Church Camp. Perhaps half the five hundred campers and staff had been affected, but no deaths had been reported. "So," I thought, lapsing quickly into my rationalist mode, "the buggers let the food go bad and then fed it to us anyhow." Christlike once more, I forgave them. As my strength came back, I ceased asking Jesus about every breath I took. My heart unburdened itself of unsaved souls in the Congo and Nigeria. My hard-won piety was all gone, along with the salmonella. I continued to go to church a few years more, but if I had been reborn at Siloam, it wasn't as a Baptist.

What I did not realize was that I had had a dangerous brush with history. Years later, in search of something else, I came across a report of an 1830s camp meeting. A great revival was sweeping the American frontier in those days, from Indiana to Kentucky to Tennessee. The reporter was Frances Trollope, the English traveller whose *Domestic Manners of the Americans*, published in 1832, was a fair account of what ruffians a brand new people can be. The food was better, and the preaching wilder in her day, but Mrs. Trollope could just as well have been reporting from Siloam Springs.

"It was in the course of this summer," she wrote, "that I found the opportunity I had long wished for, of attending a camp meeting . . . in a wild district on the confines of Indiana. The prospect of passing a night in the backwoods . . . was by no means agreeable, but I screwed my courage to the proper pitch."

When she reached the spot "on the verge of an unbroken forest," she found tents of various sizes pitched in a circle, including one for blacks. [Siloam was lily-white of course, but the early frontier Baptists and Methodists welcomed everybody.] From every tent came the sounds of "praying, preaching, singing and lamentation." What caught her eye at once was a handsome youth of about eighteen with his arms round a disheveled-looking girl, "her features working with the most violent agitation." A "tall, trim figure in black" was praying and preaching, and the young man and woman soon fell forward, twitching on the straw floor of the tent. In every tent was the same scene: "All were strewn with straw, and the distorted figures that we saw kneeling, sitting and lying among it, joined to the woeful and compulsive cries, gave to each the air of a cell in Bedlam."

"Above a hundred persons, nearly all females, came forward, uttering howlings and groans so terrible that I shall never cease to shudder when I recall them. They appeared to draw each other forward, and on the word being given, 'let us pray,' they all fell forward on their knees, but this posture was soon changed for others that permitted greater scope for the convulsive movements of their limbs; and they were soon all lying on the ground in an indescribable confusion of heads and legs . . . I felt sick with horror.

"Many of these wretched creatures were beautiful young females. The preachers moved among them at once exciting and soothing their agonies. I saw the insidious lips approach the cheeks of the unhappy girls; I heard the murmured confessions of the poor victims, and I watched their tormentors, breathing into their ears consolations that tinged the pale cheek with red."

The praying and shouting went on all night. One woman shouted, over and over, "I will hold fast to Jesus, I never will let him go; if they take me to hell, I will still hold him fast, fast, fast."

But then to Mrs. Trollope's admitted astonishment, after a brief rest at dawn, "I saw the whole camp as joyously and eagerly employed in preparing and devouring their most substantial breakfasts as if the night had been passed in dancing; and I marked many a fair but pale face, that I recognized as a demoniac of the night, simpering beside a swain, to whom she carefully administered hot coffee and eggs. The preaching saint and the howling sinners seemed alike to relish this mode of recruiting their strength."

Ending her account, Mrs. Trollope makes a tart remark about the large amounts of money hauled in by the preachers, to be spent, presumably, on Bibles, tracts, and, she snorts, "all other religious purposes." Her sympathy with the camp meeting mentality was slight. Yet she caught all the essentials. Not merely the hysteria of the women and the shouts of the preachers, but the sexuality of it—of which she vigorously disapproved. She dimly sensed the sociability; it gave the eighteen-year-olds a chance to do some serious courting. She seemed not to grasp that on the frontier this was the one true form of recreation available. It terrified her to see the people jump and shout, let alone roll around on the green earth. Then to her astonishment, what had appeared to be mass psychosis vanished with the rising sun. Saints and sinners had a decent breakfast, and Mrs. Trollope went elsewhere. So, no doubt, did everybody else, for they all had other business to look after. One cannot shout and tremble indefinitely—every party comes to an end. So, having completed a ritual that was to serve the purposes of country folk for at least another century—and in particular, I believe, the purposes of women—they hitched their teams to the wagons and drove home.

Hayden Carruth

Country Matters

Identity

FOR FORTY YEARS OR MORE MY LITERARY COLLEAGUES—WRITERS, CRITICS, EDITORS—HAVE referred to me as, in effect, a "farmer-poet." I've resented this term because almost always it has insinuated a certain degree of latent condescension, but this is a personal matter and doesn't need to be written about. What I'd like to do here is simply set the record straight—briefly, I hope humbly, and perhaps usefully. If accuracy and honesty are necessary to the arts, as I've always tried to insist, then this is a matter of some importance. Moreover showing how far artistic life now has drifted away from country life may be generally desirable. I think it is.

I am not a farmer. I never have been. In the scale of country life farmers are the elite, the landholders, the employers. Their social, political, and even aesthetic attitudes go a long way toward establishing the tone of rural existence, just as their economic and practical activities establish its material base. A few farmers are women, a few are men, but most are couples. They are mutually and equally engaged in the thousands—literally thousands—of tasks and skills required to run a farm through its seasonal changes: barnwork, fieldwork, yardwork, housework; garden work, orchard work, woods work; cooking, harvesting, and preserving; tending the hens and ducks; supervising the help—the list is variable and endless. The couples work together because they have to: otherwise the work would never be done. They are people of substance, as we say. Workers, yes, but also proprietors. And of necessity they are also people of intelligence and experience. They are responsible. They are, or at least they once were, determinative in the national consciousness.

Granted, most agricultural communities have a center, a downtown, which may be presided over by the banker and his wife, a few shopkeepers and teachers, a Catholic priest and a Protestant minister, perhaps a doctor and a lawyer, maybe even a librarian. These are the town-dwellers, few in number but often noisy, sometimes snooty. They give themselves airs. But they depend on the farmers, and in a proper community this is understood.

The rest of the country people, the nonfarmers who live outside the town, are the scroungers. They hunt and fish and wrest their livings from the soil as best they can. They have gardens. They work for the farmers, often as part-time help. They work on the road gangs, and in the old days they worked on the railroads and canals. They cut pulp in the woods; they raise a pig or two; they mow the banker's lawn; they work in the gravel pits and quarries; they whittle wooden Indian maidens for tourists and duck decoys for hunters and collectors; they make quilts and baskets; they eat fiddleheads, lambs' quarters, and milkweed in season. In the spring they work in sugarhouses, and in the fall in cider mills. They shovel snow, sand, gravel, stones, and shit.

They are full of country lore and rural speech. They know that when the yellow jackets make their nests up high, the snow will be momentous in the coming winter. They know that a green Christmas means a full graveyard at Easter. They know that the night of the full moon is always clear and cold.

In the South these people are called poor white trash, but in the North we have no equivalent, which is perhaps our good fortune. At any rate these are the people among whom I have lived and worked. In northern Vermont my holding was eleven acres, mostly nonarable, and a five-room, jerry-built house: no barn, no smithy, no toolshed. I had a small garage, a woodshed, a henhouse, and a shack where I did my writing. In rural upstate New York, where I live now, I own about twenty acres and another five-room house. These are not farms, not anywhere near. Farms are all around, of course, big ones and small, prosperous and impoverished, some working and some abandoned. But trailers, double-wides, and hovels are all around too. The extent of the rural slum ought to be obvious to anyone who takes a drive off the interstate. That's where I live.

Some farmers have liked me and appreciated the help I could give them in their work. Others disliked me and thought I was incompetent. In neither case did the facts that I had a college degree and wrote poetry in my spare time have much to do with the way I was received. A little, but not much. Mostly I was looked upon as a country jack, a guy who could do rough carpentry, help with the haying, milk cows and spread manure, clean a carburetor and repair a broken electrical fixture. I could sweat a copper joint. I sold eggs to my neighbors and hauled wood in my old 4 × 4 pickup. Sometimes I and my truck were hired to make deliveries to outlying farms in winter.

Thousands and thousands like me are living in the remote hills throughout northern North America. Many of us are inbred, brain-damaged, and schizophrenic, but many of us are healthy too. All of us are socially déclassé, to say the least.

The point here is that we are unknown. As the population of the United States has concentrated more and more in the cities, as the common entertainments have catered more and more to urban tastes, as politics has clung more and more to big business and the corporate capitalists, country people in general have been pushed out of the picture. But farmers, the landowners, still have a voice, though a small one; and they are still recognized. The rural underclass, on the other hand, has disappeared. For the vast preponderance of the American populace it simply doesn't exist.

Thoreau was a country bum. So was Robert Frost. So in her origin was even so elegant a person as Louise Bogan, and it shows in her work. People who came from the underclass or chose to assimilate themselves to it have been among the most perceptive in our history. And the reason is simple: the rural underclass is the closest to the land. Living right there in the muck and misery of it. They know more about nature than the naturalists because they know it in their lives, moment to moment. They know it accurately. And if, once in a blue moon, one of them writes about it, that writing will be as fundamental as Genesis.

Necessity in much of my life has forced me to live among these people. I have been a rural communist with a small *c*. At the limit of my life I hope I'll be forgiven if I insist, briefly, on my identity. That is to say, right now.

I Wish I Could Shimmy

People say nowadays that I am agoraphobic because I'm unwilling to fly to Ireland or San Francisco. Actually it's true; this is what a number of people have told me. But they don't know what they're talking about: they don't have an inkling.

Agoraphobia is when a stranger enters the house and you go to the attic and lie down with your face pressed into the darkest corner, under the slanting slats of the roof. It's the scream lurking in your gorge, so ready to burst that the least noise above a cat's purr makes you tremble: when the marching band from the high school practices in the street outside you sit in the back of the closet, when the March wind lashes the treetops at night you crawl behind the sofa. Agoraphobia is when every night at 2:00 A.M. for five years—that's 1,825 nights—you go out loaded with Thorazine to walk in the street beneath the dark, blank windows of the houses on either side, and you never get more than a hundred yards from your door. Agoraphobia is when you cannot say hello to your oldest friend on the phone. It is when you can converse only with your cat. It is when writing a line of poetry on paper is like squeezing hardened glue from a tube. It is when related phobias become determinative: you cannot climb to the second rung of a step-ladder without vertigo, you cannot walk into a room whose ceiling is six inches lower than the ceiling of your own room without cowering and trembling. It is when you shake like a sycamore leaf in the breeze whenever you are left alone in the house. It is when you smoke six packs of cigarettes a day. It is when you order them by the gross from the mail-order house and pay for them with borrowed money.

Agoraphobia is when night after night in loathing, in dreams or awake, you fuck yourself. Agoraphobia is when you breathe and eat the dust of oblivion.

Ten years later, recovering, you take 2,000 milligrams of Thorazine and step out of your brother's car at the curb. You walk across the sidewalk and enter the drugstore; you stand at the soda counter; you order a Coke; you drink it. Then you run for the car again. Coca-Cola is the most awful medicine in the world.

A few unfortunates will understand these words and will add to them their own horrifications. The rest of the world, the vast populace—the millions and billions, I guess—will find them only nonsense, the sheerest and most dismissible. Yet these words are, in fact, representative of the materiality of a large part of their author's life, a part that has deeply though covertly biased the rest.

> I wish I could shimmy like my sister Kate.
> She shakes it like jelly on a plate.
> My mama wanted to know last night
> Why all the boys treat Kate so nice.
> Everybody in our neighborhood
> Knows she can shake it and that's understood.
> I may be late but I'll be up to date
> When I can shake it, shake it, shake it like Kate,
> When I can shimmy like my sister Kate.

Phillip Lopate

The Dead Father
A Remembrance of Donald Barthelme

DONALD BARTHELME HAD A SQUARISH BEARD THAT MADE HIM LOOK SOMEWHAT AMISH and patriarchal, an effect enhanced by his clean-shaven upper lip. It took me a while to register that he had a beard but no mustache; and once I did, I could not stop wondering what sort of "statement" he was trying to make. On the one hand, it connoted Lincolnesque rectitude and dignity, like that of the ex–Surgeon General, C. Everett Koop. On the other hand, it seemed a double message: bearded and shaven, severe and roguish, having it both ways. Finally I got up the nerve to ask him, in a kidding way, why he shaved his mustache. He told me that he couldn't grow one because he'd had a cancerous growth removed from his lip. This reply made me aware of all I didn't, probably would never, know about the man, and of my inclination to misjudge him.

I loved to watch Donald. In a way, I could never get enough of him (which is something one says about a person who always withholds a part of himself. I know, because it has been said about me). We worked together for the last eight years of his life, and were close colleagues, friends, almost-friends—which was it? I found Barthelme to be an immensely decent, generous, courtly, and yet finally unforthcoming man. He was difficult to approach, partly because I (and I was not alone here) didn't know what to do with his formidable sadness, partly because neither did he. Barthelme would have made a good king: he had the capacity of Shakespearian tragic monarchs to project a large, self-isolating presence.

The combination of his beard, bulk, and steel-rimmed eye-glasses gave him a stern Ahab appearance that he was perfectly happy to let intimidate on occasion—only to soften it with a warm glint in his eye, like a ship's captain putting his trembling crew at ease. Having read Barthelme's whimsical miniatures, I had expected a smaller, more mercurial, puckish man, certainly not this big-shouldered, hard-drinking, John Wayne type. I couldn't get over the discrepancy between his physical solidity and the filigreed drollness of his art. Somewhere locked inside that large cowman's frame must have been a mischievous troll; and I kept stealing glances at Donald to see if the little man would put in an appearance. As time went by, however, I learned to read his jeweled sentences in the manly baritone my ear came to identify as intrinsically Barthelmean, and the sense of contradiction all but disappeared. It became natural that our fin de siècle exhaustion and cultural despair should be enunciated by a tall Texan with cowboy boots.

⚬ ⚬ ⚬

I had been teaching in the University of Houston's creative writing program for a year—the program, started by two poets, Cynthia Macdonald and Stanley Plumly, had recruited me from New York in 1980 as their first fiction writer—when the great news came down that Donald Barthelme would be joining us. Barthelme's arrival caused universal rejoicing: this would really put our program on the map, not only because Barthelme was a "name" writer but because he was one of the handful who commanded a following among graduate writing students. Indeed, probably no other short story writer was more imitated by M.F.A. students in the seventies and early eighties.

I was initially surprised that a writer of Barthelme's stature would relocate to Houston. True, he had been offered an endowed chair, a hefty salary, and regular paid sabbatical leaves, but that would not normally be enough to pry most established fiction writers from their comfortable lives. The key to the "seduction" (recruitment is the eros of academia) was that Barthelme was coming home. Though by birth a Philadelphian, he had grown up in Houston and was educated at the University of Houston, the same school that would now employ him. Barthelme was still remembered around town for his youthful cultural activities, reporting for the Houston *Post*, launching the UH literary magazine, *Forum*, directing the Contemporary Art Museum in the early sixties. Then he'd gone off to New York with regional upstart energy to make his mark (like Robert Rauschenberg, Andy Warhol, Merce Cunningham: our avant-gardists almost always seem to come from the provinces), and a few decades later was returning famous—or as famous as serious writers become in America. It was also a family move: his aging parents, his three brothers—Pete, Frederick, and Steve—and his sister Joan still lived in Houston or near enough by. Marion Knox, Donald's second wife, was pregnant, and they both thought Houston might be an easier place to raise a child than Lower Manhattan.

I had no idea what to expect from Barthelme as a colleague: whether the weight of such a star might throw off-kilter the fragile balance of our program. But Donald proved not to have an ounce of the prima donna in him. On the contrary, he was the ultimate team player, accepting his full share of the petty, annoying bureaucratic tasks, sitting on boring departmental committees, phoning our top applicants to convince them to choose our program, lobbying university bigwigs with his good-ole-boy communication skills. A would-be graphic artist ("the pleasure of cutting up and pasting together pictures, a secret vice," he once wrote), he designed all our posters and letterheads. Donald had one of the most pronounced civic consciences I have ever come across, and was fond of exhorting us with the Allen Ginsberg line: "Come, let us put our queer shoulders to the wheel."

Each Tuesday noon we would have a meeting of the creative writing staff to determine policy. These lunch meetings took place on-campus in the Galaxy Room of the School of Hotel Management; eating there was like going to a barber school for a haircut. Donald would be the first to arrive. He would order a large glass of white wine, which he would ask to have refilled several times during lunch. After we had all settled in and ordered (trial and error had convinced me that, despite poignant attempts to retool the menu, only the grilled cheese sandwich was reliable), Cynthia Macdonald, the program's founding mother and an ex–opera singer, would, with her operatic sense of urgency, alert us to the latest crisis: either our graduate students were in danger of losing their teaching stipends, or some English professor was prejudiced against our majors, or the university was hedging on its budget commitments, or a visiting writer had just called to cancel a reading.

Barthelme, who abhorred stinginess, preferred to settle the smaller crises by dipping into the "Don Fund," as the discretionary monies attached to his academic chair came to be called. He thus made it possible to circumvent the bureaucracy, save the students' literary magazine, advertise an impromptu reading, or preserve the program's honor when a visiting literary dignitary like Carlos Fuentes came to town, by taking him out to a fancy restaurant.

Sometimes, however, the problem was stickier and had to be thrashed out by Cynthia, Donald, Stanley Plumly (who left after a few years, replaced by the poet Edward Hirsch), and myself, as well as a rotating visiting cast that included Ntozake Shange, Rosellen Brown, Richard Howard, Joy Williams, Jim Robison, Mary Robison, Meg Wolitzer. In the familial dynamic that developed over the years, Cynthia and Donald were Mommy and Daddy, with the rest of us siblings contending for their favor. During heated discussions Donald would often wait until everyone else had declared a position, and then weigh in with the final word, more like an arbiter than an interested party. He was good at manipulating consensus through democratic discussion to get his way; and we made it easy for him, since everyone wanted his love and approval. At times he would inhibit opposition by indicating that any further discussion on an issue he regarded as settled was extremely dumb and ill-advised. Still, when a vote did go against him, he bowed sportingly to majority will. He often seemed to be holding back from using his full clout; he was like those professional actors who give the impression at social gatherings of saving their energy for the real performance later on.

Sometimes in the midst of the meeting, I would raise my eyes and find Donald's gaze fixed on me. What did he *see?* I wondered. He would immediately look away, not liking to be spied in the act of exercising curiosity. At other times I would catch Donald at this funny habit: he would sniff his sleeve a few inches above the wrist, taking a whiff of his arm, either because he liked the smell of his sweat or because he needed to ground himself, establish contact with his body when his mind was drifting toward Mars.

Though we usually agreed on specifics, Donald believed more fully in the mission of writing programs than I could. There was much talk about having to maintain our position as one of the top three writing programs in the country. By what standards, aside from wishful thinking, this ranking had been determined I never could ascertain: presumably it had something to do with the faculty's repute, the number of applications we received, and the publishing fortunes of our alumni. In any case, Donald was ever on guard against anything that might "dilute the quality of the program." Sometimes I would recommend bringing in visiting writers who might be less well-known but who could give our students a broader perspective stylistically or multiculturally. "But are they any *good?*" Donald would demand, and I knew what he meant: if they were any good, why hadn't he heard of them?

Donald was a man with a great sense of loyalty to family, neighborhood, academic institution, and publisher. *The New Yorker* had published him throughout his career, and he believed in the worth of those who appeared in its pages; ditto, those authors active on the executive board of PEN, the international writers organization. The other side of the coin was that he showed a massive incuriosity toward writers outside the mainstream or his personal network. If a novelist was recommended to us for a teaching post by his brother Rick—arriving under the familial mantle, as it were—he would display serious interest. But if you mentioned a good living writer he didn't know, his response was a quick veto. There was something of the air of a Mafia don about Barthelme's protection: he treated his own circle of friends (Grace Paley, Ann Beattie, Roger Angell, Susan Sontag) as family, and he proposed their names for our reading series year after year. His refusal to consider literary figures who were not inside his particular spotlight used to drive me up the wall, partly because it seemed to leave out many worthy small press/experimental writers and partly because I had not escaped the hell of anonymity so long ago or so conclusively as not to identify with these "unknown" wretches. But from Donald's point of view, I had nothing to worry about; I was good enough to be on the writing faculty team, therefore I was one of the saved.

Ironically, Barthelme was himself an experimental, iconoclastic writer, so that there was a certain contradiction between his antitraditional literary side and his involvement in rank, the Establishment, continuity. (What else is being a teacher but an assertion of belief in continuity?)

There was always a formal side to Barthelme that I associate with the English—a Victorian dryness he used to comic effect. It crops up in his earliest stories, like the "The Big Broadcast of 1938": "Having acquired in exchange for an old house that had been theirs, his and hers, a radio or more properly radio *station*, Bloomsbury could now play 'The Star Spangled Banner,' which he had always admired immoderately, on account of its finality, as often as he liked." This qualifying, donnish quality was accompanied by an equally British terseness in social situations. "I think not," he would say in response to some proposal he considered dubious, and that would be that.

Or he would signal the conversation was at an end for him by taking your arm at the elbow and guiding you off on your rounds. I was at first astonished by this gesture, which seemed like an eruption of regal impatience. At the same time, I found something reassuring in his physical steering of me, like a father picking up his child and placing him out of harm's way.

-o- -o- -o-

Much of Donald Barthelme's fiction consists of witty dialogue. Yet when I think of Donald in real life, I recall few bon mots; I remember rather his underlying silence, which has now, in death, prevailed. Silence seemed his natural condition; his speech had very little flow: you never knew when it was going to dry up. Of course, Donald talked well, in the sense that he chose his words economically and with care. His listeners would often smile at the sardonic spin he gave to well-worn figures of speech. (Among other writers, I've known only John Ashbery to take as much delight in fingering clichés.) But the pearls of wit or wisdom one might have expected from him were rare; and this was because, I think, fundamentally he did not view speech as the vehicle for expressing his inner thoughts. Rather, he treated speech as a wholly social medium, to which he subscribed as a solid, dues-paying citizen, dipping into the common fount.

What one looks for in the conversation of writers is a chance to be taken back into the kitchen where they cook up their literary surprises: a sudden flash of truth or metaphor. Around Donald, what you got was not so much the lyrical, imaginative Barthelme as the one who re-created social intercourse like a game, a tennis match, with parrying one-liners keeping the interlocutor off-balance. His remarks tended to stop rather than advance conversation.

When you waxed serious around Donald, you would expect to have your wings clipped, since he regarded getting worked up about anything in public as inappropriate. "Down, boy," he frequently mocked if I started to expatiate on a subject. These interventions felt more like a fond head-pat than anything malicious. But I never could figure out if he consistently played the referee in order to keep everyone around him at a temperature suitable for his own comfort, or out of some larger sense of group responsibility, which, in his eyes, conflicted with solo flights of enthusiasm.

Barthelme clearly considered it bad form to talk about books or the writing process in public. Perhaps he thought it too pedantic a topic to bring before intellectually mixed company. It also appeared that, toward the end of his life, he was bored with literature, much preferring the visual arts.

I had hoped, given the countless intellectual references sprinkled throughout Barthelme's stories, that the author of "Kierkegaard Unfair to Schlegel" and "Eugénie Grandet" would be as eager as I was to discuss our favorite authors. As it turned out, asking Barthelme what he thought was like demanding a trade secret, though I never gave up clumsily trying to pry loose his literary opinions. Once, at a brunch, on learning that the Swiss writer Max Frisch, who interested me, was a friend of Donald's, I immediately asked, "What do you think of Frisch's work?" I had either put the question too directly or shown too naked a desire for a glimpse at a higher circle (those writers of international stature, Frisch and Barthelme included) to let my curiosity be indulged, or Donald's feelings toward the Swiss writer were too complex or competitive for him to untangle them in public. Such speculations proliferate in the absence of a definite answer. Donald managed a grudging few syllables, to the effect that he thought Frisch's work "substantial," though "the fellow has a pretty big ego." He seemed much more comfortable discussing the rumor that Frisch might be buying an expensive loft in Soho.

This professional reticence, I should add, was by no means singular to Donald. Part of the larger loneliness of our literary life stems from the fact that writers, especially those who have reached a successful level, tend to shy away from discussing the things one would think mattered to them most—the other authors who continue to inspire them or the unsolved obstacles in their day-to-day composition—preferring instead to chatter about career moves, visiting gigs, grants, word processors, and real estate, all of which become, in effect, the language of power.

Once, when I managed to get Donald off by myself (we were driving to some forlorn suburb in outer Houston to make a fund-raising presentation), he indulged my hunger for candid literary talk. I asked him what he thought of several recent novels by Texas writers of our acquaintance. He didn't mince words; his assessments were extremely pointed and shrewd. It was exhilarating to gain admittance to the inner tabernacle of Barthelme's judgment—not to mention the fact that two writers dissecting the flaws of a third contemporary can bond them in a deliciously fratricidal way. But, to my regret, the experience was never repeated.

Perhaps because Donald had begun as a newspaperman, he still had a fair amount of the journalist left in him, which included not only a topical alertness to fashions but a heavy-drinking, hard-boiled, almost anti-intellectual downplaying of his own identity as practitioner of serious literature. I remember his boasting once that he'd dashed off a review on a *Superman* sequel, a "piece of hackwork for some glossy for a nice piece of change." Yet when the review came out, I saw that Donald had, as usual, given good weight, with an elegantly amusing, well-constructed essay. Barthelme always worked conscientiously to get the least piece of prose right. But like the A student who hates to admit he studied for a test, he preferred the pretense that he was a glorified grub working to pay the bills. I think he would have *liked* to have been a hack; it was a persistent fantasy of escape from his literary conscience. He fit into that debunking, up-from-journalism tradition of American satirists: Twain, Bierce, Ring Lardner. The problem was that his faux-hack pose made it difficult for you to take your own writing seriously in front of him, or discuss other literature with any seriousness.

Barthelme also seemed uncomfortable with psychological conversation, which was either too intimate or too tattling for his taste. His writings make it clear that he was quite astute at character analysis; and yet there was a curious antipsychological side to him, or at least a resistance to discussing such things aloud; in this he was both a gentleman of the old school and a postmodernist. One time Donald and I were talking after a meeting about one of our colleagues, who had thrown a fit over some procedural matter. I remarked with a smile that she seemed to take a certain pleasure in releasing her wrath all the way. Donald replied that he'd known people who had had temper tantrums just for the fun of it, but surely not someone as mature as our colleague. This seemed a perfect instance of Donald's loyalty: having decided that someone was a "good guy," he did not like to acknowledge that that person might still be capable of childish or self-indulgent behavior.

⋄ ⋄ ⋄

Once or twice a year Marion and Don would invite me to their house: they'd either give a dinner party or ask my girlfriend and me over for a two-couple evening. Sometimes, after a particularly happy night of warm, sparkling talk and wonderful food (both Barthelmes were superb cooks) and plentiful wine, I would think, Donald and I are actually becoming friends. I would fall under the spell of the man's gruff charm, morality, intelligence; it was like having a crush; I couldn't wait to see him again soon and take it further. But there never was any further.

I would run into him at school and say, "I really enjoyed the other evening at your house, Don."

"Well, good, good," he would reply nervously, which was his favorite way of dismissing a topic. Perhaps he was simply being modest about their hospitality; but I also thought his uneasy look expressed concern that I would start to get "mushy" on him, and make demands for a closeness he had no inclination or ability to fulfill. What I wanted was to remove the evening from the category of "dutiful community socializing that had turned out well" and place it under the file of "possible developing friendship." But the story of Barthelme's and my friendship seemed forever stalled in the early chapters; there was no accrual of intimacy from one time to the next.

In trying to account for this stasis, I often wondered if it was a question of age. Twelve years separated us, an awkward span: I was too old and set as a writer to inspire the parental fondness he bestowed on his favorite graduate students, but too young to be accepted as a peer. I was the same age, in fact, as his younger brother Frederick, who was enjoying considerable success; if anything, insurgent writers twelve years younger may have seemed to him enviable pups, breathing down his neck. Then again, the appetite for shared confidences often dwindles after fifty; at that point some writers begin to husband their secrets for the page. In any case, I sensed that he'd become used to accepting rather passively the persistent courtship by others (which is not my mode). As a woman novelist said to me: "Donald sits there on the couch and expects you to make a pass at him."

I got a deeper glimpse into his own thinking on friendship one night at a dinner party at the Barthelmes' apartment in Houston. After dinner, Donald and I settled into a rare personal conversation. I asked him if he showed his work to anyone before he sent it off for publication. He said he showed Marion; that was about it. I then inquired if he had any close friends who were his peers with whom he could talk writing. He surprised me by saying he didn't think so. He said he had had two good friends, and they had both died. One was Thomas B. Hess, the other Harold Rosenberg, both well-known art critics. "I started hanging around them in the sixties. They were older than me and they were my mentors, and it was great that we could talk about art and not necessarily about literature. They taught me a whole lot. I haven't learned anything since. I'm still working off that old knowledge. It was distressing how they both died around the same time, which left me feeling rather . . . odd," he said. "What I really want are older men, father figures who can teach *me* something. I don't want to be people's damn father figure. I want to be the baby—it's more fun. The problem is that the older you get, the harder it is to find these older role models."

A reluctant patriarch, still looking for the good father. Having been on that same search off and on, I understood some of Donald's loneliness. It doesn't matter how old you get, you still have an ache for that warm understanding. He began talking about his own father, Donald Barthelme Sr., a highly respected architect in Texas. His father, he said, had been "very uptight" with them when they were growing up: "I think he was terrified of children." As an architecture professor, Barthelme senior always tried to get the better of his students and demonstrate his superior knowledge. "Well of course we know more than our students, that's not the point!" said Donald.

I thought of his novel *The Dead Father* and wondered whether that title had irked Barthelme senior, who was (and is still) very much alive. The book is Barthelme's best novel and one of his finest achievements. In this part parody, part serious Arthurian romance, the Dead Father is an active character, boasting, complaining, demanding attention. Like a corpse that will not acknowledge its demise, this patriarch who has been "killed" (or at least put in the shade) by his more successful son seems to represent the dead weight of guilt in the Oedipal triumph. *The Dead Father* is an obsessive meditation on generational competitiveness, the division between younger and older men, and the fear of time's decaying hand.

Many of Barthelme's short stories revolve around Oedipal tensions implicit in education, mentorship, and the master-flunky tie. Take, for instance, "The King of Jazz," where Hokie Mokie blows away the young Japanese challenger in a jam session, or "Conversations with Goethe," where the narrator-flunky is triumphantly put in his place at the end:

> Critics, Goethe said, are the cracked mirror in the grand ballroom of the creative spirit. No, I said, they were, rather, the extra baggage on the great cabriolet of conceptual progress. "Eckermann," said Goethe, "*shut up.*"

I always winced when I heard Barthelme read that story aloud (as he often did), partly because of the glee he seemed to express at maintaining the upper hand and partly because of the hint—at least I took it that way—that any friendship with him would have to grow out of an inferior's flattery.

Sometimes it seemed that Donald not only was bored with everyone around him but had ceased to expect otherwise. In Houston he drew his social circle from mildly awed professionals—doctors, lawyers, etc.—who could produce a soothing harmonious patter into which he would insert an occasional barb to perk things up. Mostly Donald preferred to stand back, making sure the social machinery was running smoothly.

In his distance from us, he seemed to be monitoring some inner unease. I suppose that was partly his alcoholism. No matter how sociably engaged alcoholics are, one corner of their minds will always be taking stock of the liquor supply and plotting how to get in another drink without being too obvious about it. I never saw Donald falling-down drunk; he held his liquor, put on a good performance of sobriety; but, as he once admitted, "I'm a little drunk all the time." Sometimes, when he drank a lot, his memory blacked out.

Example: During a spring break Cynthia Macdonald delegated me to phone Donald in New York and find out which students he wanted to recommend for a prestigious fellowship. I called him around eight in the evening, and he gave his recommendations, then asked me a series of questions about departmental matters, raises, courses for next year, etc. A few days later Cynthia called him and mentioned in passing the telephone conversation he had had with me. Donald insisted he had not spoken to me in weeks. Cynthia told me to call him again, this time making sure it was before five o'clock, when the chances for sobriety were greater. The odd part is that when I did call him, we had the identical conversation: he put the same questions in the same order, with the same edgy impatience, quickly voicing one question as soon as I had answered the last. I never let on that he was repeating himself, but it struck me that he must often have been on automatic pilot, fooling the world with rote questions while his mind was clouded by alcohol.

At times he gave the impression, like a burn victim lying uncomfortably in the hospital, that there was something I was neglecting to do or figure out that might have put him at greater ease. Perhaps there is always a disappointment that an alcoholic feels in a nonalcoholic: an awareness that, no matter how sympathetic the nondrinker may seem, he will never really "get" it. That was certainly true for me: I didn't get it. I knew Donald disapproved of my not drinking—or not drinking enough. He once objected to our holding a meeting at my house, saying, "Phillip never has any liquor on hand." Which wasn't true, but interesting that he should think so. The noon meeting took place at my apartment anyhow; Donald arrived with a bottle, just in case.

I also think he disapproved, if that's the word, of my not philandering. When an artist in town began openly having an extramarital affair and most of the Houston arts community sided with his wife, Donald reassured the man that these things happened, telling him comparable experiences from his past. One of the ways Donald bonded with someone was through a shared carnal appetite—what used to be called a "vice," like drinking or womanizing.

In keeping with his Southwestern upbringing, Donald combined the strong, silent dignity of the Western male with the more polished gallantry of the South. He liked to be around women, particularly younger women, and grew more relaxed in their company. I don't think this was purely a matter of lechery, though lust no doubt played its classical part. The same enchantment showed in his delight with his older daughter, Anne, a vibrant, outgoing girl from an earlier marriage, who had been brought up largely by her mother in Scandinavia and who came to live with the Barthelmes while studying theater at the University of Houston. Given Barthelme's own (to use his phrase) "double-minded" language, hemmed in by the ironies of semantic duplicity, girl talk must have seemed a big relief. In his novel *Paradise* (1986), the hero, a middle-aged architect named Simon, shares an apartment with three beautiful young women and seems to enjoy listening in on their conversation about clothes, makeup, and jobs as much as sleeping with them.

In *The Dead Father*, Barthelme shows an awareness of the way a fifty-year-old's interest in young women might look to one's wife:

> Fifty-year-old boys . . . are boys because they don't want to be old farts, said Julie. The old fart is not cherished in this society. . . . Stumbling from the stage is anathema to them, said Julie, they want to be nuzzling new women when they are ninety.
> What is wrong with that? asked the Dead Father. Seems perfectly reasonable to me.
> The women object, she said. Violently.

Certainly some of the women in the writing program objected to what they felt was Barthelme's preference for the pretty young females in class. I ended up being a sort of confidant of the middle-aged women students, who had raised families and were finally fulfilling their dreams to become writers; several complained to me that Barthelme would make short shrift of their stories, for being too domestic and psychological. Of course, these were the very materials I had encouraged them to explore. It's true that Donald once said to me if he had to read another abortion or grandmother story, he would pack it in. I understood that what he really objected to was the solemn privileging of certain subjects over linguistic or formal invention; but I was sufficiently competitive with him for the students' love that it pleased me to hear their beefs. They also claimed that his real pets were the talented young men. This is a standard pattern in the writing program, with its hierarchies of benediction. I, too, observed how certain of our top male students would gravitate to Barthelme, and how he not only would help edit their books—and get them publishers and agents—but would invite them to hang out with him as his friend. Perhaps "jealous" is too strong a word, but I was certainly a little envious of their easy access to Donald.

In the classroom Donald could be crusty, peremptorily sitting a student down after a few pages of a story that sounded unpromising to him—a practice his favorites endorsed as honest and toughening-up; those less sure of their abilities took longer to recover. His true generosity as a teacher shone, I thought, in individual conferences, where he would go over students' manuscripts he had line-edited as meticulously as if they had been his own. Often, as I was leaving, I would see a queue waiting outside his office; he put many more hours into student conferences than I did. I sensed that in the last years his main reading was student work—or at least he led me to believe that. When I would ask Don what he'd been reading lately, he replied, "Class stories, theses. Who has time for anything else?"

Donald loved to play talent scout. When one of his graduate students finished a manuscript he thought was publishable, he would call up his agent, Lynn Nesbit, and some New York editors, maybe start a few fires at *The New Yorker*. I was reluctant to take on this role with students: both because I wasn't sure I had the power to pull it off and because I didn't like the way the writing program's success stories generated a bitter atmosphere among the unanointed. But Donald acknowledged no such side effects: to him, each book contract drew more attention to the program and simply made us "hotter." The students, whatever qualms they may have had about the hazards of Brat Pack careerism, wanted a Godfather to promote them. They were no dummies; they knew that one word from Barthelme could lead to publication.

It's embarrassing to admit, but a few times I also tried to get Donald to use his influence in my behalf. That he had a measure of power in the literary world became steadily clearer to me from remarks he would drop at our lunchtime meetings: how he had helped so-and-so receive a lucrative prize, or had worked behind the scenes at the American Academy of Arts and Letters to snare honors for the "good guys." The Prix de Rome, given out by the Academy, went to several of his protégés in the space of a few years. Well, if goodies were being handed out, what the heck, I wanted some too. Once I asked him shamelessly (trying to make it sound like a joke), "Why don't you ever recommend me for a Prix de Rome or one of those prizes?" After a stunned pause, he answered, "I think they're interested in younger men, Phillip."

Flattering as it was to be told I was past the point of needing such support, I suspected more was involved. During the eight years we taught together, two of my books were published; I sent them to Donald for advance quotes, but he always managed to misplace the galleys until long after a blurb would have done any good. By then I'd had enough good quotes; what disappointed me more was that Donald had not responded to my work.

Months after the time had passed for Donald to "blurb" my novel *The Rug Merchant*, I continued to hope that he would at least read the book and tell me honestly what he thought. I asked him a few times if he had gotten to it yet, and he said, "Regrettably, no." Finally, I must have made enough of a pest out of myself to have an effect. We were sitting together at a party, and by this point in the evening Barthelme was pretty well in his cups. His speech slurred, he said he had read my novel and "it was a good job." He was sorry the main character, Cyrus, had not gotten round to marrying the girl in the end. "Anyway—a good job," he said again, tapping my knee.

In that neurotic way we have of probing a loose tooth, I brooded that Donald didn't like my writing. More likely, he simply felt indifferent toward it. A few times he did compliment me on something I'd written, usually after having seen it in a magazine. But I was insatiable, because his approval meant so much to me—a long-awaited sign of love from the emotionally remote father. The irony is that I so longed for approval from a writer whose own work I didn't entirely accept. Our aesthetics were worlds apart: I was interested in first-person confessional writing and the tradition of psychological realism, whereas Barthelme seemed to be debunking the presumptions of realist fiction. I suppose the fact that this blessing would have come from someone who was not in my literary camp but who represented the other orthodoxy, formalism, seemed to make it all the more desirable. I imagined—craved—a reconciliation, a pure respect between his and my style in some impossible utopian space of literary exchange.

For a long while I felt secretly guilty toward Donald because I did not love his work enough. I respected it, of course, but in a detached way. When I first began reading Donald Barthelme in the sixties, he struck me as a trickster, playfully adjusting a collection of veils, impossible to pin down. Later, when I got to know Donald, I saw that almost every line of his was a disguised personal confession—if nothing else, then of inner weather and melancholy: he was masterful at casting deep shadows through just the right feints, a sort of matador courting and dodging meaning, sometimes even letting himself be gored by it for the sake of the story. Recently, the more I read him, the more I come to the conclusion that he *was* a great writer. Minor, yes, but great at his chosen scale. He could catch sorrow in a sentence. A dozen of his stories are amazing and will last.

The bulk of his best work, to my mind, was done in the sixties: we sometimes forget how energized Barthelme was by the counterculture, the politics and playful liberatory urges of that period. His peak lasted through the early seventies, up to and including *The Dead Father* (1975). After that, his fiction lost much of its emotional openness, devolving on the whole into clever, guarded pastiche. Always the professional, he could still cobble together a dazzling sentence or amusing aperçu, but he became increasingly a master of trifles. There is, however, something noble in a great talent adapting itself to diminished capacities. His 1986 novel, *Paradise,* is a sweet if thin fabrication. Between the lines of its sportive harem plot, one can read an honest admission of burnout. Donald confessed to me that he thought the book "pretty weak," and I hope I had the hypocrisy to hide my agreement. *Paradise* is honest, too, in departing from his earlier intellectual references and in reflecting the creature comforts that engaged him mentally during his last years: food, decor, and sex.

As he got older and was drawn more to comfort, Houston seemed an appropriate choice of residence. It is an easy city to live in—not as stimulating as one might like at times, but pleasant. The Barthelmes lived on the second floor of a brick Tudor house in one of the city's most beautiful areas, the oak-lined South Boulevard. Just across the street was Poe School, an excellent elementary school where his little girl, Katharine, started to go when she was old enough. Nearby were the tennis courts where Marion played regularly. In Houston the Barthelmes enjoyed more of a black-tie, upper-middle-class life than in New York, going regularly to the opera, the symphony, the ballet; Donald became a city booster, telling outsiders that the Houston performing companies were good and getting better every year. Houston proved an ideal place for him to act out his civic impulse: of the ten established writers in town, each one called upon to do his or her community share, Donald was the most famous and most cherished, being a native son. This was what his compatriots in the New York literary world, for whom his resettlement in Texas seemed a perverse self-exile, found so hard to understand.

I remember telling one of Don's Manhattan friends, who was worried that he might be wasting away down there, how packed the literary life was in Houston, how needed he was. Secretly I asked myself whether living in Houston had indeed dried up some of his creative juices. Having never known Barthelme during his "conquering years," I had no way to compare; but I suspect that Houston was not a factor. His creative crisis had already started in the late seventies, when he was still living in New York; if anything, he may have accepted the move to Texas partly in the hope of being shaken out of stagnation and personal loss.

-ᴑ-   -ᴑ-   -ᴑ-

Barthelme's sardonic, Olympian use of brand names in his fiction led me to the mistaken idea that he took a dim view of consumerism, whereas I found him to be more a happy captive of it. He would often talk to me about new types of VCRs or personal computers, a sports car he was fantasizing buying, or the latest vicissitudes with his pickup truck—assuming incorrectly that I knew as much as the typical American male about machines. He was also very interested in food: I would run into him shopping at the supermarket, wicker basket in hand, throwing in a package of tortellini; one time he began talking about the varieties of arugula and radicchio, then added that he could never leave the place without spending a fortune. "They create these needs and you can't resist. They've figured out a way to hook you," he said.

These disquisitions on arugula were not exactly what I had hoped for from Barthelme. I kept waiting for him to give me more of his innermost thoughts. But later I began to think: suppose I had been misinterpreting him all along, because of my own Brooklyn-Jewish expectations of conversation—that mixture of confiding anecdote, analytic "delving," and intellectual disputation—when in fact he was disclosing his inner self with every remark, and I was too dumb or incredulous to perceive it. Maybe he was not trying to frustrate me by holding back the goods of his interior life, but was confiding his preoccupation with things, comforts, sensual pleasures.

And why couldn't I accept that? I seemed to have to view it as a copout, a retreat into banality; I wanted him to stand up and be the staunch intellectual hero-father. Part of me responded with a line from Ernest Becker's *The Denial of Death*: "The depressed person enslaves himself to the trivial." Another part suspected that I, longtime bachelor, was merely envious of his settled domestic family life. It should be clear by now that Donald Barthelme was an enormously evocative figure for me. The difficulty is distinguishing between what was really Donald and what he evoked in me—not necessarily the same thing. If I came to regard Donald as the prisoner of a bourgeois lifestyle dedicated to discreet good taste, down to the popular Zurburán reproduction of fruit above his dining room table, this probably says less about Donald than about my own pathological attraction-repulsion vis-à-vis the Good Life, or what passes in today's world for joie de vivre.

No doubt Barthelme *was* often depressed and withdrawn, underneath all that fixation on obtainable pleasures. But he also seemed reasonably contented much of the time, at home with Marion and his two daughters. The younger Barthelme had written scornfully about married life: "The world in the evening seems fraught with the absence of promise, if you are a married man. There is nothing to do but go home and drink your nine drinks and forget about it" ("Critique de la Vie Quotidienne"). The later Barthelme, now remarried, wrote in "Chablis":

> I'm sipping a glass of Gallo Chablis with an ice cube in it, smoking, worrying. I worry that the baby may jam a kitchen knife into an electrical outlet while she's wet. I've put those little plastic plugs into all the electrical outlets but she's learned how to pop them out. I've checked the Crayolas. They've made the Crayolas safe to eat—I called the head office in Pennsylvania. She can eat a whole box of Crayolas and nothing will happen to her. If I don't get the new tires for the car I can buy the dog.

The tires, the baby, the Crayolas, the dog: the tone seems more fondly engaged with domesticity. If the later stories seem to have lost an edge, it's also possible that Donald was simply happier.

His moments of joy seemed most often connected with his child of middle age, Katharine, whom he was smitten by and who was in truth a remarkably adorable, lively, bright little girl. I remember once hailing him as he carried Katharine on his shoulders across the street. "We're just setting off for an ice cream cone," he explained, blushing to his roots as if I had come upon a guilty secret. I had indeed caught him at his most unguarded, a doting father-horsie, without his irony or gravity buckled on.

When Donald went back to New York for the summer months, he became slightly more nervous and speedy—or, as Marion put it ruefully, he "reverted to Type A"; but for that very reason, I think, I felt closer to, more in harmony with him there. In New York, also, we were removed from the demands of the writing program, and so I found it easier to pretend that we were not only colleagues but friends. The Barthelmes had retained, after protracted warfare with the landlord, their great floor-through apartment on West Eleventh Street: the walls were painted Pompeiian red; a large framed Ingres poster greeted the visitor; the radio was usually tuned to jazz; on the coffee table were oversized art books, often with texts by friends, such as Ann Beattie's *Alex Katz*. Barthelme may have been a postmodernist, but his furnishings held to the scrupulous purity of high modernism, the leather and chrome of MOMA's design galleries. As soon as you entered, Donald offered you a drink, and it was bad form to refuse, if only because your not having one undercut his pretext for imbibing. He was an extremely gracious host, perhaps overdoing the liquor refills, but otherwise attentive as a Bedouin to your comfort.

In May of 1987, by a coincidence having nothing to do with Donald, I sublet an apartment in the same brownstone on West Eleventh Street where the Barthelmes lived. Kirkpatrick and Faith Sale, their writer-editor friends, occupied the garden apartment below them, and I was two flights up in a tiny studio, sublet from an ailing Finn who had gone back to his native country for medical treatment. Though the building had more than its share of literary vibrations and timeworn, rent-stabilized charm, I quickly grew dissatisfied with my bare studio cubicle. It overlooked the street and was very noisy, especially on weekends, when the rowdy packs spilling out of Ray's Pizza on Sixth Avenue clamored up the block.

Donald knocked on my door the day he arrived in New York (I had preceded him by three weeks) and immediately began rearranging my room. "That bed doesn't belong there," he said, pointing to the Finn's futon. "The lamp's in the wrong place too." The interior decorator side of Donald took over; I became passively content to let him dictate the proper placement of objects. He insisted on loaning me some excess furniture from his apartment, and in no time at all I had an attractive Scandinavian rug, a chair ("You can borrow my Wassily chair—it's a facsimile of the Breuer"), a typewriter table, a trunk that would do as a coffee table, and some art posters for the walls. He kept running up and down stairs, hauling pieces from the basement storage.

Donald was a true good neighbor, and I could see he was delighted to have hit upon a way to help me. As long as I expected any sort of intimacy from him, it made him uncomfortable, but if I approached him as one generic human being to another, with a problem that needed fixing, he would be there instantly. If I had a flat tire, if my car engine needed a start-up, if I lacked home furnishings, I knew I could come to Donald for help. This neighborliness and common decency struck me as very Texan. Once, when my apartment in Houston had been burglarized and all my appliances stolen, Donald offered to loan me the little black-and-white television he and Marion used to keep in the kitchen for the evening news while they were preparing dinner. The generosity of this sacrifice I understood only when I returned the set three months later and saw how happy they were to get it back.

In any case, that summer Donald continued to take an active interest in my housing situation; and when I found a charming one-bedroom apartment on Bank Street, three blocks away, and signed a two-year lease, he went with me to have a look. By now I had accepted him as my habitational guru. Through his eyes I suddenly saw it as much smaller than I'd remembered, but he passed over that in silence. "Very nice. Very nice. If I were you, though, I'd have these wall stains removed," he said. "It's simple to do. I can help. Also, if you decide to paint the place, I'm good at paint jobs."

Here was a man who had barely addressed ten sentences to me during the past six months in Houston, and now he was volunteering to paint my house and wash the stains from my walls. I tabled the repainting idea, but I did enlist Donald's help in lugging my belongings the three blocks from West Eleventh to Bank Street. On the Saturday I moved, it was ninety-four degrees, naturally, and several trips were required, and we must have looked a sight, Sancho Panza and the Don with his scraggly beard, pulling boxes roped together on a small dolly. At one point it tipped over and spilled half my papers onto the sidewalk. After that, I let Donald carry the lion's share of the weight, he having a broader back and a greater liking (I told myself) for manual labor, as well as more steering ability. He was hilarious on the way over, joking about the indignity of being a beast of burden, and I must admit it tickled me to think of using one of America's major contemporary writers as a drayhorse. But why not take advantage when he seemed so proud of his strength, so indestructible, even in his mid-fifties?

When I was set up in my new apartment, I invited the Barthelmes over for Sunday brunch. It was both a return for the many dinner parties they had invited me to and a way of asserting that I was now a responsible adult entertaining on my own. Marion, who had just been in Vermont with Katharine, showed up looking radiant and tanned in a sundress. Donald was ill-at-ease that day, as though having to get through an unpleasant obligation— or else hung-over. I remember there was a direct overhead sun out on the terrace that bothered him into changing his seat several times, and made me worry about the food melting. I had overdone the spread, with so much lox and bagels, quiche, focaccia, orange juice, fruit, pie, and coffee as to leave little room for our plates. But I pulled out all the stops to be amusing, and gradually Donald began to unbend as we sat out on the terrace gabbing about the latest plays and movies and art shows and people we knew. Meanwhile, Katharine had discovered the hammock, and was having a great time bouncing in and out of it and performing "risqué" peekaboo fandangos. As usual, she and I flirted, Donald pretended to look paternally askance, and Marion was ladylike, furthering the conversation with her journalist's bright curiosity while supervising Katharine with a light hand.

⋄ ⋄ ⋄

Whenever, in the face of his opaque silence, I began wondering if I had fallen out of Barthelme's good graces, someone would reassure me: "Oh, but Don's very fond of you. He always asks after you in an interested way." During the spring semester of 1988, however, I kept having the feeling that Donald was becoming cooler toward me. Interactions that used to take up thirty-five seconds were now clipped to twelve. Nor had I been invited to the Barthelme house for their customary dinner. Had I done something to offend him? I raised the question to Ed Hirsch, who was closer to Donald than I was, and Ed told me that he had detected the same curtness in Barthelme of late—which consoled me, I must admit.

Then on April 15 we received the awful, sickening news that Donald had had to go to the hospital for throat cancer. His doctor, we learned now, had been treating it with antibiotics, but eventually decided an operation would be necessary, as the tumor turned out to be larger than originally thought. All along Donald had kept his illness secret from us, whether out of privacy or stoicism scarcely matters. I was ashamed that I had been taking his withdrawal personally. We were told he would be in the hospital anywhere from five to fourteen days, but not to visit him there, as he didn't want people seeing him in such condition.

About a week after he had come home from the hospital, and we were informed it was all right to pay a brief visit, I dropped by the Barthelme house. Knowing his love for jazz, I had bought him five archival jazz albums as a get-well present. With his newly shaven chin, Donald looked harshly exposed and rubicund. His eyes were dazed. He had a tube running from his nose to his mouth like an elephant's proboscis; its purpose was to feed him liquids, as his throat was still too sore to take in solids.

We sat in his living room, staring across at each other, having nothing to say. When I handed him the stack of jazz records, he patted them wordlessly, without bothering to examine what they were. Though I knew he must be extremely weak, I still felt hurt: wouldn't he have at least read the titles if someone he liked more had brought them? I told myself I was being ridiculous, the man was gravely ill—put ego aside for once!—and began cranking up conversation. As usual, Donald was the master of one-liners. "Demerol is great stuff." And: "I'm tired of sounding like Elmer Fudd." The tube pinching his nose did make his speech sound gurgled.

He asked testily about our having moved to offer someone a teaching position for next year while he was in the hospital. Though Donald definitely liked the writer, I sensed an under-current of breached protocol. I explained that it was an emergency and we couldn't keep the man waiting any longer. "Well, good, good," he said. I apologized for our having acted without his final input. Barthelme nodded. His daughter Katharine ran into the room, naked and wet. "Don't look at me!" she commanded. "I just took a showw-er!" Donald smiled, followed her with his eyes. I excused myself after another minute or two. A painful half hour.

The next week, though there was really no need for him to do so, Donald came to our Tuesday lunch meeting. He said he was bored hanging around the house. He also seemed to be telling us with this visit: I may be sick but it doesn't mean I'm giving up my stake in the program. Perhaps because he was up and about, and therefore one expected an improvement, his pasty, florid appearance shocked me more than when I had seen him at home. He looked bad. We wanted him to go home and lie down, not sit through our boring agenda.

I could only agree when someone said afterward, "That just wasn't Donald." Not only had he lost his beard, but his glass of white wine. The doctors had told him that from now on he was to give up all alcohol and tobacco; these two habits had probably contributed to the throat cancer in the first place.

Over the next few weeks Donald began to enjoy a remission, and we let ourselves hope that he was out of danger. That summer I moved back to New York, quitting the job at Houston, but I kept tabs on him from mutual friends. They told me he was becoming the old Donald again, except that he seemed miraculously to have given up liquor and smoking—oh, every now and then cadging a cigarette or sneaking a sip of wine at a party when Marion's back was turned.

During the spring of 1989, Barthelme went to Italy, visiting Ed Hirsch, who was there on a Prix de Rome. From all accounts, Donald was in good spirits in Rome. Passing up sightseeing, he preferred to spend his days marketing, cooking, and working on his new novel, *The King*. So in July, when I ran into someone who told me Donald was in bad shape, I wanted to argue that that was old news, no longer current. But it was current. I was stunned, yet at the same time not: when you learn that someone in remission from cancer has had a relapse, it is never a total surprise. I prayed that Donald would somehow be strong enough to pull out of it again.

A week later, waiting by the cash register for a breakfast table at the Black Labrador Inn in Martha's Vineyard, I was turning the pages of the *New York Times* and came across Donald Barthelme's obituary. There was that familiar face, staring at me with unruffled calm. It wore the same expression he wrote about in his story "Critique de la Vie Quotidienne": "you assume a thoughtful look (indeed, the same grave and thoughtful look you have been wearing all day, to confuse your enemies and armor yourself against the indifference of your friends) . . ."

I suddenly remembered the time I had written an essay on friendship for *Texas Monthly*, and I had described a "distinguished colleague" (transparently Donald) whom I liked but with whom I could never establish a real friendship. To my surprise, since Barthelme generally shunned confrontation of any sort, he confronted me on it. "I saw what you wrote about me in that *Texas Monthly* piece," he said, letting me know by his ensuing silence that if I felt there was anything needing to be cleared up, he was willing to give me the opportunity.

"Did it . . . distress you?" I asked.

"I was a bit distressed, yes. But I recognize that that's your style as a personal essayist. You write about people you know; I don't."

"Did you think that what I wrote was . . . inaccurate?"

"No, no, not necessarily. I grant you it's hard for me to make friends. Ever since my two best friends, Tom Hess and Harold Rosenberg, died . . ." and he repeated substantially what he had told me the first time.

After his death a wise man who knew us both said, "Maybe Donald couldn't be a friend, but I think he had deep feelings for all of us." It was hard for me sometimes to distinguish between the taciturnity of deep feeling and unconcern. On my side, I felt guilty for having been one of those indifferent friends who didn't take the trouble to call near the end and ask about his condition. I had told myself, Don't bother them, you're not in the inner circle anyway—a poor excuse.

I have been assessing him in these pages through the prism of my needs, hence probably misjudging him. Certainly it is perverse of me to have manufactured a drama of being rejected by Barthelme, when the objective truth is that he was almost always kind to me—distant (such was his character) but benevolent.

It has not been easy to conjure up a man who, for all his commanding presence, had something of the ghost about him even in his lifetime. My relationship to him all along was, in a sense, with a rich, shifting absence. Donald is still hovering on the page, fading, I am starting to lose him. I had hoped to hold on to him by fixing his portrait. And now I hear him knocking, like the statue of the slain Commendatore in *Don Giovanni,* warning me that I will be punished for my sins, my patricidal betrayals of his privacy.

I have one more memory to offer: the night of the first fund-raising ball for the creative writing program. When the ball had ended, I could sense an air of letdown afterward as Donald and Marion, Cynthia and I drove in the Barthelme's pickup truck to their house for a nightcap. The event had been pretty successful, but not as large a windfall financially as we had fantasized, after the year's work we had put into it. I tried a few jokes, but I could see the others had invested too much in the evening to jest about it. When we arrived, instead of sitting around having a postmortem, we—began singing songs. Cynthia has a fine trained voice, and Donald had a lovely baritone and a great memory for lyrics: Cole Porter, musical comedy, jazz ballads. It turned into a wonderfully pleasurable evening. Each of us alternated proposing songs, and the others joined in, to the best of our memories. Slowly the tension of organizing the ball seeped away. Donald seemed particularly at ease. There was no need to articulate his thoughts, except in this indirect, song-choosing fashion. It was another instance of Barthelme expressing himself most willingly through an outlet other than his chosen vocation: Donald the would-be graphic artist, the moving man, the decorator, the pop singer.

Vivian Gornick

At the University
Little Murders of the Soul

THE OTHER NIGHT AT A PARTY IN NEW YORK I RAN INTO CHARLOTTE; NEXT DAY IN A RESTAURANT I saw Daniel; the day after that in the post office Myra. I have loved these people—how I have loved them!—and all for the same reason. I am hungry for the sentence structure in their heads. It's the conversation between us that makes me love them. Responding to the shape of their sentences, my own grow full and free: thought becomes expressive, emotions clarify, and I am happy, happier than at any other time. Nothing makes me feel more alive, and in the world, than the sound of my own mind working in the presence of one that's responsive. Talking with Charlotte or Myra or Daniel the grittiness washes out. Connected to myself, I am now connected to others. Solitude is relieved. I am at peace inside my skin.

Yet in each case I could not hold onto the friendship. I failed to comfort as well as stimulate. With me *they* did not clarify. In my company each became more fragile; more complicated, more self-involved, not less. I did not give them back themselves as they wished and needed to have themselves returned. In friendship as in love peace is required as well as excitement. Unless both are present, the graft does not take. Connection remains a matter of the unreliable moment. Without steady connection the friendship has no future. In New York anything without a future is instantly flung back into the distracting surge.

Failure of connection among like-minded people is a preoccupation of mine. The people I know are all talkers: people for whom conversation is vital, the kind of people who if they're not talking don't know they're alive. Yet, many is the evening I have sat in my chair after a gathering of some sort staring into the emptiness of the past few hours, thinking about the words spoken among "people like ourselves"; words that should have opened us to ourselves but had in fact shut us down, left us feeling abstract and demoralized. Which, I wonder as I sit alone late at night, was the sentence offered as a stimulation but received as a challenge; the nuance that put Daniel off rather than drew him in; the response that scattered Charlotte's insight and flattened Myra's spirit? Why did it happen so easily, and so often? Why did we come so close, yet remain apart? Everyone in the room was decent, intelligent, literate. We all pulled the same lever in the voting booth, read the same book reviews in the *Times*. None of us was in real estate or city government. What had gone wrong here? The answer was always the same.

Good conversation is dependent on a simple but mysterious fit of mind and spirit that cannot be achieved, it just occurs. It's not a matter of mutual interests or class concerns or commonly held ideals, it's a matter of temperament; the thing that makes someone respond instinctively with an appreciative "I know just what you mean," rather than a challenging "What do you mean by that?" In the presence of shared temperament conversation almost never loses its free, unguarded flow. In its absence one is always walking on eggshells. Shared temperament is analogous to the way a set of gears works. The idea is not complicated but the mesh must be perfect. Not approximate, perfect. Otherwise the gears refuse to turn.

It's years of university teaching that have made me think about temperament. In university towns one sees countless "people like ourselves" living whole lives inside the isolation of what I've come to call the Syndrome of the Approximate Response, acclimating daily to the repeated sound of the phrase, the nuance, the sentence spoken by a colleague or a neighbor that makes one shrivel rather than expand. It is a kind of death in life to which university people become inured.

I once worked in a writing program in the South where another writer working with me was a woman my own age from New York. This department also boasted a Black Mountain poet as well as a novelist who wrote magic realism and a philosophic nature essayist. Before I left New York people said to me, "What a golden company you are fallen among. You're in for a winter of great conversation." As it turned out, none of us had very much to say to one another. The woman from New York was religious, the magic realist an alcoholic, the poet pathological on feminism, the nature writer socially autistic. By which I mean, Who knows what any of them was really like? Not I. All *I* know is that in their company I felt abstract, and in mine they felt the same.

The New York writer and I were both Jewish and we'd both been to Israel. One night at a dinner party she and I were explaining the country to the others.

"In Israel you can heal yourself of modern life," she said.

"Only in Tel Aviv do you feel like you're in the world," I said.

"The country brings you back to original values," she said.

"You feel like you're choking on nineteenth-century politics," I said.

"There you recover the power and beauty of the family," she said.

"The sexual immaturity is unbelievable," I said.

Every time I opened my mouth I heard in her response, "What do you mean by that?" as she did in mine.

We were temperamentally mismatched, all of us. We remained a collection of expatriates, isolated from one another, each of us hanging there in solitary southern space.

It was a period of exile not because of the inability to connect but because I was unable to talk about the inability to connect. Whenever I raised the matter my colleagues looked at me: first puzzled, then uneasy, then dismissive. I was making a great deal out of not very much, I was told.

"Who needs all that socializing," the magic realist said.

"It's a relief to be left alone," the essayist said.

"I don't know what you're talking about," the poet said.

-◌- -◌- -◌-

I've been teaching on and off for more than ten years now. I go out, I come back, go out and come back. These stints of mine are only a matter of three or four months—I couldn't leave New York for any real length of time—but there are more hours in four months than I could ever before have imagined. It isn't just that a weekend can last three years in a university town; after all, that can happen anywhere. In New York a good depression easily slows the raging hurry down to a dreamy sleep-walk, any day of the week. But in the city no matter how dragged out the day, the hours remain, somehow, grounded. A limit is placed on the *idea* of isolation. I may not be making love myself but the air I breath is charged; I am not doing politics, it is true, but there is politics in the daily exchange; my own appetite is without edge yet appetite is clearly the coin of the realm. When the hours grow long in a university town I walk streets that are empty of people, silent and motionless. The dreaminess thickens. Soon, there are no human reminders. I start to free-float. Sunny tree-lined streets become a moon walk.

It's the silence, especially, that gets to me. As the days and the weeks accumulate it deepens: sinks down into flesh, presses on bone, induces a pressure in the ears that comes back up buzzing. It's a silence created in streets where sex and politics die early because conversation is not a daily requirement; expressive language has passed out of common usage; people speak to transmit information, not to connect.

Mine has been a pilgrim's progress through the university. I have passed back and forth among the provincial, the respected, and the patrician where I have sometimes been welcomed, sometimes ignored, sometimes received with the civility accorded an equal. Each encounter has had its consequence. Embraced, I learned one thing, shunted aside another. But, inevitably and in all cases, I am struck by the open space into which daily exchange falls, the buzzing silence that surrounds the earnest chatter. The history of that silence is what I've learned about at school.

-◌- -◌- -◌-

Stirling, Maine, was a movie-set college town: white frame houses, hundreds of maple trees, lawns enclosed by low stone walls. Some neighborhoods were good, others better. The marginals were literally at the margin: you had to drive to the edge of town to see peeling paint and trashed front yards. From any house that an academic might be living in the world spread out in all directions: safe, gentle, prosperous. There were women on the faculty, blacks on the campus, and divorce in abundance, but a deep settled conservatism governed the atmosphere: one of working husbands, mothering wives, the politics of the world an abstraction.

I was the only visitor in the writing program that year, and nothing about me was designed to promote easy friendships among the permanent faculty—I was a woman, a New Yorker, a writer who lived primarily off her writing; they were men who had spent many years in Stirling, writers who wrote sparsely if at all, and lived academic lives—but as it turned out they were a somewhat boozy lot, eager to welcome the stranger in their midst. Every Friday afternoon the writers gathered at four o'clock in a friendly hotel bar just off campus, and one of them always stopped by my office to say, "Coming, kid?"

The words were part of a style they had all adopted. The style was an anachronism—heavy drinking, tough-guy locutions, ironic weariness—one that belonged in a World War II movie, not on an American college campus in the eighties, but it was a way these men had of separating themselves from the place in which they lived. They came together, I soon realized, on these Friday afternoons to rage like expatriates against their outcast state. I had never before heard people speak with so reckless and impassioned a contempt for the circumstance in which they passed their lives. The sentence structure of scorn grew ever more resourceful as the writers reviled themselves, and each other, for spending their lives teaching the unteachable.

One man in the writing program was made conspicuous by his absence on Friday afternoons, a novelist named Gordon Cole. Apparently, Gordon and Stanley Malin—a writer always in attendance on Friday afternoon—did not speak to each other, hadn't spoken in years. Where Gordon went Stanley failed to appear, and where Stanley presided Gordon was sure to do the same.

The disagreement between the two men had originally to do with what courses to assign writing students. Stanley had said students of writing should study everything, poetry, fiction, and nonfiction. Gordon had said nonsense. Why did a budding novelist have to waste his time learning how write an essay he was never going to write? After some years the men had quarreled violently over this philosophic difference; such an impasse had been reached that now they were unable to speak or even sit easily together in a group of their colleagues.

The quarrel, its depth and insistence, was puzzling to me, as I was repeatedly struck by how well matched these two seemed in intelligence, breadth of outlook, and literary ardor. What a pity, I often thought, that each was denied the pleasure of the other's mind. No one else in the program spoke of books and writing as freely, as vividly, as did both Gordon and Stanley, no one relished thinking out loud as much as they. Having coffee with one or the other, the entertaining high-mindedness of the conversation inevitably warmed me through and through. Yet neither could do for the other what each one so easily did for me. For each man the sentences the other spoke had become an infliction—and then a wound. Mention one to the other, and the face of the man in front of you instantly formed itself into a mask. Behind the mask neither man could be reached.

Stanley Malin was a teacher of writing in a style I remembered: an old-fashioned curmudgeon. Writing was holy and he made the girls cry. Brilliant naive, arrogant, he might stand before a class and intone, "The writer must rend his flesh. He must lay himself open to the pain. The suffering. The reader must *feel* the crucial rending of the flesh." Then suddenly he'd drop the rhetoric and announce in a voice blunt with authority, "Good writing has two characteristics. It's alive on the page and the reader is persuaded that the writer is on a voyage of discovery." When Stanley spoke in this voice anyone could learn from him.

But is was not only the girls Stanley made cry. After thirty years in Stirling he'd done that to almost everyone who had crossed his path. His mind was made in the shape of a steel trap. He had a way of encouraging people to open up quickly—the interest was penetrating, he asked many questions, one flourished in a matter of minutes—then he'd find the weak spot in the work, the argument, the personality, and he'd close in. Just as quickly, one would be made to feel a fool. You'd talked on and on, and you'd hung yourself.

His was the seductive power of an original mind coupled with a spirit of such startling negativism that people were drawn to the pleasure of his sentence structure only to find themselves wounded by the malice of his observations, and then amazed to be coming back for more. Eventually, of course, they turned away from that belittling tongue, that scorning clever mind, that excoriating need to take everyone down. Sooner or later, all men and most women walked away from Stanley feeling themselves the sum of their disabilities, and then they sought him out no more.

He was alone, and only slowly did I understand that he could do nothing to remedy his isolation. Behind the brilliant derisiveness lay a passivity of monumental proportion. Stanley Malin was a man who if the light went out in the room he remained in the dark; if he walked out in the morning and found the car had a flat tire, he turned around and went back in the house for the day; if a woman said she was leaving him unless he spoke more intimately with her, he told her to make sure the door was closed on her way out. All Stanley could do was wait for people like me to come through town. Everyone else had been used up.

Gordon Cole was as sociable as Stanley was reclusive. His wife had people to dinner once a month, and when a visiting writer or intellectual was in town she routinely produced an evening for eight or ten. These dinners had been going on for twenty years. There were one or two couples who were always in attendance, and five or six others who showed up at every second or third party. Nearly every man in the room was in the English department, and nearly every woman in the room was a faculty wife. The company ranged in age from forty to sixty and the conversation was, with rare exception, what is called civilized. Strong opinion was unwelcome at the table, and sustained exchange was experienced as tiresome.

I discovered that people introduced subjects in order to allude, not to discuss. There'd be three minutes on the headlines, seven on European travel, two on Friday night's concert. Real estate often went a good ten or fifteen minutes, and so did taxes and the cost of schooling for the children. Books never came up, and neither did the students.

Gordon was a puzzle to me at these dinners. Immensely considerate of his guests— pulling out chairs, passing dishes, refreshing drinks—his manner was uniformly affectionate. He'd sit smiling amiably when someone at the table began an anecdote full of promise, continue smiling long after it had become apparent that the point being made was too simple to be interesting, and I would see that his smile was fixed. He had stopped listening halfway through the story. His was the attentiveness of the genuinely detached. In one sense he welcomed people to his house, in another he was more of a stranger in the room than I.

Above the mantelpiece in the Cole living room stood a row of leatherbound Balzacs. Once, I began leafing through *Cousin Bette* and found myself moved by the beautifully worn pages, the absorptive thought in the marginalia. The book itself was an act of love. This was the Gordon with whom I talked when we were alone at school, a man for whom literature remained alive and life-giving. But here at the party this Gordon disappeared and in his place was a man of impenetrable politeness. Watching his masked face at the table I often wondered where he was at that moment, and in whose company. One night I realized that he was nowhere, and with no one. Gordon Cole at his own dinner table was the equivalent of Stanley Malin slumped in the dark, sitting beside a phone that no longer rang.

In time the two men became emblematic to me. In my mind's eye I saw each of them sitting alone, encircled by an isolation that spread through the silent streets across the town, out to the margin, to the peeling paint and the trashed yards neither of them ever had to look at. A tide of emotional bewilderment would rise in me. Here they were, thrown together in this small tight world, each one longing for the kind of conversation the other could supply, yet each one locked into insult and injury less than a mile apart. At that moment, the littleness of life seemed insupportable, its impact large and its consequence inevitable.

A week before I left Stirling a history teacher named Barsamian was arrested. He'd been caught slashing the tires of another history teacher, a man named Wallerstein. The incident was reported in the local paper. The memorable detail in the report was that Barsamian and Wallerstein had had a falling out (over standards) fifteen years before. The two men hadn't spoken in years.

I remember staring at the sentence, the one about them not having spoken in years. I remember thinking, Wallerstein has remained alive in Barsamian's brooding mind all this time; alive and central; an instrument of inflamed injury felt each day as they pass each other in the department corridor, sit in the same room for a committee meeting, brush past a table in the faculty club.

I was accustomed to the murderous pathologies of New York, but this was different. This was Chekhovian. These people felt violated in their souls by an atmosphere that denied them sympathetic understanding, and the violation had come to fill the inner landscape. Again bewilderment rose in me. It was inconceivable to me that intelligent, decent people should reduce themselves to eccentricity. Why was this happening?

These thoughts separated me from the people with whom I taught at Stirling, turned me into a narrator and them into characters. When I said good-bye I felt I was on one side of a human divide, they on the other. I was made of different stuff. What was in them could never be in me.

The situation was indeed Chekhovian. My turn—like that of the doctor in *Ward Six* who understands confinement only when he himself is at last imprisoned—lay just ahead.

❧   ❧   ❧

At Stirling they hadn't known Derrida from an insurance agent. At the University of the Farwest they not only knew who Derrida was, they knew the name of his publisher and the size of his last advance. Stirling was time warp: a place where everything important had occurred years ago, and people were now living with the outcome of lives long decided. At Farwest nothing was settled and no one had made peace. The department quivered with restless ambition.

Eight men and one woman taught writing here. They were novelists and poets in their mid or late fifties, many of whom had achieved a moment of fame during the sixties. I soon discovered that each of them held the place they found themselves in at a discount. One and all thought they belonged somewhere better. The atmosphere reeked of brooding courtesies and subterranean tensions. I did not for a long time understand exactly what it was I was looking at. I had never before encountered mass depression.

A graduate student picked me up at the airport on a Friday afternoon and drove to the dormitory rooms that had been secured for me. I arranged the stark little apartment to suit minimal needs and then went out for a walk. The town was calm, spacious, western, the streets wide as boulevards, the mountains cut out against the sky. Once again: houses and trees, no people. All as silent and motionless as it had been in Stirling, but here the clarity of the light and the sweetness of the air were so powerful they became a presence. It was Monday morning before I realized that, except for a few phone calls from home, I'd not spoken to a human being the entire weekend.

One by one, the following encounters took place in the course of the week:

A tall fat man stood beaming in the open doorway of my room. "My name is Dennis Mullman," he said. "I've written nineteen books and they all hate me." I laughed, and he asked how I was getting on. I told him I didn't know as I hadn't yet met anyone. "That's how they are here," he said bitterly. "No one's interested in anyone. They're all wrapped up in their own miserable selves." He withdrew, promising to be in touch soon.

"I'm Lewis Waldman," said a voice in my ear as I stood at the secretary's desk in the English office. "Oh, hello," I turned enthusiastically to face a boyish-looking man dressed in blue jeans and a tweed jacket. I recognized the name as that of the program director. "Let me know if you need anything." He waved the pipe in his hand at me and walked away.

A woman darted at me in the mailroom. "Hello hello hello," she said in a loud friendly voice. "I'm Sabina Morris. Am I glad to see *you!* Gotta get together. Talk about *Noo Yawk.* Can you buh-*lieve* this place? Twelve years I'm stuck here. Just think about *that* for a minnit." She rolled her eyes to the ceiling. "Lissen, we gotta get together." I nodded and said I had nothing but free time. "Nah," she said, pushing the air away with her hand. "Famous writer like you?" She snapped her fingers. "You'll be all booked up in a minnit. Lissen, I'll call you. We'll get together."

A cherubic-looking man—red-checked and gray-bearded, wearing blue jeans, sneakers, and a moth-eaten sweater—came toward me on the street. When he got close enough I saw the anxiety in his bright blue eyes. "Hi," he said. "I'm Sonny Coleman." He was one of the three New York novelists I knew had spent the last twenty years at Farwest. "How ya doin?" "Okay," I said hesitantly. He laughed. "Well, one good thing about this place. They leave you alone." He saluted me good-naturedly and went on his way.

A week passed, two, then three. I met my classes and walked the streets of the town. The air and the light still felt like company but on Friday afternoon of the fourth weekend I left a note in Lewis Waldman's mailbox. "I'm beginning to feel like a trespasser rather than a visitor." I wrote. "What's up?" Sunday morning, late, my phone rang. "Jeez," Waldman said. "Your note took me by surprise. I thought you were meeting people all over the place." No, I said cheerfully, that wasn't the case and since this was the fourth weekend in a row I hadn't seen anyone or gone anywhere, I thought I'd let him know. "Well," he said, "how about dinner tonight with Irwin Stoner and the woman he lives with?" Wonderful, I said, and hung up thinking, Now everything will be all right.

At seven o'clock sharp Waldman arrived in his tweed jacket and blue jeans and we drove off to a basement restaurant in an old hotel that here too served as a university meeting place. A handsome couple rose in their seats as we entered the room. The woman was tall with a headful of curly blond hair, the man of medium height with a delicate face and gray-brown hair cut so that a thick strand of it kept falling over one eye. We all shook hands and sat down.

Irwin Stoner was the writing program's Famous Person. He had written six novels in twenty-five years, all published in counterculture presses. The first three had been applauded, the second three reviewed respectfully. He'd been teaching at Farwest for years. I had looked forward to meeting him.

In the weeks that followed I tried to retrace the course that evening had taken, to see if there'd been a specific point at which we could have done it differently, but I was never able to locate the moment; and in fact I don't think there was one. We had simply been ourselves. With every set of observations made, and responses received, the distance between us had cracked wider.

"What a relief it must be to get out of New York," Stoner said.

"Not, really," I said. "It's just that I can't make a living in the city."

"It's great here. They leave you alone," Waldman said.

"I hate being left alone," I said.

"How can you write with the literary Mafia breathing down your neck?"

"I live below Fourteenth Street. The Mafia doesn't leave midtown."

"You see that establishment shit getting published all the time, it's demoralizing."

"Everything get published nowadays, not just establishment writing."

"How can you say that! Christ, if you're any good at all you can't *possibly* get a decent reading in a mainstream house."

"Are you kidding?" I said. "Never before in the history of the world has so much writing gone to print, good and bad alike."

"What are you talking about! Susan Sontag has a stranglehold on the intellectual press. Without her say-so nothing gets accepted."

"You don't really believe that, do you?"

Abigail Duffy, the Spanish teacher who lived with Stoner, laid a restraining hand on his arm—"Please, Irwin," she kept saying, "*please*"—but he shook it off. His skin was now flushed, his eyes sparking. He leaned into the provocation. I saw that my presence, certainly my perspective, was acting like an electric prod on him, making him cry out in lively anguish, putting the color back in newly angry cheeks. The thought made me lonely. My mouth closed in mid-retort. When it opened again it was to say, "Perhaps you've got a point there." I grew conciliatory, and the argument ground to a halt. After that, we worked hard to repair the torn-up atmosphere but in no time, it seemed, we were all out on the street inhaling gratefully into the cold night air.

Irwin Stoner was in advance of all that was to come.

Do what I would I could not make connection at Farwest. I had competed successfully, it seemed, for the right to visit among people none of whom wanted to know me. I had coffee, lunch, a chat at the mailbox with each person in the department, once. No disasters, no repeats. The exchanges were pleasant, even amiable, and always left me feeling abstract.

I tried to hear myself as I might have been heard, but I could not. I'd run into a writer or a teacher in the corridor or on the campus, we'd stop to chat, I'd be asked how I was and I'd answer—in three full paragraphs, as someone once said of me. Maybe it was those three paragraphs. I had always considered the fullness of my reply the only generosity I know myself to possess. But at Farwest, where people replied in one sentence, I saw eyes glaze over as I launched into the third paragraph. Those glazed eyes sank me. They cut me adrift. Once adrift, I was lost. I could learn nothing, about myself or anyone around me.

I taught my classes, read, went for long walks, sat at my desk, and spoke nearly every day with someone in New York. Yet, increasingly, I became more and more aware of those around me with whom I did *not:* talk or walk or eat. "Why doesn't *he* want to know me?" I'd find myself thinking as I collected my mail. "Why doesn't *she* want to have coffee?" walking across the campus. "Why don't *they* invite me to dinner?" in the middle of reading a student paper. The faces of my indifferent colleagues appeared in the air before me, occupying not my thoughts but a space on a field of inner vision. Gradually, these faces appeared so often they made the space shimmer, and then the field itself expanded to accommodate my unhappy concern. New York receded in imagination. My friends became voices on the telephone. Every day now the people who did not speak to me loomed larger than those who did. I began to brood.

The absence of response became a presence in my life. Out of this presence came a sense of isolation that grew steadily more pervasive. Inside the pervasiveness a vacuum formed. Inside the vacuum I began to feel not merely alone, but under quarantine: a human substance to be avoided. Possessed of an acute need to make connection I became, more than I had known myself to be, a creature of immediate experience. I was losing an inner balance whose precariousness took me by surprise.

A woman who taught seventeenth-century lit became symbolic of the rejecting world. She's one of the best, I'd been told, gracious and scholarly, an asset to literature and women's studies, a person I'd surely want to know. Friendly enough when we met, thereafter in my presence this woman did not speak. If she passed me in the hall she averted her gaze. If I walked into the lounge and she was reading a newspaper she'd glance briefly at me and, without a word or a nod, return to her paper. If she was forced to look into my face she'd manage a brief wintry smile. She had about her an air of aloofness that radiated judgment. It was a kind of behavior I had long ago shut the door on, but now at Farwest it began to invade me. Each morning when I awoke this woman's face flashed in the air before me, and angry distress flooded my heart. Once, years before, at a writers' colony a young poet who'd been feeling miserably left out of things had fantasized me at the center of a clique that was deliberately excluding her. The seventeenth-century lit teacher would have been amazed to learn that she had now become to me what I had been to the poet.

The classroom could only reflect my troubled state. The students were grave, blond, silent. I heard my voice growing thin and rhetorical. I must have said "profound," "original," and "important" fifty times an hour about books whose originality and importance would have been self-evident had I not been performing in a void.

I called a friend in New York, the wisest and most talented teacher I knew.

"They just stare at me," I told her. "I talk, and they stare."

"Darling," Ann said, "they *want* to speak, but they don't know how. It's hard for them. *Adults* don't know how. You know that. People like you and me, who are asked a question about a book, or anything else for that matter, and marshal a full response in a matter of seconds, we're rare. And these are *children*. For them it's sheer terror. They want to respond, they want to please you. They've read the book. They have feelings. But they can't find a way in to save their lives. They sit there with that puzzled frowning look on their faces. . . . The teacher who finds the questions to let them speak is setting them free for the rest of their lives. Releasing them into an articulateness their *parents* don't possess."

"Omigod," I moaned. "I can't do this."

Ann laughed straight into the receiver. "It takes years," she said. "Years."

I hung up and sat staring at the phone. A light came on in my head. I will go to the students, I thought. I will say to them, On the other side of your silence is a suffering human being. They will understand, and they will act.

Then the face of the woman who taught seventeenth-century lit intervened between me and my bright thought, and the flare of hope dimmed. If *she* could look at me week after week without a word or a nod why should *they* speak to me?

At a university reception I stood facing a scientist and a historian with a glass in my hand. The scientist was old and European, his voice resonant with the sound of one at his ease in the drawing rooms of the world, an adept at educated small talk. The historian nodded in all the appropriate places, supplying his own share of anecdotal banality. The men turned to me, inviting me to add, subtract, do what I will. I opened my mouth to speak, and nothing came out. Suddenly, I had not a thing in the world to say. At that moment I could not imagine that I had ever had anything to say, that any words of mine had ever animated an exchange, improved a conversation, given pleasure. I looked blankly into the face of each man. Then I excused myself, and walked away.

We all know that we are interesting only relatively speaking; but we don't really know it; and secretly we believe otherwise. To be faced daily with the suspicion that actually you may not be interesting *at all* is a frightening circumstance to negotiate. First you think, It must be them, it can't be me. Then you think, No, it's not them, it *is* me. Getting to the third thought, It's not them, it's not me, it's the two of us together—that takes some diving. At Farwest I shuttled back and forth between the first two, never even approaching the third.

One day, weeks after the reception, I ran into the European scientist. He asked me how things were going.

"All right," I said, perhaps ten seconds too slowly.

The scientist shifted his books from one hand to the other, adjusted his glasses, and looked at me.

"One thing you got to know about academics," he said. "Either you're too good for them, or they're too good for you."

It was my turn to look at him. I had nothing to shift of to adjust. The moment extended itself.

"You mean I'm too famous for the timid and not famous enough for the ambitious."

"You got it," he said.

"But surely the world isn't divided between the timid and the ambitious."

He made no reply. Instead he raised his hand to an invisible hat brim, saluted me, and went on his way.

I stood looking after him. Something broke loose inside, and there flared up in me a bitter torch of anger. Unjust! I cried to myself. Unjust.

Sabina Morris came hurrying down a path destined to cross mine. She was always hurrying. Once or twice a week since I'd been here she had rushed past me, halloo-ing, "Gotta get together." Today, sure enough, she called out, "I'll phone you, we'll have lunch." I put my hand out and stopped her. "Listen," I said, "it's okay to just say hello. We don't have to go through this charade whenever we run into each other." Instantly she cried out, "Do you know what it means to *live* here! You fancy visitors come out, you think all we got to do is entertain you. I work *constantly*. If I'm not teaching I'm grading papers. If I'm not grading papers I'm at committee meetings. I have no *life* here, no life at all! You don't understand! Nobody understands! We get no understanding at all!" And she rushed off.

Two days later the scientist invited me to dinner. His wife was a psychologist in the town. I told her of my encounter with Sabina Morris.

"She really believes that," the psychologist said, "that she has no time. But what it means is that she can't do anything because she has to recover every day from what it feels like to be talking *all the time* to people with whom she only rarely engages—the students, the colleagues, the deans. That's why *most* academics have no time. Only they don't know it. It's the not knowing that makes them so unhappy.

"If they knew *who* they were, and *where* they were, they'd take the bad with the good with more equanimity, and life would then be infinitely more cheerful. But as it is, they live in a continuous state of worried anxiety because this is not what they signed on for. What they signed on for was a 'life of the mind.' . . . Nobody thinks any of this out before they go plunging after tenure. . . . They all come to the university with a fantasy of intellectual gifts they expect to have nourished. But most of them, it turns out, are neither thinkers nor scholars, they're simply hardworking teachers. This, it seems, is an impossible reality to adjust to. It *feels* as though recognition of the talent within is being withheld—by all these nasty, inferior people all around them. Sabina Morris will spend the rest of her years here being eaten alive over the wrongness of her life and hating, absolutely *hating*, the students, her chairman, the provost, the chancellor. It's all because of *them*."

I found myself relishing the psychologist's words. It made me happy to see it her way, to think Sabina Morris passive and cowardly, a dream-ridden woman made small and ungenerous by self-deception. It's because *she* can neither absorb nor rise above her circumstance that things are as they are here, I thought. If *she* was different life here would be different. If *she* had more vitality, more experience, more detachment *I* would not be feeling trapped in a tight mean world. Smoldering, I realized for a moment, as much as she. But I let the moment go. The thought of Sabina Morris's moral and psychological deficiencies was giving me too much pleasure. The righteousness of my own pain burned in me, and I held the burning dear. In fact, I drew closer to the fire.

That night I lay on the couch in my sublet apartment, hands locked behind my head, gazing up at the empty square of white ceiling. I saw that I was in the grip of a humiliation I was inflicting on myself, yet I felt powerless to bring it under control. No, not powerless, unwilling. It pressed like a tumor against the inner wall of a fully fleshed chest I now thought of as narrow and bony. I needed the humiliation to fill myself in.

At midnight I understood why Barsamian had slashed Wallerstein's tires.

ᛜ   ᛜ   ᛜ

Impala U. is one of the richest schools in the country, and its writing program one of the best. The faculty publishes steadily and lives at the end of a continuous flow of invitations to readings, conferences, symposia. Sitting in the middle of the California desert, the university sparkles with green grass, stone fountains, red-tiled roofs, and palm trees. No one teaching here wishes to be somewhere else. Everyone knows this is the place to be.

At Impala there were weekly lunches, monthly readings, picnics and galas, museum openings and film festivals. The wives of doctors and lawyers had been put on a board of trustees that gave them access to the writers; they, in turn, raised money for student fellowships. The faculty was amused by the arrangement and fell in easily with organized events, as well as casual meetings around school that included students, staff, and townsfolk. A loose-knit camaraderie prevailed that sounded a note of light-hearted civility. We're secure enough, it said, to be accommodating.

Mack Dienstag, the friendly language poet who directed the program, found me an apartment, showed me around town, and gave an entertaining welcome dinner. At the dinner were Lloyd Levine and Paul Braun, a pair of poets in their late thirties; Kermit Kinnell, the program's Famous Novelist; and Carol Riceman, a critic-essayist in her forties. These people seemed to enjoy one another. Soon the banter among them picked up speed, and then direction. Within minutes it had equipped itself with a line of thought, making each of us sound intelligent in our own ears. What a good time I was having! I could not know that, for the people at the table, this dinner was obligatory. The months ahead looked promising.

The apartment was comfortable, the schedule easy, and the generic character of social life in Impala suited me well enough. I might take in a movie with one of the writers, but just as often it might be a doctor's wife or a graduate student inviting me to dinner: equally pleasing. What, after all, did I care where I got invited, or by whom, so long as I wasn't sitting home alone night after night as I had at Farwest? Yet I did remember the pleasure of that first evening and puzzled sometimes over why it failed to replicate itself.

I saw the people who'd been at the table almost every day, but in some crucial sense I didn't see them at all. Now and then I'd walk into Lloyd Levine's office to say, "Let's get together." "Definitely," he'd always reply. "This week is bad, we've got so many visitors coming, but next week for sure. Anyway, I'll see you at the department lunch on Tuesday, and at that reception on Friday afternoon. We can talk then." A day later I'd have the same exchange with Mack Dienstag or Carol Riceman and walk away feeling expectant but uneasy. The talk at lunch would inevitably be of writing program business and at the reception it was dinner party chit-chat: three minutes on the local art opening, seven on London versus New York, six on the fool in the White House. I was always left feeling tired, wanting only to get away. Meeting up with Mack or Carol or Lloyd at one of these affairs was, in a way, worse than not seeing them at all.

It was at Impala that I came to realize: when people find themselves in spirit-diluting proximity three times in a single week they have no urge to search each other out for an evening of real conversation. The memory of negative feeling lingers in the nerves and is aroused for a good twenty-four hours after by the sight of those with whom you've committed the emptiness. At none of these affairs did anyone ever suggest getting together afterward. Neither, I noticed, was the suggestion made if any of us ran into each other the next day at school. Compulsive socializing, I began to see, stirred up dissatisfactions that weren't allowed to clear out, they just kept on buzzing. Proximity was a hornet's nest.

One afternoon Sarabeth Kinnell called to say they had a visitor from New York, why didn't I come over for a drink. I was on my way to Mack Dienstag's to pick up a book I'd left at his house but sure, I said, I'd stop by. Later on at Mack's, I mentioned in passing that I'd just been at the Kinnells's. "Oh?" he said. "Are they having people over?" Something in his voice sounded a warning. Not really, I said, it had just been a spur-of-the-moment invite.

"Who was there?" he asked, carefully.

Why? I bantered, had he wanted to get out of the house?

"No," Mack said. "I hardly *ever* want to leave the house. I *love* being home." He hesitated. Then he said, "I just can't stand being left out."

"You're kidding?" I said.

"No," he laughed. "I'm not."

"What do you mean, left out?"

"It's crazy, I know. It sounds crazy even to me, but there it is. Mostly, I find gatherings a bore. I'd rather be home reading. But when I think the others are getting together, for whatever reason, and I'm not invited, I can't stand it. It preys on my mind."

"Which others?"

Mack smiled a broad, heavy smile. "The ones that count," he said, smiling ironically.

"I don't get it," I plowed on. "If you really want to stay home what does it matter who's getting together with whom? And if you *don't* want to stay home, what's the difference where you go as long as you have somewhere to go? Like Keats said, any set of people is as good as any other."

"You really believe that?" Mack said. "That any set of people is as good as any other?"

"Absolutely," I said firmly.

He sighed and handed me my book.

"You don't understand what it's like here," he said. "And it's hard for me to explain."

I found these words remarkable. At Farwest I had brooded over not being invited to dinner by people I didn't like, but here at Impala, where the company was plentiful if not ideal, I thought, What an ingrate you have to be to become neurotic over who is, or is not, inviting you to dinner. I should have known by now that to separate myself so grandly from a fellow sufferer was a guarantee I'd soon be eating my own distinction.

Impala dinner parties were, at first, a relief and a comfort. The amiability had so strong an effect on me that I was surprised my colleagues didn't feel as I felt at almost every table. I'd mention something interesting I had heard at the Dixons's, and Mack would say, "Oh, do you see them?" "Yes," I'd reply, "don't you?" "I used to," he'd say. "Used to see a lot of them. But haven't for years now." "What happened?" I'd ask. "I don't know, exactly," he'd say. "I guess we just ran out. . . ." This was a sentence I heard repeatedly. "We just ran out." Rarely, if ever, did I hear of a friendship ripening at Impala; almost always it was a tale of exhausted spirits having been arrived at.

It amused me, to hear them speak so, and then one evening—at the Dixons's, actually—the amusement suddenly evaporated. It struck me that almost every sentence I spoke that contained a piece of my mind had to be negotiated. The path leading to unimpeded thought was never clear, always clogged and strewn about with the ubiquitous "What do you mean by that?" So many exchanges seemed to bog down at the introductory stage, making the journey to a point obscure and wearying, most wearying. Why had I not seen this before? And why did I now seem to see nothing else?

It was at Impala that I first isolated the Syndrome of the Approximate Response. At the time I thought only that it was being inflicted on me. Then one night I delivered the Approximate Response myself, on a mildly grand scale, and the dynamic came clear. Things fell into place. I understood why the auditoriums during public readings grew emptier and emptier as the term progressed. I also understood why Mack Dienstag was preoccupied with being left out.

A famous Israeli poet came to read. He was handsome, self-contained, remote; a courteous smile played on his lips but he glazed over visibly when others talked. Paul Braun didn't show up at the dinner before the reading, and neither did Mack or Kermit. Serena and Lloyd Levine came, Carol and her husband, and me. Lloyd performed nonstop. He knew the poet's work by heart and had come prepared to give him the educated admiration every writer wants. The poet accepted Lloyd's deference benignly, while giving almost nothing back.

As we got up from the table Serena Levine said to me, "Isn't he sweet?" I looked at her. "No," I said, "he's not. He knows who he is at all times." Serena's eyes rested lightly on my face. "Believe me," she said, "for a man who knows who he is at all times he's sweet." I gazed at her in admiration. She *had* put in her time.

Then the poet read. From his cold mouth there issued images of beauty and of power. Throughout the reading I felt repeatedly what I had often felt here before: the extraordinary up-welling of a large spirit housed in a man of ordinary dimension. He spoke a great deal, much too much for a poet, his speech edging always toward pontification. Then he'd read a poem. Out would pour some stunning economy of insight and tenderness, and you'd be his all over again. The performance exhilarated and discomforted.

Afterward there was a reception, to which hardly anyone came. Faculty hurried away, and so did the students. None wished to submit themselves to the Great Man. Lloyd seemed exhausted, and Carol got frantic, insisting we all come back to her house for a drink. She couldn't bear for the poet to return to New York thinking Impala boring and provincial. In her living room he settled heavily into his chair, his face impassive, his eyes hooded, no longer benign. You could see, he had sung for his supper, he'd had it with the small talk, he wanted out, now.

Lloyd slumped on a couch across the room, staring at his shoes. He too had sung for his supper; he no longer knew what to do. The atmosphere infected me. I felt I had to entertain the company. I sat down on a hassock halfway between Lloyd and the poet, turning adeptly back and forth between them, and began to speak—brightly, quickly, fluently—about a trip I'd made to Israel. The poet sat back, a finger ridging his temple, his boiled eyes watching me, giving me no help at all. I spoke of Josef Brenner, saying the poet's work reminded me of Brenner's complicated feeling for Jerusalem. I explained Brenner to the others, a brilliant, early modern Hebrew novelist, little known in this country, just being rediscovered. I came to the end of my speech and turned like a good girl to the poet. He stared at me so long I thought he'd lost his English. Then he spoke.

"Actually," he said, a finger still in his temple, "Brenner's work is nothing like mine. Nothing at all. There is no resemblance whatever between us. And he is not brilliant. In fact, he is dull, quite dull. He is not being 'rediscovered.' He's been around all the time. We don't pay attention to him because we know how dull he is. But Americans come, and they make a fuss over him. They *discover* him. . . ." He shrugged and stopped talking.

The blood had left Carol's face and Lloyd was looking wild. I wanted to throw back my head and laugh out loud. The poet felt as I did when some brightly stupid person makes the same kind of sloppy-comparison mistake with me, and I'm not in the mood for a rescue mission. He wanted what I wanted: conversation that would nourish. Instead, he was getting junk food, empty calories. And so were we. I glanced over at Lloyd. His face had collapsed in weariness. None of us was getting what we needed. I saw then why the academics stop coming to these things: a sufficient number of such exchanges and the death of the heart threatens.

I also saw what led, paradoxically, to the obsession with being left out. When the meal is unsatisfactory often enough you become hooked on the idea that somewhere else people *must* be eating well. In a small, tight world, somewhere else inevitably becomes the people to your left and to your right who sat down last night at a table you were not invited to.

I found myself pitying the people around me. And then, of course, it was my turn.

One Tuesday, as the writing faculty was scattering after its weekly lunch, I heard Lloyd say, "Carol, sorry about that Proustian thing last night." "What Proustian thing?" Paul asked. Lloyd turned to him. "Remember when I called the waiter over and said to him . . ." I didn't hear the rest of the sentence. My mind had clouded over. They had dinner together, I was thinking, the three of them, they didn't invite me. They get together all the time, they never invite me. For the rest of the walk back to our offices I talked but I heard nothing: not what I said, not what anyone else said.

In the evening I lay on the couch with a book in my hands. I'd turn a page and on the page it would say, "Lloyd and Carol and Paul have dinner together all the time, they never invite me." The phone rang twice—my agent called from New York to say the book was doing well in England and a doctor's wife called to invite me to dinner. Each time I hung up, happy for a moment. Then the anxiety returned: Lloyd and Carol and Paul have dinner together, they never invite me.

I got up to make a cup of coffee. This is ri-*dic*-ulous, I said sternly to the pot of nearly boiling water. But the admonishment did no good. The brooding went on, for hours and for days. Whatever I was doing—teaching, reading, driving—suddenly I would remember 'Lloyd and Carol and Paul," and the thought was a needle in my heart. All I wanted was: *their* company, *their* attention, *their* fun. Everything else was the booby prize.

That weekend a writer I knew well came to visit, and we spent a wonderful evening together. I heard my sentences being received exactly as I sent them out. Because the ones I spoke were being responded to, I had more of them to speak. Because I had more to say I felt myself filling up. At the end of the evening I left the restaurant well fed. The hour was late. The heat had died down. I walked for a while, breathing deeply into the clear desert air. For the first time I realized that nowhere in Impala did I have the conversation that gave me back myself. I didn't need much of it, one in fact would do, but I did not have that one. I had many approximations, but not the thing itself. Hence the brooding over Lloyd-and-Carol-and-Paul.

I felt acutely the difference between the city and the small tight world. In New York if I feel bad about not being invited somewhere, the phone will ring shortly and I'm invited somewhere else just as good as the place I'm not being invited to (there, any one of six conversations will do). The brooding is a matter of minutes or an hour. I clear out quickly. I remain open, fluid, uncalculating. Here, at the university, the pain lingers. I cannot clear out. It is hard to heal. Because it is hard to heal I must defend myself: close off, grow scar tissue, thicken my hide. Speech becomes guarded. I give up expressiveness.

Or else turn into a lunatic.

I saw that I was losing it. I had thought as much, and then one day I was told as much. Serena Levine took me to lunch to let me know I was experienced as *violently* critical of: Impala, the university, the writing program. They were all, she said, beginning to feel alienated from me. My words were taken as a judgment on their lives. "You think you're only speaking your mind," she said bitterly, "but you're like the foreigner who takes you into his confidence while he trashes your country." On and on she went. I replied hotly. And then we each stopped talking at the same moment. The sun climbed high in the noon hour sky. The haze thickened and burned. Serena stared down at her plate. I looked out into the middle distance. University buildings began to shimmer. The silence between us accumulated. Here we sat, a lonely writer and an insecure faculty wife, each being made neurotic by isolation of the spirit induced at an institution in service to the life of the mind. The silence buzzed in my head. The heat became unbearable.

⚬ ⚬ ⚬

Marriage promises intimacy; when it fails to deliver the bond is destroyed.

Community promises friendship; when it fails to deliver the enterprise is dissolved.

The life of the mind promises conversation; when it fails to deliver its disciples grow eccentric.

It's easier actually to *be* alone than to be in the presence of that which arouses the need but fails to address it. For then we are in the presence of an absence and that, somehow, is not to be borne. The absence reminds us, in the worst way, that we are indeed alone: it suppresses fantasy, chokes off hope. The liveliness we start out with is stifled. We become demoralized and grow inert. The inertness is a kind of silence. The silence becomes an emptiness. One cannot really live with emptiness. The pressure is terrible; unendurable, in fact; not to be borne. Either one breaks out, or one becomes inured. To become inured is to fall into grief.

Jamaica Kincaid

A Small Place

THE ANTIGUA THAT I KNEW, THE ANTIGUA IN WHICH I GREW UP, IS NOT THE ANTIGUA YOU, a tourist, would see now. That Antigua no longer exists. That Antigua no longer exists partly for the usual reason, the passing of time, and partly because the bad-minded people who used to rule over it, the English, no longer do so. (But the English have become such a pitiful lot these days, with hardly any idea what to do with themselves now that they no longer have one quarter of the earth's human population bowing and scraping before them. They don't seem to know that this empire business was all wrong and they should, at least, be wearing sackcloth and ashes in token penance of the wrongs committed, the irrevocableness of their bad deeds, for no natural disaster imaginable could equal the harm they did. Actual death might have been better. And so all this fuss over empire—what went wrong here, what went wrong there—always makes me quite crazy, for I can say to them what went wrong: they should never have left their home, their precious England, a place they loved so much, a place they had to leave but could never forget. And so everywhere they went they turned it into England; and everybody they met they turned English. But no place could ever really be England, and nobody who did not look exactly like them would ever be English, so you can imagine the destruction of people and land that came from that. The English hate each other and they hate England, and the reason they are so miserable now is that they have no place else to go and nobody else to feel better than.) But let me show you the Antigua that I used to know.

In the Antigua that I knew, we lived on a street named after an English maritime criminal, Horatio Nelson, and all the other streets around us were named after some other English maritime criminals. There was Rodney Street, there was Hood Street, there was Hawkins Street, and there was Drake Street. There were flamboyant trees and mahogany trees lining East Street. Government House, the place where the Governor, the person standing in for the Queen, lived, was on East Street. Government House was surrounded by a high white wall—and to show how cowed we must have been, no one ever wrote bad things on it; it remained clean and white and high. (I once stood in hot sun for hours so that I could see a putty-faced Princess from England disappear behind these walls. I was seven years old at the time, and I thought, She has a putty face.) There was the library on lower High Street, above the Department of the Treasury, and it was in that part of High Street that all colonial government business took place. In that part of High Street, you could cash a cheque at the Treasury, read a book in the library, post a letter at the post office, appear before a magistrate in court. (Since we were ruled by the English, we also had their laws. There was a law against using abusive language. Can you imagine such a law among people for whom making a spectacle of yourself through speech is everything? When West Indians went to England, the police there had to get a glossary of bad West Indian words so they could understand whether they were hearing abusive language or not.) It was in that same part of High Street that you could get a passport in another government office. In the middle of High Street was the Barclays Bank. The Barclay brothers, who started Barclays Bank, were slave-traders. That is how they made their money. When the English outlawed the slave trade, the Barclay brothers went into banking. It made them even richer. It's possible that when they saw how rich banking made them, they gave themselves a good beating for opposing an end to slave trading (for surely they would have opposed that), but then again, they may have been visionaries and agitated for an end to slavery, for look at how rich they became with their banks borrowing from (through their savings) the descendants of the slaves and then lending back to them. But people just a little older than I am can recite the name of and the day the first black person was hired as a cashier at this very same Barclays Bank in Antigua. Do you ever wonder why some people blow things up? I can imagine that if my life had taken a certain turn, there would be the Barclays Bank, and there I would be, both of us in ashes. Do you ever try to understand why people like me cannot get over the past, cannot forgive and cannot forget? There is the Barclays Bank. The Barclay brothers are dead. The human beings they traded, the human beings who to them were only commodities, are dead. It should not have been that they came to the same end, and heaven is not enough of a reward for one or hell enough of a punishment for the other. People who think about these things believe that every bad deed, even every bad thought, carries with it its own retribution. So do you see the queer thing about people like me? Sometimes we hold your retribution.

And then there was another place, called the Mill Reef Club. It was built by some people from North America who wanted to live in Antigua and spend their holidays in Antigua but who seemed not to like Antiguans (black people) at all, for the Mill Reef Club declared itself completely private, and the only Antiguans (black people) allowed to go there were servants. People can recite the name of the first Antiguan (black person) to eat a sandwich at the clubhouse and the day on which it happened; people can recite the name of the first Antiguan (black person) to play golf on the golf course and the day on which the event took place. In those days, we Antiguans thought that the people at the Mill Reef Club had such bad manners, like pigs; they were behaving in a bad way, like pigs. There they were, strangers in someone else's home, and then they refused to talk to their hosts or have anything human, anything intimate, to do with them. I believe they gave scholarships to one or two bright people each year so they could go overseas and study; I believe they gave money to children's charities; these things must have made them seem to themselves very big and good, but to us there they were, pigs living in that sty (the Mill Reef Club). And what were these people from North America, these people from England, these people from Europe, with their bad behaviour, doing on this little island? For they so enjoyed behaving badly, as if there was pleasure immeasurable to be had from not acting like a human being. Let me tell you about a man; trained as a dentist, he took it on himself to say he was a doctor, specialising in treating children's illnesses. No one objected—certainly not us. He came to Antigua as a refugee (running away from Hitler) from Czechoslovakia. This man hated us so much that he would send his wife to inspect us before we were admitted into his presence, and she would make sure that we didn't smell, that we didn't have dirt under our fingernails, and that nothing else about us—apart from the colour of our skin—would offend the doctor. (I can remember once, when I had whooping cough and I took a turn for the worse, that my mother, before bundling me up and taking me off to see this man, examined me carefully to see that I had no bad smells or dirt in the crease of my neck, behind my ears, or anywhere else. Every horrible thing that a housefly could do was known by heart to my mother, and in her innocence she thought that she and the doctor shared the same crazy obsession—germs.) Then there was a headmistress of a girls' school, hired through the colonial office in England and sent to Antigua to run this school which only in my lifetime began to accept girls who were born outside a marriage; in Antigua it had never dawned on anyone that this was a way of keeping black children out of this school. This woman was twenty-six years old, not too long out of university, from Northern Ireland, and she told these girls over and over again to stop behaving as if they were monkeys just out of trees. No one ever dreamed that the word for any of this was racism. We thought these people were so ill-mannered and we were so surprised by this, for they were far away from their home, and we believed that the farther away you were from your home the better you should behave. (This is because if your bad behaviour gets you in trouble you have your family not too far off to help defend you.) We thought they were un-Christian-like; we thought they were small-minded; we thought they were like animals, a bit below human standards as we understood those standards to be. We felt superior to all these people; we thought that perhaps the English among them who behaved this way weren't English at all, for the English were supposed to be civilised, and this behaviour was so much like that of an animal, the thing we were before the English rescued us, that maybe they weren't from the real England at all but from another England, one we were not familiar with, not at all from the England we were told about, not at all from the England we could never be from, the England that was so far away, the England that not even a boat could take us to, the England that, no matter what we did, we could never be of. We felt superior, for we were so much better behaved and we were full of grace, and these people were so badly behaved and they were so completely empty of grace. (Of course, I now see that good behaviour is the proper posture of the weak, of children.) We were taught the names of the Kings of England. In Antigua, the twenty-fourth of May was a holiday—Queen Victoria's official birthday. We didn't say to ourselves, Hasn't this extremely unappealing person been dead for years and years? Instead, we were glad for a holiday. Once, at dinner (this happened in my present life), I was sitting across from an Englishman, one of those smart people who know how to run things that England still turns out but who now, since the demise of the empire, have nothing to do; they look so sad, sitting on the rubbish heap of history. I was reciting my usual litany of things I hold against England and the English, and to round things off I said, "And do you know that we had to celebrate Queen Victoria's birthday?" So he said that every year, at the school he attended in England, they marked the day she died. I said, "Well, apart from the fact that she belonged to you and so anything you did about her was proper, at least you knew she died." So that was England to us—Queen Victoria and the glorious day of her coming into the world, a beautiful place, a blessed place, a living and blessed thing, not the ugly, piggish individuals we met. I cannot tell you how angry it makes me to hear people from North America tell me how much they love England, how beautiful England is, with its traditions. All they see is some frumpy, wrinkled-up person passing by in a carriage waving at a crowd. But what I see is the millions of people, of whom I am just one, made orphans: no motherland, no fatherland, no gods, no mounds of earth for holy ground, no excess of love which might lead to the things that an excess of love sometimes brings, and worst and most painful of all, no tongue. (For isn't it odd that the only language I have in which to speak of this crime is the language of the criminal who committed the crime? And what can that really mean? For the language of the criminal can contain only the goodness of the criminal's deed. The language of the criminal can explain and express the deed only from the criminal's point of view. It cannot contain the horror of the deed, the injustice of the deed, the agony, the humiliation inflicted on me. When I say to the criminal, "This is wrong, this is wrong, this is wrong," or, "This deed is bad, and this other deed is bad, and this one is also very, very bad," the criminal understands the word "wrong" in this way: It is wrong when "he" doesn't get his fair share of profits from the crime just committed; he understands the word "bad" in this way: a fellow criminal betrayed a trust. That must be why, when I say, "I am filled with rage," the criminal says, "But why?" And when I blow things up and make life generally unlivable for the criminal (is my life not unlivable, too?) the criminal is shocked, surprised. But nothing can erase my rage—not an apology, not a large sum of money, not the death of the criminal—for this wrong can never be made right, and only the impossible can make me still: can a way be found to make what happened not have happened? And so look at this prolonged visit to the bile duct that I am making, look at how bitter, how dyspeptic just to sit and think about these things makes me. I attended a school named after a Princess of England. Years and years later, I read somewhere that this Princess made her tour of the West Indies (which included Antigua, and on that tour she dedicated my school) because she had fallen in love with a married man, and since she was not allowed to marry a divorced man she was sent to visit us to get over her affair with him. How well I remember that all of Antigua turned out to see this Princess person, how every building that she would enter was repaired and painted so that it looked brand-new, how every beach she would sun herself on had to look as if no one had ever sunned there before (I wonder now what they did about the poor sea? I mean, can a sea be made to look brand-new?), and how everybody she met was the best Antiguan body to meet, and no one told us that this person we were putting ourselves out for on such a big scale, this person we were getting worked up about as if she were God Himself, was in our midst because of something so common, so everyday: her life was not working out the way she had hoped, her life was one big mess. Have I given you the impression that the Antigua I grew up in revolved almost completely around England? Well, that was so. I met the world through England, and if the world wanted to meet me it would have to do so through England.

Are you saying to yourself, "Can't she get beyond all that, everything happened so long ago, and how does she know that if things had been the other way around her ancestors wouldn't have behaved just as badly, because, after all, doesn't everybody behave badly given the opportunity?"

Our perception of this Antigua—the perception we had of this place ruled by these bad-minded people—was not a political perception. The English were ill-mannered, not racists; the school headmistress was especially ill-mannered, not a racist; the doctor was crazy—he didn't even speak English properly, and he came from a strangely named place, he also was not a racist; the people at the Mill Reef Club were puzzling (why go and live in a place populated mostly by people you cannot stand), not racists.

⋅⊹⋅ ⋅⊹⋅ ⋅⊹⋅

Have you ever wondered to yourself why it is that all people like me seem to have learned from you is how to imprison and murder each other, how to govern badly, and how to take the wealth of our country and place it in Swiss bank accounts? Have you ever wondered why it is that all we seem to have learned from you is how to corrupt our societies and how to be tyrants? You will have to accept that this is mostly your fault. Let me just show you how you looked to us. You came. You took things that were not yours, and you did not even, for appearances' sake, ask first. You could have said, "May I have this, please?" and even though it would have been clear to everybody that a yes or no from us would have been of no consequence you might have looked so much better. Believe me, it would have gone a long way. I would have had to admit that at least you were polite. You murdered people. You imprisoned people. You robbed people. You opened your own banks and you put our money in them. The accounts were in your name. The banks were in your name. There must have been some good people among you, but they stayed home. And that is the point. That is why they are good. They stayed home. But still, when you think about it, you must be a little sad. The people like me, finally, after years and years of agitation, made deeply moving and eloquent speeches against the wrongness of your domination over us, and then finally, after the mutilated bodies of you, your wife, and your children were found in your beautiful and spacious bungalow at the edge of your rubber plantation—found by one of your many house servants (none of it was ever yours; it was never, ever yours)—you say to me, "Well, I wash my hands of all of you, I am leaving now," and you leave, and from afar you watch as we do to ourselves the very things you used to do to us. And you might feel that there was more to you than that, you might feel that you had understood the meaning of the Age of Enlightenment (though, as far as I can see, it had done you very little good); you loved knowledge, and wherever you went you made sure to build a school, a library (yes, and in both of these places you distorted or erased my history and glorified your own). But then again, perhaps as you observe the debacle in which I now exist, the utter ruin that I say is my life, perhaps you are remembering that you had always felt people like me cannot run things, people like me will never grasp the idea of Gross National Product, people like me will never be able to take command of the thing the most simpleminded among you can master, people like me will never understand the notion of rule by law, people like me cannot really think in abstractions, people like me cannot be objective, we make everything so personal. You will forget your part in the whole setup, that bureaucracy is one of your inventions, that Gross National Product is one of your inventions, and all the laws that you know mysteriously favour you. Do you know why people like me are shy about being capitalists? Well, it's because we, for as long as we have known you, *were* capital, like bales of cotton and sacks of sugar, and you were the commanding, cruel capitalists, and the memory of this is so strong, the experience so recent, that we can't quite bring ourselves to embrace this idea that you think so much of. As for what we were like before we met you, I no longer care. No periods of time over which my ancestors held sway, no documentation of complex civilisations, is any comfort to me. Even if I really came from people who were living like monkeys in trees, it was better to be that than what happened to me, what I became after I met you.

Nancy Mairs

from Waist-High in the World

BODY IN TROUBLE

"Conceptualize the body," I was instructed by the organizers of a conference at which I had been invited to speak a couple of years ago, and I balked. Something was wrong with this syntax, as though I myself—my thinking self—were no body, as though this disembodied self could speak not only for the body that it is not but for bodies in general (presumably human ones, though nothing in the directive actually debarred my corpulent corgi from my deliberations). The effect of the assignment seemed to me to divorce the speaking subject from her own corporal existence while permitting her to make free, in the chastest of senses, with the bodies of others. But why did my lecture topic—not at all an odd one at a feminist conference—strike me as so problematic?

I was squeamish about grammar in this case for at least a couple of reasons, both of which have to do with my reality as a body who has been in trouble of one sort or another for almost as long as I can remember. The first is that this construction reinforces the age-old Western dichotomy between mind, active and in control, and body, that wayward slug with which it is afflicted. Sheer knowledge of our bodies has helped dispel that myth. Before advances in medical technology began permitting us to illuminate and scrutinize our mysterious mute inner reaches, the terrain beneath the skin might well have seemed alien, even wholly separate from our "true" being. No longer. Recently, when an intestinal disturbance required my husband to have a colonoscopy, I sat in the corner and watched on a television screen as a minute camera zoomed through the glistening roseate chambers of his large bowel, thereby becoming one of the few women in the world who can truly profess that she knows and loves her partner both inside and out. In fact, since George slept through the whole procedure, I can now claim to know him more fully than he knows himself.

Over the years, as George's melanoma has moved from his skin through his lymphatic system into his belly, necessitating surgery and then chemotherapy, and as my multiple sclerosis has immobilized me, we have had to come to terms with ourselves as bodies. The physical processes of a perfectly healthy person may impinge so little on her sense of well-being that she may believe herself separate from and even in control of them. From here it's a short leap to the conviction that cerebral phenomena are of a different, generally higher, order than other bodily events and thus possess transcendent and even immortal qualities, at which point the imagined mind becomes the even more fantastic soul.

The body in trouble, becoming both a warier and a humbler creature, is more apt to experience herself all of a piece: a biochemical dynamo cranking out consciousness much as it generates platelets, feces, or reproductive cells to ensure the manufacture of new dynamos. When it became clear that the somatic basis of the depressive symptoms that had plagued me since adolescence required sustained biochemical intervention, I resisted.

"But I won't be myself if I have to take drugs!" I wailed to my therapist.

"I think," he replied, "that you're more yourself when you're medicated than when you're not." I had no self, I finally recognized, apart from my brain chemistry, but with it I had my choice of two: the self who starved and lay awake night after night and spent every conscious minute trying to postpone suicide, or the self who swallowed her pills and got on with her life. I am in every way, in my dreams as in my waking, the creature of my biochemistry. The body alone conceptualizes the body, conferring upon it, among other dubious endowments, a "mind."

But whose body? My second misgiving about my task arose from the two ways in which the phrase "the body" may be read: one reduces the speaker's flesh to a thing ("the body," not the true me), and the second suggests that one can universalize bodily experiences that may be in reality entirely idiosyncratic ("the body," not mine necessarily). For years after I began to have symptoms of MS, I used language to avoid owning them: "The left hand doesn't work anymore," I said. "There's a blurred spot in the right eye." In distancing myself from my ravaged central nervous system, I kept grief at bay; but I also banished any possibility of self-love. Only gradually have I schooled myself to speak of "my" hands, "my" eyes, thereby taking responsibility for them, though loving them ordinarily remains beyond me.

So, then: my body. And only my body. The specificity of the personal pronoun is critical to me (and to this book) because the range of bodies with disabilities is so exceptionally broad that I could not possibly speak for them all and do not wish to be perceived as trying to do so. This problem exists for any population, of course, as white middle-class academic feminists rapidly found out when they began to generalize about women, but the label "disability" masks a diversity of even more incomparable lives. What in my experience has prepared me to portray the realities of an old woman with Alzheimer's, even though we are both female; or a teenager with muscular dystrophy, even though neither of us can walk; or a young man with schizophrenia, even though I too have been confined to a mental hospital; or my niece whose eyes were removed when she was ten, even though we are blood kin? I would not presume to conceptualize their bodies. I can only represent my own experience as authentically as the tricks and vagaries of language will permit, trusting others to determine what similarities we share and make use of them as they see fit.

⊷ ⊷ ⊷

Here is my troubled body, dreaming myself into life: a guttering candle in a mound of melted wax, or a bruised pear, ripe beyond palatability, ready for the compost heap. The images, though they vary, always bear the whiff of spoliation. If there ever was a time of unalloyed love, I have long forgotten it, though I had hopes in early adolescence: that my breasts would grow magically larger and my mouth magically smaller; that I would become a strong swimmer and sailor and cyclist; that men, irresistibly drawn, would touch me and I'd burst into flame. Mostly I was, as I was trained to be, disappointed in myself. Even in the fifties, before the dazzle of shopping malls and the soft pornography of advertising for every product from fragrance to bed linen, a girl learned to compare herself unfavorably to an ideal flashed at her on glossy magazine covers and cinema screens and then to take measures to rectify her all too glaring deficiencies. I started painting my lips with Tangée when I was eleven, polishing my fingernails as soon as I stopped biting them, for my first great love at thirteen, plucking my eyebrows and wearing green eye-shadow at sixteen. I strapped on padded bras and squeezed into pantiegirdles to ac-centuate the positive and e-liminate the negative. I could not imagine a body that didn't require at least minor structural modification.

I still can't, and neither can any other woman I know. Not long ago, my mother and I shared a mirror as we put on faces for a festive evening. "I hate these," she said drawing her fingers down the lines from the corners of her mouth, "and this," patting the soft sag of flesh under her chin. I didn't try to protest, though she is a pretty woman, because I hate the same features now developing in my own face. One sister's breasts hang down, she laments, and the other's hips are too broad; my mother-in-law's bosom is too ample; even my daughter, possessed of a body too shapely for complaint, rues her small round nose. All these women, ranging in age from thirty to eighty-four, are active and fit, and fortunately they are too absorbed by their demanding lives to dwell upon whatever defects they perceive themselves to display. None could be considered vain. Not one has mutilated herself with rhinoplasty or liposuction or any of the other measures cosmetic surgeons have developed for emptying women's pockets into their own. Their dissatisfaction with their bodies seems as natural to them as their menses or hot flashes, simply an element of womanly existence.

Even if I hadn't developed MS, then, I would probably view myself with some distaste. But by the time I was thirty, I walked with a limp and used a cane. By forty, I wore a brace on my left leg and used a motorized scooter to cover all but short distances. Now, in my fifties, I divide my time between wheelchair and bed, my belly and feet are swollen from forced inactivity, my shoulders slump, and one of my arms is falling out of its socket.

The other day, when my husband opened a closet door, I glimpsed myself in the mirror recently installed there. "Eek," I squealed, "a cripple!" I was laughing, but as is usually the case, my humor betrayed a deeper, darker reaction. We have almost as many mirrors as a fun house, to give our small quarters an illusion of space, but I avoid looking into them straight on, and I dislike the objective evidence of photos as well. ("If I don't see you," my sister used to tease, her hands over her eyes, "you can't be you!") I love my wheelchair, a compact electric model called a Quickie P100, and I've spent so much time in it, and become so adept at maneuvering it, that I have literally incorporated it—made it part of my body—and its least ailment sends me into a greater tizzy than my own headaches. But the wheel-chair I experience is not "out there" for me to observe, any more than the rest of my body is, and I'm invariably shocked at the sight of myself hunched in its black framework of aluminum and plastic.

Although—or perhaps because—I am appalled by my own appearance, I devote an absurd amount of time and expense to its decoration. "Not for Mom peignoirs and pillows as she takes to her bed," my daughter points out. "No, she still likes to get out and find just the right color turtleneck or the perfect pair of black leggings." The green eyeshadow of youth has proliferated into every color of the rainbow, as well as a number that don't appear there, and been joined by foundation, mascara, blusher, and lipstick, not to mention the creams and lotions used to prepare the relentlessly wrinkling surface for this palette. I dread the day when my fingers become so weak that I have to go into the world with my bare face hanging out.

Already I can no longer dress myself, and I quip about moving to a climate so temperate that I wouldn't need any clothing at all, but in truth, of course, I could bear to hang out my bare body even less than my bare face. I buy garment after garment in the hope of finding one that will fit well enough to clothe me in some tatter of grace. Designers conceive tall bony pubescent bodies swinging down runways to some hectic beat on skinny but serviceable legs, and even the apparel that makes it to the outlet stores where I shop is cut for a lithe erect form in motion. This is who I want to be, of course, and so I cruise the aisles searching for a magic cloak that will transform me into her.

◦ ◦ ◦

The "her" I never was and am not now and never will become. In order to function as the body I am, I must forswear her, seductive though she may be, or make myself mad with self-loathing. In this project, I get virtually no cultural encouragement. Illness and deformity, instead of being thought of as human variants, the consequence of cosmic bad luck, have invariably been portrayed as deviations from the fully human condition, brought on by personal failing or by divine judgment. The afflicted body is never simply that—a creature that suffers, as all creatures suffer from time to time. Rather, it is thought to be "broken," and thus to have lost its original usefulness; or "embattled," and thus in need of militaristic response, its own or someone else's, to whip it back into shape; or "spoiled," and thus a potential menace to the bodies around it. In any case, it is not the sort of thing your average citizen would like to wake up next to tomorrow morning.

To embrace such a self requires a sense of permission some people achieve more readily than others. George's body, like mine, has been battered by aging and illness. Liver spots have appeared on the backs of his hands and crow's feet at the corners of his eyes and white hairs in his beard. He bears a puckered scar on his right upper arm. A second scar, in his right armpit, is invisible, but his right breast sags where the muscles were severed. A third runs the length of his abdomen; the surgeon boasted of his handiwork, but frankly George's reconstructed navel looks a little improvised. For several years now he has been impotent, and although I miss his erections sadly, he does not. "I'm at peace with my body," he says. I am at a loss to explain his complacency except as the habit of a lifetime of believing that whatever way he is is as he ought to be, a confidence that seems to arise in part from the possession of a penis, whether that organ itself still rises or does not. He senses himself to be "all right," revising his self-image as necessary to maintain this equilibrium, just as reflexively as I feel myself to be "all wrong."

In fact, he is also at peace with my body in a way that I am not. He always has been, and now that I can do little for myself, he rubs in lotion and sprays on scent, clips nails and stray hairs, wrestles stockings onto my rubbery legs, lifts me off toilets in women's rooms from Los Angeles to London. His ministrations, combining skill with sensuality, reassure me that this is the body he has loved since he first set eyes (or, if recent research is correct, nose) on it thirty-five years ago. Not long ago, a young clerk in a Victoria's Secret shop, joining in our deliberations over assorted styles and colors of underpants, was clearly startled by George's experienced and critical eye. Settling on a couple of briefs, in a sensible cut but a sexy fabric, he explained that he was the one who had to get me into them, but she still seemed to find his expertise—so patently nonprurient, rather like my grandmother's—a little kinky. Which was, he'd doubtless point out, her problem, not his. The peace he feels with his body has rendered him secure enough in his sexual identity that he enters and exits feminine space with aplomb. George's attentive and affectionate presence provides proof against the revulsion with which I am all too apt to greet myself; and even his easier peace depends in part, I am sure, on the fact that my body has remained crazy about his body throughout its vicissitudes.

I doubt that any body, whether in trouble or out, can fully conceive a self without an other to stroke it—with fingertips and lips, with words and laughter—into being and well-being. Research has demonstrated that infants deprived of touch fail to thrive, and that blood pressure is lowered and spirits are raised in elderly people given pets to caress. If physical stimulation is wholesome—even lifesaving—at the extremes of life, why should we suppose the middle to be any different? Our bodies conceptualize not only themselves but also each other, murmuring: Yes, you are there; yes, you are you; yes, you can love and be loved.

❧   ❧   ❧

I have been fortunate, as many people with disabilities are not, to have had throughout my adult life someone who loves me into being in just this way. Recently, when George and I were sharing memories of a friend with rheumatoid arthritis who had just died unexpectedly, I recalled an April morning years ago at the school where the three of us, close contemporaries, were teaching. "It's spring," Jill sighed as she thumped into the chair beside mine in the faculty room. "How I wish I had someone to love!" I was startled by this revelation. Still newly and mildly disabled myself, I hadn't yet given much thought to the sexual predicament in which a crippled body may find herself. Jill had developed arthritic symptoms in infancy, although not until she was in college did the damage to her joints really limit her mobility. She might not have been a pretty woman even without arthritis; as it was, she had the receding chin and twisted fingers characteristic of this disease, together with the "moon" face caused by anti-inflammatory drugs, and she moved slowly, stifflegged, on crutches. Outgoing and energetic, she could on occasion overwhelm those around her with criticisms or demands, but despite her prickliness, she was warm and funny and had many devoted friends. I don't suppose she ever had the lover she wished for, though.

Desire depends very little on physical perfection or prowess. Desirability, alas, depends on these a great deal. Perhaps the sociobiologists are correct in theorizing that we are attracted to those who appear most fit for reproduction; or perhaps we merely want whatever we are trained to want. Regardless of origin, standards of beauty and sources of arousal may vary from culture to culture, but every culture has them; and ours, at least, rigorously excludes most physical defects. A man with a slight limp or a patch over one eye, suggesting a wound from some heroic action, might still be considered dashing (though so many years have passed since the last "honorable" war that this effect may have worn off), but if he requires a wheelchair or a guide dog, he is likely to be viewed as a problem rather than a sex object. And although a condition that doesn't cause outright disfigurement, such as deafness, may be tolerated in a woman, I can't think of a single sign of injury or illness that would actually confer cachet.

On the contrary, the general assumption, even among those who might be expected to know better, is that people with disabilities are out of the sexual running. Not one of my doctors, for example, has ever asked me about my sex life. Most people, in fact, deal with the discomfort and even distaste that a misshapen body arouses by dissociating that body from sexuality in reverie and practice. "They" can't possibly do it, the thinking goes; therefore, "they" mustn't even want it; and that is *that*. The matter is closed before a word is uttered. People with disabilities can grow so used to unstated messages of consent and prohibition that they no longer "hear" them as coming from the outside, any more than the messengers know they are "speaking" them. This vast conspiracy of silence surrounding the sexuality of the disabled consigns countless numbers to sexual uncertainty and disappointment.

Many years ago, I concluded an essay called "On Not Liking Sex" with the speculation that I might one day write another on liking sex. This, I guess, constitutes that long-deferred essay. I really do like sex. A lot. Especially now that the issues of power and privacy that vexed me then have resolved themselves with time. Unfortunately, I like intercourse best of all, and the knowledge that I will never experience that again shrouds me in sexual sadness. I have elected, after years of struggle, to remain faithful now to George; but even if I had not, I am aware that men no longer look at me "that way." This might well be so even if I weren't crippled, since a woman in her fifties does not arouse most men to passion, but my wheelchair seals my chastity. Men may look at me with pity, with affection, with amusement, with admiration, but never with lust. To be truthful, I have so internalized the social proscription of libido in my kind that if a man did come on to me, I'd probably distrust him as at least a little peculiar in his erotic tastes.

Anyway, except for George, I no longer look at men "that way" either. Whatever complicated motives—and the urge to prove that I was still desirable even though disabled certainly lurked among them—drove me in my twenties and thirties into the arms of a series of men have long since lost their force. I still like sex, but only with George, who cannot give me intercourse. But on this of all days, the fifth anniversary of his last cancer surgery, when against all odds he is not merely alive but well, when he will soon return from a full day's work and take me out for a celebratory dinner, I am mindful that sorrow, sexual or otherwise, does not necessarily bleed away life's sweetness. In fact, the consequences of George's impotence have been surprisingly mixed, since in precluding intercourse it has forced us to discover alternative means to intimacy.

Oddly and ironically, my disability provides one of these. I've heard it said that a sexual relationship cannot be sustained when one partner provides routine care to the disabled other. Perhaps so, if the relationship depends heavily on glamour, as I suppose a good many do. After thirty-five years of acquaintance, and with two catastrophic illnesses, if we demanded enchantment, we'd be sorely let down. Our bodies hold few mysteries for each other. Once you've helped your wife change her wet pants, or watched the surgeon pop a colony of E. coli from the healing wound in your husband's belly, you have seen behind all the veils. I don't know what the sexual bond between us relies on, but it's not sorcery. The routine of caregiving doesn't seem to diminish our attraction; George's impotence, which has a physiological rather than a psychological basis, doesn't usually discourage either of us from lovemaking. And because we have grown so familiar with each other's physical realities, we love each other more unabashedly and inventively as time goes on.

Whether for making love or not, our bodies—one twisted and nearly inert, the other scarified, both softening now with age and indulgence—instinctively seek each other out. Even our most mundane interactions bear an erotic charge. I don't mean that we pant and grope every time he tugs my sweater over my head or adjusts my bedclothes. Rutting adolescence lies many years in our wake. But he may stroke my neck when he brings me a cup of coffee. And since my wheelchair places me just at the height of his penis (though *Cock-High in the World* struck me as just too indecorous a book title), I may nuzzle it in return. We carry on a constant, often hardly conscious, corporeal conversation regardless of our other pursuits and preoccupations. Without my disability to throw us together thus habitually, our bodies might spend their days racing separately from one activity to another, coming across each other only in time to tumble into sleep.

❖   ❖   ❖

The panic George's illness arouses in me stems in part from dread of the day when, without his steady and tender regard, I will have to keep my self going. Increasingly, as a body, I am turning into a set of problems: a bulk to be raised from the bed and maneuvered from one location to another; long, awkward arms and legs to be thrust into sleeves and pantlegs, stockings, shoes; a stomach to be filled time and time again; hair and teeth to be kept clean and nails to be pared; bladder and kidneys to be kept free from infection; buttocks to be monitored for signs of decubiti. Made not just of flesh and blood but of metal and rubber, I must be loaded into the van, tied down, seatbelt fastened in order to be transported anywhere, then unfastened, untied, unloaded at my destination. The absence of curb cuts, the presence of even one step, too narrow a door—all present obstacles.

No one but George, I fear, has reason to see me as more than the sum of my problems. Without him I would feel reduced to my nuisance value. I am terrified, against all reason, of being abused in retaliation. No one has ever, except by accident, hurt me. Matthew himself recalls most poignantly "The Day I Knocked Mom Down": "We were all arguing around the dining room table, raised voices, red faces, the whole deal. Hell, I can't even remember what we were going on about, something to do with my latest badness I suppose, but at any rate, fuses were short and I was leaving the realm of rational thought. Then my mother, innocently enough, tried to leave the table; god knows what I was thinking or why it was so important to finish my point, but I did try to shove her back into her chair. And those next few seconds will certainly follow me forever. The look of shock on her face as she collapsed, missing the chair entirely, the pure anger emanating from my dad (angriest I've ever seen him), the knowledge that I really had to go now and that something had changed forever and that there would be no returning from this event, these are the impressions that remain of that moment."

He can't have been more than sixteen, a hot-headed clumsy adolescent, and I would give anything to eradicate this mischance from his memory. Too much time has passed for it to serve us. For a while it made me wary of him, true, in the way that I was nervous about driving after a car bashed the rear end of my Kharmann Ghia when I braked at a yellow light in 1964. I drove for twenty-five more years, though. I go on mothering Matthew with the same ease.

He does not pose the threat I feel. Instead, I have visions of enduring life at the hands of strangers: refused food or drink, shoved roughly into bed, allowed to slip from my wheelchair and abandoned in a puddle of my own urine. These horrors, arising naturally, if irrationally, from physical helplessness, reflect an utter lack of self-regard. This is not what George has taught me. If I don't want to be reduced to a constellation of problems, I must imagine my body as something other than problematic: a vehicle for enmeshing the life I have been given into the lives of others. Easy enough to say. But to do? Who will have me? And on what terms?

⟡ ⟡ ⟡

In biblical times, physical and mental disorders were thought to signify possession by demons. In fact, Jesus's proficiency at casting these out accounted for much of his popularity among the common folk (though probably not among swine). People who were stooped or blind or subject to seizures were clearly not okay as they were but required fixing, and divine intervention was the only remedy powerful enough to cleanse them of their baleful residents.

Theologically as well as medically, this interpretation of the body in trouble now seems primitive, and yet we perpetuate the association underlying it. A brief examination of "dead" metaphors (those which have been so thoroughly integrated into language that we generally overlook their analogical origins) demonstrates the extent to which physical vigor equates with positive moral qualities. "Keep your chin up," we say (signifying courage), "and your eyes open" (alertness); "stand on your own two feet" (independence) "and tall" (pride); "look straight in the eye" (honesty) or "see eye to eye" (accord); "run rings around" (superiority). By contrast, physical debility connotes vice, as in "sit on your ass" (laziness), "take it lying down" (weakness), "listen with half an ear" (inattention), and get left "without a leg to stand on" (unsound argument). The way in which the body occupies space and the quality of the space it occupies correlate with the condition of the soul: it is better to be admired as "high-minded" than "looked down on" for one's "low morals," to be "in the know" than "out of it," to be "up front" than "back-handed," to be "free as a bird" than "confined to a wheelchair."

Now, the truth is that, unless you are squatting or six years old, I can never look you straight in the eye, and I spend all my time sitting on my ass except when I'm taking it lying down. These are the realities of life in a wheelchair (though in view of the alternatives—bed, chair, or floor—"confinement" is the very opposite of my condition). And the fact that the soundness of the body so often serves as a metaphor for its moral health, its deterioration thus implying moral degeneracy, puts me and my kind in a quandary. How can I possibly be "good"? Let's face it, wicked witches are not just ugly (as sin); they're also bent and misshapen (crooked). I am bent and misshapen, therefore ugly, therefore wicked. And I have no way to atone.

It is a bind many women, not just the ones with disabilities, have historically found themselves in by virtue of their incarnation in a sociolinguistic system over which they have had relatively little power. (Notice how virile the virtues encoded in the examples above.) Female bodies, even handsome and wholesome ones, have tended to give moralists fits of one sort or another (lust, disgust, but seldom trust). As everyone who has read the *Malleus Maleficarum* knows, "All witchcraft comes from carnal Lust which is in Women insatiable." If a good man is hard to find, a good woman is harder, unless she's (1) prepubescent, (2) senile, or (3) dead; and even then, some will have their doubts about her. It is tricky enough, then, trying to be a good woman at all, but a crippled woman experiences a kind of double jeopardy. How can she construct a world that will accommodate her realities, including her experience of her own goodness, while it remains comprehensible to those whose world-views are founded on premises alien or even inimical to her sense of self?

Disability is at once a metaphorical and a material state, evocative of other conditions in time and space—childhood and imprisonment come to mind—yet "like" nothing but it-self. I can't live it or write about it except by conflating the figurative and the substantial, the "as if" with the relentlessly "what is." Let me illustrate with an experience from a couple of years ago, when George and I went to a luncheon honoring the Dalai Lama held at a large resort northwest of Tucson. Although we were not enrolled in the five-day workshop he had come here to lead, we found ourselves in the hallway when the meeting room disgorged the workshop participants—all fourteen hundred of them—into a narrow area further con-stricted by tables laden with bells, beads, and brochures. And let me tell you, no matter how persuaded they were of the beauty and sacredness of all life, not one of them seemed to think that any life was going on below the level of her or his own gaze. "Down here!" I kept whimpering at the hips and buttocks and bellies pressing my wheelchair on all sides. "Down here! There's a person down here!" My only recourse was to roll to one side and hug a wall.

Postmodern criticism, feminist and otherwise, makes a good deal of the concept of wall-hugging, or marginality, which is meant to suggest that some segment of the popula-tion—black, brown, yellow, or red, poor, female, lesbian, what have you—is shouldered to the side, heedlessly or not, by some perhaps more numerous and certainly more powerful segment, most frequently wealthy, well-educated Euro-American males. Regardless of the way marginality is conceived, it is never taken to mean that those on the margin occupy a physical space literally outside the field of vision of those in the center, so that the latter trip unawares and fall into the laps of those they have banished from consciousness unless these scoot safely out of the way. "Marginality" thus means something altogether different to me from what it means to social theorists. It is no metaphor for the power relations between one group of human beings and another but a literal description of where I stand (figura-tively speaking): over here, on the edge, out of bounds, beneath your notice. I embody the metaphors. Only whether or not I like doing so is immaterial.

It may be this radical materiality of my circumstances, together with the sense I men-tioned earlier that defect and deformity bar me from the ranks of "good" women, which have spurred me in the past, as they no doubt will go on doing, to put the body at the cen-ter of all my meditations, my "corpus," if you will. Not that I always write *about* the body, though I often do, but that I always write, consciously, *as* a body. (This quality more than any other, I think, exiles my work from conventional academic discourse. The guys may be writing with the pen/penis, but they pretend at all times to keep it in their pants.) And it is this—my—crippled female body that my work struggles to redeem through that most fig-urative of human tools: language. Because language substitutes a no-thing for a thing, whereas a body is pure thing through and through, this task must fail. But inevitable disap-pointment does not deprive labor of its authenticity.

And so I use inscription to insert my embodied self into a world with which, over time, I have less and less in common. Part of my effort entails reshaping both that self and that world in order to reconcile the two. We bear certain responsibilities toward each other, the world and I, and I must neither remove myself from it nor permit it to exclude me if we are to carry these out. I can't become a "hopeless cripple" without risking moral paralysis; nor can the world, except to its own diminishment, refuse my moral participation.

But is a woman for whom any action at all is nearly impossible capable of right action, or am I just being morally cocky here? After all, if I claim to be a good woman, I leave myself open to the question: Good for what? The most straightforward answer is the most tempting: Good for nothing. I mean really. I can stand with assistance but I can't take a step; I can't even spread my own legs for sex anymore. My left arm doesn't work at all, and my right one grows weaker almost by the day. I am having more and more trouble raising a fork or a cup to my lips. (It is possible, I've discovered, though decidedly odd, to drink even coffee and beer through a straw.) I can no longer drive. I lack the stamina to go out to work. If I live to see them, I will never hold my own grandchildren. These incapacities constitute a stigma that, according to social scientist Erving Goffman, removes me from normal life into a "discredited" position in relation to society.

From the point of view of the Catholic Church, to which I belong, however, mine must be just about the ideal state: too helpless even for the sins other flesh is heir to. After all, parties aren't much fun now that I meet the other revelers eye to navel, and getting drunk is risky since I can hardly see straight cold sober. No matter how insatiable my carnal Lust, nobody's likely to succumb to my charms and sully my reputation. But I am, by sympathy at least, a Catholic *Worker*, part of a community that wastes precious little time fretting about the seven deadlies, assuming instead that the moral core of being in the world lies in the care of others, in *doing* rather than *being* good. How can a woman identify herself as a Catholic Worker if she can't even cut up carrots for the soup or ladle it out for the hungry people queued up outside the kitchen door? Physical incapacity certainly appears to rob such a woman of moral efficacy.

Well, maybe moral demands should no longer be placed on her. Perhaps she ought simply to be "excused" from the moral life on the most generous of grounds: that she suffers enough already, that she has plenty to do just to take care of herself. This dismissive attitude tends to be reinforced when the woman lives at the height of your waist. Because she "stands" no higher than a six-year-old, you may unconsciously ascribe to her the moral development of a child (which, in view of Robert Coles's findings, you will probably underestimate) and demand little of her beyond obedience and enough self-restraint so that she doesn't filch candy bars at the checkout counter while you're busy writing a check. (God, I can't tell you how tempting those brightly wrapped chunks are when they're smack up against your nose.) "Stature" is an intrinsic attribute of moral life, and the woman who lacks the one may be judged incapable of the other.

I am exaggerating here, of course, but only a little. Beyond cheerfulness and patience, people don't generally expect much of a cripple's character. And certainly they presume that care, which I have placed at the heart of moral experience, flows in one direction, "downward": as from adult to child, so from well to ill, from whole to maimed. This condescension contributes to what Goffman calls "spoiled identity," though he does not deal satisfactorily with the damage it inflicts: without reciprocity, the foundation of any mature moral relationship, the person with a defect cannot grow "up" and move "out" into the world but remains constricted in ways that make being "confined to a wheelchair" look trivial. And so I would say that while it is all right to excuse me from making the soup (for the sake of the soup, probably more than "all right"), you must never—even with the best intentions, even with my own complicity—either enable or require me to withdraw from moral life altogether.

So much for carrot-cutting, then, or any other act involving sharp instruments. But wait! On sharp instrument is left me: my tongue. (Here's where metaphor comes in handy.)

And my computer keyboard is . . . just waist high. With these I ought to be able to concoct another order of soup altogether (in which I'll no doubt find myself up to my ears). In other words, what I can still *do*—so far—is write books. Catholic Workers being extraordinarily tolerant of multiplicity, on the theory that it takes all kinds of parts to form a body, this activity will probably be counted good enough.

The world to which I am a material witness is a difficult one to love. But I am not alone in it now; and as the population ages, more and more people—a significant majority of them women—may join me in it, learning to negotiate a chill and rubble-strewn landscape with impaired eyesight and hearing and mobility, searching out some kind of home there. Maps render foreign territory, however dark and wide, fathomable. I mean to make a map. My infinitely harder task, then, is to conceptualize not merely a habitable body but a habitable world: a world that wants me in it.

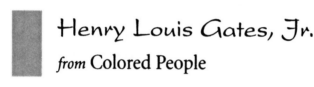

Henry Louis Gates, Jr.
from Colored People

CURRENT EVENTS

LESS THAN FOUR YEARS AFTER MY BIRTH, SOMETHING HAPPENED THAT WOULD INDELIBLY mark me and my peers for life—something that would open up another world to us, a world our parents could never have known. *Brown v. Board* was decided in 1954.

I entered the Davis Free Elementary School in 1956, just one year after it was integrated. There are many places where the integration of the schools lagged behind that of other social institutions. The opposite was true of Piedmont. What made the Supreme Court decision so determining for us was that school was for many years after 1955 virtually the only integrated arena in Piedmont.

To their credit, Mr. Harley Dixon and the other commissioners of the county school board responded quickly to the new judicial order. Otherwise it might have taken us a hundred more years to integrate, because everybody colored was devoted to Howard High School. They liked the teachers, they liked the principal, they liked the building and the basketball team. They liked its dignity and pride. They did not like its worn-down textbooks, the ones sent up by the board of education when the white schools got tired of them or when they were outdated. Other than that, Howard High was quite fine, thank you very much, your ticket to ride if you worked hard enough.

When I started at the white school in 56, everybody I knew was excited about integration, and everybody was scared. Mama would grill us every day about who said what and *how*. Mama did not play when it came to her boys, and she wasn't going to let any white woman or man step on her babies' dreams.

❧ ❧ ❧

In the newly integrated school system, race was like an item of apparel that fitted us up all tight, like one of Mama's girdles or the garters that supported her hose. Nobody ever *talked* about race, but it was there in the lines drawn around socializing. Look, but don't touch.

Don't even think about asking that white girl to dance. Obey that rule and everything will be fine. We'll all get along. Colored go with colored; white with white.

School—the elementary school at the top of Kenny House Hill and the high school over in the Orchard—was a fairly constant clash of cultures, especially for the older kids, who had had a segregated education all those years and had lived rigidly segregated lives for so very long. Cultural clashes, like the time that Mr. Staggers, the principal, asked Arthur Galloway what he had done to his hair, and Audie said he had gotten a process. And Mr. Staggers asked him what a process was. And Audie told him the truth, explaining about a mixture of mashed potatoes, eggs, and lye, and how you smear it on your hair with a paintbrush, and how it burns the kink right out. And Mr. Staggers interrupted Audie, accused him of lying, and took him to the office to impose corporal punishment on his behind with his favorite paddle, "Mr. Walnut," specially made with holes in it for improved aerodynamics. Or the day that Mr. Staggers asked one of the colored kids if he knew any poetry, and the fool said yes, "Shine and the Titanic," and Mr. Staggers asked that he recite a verse or two, only to halt the student, alarmed and panicked, when he got to the part about Mrs. Astor raising her dress and offering to trade sex for her survival. Daddy would say that people who could barely remember their names could recite twenty verses of "The Signifying Monkey" and "Shine and the Titanic":

> "Shine, Shine, save poor me—
> I'll make you as rich as a shine can be."
> And Shine said:
> Money's good but money don't last—
> Shine's gonna save his own black ass.
> And Shine swam on.

The two-week suspension was all anybody talked about down at the colored Legion in Keyser.

By the time I showed up at the "white school" (as we still thought of it), they were expecting me. Mama used to clean the houses of my teachers, Mrs. Mellor and Mrs. Bell, and they respected her. One time I referred to Mama as "she," and Mrs. Bell lectured me in front of the entire fourth-grade class about referring to someone like my mother with a pronoun. Your mother is a lady, a real lady. What is wrong with you? she asked. Have you bumped your head? It made me feel good, this white woman talking about my mama like that, in front of the other kids.

From the first day of first grade, I was marked out to excel. My brother's performance had been outstanding the year before, and I had shone in the preschool test. I was quiet, I was smart, I had a good memory, I already knew how to read and write, and I was blessed with the belief that I could learn anything. I was all set to become the little prince of that almost all-white school. The little brown prince with a stocking cap for a crown.

The teachers, in turn, pushed me and encouraged me. Except for Mrs. Sheetz, my first-grade teacher, who accused me of stealing her scissors. Why? Because I had laughed when, in her inquisition of the class, going down each row of desks, pupil to pupil, she finally got to me. I was so astonished at the idea that I laughed some more, which hung a cloud of accusation over my head until I got home with her note. Did you take her scissors? Mama asked. All I want to know, Daddy interrupted Mama, is, Did you take the scissors? Just tell us the truth and we're behind you. I laughed again, aching with the laughter. No, I don't have her scissors. Why would I do a thing like that? Bonnie Gilroy had the scissors; Bonnie Gilroy, the trashiest of the white trash, had had those scissors all along. She used to bring plastic bleach jugs up to our house, and we'd fill them with water for drinking. She was scrawny and scraggly, greasy, dirty, and dumb. I'd have looked at Bonnie first, had I been Mrs. Sheetz. After that I hated Mrs. Sheetz with all my injured pride and delighted in scoring all A's in her class for the rest of that first year.

By second grade, it was entirely my world; there wasn't anything I couldn't learn. I loved the way Mrs. Mellor said my name Louis, as I was called (thank God nobody used my middle name, Smith, which I hated and longed to change). They gave me a test in the middle of the year, and I got 489 answers right out of 500. The other teachers had come down to Mrs. Mellor's room at the end of the hall, to the right of the boys' bathroom, and stared at the score sheet she was holding and then at me. I took to wearing a white cotton boatneck sweatshirt with a chessboard on its front, like a personal coat of arms. These teachers were serious about learning, and about school. Piedmont had turned out most of the county's doctors. In a school of six grades and only 250 or so kids, that is quite something.

If I was the school's prince, my princess was Linda Hoffman. It was inevitable. Linda and I were the best students in our class. Linda and I were soul mates, or so I fantasized. She ate books. She read more books more quickly and with greater comprehension than anybody I knew. Total concentration was her gift. We were an item: long, deep stares into her eyes, lots of times, every day. She called me Gates, just like Mama called Daddy, and I called her Hoffman, or Linda H. We exchanged pictures every year and gave each other an extra valentine in the brown-bag "mailboxes" we made for the occasion. The teachers often paired us together, because our combined magic was so powerful.

I revered Linda H. I used to walk half a mile out of my way just so I could pass her house and maybe catch a glimpse of her. One day when I was in fourth grade, a traveling magician came to town. The entire six grades assembled, to walk two abreast down Kenny House Hill, across the tracks, over to the Orchard, and past the pool to the high school, where special assemblies were held. At some point in his act, the magician asked for a student volunteer, and somehow he chose Hoffman.

Pick your little boyfriend, honey, he said. I want Skippy, was all I heard Linda say, before the whole auditorium erupted in surprise and nervous laughter. I felt chagrined and maybe a little proud as I joined her on the stage.

Well, that didn't play. In that school, no white girl and colored boy had yet stood onstage together. I thought that Mr. Magician would do his World-Famous Disappearing Act. He managed to do his trick, whatever it was, but it was clear that he was flustered, and he shooed us off as soon as he could. Thank God he hadn't tried to make my hair stand on end with a static-electricity machine.

"I want Skippy, I want Skippy"—that's all I heard from the older colored kids, over and over again. Interracial dating was taboo in Piedmont. Like Booker T. Washington had said in 1895 in Atlanta, in all things educational we were as one, like a clenched fist, but in all things social we were the five separate fingers. Colored danced with colored, white danced with white. At the operettas and the Junior Fair, they'd make two colored boys or two white boys or girls dance together, if the numbers of boys to girls was uneven. Or a colored boy and a white boy, if that was absolutely essential to the artistic success of our rinky-dink productions. But never cross the line of race *and* gender. You couldn't even think about that.

Which is probably why we thought about it all the time. But things could be no other way. The school board had worked out all sorts of compromises to enable integration in the county to proceed. No dating, of course, no holding hands, no dancing. Not too many colored on the starting lineup of the basketball teams. One colored cheerleader, max. Hire one colored elementary teacher, one in the high school (make that one the former principal of the colored school). Put most of the colored in the B track, vocational, but treat the A group fairly. Corporal punishment to be meted out for racial infractions. Give regular lectures on hygiene. Don't rock the social boat. You'll get along as long as you abide by the rules.

Rocky's friends and my friends—the ones we invited to our home, I mean—were all colored. My friend Rodney would stay over a lot. So would Jerry and Roland. But I didn't have overnight white friends, ever. In eighteen years of living in Piedmont, going to school with white kids for twelve, I never had a single white friend over for dinner. Nor would anyone white have ever invited me. And I had some good white friends, too. Like Johnny DiPilato.

I went to Johnny's house several times, but only for a hot minute or two. Like I said, I never got invited for dinner. Yet his mom was very nice to me, genuinely nice, not with one of those tight smiles that say: What are you doing in my house, you little nigger boy, and how soon are you going to get your little colored ass offa my sofa? She called Mama Mrs. Gates, and Mama called her Mrs. DiPilato. That was rare in Piedmont. Colored people might call each other Miss, Mrs., or Mr., to show respect. But colored people continued to call white people Miss or Mrs. or Mr. even when those white people addressed them by their Christian names. I guess Johnny Dip was always slightly off-center because his father had a thick Italian accent, which was easily imitated. Skeep, he'd call me. Johnny was ashamed of his father's accent. You could see it in his face and in the way he'd defy his father and say rude things right in front of him.

I used to go over to Pat Amoroso's house in the Orchard and sit in his kitchen or on his steps, but only if his father was asleep or wasn't home. His father hated niggers. It was as simple as that. Nobody colored much minded. He had a right, people said. I'd hate niggers, too, if . . . That's how people would explain him away. What he really hated was the fact that his son, Donny, had been killed late one night in a hit-and-run accident right at the crest of old Snaky. And Gerry Washington had been driving. Driving drunk, on the wrong side of the road, up over the hill. Then he had run down the tracks to hide, before they caught his black ass. So instead of mourning like a normal person, Mr. Amoroso decided to hate niggers. It was his way of bearing witness, of remembering his son, of showing his love and his grief. Actually, he could be pretty nice when he forgot you were a nigger. We all felt sorry for Mr. Amoroso. We all understood. Two years ago, Gerry Washington got killed in a car in D.C. or somewhere. "Just like he killed that Amoroso boy," the town said. Everybody understood why he had to die like he did.

An eye for an eye is a major precept in Piedmont, though most people prefer retributive woofing to retributive justice. *Somethin' bad gonna happen to that nigger, and God don't like ugly.*

◆   ◆   ◆

One factor that eased my passage in school was the fact that Rocky was the pioneer, so he got the brunt of the problems that lay in wait. There was the time when Mrs. Bright told Rocky that he didn't need coaching for the literary competition, he was already perfect, so Mama coached him every night till he got James Weldon Johnson's great poem, "The Creation," right. Rocky stepped out on that stage and, with the power and force of Mama's coaching, blew the Drane girl to Timbuktu. Mrs. Bright almost fainted because she had wanted that Drane girl to demolish my brother.

It was Mama who took the battle to them, Mama who showed us how to fight. We didn't always win, of course. In eighth grade, Rocky couldn't be awarded West Virginia's most coveted prize for excellence in state history, a Golden Horseshoe, one of Daddy's white friends told us, because the hotel where we would have had to stay in the state capital was segregated. Hell, they'd just denied entry to Elgin Baylor, the star forward of the Minneapolis Lakers. Rocky had missed winning by "half a point," they said. He had misspelled a word, they said. Too bad, they said. Sometimes it seems Rocky's childhood ended that day, the day he found out why he had not won. Now, a Golden Horseshoe is the Nobel Prize of eighth graders in West Virginia. Your entire education has prepared you for this competition. Four winners per county. Meeting the governor. Fame. Glory.

One half point. A misspelled word. How it haunted Rocky! Then Elmer Shaver—the white man who was Daddy's boss at the phone company and one of his best friends—came up one night, late, and explained the whole thing in a whispered voice, while Rocky and I sat on our bunks in our bedroom, listening to John R. out of *Randy's Record Shop* in Gallatin, Tennessee. And then, after Mr. Shaver left, Mama tried to find the voice to tell it, to tell the awful truth of what those crackers did. How relieved Rocky was that it was not his fault, that he had not blown the chance of a lifetime to be the first colored Golden Horseshoe winner by transposing some letters.

But then, as soon as you let yourself feel relief, this next wave came crashing over you, larger and more dangerous than the first wave, of guilt and responsibility, and this wave was the terrible one, this wave crushing and inexorable: no matter what you did or how you did it, it didn't matter because it was their world, their sea, and their tide, and your little black ass was about as significant as a grain of yellow sand.

Something died inside, the part that spells the difference between hoping and doing, between casting wide or casting close, between wearing the horizon like a shawl around your shoulders or allowing it to choke you to death like one of those plastic dry cleaner's bags that warn of suffocation in dire blue letters. And something happened to Rocky when that county school board lied and told him that he had almost won, that he should have worked just a little harder, that he transposed two letters. That it could have happened to anyone, boy—but especially to you, *boy.*

I saw him nursing the injury in silence, unable to speak of it, unwilling to shed it. Paltry as it may seem from the vantage of adulthood, the knowledge of that deception cast a shadow over his life. That same knowledge drove me to win a Golden Horseshoe six years later.

Rocky kept tripping over those rules that you didn't know existed until you broke them. Like being selected in the eleventh grade by the school for Boys State, whereupon the white American Legion, led by Frank Price, informed the board that they preferred a white boy. Mr. Staggers, the principal, had to inform Frank Price that they'd take Paul Gates or send no one at all. He went, and we all rejoiced at another victory for the Negro race. But Rocky hurt from this sort of thing.

Rocky was five years and six grades ahead of me, so I tracked him through the school system quietly, stealthily, avoiding his pitfalls and false starts, emulating him but at a distance. It was a role I liked. The younger, the disciple, the pupil, the neophyte, the ephebe, the apprentice: that's a position people describe as one of confinement. To me, they have it exactly wrong. They don't see that it carries a kind of freedom: no anxiety about finding the path, just the determination to keep your feet on the path. Most of the time, I've found that challenge enough.

◦ ◦ ◦

In 1960, when I was in fifth grade, we started to hear about Africa as part of current events, for the independence movement was sweeping that continent. At home, stories about Africa and Africans started turning up on TV. We used to make jokes about Ubangi lips, and poke ours out as far as we could. The older boys would talk about them, too, in marvelling tones: Black Africans, man, those Africans are *black*, blue-black. Blacker than Ray or Lawson. Yeah, and those French women like those Africans too, boy. I saw them arm in arm, walking down the streets in Paris like it was the most natural thing in the world—kinky, beady-headed too. Um, um, um. And they don't want you over there, either. They don't want you. Dem Africans. They say they're not Negroes; they are Africans, and don't you call me black. Big-dick motherfuckers too, swing in trees and shit, living in grass huts.

For my part, I used to watch *Ramar of the Jungle* every Saturday morning. Ramar was a doctor who looked a lot like Omar Sharif. His black sidekick, Willy, who looked like Delton Allen, had a pet monkey that perched on his shoulder. Ramar was always being trapped by some witch doctor or medicine man, who was worried because his dances and chants were not reversing the fever of the chief's son. Just one little shot of this, Ramar would tell the chief, and things will be OK. White man's poison, the medicine man would say. Willy, Tom that he was, would betray his people and free Ramar, and the chief's son would live. Ramar would send the son to England to attend medical school. It was *hot* in that jungle too, and the natives would be sweating like crazy, but Ramar in his perma-pressed khaki suit and safari hat would always be clean. Ramar was *bad*. So was Willy's pet monkey.

In school, I was busy learning how to say the names of the leaders of the new African nations: Moise Tshombe, Patrice Lumumba, Kwame Nkrumah, Sékou Touré, Jomo Kenyatta. I'd listen to how Edward R. Murrow or Walter Cronkite said them, then I'd practice in my head. We'd get large current affairs maps each week, with a flat colored map of the world at the top, then a dozen or so news stories numbered to match places on the map. There was a quiz each Friday. I think it was this class that influenced me most to go to Africa when I was nineteen, to live in the bush in a socialist village in Tanzania for a year, and then (with a kid I met from Harvard) to hitchhike across the equator, from the Indian Ocean to the Atlantic Ocean, without leaving the ground.

I lived for that map each week. I loved globes and maps and geography. History too. The only problem with history class was that they'd bring up slavery—for a minute or two at the end of the Civil War section, which was a minute or two of mutual embarrassment. The Africans had been primitive savages, swinging in trees and eating bananas, worshiping rocks and stones and trees, until the White Man came to set them free by granting them admission to the University of Slavery. John Brown was a crazy troublemaker; the first man to get killed at Harpers Ferry was colored. That showed how very evil it was. Mr. Lincoln got assassinated because he freed the slaves.

Now, that always made me feel bad. Every time one of them tries to help you people too much, Daddy would say, laughing, he gets shot. First was Kennedy—King would be next, he reckoned. The oddest thing about the assassination of President Kennedy, to me—once you got over your shock and tears about him being dead—was the first question that the colored people asked when they heard the news. "Was he colored?" they asked, referring to the President's assassin. My grandparents, my parents, and I would ask that same question, in that same way, upon hearing the news of any tragedy of major dimensions that could implicate the entire race. "Was he colored?" we'd ask, hoping against hope, expecting the worst. "Was he colored?"

Thomas Lynch
The Undertaking

EVERY YEAR I BURY A COUPLE HUNDRED OF MY TOWNSPEOPLE. ANOTHER TWO OR THREE dozen I take to the crematory to be burned. I sell caskets, burial vaults, and urns for the ashes. I have a sideline in headstones and monuments. I do flowers on commission.

Apart from the tangibles, I sell the use of my building: eleven thousand square feet, furnished and fixtured with an abundance of pastel and chair rail and crown moldings. The whole lash-up is mortgaged and remortgaged well into the next century. My rolling stock includes a hearse, two Fleetwoods, and a minivan with darkened windows our pricelist calls a service vehicle and everyone in town calls the Dead Wagon.

I used to use the *unit pricing method*—the old package deal. It meant that you had only one number to look at. It was a large number. Now everything is itemized. It's the law. So now there is a long list of items and numbers and italicized disclaimers, something like a menu or the Sears Roebuck Wish Book, and sometimes the federally-mandated options begin to look like cruise control or rear-window defrost. I wear black most of the time, to keep folks in mind of the fact we're not talking Buicks here. At the bottom of the list there is still a large number.

In a good year the gross is close to a million, five percent of which we hope to call profit. I am the only undertaker in this town. I have a corner on the market.

The market, such as it is, is figured on what is called *the crude death rate*—the number of deaths every year out of every thousand persons.

Here is how it works.

Imagine a large room into which you coax one thousand people. You slam the doors in January, leaving them plenty of food and drink, color TVs, magazines, and condoms. Your sample should have an age distribution heavy on baby boomers and their children—1.2 children per boomer. Every seventh adult is an old-timer, who, if he or she wasn't in this big room, would probably be in Florida or Arizona or a nursing home. You get the idea. The group will include fifteen lawyers, one faith healer, three dozen real-estate agents, a video technician, several licensed counselors, and a Tupperware distributor. The rest will be between jobs, middle managers, ne'er-do-wells, or retired.

Now for the magic part—come late December when you throw open the doors, only 991.6, give or take, will shuffle out upright. Two hundred and sixty will now be selling Tupperware. The other 8.4 have become the crude death rate.

Here's another stat.

Of the 8.4 corpses, two-thirds will have been old-timers, five percent will be children, and the rest (slightly less than 2.5 corpses) will be boomers—realtors and attorneys likely—one of whom was, no doubt, elected to public office during the year. What's more, three will have died of cerebral-vascular or coronary difficulties, two of cancer, one each of vehicular mayhem, diabetes, and domestic violence. The spare change will be by act of God or suicide—most likely the faith healer.

The figure most often and most conspicuously missing from the insurance charts and demographics is the one I call The Big One, which refers to the number of people out of every hundred born who will die. Over the long haul, The Big One hovers right around . . . well, dead nuts on one hundred percent. If this were on the charts, they'd call it *death expectancy* and no one would buy futures of any kind. But it is a useful number and has its lessons. Maybe you will want to figure out what to do with your life. Maybe it will make you feel a certain kinship with the rest of us. Maybe it will make you hysterical. Whatever the implications of a one hundred percent death expectancy, you can calculate how big a town this is and why it produces for me a steady if unpredictable labor.

⚬   ⚬   ⚬

They die around the clock here, without apparent preference for a day of the week, month of the year; there is no clear favorite in the way of season. Nor does the alignment of the stars, fullness of moon, or liturgical calendar have very much to do with it. The whereabouts are neither here nor there. They go off upright or horizontally in Chevrolets and nursing homes, in bathtubs, on the interstates, in ERs, ORs, BMWs. And while it may be that we assign more equipment or more importance to deaths that create themselves in places marked by initials—ICU being somehow better than Greenbriar Convalescent Home—it is also true that the dead don't care. In this way, the dead I bury and burn are like the dead before them, for whom time and space have become mortally unimportant. This loss of interest is, in fact, one of the first sure signs that something serious is about to happen. The next thing is they quit breathing. At this point, to be sure, a *gunshot wound to the chest* or *shock and trauma* will get more ink than a CVA or ASHD, but no cause of death is any less permanent than the other. Any one will do. The dead don't care.

Nor does *who* much matter, either. To say, "I'm OK, you're OK, and by the way, he's dead!" is, for the living, a kind of comfort.

It is why we drag rivers and comb plane wrecks and bomb sites.

It is why MIA is more painful than DOA.

It is why we have open caskets and all read the obits.

Knowing is better than not knowing, and knowing it is you is terrifically better than knowing it is me. Because once I'm the dead guy, whether you're OK or he's OK, won't much interest me. You can all go bag your asses, because the dead don't care.

Of course, the living, bound by their adverbs and their actuarials, still do. Now, there is the difference and why I'm in business. The living are careful and oftentimes caring. The dead are careless, or maybe it's care-less. Either way, they don't care. These are unremarkable and verifiable truths.

⚬   ⚬   ⚬

My former mother-in-law, herself an unremarkable and verifiable truth, was always fond of holding forth with Cagneyesque bravado—to wit: "When I'm dead, just throw me in a box and throw me in a hole." But whenever I would remind her that we did substantially that with everyone, the woman would grow sullen and a little cranky.

Later, over meatloaf and green beans, she would invariably give out with: "When I'm dead just cremate me and scatter the ashes."

My former mother-in-law was trying to make carelessness sound like fearlessness. The kids would stop eating and look at each other. The kids' mother would plead, "Oh Mom, don't talk like that." I'd take out my lighter and begin to play with it.

In the same way, the priest that married me to this woman's daughter—a man who loved golf and gold ciboria and vestments made of Irish linen; a man who drove a great black sedan with a wine-red interior and who always had his eye on the cardinal's job—this same fellow, leaving the cemetery one day, felt called upon to instruct me thus: "No bronze coffin for me. No sir! No orchids or roses or limousines. The plain pine box is the one I want, a quiet Low Mass and the pauper's grave. No pomp and circumstance."

He wanted, he explained, to be an example of simplicity, of prudence, of piety and austerity—all priestly and, apparently, Christian virtues. When I told him that he needn't wait, that he could begin his ministry of good example even today, that he could quit the country club and do his hacking at the public links and trade his brougham for a used Chevette; that free of his Florsheims and cashmeres and prime ribs, free of his bingo nights and building funds, he could become, for Christ's sake, the very incarnation of Francis himself, or Anthony of Padua; when I said, in fact, that I would be willing to assist him in this, that I would gladly distribute his savings and credit cards among the worthy poor of the parish, and that I would, when the sad duty called, bury him for free in the manner he would have, by then, become accustomed to; when I told your man these things, he said nothing at all, but turned his wild eye on me in the way that the cleric must have looked on Sweeney years ago, before he cursed him, irreversibly, into a bird.

What I was trying to tell the fellow was, of course, that being a dead saint is no more worthwhile than being a dead philodendron or a dead angelfish. Living is the rub, and always has been. Living saints still feel the flames and stigmata of this vale of tears, the ache of chastity and the pangs of conscience. Once dead, they let their relics do the legwork, because, as I was trying to tell this priest, the dead don't care.

Only the living care.

And I am sorry to be repeating myself, but this is the central fact of my business—that there is nothing, once you are dead, that can be done *to you* or *for you* or *with you* or *about you* that will do you any good or any harm; that any damage or decency we do accrues to the living, to whom your death happens, if it really happens to anyone. The living have to live with it. You don't. Theirs is the grief or gladness your death brings. Theirs is the loss or gain of it. Theirs is the pain and the pleasure of memory. Theirs is the invoice for services rendered and theirs is the check in the mail for its payment.

And there is the truth, abundantly self-evident, that seems, now that I think of it, the one most elusive to the old in-laws, the parish priest, and to perfect strangers who are forever accosting me in barber-shops and cocktail parties and parent-teacher conferences, hellbent or duty-bound to let me in on what it is they want done with them when they are dead.

Give it a rest is the thing I say.

Once you are dead, put your feet up, call it a day, and let the husband or the missus or the kids or a sibling decide whether you are to be buried or burned or blown out of a cannon or left to dry out in a ditch somewhere. It's not your day to watch it, because the dead don't care.

⟡   ⟡   ⟡

Another reason people are always rehearsing their obsequies with me has to do with the fear of death that anyone in their right mind has. It is healthy. It keeps us from playing in traffic. I say it's a thing we should pass on to the kids.

There is a belief—widespread among the women I've dated, local Rotarians, and friends of my children—that I, being the undertaker here, have some irregular fascination with, special interest in, inside information about, even attachment to, *the dead.* They assume, these people, some perhaps for defensible reasons, that I want their bodies.

It is an interesting concept.

But here is the truth.

Being dead is one—the worst, the last—but only one in a series of calamities that afflicts our own and several other species. The list may include, but is not limited to, gingivitis, bowel obstruction, contested divorce, tax audit, spiritual vexation, cash flow problems, political upheaval, and on and on and on some more. There is no shortage of misery. And I am no more attracted to the dead than the dentist is to your bad gums, the doctor to your rotten innards, or the accountant to your sloppy expense records. I have no more stomach for misery that the banker or the lawyer, the pastor or the politico—because misery is careless and is everywhere. Misery is the bad check, the ex-spouse, the mob in the street, and the IRS—who, like the dead, feel nothing and, like the dead, *don't care.*

⋅ᴑ ⋅ᴑ ⋅ᴑ

Which is not to say that the dead do not matter.

They do. They do. Of course they do.

Last Monday morning Milo Hornsby died. Mrs. Hornsby called at 2 A.M. to say that Milo had *expired* and would I take care of it, as if his condition were like any other that could be renewed or somehow improved upon. At 2 A.M., yanked from my REM sleep, I am thinking, put a quarter into Milo and call me in the morning. But Milo is dead. In a moment, in a twinkling, Milo has slipped irretrievably out of our reach, beyond Mrs. Hornsby and the children, beyond the women at the laundromat he owned, beyond his comrades at the Legion Hall, the Grand Master of the Masonic Lodge, his pastor at First Baptist, beyond the mailman, zoning board, town council, and Chamber of Commerce; beyond us all, and any treachery or any kindness we had in mind for him.

Milo is dead.

X's on his eyes, lights out, curtains.

Helpless, harmless.

Milo's dead.

Which is why I do not haul to my senses, coffee and quick shave, Homburg and great coat, warm up the Dead Wagon, and make for the freeway in the early o'clock for Milo's sake. Milo doesn't have any sake anymore. I go for her—for she who has become, in the same moment and the same twinkling, like water to ice, the Widow Hornsby. I go for her—because she still can cry and care and pray and pay my bill.

⋅ᴑ ⋅ᴑ ⋅ᴑ

The hospital that Milo died in is state-of-the-art. There are signs on every door declaring a part or a process or bodily function. I like to think that, taken together, the words would add up to The Human Condition, but they never do. What's left of Milo, the remains, are in the basement, between SHIPPING & RECEIVING and LAUNDRY ROOM. Milo would like that if he were still liking things. Milo's room is called PATHOLOGY.

The medical-technical parlance of death emphasizes disorder.

We are forever dying of failures, of anomalies, of insufficiencies, of dysfunctions, arrests, accidents. These are either chronic or acute. The language of death certificates—Milo's says "Cardiopulmonary Failure"—is like the language of weakness. Likewise, Mrs. Hornsby, in her grief, will be said to be breaking down or falling apart or going to pieces, as if there were something structurally awry with her. It is as if death and grief were not part of The Order of Things, as if Milo's failure and his widow's weeping were, or ought to be, sources of embarrassment. "Doing well" for Mrs. Hornsby would mean that she is bearing up, weathering the storm, or being strong for the children. We have willing pharmacists to help her with this. Of course, for Milo, doing well would mean he was back upstairs, holding his own, keeping the meters and monitors bleeping.

But Milo is downstairs, between SHIPPING & RECEIVING and LAUNDRY ROOM, in a stainless-steel drawer, wrapped in white plastic top to toe, and—because of his small head, wide shoulders, ponderous belly, and skinny legs, and the trailing white binding cord from his ankles and toe tag—he looks, for all the world, like a larger than life-size sperm.

I sign for him and get him out of there. At some level, I am still thinking Milo gives a shit, which by now, of course, we all know he doesn't—because the dead don't care.

Back at the funeral home, upstairs in the embalming room, behind a door marked PRI-VATE, Milo Hornsby is floating on a porcelain table under florescent lights. Unwrapped, out-stretched, Milo is beginning to look a little more like himself—eyes wide open, mouth agape, returning to our gravity. I shave him, close his eyes, his mouth. We call this *setting the features*. These are the features—eyes and mouth—that will never look the way they would have looked in life when they were always opening, closing, focusing, signaling, telling us something. In death, what they tell us is that they will not be doing anything anymore. The last detail to be managed is Milo's hands—one folded over the other, over the umbilicus, in an attitude of ease, of repose, of retirement.

They will not be doing anything anymore, either.

I wash his hands before positioning them.

When my wife moved out some years ago, the children stayed here, as did the dirty laundry. It was big news in a small town. There was the gossip and the goodwill that places like this are famous for. And while there was plenty of talk, no one knew exactly what to say to me. They felt helpless, I suppose. So they brought casseroles and beef stews, took the kids out to the movies or canoeing, brought their younger sisters around to visit me. What Milo did was send his laundry van around twice a week for two months, until I found a house-keeper. Milo would pick up five loads in the morning and return them by lunchtime, fresh and folded. I never asked him to do this. I hardly knew him. I had never been in his home or his laundromat. His wife had never known my wife. His children were too old to play with my children.

After my housekeeper was installed, I went to thank Milo and pay the bill. The invoices detailed the number of loads, the washers and the dryers, detergent, bleaches, fabric soften-ers. I think the total came to sixty dollars. When I asked Milo what the charges were for pick-up and delivery, for stacking and folding and sorting by size, for saving my life and the lives of my children, for keeping us in clean clothes and towels and bed linen, "Never mind that" is what Milo said. "One hand washes the other."

I place Milo's right hand over his left hand, then try the other way. Then back again. Then I decide that it doesn't matter. One hand washes the other either way.

The embalming takes me about two hours.

It is daylight by the time I am done.

Every Monday morning, Ernest Fuller comes to my office. He was damaged in some profound way in Korea. The details of his damage are unknown to the locals. Ernest Fuller has no limp or anything missing so everyone thinks it was something he saw in Korea that left him a little simple, occasionally perplexed, the type to draw rein abruptly in his day-long walks, to consider the meaning of litter, pausing over bottle caps and gum wrappers. Ernest Fuller has a nervous smile and a dead-fish handshake. He wears a baseball cap and thick eyeglasses. Every Sunday night Ernest goes to the supermarket and buys up the tabloids at the checkout stands with headlines that usually involve Siamese twins or movie stars or UFOs. Ernest is a speed reader and a math whiz but because of his damage, he has never held a job and never applied for one. Every Monday morning, Ernest brings me clippings of stories under headlines like: 601 LB MAN FALLS THRU COFFIN—A GRAVE SITUATION or EMBALMER FOR THE STARS SAYS ELVIS IS FOREVER. The Monday morning Milo Hornsby died, Ernest's clipping had to do with an urn full of ashes, somewhere in East Anglia, that made grunting and groaning noises, that whistled sometimes, and that was expected to begin talking. Certain scientists in England could make no sense of it. They had run several tests. The ashes' widow, however, left with nine children and no estate, is convinced that her dearly beloved and greatly reduced husband is trying to give her winning numbers for the lottery. "Jacky would never leave us without good prospects," she says. "He loved his family more than anything." There is a picture of the two of them, the widow and the urn, the living and the dead, flesh and bronze, the Victrola and the Victrola's dog. She has her ear cocked, waiting.

We are always waiting. Waiting for some good word or the winning numbers. Waiting for a sign or wonder, some signal from our dear dead that the dead still care. We are gladdened when they do outstanding things, when they arise from their graves or fall through their caskets or speak to us in our waking dreams. It pleases us no end, as if the dead still cared, had agendas, were yet alive.

But the sad and well-known fact of the matter is that most of us will stay in our caskets and be dead a long time, and that our urns and graves will never make a sound. Our reason and requiems, our headstones or High Masses, will neither get us in nor keep us out of heaven. The meaning of our lives, and the memories of them, belong to the living, just as our funerals do. Whatever being the dead have now, they have by the living's faith alone.

We heat graves here for winter burials, as a kind of foreplay before digging in, to loosen the frost's hold on the ground before the sexton and his backhoe do the opening. We buried Milo in the ground on Wednesday. The mercy is that what we buried there, in an oak casket, just under the frost line, had ceased to be Milo. Milo had become the idea of himself, a permanent fixture of the third person and past tense, his widow's loss of appetite and trouble sleeping, the absence in places where we look for him, our habits of him breaking, our phantom limb, our one hand washing the other.

Jane Shapiro
This Is What You Need for a Happy Life

I WANT TO BE MARRIED TO ONE MAN FOR LIFE. SO FAR THIS HAS ELUDED ME—THAT'S THE way I think about it: *so far.* As if, after two marriages and two divorces and many quick, interesting years alone—during which years I've lived exactly as I wanted—it could still happen now. I'll be twenty-one and my sexy, considerate boyfriend and I will marry on a blue day, surrounded by an elaborate, loving, familial community that will ratify and then proceed to sustain our union, and he and I will live productively side by side for six decades, growing daily more tranquil and enmeshed. We'll move to a hot climate and sit in twin lawn chairs and telephone our many grown children. Our gold rings will wear and our fingers will shrink. We'll die married! Still this story seems so real to me.

⊷ ⊷ ⊷

One way I've been thinking about divorce these days has been in discussion with Raoul Lionel Felder, the famous New York divorce lawyer, whose matrimonial firm is the largest and most successful in the country.

Q: Do people first arrive in your office with great ambivalence about divorcing?

A: Not really. Because by the time they come here, they've been to the priest, the minister, psychiatrist, psychologist, the yenta next door—all these people. So while it's not a Rubicon beyond which they can't step back, the fact is they've usually played out all their hands.

Q: So you don't see people who aren't sure—

A: I see them. I see them. But that's not the profile of the majority of clients, no. Because even the people who say "I just want information"—they don't want information, they want to see if they can get up enough courage, or enough money, and so forth.

Q: Have you often thought "These two people should not get divorced"?

A: What I have seen is two misfits. Where you say "Jesus, they're made for each other in heaven! Why are these people ever getting divorced? Who would want to put up with either one of them?"

⊷ ⊷ ⊷

Fifteen years back in time, Ed's and my divorce is imminent. He phones, from a resort in South Carolina. "It's terrific here!" Ed cries, forgetting he and I are estranged. There are 125 tennis courts. There are lavish plants and lawns. Meanwhile I'm thinking: This guy owes me money. Ed has been my second husband—my real one, as I think of him; every divorced woman has had one real husband. Before the kids get to the phone, Ed has filled me in on the layout of his suite. Two giant bedrooms, a living room, a dining room, and an immaculate, gargantuan terrace now house my lonely future ex-husband as he struggles in South Carolina to get perspective on his confusing, tangled, ongoing life with me.

Divorce, like other traumatic events, causes time traveling—like me, many divorcing people, I imagine, find themselves vividly living in other time places: years ago, or years from now when all this will be over, when what is broken will be fixed. Or you feel like two people at once—an old woman who has lost everyone and a girl whose life is beginning at last.

I'm an ordinary divorcée, vivaciously mourning. I rise in the morning peppy and sanguine; only hours later, a heaviness grows in my chest and I'm near sobbing. I weep for hours, fall asleep still snuffling, then wake in the night with tears running into my ears. The next day, I'm shaky and refreshed; at midnight, I can't sleep because I'm excited, planning my moves.

I call my friends to make crude jokes, talk urgently, over-explain and guffaw; I keep them on the phone too long and call again too soon. Daily, I have ideas! I impulsively introduce myself to new people, make plans to change careers or adopt some children or leave town, write sudden letters to friends from high school, sleep with wrong men: a merry widow, every day.

᠂᠔ ᠂᠔ ᠂᠔

Ed takes the kids for the weekend. I can't bear two days without the kids. So I travel to Fire Island to see Benjy, my childhood friend, and his wife and their children—to visit them and their family-ness. On Ben and Alice's redwood deck, in hazy sun and wet air, I know I've been cast off the planet. How can I be among that vast company, the divorcing or divorced, and be so alone? Morosely, Ben introduces me to three sunburned couples: "*This lady is estranged, poor woman.*"

All fall, when not working or cooking, I look at television. A week before our divorce is final, a Tuesday evening finds me intently watching the interviewing of some cover girls. Outside, it's darkening fast. The phone rings and I grab for it—could be my husband. But the line is dead. In pearly voices, the cover girls unanimously maintain that having your image appear in a magazine does not change your life.

I have never understood this construct: does not change your life. If these women are right, then divorce doesn't change your life either. I try saying this to myself, but with a convincing sense that my life is (for the second time, this being my second divorce) about to be over.

People who have gone from poverty and obscurity and struggle and despair to being famous movie actors and bestselling authors will say this too: It doesn't change your life. When patently it does. When anyone can see your life is changed beyond recognition.

᠂᠔ ᠂᠔ ᠂᠔

The imminence of Eddie's and my divorce brings back to me my old tormenting feeling of not belonging to any group, family, or clan. A raucous call from a divorced girlfriend reminds me I'll soon be joining a new family—that of women alone, making bawdy jokes, asserting their exhilaration at controlling their lives, and looking, wherever they want, whenever they choose, for fresh mates.

I want to steal some husbands.

I imagine some married women—my closest friends—dying. Right now they're young, lovely, strong. Suddenly they get painless illnesses and swiftly succumb. Their bereaved husbands and I, linked in shock and grief, begin having dinners together. Helpless, in extremis, each husband and I tell many truths. In a dignified way, we bond. At last, hesitantly, then robustly, he and I have brave, profound, elegiac, joyful sex; tears drop from our four overinformed eyes onto afternoon sheets. *Astonishing, life's bounty. We have found each other.* Except that the identity of the widower changes daily, my fantasy is almost pornographic in its extreme specificity: We take our several children to the Phoenix Garden, and then to the movies on Greenwich Avenue, where we chew jujubes and hold hands in the flickering dark and light. We borrow an eight-room condo at Sugarbush, ski hard and eat chili for lunch; at night the kids sleep curled together like pups.

I actually sit at married couples' tables around town, indefatigable in my frantic loneliness, accepting condolences and advice, and thinking, Do I want him? As if I might slip poisoned powder into my beloved girlfriends' Cabernets.

I see what this is: I don't want to have to begin again and set out and endure trial and error and finally make a husband out of an actual person loose in the world. I want someone who *already is* a husband.

⋅♦⋅ ⋅♦⋅ ⋅♦⋅

I ask Raoul Felder if he has in mind a profile of the ideal client.

A: No, *I* don't. But generally a divorce lawyer would like a stupid rich woman. A stupid *compliant* rich woman. It doesn't mean the woman is going to be exploited. It means that there's enough money to get well paid, that the client isn't going to question you, and that the client will follow your advice. It's not pejorative, it doesn't mean you'll do something bad for your client—actually, it's the reverse, you'll do better for her; you'll just do your job and not be bothered. You can't blame a lawyer for wanting those three attributes.

⋅♦⋅ ⋅♦⋅ ⋅♦⋅

Months pass and I am still thirty-eight—still young. While waiting for my best friends to die, I start dating.

When you first turn your attention from your husband, your judgment is wild and you can't tell potentially suitable people from entirely wrong ones. As we've learned, there are days almost any man (or woman) in the known world looks like a real possibility.

I find a man. I think he's a possibility. I support this idea with the contention that he and I are culturally similar. Our fathers both went (before the Second World War) to Harvard; the new man and I share a longing and admiration for our dead fathers, those darkly handsome, clever boys bucking the quota up there in foreign Cambridge so long ago. The correspondences between the new man and I are so unlikely as to appear significant: We are grandchildren of Latvian Jews who settled in Newark and sold rags until they got ideas and promptly made, in dental equipment and real estate respectively, two modest fortunes. The new man and I get stoned in his Jacuzzi and I make a fool of myself crying, "*From rags to riches!* I never understood what it meant!"

He's a surgeon and I'm ready for a lover; watching him cut a bite of steak is pretty much a sexual thing. We love meeting in the hospital lobby and rushing to a restaurant. All summer we sit on banquettes in chilled air, plates of pasta before us, trying to get to know each other, not too fast and not too much. We watch ourselves dialing for reservations, chatting at the theater, moving confidently through a lavish world, availing ourselves, without guilt or regret, of its pleasures—he and I share some romantic dream of being well-heeled grown-ups. This makes us appear to be in love.

The new man is great—competent, energetic, alternately solicitous and remote, well paid. After a couple of months, he suddenly appears distracted and says we are not the lovers I had assumed we had become. He needs to think. He wants time off. You are a passive-aggressive shit, I tell him, and our shared passion vanishes like day breaking.

I sob to a friend about our breakup. She says: "This always happens. This is a typical opening salvo: doesn't hit the target, just starts to define where it is."

My friend Ben, though married, knows many single men. When I beg him, he tries to think up a guy for me, suggesting in quick succession two rich, sentimental drug dealers and a never-married mathematician with a heart condition.

Not long after this, I stopped worrying about remarrying and promptly enjoyed fifteen interesting single years.

⋄ ⋄ ⋄

I ask Raoul Felder: is there a difference between a man's divorce and a woman's divorce?

A: The dynamics are different if you represent a man.

Q: There's probably more crying with a woman—?

A: More crying. There's more emotionality in a woman's divorce and less punching numbers in a computer. It's much harder when you represent a woman. Because today, in divorce in America, the business is at stake. If you represent a man, you're sitting with a party who has all the records, knows what he's doing, has the business accounts in his control. With a woman, you're outside knocking on the door, trying to get in.

Q: Has a woman ever come in to see you and not cried?

A: Oh, sure. *Sure.*

Q: Who? Women who are just completely fed up and finished?

A: [Looks at me sympathetically] Oh, there are fortune hunters and adventuresses in the world.

⋄ ⋄ ⋄

Just this year—just this month—I woke early, in darkness, with the fully formed intention to talk to my first husband. Since our parting thirty years ago, I've laid eyes on him three times: twice, we spoke awhile; once, I happened to see him run past in the Boston Marathon (even before I recognized his face, I felt an access of pride: his legs were springy and he was breathing well). My first husband and I had never discussed our divorce, as we had never discussed our marriage—we've never mentioned what we were doing all those years ago. Recently, I gave him a call.

JANE: I have very little recollection of what happened when we got divorced. Do you?

DAVID: Well, I've always had three important recollections. I recall coming home from work one day and the apartment was cleared out: not only you and the baby but also furniture.

JANE: What furniture?

DAVID: Not a lot. We had some furniture. One of your father's trucks came for it.

JANE: I didn't take the furniture!

DAVID: The baby's furniture. And I remember a knock on the door about seven at night, I don't know what month. Two cops were there, and I remember the shine, the light reflecting off their leather jackets. And they handed me something—I think it was a court order.

JANE: It's not in your divorce folder?

DAVID: I couldn't find it. But I deduced that the court order was to pay child support of 125 dollars per—must've been a week.

JANE: Could've been a month. It was 1966.

DAVID: Yeah, it could've—

JANE: Sounds like a month.

DAVID: And I also remember going to New York and not being able to see the kids. Those are the three recollections that have stuck with me over the years.

JANE: Why couldn't you see the kids?

DAVID: One time you weren't there when you were supposed to be. And another time—

JANE: You mean I knew in advance you were coming?

DAVID: Oh yeah. In the folder I found a log, it was interesting, of when I went to see them. Strange pieces of paper, with dates. It says: "January: Jane to Europe. February: Jane asked to delay visitation because of her marriage." And then apparently I saw the kids March 22nd, 1969. And then: "April: Delayed because of death." I have no idea whose death it was—

JANE: My father's.

DAVID: That was your father's death, in sixty-nine?

JANE: Yeah, I got married in February and my father died in April.

DAVID: And then that May: "Not there." You weren't there. I remember knocking and there was no answer. And then in June: "Jane said no because of erratic behavior."

JANE: Whose? [laughing]

DAVID: Well, I don't know! I assume you had determined that my behavior was erratic—

JANE: Oh, this is terrible, this is—

DAVID: And then the visitation stops. I think you were still living then in Washington Square. And the Mexican divorce had been—

JANE: Yes, when was that? When *was* the Mexican divorce?

DAVID: I have a copy of it, so I assume you must have the original.

JANE: I don't have the original of anything.

DAVID: And I've also got all these papers from Ephraim London and all your high-powered—

JANE: He was a civil rights lawyer, I don't know why he—

DAVID: He was your attorney! You had all Park Avenue—

JANE: I know. London had an elegant office. I mainly remember the dresses I wore when I went to see him. I have a sartorial record of that time, nothing else—it's really embarrassing. But I went to Juárez, I had to fly to El Paso, so—

DAVID: I know that.

JANE: Well, when did—when was that?

DAVID: Hold on. I've got it here—

JANE: [laughing] I'm pretty excited about this—

DAVID: You're "excited." This is just like a reunion then, isn't it?

JANE: This is great!

DAVID: "This is *grreatt.*" Is it?

JANE: No, but it's—it's important, for me anyway, because who's going to be able to tell me about my life?

DAVID: I'll tell you about your life.

⟡ ⟡ ⟡

DAVID: Yeah, after reading these papers over the weekend, I had so many strange feelings. Okay. How do you want to proceed?

JANE: Well, we *are* proceeding. My memories from that time are so hazy. And one reason I don't remember much, I think, was that I'd been suddenly thrust into another, completely consuming life. Because of course when I left I had one baby and I was pregnant, and then soon I had two babies, and I moved alone to New York, where I got no sleep, I didn't have time to eat, I got up at five in the morning and took care of the babies and I went to school at night. So I was hurled out of the life I had lived with you, you know?

DAVID: Yes.

JANE: Into another life, all alone. I just don't remember a lot from that time. Do you recall anything about our marriage? I mean—how did we *decide* to get married? And who brought it up? And how did—

DAVID: You brought it up.

JANE: I did?

DAVID: You brought it up.

JANE: That's what I figured.

DAVID: One day, I think, you called and said Let's get married. So we did.

JANE: Sounds plausible.

DAVID: Late December.

JANE [GLOOMILY]: I know we had anemone and ranunculus.

DAVID: Do you want the Hebrew date?

JANE: Yeah, I'd love that.

DAVID: The sixth of—either "Teves" or "Jeves."

JANE: Probably a *T,* don't you think?

DAVID: Rabbi Stanley Yedwab.

JANE: Doesn't Yedwab sound like one of those invented words, or like a name backwards?

DAVID: Absolutely.

JANE: "B-A-W-D-E-Y," IT IS, backwards.

DAVID: Bawdy. We said that at the time.

JANE: Oh! We did? At the time? So that was a memory, what I just said?

DAVID: It was a memory.

JANE: Now, do you remember anything about our marriage?

DAVID: Uhh. I—

JANE: I mean, did we have fights? Probably did.

DAVID: I don't remember fights.

JANE: I don't remember *any*.

DAVID: None. I remember feeling pressure from your father and, less so, from you: "What are you gonna do with your life?"

JANE: But you were in graduate school.

DAVID: No.

JANE: Oh.

DAVID: I was only in school when we first got married, in Ithaca.

JANE: Well, how long did we live in Ithaca?

DAVID: Two semesters. A calendar year.

JANE: I've often wondered. Well, what was our—did we have any relationship, that you recall? I know we did, but do you specifically recall anything about it?

DAVID: I remember a dock we used to walk to. On Cooper River.

JANE: Do you remember having discussions about anything, ever?

DAVID: About me: "What are you going to do that's respectable?"

JANE: That was scapegoating—it seems so now. It was neatly structured. I was sinking and dying. And nobody was saying to *me*, "What're you gonna do?" Also, when I got pregnant, nobody said "Gee, isn't it a little early?" In those days, y'know, it seemed sensible.

DAVID: Well, I don't recall if you were taking birth control pills. I think you were, weren't you?

JANE: Well, obviously at some point I must not've been.

DAVID: It was a conscious choice, therefore, not to continue with birth control. Okay.

❧ ❧ ❧

DAVID: I would have to say I did not know the kind of turmoil you were going through. I had no idea of the psychological pain you felt.

JANE: Did I ever mention anything? I can imagine I didn't. I'm just wondering.

DAVID: I don't think so. But it could've been my insensitivity.

JANE: Oh no no no, I doubt I did mention it, actually. Did I talk much? I think I was silent.

DAVID: You were quiet.

JANE: Did I attack you? I can imagine that too.

DAVID: Attack me? Physically?

JANE: Emotionally. I mean did I get mad?

DAVID: I still don't recall *ever* having an argument.

JANE: Isn't that interesting. I don't either.

DAVID: And that was part of the difficulty I had in understanding why there was a breakup. I suppose retrospectively it seems our marriage was meant to be an escape for you.

JANE: Yes, it was.

DAVID: I was a way out.

JANE: Well, I didn't know what else to do with my life. I didn't *have anything* I could possibly do with my life. And I couldn't work, I couldn't study, I couldn't think. There was this blind pain in my head. For many years. And I guess—it was a desperate thing: "Okay, I'll get married, what else can I do. Because I can't think straight."

DAVID: It's a shame we have to have our conversation by phone. There's so much here, real and imagined. And maybe the prelude to your writing about our marriage and divorce is for us to—

JANE: Well, y'know, I'm not writing about *our* divorce. I'm doing a piece about divorce generally. Which is just one of those things in my professional life. And I could imagine our conversation might end up a paragraph, or a sentence. And I'll interview Raoul Felder, the big divorce lawyer, and that'll be another paragraph. And I'll write some very emotional thing about—maybe what I recall of Juárez (which is almost nothing).

But really, the main thing is, this is about thirty years later. Our lives are moving fast. I thought I'd like to—know what happened.

⚬ ⚬ ⚬

Q FOR RAOUL FELDER: What qualities make an excellent divorce lawyer?

A: Well, the field attracts a mixed bag. Some of them are good lawyers—very few—and some are just cesspool types. Some are control freaks and some are exploitation people. It attracts the worst. (And sometimes some of the best, but very few.) It's not a complicated area of law. I think it's fair to say of most divorce lawyers that you wouldn't want to have a cup of tea with them. And you wouldn't want to kiss them. There's just nobody home.

Q: So it attracts an unsavory group?

A: "Unsavory" is a strong word. A needy group of people. And when you marry need with mediocrity, you get an awful hybrid.

⚬ ⚬ ⚬

As David and I reminded ourselves, I secured our divorce in Juárez. At once, I forgot it; decades later when I tried to remember, what returned so strongly was an odd constellation of things—heat and pale sunlight and dust blowing, and a grim feeling of timelessness and urgency and sadness, and air-conditioning and the scent of martinis and whiskey sours transpiring from iced glasses. I remember the experience both vaguely and intensely, as if this divorce had been a childhood milestone, which of course it almost was—I was twenty-four.

My younger sister flew down with me to El Paso. (The family, I think, assigned her to do this; it's still astonishing to me that she was there. My sister must've stayed in a motel with me and the next morning ridden with me across the border along with the other charges of our local Mexican lawyer. Down in El Paso, we were this morning's bunch of New Yorkers about to be unhitched fast, in concert, in Spanish. We crossed and recrossed the border in a van, through clouds of dust that hung in Texan, then Mexican, then Texan air.

Later, I think our group drank cocktails in a freezing hotel bar in the middle of the afternoon, me and my sister and the other divorced people. Dark red glow of the bar's interior, relief and camaraderie and pain. The others were older than I and either hectically pleased to be unencumbered or despondent about it or both. In farewell, our lawyer said to my sister, who was twenty-one and engaged to be married: "I'll see you in a couple of years."

᭸ ᭸ ᭸

I ask Raoul Felder how many years he has been married.

A: Thirty—I don't know, thirty-one years, something like that.

Q: Could you imagine getting a divorce?

A: I'm not a divorce person myself. I'm not a divorcing kind of person. If people leave me alone, I leave them alone.

Q: But let's say yours and your wife's paths diverged?

A: Things don't bother me, I'm into my own head. I don't get bothered if somebody makes a lousy meal—so you eat out. You don't like the perfume—so you sniff other people's perfume. That's all. It's a simple life.

Q: Right. So why is it that other people are coming in this office, their paths have diverged and they've got to—

A: Because most of the time, I think, people are narrow intellectually; they've put too much investment in marriage. You put a lot of investment in marriage, it doesn't work out. You don't put a lot of investment, you roll with it as it comes.

Q: Like anything else. If your expectation is at the correct level, it's going to work?

A: That's right.

1995

My Lover and his former wife still own together, for tax reasons, the house he lives in. When we met, this seemed okay—sensible and modern. But my lover sleeps on the futon they shared, under his wife's childhood counterpane; nearby sits her dressing table, holding makeup and combs and perfume; on his desk is a silver box with bracelets and earrings inside. The bathroom (dual sinks) is a gallery of photographs: They have no children, so over and over, in black-and-white and color, it's just them. She graduates from law school, he catches a fish. Every time you step out of the shower, you meet again the annoyingly fresh-faced couple at their wedding in 1978. One of the pictures is so prized that a duplicate appears in his study, pinned as if casually on the wall. They are splashing in the Caribbean sea! Enjoying honeymoon water play! My lover says: "That picture is not characteristic of us. I don't know who stuck it there. I never look at it." He says about her clothes in the closet: "I don't notice them."

"Well, do you notice when she's sleeping with you?"

This is a tough one. Sometimes she drives the two hours from the city and sleeps in their former bed at his side. It isn't often, but it does happen. They don't make love, or touch at all. (I believe this; they hadn't had wholehearted sex in years anyway; why would he need to invent this, after the amazing stuff he's cheerfully confessed?) They just lie there. Probably he clings to the futon's edge and immediately drops unconscious. Maybe she falls quickly into her own dreamless sleep and wakes wondering where she is. She walked out of this house, for somebody else, five years ago.

Well, it turns out they're not divorced yet—haven't gotten around to it. Almost every day, some of the mail that arrives is addressed to his wife. "Do you notice her mail?" I demand. "Not this again," he says. "No. I don't. It's an occasional piece of *mail.*"

And of course she used to cook once in awhile, and his kitchen is still hung with her omelette pans, and her spices are lined up, alphabetized and fading, above the sink. One night while I'm standing under the copper-pot ceiling, the phone rings, and he cries, "Don't answer it!" I answer it. She asks for him: "This is his wife." When, midsentence, she realizes who I am, she hangs up. So is she gone?

He's sick of me. He says *Yes, sue me, I was sad when she left.* He says she left regretfully but irrevocably. He says their interdependence is the merest vestigial convenience, their emotional contact nil. (On alternate days, he says she's his best friend for life.) He says the distance between them is vast and unvarying and immutable and he's so fucking tired of being badgered. He says it means less than nothing that they're not divorced yet; not being divorced yet is fundamentally a clerical oversight; of course they plan to divorce, they can divorce any time.

"How about now?"

"Man, you make trouble, don't you?"

Anybody can see I'm stupid in romance and inclined to believe just about anything. We both want me to think my lover's story adds up. Still, I've learned a simple thing in my complicated travels: If you're not divorced yet, you're married.

⌀   ⌀   ⌀

DAVID: You gonna interview your second husband too?

JANE [PUZZLED]: Of course not. I know what happened with him. I talk to him once a week.

⌀   ⌀   ⌀

Raoul Felder tells me: In the beginning when you married somebody you were twenty-five, all you did was pound away; you're two sweaty bodies—that's what the marriage is. And then you realize, "Why'd I marry this one?"

Q: So you meet someone else, or you just decide to leave.

A: And most of the time people end up marrying the same people. A little younger, or sexier, or richer, or this or that. But basically the same people again.

Q: Have clients come back to you repeatedly?

A: Of course! As many as four times—a man I talked to this morning, I've done three divorces for. [Pauses. Reflects.] Give 'em a nice divorce, they keep coming.

Q: That's very interesting—it makes the divorce sound nicer than the wedding.

A: It's more expensive but sometimes nicer. You're giving them freedom. At the wedding, they're selling themselves into bondage. With the divorce, you're giving them happiness, release, a chance to make a better life for themselves. How many times can you say to someone, "Here: This is what you need for a happy life. Go. [glumly] Have a happy life."

⌀   ⌀   ⌀

Divorce has left me high and dry. The other day, after, as I've said, many years of excellent single living, I surprised myself with that thought.

I tell my married friends: "I've changed my mind—I want to live with a man." They all say the same thing: "No you don't."

Whenever I have dinner with another single woman, after a decent interval we say what we want in a husband. We name popular qualities, always the same ones, as if men were truly commodities. Potent, we say. Rich, we say. We all claim to want to mate with independent, mature men, and later in the evening all claim to want younger, gentler, more passionate and malleable ones with beautiful arms and legs.

Everybody always says her cherished fantasy is to be *with* a man but to live in a separate house. Okay, maybe that's impossible. So everybody rushes to say she wants a man who is "very busy." This is a universal wish: busy. I am often the first to assert that I want a busy man—somebody who has his "own life," who doesn't "cling," who will leave me alone and so on. Who can sit nearby without leaning into the edge of my vision or even glancing my way. Of course we don't want to marry a cold or hard or distant man, but somebody as anomalous, fantastic, as a satyr or unicorn: so independent, so warm. And we'll live with him forever—we'll never divorce.

Rich, we say.

Let him live across town, we say.

We are hard-hearted hannahs. We laugh like maniacs and order more wine.

Nobody says: somebody to care for me alone in the world.

Joy Williams
Save the Whales, Screw the Shrimp

I DON'T WANT TO TALK ABOUT *ME*, OF COURSE, BUT IT SEEMS AS THOUGH FAR TOO MUCH ATtention has been lavished on *you* lately—that your greed and vanities and quest for self-fulfillment have been catered to far too much. You just want and want and want. You haven't had a mandala dream since the eighties began. To have a mandala dream you'd have to instinctively know that it was an attempt at self-healing on the part of Nature, and you don't believe in Nature anymore. It's too isolated from you. You've abstracted it. It's so messy and damaged and sad. Your eyes glaze as you travel life's highway past all the crushed animals and the Big Gulp cups. You don't even take pleasure in looking at nature photographs these days. Oh, they can be just as pretty, as always, but don't they make you feel increasingly . . . anxious? Filled with more trepidation than peace? So what's the point? You see the picture of the baby condor or the panda munching on a bamboo shoot, and your heart just sinks, doesn't it? A picture of a poor old sea turtle with barnacles on her back, all ancient and exhausted, depositing her five gallons of doomed eggs in the sand hardly fills you with joy, because you realize, quite rightly, that just outside the frame falls the shadow of the condo. What's cropped from the shot of ocean waves crashing on a pristine shore is the plastics plant, and just beyond the dunes lies a parking lot. Hidden from immediate view in the butterfly-bright meadow, in the dusky thicket, in the oak and holly wood, are the surveyors' stakes, for someone wants to build a mall exactly there—some gas stations and supermarkets, some pizza and video shops, a health club, maybe a bulimia treatment center. Those lovely pictures of leopards and herons and wild rivers, well, you just know they're going to be accompanied by a text that will serve only to bring you down. You don't want to think about it! It's all so un-cool. And you don't want to feel guilty either. Guilt is uncool. Regret maybe you'll consider. *Maybe.* Regret is a possibility, but don't push me, you say. Nature photographs have become something of a problem, along with almost everything else. Even though they leave the bad stuff out—maybe because you *know* they're leaving all the bad stuff out—such pictures are making you increasingly aware that you're a little too late for Nature. Do you feel that? Twenty years too late, maybe only ten? Not *way* too late, just a little too late? Well, it appears that you are. And since you are, you've decided you're just not going to attend this particular party.

◦ ◦ ◦

Pascal said that it is easier to endure death without thinking about it than to endure the thought of death without dying. This is how you manage to dance the strange dance with that grim partner, nuclear annihilation. When the U.S. Army notified Winston Churchill that the first atom bomb had been detonated in New Mexico, it chose the code phrase BA-BIES SATISFACTORILY BORN. So you entered the age of irony, and the strange double life you've been leading with the world ever since. Joyce Carol Oates suggests that the reason writers—*real* writers, one assumes—don't write about Nature is that it lacks a sense of humor and registers no irony. It just doesn't seem to be of the times—these slick, sleek, knowing, objective, indulgent times. And the word *Environment.* Such a bloodless word. A flat-footed word with a shrunken heart. A word increasingly disengaged from its association with the natural world. Urban planners, industrialists, economists, and developers use it. It's a lost word, really. A cold word, mechanistic, suited strangely to the coldness generally felt toward Nature. It's their word now. You don't mind giving it up. As for *Environmentalist*, that's one that can really bring on the yawns, for you've tamed and tidied it, neutered it quite nicely. An environmentalist must be calm, rational, reasonable, and willing to compromise, otherwise you won't listen to him. Still, his beliefs are *opinions* only, for this is the age of rad-ical subjectivism. Not long ago, Barry Commoner spoke to the Environmental Protection Agency. He scolded them. They loved it. The way they protect the environment these days is apparently to find an "acceptable level of harm from a pollutant and then issue rules allow-ing industry to pollute to that level." Commoner suggested that this was inappropriate. An EPA employee suggested that any other approach would place limits on economic growth and implied that Commoner was advocating this. Limits on economic growth! Commoner vigorously denied this. Oh, it was a healthy exchange of ideas, healthier certainly than our air and water. We needed that little spanking, the EPA felt. It was refreshing. The agency has recently lumbered into action in its campaign to ban dinoseb. You seem to have liked your dinoseb. It's been a popular weed killer, even though it has been directly linked with birth defects. You must hate weeds a lot. Although the EPA appears successful in banning the poi-son, it will still have to pay the disposal costs and compensate the manufacturers for the market value of the chemicals they still have in stock.

That's ironic, you say, but farmers will suffer losses, too, oh dreadful financial losses, if herbicide and pesticide use is restricted.

Farmers grow way too much stuff anyway. They grow surplus crops with subsidized water created by turning rivers great and small into a plumbing system of dams and canals. Rivers have become *systems.* Wetlands are increasingly being referred to as *filtering systems*—things deigned *useful* because of their ability to absorb urban run-off, oil from roads, et cetera.

We know that. We've known that for years about farmers. We know a lot these days.

We're very well informed. If farmers aren't allowed to make a profit by growing surplus crops, they'll have to sell their land to developers, who'll turn all that *arable land* into office parks. Arable land isn't Nature anyway, and besides, we like those office parks and shopping plazas, with their monster supermarkets open twenty-four hours a day with aisle after aisle after aisle of *products*. It's fun. Products are fun.

⚬ ⚬ ⚬

Farmers like their poisons, but ranchers like them even more. There are well-funded predominantly federal and cooperative programs like the Agriculture Department's Animal Damage Control Unit that poison, shoot, and trap several thousand animals each year. This unit loves to kill things. It was created to kill things—bobcats, foxes, black bears, mountain lions, rabbits, badgers, countless birds—all to make this great land safe for the string bean and the corn, the sheep and the cow, even though you're not consuming as much cow these days. A burger now and then, but burgers are hardly cows at all, you feel. They're not all *our* cows in any case, for some burger matter is imported. There's a bit of Central American burger matter in your bun. Which is contributing to the conversion of tropical rain forest into cow pasture. Even so, you're getting away from meat these days. You're eschewing cow. It's seafood you love, shrimp most of all. And when you love something, it had better watch out, because you have a tendency to love it to death. Shrimp, shrimp, shrimp. It's more common on menus than chicken. In the wilds of Ohio, far, far from watery shores, four out of the six entrées on a menu will be shrimp, for some modest sum. Everywhere, it's all the shrimp you can eat or all you *care* to eat, for sometimes you just don't feel like eating all you *can*. You are intensively *harvesting* shrimp. Soon there won't be any left and then you can stop. It takes that, often, to make you stop. Shrimpers shrimp, of course. That's their *business*. They put out these big nets and in these nets, for each pound of shrimp, they catch more than ten times that amount of fish, turtles, and dolphins. These, quite the worse for wear, they dump back in. There is an object called TED (Turtle Excluder Device), which would save thousands of turtles and some dolphins from dying in the nets, but the shrimpers are loath to use TEDs, as they say it would cut the size of their shrimp catch.

We've heard about TED, you say.

They want you, all of you, to have all the shrimp you can eat and more. At Kiawah Island, off the coast of South Carolina, visitors go out on Jeep "safaris" through the part of the island that hasn't been developed yet. ("Wherever you see trees," the guide says, "really, that's a lot.") The safari comprises six Jeeps, and these days they go out at least four times a day, with more trips promised soon. The tourists drive their own Jeeps and the guide talks to them by radio. Kiawah has nice beaches, and the guide talks about turtles. When he mentions the shrimpers' role in the decline of the turtle, the shrimpers, who share the same frequency, scream at him. Shrimpers and most commercial fishermen (many of them working with drift and gill nets anywhere from six to thirty miles long) think of themselves as an *endangered species*. A recent newspaper headline said, "Shrimpers Spared Anti-Turtle Devices." Even so, with the continuing wanton depletion of shrimp beds, they will undoubtedly have to find some other means of employment soon. They might, for instance, become part of that vast throng laboring in the *tourist industry*.

⚬ ⚬ ⚬

Tourism has become an industry as destructive as any other. You are no longer benign in your traveling somewhere to look at the scenery. You never thought there was much gain in just looking anyway, you've always preferred to *use* the scenery in some manner. In your desire to get away from what you've got, you've caused there to be no place to get away *to*. You're just all bumpered up out there. Sewage and dumps have become prime indicators of America's lifestyle. In resort towns in New England and the Adirondacks, measuring the flow into the sewage plant serves as a business barometer. Tourism is a growth industry. You believe in growth. *Controlled* growth, of course. Controlled exponential growth is what you'd really like to see. You certainly don't want to put a moratorium or a cap on anything. That's illegal, isn't it? Retro you're not. You don't want to go back or anything. Forward. Maybe ask directions later. Growth is *desirable* as well as being *inevitable*. Growth is the one thing you seem to be powerless before, so you try to be realistic about it. Growth is—it's weird—it's like cancer or something.

Recently you, as tourist, have discovered your national parks and are quickly *overburdening* them. Spare land and it belongs to you! It's exotic land too, not looking like all the stuff around it that looks like everything else. You want to take advantage of this land, of course, and use it in every way you can. Thus the managers—or *stewards*, as they like to be called—have developed *wise* and *multiple-use* plans, keeping in mind exploiters' interests (for they have their needs, too) as well as the desires of the backpackers. Thus mining, timbering, and ranching activities take place in the national forests, where the Forest Service maintains a system of logging roads eight times larger than the interstate highway system. The national parks are more of a public playground and are becoming increasingly Europeanized in their look and management. Lots of concessions and motels. You deserve a clean bed and a hot meal when you go into the wilderness. At least your stewards think that you do. You keep your stewards busy. Not only must they cater to your multiple and conflicting desires, they have to manage your wildlife *resources*. They have managed wildfowl to such an extent that the reasoning has become, If it weren't for hunters, ducks would disappear. Duck stamps and licensing fees support the whole rickety duck-management system. Yes! If it weren't for the people who killed them, wild ducks wouldn't exist! Managers are managing all wild creatures, not just those that fly. They track and tape and tag and band. They relocate, restock, and reintroduce. They cull and control. It's hard to keep it all straight. Protect or poison? Extirpate or just mostly eliminate? Sometimes even the stewards get mixed up.

❧ ❧ ❧

This is the time of machines and models, hands-on management and master plans. Don't you ever wonder as you pass that billboard advertising another MASTER-PLANNED COMMUNITY just what master they are actually talking about? Not the Big Master, certainly. Something brought to you by one of the tiny masters, of which there are many. But you like these tiny masters and have even come to expect and require them. In Florida they've just started a ten-thousand-acre city in the Everglades. It's a *megaproject*, one of the largest ever in the state. Yes, they must have thought you wanted it. No, what you thought of as the Everglades, the Park, is only a little bitty part of the Everglades. Developers have been gnawing at this irreplaceable, strange land for years. It's like they just *hate* this ancient sea of grass. Maybe you could ask them about this sometime. Roy Rogers is the senior vice president of strategic planning, and the old cowboy says that every tree and bush and inch of sidewalk in the project has been planned. Nevertheless, because the whole thing will take twenty-five years to complete, the plan is going to be constantly changed. You can understand this. The important thing is that there be a blueprint. You trust a blueprint. The tiny masters know what you like. You like *a secure landscape* and *access to services*. You like grass—that is, lawns. The ultimate lawn is the golf course, which you've been told has "some ecological value." You believe this! Not that it really matters, you just like to play golf. These golf courses require a lot of watering. So much that the more inspired of the masters have taken to watering them with effluent, *treated* effluent, but yours, from all the condos and villas built around the stocked artificial lakes you fancy.

I really don't want to think about sewage, you say, but it sounds like progress.

It is true that the masters are struggling with the problems of your incessant flushing. Cuisine is also one of their concerns. Advances in sorbets—sorbet intermezzos—in their clubs and fine restaurants. They know what you want. You want A HAVEN FROM THE ORDINARY WORLD. If you're A NATURE LOVER in the West you want to live in a $200,000 home in A WILD ANIMAL HABITAT. If you're eastern and consider yourself more hip, you want to live in new towns—brand-new reconstructed-from-scratch towns—in a house of NINETEENTH-CENTURY DESIGN. But in these new towns the masters are building, getting around can be confusing. There is an abundance of curves and an infrequency of through streets. It's the new wilderness without any trees. You can get lost, even with all the "mental bread crumbs" the masters scatter about as visual landmarks—the windmill, the water views, the various groupings of landscape "material." You *are* lost, you know. But you trust a Realtor will show you the way. There are many more Realtors than tiny masters, and many of them have to make do with less than a loaf—that is, trying to sell stuff that's already been built in an environment already "enhanced" rather than something being planned—but they're everywhere, willing to show you the path. If Dante returned to Hell today, he'd probably be escorted down by a Realtor, talking all the while about how it was just another level of Paradise.

> When have you last watched a sunset? Do you remember where you were? With whom?
> At Loews Ventana Canyon Resort, the Grand Foyer will provide you with that opportunity through lighting which is computerized to diminish with the approaching sunset!

The tiny masters are willing to arrange Nature for you. They will compose it into a picture that you can look at at your leisure, when you're not doing work or something like that. Nature becomes scenery, a prop. At some golf courses in the Southwest, the saguaro cacti are reported to be repaired with green paste when balls blast into their skin. The saguaro can attempt to heal themselves by growing over the balls, but this takes time, and the effect can be somewhat . . . baroque. It's better to get out the pastepot. Nature has become simply a visual form of entertainment, and it had better look snappy.

Listen, you say, we've been at Ventana Canyon. It's in the desert, right? It's very, very nice, a world-class resort. A totally self-contained environment with everything that a person could possibly want, on more than a thousand acres in the middle of zip. It sprawls but nestles, like. And they've maintained the integrity of as much of the desert ecosystem as possible. Give them credit for that. *Great* restaurant, too. We had baby bay scallops there. Coming into the lobby there are these two big hand-carved coyotes, mutely howling. And that's the way we like them, *mute*. God, why do those things howl like that?

⌖   ⌖   ⌖

Wildlife is a personal matter, you think. The attitude is up to you. You can prefer to see it dead or not dead. You might want to let it mosey about its business or blow it away. Wild things exist only if you have the graciousness to allow them to. Just outside Tucson, Arizona, there is a brand-new structure modeled after a French foreign legion outpost. It's the *International Wildlife Museum,* and it's full of dead animals. Three hundred species are there, at least a third of them—the rarest ones—killed and collected by one C. J. McElroy, who enjoyed doing it and now shares what's left with you. The museum claims to be educational because you can watch a taxidermist at work or touch a lion's tooth. You can get real close to these dead animals, closer than you can in a zoo. Some of you prefer zoos, however, which are becoming bigger, better, and bioclimatic. New-age zoo designers want the animals to *flow right out into your space.* In Dallas there will soon be a Wilds of Africa exhibit; in San Diego there's a simulated rain forest, where you can thread your way "down the side of a lush canyon, the air filled with a fine mist from 300 high-pressure nozzles"; in New Orleans you've constructed a swamp, the real swamp not far away on the verge of disappearing. Animals in these places are abstractions—wandering relics of their true selves, but that doesn't matter. Animal behavior in a zoo is nothing like natural behavior, but that doesn't really matter, either. Zoos are pretty, contained, and accessible. These new habitats can contain one hundred different species—not more than one or two of each thing, of course—on seven acres, three, one. You don't want to see *too much* of anything, certainly. An *example* will suffice. Sort of like a biological Crabtree & Evelyn basket selected with *you* in mind. You like things reduced, simplified. It's easier to take it all in, park it in your mind. You like things inside better than outside anyway. You are increasingly looking at and living in proxy environments created by substitution and simulation. *Resource economists* are a wee branch in the tree of tiny masters, and one, Martin Krieger, wrote, "Artificial prairies and wildernesses have been created, and there is no reason to believe that these artificial environments need be unsatisfactory for those who experience them. . . . We will have to realize that the way in which we experience nature is conditioned by our society—which more and more is seen to be receptive to responsible intervention."

Nature has become a world of appearances, a mere source of materials. You've been editing it for quite some time; now you're in the process of deleting it. Earth is beginning to look like not much more than a launching pad. Back near Tucson, on the opposite side of the mountain from the dead-animal habitat, you're building Biosphere II (as compared with or opposed to Biosphere I, more commonly known as Earth)—a 2 1/2-acre terrarium, an artificial ecosystem that will include a rain forest, a desert, a thirty-five-foot ocean, and several thousand species of life (lots of microbes), including eight human beings, who will cultivate a bit of farmland. You think it would be nice to colonize other worlds after you've made it necessary to leave this one.

Hey, that's pretty good, you say, all that stuff packed into just 2 1/2 acres. That's only about three times bigger than my entire *house.*

It's small all right, but still not small enough to be, apparently, useful. For the purposes of NASA, say, it would have to be smaller, oh much smaller, and energy-efficient too. Fiddle, fiddle, fiddle. You support fiddling, as well as meddling. This is how you learn. Though it's quite apparent the environment has been grossly polluted and the natural world abused and defiled, you seem to prefer to continue pondering effects rather than preventing causes. You want proof, you insist on proof. A Dr. Lave from Carnegie-Mellon—and he's an expert, an economist, and an environmental *expert*—says that scientists will have to prove to you that you will suffer if you don't become less of a "throwaway society." *If you really want me to give up my car or my air conditioner, you'd better prove to me first that the earth would otherwise be uninhabitable,* Dr. Lave says. *Me* is *you,* I presume, whereas *you* refers to them. You as in me—that is, *me, me, me*—certainly strike a hard bargain. Uninhabitable the world has to get before you rein in your requirements. You're a consumer after all, *the* consumer upon whom so much attention is lavished, the ultimate user of a commodity that has become, these days, everything. To try to appease your appetite for proof, for example, scientists have been leasing for experimentation forty-six pristine lakes in Canada.

They don't want to *keep* them, they just want to *borrow* them.

They've been intentionally contaminating many of the lakes with a variety of pollutants dribbled into the propeller wash of research boats. It's *one of the boldest experiments in lake ecology ever conducted.* They've turned these remote lakes into huge *real-world test tubes.* They've been doing this since 1976! And what they've found so far in these *preliminary* studies is that pollutants are really destructive. The lakes get gross. Life in them ceases. It took about eight years to make this happen in one of them, everything carefully measured and controlled all the while. Now the scientists are slowly reversing the process. But it will take hundreds of years for the lakes to recover. They think.

◦❧ ◦❧ ◦❧

Remember when you used to like rain, the sound of it, the feel of it, the way it made the plants and trees all glisten. We needed that rain, you would say. It looked pretty too, you thought, particularly in the movies. Now it rains and you go, Oh-oh. A nice walloping rain these days means *overtaxing our sewage treatment plants.* It means *untreated waste discharged directly into our waterways.* It means . . .

Okay. Okay.

Acid rain! And we all know what this is. Or most of us do. People of power in government and industry still don't seem to know what it is. Whatever it is, they say, they don't want to curb it, but they're willing to study it some more. Economists call air and water pollution "externalities" anyway. Oh, acid rain. You do get so sick of hearing about it. The words have already become a white-noise kind of thing. But you think in terms of *mitigating* it maybe. As for *the greenhouse effect,* you think in terms of *countering* that. One way that's been discussed recently is the planting of new forests, not for the sake of the forests alone, oh my heavens, no. Not for the sake of majesty and mystery or of Thumper and Bambi, are you kidding me, but because, as every schoolchild knows, trees absorb carbon dioxide. They just soak it up and store it. They just love it. So this is the plan: you plant millions of acres of trees, and you can go on doing pretty much whatever you're doing—driving around, using staggering amounts of energy, keeping those power plants fired to the max. Isn't Nature remarkable? So willing to serve? You wouldn't think it had anything more to offer, but it seems it does. Of course these "forests" wouldn't exactly be forests. They would be more like trees. *Managed* trees. The Forest Service, which now manages our forests by cutting them down, might be called upon to evolve in their thinking and allow these trees to grow. They would probably be patented trees after a time. Fast-growing, uniform, genetically-created-to-be-toxin-eating *machines.* They would be *new-age* trees, because the problem with planting the old-fashioned variety to *combat* the greenhouse effect, which is caused by pollution, is that they're already dying from it. All along the crest of the Appalachians from Maine to Georgia, forests struggle to survive in a toxic soup of poisons. They can't *help* us if we've killed them, now can they?

◦❧ ◦❧ ◦❧

All right, you say, wow, lighten up will you? Relax. Tell about yourself.

Well, I say, I live in Florida . . .

Oh my God, you say. Florida! Florida is a joke! How do you expect us to take you seriously if you still live there! Florida is crazy, it's pink concrete. It's paved, it's over. And a little girl just got eaten by an alligator down there. It came out of some swamp next to a subdivision and just carried her off. That set your Endangered Species Act back fifty years, you can bet.

I . . .

Listen, we don't want to hear any more about Florida. We don't want to hear about Phoenix or Hilton Head or California's Central Valley. If our wetlands—our *vanishing* wetlands—are mentioned one more time, we'll scream. And the talk about condors and grizzlies and wolves is becoming too de trop. We had just managed to get whales out of our minds when those three showed up under the ice in Alaska. They even had *names*. Bone is the dead one, right? It's almost the twenty-first century! Those last condors are *pathetic*. Can't we just get this over with?

Aristotle said that all living beings are ensouled and striving to participate in eternity.

Oh, I just bet he said that, you say. That doesn't sound like Aristotle. He was a humanist. We're all humanists here. This is the age of humanism. And it has been for a long time.

◦ ◦ ◦

You are driving with a stranger in the car, and it is the stranger behind the wheel. In the back seat are your pals for many years now—DO WHAT YOU LIKE and his swilling sidekick, WHY NOT. A deer, or some emblematic animal, something from that myriad natural world you've come from that you now treat with such indifference and scorn—steps from the dimming woods and tentatively upon the highway. The stranger does not decelerate or brake, not yet, maybe not at all. The feeling is that whatever it is *will get out of the way*. Oh, it's a fine car you've got, a fine machine, and oddly you don't mind the stranger driving it, because in a way, everything has gotten too complicated, way, way out of your control. You've given the wheel to the masters, the managers, the comptrollers. Something is wrong, *maybe*, you feel a little sick, *actually*, but the car is luxurious and fast and you're *moving*, which is the most important thing by far.

◦ ◦ ◦

Why make a fuss when you're so comfortable? Don't make a fuss, make a baby. Go out and get something to eat, build something. Make *another* baby. Babies are cute. Babies show you have faith in the future. Although faith is perhaps too strong a word. They're everywhere these days, in all the crowds and traffic jams, there are the babies too. You don't seem to associate them with the problems of population increase. They're just babies! And you've come to believe in them again. They're a lot more tangible than the afterlife, which, of course, you haven't believed in in ages. At least not for yourself. The afterlife now belongs to plastics and poisons. Yes, plastics and poisons will have a far more extensive afterlife than you, that's known. A disposable diaper, for example, which is all plastic and wood pulp—you like them for all those babies, so easy to use and toss—will take around four centuries to degrade. Almost all plastics do, centuries and centuries. In the sea, many marine animals die from ingesting or being entangled in discarded plastic. In the dumps, plastic squats on more than 25 percent of dump space. But your heart is disposed toward plastic. Someone, no doubt the plastics industry, told you it was convenient. This same industry is now looking into recycling in an attempt to get the critics of their nefarious, multifarious products off their backs. That should make you feel better, because *recycling* has become an honorable word, no longer merely the hobby of Volvo owners. The fact is that people in plastics are born obscurants. Recycling (practically impossible) won't solve the plastic glut, only reduction of production will, and the plastics industry isn't looking into that, you can be sure. Waste is not just the stuff you throw away, of course, it's the stuff you use to excess. With the exception of *hazardous waste*, which you do worry about from time to time, it's even thought you have a declining sense of emergency about the problem. Builders are building bigger houses because you want bigger. You're trading up. Utility companies are beginning to worry about your constantly rising consumption. Utility companies! You haven't entered a new age at all but one of upscale nihilism, deluxe nihilism.

❧   ❧   ❧

In the summer, particularly in *the industrial Northeast,* you did get a little excited. The filth cut into your fun time. Dead stuff floating around. Sludge and bloody vials. Hygienic devices—appearing not quite so hygienic out of context—all coming in on the tide. The air smelled funny, too. You tolerate a great deal, but the summer of '88 was truly creepy. It was even thought for a moment that the environment would become a political issue. But it didn't. You didn't want it to be, preferring instead to continue in your politics of subsidizing and advancing avarice. The issues were the same as always—jobs, defense, the economy, maintaining and improving the standard of living in this greedy, selfish, expansionistic, industrialized society.

You're getting a little shrill here, you say.

You're pretty well off. You expect to be better off soon. You do. What does this mean? More software, more scampi, more square footage? You have created an ecological crisis. The earth is infinitely variable and alive, and you are killing it. It seems safer this way. But you are not safe. You want to find wholeness and happiness in a land increasingly damaged and betrayed, and you never will. More than material matters. You must change your ways.

What is this? *Sinners in the Hands of an Angry God?*

The ecological crisis cannot be resolved by politics. It cannot be solved by science or technology. It is a crisis caused by culture and character, and a deep change in personal consciousness is needed. Your fundamental attitudes toward the earth have become twisted. You have made only brutal contact with Nature, you cannot comprehend its grace. You must change. Have few desires and simple pleasures. Honor nonhuman life. Control yourself, become more authentic. Live lightly upon the earth and treat it with respect. Redefine the word *progress* and dismiss the managers and masters. Grow inwardly and with knowledge become truly wiser. Make connections. Think differently, behave differently. For this is essentially a moral issue we face and moral decisions must be made.

A *moral issue!* Okay, this discussion is now toast. A *moral* issue . . . And who's this *we* now? Who are *you* is what I'd like to know. You're not me, anyway. I admit, someone's to blame and something should be done. But I've got to go. It's getting late. That's dusk out there. That is dusk, isn't it? It certainly doesn't look like any dawn I've ever seen. Well, take care.

Ntozake Shange

What Is It We Really Harvestin' Here?

We got a sayin', "The blacker the berry, the sweeter the juice," which is usually meant as a compliment. To my mind, it also refers to the delectable treats we as a people harvested for our owners and for our own selves all these many years, slave or free. In fact, we knew something about the land, sensuality, rhythm and ourselves that has continued to elude our captors—puttin' aside all our treasures in the basement of the British Museum, or the Met, for that matter. What am I talkin' about? A different approach to the force of gravity, to our bodies, and what we produce: a reverence for the efforts of the group and the intimate couple. Harvest time and Christmas were prime occasions for courtin'. A famine, a drought, a flood or Lent do not serve as inspiration for couplin', you see.

The Juba, a dance of courtin' known in slave quarters of North America and the Caribbean, is a phenomenon that stayed with us through the jitterbug, the wobble, the butterfly, as a means of courtin' that's apparently very colored, and very "African." In fact we still have it and we've never been so "integrated"—the *Soul Train* dancers aren't all black anymore, but the dynamic certainly is. A visitor to Cuba in Lynne Fauley Emery's "Dance Horizon Book" described the Juba as a series of challenges.

> A woman advances and commencing a slow dance, made up of shuffling of the feet and various contortions of the body, thus challenges a rival from among the men. One of these, bolder than the rest, after a while steps out, and the two then strive which shall tire the other; the woman performing many feats which the man attempts to rival, often excelling them, amid the shouts of the rest. A woman will sometimes drive two or three successive beaux from the ring, yielding her place at length to some impatient belle.

John Henry went up against a locomotive, but decades before we simply were up against ourselves and the elements. And so we are performers in the fields, in the kitchens, by kilns, and for one another. Sterling Stuckey points out, in "Slave Culture," however, that by 1794 "it was illegal to allow slaves to dance and drink on the premises . . . without the written consent of their owners," the exceptions being Christmas and the burials, which are communal experiences. And what shall we plant and harvest, so that we might "Hab big times duh fus hahves, and duh fus ting wut growed we take tuh duh church so as ebrybody could hab a pieces ub it. We pray over it and shout. Wen we hab a dance, we use tuh shout in a rinig. We ain't have wutyuh call a propuh dance tuday."

Say we've gone about our owners' business. Planted and harvested his crop of sugar cane, remembering that the "ration of slaves/sugar was ten times that of slaves/tobacco and slaves/cotton." That to plant a sugar crop we have to dig a pit 3 feet square and a few inches deep into which one young plant is set. Then, of course, the thing has to grow. A mature sugar-cane plant is 3–9 feet tall. That's got to be cut at exactly the right point. Then we've got to crush it, boil it, refine it, from thick black syrup to fine white sugar, to make sure, as they say in Virginia, that we "got the niggah out." Now it's time to tend to our own gardens. Let's grow some sweet potatoes to "keep the niggah alive."

Sweet Potatoes

Like everything else, we have to start with something. Now we need a small piece of potato with at least one of those scraggly roots hanging about for this native Central American tuber. This vegetable will stand more heat than almost any other grown in the United States. It does not take to cool weather, and any kind of frost early or seasonal will kill the leaves, and if your soil gets cold the tubers themselves will not look very good. Get your soil ready at least two weeks before planting, weeding, turning, and generally disrupting the congealed and solid mass we refer to as dirt, so that your hands and the tubers may move easily through the soil, as will water and other nutrients.

Once the soil is free of winter, two weeks after the last frost, plant the potato slips in 6–12-inch ridges, 3–4.5 feet apart. Separate the plants by 9–12 inches. If we space the plants more than that, our tubers may be grand, but way too big to make good use of in the kitchen. We should harvest our sweet potatoes when the tubers are not quite ripe, but of good size, or we can wait until the vines turn yellow. Don't handle our potatoes too roughly, which could lead to bruising and decay. If a frost comes upon us unexpectedly, take those potatoes out the ground right away. Our potatoes will show marked improvement during storage, which allows the starch in them to turn to sugar. Nevertheless let them lie out in the open for 2 to 3 hours to fully dry. Then move them to a moist and warm storage space. The growing time for our crop'll vary from 95 to 125 days.

The easiest thing to do with a sweet potato is to bake it. In its skin. I coat the thing with olive oil, or butter in a pinch. Wrap it in some aluminum foil, set it in the oven at 400 degrees. Wait till I hear sizzling, anywhere from 45 minutes to an hour after, in a very hot oven. I can eat it with my supper at that point or I can let it cool off for later. (One of the sexiest dates I ever went on was to the movies to see "El Mariachi." My date brought along chilled baked sweet potatoes and ginger beer. Much nicer than canola-sprayed "buttered" popcorn with too syrupy Coca-Cola, wouldn't you say?)

Mustard Greens

No, they are not the same as collards. We could say they, with their frilly edges and sinuous shapes, have more character, are more flirtatious, than collards. This green can be planted in the spring or the fall, so long as the soil is workable (not cold). It's not a hot weather plant, preferring short days and temperate climates. We can use the same techniques for mustard greens that we use for lettuce. Sowing the seeds in rows 12–18 inches apart, seedlings 4–8 inches apart. These plants should get lots of fertilizer to end up tender, lots of water, too. They should be harvested before they are fully mature. Now, you've got to be alert, because mustard greens grow fast, 25–40 days from the time you set them in the soil to harvest. When it comes time to reap what you've sown, gather the outer leaves when they are 3–4 inches long, tender enough; let the inner leaves then develop more or wait till it's hot and harvest the whole plant.

Now we cook the mustard greens just like the collards, or we don't have to cook it at all. This vegetable is fine in salads or on sandwiches and soups. If you shy away from pungent tastes, mix these greens with some collards, kale, or beet greens. That should take some of the kick out of them. I still like my peppers and vinegar, though. If we go back, pre-Columbus, the Caribs did, too. According to Spanish travelers, the Caribs, who fancied vegetables, added strong peppers called aji-aji to just about everything. We can still find aji-aji on some sauces from Spanish-speaking countries if we read the labels carefully. Like "La Morena." So appropriate.

Watermelon

The watermelon is an integral part of our actual life as much as it is a feature of our stereotypical lives in the movies, posters, racial jokes, toys, and early American portraits of the "happy darky." We could just as easily been eatin' watermelon in D.W. Griffith's "Birth of a Nation" as chicken legs. The implications are the same. Like the watermelon, we were a throwback of "African" pre-history, which isn't too off, since Lucy, the oldest Homo sapiens currently known is from Africa, too.

But I remember being instructed not to order watermelon in restaurants or to eat watermelon in any public places because it makes white people think poorly of us. They already did that, so I don't see what the watermelon was going to precipitate. Europeans brought watermelon with them from Africa anyway. In Massachusetts by 1629 it was recorded as "abounding." In my rebelliousness as a child, I got so angry about the status of the watermelon, I tried to grow some in the flower box on our front porch in Missouri. My harvest was minimal to say the least.

Here's how you can really grow you some watermelon. They like summer heat, particularly sultry, damp nights. If we can grow watermelons, we can grow ourselves almost any other kind of melon. The treatment is the same. Now, these need some space, if we're looking for a refrigerator-sized melon or one ranging from 25–30 pounds. Let them have a foot between plants in between rows 4–6 feet apart. They need a lot of fertilizer, especially if the soil is heavy and doesn't drain well. When the runners (vines) are a foot to a foot-and-a-half long, fertilize again about 8 inches from the plant itself. Put some more fertilizer when the first melons appear. Watermelons come in different varieties, but I'm telling you about the red kind. I have no primal response to a golden or blanched fleshed melon. Once your melons set on the vines and start to really take up some space, be sure not to forget to water the vines during the ripening process.

When is your watermelon ripe? You can't tell by thumping it nor by the curly tail at the point where the melon is still on the vine. The best way to know if your melon is ready is by looking at the bottom. The center turns from a light yellow to deep amber. Your melon'll have a powdery or mushy tasteless sorta taste if you let it ripen too long.

Surely you've seen enough pictures or been to enough picnics to know how to eat a watermelon, so I won't insult you with that information. However, there is a fractious continuing debate about whether to sprinkle sugar or salt on your watermelon slice. I am not going to take sides in this matter.

⟡   ⟡   ⟡

Some of us were carried to the New World specifically because we knew 'bout certain crops, knew 'bout the groomin' and harvestin' of rice, for instance.

> Plantation owners were perfectly aware of the superiority . . . of African slaves from rice country. Littlefield (journalist) writes that "as early as 1700 ships from Carolina were reported in the Gambia River." . . . In a letter dated 1756, Henry Laurens, a Charleston merchant, wrote, "The slaves from the River Gambia are prefer'd to all others with us save the Gold Coast." The previous year he had written: "Gold Coast or Gambias are best; next to them the Windward Coast are prefer'd to Angolas."

These bits of information throw an entirely different, more dignified light on "colored" cuisine, for me. Particularly since I was raised on rice and my mother's people on both sides are indefatigable Carolinians, South, to be exact, South Carolinians. To some, our "phrenologically immature brains" didn't have consequence until our mastery of the cultivation of "cargo," "patna," "joponica," and finally Carolina rice, "small-grained, rather long and wiry, and remarkably white" was transferred to the books and records of our owners. Nevertheless, our penchant for rice was not dampened by its relationship to our bondage. Whether through force or will, we held on to our rice-eatin' heritage. I repeat, I was raised on rice. If I was Joe Williams, instead singin' "Every day, every day, I sing the blues," I'd be sayin', "Oh, every day, almost any kinda way, I get my rice."

My poor mother, Eloise, Ellie, for short, made the mistake of marrying a man who was raised by a woman from Canada. So every day, he wanted a potato, some kinda potato, mashed, boiled, baked, scalloped, fried, just a potato. Yet my mother was raising a sixth generation of Carolinians, which meant we had to eat some kinda rice. Thus, Ellie was busy fixing potato for one and rice for all the rest every day, until I finally learnt how to do one or the other and gave her a break. I asked Ellie Williams how her mother, Viola, went about preparing the rice for her "chirren"—a Low-country linguistic lapse referring to off-spring like me. Anyway, this is what Mama said.

Mama's Rice

"We'd buy some rice in a brown paper bag (this is in The Bronx). Soak it in a bit of water. Rinse it off and cook it the same way we do now." "How is that, Ma?" I asked. "Well, you boil a certain amount of water. Let it boil good. Add your rice and let it boil till tender. Stirring every so often because you want the water to evaporate. You lift your pot. You can tell if your rice is okay because there's no water there. Then you fluff it with a fork. You want every kind, extra, extra, what you call it. No ordinary olive oil will do.

"Heat this up. Just a little bit of it. You don't want no greasy rice, do you? Heat this until, oh, it is so hot that the smoke is coming quick. Throw in 3–4 cloves garlic, maybe 1 cup chopped onion too, I forget. Let that sizzle and soften with 1/2 cup each cilantro, pimiento, and everything. But don't let this get burned, no. So add your 4 cups water and 2 cups rice. Turn up the heat some more till there's a great boiling of rice, water, seasonings. The whole thing. Then leave it alone for a while with the cover on so all the rice cooks even. Now, when you check and see there's only a small bit of water left in the bottom of the pot, stir it all up. Turn the heat up again and wait. When there's no water left at all, at all. Just watch the steam coming up. Of course you should have a good pegau by now, but the whole pot of your rice should be delicioso, ready even for my table. If you do as I say."

⋅❦⋅ ⋅❦⋅ ⋅❦⋅

For North Americans, a pot with burnt rice on the bottom is a scary concept. But all over the Caribbean, it's a different story entirely. In order to avoid making asopao—a rice moist and heavy with the sofrito or tomato-achiote mixture, almost like a thick soup where the rice becomes one mass instead of standing, each grain on its own—it is necessary to let the rice on the bottom of the pot get a crustlike bottom, assuring that all moisture has evaporated. My poor North American mother, Ellie, chastises me frequently for "ruining" good rice with all this spice. Then I remind her that outside North America we Africans were left to cook in ways that reminded us of our mother's cooking, not Jane Austen's characters. The rice tastes different, too. But sometimes I cheat and simply use Goya's Sazon—after all, I'm a modern woman. I shouldn't say that too loudly, though. Mathilde can hear all the way from her front porch any blasphemous notion I have about good cooking. No, it is her good cooking that I am to learn. I think it is more than appropriate that we know something about some of the crops that led to most of us African descendants of the Diaspora, being here, to eat anything at all.

But rather than end on a sour note, I am thinking of my classes with the great Brazilian dancer, choreographer and teacher Mercedes Baptista at the now legendary Clark Center. We learned a harvest dance, for there are many, but the movements of this celebratory ritual were lyrical and delicate, far from the tortured recounts of Euro-Americans to our "jigaboo" gatherings; no gyrations, repetitive shuffling that held no interest. Indeed, the simple movement of the arms, which we worked on for days until we got it, resembled a tropical port-a-bras worthy of any ballerina. Our hip movements, ever so subtle, with four switches to the left, then four to the right, all the while turning and covering space. The head leaning in the direction of the hips, the arms moving against it, till the next hip demanded counterpoint.

A healthy respect for the land, for what we produce for the blessing of a harvest begot dances of communal joy. On New Year's Eve in the late fifties, we danced the Madison; today it's a burning rendition of "The Electric Slide." Eighty-year-olds jammin' with toddlers after the weddin' toast. No, we haven't changed so much.

Stanton Michaels
How to Write a Personal Essay

THE EASIEST WAY TO WRITE A PERSONAL ESSAY IS TO USE THE STANDARD FORM TAUGHT IN Composition 101: an introductory paragraph followed by three paragraphs outlining three main points and a final summary paragraph. But instead of just blathering about yourself, describe vivid scenes and what they mean to you, such as when your 2-year-old son, Jordan, solemnly declares from the bathtub "I can't swim—my penis is hard" and you tell him it's OK, it's normal, knowing it'll subside and he'll be able to swim soon, but you don't tell him that teeny little weenie he's holding will be the source of the most intense worries, sorrows, and pleasures he'll ever experience, and you wonder if you'll ever be able to tell him the truth. You could follow this thought with the trials and tribulations of your own penis, unless you're a woman—but of course females are involved with love, sex, and life built around their own body parts, which can provide many interesting topics. The key to maintaining reader interest is to be open and honest, displaying your concerns and fears through specific, true-life examples rather than abstract concepts about how you think sex education is important because you learned the hard way on your own and you doubt you'll explain things any better than your own father did. Follow this format and, while you may not become a world-renowned author, you will be able to complete a personal essay.

Use five sentences in each paragraph. Some authors, like Faulkner, write immensely long sentences that drift into nooks and crannies of life, enlightening the reader about how, at age 16, you were tricked by a girl into trying on ring sets from her mom's jewelry-making equipment to find your ring size and later presented with a black onyx and silver ring you were too scared to wear because it implied going steady, which leads to sex, and Dad had just given you and your brother a box of Trojans the week before when Mom and Brooke had gone shopping at Sears for dresses and you were as uncomfortable as Dad when he grunted out his heart-to-heart "Use these to be safe," especially since you'd recently calculated and realized he'd knocked Mom up with you when she was 16 and he was out of the army after a four-year hitch and you figured it must have happened by accident since their meeting was accidental, him picking her and her sisters up at a railroad crossing in the rain on Halloween and giving them a ride home, coming later to visit, finally getting down in April without a condom or maybe with one that broke and there you are in December but at least they'd gotten married over the summer and you realize it's April now and you stare at the ring and finally throw it away and tell her later you don't wear jewelry. Tough guys like Hemingway write short, straightforward sentences, such as: "The author stopped typing. His thick fingers lay bare on the keyboard. Although he's been married for eight years, his ring finger is naked. His wife knows he doesn't wear jewelry. Ever." Yet other writers like to mix up the lengths of their sentences, using long, compound run-ons that begin with one thought then drive on to others but eventually circle back for completion, then follow with a short, crisp, prissy sentence that would satisfy an eighth-grade grammar teacher. Not me.

Write about things you've done or people you know, introducing your first true love or your first sexual encounter at age 17 crammed in the back of a Volkswagen Beetle with Danielle who will do it for free cause she has a crush on you and you need the experience to be ready for your true first time with Julie whom you love and can't get off your mind while you're wedged against the cold side window, remembering Julie's taste, the force of her tongue in your mouth, the way she holds your hard-on like she knows what she wants and you need to be sure how to do it exactly right so here you are pumping away feeling cheap and drunk and ashamed and excited and sore and thinking sex should be a lot more fun or magical than this floundering on the back seat. You can write in sober first person ("I found later with Julie I didn't need the practice session with Danielle"), but some feel this is self-serving and others, such as myself, need the safe distance from slivers of memory provided by humor, misdirection, and second or even third person ("At least he wore a condom both times"). Don't take examples from television or books or newspapers unless they have an effect on you. Don't write about Kurt Cobain's suicide after achieving fatherhood or Jimi and Janis overdosing when you were a teen unless you're a musician—even a part-time folk-rock banjo-picker—wondering how you ever made it out of adolescence since you were so horny yet scared of sex you could only function by smoking a joint first thing in the morning to slow down your thoughts yet still dragged home at midnight after playing a party and jerked off into a dark toilet bowl before passing out in bed worried if you'd wake the next morning and mostly hoping you wouldn't, having all these memories from those horrid nights years ago cascade through your mind when you returned home from a jam session last Wednesday night a little drunk and then—after checking on Jordan and his sister sleeping peacefully—crying for Kurt who'll never know his own child and crying for Jim Morrison and Carla Hill and Randy Batson who died in a car accident in high school and all the others you remember, knowing it was just luck you made it and they didn't, finally wiping away the tears as you piss tequila residue into a murky toilet before going to sleep knowing you're gonna drag tomorrow at work but sure you'll wake up in time as you always do. Write about universal themes you've experienced personally and others can relate to, like love, fear, and death—or sex, drugs, and rock 'n' roll.

Use specific examples that stick to one theme. Don't write generically about how condoms might break when you can write specifically about the first time with Melanie who'd just gotten over an abortion and her new IUD wasn't ready yet so you ran back to your cabin at the summer camp where you were both counselors to get the jet-black, ribbed Love Machine you'd bought in a gas station in North Carolina and carried for two years for just such an occasion but after shredded pieces of black latex dripping with semen fell onto the rumpled sheets and Melanie stared like it was a loaded shotgun pointed right at her belly and all you could do was shrug "Sorry" and the only worry on your mind was when your next day off was so you could get to town and buy some that worked because this first time with her was what you'd always hoped sex would finally turn out to be—a fun, relaxed sharing of talk, laughter, and touch. Stick to one theme. Don't write about Carla Hill in ninth grade when you were 14 if you're writing about your sex life because she was murdered before anything happened, her throat cut in her own bed during an attempted rape the night before you'd finally mustered up enough courage to ask her to go steady and your buddies had helped you out by sitting in all the seats in the front, right-hand side of the bus where she always sat, leaving the only open space right next to you so she'd just have to sit there and you had your name bracelet all ready but she never got on and everyone else was sobbing, telling you about it. I feel that stories like that, despite being of possible interest, lack relevance to the major themes of "your sex life" in this essay and should be saved for some other piece of writing—unless, of course, you can tie the story in using a new focus, perhaps discovered while writing the essay, such as maybe realizing your refusal to wear jewelry has nothing to do with your dad, condoms, and pregnancy but is instead related somehow to your first attempt at commitment that went totally sour and you simply compensated in the best way your 14-year-old mind could think of.

Personal essays come in all kinds. Some are forms of reportage, such as those by John McPhee or Tracy Kidder, telling the truths about people they've interviewed yet injecting the honesty of the reporter's perception rather than trying to pretend a writer has no slant that skews a story. Other essays deal with decisions made, such as when you finally decide to make a baby and Cheryl leaves her diaphragm out for the first time in 14 years and you laugh as you remember getting sick of her mom asking about grandkids and telling her you both wanted to get really good at sex before doing it for real and now here you are for real and scared if you'll be good enough, and you're not talking just about sex now. Essays can also be speculative: questions about found objects, thoughts about missed opportunities and things that never were, or memories that haunt you such as Lindsey in Washington, D.C., who lived in an all-women's house that banned men and made you stand outside in the snow when you came over to get some banjo books abandoned by a former tenant but something happened and Lindsey moved into your room the weekend you hitched down to North Carolina as bodyguard and companion to her friend Rose and stayed when you got back to hump you two or three times a night until you got so raw you could hardly walk and with no talk or even real emotion of love or commitment to prevent you leaving a month later, but now you remember how there also wasn't any talk of contraception because you'd assumed she took care of it since she was so much older, yet now you jerk awake in the middle of the night years later with the stark realization that a lesbian has no need of IUDs or diaphragms or the pill but she does need something to make a baby of her own and maybe there's a little Stan Junior walking around someplace who is 6 years older now than you were then and you wonder if he's as naive as you suddenly discover you were (probably still are) and the only minuscule iota of relief you can find is that at least you'll never have to give him that man-to-man about the birds and bees. By baring your life, using concrete situations and honest thoughts, and following the basic rules of grammar and composition, you too can write a personal essay in 25 sentences.

4

Literary Journalism

The traditional journalist, God bless him, is a "Just the facts, Ma'am" kind of guy. Not for him the squishy-squashy territory of subjective experience, or wishy-washy questions about his objectivity, or longhaired worries over whether his work will last. He sees both sides of every issue, talks to both camps, reports. To the best of his abilities, he writes without bias. All of his stories are other people's stories. His language is always like the next reporter's language, and this is a good thing: we don't need personality on the front page—we need to know what happened, who what where when how and why, and we want it in the disembodied, generalized, authoritative voice of the newspaper in hand.

Not for our traditional journalist fancy language and ten-dollar words and sentences longer than your leg: he wants all his employer's readers to understand him utterly, from the callow kid in seventh grade to the professor at the local college, from the sisters at the abbey to the regulars at Joe's Bar and Grill. And he wants to offend none of them, but only to inform their opinions. He thinks in column inches and sources, and not in paragraphs and people. He brings the facts to light, and leaves interpretation to others. If his employer and his prejudices and safety let him, he provides one of the crucial services in the preservation of freedom and democracy: the transmission of untainted information. Hail the traditional journalist!

But let's face it, the traditional journalist does not aspire to art. He aspires to the scoop, and to the facts, and to the story of the day, and finds unbounded excellence in this way. His editors, journalists themselves, reserve for themselves and for selected columnists the right to express opinion. In this expression of opinion, the traditional journalism aspires to influence. But influence is not art, either. On the features page, traditional newspaper does start to tell stories, but they are stories about strangers brought briefly to light, stories that any one of the excellent reporters in the pool of features writers could go out and get and then write competently to the specifications of the features editor.

Literary journalism aspires to art. It may aspire to other things, as well, but artfulness is the crucial ingredient. And art requires an artist, that is, an individual working to her own

303

ends for her own reasons to create something that wasn't there when she started, something no one but the artist knew was necessary until it appeared, something that only the artist could have made in that exact way, or perhaps at all.

The literary journalist may not go around thinking of making art or of being an artist, but in using the language in fresh ways, making characters out of her people (very often including herself), in showing readers the drama of the factual, in having an opinion, in treating her bias as a virtue, in writing for both present and future, in having a very human voice, in presenting her subjects in ways no one else could, in making free use of the conventions of storytelling (dialogue instead of quotation, scene instead of declaration, plot instead of event, point-of-view instead of impartiality, deep involvement instead of professional detachment), she is making literary art at least possible.

Literary journalism is not particularly new, though the label is. Many critics have pointed to George Orwell as a literary journalist, and writers in English well before him like Addison and Steele (Joseph and Richard, respectively), William Hazlitt the elder, James Boswell, and even Robert Louis Stevenson wrote at times in the form before anyone thought to name it, bringing voice and first-person sensibility and unhidden subjectivity (including fierce opinion) and careful language to what was essentially reportage, building a kind of bridge between the essay and the news report.

In the twentieth-century United States, glossy, high-budget magazines gave certain nonfiction writers the benefit of comparatively long and leisurely weekly and monthly deadlines and wider columns for paragraphs to grow in. Audiences got used to reading fiction in these fancy magazines, and came to expect drama and characters and elegant structure and poetry and surprises from the nonfiction, as well. Readers began to respond to writers who told them what it *felt* like to be a soldier, for example, what it *felt* like to be poor. They wanted the smells, sights, sounds, pains and caresses, and tastes of life itself, wanted the writing so vivid that as readers they might feel the emotions of the people they read about, and, more and more, feel the emotions and therefore the humanity of the writers themselves.

I include a chapter from John Hersey's *Hiroshima* here (it's a stretch, I admit, to call it contemporary, though Mr. Hersey is still alive) because *Hiroshima* is one of the first widely read works of journalism to use the novelist's techniques. Like nearly all the selections I reproduce here, *Hiroshima* appeared first in a periodical, in this case *The New Yorker,* whose editor at the time, Harold Ross in 1946, devoted a whole issue to the piece, an unheard-of move. In a letter to the writer, the famously irascible and understated Ross said, "Those fellows who said 'Hiroshima' was the story of the year, etc., underestimated it. It is unquestionably the story of my time, if not of all time. Nor have I heard of anything like it." Of course, humanizing the Japanese victims of the atomic bomb was deeply controversial—but Hersey's conscience became the world's conscience, and his technique made *people* of what had been mere front page statistics.

Many critics have pointed out that Truman Capote's *In Cold Blood* (subtitled *A True Account of a Multiple Murder and Its Consequences* and published in 1965) is only possible because of the pioneering done by Hersey in *Hiroshima,* not only in technique, but in style and structure. And continuing controversy has surrounded the issue of Capote's accuracy. Did he slip and slide with the facts (especially in the matter of dialogue, and scenes only the dead could remember) in his pursuit of the truth and drama? He called his book a nonfiction novel, causing riots of discussion and argument.

The stage was now set for what Tom Wolfe called the New Journalists, tooting his own rather loud horn while declaring rightly or wrongly that nonfiction writers were taking the literary high ground that novelists had abandoned.

Michael Herr had more to say about war in Vietnam than he'd been able to report back to newspapers—his work in *Dispatches* gives the real picture of a journalist's life and work in war, emotion and regret included.

Norman Mailer's *Executioner's Song,* which he subtitled *A True Novel,* tells the story of Gary Gilmore, the first man executed after the Supreme Court lifted its ban on capital punishment, back in the 1970s. Mikal Gilmore gives his own version in *Shot in the Heart,* published later. Mikal is not only a fine reporter, but Gary's little brother. How does the personal angle figure into the search for the truth in this case?

And all the writers in this section dedicated themselves to the stories they wanted to tell, light-years beyond the limits of traditional journalism, lived inside their stories until they themselves were inextricable from these stories—that is, only one writer, the artist at the center of the telling, could have done the job at hand.

Readers interested in further immersion in literary journalism should find two excellent volumes helpful indeed: *The Literary Journalists,* edited by Norman Sims, and *The Literature of Reality,* edited by Gay Talese and Barbara Lounsberry. And get hold of any one or more of John McPhee's books, all of which are among the best examples of contemporary literary nonfiction available. I've included Mr. McPhee later in this volume—but if there were unlimited room, I would have included him here, too (and in the essay section, and in the memoir section): he's that important.

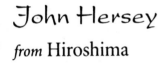

John Hersey

from Hiroshima

THE FIRE

IMMEDIATELY AFTER THE EXPLOSION, THE REVEREND MR. KIYOSHI TANIMOTO, HAVING RUN wildly out of the Matsui estate and having looked in wonderment at the bloody soldiers at the mouth of the dugout they had been digging, attached himself sympathetically to an old lady who was walking along in a daze, holding her head with her left hand, supporting a small boy of three or four on her back with her right, and crying, "I'm hurt! I'm hurt! I'm hurt!" Mr. Tanimoto transferred the child to his own back and led the woman by the hand down the street, which was darkened by what seemed to be a local column of dust. He took the woman to a grammar school not far away that had previously been designated for use as a temporary hospital in case of emergency. By this solicitous behavior, Mr. Tanimoto at once got rid of his terror. At the school, he was much surprised to see glass all over the floor and fifty or sixty injured people already waiting to be treated. He reflected that, although the all-clear had sounded and he had heard no planes, several bombs must have been dropped. He thought of a hillock in the rayon man's garden from which he could get a view of the whole of Koi—of the whole of Hiroshima, for that matter—and he ran back up to the estate.

From the mound, Mr. Tanimoto saw an astonishing panorama. Not just a patch of Koi, as he had expected, but as much of Hiroshima as he could see through the clouded air was giving off a thick, dreadful miasma. Clumps of smoke, near and far, had begun to push up through the general dust. He wondered how such extensive damage could have been dealt out of a silent sky; even a few planes, far up, would have been audible. Houses nearby were burning, and when huge drops of water the size of marbles began to fall, he half thought that they must be coming from the hoses of firemen fighting the blazes. (They were actually drops of condensed moisture falling from the turbulent tower of dust, heat, and fission fragments that had already risen miles into the sky above Hiroshima.)

Mr. Tanimoto turned away from the sight when he heard Mr. Matsuo call out to ask whether he was all right. Mr. Matsuo had been safely cushioned within the falling house by the bedding stored in the front hall and had worked his way out. Mr. Tanimoto scarcely answered. He had thought of his wife and baby, his church, his home, his parishioners, all of them down in that awful murk. Once more he began to run in fear—toward the city.

❧   ❧   ❧

Mrs. Hatsuyo Nakamura, the tailor's widow, having struggled up from under the ruins of her house after the explosion, and seeing Myeko, the youngest of her three children, buried breast-deep and unable to move, crawled across the debris, hauled at timbers, and flung tiles aside, in a hurried effort to free the child. Then, from what seemed to be caverns far below, she heard two small voices crying, "*Tasukete! Tasukete!* Help! Help!"

She called the names of her ten-year-old son and eight-year-old daughter: "Toshio! Yaeko!"

The voices from below answered.

Mrs. Nakamura abandoned Myeko, who at least could breathe, and in a frenzy made the wreckage fly above the crying voices. The children had been sleeping nearly ten feet apart, but now their voices seemed to come from the same place. Toshio, the boy, apparently had some freedom to move, because she could feel him undermining the pile of wood and tiles as she worked from above. At last she saw his head, and she hastily pulled him out by it. A mosquito net was wound intricately, as if it had been carefully wrapped, around his feet. He said he had been blown right across the room and had been on top of his sister Yaeko under the wreckage. She now said, from underneath, that she could not move, because there was something on her legs. With a bit more digging, Mrs Nakamura cleared a hole above the child and began to pull her arm. "*Itai!* It hurts!" Yaeko cried. Mrs. Nakamura shouted, "There's no time now to say whether it hurts or not," and yanked her whimpering daughter up. Then she freed Myeko. The children were filthy and bruised, but none of them had a single cut or scratch.

Mrs. Nakamura took the children out into the street. They had nothing on but underpants, and although the day was very hot, she worried rather confusedly about their being cold, so she went back into the wreckage and burrowed underneath and found a bundle of clothes she had packed for an emergency, and she dressed them in pants, blouses, shoes, padded-cotton air-raid helmets called *bokuzuki,* and even, irrationally, overcoats. The children were silent, except for the five-year-old, Myeko, who kept asking questions: "Why is it night already? Why did our house fall down? What happened?" Mrs. Nakamura, who did not know what had happened (had not the all-clear sounded?), looked around and saw through the darkness that all the houses in her neighborhood had collapsed. The house next door, which its owner had been tearing down to make way for a fire lane, was now very thoroughly, if crudely, torn down; its owner, who had been sacrificing his home for the community's safety, lay dead. Mrs. Nakamoto, wife of the head of the local air-raid-defense Neighborhood Association, came across the street with her head all bloody, and said that her baby was badly cut; did Mrs. Nakamura have any bandage? Mrs. Nakamura did not, but she crawled into the remains of her house again and pulled out some white cloth that she had been using in her work as a seamstress, ripped it into strips, and gave it to Mrs. Nakamoto. While fetching the cloth, she noticed her sewing machine; she went back in for it and dragged it out. Obviously, she could not carry it with her, so she unthinkingly plunged her symbol of livelihood into the receptacle which for weeks had been her symbol of safety—the cement tank of water in front of her house, of the type every household had been ordered to construct against a possible fire raid.

A nervous neighbor, Mrs. Hataya, called to Mrs. Nakamura to run away with her to the woods in Asano Park—an estate, by the Kyo River not far off, belonging to the wealthy Asano family, who once owned the Toyo Kisen Kaisha steamship line. The park had been designated as an evacuation area for their neighborhood. Seeing fire breaking out in a nearby ruin (except at the very center, where the bomb itself ignited some fires, most of Hiroshima's citywide conflagration was caused by inflammable wreckage falling on cookstoves and live wires), Mrs. Nakamura suggested going over to fight it. Mrs. Hataya said, "Don't be foolish. What if planes come and drop more bombs?" So Mrs. Nakamura started out for Asano Park with her children and Mrs. Hataya, and she carried her rucksack of emergency clothing, a blanket, an umbrella, and a suitcase of things she had cached in her air-raid shelter. Under many ruins, as they hurried along, they heard muffled screams for help. The only building they saw standing on their way to Asano Park was the Jesuit mission house, alongside the Catholic kindergarten to which Mrs. Nakamura had sent Myeko for a time. As they passed it, she saw Father Kleinsorge, in bloody underwear, running out of the house with a small suitcase in his hand.

⊹ ⊹ ⊹

Right after the explosion, while Father Wilhelm Kleinsorge, S. J., was wandering around in his underwear in the vegetable garden, Father Superior LaSalle came around the corner of the building in the darkness. His body, especially his back, was bloody; the flash had made him twist away from his window, and tiny pieces of glass had flown at him. Father Kleinsorge, still bewildered, managed to ask, "Where are the rest?" Just then, the two other priests living in the mission house appeared—Father Cieslik, unhurt, supporting Father Schiffer, who was covered with blood that spurted from a cut above his left ear and who was very pale. Father Cieslik was rather pleased with himself, for after the flash he had dived into a doorway, which he had previously reckoned to be the safest place inside the building, and when the blast came, he was not injured. Father LaSalle told Father Cieslik to take Father Schiffer to a doctor before he bled to death, and suggested either Dr. Kanda, who lived on the next corner, or Dr. Fujii, about six blocks away. The two men went out of the compound and up the street.

The daughter of Mr. Hoshijima, the mission catechist, ran up to Father Kleinsorge and said that her mother and sister were buried under the ruins of their house, which was at the back of the Jesuit compound, and at the same time the priests noticed that the house of the Catholic-kindergarten teacher at the front of the compound had collapsed on her. While Father LaSalle and Mrs. Murata, the mission housekeeper, dug the teacher out, Father Kleinsorge went to the catechist's fallen house and began lifting things off the top of the pile. There was not a sound underneath; he was sure the Hoshijima women had been killed. At last, under what had been a corner of the kitchen, he saw Mrs. Hoshijima's head. Believing her dead, he began to haul her out by the hair, but suddenly she screamed, "*Itai! Itai!* It hurts!

It hurts!" He dug some more and lifted her out. He managed, too, to find her daughter in the rubble and free her. Neither was badly hurt.

A public bath next door to the mission house had caught fire, but since there the wind was southerly, the priests thought their house would be spared. Nevertheless, as a precaution, Father Kleinsorge went inside to fetch some things he wanted to save. He found his room in a state of weird and illogical confusion. A first-aid kit was hanging undisturbed on a hook on the wall, but his clothes, which had been on other hooks nearby, were nowhere to be seen. His desk was in splinters all over the room, but a mere papier-mâché suitcase, which he had hidden under the desk, stood handle-side up, without a scratch on it, in the doorway of the room, where he could not miss it. Father Kleinsorge later came to regard this as a bit of Providential interference, inasmuch as the suitcase contained his breviary, the account books for the whole diocese, and a considerable amount of paper money belonging to the mission, for which he was responsible. He ran out of the house and deposited the suitcase in the mission air-raid shelter.

At about this time, Father Cieslik and Father Schiffer, who was still spurting blood, came back and said that Dr. Kanda's house was ruined and that fire blocked them from getting out of what they supposed to be the local circle of destruction to Dr. Fujii's private hospital, on the bank of the Kyo River.

❧   ❧   ❧

Dr. Masakazu Fujii's hospital was no longer on the bank of the Kyo River; it was in the river. After the overturn, Dr. Fujii was so stupefied and so tightly squeezed by the beams gripping his chest that he was unable to move at first, and he hung there about twenty minutes in the darkened morning. Then a thought which came to him—that soon the tide would be running in through the estuaries and his head would be submerged—inspired him to fearful activity; he wriggled and turned and exerted what strength he could (though his left arm, because of the pain in his shoulder, was useless), and before long he had freed himself from the vise. After a few moments' rest, he climbed onto the pile of timbers and, finding a long one that slanted up to the river-bank, he painfully shinnied up it.

Dr. Fujii, who was in his underwear, was now soaking and dirty. His undershirt was torn, and blood ran down it from bad cuts on his chin and back. In this disarray, he walked out onto Kyo Bridge, beside which his hospital had stood. The bridge had not collapsed. He could see only fuzzily without his glasses, but he could see enough to be amazed at the number of houses that were down all around. On the bridge, he encountered a friend, a doctor named Machii, and asked in bewilderment, "What do you think it was?"

Dr. Machii said, "It must have been a *Molotoffano hanakago*"—a Molotov flower basket, the delicate Japanese name for the "bread basket," or self-scattering cluster of bombs.

At first, Dr. Fujii could see only two fires, one across the river from his hospital site and one quite far to the south. But at the same time, he and his friend observed something that puzzled them, and which, as doctors, they discussed: although there were as yet very few fires, wounded people were hurrying across the bridge in an endless parade of misery, and many of them exhibited terrible burns on their faces and arms. "Why do you suppose it is?" Dr. Fujii asked. Even a theory was comforting that day, and Dr. Machii stuck to his. "Perhaps because it was a Molotov flower basket," he said.

There had been no breeze earlier in the morning when Dr. Fujii had walked to the railway station to see his friend off, but now brisk winds were blowing every which way; here on the bridge the wind was easterly. New fires were leaping up, and they spread quickly, and in a very short time terrible blasts of hot air and showers of cinders made it impossible to stand on the bridge any more. Dr. Machii ran to the far side of the river and along a still unkindled street. Dr. Fujii went down into the water under the bridge, where a score of people had already taken refuge, among them his servants, who had extricated themselves from the wreckage. From there, Dr. Fujii saw a nurse hanging in the timbers of his hospital by her legs, and then another painfully pinned across the breast. He enlisted the help of some of the others under the bridge and freed both of them. He thought he heard the voice of his niece for a moment, but he could not find her; he never saw her again. Four of his nurses and the two patients in the hospital died, too. Dr. Fujii went back into the water of the river and waited for the fire to subside.

◆　◆　◆

The lot of Drs. Fujii, Kanda, and Machii right after the explosion—and, as these three were typical, that of the majority of the physicians and surgeons of Hiroshima—with their offices and hospitals destroyed, their equipment scattered, their own bodies incapacitated in varying degrees, explained why so many citizens who were hurt went untended and why so many who might have lived died. Of a hundred and fifty doctors in the city, sixty-five were already dead and most of the rest were wounded. Of 1,780 nurses, 1,654 were dead or too badly hurt to work. In the biggest hospital, that of the Red Cross, only six doctors out of thirty were able to function, and only ten nurses out of more than two hundred. The sole uninjured doctor on the Red Cross Hospital staff was Dr. Sasaki. After the explosion, he hurried to a storeroom to fetch bandages. This room, like everything he had seen as he ran through the hospital, was chaotic—bottles of medicines thrown off shelves and broken, salves spattered on the walls, instruments strewn everywhere. He grabbed up some bandages and an unbroken bottle of mercurochrome, hurried back to the chief surgeon, and bandaged his cuts. Then he went out into the corridor and began patching up the wounded patients and the doctors and nurses there. He blundered so without his glasses that he took a pair off the face of a wounded nurse, and although they only approximately compensated for the errors of his vision, they were better than nothing. (He was to depend on them for more than a month.)

Dr. Sasaki worked without method, taking those who were nearest him first, and he noticed soon that the corridor seemed to be getting more and more crowded. Mixed in with the abrasions and lacerations which most people in the hospital had suffered, he began to find dreadful burns. He realized then that casualties were pouring in from outdoors. There were so many that he began to pass up the lightly wounded; he decided that all he could hope to do was to stop people from bleeding to death. Before long, patients lay and crouched on the floors of the wards and the laboratories and all the other rooms, and in the corridors, and on the stairs, and in the front hall, and under the portecochère, and on the stone front steps, and in the driveway and courtyard, and for blocks each way in the streets outside. Wounded people supported maimed people; disfigured families leaned together. Many people were vomiting. A tremendous number of schoolgirls—some of those who had been taken from their classrooms to work outdoors, clearing fire lanes—crept into the hospital. In a city of two hundred and forty-five thousand, nearly a hundred thousand people had been killed or doomed at one blow; a hundred thousand more were hurt. At least ten thousand of the wounded made their way to the best hospital in town, which was altogether unequal to such a trampling, since it had only six hundred beds, and they had all been occupied. The people in the suffocating crowd inside the hospital wept and cried, for Dr. Sasaki to hear, "*Sensei!* Doctor!," and the less seriously wounded came and pulled at his sleeve and begged him to go to the aid of the worse wounded. Tugged here and there in his stockinged feet, bewildered by the numbers, staggered by so much raw flesh, Dr. Sasaki lost all sense of profession and stopped working as a skillful surgeon and a sympathetic man; he became an automaton, mechanically wiping, daubing, winding, wiping, daubing, winding.

⚬ ⚬ ⚬

Some of the wounded in Hiroshima were unable to enjoy the questionable luxury of hospitalization. In what had been the personnel office of the East Asia Tin Works, Miss Sasaki lay doubled over, unconscious, under the tremendous pile of books and plaster and wood and corrugated iron. She was wholly unconscious (she later estimated) for about three hours. Her first sensation was of dreadful pain in her left leg. It was so black under the books and debris that the borderline between awareness and unconsciousness was fine; she apparently crossed it several times, for the pain seemed to come and go. At the moments when it was sharpest, she felt that her leg had been cut off somewhere below the knee. Later, she heard someone walking on top of the wreckage above her, and anguished voices spoke up, evidently from within the mess around her: "Please help! Get us out!"

⚬ ⚬ ⚬

Father Kleinsorge stemmed Father Schiffer's spurting cut as well as he could with some bandage that Dr. Fujii had given the priests a few days before. When he finished, he ran into the mission house again and found the jacket of his military uniform and an old pair of gray trousers. He put them on and went outside. A woman from next door ran up to him and shouted that her husband was buried under her house and the house was on fire; Father Kleinsorge must come and save him.

Father Kleinsorge, already growing apathetic and dazed in the presence of the cumulative distress, said, "We haven't much time." Houses all around were burning, and the wind was now blowing hard. "Do you know exactly which part of the house he is under?" he asked.

"Yes, yes," she said. "Come quickly."

They went around to the house, the remains of which blazed violently, but when they got there, it turned out that the woman had no idea where her husband was. Father Kleinsorge shouted several times, "Is anyone there?" There was no answer. Father Kleinsorge said to the woman, "We must get away or we will all die." He went back to the Catholic compound and told the Father Superior that the fire was coming closer on the wind, which had swung around and was now from the north; it was time for everybody to go.

Just then, the kindergarten teacher pointed out to the priests Mr. Fukai, the secretary of the diocese, who was standing in his window on the second floor of the mission house, facing in the direction of the explosion, weeping. Father Cieslik, because he thought the stairs unusable, ran around to the back of the mission house to look for a ladder. There he heard people crying for help under a nearby fallen roof. He called to passers-by running away in the street to help him lift it, but nobody paid any attention, and he had to leave the buried ones to die. Father Kleinsorge ran inside the mission house and scrambled up the stairs, which were awry and piled with plaster and lathing, and called to Mr. Fukai from the doorway of his room.

Mr. Fukai, a very short man of about fifty, turned around slowly, with a queer look, and said, "Leave me here."

Father Kleinsorge went into the room and took Mr. Fukai by the collar of his coat and said, "Come with me or you'll die."

Mr. Fukai said, "Leave me here to die."

Father Kleinsorge began to shove and haul Mr. Fukai out of the room. Then the theological student came up and grabbed Mr. Fukai's feet, and Father Kleinsorge took his shoulders, and together they carried him downstairs and outdoors. "I can't walk!" Mr. Fukai cried. "Leave me here!" Father Kleinsorge got his paper suitcase with the money in it and took Mr. Fukai up pickaback, and the party started for the East Parade Ground, their district's "safe area." As they went out of the gate, Mr. Fukai, quite childlike now, beat on Father Kleinsorge's shoulders and said, "I won't leave. I won't leave." Irrelevantly, Father Kleinsorge turned to Father LaSalle and said, "We have lost all our possessions but not our sense of humor."

The street was cluttered with parts of houses that had slid into it, and with fallen telephone poles and wires. From every second or third house came the voices of people buried and abandoned, who invariably screamed, with formal politeness, "*Tasukete kure!* Help, if you please!" The priests recognized several ruins from which these cries came as the homes of friends, but because of the fire it was too late to help. All the way, Mr. Fukai whimpered, "Let me stay." The party turned right when they came to a block of fallen houses that was one flame. At Sakai Bridge, which would take them across to the East Parade Ground, they saw that the whole community on the opposite side of the river was a sheet of fire; they dared not cross and decided to take refuge in Asano Park, off to their left. Father Kleinsorge, who had been weakened for a couple of days by his bad case of diarrhea, began to stagger under his protesting burden, and as he tried to climb up over the wreckage of several houses that blocked their way to the park, he stumbled, dropped Mr. Fukai, and plunged down, head over heels, to the edge of the river. When he picked himself up, he saw Mr. Fukai running away. Father Kleinsorge shouted to a dozen soldiers, who were standing by the bridge, to stop him. As Father Kleinsorge started back to get Mr. Fukai, Father LaSalle called out, "Hurry! Don't waste time!" So Father Kleinsorge just requested the soldiers to take care of Mr. Fukai. They said they would, but the little, broken man got away from them, and the last the priests could see of him, he was running back toward the fire.

⋅०⋅   ⋅०⋅   ⋅०⋅

Mr. Tanimoto, fearful for his family and church, at first ran toward them by the shortest route, along Koi Highway. He was the only person making his way into the city; he met hundreds and hundreds who were fleeing, and every one of them seemed to be hurt in some way. The eyebrows of some were burned off and skin hung from their faces and hands. Others, because of pain, held their arms up as if carrying something in both hands. Some were vomiting as they walked. Many were naked or in shreds of clothing. On some undressed bodies, the burns had made patterns—of undershirt straps and suspenders and, on the skin of some women (since white repelled the heat from the bomb and dark clothes absorbed it and conducted it to the skin), the shapes of flowers they had had on their kimonos. Many, although injured themselves, supported relatives who were worse off. Almost all had their heads bowed, looked straight ahead, were silent, and showed no expression whatever.

After crossing Koi Bridge and Kannon Bridge, having run the whole way, Mr. Tanimoto saw, as he approached the center, that all the houses had been crushed and many were afire. Here the trees were bare and their trunks were charred. He tried at several points to penetrate the ruins, but the flames always stopped him. Under many houses, people screamed for help, but no one helped; in general, survivors that day assisted only their relatives or immediate neighbors, for they could not comprehend or tolerate a wider circle of misery. The wounded limped past the screams, and Mr. Tanimoto ran past them. As a Christian he was filled with compassion for those who were trapped, and as a Japanese he was overwhelmed by the shame of being unhurt, and he prayed as he ran, "God help them and take them out of the fire."

He thought he would skirt the fire, to the left. He ran back to Kannon Bridge and followed for a distance one of the rivers. He tried several cross streets, but all were blocked, so he turned far left and ran out to Yokogawa, a station on a railroad line that detoured the city in a wide semicircle, and he followed the rails until he came to a burning train. So impressed was he by this time by the extent of the damage that he ran north two miles to Gion, a suburb in the foothills. All the way, he overtook dreadfully burned and lacerated people, and in his guilt he turned to right and left as he hurried and said to some of them, "Excuse me for having no burden like yours." Near Gion, he began to meet country people going toward the city to help, and when they saw him, several exclaimed, "Look! There is one who is not wounded." At Gion, he bore toward the right bank of the main river, the Ota, and ran down it until he reached fire again. There was no fire on the other side of the river, so he threw off his shirt and shoes and plunged into it. In midstream, where the current was fairly strong, exhaustion and fear finally caught up with him—he had run nearly seven miles—and he became limp and drifted in the water. He prayed, "Please. God, help me to cross. It would be nonsense for me to be drowned when I am the only uninjured one." He managed a few more strokes and fetched up on a spit downstream.

Mr. Tanimoto climbed up the bank and ran along it until, near a large Shinto shrine, he came to more fire, and as he turned left to get around it, he met, by incredible luck, his wife. She was carrying their infant son. Mr. Tanimoto was now so emotionally worn out that nothing could surprise him. He did not embrace his wife; he simply said, "Oh, you are safe." She told him that she had got home from her night in Ushida just in time for the explosion; she had been buried under the parsonage with the baby in her arms. She told how the wreckage had pressed down on her, how the baby had cried. She saw a chink of light, and by reaching up with a hand, she worked the hole bigger, bit by bit. After about half an hour, she heard the crackling noise of wood burning. At last the opening was big enough for her to push the baby out, and afterward she crawled out herself. She said she was now going out to Ushida again. Mr. Tanimoto said he wanted to see his church and take care of the people of his Neighborhood Association. They parted as casually—as bewildered—as they had met.

Mr. Tanimoto's way around the fire took him across the East Parade Ground, which, being an evacuation area, was now the scene of a gruesome review: rank on rank of the burned and bleeding. Those who were burned moaned, "*Mizu, mizu!* Water, water!" Mr. Tanimoto found a basin in a nearby street and located a water tap that still worked in the crushed shell of a house, and he began carrying water to the suffering strangers. When he had given drink to about thirty of them, he realized he was taking too much time. "Excuse me," he said loudly to those nearby who were reaching out their hands to him and crying their thirst. "I have many people to take care of." Then he ran away. He went to the river again, the basin in his hand, and jumped down onto a sandspit. There he saw hundreds of people so badly wounded that they could not get up to go farther from the burning city. When they saw a man erect and unhurt, the chant began again: "*Mizu, mizu, mizu.*" Mr. Tanimoto could not resist them; he carried them water from the river—a mistake, since it was tidal and brackish. Two or three small boats were ferrying hurt people across the river from Asano Park, and when one touched the spit, Mr. Tanimoto again made his loud, apologetic speech and jumped into the boat. It took him across to the park. There, in the underbrush, he found some of his charges of the Neighborhood Association, who had come there by his previous instructions, and saw many acquaintances, among them Father Kleinsorge and the other Catholics. But he missed Fukai, who had been a close friend. "Where is Fukai-*san?*" he asked.

"He didn't want to come with us," Father Kleinsorge said. "He ran back."

٭٭ ٭٭ ٭٭

When Miss Sasaki heard the voices of the people caught along with her in the dilapidation at the tin factory, she began speaking to them. Her nearest neighbor, she discovered, was a high-school girl who had been drafted for factory work, and who said her back was broken. Miss Sasaki replied, "I am lying here and I can't move. My left leg is cut off."

Some time later, she again heard somebody walk overhead and then move off to one side, and whoever it was began burrowing. The digger released several people, and when he had uncovered the high-school girl, she found that her back was not broken, after all, and she crawled out. Miss Sasaki spoke to the rescuer, and he worked toward her. He pulled away a great number of books, until he had made a tunnel to her. She could see his perspiring face as he said, "Come out, Miss." She tried. "I can't move," she said. The man excavated some more and told her to try with all her strength to get out. But books were heavy on her hips, and the man finally saw that a bookcase was leaning on the books and that a heavy beam pressed down on the bookcase. "Wait," he said. "I'll get a crowbar."

The man was gone a long time, and when he came back, he was ill-tempered, as if her plight were all her fault. "We have no men to help you!" he shouted in through the tunnel. "You'll have to get out by yourself."

"That's impossible," she said. "My left leg . . ." The man went away.

Much later, several men came and dragged Miss Sasaki out. Her left leg was not severed, but it was badly broken and cut and it hung askew below the knee. They took her out into a courtyard. It was raining. She sat on the ground in the rain. When the downpour increased, someone directed all the wounded people to take cover in the factory's air-raid shelters. "Come along," a torn-up woman said to her. "You can hop." But Miss Sasaki could not move, and she just waited in the rain. Then a man propped up a large sheet of corrugated iron as a kind of lean-to, and took her in his arms and carried her to it. She was grateful until he brought two horribly wounded people—a woman with a whole breast sheared off and a man whose face was all raw from a burn—to share the simple shed with her. No one came back. The rain cleared and the cloudy afternoon was hot; before nightfall the three grotesques under the slanting piece of twisted iron began to smell quite bad.

٭٭ ٭٭ ٭٭

The former head of the Nobori-cho Neighborhood Association to which the Catholic priests belonged was an energetic man named Yoshida. He had boasted, when he was in charge of the district air-raid defenses, that fire might eat away all of Hiroshima but it would never come to Nobori-cho. The bomb blew down his house, and a joist pinned him by the legs, in full view of the Jesuit mission house across the way and of the people hurrying along the street. In their confusion as they hurried past, Mrs. Nakamura, with her children, and Father Kleinsorge, with Mr. Fukai on his back, hardly saw him; he was just part of the general blur of misery through which they moved. His cries for help brought no response from them; there were so many people shouting for help that they could not hear him separately. They and all the others went along. Nobori-cho became absolutely deserted, and the fire swept through it. Mr. Yoshida saw the wooden mission house—the only erect building in the area—go up in a lick of flame, and the heat was terrific on his face. Then flames came along his side of the street and entered his house. In a paroxysm of terrified strength, he freed himself and ran down the alleys of Nobori-cho, hemmed in by the fire he had said would never come. He began at once to behave like an old man; two months later his hair was white.

·❖· ·❖· ·❖·

As Dr. Fujii stood in the river up to his neck to avoid the heat of the fire, the wind blew stronger and stronger, and soon, even though the expanse of water was small, the waves grew so high that the people under the bridge could no longer keep their footing. Dr. Fujii went close to the shore, crouched down, and embraced a large stone with his usable arm. Later it became possible to wade along the very edge of the river, and Dr. Fujii and his two surviving nurses moved about two hundred yards upstream, to a sandpit near Asano Park. Many wounded were lying on the sand. Dr. Machii was there with his family; his daughter, who had been outdoors when the bomb burst, was badly burned on her hands and legs but fortunately not on her face. Although Dr. Fujii's shoulder was by now terribly painful, he examined the girl's burns curiously. Then he lay down. In spite of the misery all around, he was ashamed of his appearance, and he remarked to Dr. Machii that he looked like a beggar, dressed as he was in nothing but torn and bloody underwear. Later in the afternoon, when the fire began to subside, he decided to go to his parental house, in the suburb of Nagatsuka. He asked Dr. Machii to join him, but the Doctor answered that he and his family were going to spend the night on the spit, because of his daughter's injuries. Dr. Fujii, together with his nurses, walked first to Ushida, where, in the partially damaged house of some relatives, he found first-aid materials he had stored there. The two nurses bandaged him and he them. They went on. Now not many people walked in the streets, but a great number sat and lay on the pavement, vomited, waited for death, and died. The number of corpses on the way to Nagatsuka was more and more puzzling. The Doctor wondered: Could a Molotov flower basket have done all this?

Dr. Fujii reached his family's house in the evening. It was five miles from the center of town, but its roof had fallen in and the windows were all broken.

·❖· ·❖· ·❖·

All day, people poured into Asano Park. This private estate was far enough away from the explosion so that its bamboos, pines, laurel, and maples were still alive, and the green place invited refugees—partly because they believed that if the Americans came back, they would bomb only buildings; partly because the foliage seemed a center of coolness and life, and the estate's exquisitely precise rock gardens, with their quiet pools and arching bridges, were very Japanese, normal, secure; and also partly (according to some who were there) because of an irresistible, atavistic urge to hide under leaves. Mrs. Nakamura and her children were among the first to arrive, and they settled in the bamboo grove near the river. They all felt terribly thirsty, and they drank from the river. At once they were nauseated and began vomiting, and they retched the whole day. Others were also nauseated; they all thought (probably because of the strong odor of ionization, an "electric smell" given off by the bomb's fission) that they were sick from a gas the Americans had dropped. When Father Kleinsorge and the other priests came into the park, nodding to their friends as they passed, ka-muras were all sick and prostrate. A woman named Iwasaki, who lived in the neighborhood of the mission and who was sitting near the Nakamuras, got up and asked the priests if she should stay where she was or go with them. Father Kleinsorge said, "I hardly know where the safest place is." She stayed there, and later in the day, though she had no visible wounds or burns, she died. The priests went farther along the river and settled down in some un-derbrush. Father LaSalle lay down and went right to sleep. The theological student, who was wearing slippers, had carried with him a bundle of clothes, in which he had packed two pairs of leather shoes. When he sat down with the others, he found that the bundle had broken open and a couple of shoes had fallen out and now he had only two lefts. He retraced his steps and found one right. When he rejoined the priests, he said, "It's funny, but things don't matter any more. Yesterday, my shoes were my most important possessions. Today, I don't care. One pair is enough."

Father Cieslik said, "I know. I started to bring my books along, and then I thought, 'This is no time for books.'"

When Mr. Tanimoto, with his basin still in his hand, reached the park, it was very crowded, and to distinguish the living from the dead was not easy, for most of the people lay still, with their eyes open. To Father Kleinsorge, an Occidental, the silence in the grove by the river, where hundreds of gruesomely wounded suffered together, was one of the most dreadful and awesome phenomena of his whole experience. The hurt ones were quiet; no one wept, much less screamed in pain; no one complained; none of the many who died did so noisily; not even the children cried; very few people even spoke. And when Father Klein-sorge gave water to some whose faces had been almost blotted out by flash burns, they took their share and then raised themselves a little and bowed to him, in thanks.

Mr. Tanimoto greeted the priests and then looked around for other friends. He saw Mrs. Matsumoto, wife of the director of the Methodist School, and asked her if she was thirsty. She was, so he went to one of the pools in the Asanos' rock gardens and got water for her in his basin. Then he decided to try to get back to his church. He went into Nobori-cho by the way the priests had taken as they escaped, but he did not get far; the fire along the streets was so fierce that he had to turn back. He walked to the riverbank and began to look for a boat in which he might carry some of the most severely injured across the river from Asano Park and away from the spreading fire. Soon he found a good-sized pleasure punt drawn up on the bank, but in and around it was an awful tableau—five dead men, nearly naked, badly burned, who must have expired more or less all at once, for they were in atti-tudes which suggested that they had been working together to push the boat down into the river. Mr. Tanimoto lifted them away from the boat, and as he did so, he experienced such horror at disturbing the dead—preventing them, he momentarily felt, from launching their craft and going on their ghostly way—that he said out loud, "Please forgive me for taking this boat. I must use it for others, who are alive." The punt was heavy, but he managed to slide it into the water. There were no oars, and all he could find for propulsion was a thick bamboo pole. He worked the boat upstream to the most crowded part of the park and began to ferry the wounded. He could pack ten or twelve into the boat for each crossing, but as the river was too deep in the center to pole his way across, he had to paddle with the bamboo, and consequently each trip took a very long time. He worked several hours that way.

Early in the afternoon, the fire swept into the woods of Asano Park. The first Mr. Tani-moto knew of it was when, returning in his boat, he saw that a great number of people had moved toward the riverside. On touching the bank, he went up to investigate, and when he

...e shouted, "All the young men who are not badly hurt come with me!" Father ...moved Father Schiffer and Father LaSalle close to the edge of the river and asked ...there to get them across if the fire came too near, and then joined Tanimoto's volunteers. Mr. Tanimoto sent some to look for buckets and basins and told others to beat the burning underbrush with their clothes; when utensils were at hand, he formed a bucket chain from one of the pools in the rock gardens. The team fought the fire for more than two hours, and gradually defeated the flames. As Mr. Tanimoto's men worked, the frightened people in the park pressed closer and closer to the river, and finally the mob began to force some of the unfortunates who were on the very bank into the water. Among those driven into the river and drowned were Mrs. Matsumoto, of the Methodist School, and her daughter.

When Father Kleinsorge got back after fighting the fire, he found Father Schiffer still bleeding and terribly pale. Some Japanese stood around and stared at him, and Father Schiffer whispered, with a weak smile, "It is as if I were already dead." "Not yet," Father Kleinsorge said. He had brought Dr. Fujii's first-aid kit with him, and he had noticed Dr. Kanda in the crowd, so he sought him out and asked him if he would dress Father Schiffer's bad cuts. Dr. Kanda had seen his wife and daughter dead in the ruins of his hospital; he sat now with his head in his hands. "I can't do anything," he said. Father Kleinsorge bound more bandage around Father Schiffer's head, moved him to a steep place, and settled him so that his head was high, and soon the bleeding diminished.

The roar of approaching planes was heard about this time. Someone in the crowd near the Nakamura family shouted, "It's some Grummans coming to strafe us!" A baker named Nakashima stood up and commanded, "Everyone who is wearing anything white, take it off." Mrs. Nakamura took the blouses off her children, and opened her umbrella and made them get under it. A great number of people, even badly burned ones, crawled into bushes and stayed there until the hum, evidently of a reconnaissance or weather run, died away.

It began to rain. Mrs. Nakamura kept her children under the umbrella. The drops grew abnormally large, and someone shouted, "The Americans are dropping gasoline. They're going to set fire to us!" (This alarm stemmed from one of the theories being passed through the park as to why so much of Hiroshima had burned: it was that a single plane had sprayed gasoline on the city and then somehow set fire to it in one flashing moment.) But the drops were palpably water, and as they fell, the wind grew stronger and stronger, and suddenly—probably because of the tremendous convection set up by the blazing city—a whirlwind ripped through the park. Huge trees crashed down; small ones were uprooted and flew into the air. Higher, a wild array of flat things revolved in the twisting funnel—pieces of iron roofing, papers, doors, strips of matting. Father Kleinsorge put a piece of cloth over Father Schiffer's eyes, so that the feeble man would not think he was going crazy. The gale blew Mrs. Murata, the mission housekeeper, who was sitting close by the river, down the embankment at a shallow, rocky place, and she came out with her bare feet bloody. The vortex moved out onto the river, where it sucked up a water-spout and eventually spent itself.

After the storm, Mr. Tanimoto began ferrying people again, and Father Kleinsorge asked the theological student to go across and make his way out to the Jesuit Novitiate at Nagatsuka, about three miles from the center of town, and to request the priests there to come with help for Fathers Schiffer and La-Salle. The student got into Mr. Tanimoto's boat and went off with him. Father Kleinsorge asked Mrs. Nakamura if she would like to go out to Nagatsuka with the priests when they came. She said she had some luggage and her children were sick—they were still vomiting from time to time, and so, for that matter, was

e—and therefore she feared she could not. He said he thought th. 'thers from the Novi-
te could come back the next day with a pushcart to get her.

Late in the afternoon, when he went ashore for a while, Mr. Tanimto, upon whose en-
gy and initiative many had come to depend, heard people begging fc food. He consulted
ther Kleinsorge, and they decided to go back into town to get som rice from Mr. Tani-
oto's Neighborhood Association shelter and from the mission shelt. Father Cieslik and
'o or three others went with them. At first, when they got among e rows of prostrate
uses, they did not know where they were; the change was too sudda, from a busy city of
'o hundred and forty-five thousand that morning to a mere patter. of residue in the af-
rnoon. The asphalt of the streets was still so soft and hot from th fires that walking was
comfortable. They encountered only one person, a woman, wb said to them as they
ssed, "My husband is in those ashes." At the mission, where Mr. animoto left the party,
ther Kleinsorge was dismayed to see the building razed. In the g rden, on the way to the
elter, he noticed a pumpkin roasted on the vine. He and Father Cieslik tasted it and it was
od. They were surprised at their hunger, and they ate quite a bit. hey got out several bags
rice and gathered up several other cooked pumpkins and dug up some potatoes that were
icely baked under the ground, and started back. Mr. Tanimoto rejoined them on the way.
ne of the people with him had some cooking utensils. In the park, Mr. Tanimoto organ-
ed the lightly wounded women of his neighborhood to cook. Father Kleinsorge offered the
akamura family some pumpkin, and they tried it, but they could not keep it on their stom-
chs. Altogether, the rice was enough to feed nearly a hundred people.

Just before dark, Mr. Tanimoto came across a twenty-year-old girl, Mrs. Kamai, the
animoto's next-door neighbor. She was crouching on the ground with the body of her in-
nt daughter in her arms. The baby had evidently been dead all day. Mrs. Kamai jumped
p when she saw Mr. Tanimoto and said, "Would you please try to locate my husband?"

Mr. Tanimoto knew that her husband had been inducted into the Army just the day be-
ore; he and Mrs. Tanimoto had entertained Mrs. Kamai in the afternoon, to make her for-
et. Kamai had reported to the Chugoku Regional Army Headquarters—near the ancient
astle in the middle of town—where some four thousand troops were stationed. Judging by
he many maimed soldiers Mr. Tanimoto had seen during the day, he surmised that the bar-
acks had been badly damaged by whatever it was that had hit Hiroshima. He knew he
adn't a chance of finding Mrs. Kamai's husband, even if he searched, but he wanted to
umor her. "I'll try," he said.

"You've got to find him," she said. "He loved our baby so much. I want him to see her
nce more."

Truman Capote
from In Cold Blood

ON AN ARIZONA HIGHWAY, A TWO-CAR CARAVAN IS FLASHING ACROSS SAGEBRUSH COUN-
try—the mesa country of hawks and rattlesnakes and towering red rocks. Dewey is driving
the lead car, Perry Smith sits beside him, and Duntz is sitting in the back seat. Smith is handcuffed, and the handcuffs are attached to a security belt by a short length of chain—an

arrangement so resting his movements that he cannot smoke unaided. When he wants a cigarette, Dewey must light it for him and place it between his lips, a task that the detective finds "repelle' for it seems such an intimate action—the kind of thing he'd done while he was courg his wife.

On the whole prisoner ignores his guardians and their sporadic attempts to goad him by repeating ts of Hickock's hour-long tape-recorded confession: "He says he tried to stop you, Perry. it says he couldn't. Says he was scared you'd shoot him too," and "Yes, sir, Perry. It's all yo fault. Hickock himself, he says he wouldn't harm the fleas on a dog." None of this—outwdly, at any rate—agitates Smith. He continues to contemplate the scenery, to read Burm-Shave doggerel, and to count the carcasses of shotgunned coyotes festooning ranch fence.

Dewey, not anticipating any exceptional response, says, "Hickock tells us you're a natural-born killer. Says it doesn't bother you a bit. Says one time out there in Las Vegas you went after a colored man witha bicycle chain. Whipped him to death. For fun."

To Dewey's surprise, the prisoner gasps. He twists around in his seat until he can see, through the rear window, the motorcade's second car, see inside it: "The tough boy!" Turning back, he stares at te dark streak of desert highway. "I thought it was a stunt. I didn't believe you. That Dick let fly. The tough boy! Oh, a real brass boy. Wouldn't harm the fleas on a dog. Just run over the dog." He spits. "I never killed any nigger." Duntz agrees with him; having studied the files on unsolved Las Vegas homicides, he knows Smith to be innocent of this particular deed. "I never killed any niggers. But he thought so. I always knew if we ever got caught, if Dick ever really let fly, dropped his guts all over the goddam floor—I knew he'd tell about the nigger." He spits again. "So Dick was afraid of me? That's amusing. I'm very amused. What he don't know is, I almost did shoot him."

Dewey lights two cigarettes, one for himself, one for the prisoner. "Tell us about it, Perry."

Smith smokes with closed eyes, and explains, "I'm thinking. I want to remember this just the way it was." He pauses for quite a while. "Well, it all started with a letter I got while I was out in Buhl, Idaho. That was September or October. The letter was from Dick, and he said he was on to a cinch. The perfect score. I didn't answer him, but he wrote again, urging me to come back to Kansas and go partners with him. He never said what kind of score it was. Just that it was a 'sure-fire cinch.' Now, as it happened, I had another reason for wanting to be in Kansas around about that time. A personal matter I'd just as soon keep to myself—it's got nothing to do with this deal. Only that otherwise I wouldn't have gone back there. But I did. And Dick met me at the bus station in Kansas City. We drove out to the farm, his parents' place. But they didn't want me there. I'm very sensitive; I usually know what people are feeling.

"Like you." He means Dewey, but does not look at him. "You hate handing me a butt. That's your business. I don't blame you. Any more than I blamed Dick's mother. The fact is, she's a very sweet person. But she knew what I was—a friend from The Walls—and she didn't want me in her house. Christ, I was glad to get out, go to a hotel. Dick took me to a hotel in Olathe. We bought some beer and carried it up to the room, and that's when Dick outlined what he had in mind. He said after I'd left Lansing he celled with someone who'd once worked for a wealthy wheat grower out in western Kansas. Mr. Clutter. Dick drew me a diagram of the Clutter house. He knew where everything was—doors, halls, bedrooms. He said one of the ground-floor rooms was used as an office, and in the office there was a safe— a wall safe. He said Mr. Clutter needed it because he always kept on hand large sums of cash.

Never less than ten thousand dollars. The plan was to rob the safe, and if we were seen—well, whoever saw us would have to go. Dick must have said it a million times: 'No witnesses.'"

Dewey says, "How many of these witnesses did he think there might be? I mean, how many people did he expect to find in the Clutter house?"

"That's what I wanted to know. But he wasn't sure. At least four. Probably six. And it was possible the family might have guests. He thought we ought to be ready to handle up to a dozen."

Dewey groans, Duntz whistles, and Smith, smiling wanly, adds, "Me, too. Seemed to me that was a little off. Twelve people. But Dick said it was a cinch. He said, 'We're gonna go in there and splatter those walls with hair.' The mood I was in, I let myself be carried along. But also—I'll be honest—I had faith in Dick; he struck me as being very practical, the masculine type, and I wanted the money as much as he did. I wanted to get it and go to Mexico. But I hoped we could do it without violence. Seemed to me we could if we wore masks. We argued about it. On the way out there, out to Holcomb, I wanted to stop and buy some black silk stockings to wear over our heads. But Dick felt that even with a stocking he could still be identified. Because of his bad eye. All the same, when we got to Emporia—"

Duntz says, "Hold on, Perry. You're jumping ahead. Go back to Olathe. What time did you leave there?"

"One. One-thirty. We left just after lunch and drove to Emporia. Where we bought some rubber gloves and a roll of cord. The knife and shotgun, the shells—Dick had brought all that from home. But he didn't want to look for black stockings. It got to be quite an argument. Somewhere on the outskirts of Emporia, we passed a Catholic hospital, and I persuaded him to stop and go inside and try and buy some black stockings from the nuns. I knew nuns wear them. But he only made believe. Came out and said they wouldn't sell him any. I was sure he hadn't even asked, and he confessed it; he said it was a puky idea—the nuns would've thought he was crazy. So we didn't stop again till Great Bend. That's where we bought the tape. Had dinner there, a big dinner. It put me to sleep. When I woke up, we were just coming into Garden City. Seemed like a real dead-dog town. We stopped for gas at a filling station—"

Dewey asks if he remembers which one.

"Believe it was a Phillips 66."

"What time was this?"

"Around midnight. Dick said it was seven miles more to Holcomb. All the rest of the way, he kept talking to himself, saying this ought to be here and that ought to be there—according to the instructions he'd memorized. I hardly realized it when we went through Holcomb, it was such a little settlement. We crossed a railroad track. Suddenly Dick said, 'This is it, this has to be it.' It was the entrance to a private road, lined with trees. We slowed down and turned off the lights. Didn't need them. Account of the moon. There wasn't nothing else up there—not a cloud, nothing. Just that full moon. It was like broad day, and when we started up the road, Dick said, 'Look at this spread! The barns! That house! Don't tell me this guy ain't loaded.' But I didn't like the setup, the atmosphere; it was sort of *too* impressive. We parked in the shadows of a tree. While we were sitting there, a light came on—not in the main house but a house maybe a hundred yards to the left. Dick said it was the hired man's house; he knew because of the diagram. But he said it was a damn sight nearer the Clutter house than it was supposed to be. Then the light went off. Mr. Dewey—the witness you mentioned. Is that who you meant—the hired man?"

"No. He never heard a sound. But his wife was nursing a sick baby. He said they were up and down the whole night."

"A sick baby. Well, I wondered. While we were still sitting there, it happened again—a light flashed on and off. And that really put bubbles in my blood. I told Dick to count me out. If he was determined to go ahead with it, he'd have to do it alone. He started the car, we were leaving, and I thought, Bless Jesus. I've always trusted my intuitions; they've saved my life more than once. But halfway down the road Dick stopped. He was sore as hell. I could see he was thinking, Here I've set up this big score, here we've come all this way, and now this punk wants to chicken out. He said, 'Maybe you think I ain't got the guts to do it alone. But, by God, I'll show you who's got guts.' There was some liquor in the car. We each had a drink, and I told him, 'O.K., Dick. I'm with you.' So we turned back. Parked where we had before. In the shadows of a tree. Dick put on gloves; I'd already put on mine. He carried the knife and a flashlight. I had the gun. The house looked tremendous in the moonlight. Looked empty. I remember hoping there was nobody home—"

Dewey says, "But you saw a dog?"

"No."

"The family had an old gun-shy dog. We couldn't understand why he didn't bark. Unless he'd seen a gun and bolted."

"Well, I didn't see anything or nobody. That's why I never believed it. About an eyewitness."

"Not *eye*witness. Witness. Someone whose testimony associates you and Hickock with this case."

"Oh. Uh-huh. Uh-huh. Him. And Dick always said he'd be too scared. Ha!"

Duntz, not to be diverted, reminds him, "Hickock had the knife. You had the gun. How did you get into the house?"

"The door was unlocked. A side door. It took us into Mr. Clutter's office. Then we waited in the dark. Listening. But the only sound was the wind. There was quite a little wind outside. It made the trees move, and you could hear the leaves. The one window was curtained with Venetian blinds, but moonlight was coming through. I closed the blinds, and Dick turned on his flashlight. We saw the desk. The safe was supposed to be in the wall directly behind the desk, but we couldn't find it. It was a paneled wall, and there were books and framed maps, and I noticed, on a shelf, a terrific pair of binoculars. I decided I was going to take them with me when we left there."

"Did you?" asks Dewey, for the binoculars had not been missed.

Smith nods. "We sold them in Mexico."

"Sorry. Go on."

"Well, when we couldn't find the safe, Dick doused the flashlight and we moved in darkness out of the office and across a parlor, a living room. Dick whispered to me couldn't I walk quieter. But he was just as bad. Every step we took made a racket. We came to a hall and a door, and Dick, remembering the diagram, said it was a bedroom. He shined the flashlight and opened the door. A man said, 'Honey?' He'd been asleep, and he blinked and said, 'Is that you, honey?' Dick asked him, 'Are you Mr. Clutter?' He was wide awake now; he sat up and said, 'Who is it? What do you want?' Dick told him, very polite, like we were a couple of door-to-door salesmen, 'We want to talk to you, sir. In your office, please.' And Mr. Clutter, barefoot, just wearing pajamas, he went with us to the office and we turned on the office lights.

"Up till then he hadn't been able to see us very good. I think what he saw hit him hard.

Dick says, 'Now, sir, all we want you to do is show us where you keep that safe.' But Mr. Clutter says, 'What safe?' He says he don't have any safe. I knew right then it was true. He had that kind of face. You just knew whatever he told you was pretty much the truth. But Dick shouted at him, 'Don't lie to me, you sonofabitch! I know goddam well you got a safe!' My feeling was nobody had ever spoken to Mr. Clutter like that. But he looked Dick straight in the eye and told him, being very mild about it—said, well, he was sorry but he just didn't have any safe. Dick tapped him on the chest with the knife, says, 'Show us where that safe is or you're gonna be a good bit sorrier.' But Mr. Clutter—oh, you could see he was scared, but his voice stayed mild and steady—he went on denying he had a safe.

"Sometime along in there, I fixed the telephone. The one in the office. I ripped out the wires. And I asked Mr. Clutter if there were any other telephones in the house. He said yes, there was one in the kitchen. So I took the flashlight and went to the kitchen—it was quite a distance from the office. When I found the telephone, I removed the receiver and cut the line with a pair of pliers. Then, heading back, I heard a noise. A creaking overhead. I stopped at the foot of the stairs leading to the second floor. It was dark, and I didn't dare use the flashlight. But I could tell there was someone there. At the top of the stairs, silhouetted against a window. A figure. Then it moved away."

Dewey imagines it must have been Nancy. He'd often theorized, on the basis of the gold wristwatch found tucked in the toe of a shoe in her closet, that Nancy had awakened, heard persons in the house, thought they might be thieves, and prudently hidden the watch, her most valuable property.

"For all I knew, maybe it was somebody with a gun. But Dick wouldn't even listen to me. He was so busy playing tough boy. Bossing Mr. Clutter around. Now he'd brought him back to the bedroom. He was counting the money in Mr. Clutter's billfold. There was about thirty dollars. He threw the billfold on the bed and told him, 'You've got more money in this house than that. A rich man like you. Living on a spread like this.' Mr. Clutter said that was all the cash he had, and explained he always did business by check. He offered to write us a check. Dick just blew up—'What kind of Mongolians do you think we are?'—and I thought Dick was ready to smash him, so I said, 'Dick. Listen to me. There's somebody awake upstairs.' Mr. Clutter told us the only people upstairs were his wife and a son and daughter. Dick wanted to know if the wife had any money, and Mr. Clutter said if she did, it would be very little, a few dollars, and he asked us—really kind of broke down—please not to bother her, because she was an invalid, she'd been very ill for a long time. But Dick insisted on going upstairs. He made Mr. Clutter lead the way.

"At the foot of the stairs, Mr. Clutter switched on lights that lighted the hall above, and as we were going up, he said, 'I don't know why you boys want to do this. I've never done you any harm. I never saw you before.' That's when Dick told him, 'Shut up! When we want you to talk, we'll tell you.' Wasn't anybody in the upstairs hall, and all the doors were shut. Mr. Clutter pointed out the rooms where the boy and girl were supposed to be sleeping, then opened his wife's door. He lighted a lamp beside the bed and told her, 'It's all right, sweetheart. Don't be afraid. These men, they just want some money.' She was a thin, frail sort of woman in a long white nightgown. The minute she opened her eyes, she started to cry. She says, talking to her husband, 'Sweetheart, I don't have any money.' He was holding her hand, patting it. He said, 'Now, don't cry, honey. It's nothing to be afraid of. It's just I gave these men all the money I had, but they want some more. They believe we have a safe somewhere in the house. I told them we don't.' Dick raised his hand, like he was going to crack him across the mouth. Says, 'Didn't I tell you to shut up?' Mrs. Clutter said, 'But my husband's telling you the God's truth. There isn't any safe.' And Dick answers back, 'I know goddam well you got a safe. And I'll find it before I leave here. Needn't worry that I won't.' Then he asked her where she kept her purse. The purse was in a bureau drawer. Dick turned it inside out. Found just some change and a dollar or two. I motioned to him to come into the hall. I wanted to discuss the situation. So we stepped outside, and I said—"

Duntz interrupts him to ask if Mr. and Mrs. Clutter could overhear the conversation.

"No. We were just outside the door, where we could keep an eye on them. But we were whispering. I told Dick, 'These people are telling the truth. The one who lied is your friend Floyd Wells. There isn't any safe, so let's get the hell out of here.' But Dick was too ashamed to face it. He said he wouldn't believe it till we searched the whole house. He said the thing to do was tie them all up, then take our time looking around. You couldn't argue with him, he was so excited. The glory of having everybody at his mercy, that's what excited him. Well, there was a bathroom next door to Mrs. Clutter's room. The idea was to lock the parents in the bathroom, and wake the kids and put them there, then bring them out one by one and tie them up in different parts of the house. And then, says Dick, after we've found the safe, we'll cut their throats. Can't shoot them, he says—that would make too much noise."

Perry frowns, rubs his knees with his manacled hands. "Let me think a minute. Because along in here things begin to get a little complicated. I remember. Yes. Yes, I took a chair out of the hall and stuck it in the bathroom. So Mrs. Clutter could sit down. Seeing she was said to be an invalid. When we locked them up, Mrs. Clutter was crying and telling us, 'Please don't hurt anybody. Please don't hurt my children.' And her husband had his arms around her, saying, like, 'Sweetheart, these fellows don't mean to hurt anybody. All they want is some money.'

"We went to the boy's room. He was awake. Lying there like he was too scared to move. Dick told him to get up, but he didn't move, or move fast enough, so Dick punched him, pulled him out of bed, and I said, 'You don't have to hit him, Dick.' And I told the boy—he was only wearing a T-shirt—to put on his pants. He put on a pair of blue jeans, and we'd just locked him in the bathroom when the girl appeared—came out of her room. She was all dressed, like she'd been awake some while. I mean, she had on socks and slippers, and a kimono, and her hair was wrapped in a bandanna. She was trying to smile. She said, 'Good grief, what is this? Some kind of joke?' I don't guess she thought it was much of a joke, though. Not after Dick opened the bathroom door and shoved her in . . ."

Dewey envisions them: the captive family, meek and frightened but without any premonition of their destiny. Herb *couldn't* have suspected, or he would have fought. He was a gentle man but strong and no coward. Herb, his friend Alvin Dewey felt certain, would have fought to the death defending Bonnie's life and the lives of his children.

"Dick stood guard outside the bathroom door while I reconnoitred. I frisked the girl's room, and I found a little purse—like a doll's purse. Inside it was a silver dollar. I dropped it somehow, and it rolled across the floor. Rolled under a chair. I had to get down on my knees. And just then it was like I was outside myself. Watching myself in some nutty movie. It made me sick. I was just disgusted. Dick, and all his talk about a rich man's safe, and here I am crawling on my belly to steal a child's silver dollar. One dollar. And I'm crawling on my belly to get it."

Perry squeezes his knees, asks the detectives for aspirin, thanks Duntz for giving him one, chews it, and resumes talking. "But that's what you do. You get what you can. I frisked the boy's room, too. Not a dime. But there was a little portable radio, and I decided to take it. Then I remembered the binoculars I'd seen in Mr. Clutter's office. I went downstairs to get them. I carried the binoculars and the radio out to the car. It was cold, and the wind and the cold felt good. The moon was so bright you could see for miles. And I thought, Why don't I walk off? Walk to the highway, hitch a ride. I sure Jesus didn't want to go back in that house. And yet—How can I explain this? It was like I wasn't part of it. More as though I was reading a story. And I had to know what was going to happen. The end. So I went back upstairs. And now, let's see—uh-huh, that's when we tied them up. Mr. Clutter first. We called him out of the bathroom, and I tied his hands together. Then I marched him all the way down to the basement—"

Dewey says, "Alone and unarmed?"

"I had the knife."

Dewey says, "But Hickock stayed guard upstairs?"

"To keep them quiet. Anyway, I didn't need help. I've worked with rope all my life."

Dewey says, "Were you using the flashlight or did you turn on the basement lights?"

"The lights. The basement was divided into two sections. One part seemed to be a play-room. Took him to the other section, the furnace room. I saw a big cardboard box leaning against the wall. A mattress box. Well, I didn't feel I ought to ask him to stretch out on the cold floor, so I dragged the mattress box over, flattened it, and told him to lie down."

The driver, via the rear-view mirror, glances at his colleague, attracts his eye, and Duntz slightly nods, as if in tribute. All along Dewey had argued that the mattress box had been placed on the floor for the *comfort* of Mr. Clutter, and taking heed of similar hints, other fragmentary indications of ironic, erratic compassion, the detective had conjectured that at least one of the killers was not altogether uncharitable.

"I tied his feet, then tied his hands to his feet. I asked him was it too tight, and he said no, but said would we please leave his wife alone. There was no need to tie her up—she wasn't going to holler or try to run out of the house. He said she'd been sick for years and years, and she was just beginning to get a little better, but an incident like this might cause her to have a setback. I know it's nothing to laugh over, only I couldn't help it—him talking about a 'setback.'

"Next thing, I brought the boy down. First I put him in the room with his dad. Tied his hands to an overhead steampipe. Then I figured that wasn't very safe. He might somehow get loose and undo the old man, or vice versa. So I cut him down and took him to the play-room, where there was a comfortable-looking couch. I roped his feet to the foot of the couch, roped his hands, then carried the rope up and made a loop around his neck, so if he struggled he'd choke himself. Once, while I was working, I put the knife down on this—well, it was a freshly varnished cedar chest; the whole cellar smelled of varnish—and he asked me not to put my knife there. The chest was a wedding present he'd built for somebody. A sister, I believe he said. Just as I was leaving, he had a coughing fit, so I stuffed a pillow under his head. Then I turned off the lights—"

Dewey says, "But you hadn't taped their mouths?"

"No. The taping came later, after I'd tied both the women in their bedrooms. Mrs. Clutter was still crying, at the same time she was asking me about Dick. She didn't trust him, but said she felt I was a decent young man. I'm *sure* you are, she says, and made me promise I wouldn't let Dick hurt anybody. I think what she really had in mind was her daughter. I was worried about that myself. I suspected Dick was plotting something, something I wouldn't stand for. When I finished tying Mrs. Clutter, sure enough, I found he'd taken the girl to her bedroom. She was in the bed, and he was sitting on the edge of it talking to her. I stopped that; I told him to go look for the safe while I tied her up. After he'd gone, I roped her feet together and tied her hands behind her back. Then I pulled up the covers, tucked her in till just her head showed. There was a little easy chair near the bed, and I thought I'd rest a minute; my legs were on fire—all that climbing and kneeling. I asked Nancy if she had a boy friend. She said yes, she did. She was trying hard to act casual and friendly. I really liked her. She was really nice. A very pretty girl, and not spoiled or anything. She told me quite a lot about herself. About school, and how she was going to go to a university to study music and art. Horses. Said next to dancing what she liked best was to gallop a horse, so I mentioned my mother had been a champion rodeo rider.

"And we talked about Dick; I was curious, see, what he'd been saying to her. Seems she'd asked him why he did things like this. Rob people. And, wow, did he toss her a tearjerker—said he'd been raised an orphan in an orphanage, and how nobody had ever loved him, and his only relative was a sister who lived with men without marrying them. All the time we were talking, we could hear the lunatic roaming around below, looking for the safe. Looking behind pictures. Tapping the walls. Tap tap tap. Like some nutty woodpecker. When he came back, just to be a real bastard I asked had he found it. Course he hadn't, but he said he'd come across another purse in the kitchen. With seven dollars."

Duntz says, "How long now had you been in the house?"

"Maybe an hour."

Duntz says, "And when did you do the taping?"

"Right then. Started with Mrs. Clutter. I made Dick help me—because I didn't want to leave him alone with the girl. I cut the tape in long strips, and Dick wrapped them around Mrs. Clutter's head like you'd wrap a mummy. He asked her, 'How come you keep on crying? Nobody's hurting you,' and he turned off the bedside lamp and said, 'Good night, Mrs. Clutter. Go to sleep.' Then he says to me, as we're heading along the hall toward Nancy's room, 'I'm gonna bust that little girl.' And I said, 'Uh-huh. But you'll have to kill me first.' He looked like he didn't believe he'd heard right. He says, 'What do you care? Hell, you can bust her, too.' Now, that's something I despise. Anybody that can't control themselves sexually. Christ, I hate that kind of stuff. I told him straight, 'Leave her alone. Else you've got a buzz-saw to fight.' That really burned him, but he realized it wasn't the time to have a flat-out free-for-all. So he says, 'O.K., honey. If that's the way you feel.' The end of it was we never even taped her. We switched off the hall light and went down to the basement."

Perry hesitates. He has a question but phrases it as a statement: "I'll bet he never said anything about wanting to rape the girl."

Dewey admits it, but he adds that except for an apparently somewhat expurgated version of his own conduct, Hickock's story supports Smith's. The details vary, the dialogue is not identical, but in substance the two accounts—thus far, at least—corroborate one another.

"Maybe. But I knew he hadn't told about the girl. I'd have bet my shirt."

Duntz says, "Perry, I've been keeping track of the lights. The way I calculate it, when you turned off the upstairs light, that left the house completely dark."

"Did. And we never used the lights again. Except the flashlight. Dick carried the flashlight when we went to tape Mr. Clutter and the boy. Just before I taped him, Mr. Clutter asked me—and these were his last words—wanted to know how his wife was, if she was all right, and I said she was fine, she was ready to go to sleep, and I told him it wasn't long till morning, and how in the morning somebody would find them, and then all of it, me and Dick and all, would seem like something they dreamed. I wasn't kidding him. I didn't want to harm the man. I thought he was a very nice gentleman. Soft-spoken. I thought so right up to the moment I cut his throat.

"Wait. I'm not telling it the way it was." Perry scowls. He rubs his legs; the handcuffs rattle. "After, see, after we'd taped them, Dick and I went off in a corner. To talk it over. Remember, now, there were hard feelings between us. Just then it made my stomach turn to think I'd ever admired him, lapped up all that brag. I said, 'Well, Dick. Any qualms?' He didn't answer me. I said, 'Leave them alive, and this won't be any small rap. Ten years the very least.' He still didn't say anything. He was holding the knife. I asked him for it, and he gave it to me, and I said, 'All right, Dick. Here goes.' But I didn't mean it. I meant to call his bluff, make him argue me out of it, make him admit he was a phony and a coward. See, it was something between me and Dick. I knelt down beside Mr. Clutter, and the pain of kneeling—I thought of that goddam dollar. Silver dollar. The shame. Disgust. And *they'd* told me never to come back to Kansas. But I didn't realize what I'd done till I heard the sound. Like somebody drowning. Screaming under water. I handed the knife to Dick. I said, 'Finish him. You'll feel better.' Dick tried—or pretended to. But the man had the strength of ten men—he was half out of his ropes, his hands were free. Dick panicked. Dick wanted to get the hell out of there. But I wouldn't let him go. The man would have died anyway, I know that, but I couldn't leave him like he was. I told Dick to hold the flashlight, focus it. Then I aimed the gun. The room just exploded. Went blue. Just blazed up. Jesus, I'll never understand why they didn't hear the noise twenty miles around."

Dewey's ears ring with it—a ringing that almost deafens him to the whispery rush of Smith's soft voice. But the voice plunges on, ejecting a fusillade of sounds and images: Hickock hunting the discharged shell; hurrying, hurrying, and Kenyon's head in a circle of light, the murmur of muffled pleadings, then Hickock again scrambling after a used cartridge; Nancy's room, Nancy listening to boots on hardwood stairs, the creak of the steps as they climb toward her, Nancy's eyes, Nancy watching the flashlight's shine seek the target ("She said, 'Oh, no! Oh, please. No! No! No! No! Don't! Oh, please don't! Please!' I gave the gun to Dick. I told him I'd done all I could do. He took aim, and she turned her face to the wall"); the dark hall, the assassins hastening toward the final door. Perhaps, having heard all she had, Bonnie welcomed their swift approach.

"That last shell was a bitch to locate. Dick wiggled under the bed to get it. Then we closed Mrs. Clutter's door and went downstairs to the office. We waited there, like we had when we first came. Looked through the blinds to see if the hired man was poking around, or anybody else who might have heard the gunfire. But it was just the same—not a sound. Just the wind—and Dick panting like wolves were after him. Right there, in those few seconds before we ran out to the car and drove away, that's when I decided I'd better shoot Dick. He'd said over and over, he'd drummed it into me: *No witnesses.* And I thought, *He's* a witness. I don't know what stopped me. God knows I should've done it. Shot him dead. Got in the car and kept on going till I lost myself in Mexico."

A hush. For ten miles and more, the three men ride without speaking.

Sorrow and profound fatigue are at the heart of Dewey's silence. It had been his ambition to learn "exactly what happened in that house that night." Twice now he'd been told, and the two versions were very much alike, the only serious discrepancy being that Hickock attributed all four deaths to Smith, while Smith contended that Hickock had killed the two women. But the confessions, though they answered questions of how and why, failed to satisfy his sense of meaningful design. The crime was a psychological accident, virtually an impersonal act; the victims might as well have been killed by lightning. Except for one thing: they had experienced prolonged terror, they had suffered. And Dewey could not forget their sufferings. Nonetheless, he found it possible to look at the man beside him without anger— with, rather, a measure of sympathy—for Perry Smith's life had been no bed of roses but pitiful, an ugly and lonely progress toward one mirage and then another. Dewey's sympathy, however, was not deep enough to accommodate either forgiveness or mercy. He hoped to see Perry and his partner hanged—hanged back to back.

Duntz asks Smith, "Added up, how much money did you get from the Clutters?"

"Between forty and fifty dollars."

Michael Herr

from Dispatches

ILLUMINATION ROUNDS

We were all strapped into the seats of the Chinook, fifty of us, and something, someone was hitting it from the outside with an enormous hammer. How do they do that? I thought, we're a thousand feet in the air! But it had to be that, over and over, shaking the helicopter, making it dip and turn in a horrible out-of-control motion that took me in the stomach. I had to laugh, it was so exciting, it was the thing I had wanted, almost what I had wanted except for that wrenching, resonant metal-echo; I could hear it even above the noise of the rotor blades. And they were going to fix that, I knew they would make it stop. They had to, it was going to make me sick.

They were all replacements going in to mop up after the big battles on Hills 875 and 876, the battles that had already taken on the name of one great battle, the battle of Dak To. And I was new, brand new, three days in-country, embarrassed about my boots because they were so new. And across from me, ten feet away, a boy tried to jump out of the straps and then jerked forward and hung there, his rifle barrel caught in the red plastic webbing of the seat back. As the chopper rose again and turned, his weight went back hard against the webbing and a dark spot the size of a baby's hand showed in the center of his fatigue jacket. And it grew—I knew what it was, but not really—it got up to his armpits and then started down his sleeves and up over his shoulders at the same time. It went all across his waist and down his legs, covering the canvas on his boots until they were dark like everything else he wore, and it was running in slow, heavy drops off his fingertips. I thought I could hear the drops hitting the metal strip on the chopper floor. Hey! . . . Oh, but this isn't anything at all, it's not real, it's just some *thing* they're going through that isn't real. One of the door gunners was heaped up on the floor like a cloth dummy. His hand had the bloody raw look of a pound of liver fresh from the butcher paper. We touched down on the same lz we had just left a few minutes before, but I didn't know it until one of the guys shook my shoulder, and then I couldn't stand up. All I could feel of my legs was their shaking, and the guy thought I'd been hit and helped me up. The chopper had taken eight hits, there was shattered plastic all over the floor, a dying pilot up front, and the boy was hanging forward in the straps again, he was dead, but not (I knew) really dead.

It took me a month to lose that feeling of being a spectator to something that was part game, part show. That first afternoon, before I'd boarded the Chinook, a black sergeant had tried to keep me from going. He told me I was too new to go near the kind of shit they were throwing around up in those hills. ("You a reporter?" he'd asked, and I'd said, "No, a writer," dumbass and pompous, and he'd laughed and said, "Careful. You can't use no eraser up where you wanna go.") He'd pointed to the bodies of all the dead Americans lined in two long rows near the chopper pad, so many that they could not even cover all of them decently. But they were not real then, and taught me nothing. The Chinook had come in, blowing my helmet off, and I grabbed it up and joined the replacements waiting to board. "Okay, man," the sergeant said. "You gotta go, you gotta go. All's I can say is, I hope you get a clean wound."

◦ ◦ ◦

The battle for Hill 875 was over, and some survivors were being brought in by Chinook to the landing strip at Dak To. The 173rd Airborne had taken over 400 casualties, nearly 200 killed, all on the previous afternoon and in the fighting that had gone on all through the night. It was very cold and wet up there, and some girls from the Red Cross had been sent up from Pleiku to comfort the survivors. As the troops filed out of the helicopters, the girls waved and smiled at them from behind their serving tables. "Hi, soldier! What's your name?" "Where you from, soldier?" "I'll bet some hot coffee would hit the spot about now."

And the men from the 173rd just kept walking without answering, staring straight ahead, their eyes rimmed with red from fatigue, their faces pinched and aged with all that had happened during the night. One of them dropped out of line and said something to a loud, fat girl who wore a Peanuts sweatshirt under her fatigue blouse and she started to cry. The rest just walked past the girls and the large, olive-drab coffee urns. They had no idea of where they were.

◦ ◦ ◦

A senior NCO in the Special Forces was telling the story: "We was back at Bragg, in the NCO Club, and this schoolteacher comes in an' she's real good-lookin'. Dusty here grabs her by the shoulders and starts runnin' his tongue all over her face like she's a fuckin' ice-cream cone. An' you know what she says? She says, 'I like you. You're different.'"

◦ ◦ ◦

At one time they would have lighted your cigarette for you on the terrace of the Continental Hotel. But those days are almost twenty years gone, and anyway, who really misses them? Now there is a crazy American who looks like George Orwell, and he is always sleeping off his drinks in one of the wicker chairs there, slumped against a table, starting up with violence, shouting and then going back to sleep. He makes everyone nervous, especially the waiters; the old ones who had served the French and the Japanese and the first American journalists and OSS types ("those noisy bastards at the Continental," Graham Greene called them) and the really young ones who bussed the tables and pimped in a modest way. The little elevator boy still greets the guests each morning with a quiet "*Ca va?*" but he is seldom answered, and the old baggage man (he also brings us grass) will sit in the lobby and say, "How are you tomorrow?"

"Ode to Billy Joe" plays from speakers mounted on the terrace's corner columns, but the air seems too heavy to carry the sound right, and it hangs in the corners. There is an exhausted, drunk master sergeant from the 1st Infantry Division who has bought a flute from the old man in khaki shorts and pith helmet who sells instruments along Tu Do Street. The old man will lean over the butt-strewn flower boxes that line the terrace and play "Frère Jacques" on a wooden stringed instrument. The sergeant has brought the flute, and he is playing it quietly, pensively, badly.

The tables are crowded with American civilian construction engineers, men getting $30,000 a year from their jobs on government contracts and matching that easily on the black market. Their faces have the look of aerial photos of silicone pits, all hung with loose flesh and visible veins. Their mistresses were among the prettiest, saddest girls in Vietnam. I always wondered what they had looked like before they'd made their arrangements with the engineers. You'd see them at the tables there, smiling their hard, empty smiles into those rangy, brutal, scared faces. No wonder those men all looked alike to the Vietnamese. After a while they all looked alike to me. Out on the Bien Hoa Highway, north of Saigon, there is a monument to the Vietnamese war dead, and it is one of the few graceful things left in the country. It is a modest pagoda set above the road and approached by long flights of gently rising steps. One Sunday, I saw a bunch of these engineers gunning their Harleys up those steps, laughing and shouting in the afternoon sun. The Vietnamese had a special name for them to distinguish them from all other Americans: it translated out to something like "The Terrible Ones," although I'm told that this doesn't even approximate the odium carried in the original.

◦ ◦ ◦

There was a young sergeant in the Special Forces, stationed at the C Detachment in Can Tho, which served as the SF headquarters for IV Corps. In all, he had spent thirty-six months in Vietnam. This was his third extended tour, and he planned to come back again as soon as he possibly could after this current hitch was finished. During his last tour he had lost a finger and part of a thumb in a fire-fight, and he had been generally shot up enough times for the three Purple Hearts which mean that you don't have to fight in Vietnam anymore. After all that, I guess they thought of him as a combat liability, but he was such a hard charger that they gave him the EM Club to manage. He ran it well and seemed happy, except that he had gained a lot of weight in the duty, and it set him apart from the rest of the men. He loved to horse around with the Vietnamese in the compound, leaping on them from behind, leaning heavily on them, shoving them around and pulling their ears, sometimes punching them a little hard in the stomach, smiling a stiff small smile that was meant to tell them all that he was just being playful. The Vietnamese would smile too, until he turned to walk away. He loved the Vietnamese, he said, he really *knew* them after three years. As far as he was concerned, there was no place in the world as fine as Vietnam. And back home in North Carolina he had a large, glass-covered display case in which he kept his medals and decorations and citations, the photographs taken during three tours and countless battles, letters from past commanders, a few souvenirs. The case stood in the center of the living room, he said, and every night his wife and three kids would move the kitchen table out in front of it and eat their dinner there.

◦ ◦ ◦

At 800 feet we knew we were being shot at. Something hit the underside of the chopper but did not penetrate it. They weren't firing tracers, but we saw the brilliant flickering blips of light below, and the pilot circled and came down very fast, working the button that released fire from the flex guns mounted on either side of the Huey. Every fifth round was a tracer, and they sailed out and down, incomparably graceful, closer and closer, until they met the tiny point of light coming from the jungle. The ground fire stopped, and we went on to land at Vinh Long, where the pilot yawned and said, "I think I'll go to bed early tonight and see if I can wake up with any enthusiasm for this war."

⊹ ⊹ ⊹

A twenty-four-year-old Special Forces captain was telling me about it. "I went out and killed one VC and liberated a prisoner. Next day the major called me in and told me that I'd killed fourteen VC and liberated six prisoners. You want to see the medal?"

⊹ ⊹ ⊹

There was a little air-conditioned restaurant on the corner of Le Loi and Tu Do, across from the Continental Hotel and the old opera house which now served as the Vietnamese Lower House. Some of us called it the Graham Greene Milk Bar (a scene in *The Quiet American* had taken place there), but its name was Givral. Every morning they baked their own baguettes and croissants, and the coffee wasn't too bad. Sometimes, I'd meet there with a friend of mine for breakfast.

He was a Belgian, a tall, slow-moving man of thirty who'd been born in the Congo. He professed to know and love war, and he affected the mercenary sensibility. He'd been photographing the Vietnam thing for seven or eight years now, and once in a while he'd go over to Laos and run around the jungles there with the government, searching for the dreaded Pathet Lao, which he pronounced "Paddy Lao." Other people's stories of Laos always made it sound like a lotus land where no one wanted to hurt anyone, but he said that whenever he went on ops there he always kept a grenade taped to his belly because he was a Catholic and knew what the Paddy Lao would do to him if he were captured. But he was a little crazy that way, and tended to dramatize his war stories.

He always wore dark glasses, probably even during operations. His pictures sold to the wire services, and I saw a few of them in the American news magazines. He was very kind in a gruff, offhanded sort of way, kindness embarrassed him, and he was so graceless among people, so eager to shock, that he couldn't understand why so many of us liked him. Irony was the effect he worked for in conversation, that and a sense of how exquisite the war could be when all of its machinery was running right. He was explaining the finish of an operation he'd just been on in War Zone C, above Cu Chi.

"There were a lot of dead VC," he said. "Dozens and dozens of them! A lot of them were from the same village that has been giving you so much trouble lately. VC from top to bottom—Michael, in that village the fucking *ducks* are VC. So the American commander had twenty or thirty of the dead flown up in a sling load and dropped into the village. I should say it was a drop of at least two hundred feet, all those dead Viet Congs, right in the middle of the village."

He smiled (I couldn't see his eyes).

"Ah, Psywar!" he said, kissing off the tips of his fingers.

⊹ ⊹ ⊹

Bob Stokes of *Newsweek* told me this: In the big Marine hospital in Danang they have what is called the "White Lie Ward," where they bring some of the worst cases, the ones who can be saved but who will never be the same again. A young marine was carried in, still unconscious and full of morphine, and his legs were gone. As he was being carried into the ward, he came out of it briefly and saw a Catholic chaplain standing over him.

"Father," he said, "am I all right?"

The chaplain didn't know what to say. "You'll have to talk about that with the doctors, son."

"Father, are my legs okay?"

"Yes," the chaplain said. "Sure."

By the next afternoon the shock had worn off and the boy knew all about it. He was lying on his cot when the chaplain came by.

"Father," the Marine said, "I'd like to ask you for something."

"What, son?"

"I'd like to have that cross." And he pointed to the tiny silver insignia on the chaplain's lapel.

"Of course," the chaplain said. "But why?"

"Well, it was the first thing I saw when I came to yesterday, and I'd like to have it."

The chaplain removed the cross and handed it to him. The Marine held it tightly in his fist and looked at the chaplain.

"You lied to me, Father," he said. "You cocksucker. You lied to me."

⚬   ⚬   ⚬

His name was Davies, and he was a gunner with a helicopter group based at Tan Son Nhut airport. On paper, by the regulations, he was billeted in one of the big "hotel" BEQ's in Cholon, but he only kept his things there. He actually lived in a small two-story Vietnamese house deeper inside of Cholon, as far from the papers and the regulations as he could get. Every morning he took an Army bus with wire-grille windows out to the base and flew missions, mostly around War Zone C, along the Cambodian border, and most nights he returned to the house in Cholon where he lived with his "wife" (whom he'd found in one of the bars) and some other Vietnamese who were said to be the girl's family. Her mamma-san and her brother were always there, living on the first floor, and there were others who came and went. He seldom saw the brother, but every few days he would find a pile of labels and brand names torn from cardboard cartons, American products that the brother wanted from the PX.

The first time I saw him he was sitting alone at a table on the Continental terrace, drinking a beer. He had a full, drooping mustache and sharp, sad eyes, and he was wearing a denim workshirt and wheat jeans. He also carried a Leica and a copy of *Ramparts*, and I just assumed at first that he was a correspondent. I didn't know then that you could buy *Ramparts* at the PX, and after I'd borrowed and returned it we began to talk. It was the issue that featured left-wing Catholics like Jesus Christ and Fulton Sheen on the cover. "*Catholique?*" one of the bar girls said later that night. "*Moi aussi,*" and she kept the magazine. That was when we were walking around Cholon in the rain trying to find Hoa, his wife. Mamma-san had told us that she'd gone to the movies with some girlfriends, but Davies knew what she was doing.

"I hate that shit," he said. "It's so uncool."

"Well, don't put up with it."

"Yeah."

Davies' house was down a long, narrow alley that became nothing more than a warren at the end, smelling of camphor smoke and fish, crowded but clean. He would not speak to Mamma-san, and we walked straight up to the second floor. It was one long room that had a sleeping area screened off in an arrangement of filmy curtains. At the top of the stairs there was a large poster of Lenny Bruce, and beneath it, in a shrine effect, was a low table with a Buddha and lighted incense on it.

"Lenny," Davies said.

Most of one wall was covered with a collage that Davies had done with the help of some friends. It included glimpses of burning monks, stacked Viet Cong dead, wounded Marines screaming and weeping, Cardinal Spellman waving from a chopper, Ronald Reagan, his face halved and separated by a stalk of cannabis; pictures of John Lennon peering through wire-rimmed glasses, Mick Jagger, Jimi Hendrix, Dylan, Eldridge Cleaver, Rap Brown; coffins draped with American flags whose stars were replaced by swastikas and dollar signs; odd parts clipped from *Playboy* pictures, newspaper headlines (FARMERS BUTCHER HOGS TO PROTEST PORK PRICE DIP), photo captions (*President Jokes with Newsmen*), beautiful girls holding flowers, showers of peace symbols; Ky standing at attention and saluting, a small mushroom cloud forming where his genitalia should have been; a map of the western United States with the shape of Vietnam reversed and fitted over California and one large, long figure that began at the bottom with shiny leather boots and rouged knees and ascended in a microskirt, bare breasts, graceful shoulders and a long neck, topped by the burned, blackened face of a dead Vietnamese woman.

By the time Davies' friends showed up, we were already stoned. We could hear them below, laughing and rapping with Mama, and then they came up the stairs, three spades and two white guys.

"It sure do smell *peculiar* up here," one of them said.

"Hi, you freaky li'l fuckers."

"This grass is Number Ten," Davies said. "Every time I smoke this grass over here it gives me a bad trip."

"Ain' nuthin' th' matter with that grass," someone said. "It ain't the grass."

"Where's Hoa?"

"Yeah, Davies, where's your ole lady at?"

"She's out hustling Saigon tea, and I'm fucking sick of it." He tried to look really angry, but he only looked unhappy.

One of them handed off a joint and stretched out. "Hairy day today," he said.

"Where'd you fly?"

"Bu Dop."

"Bu Dop!" one of the spades said, and he started to move toward the joint, jiving and working his shoulders, bopping his head. "Bu Dop, budop, bu dop dop *dop!*"

"Funky funky Bu Dop."

"Hey, man, can you OD on grass?"

"I dunno, baby. Maybe we could get jobs at the Aberdeen Proving Grounds smokin' dope for Uncle Sugar."

"Wow, I'm stoned. Hey, Davies, you stoned?"

"Yeah," Davies said.

It started to rain again, so hard that you couldn't hear drops, only the full force of the water pouring down on the metal roof. We smoked a little more, and then the others started to leave. Davies looked like he was sleeping with his eyes open.

"That goddamn pig," he said. "Fuckin' whore. Man, I'm paying out all this bread for the house and those people downstairs. I don't even know who they are, for Christ's sake. I'm really . . . I'm getting sick of it."

"You're pretty short now," someone said. "Why don't you cut out?"

"You mean just split?"

"Why not?"

Davies was quiet for a long time.

"Yeah," he finally said. "This is bad. This is really bad. I think I'm going to get out of here."

—◦— —◦— —◦—

A bird colonel, commanding a brigade of the 4th Infantry Division: "I'll bet you always wondered why we call 'em Dinks up in this part of the country. I thought of it myself. I'll tell you, I never *did* like hearing them called Charlie. See, I had an uncle named Charlie, and I liked him too. No, Charlie was just too damn good for the little bastards. So I just thought, What are they *really* like? and I came up with rinky-dink. Suits 'em just perfect, Rinky-Dink. 'Cept that was too long, so we cut it down some. And that's why we call 'em Dinks."

—◦— —◦— —◦—

One morning before dawn, Ed Fouhy, a former Saigon bureau chief for CBS, went out to 8th Aerial Port at Tan Son Nhut to catch the early military flight to Danang. They boarded as the sun came up, and Fouhy strapped in next to a kid in rumpled fatigues, one of those soldiers you see whose weariness has gone far beyond physical exhaustion, into that state where no amount of sleep will ever give him the kind of rest he needs. Every torpid movement they make tells you that they are tired, that they'll stay tired until their tours are up and the big bird flies them back to the World. Their eyes are dim with it, their faces almost puffy, and when they smile you have to accept it as a token.

There was a standard question you could use to open a conversation with troops, and Fouhy tried it. "How long you been in-country?" he asked.

The kid half lifted his head; that question could *not* be serious. The weight was really on him, and the words came slowly.

"All fuckin' day," he said.

—◦— —◦— —◦—

"You guys out to do a story on me suntahm," the kid said. He was a helicopter gunner, six-three with an enormous head that sat in bad proportion to the rest of his body and a line of picket teeth that were always on show in a wet, uneven smile. Every few seconds he would have to wipe his mouth with the back of his hand, and when he talked to you his face was always an inch from yours, so that I had to take my glasses off to keep them dry. He was from Kilgore, Texas, and he was on his seventeenth consecutive month in-country.

"Why should we do a story about you?"

"'Cause I'm so fuckin' good," he said, "'n' that ain' no shit, neither. Got me one hunnert 'n' fifty-se'en gooks kilt. 'N' fifty caribou." He grinned and stanched the saliva for a second. "Them're all certified," he added.

The chopper touched down at Ba Xoi and we got off, not unhappy about leaving him. "Lis'n," he said laughing, "you git up onna ridgeline, see y' keep yer head down. Y'heah?"

—◦— —◦— —◦—

"Say, how'd you get to be a co-respondent an' come ovah to this raggedly-ass mother-fucker?"

He was a really big spade, rough-looking even when he smiled, and he wore a gold nose-bead fastened through his left nostril. I told him that the nose-bead blew my mind, and he said that was all right, it blew everybody's mind. We were sitting by the chopper pad of an lz above Kontum. He was trying to get to Dak To, I was heading for Pleiku, and we both wanted to get out of there before nightfall. We took turns running out to the pad to check the choppers that kept coming in and taking off, neither of us having any luck, and after we'd talked for an hour he laid a joint on me and we smoked.

"I been here mor'n eight months now," he said. "I bet I been in mor'n twenny firefights. An' I ain' hardly fired back once."

"How come?"

"Shee-it, I go firin' back, I might kill one a th' Brothers you dig it?"

I nodded, no Viet Cong ever called *me* honky, and he told me that in his company alone there were more than a dozen Black Panthers and that he was one of them. I didn't say anything, and then he said that he wasn't just a Panther; he was an agent for the Panthers, sent over here to recruit. I asked him what kind of luck he'd been having, and he said fine, real fine. There was a fierce wind blowing across the lz, and the joint didn't last very long.

"Hey, baby," he said, "that was just some shit I tol' you. Shit, I ain't no Panther. I was just fuckin' with you, see what you'd say."

"But the Panthers have guys over here. I've met some."

"Tha' could be," he said, and he laughed.

A Huey came in, and he jogged out to see where it was headed. It was going to Dak To, and he came back to get his gear. "Later, baby," he said. "An' luck." He jumped into the chopper, and as it rose from the strip he leaned out and laughed, bringing his arm up and bending it back toward him, palm out and the fist clenched tightly in the Sign.

⌀ ⌀ ⌀

One day I went out with the ARVN on an operation in the rice paddies above Vinh Long, forty terrified Vietnamese troops and five Americans, all packed into three Hueys that dropped us up to our hips in paddy muck. I had never been in a rice paddy before. We spread out and moved toward the marshy swale that led to the jungle. We were still twenty feet from the first cover, a low paddy wall, when we took fire from the treeline. It was probably the working half of a crossfire that had somehow gone wrong. It caught one of the ARVN in the head, and he dropped back into the water and disappeared. We made it to the wall with two casualties. There was no way of stopping their fire, no room to send a flanking party, so gunships were called and we crouched behind the wall and waited. There was a lot of fire coming from the trees, but we were all right as long as we kept down. And I was thinking, Oh man, so this is a rice paddy, yes, wow! when I suddenly heard an electric guitar shooting right up in my ear and a mean, rapturous black voice singing, coaxing, "Now c'mon baby, stop actin' so crazy," and when I got it all together I turned to see a grinning black corporal hunched over a cassette recorder. "Might's well," he said. "We ain' goin' *no*where till them gunships come."

That's the story of the first time I ever heard Jimi Hendrix, but in a war where a lot of people talked about Aretha's "Satisfaction" the way other people speak of Brahms' Fourth, it was more than a story; it was Credentials. "Say, that Jimi Hendrix is my main man," someone would say. "He has *definitely* got his shit together!" Hendrix had once been in the 101st Airborne, and the Airborne in Vietnam was full of wiggy-brilliant spades like him, really mean and really good, guys who always took care of you when things got bad. That music meant a lot to them. I never once heard it played over the Armed Forces Radio Network.

◆ ◆ ◆

I met this kid from Miles City, Montana, who read the *Stars and Stripes* every day, checking the casualty lists to see if by some chance anybody from his town had been killed. He didn't even know if there was anyone else from Miles City in Vietnam, but he checked anyway because he knew for sure that if there *was* someone else and they got killed, he would be all right. "I mean, can you just see *two* guys from a raggedy-ass town like Miles City getting killed in Vietnam?" he said.

The sergeant had lain out near the clearing for almost two hours with a wounded medic. He had called over and over for a medevac, but none had come. Finally, a chopper from another outfit, a LOH, appeared, and he was able to reach it by radio. The pilot told him that he'd have to wait for one of his own ships, they weren't coming down, and the sergeant told the pilot that if he did not land for them he was going to open fire from the ground and fucking well *bring* him down. So they were picked up that way, but there were repercussions.

The commander's code name was Mal Hombre, and he reached the sergeant later that afternoon from a place with the call signal Violent Meals.

"God *damn* it, Sergeant," he said through the static, "I thought you were a professional soldier."

"I waited as long as I could, Sir. Any longer, I was gonna lose my man."

"This outfit is perfectly capable of taking care of its own dirty laundry. Is that clear, Sergeant?"

"Colonel, since when is a wounded trooper 'dirty laundry'?"

"At ease, Sergeant," Mal Hombre said, and radio contact was broken.

◆ ◆ ◆

There was a spec 4 in the Special Forces at Can Tho, a shy Indian boy from Chinle, Arizona, with large, wet eyes the color of ripe olives and a quiet way of speaking, a really nice way of putting things, kind to everyone without ever being stupid or soft about it. On the night that the compound and the airstrip were hit, he came and asked me if there was a chaplain anywhere around. He wasn't very religious, he said, but he was worried about tonight. He'd just volunteered for a "suicide squad," two jeeps that were going to drive across the air-strip with mortars and a recoilless rifle. It looked bad, I had to admit; there were so few of us in the compound that they'd had to put me on the reaction force. It might be bad. He just had a feeling about it, he'd seen what always happened to guys whenever they got that feeling, at least he *thought* it was that feeling, a bad one, the worst he'd ever had.

I told him that the only chaplains I could think of would be in the town, and we both knew that the town was cut off.

"Oh," he said. "Look, then. If I get it tonight . . ."

"It'll be okay."

"Listen, though. If it happens . . . I think it's going to . . . will you make sure the colonel tells my folks I was looking for a chaplain anyway?"

I promised, and the jeeps loaded and drove off. I heard later that there had been a brief firefight, but that no one had been hurt. They didn't have to use the recoilless. They all drove back into the compound two hours later. The next morning at breakfast he sat at another table, saying a lot of loud, brutal things about the gooks, and he wouldn't look at me. But at noon he came over and squeezed my arm and smiled, his eyes fixed somewhere just to the right of my own.

⟡ ⟡ ⟡

For two days now, ever since the Tet Offensive had begun, they had been coming by the hundreds to the province hospital at Can Tho. They were usually either very young or very old or women, and their wounds were often horrible. The more lightly wounded were being treated quickly in the hospital yard, and the more serious cases were simply placed in one of the corridors to die. There were just too many of them to treat, the doctors had worked without a break, and now, on the second afternoon, the Viet Cong began shelling the hospital.

One of the Vietnamese nurses handed me a cold can of beer and asked me to take it down the hall where one of the Army surgeons was operating. The door of the room was ajar, and I walked right in. I probably should have looked first. A little girl was lying on the table, looking with wide dry eyes at the wall. Her left leg was gone, and a sharp piece of bone about six inches long extended from the exposed stump. The leg itself was on the floor, half wrapped in a piece of paper. The doctor was a major, and he'd been working alone. He could not have looked worse if he'd lain all night in a trough of blood. His hands were so slippery that I had to hold the can to his mouth for him and tip it up as his head went back. I couldn't look at the girl.

"Is it all right?" he said quietly.

"It's okay now. I expect I'll be sick as hell later on."

He placed his hand on the girl's forehead and said, "Hello, little darling." He thanked me for bringing the beer. He probably thought that he was smiling, but nothing changed anywhere in his face. He'd been working this way for nearly twenty hours.

⟡ ⟡ ⟡

The Intel report lay closed on the green field table, and someone had scrawled "What does it all mean?" across the cover sheet. There wasn't much doubt about who had done that; the S-2 was a known ironist. There were so many like him, really young captains and majors who had the wit to cut back their despair, a wedge to set against the bitterness. What got to them sooner or later was an inability to reconcile their love of service with their contempt for the war, and a lot of them finally had to resign their commissions, leave the profession.

We were sitting in the tent waiting for the rain to stop, the major, five grunts and myself. The rains were constant now, ending what had been a dry monsoon season, and you could look through the tent flap and think about the Marines up there patrolling the hills. Someone came in to report that one of the patrols had discovered a small arms cache.

"An arms cache!" the major said. "What happened was, one of the grunts was out there running around, and he tripped and fell down. That's about the only way we ever find any of this shit."

He was twenty-nine, young in rank, and this was his second tour. The time before, he had been a captain commanding a regular Marine company. He knew all about grunts and patrols, arms caches and the value of most Intelligence.

It was cold, even in the tent, and the enlisted Marines seemed uncomfortable about lying around with a stranger, a correspondent there. The major was a cool head, they knew that; there wasn't going to be any kind of hassle until the rain stopped. They talked quietly among themselves at the far end of the tent, away from the light of the lantern. Reports kept coming in: reports from the Vietnamese, from recon, from Division, situation reports, casualty reports, three casualty reports in twenty minutes. The major looked them all over.

"Did you know that a dead Marine costs eighteen thousand dollars?" he said. The grunts all turned around and looked at us. They knew how the major had meant that because they knew the major. They were just seeing about me.

The rain stopped, and they left. Outside, the air was still cool, but heavy, too, as though a terrible heat was coming on. The major and I stood by the tent and watched while an F-4 flew nose-down, released its load against the base of a hill, leveled and flew upward again.

"I've been having this dream," the major said. "I've had it two times now. I'm in a big examination room back at Quantico. They're handing out questionnaires for an aptitude test. I take one and look at it, and the first question says, 'How many kinds of animals can you kill with your hands?'"

We could see rain falling in a sheet about a kilometer away. Judging by the wind, the major gave it three minutes before it reached us.

"After the first tour, I'd have the goddamndest nightmares. You know, the works. Bloody stuff, bad fights, guys dying, *me* dying . . . I thought they were the worst," he said. "But I sort of miss them now."

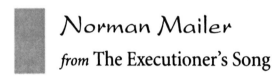

Norman Mailer

from The Executioner's Song

THE TURKEY SHOOT

1

IN THE MINIMUM SECURITY ROOM TO WHICH SCHILLER HAD BEEN ESCORTED BY THE guards were a lot of people he didn't recognize. One by one, they would pass in, try not to look confused, take a folding chair and sit down. Nobody was talking to anyone else. It did not have the atmosphere of a funeral, but there was an utter and polite calm.

Then Toni Gurney walked in. For the first time, Larry saw somebody he could say hello to and chatted with her. It was not so much that he was the man who broke the ice, but at least one conversation had begun, and soon a lot of people began to converse.

After a while, Vern came over and pointed out a fellow Schiller had noticed, a rather icy-looking man, wearing an obvious toupee, accompanied by two severe-looking women. Schiller assumed the fellow was a mortician, but Vern said, "That's the doctor who's going to take Gary's eyes out."

Then Stanger came into the room and he was furious. Judge Bullock had delayed the order. Now, Gary could be executed at any time during the day. "Would you believe that, Larry?" Schiller could see that Stanger didn't want Gary to be executed, and, in fact, when Moody came up, Ron still maintained that this would be another dry run. The execution was simply not going to come down. Schiller heard someone in the corner say, "They may keep us here three hours."

⋄   ⋄   ⋄

Just then a guard came running in from the back door and yelled some words over his shoulder. "Overturned," he cried out. "It's on." At that moment, Stanger, for the first time, understood that Gary Gilmore was going to be shot. It went through him like he had been kicked in the chest. Then he felt chilled. It was an appalling sensation. The strangeness of the reaction went all through him. For the first time in his life, Ron could feel the ends of his nerves. His heart could have been caked in ice. he looked over at Schiller taking notes on the back of some paper and thought, "I'm sure glad he's recording all this, because I can't even move. I don't know if I can walk."

⋄   ⋄   ⋄

Then they started to transfer the guests. As they led him to the car, Stanger knew he must look ready to throw up. He felt as close to death as breathing, and wondered if he were going mad, because he would have bet a million Gary Gilmore would never be executed. It had made his job easy. He had never felt any moral dilemma in carrying out Gary's desires. In fact, he couldn't have represented him if he really believed the State would go through with it all. It had been a play. He had seen himself as no more important than one more person on the stage.

2

Out in the parking lot, the reporters were being awakened. There was a lot of banging on the doors of vans. "The firing squad is coming," someone shouted.

⋄   ⋄   ⋄

Robert Sam Anson, covering it for *New Times,* was taking notes:

> Once again, everyone is running. A hundred yards away, in Maximum, a police car, followed by a van, has pulled close to the gate. Now Sam Smith strides toward the building, erect, determined, coatless, oblivious to the cold. At 7:47, a small party of people emerges from the Maximum door; even at this distance, Gilmore can be seen quite distinctly. He is wearing white pants and a black T-shirt. . . . "It all looks pretty good," one of the guards comments. "All that's left now is the paper work," his partner answers.
>
> With the appearance of Gilmore, the reporters become a mob, a herd spooked into stampede. Camera lights tilt crazily up into the air as their bearers struggle to shift them into position. Producers are shouting orders. Directly in front of the prison building, Geraldo Rivera, attired in black leather jacket and jeans and looking cool, the way only Geraldo Rivera can look cool, is shouting into his mike. "Kill the Rona segment. Get rid of it. Give me air. You'll be able to hear the shots. I promise. You'll be able to hear the shots."

When Gary came out of Maximum Detention, he was escorted to the van and seated behind the driver. Meersman sat next to him and then Warden Smith came in, and three new guards. The van drove slowly with the seven men, the only car moving in all that quarter mile of prison streets from Maximum Detention to the cannery.

❧ ❧ ❧

As soon as they started, Gary reached in with both manacled hands to a pocket of his pants and took out a folded piece of paper and put it on his knee so that he could look at it. It was a picture of Nicole clipped from a magazine, and he stared at it.

When the driver of the van turned the key for the motor, the radio, having been on before, now went on again. The tension in the van was sufficient that everyone jumped. Then the words of a song were heard. The driver immediately reached down to turn the radio off, but Gary looked up and said, "Please leave it on." So they began to drive and there was music coming from the radio. The words of the song told of the flight of a white bird. "Una paloma blanca," went the refrain, "I'm just a bird in the sky. Una paloma blanca, over the mountains I fly."

❧ ❧ ❧

The driver said again, "Would you like me to leave the radio on?" Again Gary said, "Yes." "It's a new day, it's a new way," said the words, "and I fly up to the sun."

❧ ❧ ❧

As they drove along slowly, and the song played, Father Meersman noticed that Gary no longer looked at the picture. It was as if the words had become more important.

> Once I had my share of losing,
> Once they locked me on a chain,
> Yes, they tried to break my power,
> Oh, I still can feel the pain.

No one spoke any longer and the song played through.

> No one can take my freedom away,
> Yes, no one can take my freedom away.

When it was done, they drove in silence and got out at the cannery, one by one, disembarking in the way they had practiced in the early hours of the morning when these same prison guards had walked through the scene with a model standing in for Gary. Now, they brought him into the cannery, very, very smoothly. Meersman felt that the practice had paid big dividends.

> Last nite I flew in my dream
> like a white bird through the window . . .
> Tonite i will tell my soul to fly me to you.

3

All through the trip from Maximum to the cannery, all the while "La Paloma Blanca" was playing, Father Meersman did not have any particular feelings as such. Like anything else, one had to proceed to each particular stage in order that it all run smoothly. That was the uppermost thing in his mind, to be thinking ahead to the next step, so that even getting into the van, there wouldn't be any stumbling.

❧   ❧   ❧

It had been beautifully planned, Father Meersman thought. Even to the care with which they had arranged that as the vehicle with Gary Gilmore in it moved from Maximum to the cannery, all the traffic in the prison compound would stop with no vehicles moving while this one vehicle made its way, so that for the purposes of security, everything was protected. The authorities had timed this transfer with a stopwatch whereby they knew as far as you can humanly know how long it would take for the van to go to this corner and then to that corner, and Father Meersman had occupied himself so intensely in the logic of these steps that he did not have a feeling he could really reflect on other than his paramount concern that Gary Gilmore not be upset in any way through this whole thing. It was Gary Gilmore's calm frame of mind he wanted to carry through the procedure smoothly and have finished smoothly, and on the flow of such quiet thoughts, his black wintertime coat wrapped around him. Father Meersman arrived with the others at the cannery.

❧   ❧   ❧

Now, it was important to make sure that the van be as close to the steps as possible. Gary would be wearing shackles, and uppermost in Father Meersman's mind was that he should not have a long slow, painful walk. In fact, Father Meersman did not take his mind away from the mechanics of these activities until the entire procedure had come to its conclusion and they had mounted the nine or ten wooden steps that would take them into the room of execution and Gilmore was set in that chair. Then Father Meersman felt they were home, and everything would go smoothly.

❧   ❧   ❧

Noall Wootton left the Warden's office to walk over to the cannery. He was taking his time. With luck, it might all be over before he got there, but the Utah County Sheriff made a point of stopping to pick him up, and they drove to a door in a warehouse where the Assistant Warden, Leon Hatch, waved Wootton in. It was a big room with gray cement-block walls. That was all he could see, for he went immediately to the rear. Noall was struck with how many people were there. A lot of huge guys were in front of him. Wootton couldn't see a thing. That was fine. He didn't want to get in anybody's way. He just stayed in the back with the empty paint cans, the old tires, and the discarded machinery.

4

Out in Denver, Earl Dorius was wandering down the corridor when he noticed Jack Ford of KSL on the telephone. As soon as Jack came out of the booth, Earl inquired what was going on at the prison, and heard that they were proceeding, and the car carrying Gilmore had just reached the cannery.

❧   ❧   ❧

This was the first time, during what Earl thought of as the entire ordeal, that it became real a man was about to be killed. Now he felt in his own nerves the tension that Gordon

Richards had felt when Earl first gave him the message, and these feelings also gave Earl a clue to the sentiments of the prison personnel. He passed through a very heavy feeling of anguish for the Warden. It would not be easy for his friend, Sam Smith, to order the execution of a man.

⚬ ⚬ ⚬

Earl decided that he, however, really did not feel any pity for Gilmore. The impact this man had had on the families of his victims, even the vastly lesser impact on Earl's own life these last few months when he hardly saw his children, was not conducive to feeling much compassion. Only sorrow for the Warden.

⚬ ⚬ ⚬

After Judith Wolbach left the courtroom, she looked down from a high window in the corridor at the gray dawn coming in, and became aware of an emotional void in herself. The thing most disturbing to Judith at this moment was that she felt so dirty. She hadn't even had a chance to go home that night or change her shirt. Just felt sweaty and tired and really disgusted. It shocked her that she had no other reaction. She thought the Bench had exhibited despicable behavior, and she felt nasty about Dorius, and that was it.

5

Outside Minimum Security, cars were waiting for the people who would witness the execution, and at the end of a short drive, Schiller saw a camper back up against the cement-brick building they called the cannery and he said to himself, "That's the executioners." Then he heard a noise above and was startled. The press release put out by the prison had stated that the air space above the prison up to 1,500 feet was going to be off limits. But there was a copter directly overhead. Later, Schiller found out that a newspaper had been able to get away with it and take pictures of Gilmore being transferred, because the release had specified airplanes, not helicopters.

⚬ ⚬ ⚬

Just in back of the cannery, Schiller saw a black canvas structure that had been built out on the loading platform like an extra room, and he realized the executioners must be waiting in there. Then his car went around another corner of the building, and he saw Vern, Moody, and Stanger get out of the automobile ahead and go up the entrance steps. When it was his turn to walk through the door, Schiller could see from the corner of his eye that Gary was to his right and strapped in a chair. What hit him before he even took a true look, was that Gary's end of the room was lit, not brightly like a movie set, but lights were on him, and the rest of the room was dark. He was up on a little platform. It was like a stage. With the chair so prominent, it felt more as if an electrocution was going to take place than a shooting.

⚬ ⚬ ⚬

As Schiller walked forward, the rear view of Gary's head changed to a profile, and then he was able to see a little of his face. At that point, Gilmore acknowledged his presence, and Schiller nodded back. The next thing he noticed was that Gilmore was not strapped tightly into the chair. It was the first detail that really hit him. Everything was loose.

❧   ❧   ❧

There were straps around his arms and legs, but they all had a good inch of slack. He could have pulled his hands right out of their restraints. Then, as Schiller continued to move forward, he saw a painted line before him on the floor, and an official said, "Stand behind that," so he wheeled and faced the chair. Now, with Gilmore again on his right, Schiller could see to his left a black blind with slots in it, and he estimated the distance at twenty-five feet from himself and about the same distance from Gilmore. Then, he took a good look.

❧   ❧   ❧

It was the first time Schiller had seen Gary in person since December. At this moment, he looked tired, depleted, thin, older than Schiller had ever seen him, and a little glassy-eyed. A tired old bird with very bright eyes.

❧   ❧   ❧

The next thing to impress Schiller was that Gary was still in control. He was carrying on conversations, not loud enough to hear, but saying something to the guards strapping him, to the Warden, and to the priest. Maybe there were eight people around him in maroon jackets. Schiller was about to put down in his notes that they were prison officials, but that was exactly what he wished to guard against. No journalistic assumptions. So he would not suppose they were prison officials. Just people in red coats. Then, as his photographer's eye grew accustomed to the scene, he could not quite believe what he next observed. For the seat of execution was no more than a little old office chair, and behind it was an old filthy mattress backed up by sandbags and the stone wall of the cannery. They had rammed that mattress between the chair and the sandbags, a last-minute expedient, no doubt, as if, sometime during the night, they had decided that the sandbags weren't enough and bullets might go through, hit the wall, and ricochet. But the dirty mattress repelled Schiller. He said to himself, My God, they stitched the black canvas neatly around the rifle slots for the assassins. Then he realized the word he was using.

❧   ❧   ❧

Still, you could not ignore the contrast between the meticulous preparation of the blind, and Gary's chair with its filthy ramshackle backdrop. Even the bindings around his arms looked to be made out of cheap webbing.

6

Ron Stanger's first impression was how many people were in the room. God, the number of spectators. Executions must be a spectator sport. It really hit him even before his first look at Gary, and then he was thankful the hood was not on yet. That was a relief. Gilmore was still a human being, not a hooded, grotesque thing, and Ron realized how he had been preparing himself for the shock of seeing Gary with his face concealed in a black bag. But, no, there was Gary staring at the crowd with an odd humor in his face. Stanger knew what he was thinking. "Anybody who knows somebody is going to get an invite to the turkey shoot."

❧   ❧   ❧

Stanger hadn't thought there would be anybody here to speak of, but there must have been fifty people behind the white line. Any cop or bureaucrat who had a little pull had gotten in. Stanger could hear Bob Moody's words about Sam Smith, so often repeated. "He's a very sincere man. It's just that he's incompetent. Totally incompetent." Here were all these Sheriffs and County Troopers Stanger had never seen before, come right out of the woodwork—how could you be respected in your profession if you weren't here?

Moody also felt anger at all the people who had been invited. Sam Smith had given them such fuss whether it would be five or seven guests. Now there were all these needless people pressed behind the line, and the executioners back of the screen talking. You couldn't hear what they were saying, but you could hear them, and it incensed Bob that Ernie Wright, Director of Corrections, was dancing around greeting people, practically gallivanting with his big white cowboy hat, looking like a Texas bureaucrat.

⚬ ⚬ ⚬

Moody had the feeling that the riflemen behind the blind were purposely not looking at Gary, but keeping their backs to him, chatting away in a group, and would only turn around at the last minute when given the order. Ron Stanger, situated next to Bob Moody, wanted to get up and say to all, "Here, bless your heart, you wouldn't give this man a piece of pizza before you blow his guts out." That's what he wanted to say, but he didn't dare. It would have been too hysterical. Couldn't let the man, he would have shouted, have his pizza and a six-pack of beer. Rather have it wind up in a correctional belly, wouldn't you?

Cline Campbell's first thought when he walked into the room was, my goodness, do they sell tickets to this? All the same, Campbell could feel how everybody was scared to death. It hung over the execution. The good old bureaucratic fear that somebody in an official place was going to forget something. Then there'd be all political or legal hell to pay. Campbell just contented himself with saying to Gary, "How are you doing?" and then he stood to one side of the chair and Father Meersman to the other, and Father Meersman got a cup of water and Gilmore took a sip of it as the priest held it to his mouth.

⚬ ⚬ ⚬

An official came up to Vern and said Gary wanted to speak to him. Vern walked over into the light that was on Gary, and his nephew looked up at him with those baby-blue eyes of his, and Vern felt he'd like to pull him out of that chair, just pull him out of that chair and make him free again. Vern was feeling a great deal of emotion. He didn't want him in that chair, really.

⚬ ⚬ ⚬

Gary said, "Look, take this watch. I don't want anybody to have it but Nicole." He had broken it and taped it with the hands set at 7:49. Now, he handed it to Vern. Must have been holding it all this while. Then Gary said, "I want you to promise you'll see to it that Nicole is taken care of." How in the world Gary figured he could take care of her, Vern didn't know, but Gary had to ask somebody. They shook hands and Gary started to squeeze his hand, right there in the chair as if he could crush Vern's knuckles. He said to Vern, "Come on, I'll give you a go," and Vern said, "Gary, I could pull you right out of that chair if I wanted to."

Gary said, "Would you?"

Vern went back to his place behind the line and thought of the conversation he'd had weeks before when Gary asked him and Ida to be witnesses, and Vern had said, "I don't want Ida to see it," and Gary said, "but I want *you* there, Vern."

"I don't know whether I can take it or not," Vern had said, "I don't think I can." Gary had said, "Well, I want you there."

"Why?" Vern asked. "Why do you want me?"

"Well, Vern," Gary said, "I want to show you. I've already shown you how I live"—he gave his most mocking smile—"and I'd like to show you how I can die." Vern thought all this now must be part of what he had said then because, back behind the line, feeling Gary's hand still on his, Vern wanted to tell him, "That was so good, Gary, what you just did."

⊸ ⊸ ⊸

Bob Moody came next, and he shook hands. Gary had a smaller hand than Bob had expected, but neither cold nor feverishly warm, just a shock, for it was a warm, living hand like any other. Gary looked at him and said, "Well, Moody, I'm going to leave you my hair. You need it worse than I do."

⊸ ⊸ ⊸

Schiller was next. As he walked up, he kept worrying about the right thing to say. But when he got there, he was dazed by the immensity of it all. It was as if he was saying good-bye to a man who was going to step into a cannon and be fired to the moon, or dropped in an iron chamber to the bottom of the sea, a veritable Houdini. He grasped both of Gilmore's hands and it didn't matter if the man was a murderer, he could just as well have been a saint, for either at this moment seemed equally beyond Schiller's way of measure—and he said, he heard it come out of him, "I don't know what I'm here for."

⊸ ⊸ ⊸

Gilmore replied, "You're going to help me escape." Schiller looked at him sitting in the chair and said, "I'll do it the best way that's humanly possible," and was thinking by that, he would treat it all in the most honest way, and Gilmore smiled back at him with that funny tight grin of his, just a little expression in the upper lip, as if he alone knew the meaning of what had just been said, and then the grin broadened into that thin-lipped smile he showed on occasion, evil as a jackal, subtly jeering, the last facial expression Schiller would have to remember of Gilmore. They shook hands, Gilmore's grip kind of weak, and Schiller walked away not knowing whether he had handled the moment the way he should. Didn't even know if it was a moment to be handled. He felt like he had no real relationship to Gilmore.

⊸ ⊸ ⊸

Vern had gone first because he was the patriarch, then Bob Moody, but Schiller had tried to be last. Stanger had thought, "You've got to be kidding, you're even doing it now," and won the maneuvering. Larry went ahead. When it came Stanger's turn, he couldn't think of anything to say. Just murmured, "Hang in there. Stick with it." Gary didn't look very tough. Wan, in fact. His eye showed the effect of all those drugs wearing off. He was trying to be brave, but just said, "Cool," like it wasn't that easy anymore to get the words out, and they shook hands. Gary squeezed real hard, and Stanger put his arm around his shoulder, and Gary moved the hand that was loose in the straps to touch Ron's arm. Stanger kept thinking that Gilmore's hands were skinnier than you'd think they'd be. And they looked in each other's eyes, kind of a final embrace.

⊷   ⊷   ⊷

As soon as Ron returned to his position behind the line, a prison official came up to ask if he wanted cotton for his ears. Then Ron noticed that everybody was taking cotton, so he stuffed some into his head, and watched Sam Smith walk over to the back of the room where a red telephone was on a chair. Then Sam Smith made a phone call, and walked back and came up to Gary and started to read a declaration.

⊷   ⊷   ⊷

Schiller, trying to listen, decided it was some official document. Not the sort, by the sound of it, that he would listen to normally but, through the cotton he could hear Sam Smith going blah, blah, blah. All the while, Gary was not looking at the Warden, but rather, leaning in his chair from side to side in order to stare around the large body of Sam Smith, practically tipping that chair over trying to see the faces behind the executioner's blind, catch a glint of their expression.

⊷   ⊷   ⊷

Then the Warden said, "Do you have anything you'd like to say?" and Gary looked up at the ceiling and hesitated, then said, "Let's do it." That was it. The most pronounced amount of courage, Vern decided, he'd ever seen, no quaver, no throatiness, right down the line. Gary had looked at Vern as he spoke.

⊷   ⊷   ⊷

The way Stanger heard it, it came out like Gary wanted to say something good and dignified and clever, but couldn't think of anything profound. The drugs had left him too dead. Rather than say nothing, he did his best to say it very clear, "Let's do it."

⊷   ⊷   ⊷

That was about what you'd expect of a man who'd been up for more than twenty-four hours and had taken everything and now was hung over, and coming down, and looking older than Ron had ever seen him. Ah, he was drained out. Ron could see deep lines in his face for the first time. Gilmore looked as white as the day the lawyers first met him after the suicide attempt.

⊷   ⊷   ⊷

Father Meersman walked up to give the last rites, and Noall Wootton braced himself and took a peep between the shoulders of some of the big men in front of him, and remembered Gary when he had come to the Board of Pardons Hearing, very confident that day, like he was holding all the cards, the ace and everything else you might need. Now, in Wootton's opinion, he didn't have it.

⊷   ⊷   ⊷

And Schiller, looking at the same man, thought he was resigned in his appearance, but with presence, and what you could call a certain authority.

⊷   ⊷   ⊷

Father Meersman finished giving Gary Gilmore the last rites. As they came forward with the hood, Gilmore said to him, "Dominus vobiscum." Father Meersman didn't know how to describe his emotion. Gary couldn't have said anything that brought back more of an automatic response. This was the greeting Father Meersman had given to the people again and again over the ten years and twenty and thirty since he had become a priest. "Dominus vobiscum," he would say at Mass and the response would come back, "Et cum spiritu tuo."

So now, when Gilmore said Dominus vobiscum, Father Meersman answered like an altar boy, "Et cum spiritu tuo," and as the words came out of his mouth, Gary kind of grinned and said, "There'll always be a Meersman."

❧ ❧ ❧

"He wants to say," said Father Meersman to himself, "that there will always be a priest present at a time like this."

❧ ❧ ❧

Three or four men in red coats came up and put the hood on Gilmore's head. Nothing was said after that.

❧ ❧ ❧

Absolutely nothing said. They put a waist strap on Gilmore, and a head strap, and Father Meersman began to think of how when they were first strapping him in the chair, Gilmore had wanted water and Father Meersman had given him water for the throat that was too dry. Then he had wanted another drink.

❧ ❧ ❧

Now, the doctor was beside him, pinning a white circle on Gilmore's black shirt, and the doctor stepped back. Father Meersman traced the big sign of the cross, the last act he had to perform. Then, he, too, stepped over the line, and turned around, and looked back at the hooded figure in the chair. The phone began to ring.

❧ ❧ ❧

Noall Wootton's first reaction was, God, it's just like in the movies, it isn't going to happen. Schiller was taking notes on the checks he'd been careful to remove from the checkbook holder, and he noted that the hood came down loosely like a square carton over Gary's head. Not form fitting in any way. You could not have a sense of his features beneath the sack.

❧ ❧ ❧

Stanger, listening to the phone, thought, "It is a final confirmation of some kind." Then Sam Smith hung up, and walked back to his place behind the line, and it happened to be next to Schiller. He handed Larry more cotton and they looked into each other's eyes. Then, Schiller didn't know if Sam Smith made a movement with his arm, or didn't, but he felt as if he saw something in the Warden's shoulder move, and Ron and Bob Moody and Cline Campbell heard a countdown begin, and Noall Wootton put his fingers in his ears on top of the cotton, and Gary's body looked calm to Campbell. Cline could not believe the calm he saw in that man. Gilmore was so strong in his desire to die right, that he didn't clench his fist as the count began.

❧ ❧ ❧

Stanger said to himself, "I hope I don't fall down." He had his hand up to protect his head somehow. Right through the cotton, he heard the sound of heavy breathing and saw the barrels of the rifles projecting from the slits of the blind. He was shocked at how close those muzzles were to the victim. They sure didn't want to miss. Then it all got so quiet your attention was called to it. Right through the cotton, Ron heard these whispers, "One," and "Two," and they never got to say, "Three" before the guns went, "Bam. Bam. Bam." So loud it was terrifying. A muscle contracted from Ron's shoulder down to his lower back. Some entire school of muscles in a spasm.

⋆ ⋆ ⋆

Schiller heard three shots, expecting four. Gary's body did not jerk nor the chair move, and Schiller waited for the fourth shot and found out later that two must have come out simultaneously. Noall Wootton tried to look at Gary at that point, but couldn't see anything from the rear of the crowd and went out the door before anyone else, and straight to his car which was up by Minimum Security, got in it, drove out. There were reporters interviewing people and photographers, but he didn't stop. He didn't want to talk to anybody.

7

Vern just heard a great big *WHAM!* When it happened, Gary never raised a finger. Didn't quiver at all. His left hand never moved, and then, after he was shot, his head went forward, but the strap held his head up, and then the right hand slowly rose in the air and slowly went down as if to say, "That did it, gentlemen." Schiller thought the movement was as delicate as the fingers of a pianist raising his hand before he puts it down on the keys. The blood started to flow through the black shirt and came out onto the white pants and started to drop on the floor between Gary's legs, and the smell of gunpowder was everywhere. Then, the lights went down, and Schiller listened to the blood drip. He was not certain he could hear it drip, but he felt it, and with that blood, the life in Gilmore's body seemed to lift off him like smoke. Ron Stanger, feeling dizzy, said to himself, "You're the only one that's going to pass out, and it will be embarrassing to end on the ground with all these people here," and he staggered backward from the force of the contraction in his back, put his arms out, grabbed hold of somebody to steady himself, and turned back to get another look at the body. That was when he saw Gilmore's right hand lift.

⋆ ⋆ ⋆

Ron closed his eyes and when he opened them again, the blood was a pool in Gary's lap, running to his feet and covering his tennis shoes, those crazy red, white and blue tennis shoes he always wore in Maximum. The shoelaces were now blooded over.

⋆ ⋆ ⋆

A doctor came along with a stethoscope and shook his head. Gilmore wasn't dead yet.

⋆ ⋆ ⋆

Ron thought of the day when Gary was in Fagan's office for a moment, and in that ten seconds Gary was all over his desk like a butterfly. He opened the desk drawer and took out a spoon, and shoelaces, went through everything like a guy leading an orchestra. It was beautiful. Gilmore was a *talented* thief, after all, and finished just as Fagan said, "Yeah, okay, Joe." By the time the Lieutenant turned around, old Gary was sitting there calm as a nodding owl, and Stanger on the other side of the glass had his eyes wide open.

⋄ ⋄ ⋄

Gary made jokes about the shoelaces after that. They were good enough to hang himself by, he would tell Ron, and now the hand that had done the stealing moved up in the air and came down. It could have been pointing at the blood on the shoelaces.

⋄ ⋄ ⋄

They waited about twenty seconds. Then the doctor went up again, and Father Meersman came up, and Sam Smith, and the doctor put the stethoscope to Gary's arm once more, turned to Sam, and nodded. Sam Smith unloosened the waist strap, slid Gilmore out from underneath the head strap, and looked behind the body at the shot pattern where the holes came through.

Stanger was furious. The moment Gilmore was shot, everybody should have been walked out, and not served for a party to all this. Even as Sam was examining the body, Gary fell over into Meersman's hands. The padre had to hold the head while Sam went fishing all over Gilmore's back to locate the exit wounds. Blood started coming onto Meersman's hands, and dripped through his fingers, and Vern began to weep. Then Father Meersman wept. An officer finally came around and said to the people standing behind the line. "Time for you to leave." Schiller walked out saying to himself. "What have we accomplished? There aren't going to be less murders."

⋄ ⋄ ⋄

All the while Father Meersman and Cline Campbell were unbuckling Gilmore's arms and legs. Campbell kept thinking of the importance of the eyes. He said to himself. "Why doesn't somebody move? We've got to save the eyes."

8

Over at the Warden's office, just a few minutes earlier. Gordon Richards had received a phone call from an Assistant Clerk in the U.S. Supreme Court, who was saying that the full Court—with Justice Brennan not participating—had just acted on the application for a Stay from the ACLU and had denied it. Richards got a little upset. This Clerk who was named Peter Beck had been told nothing about "Mickey from Wheeling, West Virginia." Well, did Mr. Beck know, Richards asked, where Mr. Rodak was born and what his nickname was? "Is it Mike?" said Beck. Richards then asked if Mr. Rodak could call him. Before he knew it, he got put on hold. "Hurry, please," Richards called out to Beck, "it's crucial." There he was sitting with unconfirmed information from the Supreme Court. So he called out to the prison officials there with him in the Warden's office. "Tell them to hold at the cannery." The officials shook their heads, however. The execution had just been carried out.

⋄ ⋄ ⋄

Three minutes later, Rodak came on the line. Richards asked for his nickname and his birthplace. The nickname was Mickey, he said, but he had been born in Smock, Pennsylvania.

"What about West Virginia?" asked Richards. "I was born in Smock," said Rodak, "but I went to West Virginia. I'm a member of the West Virginia Bar."

Had he offered this information to Earl Dorius? asked Richards. Didn't think so, said

Rodak. Finally, he remembered. "Oh, yes, the fellow wanted to make sure that he didn't get any false telephone calls." Right. "Is," asked Rodak, "the execution over yet?"

"Wouldn't it have been horrible," said Richards to one of the officials, as he hung up, "if that had been simultaneous calls?"

9

Vern, Bob Moody, Ron Stanger, and Larry Schiller got into a car and drove over to the Administration Building. During that minute, they discussed whether or not to issue a press statement ahead of the Warden.

﹡   ﹡   ﹡

Stanger said, "I think we ought to. What do you say, Larry?" Schiller replied, "We have no obligation. The first person who gets there is the first person the press will talk to," and Stanger said, "Let's beat the Warden to the punch."

Vern said, "Can you answer questions about the execution, Larry? I don't want to talk about that."

﹡   ﹡   ﹡

The press conference was being held on the second floor of the Administration Building in a large conference chamber that looked like a courtroom. It was already as crowded as the Board of Pardons Hearing, same bedlam of media, cameras and crazy white light, people pushing to get in, close to 100 degrees inside. No room to breathe.

﹡   ﹡   ﹡

Trying to get upstairs, they were buffeted every way. Some TV guy was working with a couple of electric cables in front of Bob Moody, and got so rude about letting Moody pass that Bob just grabbed a male-female connection crossing his path and yanked it apart. The TV man cried out, "My God, I've lost power, lost power," as Moody went by.

﹡   ﹡   ﹡

When they reached the stage, Schiller said to Vern, "Why don't you talk first?" and Vern sat on a chair to rest his aching leg.

He did not speak long. "It was very upsetting to me," Vern said, "but he got his wish, he did die . . . and he died in dignity. That's all I have to say."

﹡   ﹡   ﹡

Bob Moody told them. "I think it's a very brutal, cruel kind of a thing, that I would only hope that we could take a good and better look at ourselves, our society and our systems. Thank you."

Ron said, "He was always trying to keep the spirit light because he made the statement he had received a gift, and that gift was he knew he was going to die, and he could make the arrangements and, therefore, he was indeed fortunate. He always said that he looked forward to the time when he could have quiet, when he could meditate, and today, Gary Gilmore has quiet, and he has quiet through eternity."

﹡   ﹡   ﹡

Schiller said, "I'm not here to express any of my personal feelings, but after Vern has left, I'll be more than glad to relate any of the facts anybody here would like to know. I don't think it would be proper to relay them in Vern's presence, but I will answer your questions then." He threw a look around the room and the only smile that came back was from David Johnston of the *L.A. Times* and the Orem TraveLodge. Then Gus Sorensen gave a wink.

ANNOUNCER FOR THE TV POOL

Leaving the platform now are Ron Stanger and Robert Moody, two attorneys who have helped Gary Gilmore in the last couple of months to get the wish that he said he wanted at that time, that he wanted to die, these men helped to see that he got there. Also leaving, Vern Damico, Gilmore's uncle from Provo, Utah, the man who took Gilmore in after he was paroled from a prison. And now, Lawrence Schiller, a literary agent/film-maker who's been involved in this case for some time.

           ❧   ❧   ❧

Dave Johnston, watching Schiller, decided to give points to the guy's cool. Here, at this press conference with everybody hating his guts for tieing up the story, Schiller was still doing a real reporter's job. His adrenalin had to be high enough to make his frame shake, thought Johnston, yet not a quiver was showing.

           ❧   ❧   ❧

Schiller spoke of the yellow line and the black hood and the black T-shirt Gary was wearing and the white pants, and the shots. ". . . Slowly, red blood emerged from under the black T-shirt and onto the white slacks. It seemed to me that his body still had a movement, for approximately fifteen to twenty seconds, it is not for me to determine whether it was an after-death or prior-to-death movement. The minister and the doctor proceeded towards Gary," Schiller said, and kept on speaking in slow, clear sentences, trying to make the note-taking easy for tired reporters.
    Then it was Sam Smith's turn.

SAM SMITH: I have no formal statement. I think Mr. Schiller pretty well covered the detail. I will respond to questions.
    QUESTION: What was the official time, Warden?
    SAM SMITH: The official time was 8:07.
    QUESTION: How did you give the signal?
    SAM SMITH: I didn't really give the signal. I indicated all was in readiness.
    QUESTION: How did you do that?
    SAM SMITH: Just by a motion.
    QUESTION: Was there a squad leader?
    SAM SMITH: Yes, there was.
    QUESTION: Did the squad leader give the signal?
    SAM SMITH: What happened inside of there. I have no knowledge.
    QUESTION: Who were the forty people present?

SAM SMITH: Well, I didn't count the same as Mr. Schiller.

QUESTION: But you disagree with his figure of forty, though, Warden?

SAM SMITH: Yes, I would definitely disagree with that figure.

QUESTION: How many were there?

SAM SMITH: Less.

QUESTION: Thirty? Twenty?

SAM SMITH: I wouldn't give you an exact number.

QUESTION: Warden, can we inspect the site now?

SAM SMITH: As soon as we find out that everything is clear and that we can handle the traffic.

When Sam Smith stepped off, Johnston went up to Schiller and said, "You amaze me. You really are a journalist."

Schiller got a glint in his eye. Johnston could see the compliment go all the way in. "Yes, it was swell," said Johnston, "but why did you give it all away?" Larry cocked his head, and got a sly grin like a big German shepherd who is lolling its tongue. He said. "I didn't give away anything that mattered."

But he couldn't keep it in. "Gilmore's last words," Schiller confessed, "were not what I said they were."

Johnston laughed. He had a feeling there was more to the story. "Larry, there are some," he said, "who might look on that as a lie."

"No," said Schiller, "'Let's do it' was the last thing everybody heard."

Johnston said to himself, "This is one secret he'll have to tell. He's like a kid who'll have to tell one person anyway."

"Well," said Larry, and swore him to secrecy, "Gary spoke in Latin to the priest."

"He did? What were his words?"

"If I knew them, I couldn't pronounce them," said Schiller, and gave his sly grin again. "But I'll find out."

⭒   ⭒   ⭒

They drove over together to the execution site. When they got inside the cannery, Schiller couldn't believe what he now saw. His description of the events had been accurate in every way but one. He had gotten the colors wrong. The black cloth of the blind was not black but blue, the line on the floor was not yellow but white, and the chair was not black, but dark green. He realized that during the execution something had altered in his perception of color.

⭒   ⭒   ⭒

He left the place of execution a second time with a memory of reporters swarming over the chair, the sandbags and the holes in the mattress, creatures of an identical species feeding, all feeding, in the same place. As he went out the door, one man was explaining to another that steel-jacketed bullets had been used so they would make no larger hole in the rear than in the front, which would avoid, thereby, the worst of the mess, and the body jumping from the impact.

Mikal Gilmore

from Shot in the Heart

LAST WORDS

In the first week of January, Anthony Amsterdam, negotiating through Gary's attorneys—Robert Moody and Ronald Stanger—and prison officials, arranged for me and my brother Frank to visit Gary. My mother's physical condition prohibited her traveling. Richard Giauque, a Salt Lake City attorney who had acted on Amsterdam's and the family's behalf in Utah, was to meet us at the airport. As far as we knew, it was a "one time only, no physical contact" visit.

On Tuesday morning, January 11, Frank and I caught a plane into Salt Lake. We tried talking for a while on the flight, but after a bit my brother lapsed into a brooding silence. I could tell he was in deep pain over what would be facing us.

His silence gave me a chance to think about some things I hadn't wanted to think about. I was heading into Utah to confront a man, a blood relative, whom I had never really known, and whom I now had a bitter relationship with. I could tell myself we were very different people—I *had* told myself that for years—and in certain ways, that was true. Gary was a killer, I was not. But in truth, on this day we were both monsters, each determined to get his own way, despite what would likely be mortal consequences for others.

I was prepared and willing to do whatever was necessary to stop Gary's execution. I could tell myself I was doing this for good moral purposes—I did not believe in the death penalty, and certainly Gary's execution would hasten its return—but I had other reasons that were less generous. I did not want Gary to die this way because I did not want his death to ruin my life or what remained of the lives of my family. I did not want to live with the ruin and stigma of being a brother to the man who had brought capital punishment back to America. I had rights to my own hopes, I told myself, and those hopes could never come to be, as long as I was a blood relation to such shame and infamy. I already knew that part of the world would judge me for Gary's actions, and I did not want to share his condemnation. I still had my whole life ahead of me.

To get my way, to win this battle, I would have to impose my will on the situation and on my brother. I would have to take legal action that might forestall his execution, maybe even for years. I knew that if I did so, I would be robbing him of this strange moment he had seized in history. Worse, I would likely be condemning him to another form of suffering—a waiting for a slower death, within the hell of prison—and despite the horrible things Gary had done, I had little doubt that he had suffered much in recent months and that his waiting for the moment of his death could not be an easy thing. But if I didn't make Gary suffer, then the rest of us would have to. I would have to be with my mother and see the look on her face when we heard the news that the execution had been carried out. More than anything else, I did not want to see my mother go through that moment.

Even though I was hoping to save my brother's life in the course of this visit (And what the hell did *that* mean? How could you save the life of a man whose soul was already lost?), I did not feel in any sense like a good person on this morning. In fact, I would never again feel like a good person. That possibility, much less that certainty, got left somewhere up there in the sky during that flight. When the plane landed, I was in a place where people decided who would live and who would have to die. It was both a physical and spiritual place, and it was a place I'd been the drama we had been assigned to play.

Once you arrived at such a place, the stain of blood would wash upon your hands and would never be cleansed or forgotten.

No, I was not a good person and I never could be again. The momentum of my blood history had taken that possibility away from me.

-⊕-   -⊕-   -⊕-

When we arrived in Salt Lake City, Richard Giauque met us at the airport with a Rolls-Royce. He apologized immediately for its "gaudiness"—he'd had to borrow his law partner's car at the last minute, he said. En route to Draper, Giauque explained that it was possible to achieve a stay until the constitutionality of Utah's death penalty had been determined.

Draper Prison is located at a place in the Salt Lake Valley known as the "Point of the Mountain." Because of the heavy pollution in the valley, one doesn't even become aware of the mountains until the final, winding approach to the prison. It rests at the center of a flat basin, surrounded by tall, sharply-inclined snowy slopes. It is perhaps the most beautiful vista in the entire valley.

The car had to stop at a central tower, where a guard gave us clearance to drive down the narrow road to maximum security, a small building surrounded by another tower and two barbed-wire fences. We were told we would be allowed a ninety-minute, uninterrupted visit. Gary was still under maximum restrictions at this point and technically wasn't even allowed visitors, except for his attorneys. This family visit was an "exception." We were led into an open triangular room where no guards were present and informed that we would be allowed a physical contact visit.

Gary strolled in through sliding doors dressed in prison whites and red, white, and blue sneakers, twirling a comb and smiling broadly. For so long, I'd seen only the grim, cold-looking photos and film clips that I'd forgotten how charming he could be. "You're looking as fit as ever," he said to Frank, and to me: "And you're just as damn skinny as ever."

He rearranged the benches in front of the guard-room window. "So those poor fools can keep an eye on me," he said.

For the first few minutes we exchanged small talk, trying to get comfortable with the surroundings and to approach the inevitable subject. Gary's face narrowed as we mentioned the decision of Robert Excell White—a condemned man in Texas whose request for execution had occurred at about the same time as Gary's—to fight for his life. He shrugged. "Yeah, I guess you could say he equivocated. Well, that has nothing to do with me. You see, for a while I felt guilty about this whole capital punishment thing, and that's partially why I tried to kill myself. But I'm tired of everybody pinning that on me. I don't care what happens to all these rapists and torturers. They can take them out and shoot them tomorrow. What happens to me won't affect them; their cases will be judged on their own merits."

I broached the prospect of intervention, but Gary cut it off right away. "Look, I don't want anybody interfering, no outside causes, no lawyers like Amsterdam." He reached out and took hold of my chin, staring me in the eyes. "He's out of this, I hope." Before I had a chance to reply, the visitors' door rolled open and in walked Uncle Vernon and Aunt Ida. We had been assured a private visit. As far as I knew, this was our only time with Gary, and here we were, fifteen minutes into what we expected to be our last conversation with our brother, and in walk Uncle Vernon and Aunt Ida, like it's old folks' week. Uncle Vernon and Aunt Ida, who stood to be richer than they had ever been before if Gary would just sit down in a large wooden chair one week from now and allow five strangers to pump bullets into his heart.

That Vernon and Ida—our uncle, our aunt. I was so furious, I wanted to rip the cheery, familial smiles off their fucking faces and turn them upside down.

The rest of the visit was aggravating. Gary and Vernon did most of the talking, discussing numerous people Gary wanted to leave some money to and cracking an occasional macabre joke. Vernon had brought along a bag of green T-shirts adorned with the legend GILMORE—DEATH WISH and a computerized photo of Gary. Apparently the shirts had been ordered by either Gary or Vernon. They talked about the possibility of Gary wearing one on the execution morning, and then auctioning it off to the highest bidder. I felt bilious. After the ninety minutes, the visit was terminated.

As we were leaving, Gary offered me a T-shirt. "I'm not sure it would be of much use to me, Gary."

"Well," he drawled, smiling, "it's a little big for you, but I think you can grow into it." I accepted the shirt.

"Is there anything I can do for you while you're in town?" Vernon asked. I replied that I wanted him to arrange a meeting with Gary's attorneys, Ron Stanger and Moody, and with Larry Schiller.

Back in Salt Lake City, I decided to stay for a couple of days and attempt to visit Gary on my own. At Giauque's office, I told him of my ambivalence over the situation—how, on one hand, I was firmly opposed to capital punishment, no matter the crime or the wishes of the condemned, but also how I felt it was important not to take any action without giving Gary fair warning—that I wasn't prepared to save Gary's life when it might only result in providing the impetus for a final suicide attempt.

I asked Giauque if he could tell me the names of some of the journalists who were in town covering this affair. I thought that a well-connected reporter might be able to apprise me of what was going on behind the scenes in this complex situation. Most of the names he mentioned—journalists like Geraldo Rivera—were people I had no interest in talking to. Then he mentioned Bill Moyers, the former press aide to President Lyndon B. Johnson, and a writer and journalist I had much respect for.

"Can you put me together with Moyers?" I asked.

A couple of hours later I was having dinner and a much-needed drink or two with Moyers at his hotel. He clearly had some misgivings about the moral dimensions of covering this story, and he was not glad to see the death penalty returning to America. He agreed to talk with me and tell me what he knew, and he assured me that he would never use any of the information I gave him in his reporting unless he cleared it with me. He told me that I should be cautious about the advice that any legal, business, or journalistic people might give me in the days ahead—that instead, I should try to come to terms with my own conscience and try to reconcile that with the communications that would go on between me and Gary. Even now, all these years later, I remain certain that Bill Moyers's gentle concern was a key influence in helping me hold on to my sanity during that week.

⋆ ⋆ ⋆

At nine o'clock that night I called Vernon to ask if any arrangements had been made for a meeting with Moody and Stanger. The lawyers were unavailable at the time, but Schiller was flying in from Los Angeles and was willing to meet me at the Salt Lake Hilton at one in the morning. I was a little drunk and in need of sleep, but I didn't want to pass up a meeting with Gary's keeper.

At the Hilton, I recognized Schiller from his picture in the December 20th *New West* article, "The Merchandising of Gary Gilmore," by Barry Farrell (who later became one of Schiller's researchers and collaborators); he recognized me because of my resemblance to Gary. I had wanted to meet Schiller—who had something of a reputation as a death-minded entrepreneur for his interviews for Albert Goldman's infamous Lenny Bruce biography, and for his handling of projects and stories involving Marilyn Monroe, Jack Ruby, and Sharon Tate murderer Susan Atkins—because it occurred to me that he might be trying to exploit this execution for his own ends. Also, I realized that to deal with Gary at this stage, I would also have to deal with the man who owned Gary's story.

Schiller and I talked for nearly two hours. Each of us asked pointed questions about what we were doing in Utah and about our interests in Gary. I spoke frankly of my concerns about Gary's choices and their possible ramifications, and Schiller responded sympathetically to those concerns, but stopped short of professing to share them. Finally I asked Schiller what I considered an inescapable question: Was Gary worth more to him dead than alive?

Schiller hesitated for a few moments, then said: "Many years ago, when I was working as a news photographer, I was sent out to cover a fire. There were firemen carrying a person through a window, and I had to ask myself whether I should take a picture of that moment, or put down my camera and go help them drag that person to safety. I chose to take the picture. I decided then it was my obligation as a journalist to preserve what existed.

"To answer your question, I'm here to record history, not to make it."

At the end of the session, Schiller had impressed me with his forth-rightness. Also, I trusted his intentions toward the Bushnell and Jensen families, and felt I could believe him when he promised to keep our conversations confidential. He drove me back to my hotel and, as I was getting out of his rental car, he made a curious comment.

"What's your middle name?" he asked. I told him. He jotted it down in a notebook and then wrote out a phone number and handed it to me. "This is where you can leave a message for me if you need to get in touch and can't find me at either the Hilton or the Travelodge in Orem. But just use your middle name and not your last. That's Stranger's office and you shouldn't tip him off about where you're staying. Gary doesn't have the best attorneys in town, but then I didn't choose them."

❖ ❖ ❖

I tried to call Frank at his hotel the next afternoon, but he had checked out. I called my mother back in Oregon to see if Frank had headed home, but as far as she knew, he was still in the Salt Lake area. This time, I would have to see Gary alone.

When I was signing the visitors log at Draper, I noticed that Moody and Stanger had signed in just before me. I glanced over to the phone cubicle and could see them talking to Gary. I explained to the officer in charge that I wanted to speak with my brother privately. He said he would do his best, and let me in the same triangular room I'd been in the day before. I sat in the far corner, away from the phone cage. Moments later a guard came in and told Stanger that the watch commander wanted to see him for a minute. After Stanger disappeared through the rolling bars, Moody asked Gary how the family visit had been. I couldn't hear my brother's reply. "Listen, Gary," Moody continued, "Schiller met with your brother late last night at the Hilton. He thinks Mikal might try to stop the execution."

I couldn't believe what I was hearing. I moved over to the bench next to the cage. "Did you know that Giauque brought your brothers out here in a Rolls-Royce yesterday?" I couldn't hear the next sentence but it included a mention of the hotel where I was registered.

The guard reentered. "Mr. Moody, will you come with me for a minute?" As he got up to leave, Moody glanced at me, then did a double take. "Who is that?" I heard him ask, farther down the corridor. I had to wait about thirty minutes before Gary came in, spinning a Scotsman's cap on his finger and wearing a black sleeveless sweatshirt. Stanger and Moody were standing behind him. Gary introduced us. "Sorry we have to meet under these circumstances," said Stanger, "but if there's anything we can do for you, just give us a call." I nodded.

"Uh, I'm glad you came back," said Gary, after Moody and Stanger had left. Gary took a seat on the back of the bench.

"Gary, I don't want to play any games with you. I overheard what your lawyers said and, yes, it's true. I did meet with Schiller last night. I am thinking of seeking a stay."

The smile on Gary's face fell away; in its place I saw the stern stare I'd come to know from newspaper and magazine photos. "Is it true that Giauque brought you out here in a Rolls-Royce yesterday?" Schiller had asked me the same question the night before. The Rolls had become a symbol of powerful, outside intervention, I surmised, yet it seemed so trivial. I explained the situation to Gary. He spoke angrily: "Amsterdam and Giauque are cumsucking nigger-fuckers who are just trying to use you for some cause. Why do they want to meddle with my life? Because they're opposed to capital punishment? Does that make them special, or holy men? I was given a sentence to die. Now is that some kind of joke? I don't want that over my head."

I decided to avoid a discussion of legal ethics or lawyers. "If you want to believe all that shit about Giauque and Amsterdam, then go ahead," I replied, "but it doesn't have anything to do with you and me. I could take action independently that might achieve a stay, that could result in a commutation of your sentence."

Gary shook his head. "That's impossible," he declared. "I couldn't even stop this thing if I wanted to." He paused for several moments. "Could you really do that?"

I replied that I believed I could. Gary stood up and started to walk around the room.

"They'd never let me free, man, and I've spent too much time in jail. I don't have anything left to me." He came face to face. "I killed two men. I don't want to spend the rest of my life in jail. If some fucker gets me set free, then I'm going to go get a gun and kill a few of those damn lawyers who keep interfering. Then I'll say to you, 'See what your meddling accomplished? Are you proud?'"

"Time's up," announced a voice from the guard's nest.

Gary tried to flash a relaxed-looking smile. "Come back and talk to me some more about this tomorrow," he said. As I was passing through the door, he called: "Where were you ten years ago when I needed you?" All the way back to Salt Lake those final words reverberated in my head. I felt confused and broken. An hour earlier, I thought that the only right decision was to argue for a stay, to choose life over death. But I couldn't make that choice for Gary. I wanted to disappear, to fold up into a void where choices and conscience didn't exist. Where I could forget the look in Gary's eyes.

ᛏ   ᛏ   ᛏ

That night I had dinner with Moyers again. I told him about my conversation with Gary. After listening, Moyers asked me if I thought there was any chance he might be able to visit and speak with Gary. I told him that Schiller had an exclusive deal with my brother, and that no other journalists could talk to him. Moyers said he was willing to assure me and Gary and Schiller that he would not use the conversation for journalistic purposes. He did not want to tape it or film it, and unless he had the appropriate consent of those involved, he would not disclose the contents of the conversation in his report. He just thought that, since both he and Gary were men who had been born in Texas, they might have some common ground for talking. He also thought he might have a philosophical view or two to offer about Gary's situation that my brother might find interesting, maybe even persuasive. I trusted Moyers and told him I would see what could be done.

I went on a long walk around the cold, snow-covered streets of Salt Lake that night. I was walking over by the Mormon Temple when I ran into Frank. At first he didn't see me. He was going along with his hands jammed into his pockets, staring at the ground. I called his name.

I told him I'd been to see Gary, and I told him what we had discussed. I also said that Frank could go back and visit with Gary some more himself, either with or without me. Apparently the prison's stipulation of a one-time visit had been forgotten.

"No," said Frank, "I can't do that. I can't go see him again." And then, as the tears began to fall from his eyes, my brother turned and walked off into the cold night.

Fifteen years later, Frank and I visited Salt Lake together, to try to reestablish some family contacts and to make sense of some of what had happened all those years before. One afternoon, Frank took me over to Liberty Park. It was here, when we were all children and were living with my parents in the haunted house in Salt Lake, that Frank and Gary used to come nearly every afternoon to play. They would run around, play ball, pull pranks on the stodgy Mormons. Frank thought it was maybe the happiest hours the two of them ever spent together. All this was just before Gary began stealing things and hiding them in the garage—before he changed forever into a bad boy.

As we sat there in the park that day, Frank explained to me why he had decided, those years before, not to visit Gary anymore at Draper. After seeing him that one time, Frank said, he came to this park and sat where we were now sitting, and he gave some long thought to what had happened, and what would yet happen.

"I hated what Gary had done," Frank said to me. "What he did was hideous. But I also hate what had been done to him.

"Do you think if Gary hadn't been in prison for twenty-two years, he would have shot that one man in the back of the head in front of his pregnant wife and little kid? What about the other guy? He shot him in the gas station and they say he didn't die for hours. That's the story I heard. That he didn't die for hours and he suffered, suffered to death. I am convinced that the twenty-two years of training that Gary got from the animalistic prison society he had lived in turned him into the animal that brought on those tragedies.

"He'd seen things in prison. He told me about those things. He had seen people maimed—he saw a man get his hands cut off—and he had seen men murdered. He'd seen so fucking many assaults, and when he was younger, he himself had been assaulted. Beaten. Raped. Terrorized. But he learned to go with it. As he got older and bigger and meaner, he became the assaulter. After that, they had nothing they could scare him with. It was like being in Vietnam for twenty-two years. He'd been the victim and the victimizer of so many hideous things. He could say, 'Yes, I've been destroyed, but now I'm the one who does the destroying.'

"You'll find thousands and thousands of men in this country that lived a similar life, and many of those men would probably make the same kinds of choices as Gary—the same ways of killing and dying. All those years in the horror and brutality of prison changes them. They reach a point of no return. They sort of live a day at a time, and to them, after a while, death starts to look like a way out of life, which is what it is—a way out of everything. They're afraid of almost everything but dying, some of those guys. And they become really dangerous. You can't lock them up, because that's home to them. You can't kill them, because they want that. They are your truly dangerous people, and there are thousands of them in this country walking around, because of our jails and prisons, who are exactly like Gary. Take some kid that has problems—maybe emotional problems, maybe family problems—put him in these outrageous horror house reformatories and prisons, and chances are, eventually, that kid will become like our brother.

"Gary had reached that point of no return. He wanted the release of death. That's one reason I didn't go back and visit him again. I knew he really wanted it, and it bothered me. Not only did he want it, it was like it was a holiday. He was celebrating. He was trying to be set free. It was his exodus.

"That last time I saw him—he was so different from the brooding man I visited throughout the years. This time, he sat there and he was snapping his fingers, he was laughing and he was making jokes. It was like Christmas Eve. He had found the perfect way to beat the system by having them kill him. Then he's out of it. It's over. In his way of thinking, I'm convinced he believed he had won. Most of us couldn't win the way he did. But that was his idea of freedom, and, of course, it was the only freedom he had left. That's the reason I stood back. I know you and Mom wanted to save him, and I never held that against the two of you. But I had to stand back because if I had gone on and done something, if they had kept him locked up in that hell, I would have felt to blame for it.

"I don't think I slept two minutes that night, after seeing him. I knew I wasn't going back anymore. I couldn't watch him suffer, and I couldn't watch him die. I sat here in the park that day and I thought: 'I don't want to see him again. I'm going to try to keep him in my heart and mind as that boy I used to play with here—the little brother that I loved, before he got ruined.' The only thing that bothers me about my decision is, I don't think Gary knew that I actually liked him. I don't think he ever knew in his life that I actually did care about him, that I really felt for him. But there was nothing more that could be done for him. It was all over for Gary. He had no chance. And I think that's what he was trying to tell you."

⋅๏⋅ ⋅๏⋅ ⋅๏⋅

The morning after I had run into Frank on the street, I phoned Schiller in Orem. I told him of the remarks I heard Moody make and expressed my disappointment in having any portion of what I'd understood to be a confidential conversation relayed to others.

"I didn't tell Moody or Stanger of our conversation," he replied.

"Who did?"

"Well, I told your Uncle Vernon a couple of things, but just because I assumed he was your main contact here and you would want to stay in touch with him. Now he may have passed some of that along to Moody or Stanger, but anything else you heard was projection on their part." He apologized if he had violated my trust and then offered me some final advice: "Don't call the prison before going out. Information gets passed out of there pretty easily, and a lot of people, including myself, know the minute you enter that maximum-security compound."

After making a couple of calls, though, I learned that visits had to be authorized in advance. I made arrangements for a late-afternoon visit, then sat down and wrote Gary a long letter. It was easy to forget what I wanted to say to him when I was face to face with him and his anger. I wrote him that whatever choice I made, it was a matter of love, an issue between him and me, and not the courts or the newspapers. I told him that I thought redemption was more possible in the choice of life over death, and confessed that for years he'd frightened and confused me because of his violent whims. If time enough existed, I wanted to lift that barrier.

That afternoon at the prison was the first day Gary was officially authorized to have visitors, which meant, ironically, I had to talk to him over the phone. After looking through my letter, a guard gave it to Gary. He read it quietly, pensively. When he was finished he managed a smile. "Well put," he said. "Are you familiar with Nietzsche? He once wrote that a time comes when a man should rise to meet the occasion. That's what I'm trying to do, Mikal . . . Look," he said, suddenly changing the subject, "I was thinking about what I said yesterday, about 'where were you.' I realized that was unfair. I wasn't around much when you were a kid. I don't hate you, although I've tried to act that way lately. You're my brother. I know what that means. I've been angry with you, but I've never hated you."

I forced myself to ask the question I'd been building up to for the last few days: "What would you do if I tried to stop this?"

He winced. "I don't want you to do that," he said evenly.

"That doesn't answer my question."

"Please don't."

"Gary, what would you do? All you've said is that you wanted the sentence of the court carried out. What if that sentence were commuted?"

"I'd kill myself. Look, I'm not watched that closely in this place, no matter what you hear. I could've killed myself any time in the last two weeks, but I don't want to do that. You see, I want some good to come from all this. If I commit suicide, then I can't be a donor—to people who have more right to life than I do—and my whole will could become suspect . . . Besides, if a person's dumb enough to murder and get caught, then, he shouldn't snivel about what he gets."

From there, Gary talked about prison reality, telling me some of the brutality he had witnessed and some that he had fostered. He was terrified of a life in prison, he said. "Maybe you could have my sentence commuted, but you wouldn't have to live that sentence or be around when I killed myself." The fear in his eyes was always most discernible when he spoke about prison, far more than when he spoke about his own impending death. Maybe because one was an ever-present concrete reality and the other an abstraction. "I don't think death will be anything new or frightening for me. I think I've been there before."

We talked for hours, or rather Gary talked. I'd already missed a flight back home and had forgotten about the person waiting out in the parking lot for me. This was the first real communication we'd shared in years; neither of us wanted to let go. Gary asked me to return the next day and, in turn, I asked if he would be willing to meet with Bill Moyers, for the purpose of a conversation, not an interview. Gary readily agreed, as long as it was off the record, because of his deal with Schiller.

Later that night Schiller himself called Moyers and indicated that any communication with Gary was unlikely. I didn't bring up the subject the next day, Friday, but Gary did. "Schiller won't let me see your friend. He wants to guard his 'exclusivity.' Sometimes that son of a bitch acts like he owns me, like he can run my life. He did this to me once before, when I asked him to recover some of my private letters to Nicole. I didn't like seeing that shit in print; the drawings didn't bother me so much, but the letters were nobody's business. And, contrary to my wishes, Schiller read them. I felt like firing him right then, and I probably still should, but it's too late to find anybody else. What I should do, though, is revoke his invitation to the execution." I didn't offer any opinion. I didn't want to get caught up in a feud between Gary and Schiller.

I told Gary that I should leave that night, to go back home and spend the rest of the weekend with Mother.

"Can't you stay one more day?" he asked. "I'd like to see you again, and I have this book Johnny Cash sent me; I want you to give it to Mom."

I agreed to return the next day—Saturday—but before I left he wanted to tell me one more thing. "You know I've said a lot of stuff about how I don't care what people think about me, but that's not completely true. I don't like it when they say I'm jittery and stuff. I've never told anybody this before, but I don't know what Monday's going to be like. Maybe that's why I need Schiller there, so I'll keep cool . . . I know you don't believe this, but I didn't mean for this to become such a big thing. I never expected the books or movies, maybe a few articles."

We pressed our hands against the glass between us and said good-bye.

⋆ ⋆ ⋆

Imagine the impossible leaps and borders your heart must cross when you're arguing with a man about his own death. There was a logic, a congruity to Gary's choice, I had to admit, but none of that changed my desire for him to stay alive. But just as you try to convince the lover who no longer loves you to love you nonetheless—because you cannot imagine going on in your life, living it, without the presence or thing that you need and love most—in the same moment that you make your argument, and try to convince the person to stay and love you all over again, you also know that your argument is already lost, and along with it, a version of your future.

When you are arguing with somebody who is hell-bent on dying, you realize that if you lose the argument, there is no more chance for further argument, that you will have seen that person for the last time. I could not believe that I was in that place in my life, that I could possibly be caught up in such an argument. Death is one thing we almost never get to argue with. You can't argue with the disease that takes your loved one or yourself, or the car accident or the killer that snuffs out a life without warning. But a man who *wants* to die . . . When I argued with Gary, I was arguing with death itself—he was death, wanting itself as its only possible fulfillment—and I learned that you cannot win, that this thing which will ruin your heart the most cannot be resisted or stopped, that you will lose this person, and you will have to live with that loss forever. And you will not have lost them to cancer or to the cruelty of another's actions; you will have lost them to the abyss of their own soul, and you will be afraid that maybe their surrender to that abyss is, after all, the only act that makes sense. But mainly, you know that you will never see them again—that you pleaded with them to stay and that there was nothing you could do—it was too late to do anything that would make a difference. Maybe in that moment, you will want to go where they're going, because it can't possibly hurt so much or look so goddamn fucking eternal as the prospect of spending the rest of your life accommodating a loss that no sane heart could ever possibly afford or hope to accommodate without letting ruin so deep inside that it becomes an ineradicable part of your deepest self.

⋆ ⋆ ⋆

I spoke with Giauque the same day and informed him that I had decided not to intervene. Telling him was almost as hard as making the decision. I could have sought a stay, signed the necessary documents and returned home feeling that I had made the right decision, the moral choice. But I didn't have to bear the weight of that decision. Gary did. Had he chosen suicide, I could rightfully claim that I was not responsible for his choice, only my own. If I could have chosen for Gary to live, I would have.

I had several helpful conversations with Bill Moyers during that week, and at one point he told me that if we are confronted with a choice between life and death and choose anything short of life, then we choose short of humanity. That made it all seem so clear-cut. I wrestled with the decision and finally realized that I couldn't choose life for Gary, and he wouldn't. He had worked out what he reasoned to be some sort of atonement. He wanted death, his final scenario of redemption, his final release from the law. To Gary the greatest irony was that the law—which in his eyes had always sought to break him—finally wanted to save him, when he no longer wanted salvation. In order to beat the law, he had to lose everything—everything except his own unswerving definition of dignity.

I couldn't reason with that, I couldn't change that. And in the end, I couldn't take it away from him.

As a result, I now had a role in this story I had never wanted and had never bargained for: I had become a chooser. I had made decisions that would have consequences. Maybe these consequences wouldn't stop here—maybe other men would now die because we had decided not to challenge history or justice at this point, or maybe there would be numerous other people whose lives would be affected, stopped or turned upside down as a result of these last few days. Maybe the spirit of the nation itself would now be different—bloodier, and more pitiless. The effects, I thought, were incalculable. They could ripple through our lives forever, and into the lives of our children.

What a difference a killing can make.

◆ ◆ ◆

On Saturday, January 15, I visited Gary for the last time. By then, camera crews were camped all over the town of Draper, preparing for the finale.

During our previous meetings that week, Gary had always opened with some friendly remarks, a joke or even a handstand. This day, though, he seemed nervous, though he denied it. "Naw, the noise in this place gets to me sometimes, but I'm as cool as a cucumber," he said, holding up a steady hand. The muscles in his wrists and arms, though, were taut and thick as rope.

Gary started to show me letters and pictures he'd received, mostly from children and teenage girls. He said he always tried to answer the ones from kids first, and then he read one from a boy who claimed to be eight years old: "I hope they put you someplace and make you live forever for what you did. You have no right to die. With all the malice in my heart, (name)."

"Man, that one shook me up for a long time," he said.

I asked him if he'd replied to it. "Yeah. I wrote, 'You're too young to have malice in your heart. I had it in mine at a young age and look what it did for me.'"

He had a guard bring the book that Johnny Cash had sent. It was his autobiography, *The Man in Black*, which Gary wanted left with our mother.

"I'd really like to give you something or leave something for you. Why don't you let me leave you some money? Everybody needs money." I declined, suggesting that he give it to the Bushnell and Jensen families instead. "There's no way money can buy back what I did to those people," he said, shaking his head.

Gary's eyes nervously scanned the letters and pictures in front of him, finally falling on one that made him smile. He held it up. A picture of Nicole. "She's pretty, isn't she?" I agreed. "I look at this picture every day. I took it myself. It's the one I made the drawing from. Would you like to have it?"

I said I would be pleased to have it.

Finally I had a last question to ask: "Gary, remember the night you were arrested, when you were on your way to the airport?"

He nodded.

"Where would you have gone had you made it to the airport?"

"Um, Portland."

"But certainly you knew that was the first place they would have looked for you. Why would you want to go there?"

Gary studied the shelf top in front of him for a few seconds. "I don't really want to talk about that night anymore," he said. "There's no *point* in talking about it."

"Please, Gary, I'd like to know: What would you have done in Portland?"

"Mikal, don't."

"Please. I have to know. What would you have done? Would you have come to see me?"

Again, he nodded.

"And . . . ?"

He sighed and looked straight at me, and for a moment his eyes flashed an old anger. "And what would *you* have done if I had come to you?" he asked. "If I had come and said I was in trouble and needed help, needed a place to stay? Would *you* have taken me in? Would you have hidden me?"

I couldn't reply. The question had been turned back on me, and suddenly I could not stand the awfulness of my own answers. Gary sat there for long moments, holding me with his eyes, then said steadily: "I think I was coming to kill you. I think that's what would have happened. There simply may have been no choice for you, and no choice for me." His eyes softened and he gave me a tender smile. It was filled with the sad brokenness of our common history. "Do you understand why?" he asked.

I nodded back. Of course I understood why. I had escaped the family, or at least thought I had. Gary had not.

At that moment, I felt a certain terror. I knew that what Gary had said was true. I knew that death could have been my past, which would mean I would now have no present. In fact, it felt like it had come close to happening, just for the conception of that possibility. And so I felt not just some terror, but also some relief. Jensen's and Bushnell's death, and Gary's own impending death, had added up to my own safety, and as soon as I realized that, my relief was shot through with guilt. And remorse. I thought of all the other things that might have happened in our home or in our love that maybe could have changed this moment, so we would not be sitting here, in this awful place, at this awful time.

Oddly, though, I also felt closer to Gary in that moment than I'd ever felt before. For just that second, I understood completely why he wanted to die.

At that point, Warden Samuel Smith entered Gary's room. They discussed whether Gary would have to wear a hood on Monday morning. I put down the phone. Minutes passed. When I picked up the phone again, Smith was telling Gary that Schiller wouldn't be allowed to visit with Gary in the final hours before the execution.

I rapped on the glass. I would have to leave soon and I asked if the warden would allow us a final handshake. At first Smith refused, but he assented after Gary explained it was our final visit, on the condition I agree to a skin search. I agreed. After the search, conducted by two guards, two other guards brought Gary in. They said I would have to roll up my sleeve past my elbow, and that we could not touch beyond a handshake. Gary grasped my hand, squeezed tight, and said, "Well, I guess this is it." He leaned over and kissed me on the cheek. "See you in the darkness beyond."

I pulled my eyes away from his. I knew I couldn't stop crying at this point, and I didn't want him to see it. "Are you okay?" he asked. I bit my lip and nodded. A guard handed me the book and the picture of Nicole and started to walk with me to the rolling-bar doors. Gary watched me pass through them. "Give my love to Mom," he called. "And put on some weight. You're still too skinny."

The guard walked with me through the two fence gates and patted me on the back as I left. "Take it easy, fella," he said.

❖   ❖   ❖

I went back home, and left Gary to his fate. I hated myself. I felt like I had inadvertently taken sides with the death penalty—a brutal social ethos that I despised. At the same time, I guess I decided that Gary was better off dead. I had little doubt that if he was kept alive, he would kill himself, and perhaps others as well. I didn't want to live with having taken an action that might have resulted in such consequences. I hated living with any of these choices—I hated finding myself in a place where any action or non-action would result in the certainty of death.

The night before Gary's execution, I visited my mother and Frank. I had called the prison earlier in the day and arranged for us all to have a last brief conversation with him on the phone. His last words to my mother were: "Don't cry, Mom. I love you. I want you to go on with your life." And her last words were: "Gary, I'm going to stay brave for you until tomorrow, but I know I'll never stop crying. I'll cry every day for the rest of my life."

She handed the phone to me. Gary told me he had talked with his biggest hero, Johnny Cash, earlier that evening. I asked him what Cash had said. "When I picked up the phone I said, 'Is this the *real* Johnny Cash?' And he said: 'Yes it is.' And I said: 'Well, this is the real Gary Gilmore.'"

Gary told me he had to get off the phone. "I'll miss you, Gary," I said. "We're all proud of you."

"Don't be proud of me," he said. "What's there to be proud of? I'm just going to be shot to death, for something that should never have happened."

Those were our last words.

❖   ❖   ❖

On Monday morning, January 17, in a cannery warehouse out behind Utah State Prison, Gary met his firing squad. I was with my mother and brother and girlfriend when it happened. Just moments before, we had seen the morning newspaper with the headline EXECUTION STAYED, and turned on the television for more news. *Good Morning America* was on, and there was a press conference: They were announcing that Gary was dead.

There was no way to be braced for that last seesawing of emotion. One moment you're forcing yourself to live through the hell of knowing that somebody you love is going to die in a known way, at a specific time and place, and that not only is there nothing you can do to change that, but that for the rest of your life, you will have to move around in a world that wanted this death to happen. You will have to walk past people every day who were heartened by the killing of somebody in your family—somebody who had long ago been himself murdered emotionally. You will have to live in this world and either hate it or make peace with it, because it is the only world you will have available to live in. It is the only world that *is*.

The next moment, you see a headline that holds the possibility of a reprieve. Maybe, you think, the courts are seizing control of this matter, wresting it from the momentum of this crazy, eerie inevitability. Maybe they will not allow the death penalty to be applied here so hurriedly—and maybe *that* will be enough to break the back of this horror, to diffuse all this madness. Maybe it would prove a reprieve not just for Gary and his indomitable will to die, but also a reprieve for what was left of this family. Maybe now we would not have to live in a world that had killed one of us without any misgiving.

And then, as soon as you've allowed yourself that impossible hope, you turn on the television, and there is Larry Schiller—the only journalist who was allowed to witness the shooting—and he is telling you how the warden put a black hood over Gary's head and pinned a small, circular cloth target above his chest, and then how five men pumped a volley of bullets into that target. He is telling you how the blood flowed from Gary's devastated heart and down his chest, down his legs, staining his white pants scarlet and dripping to the warehouse floor. He is telling you how Gary's arm rose slowly at the moment of the impact, how his fingers seemed to wave, to send a sign of departure as his life left him, as if he were finally trying to bid a gentle good-bye to a hard life.

One moment, hope has come from nowhere. The next moment, you learn that the horror has already happened—and you know you will always have to live with the details of that horror. You will have to try to find a way to live with the sorrow that will now always be at the heart of your heart. You will have to try to find a way to live in this world, in this life, and not hate it—and you will have to try despite the impossibility of such a task.

I thought all this, and then I looked over at my mother, and I saw her face crack, and I heard her wail: "My God, Gary, where are you? Where have you gone to?"

⋅❦⋅   ⋅❦⋅   ⋅❦⋅

Following my brother's execution, an outcry arose in Utah against what many people (including several death penalty advocates) saw as the unnecessarily bloody and "old West" aspect of Utah's mode of capital punishment. Why hold on to such gruesome conventions, the reformists argued, when an increasing number of other states were opting for the comparatively "humane" method of putting the condemned to death by lethal injection? In a fairly brilliant act of legal and moral sleight-of-hand, the Utah legislature managed to accommodate both the traditions of their region and the reformists' pressure for change. As of 1980, hanging—an old West practice if ever there was one—would no longer be an option for execution (nobody ever chose it anyway), and in its place, Utah now offered the alternative of lethal injection. However, under what was rumored to be a tremendous amount of backroom ecclesiastical pressure, the state also retained the firing squad option, in case the man who was going to die wanted his blood to be shed, as a bid for salvation. In the years since, nobody has opted for the choice of being shot, and it is not likely that many will ever again take that course. Chances are, Gary Gilmore will remain the last man to die before a firing squad in America, as well as the last man to pay the Mormons' rigorous cost of Blood Atonement.

⋅❦⋅   ⋅❦⋅   ⋅❦⋅

Years later, I would learn what my brother's last words were. They stunned me when I heard them, they haunt me still. Gary Gilmore's final words, before the life was shot out of him, were these: "There will always be a father."

Joyce Johnson

from What Lisa Knew

NOVEMBER 1987

Hate is not the opposite of love, apathy is. The opposite of will is not indecision—
which actually may represent the struggle of the *effort* to decide, as in William
James—but being uninvolved, detached, unrelated to the significant events. Then
the issue of will never can arise.

—*Rollo May,* Love and Will, *1969*

THERE WAS AN ABSENCE OF LIGHT, ALTHOUGH THE ELECTRICAL CURRENT WAS ON IN THAT
one-bedroom brownstone apartment in Greenwich Village, where Hedda Nussbaum, a former writer and editor of children's books, had lived for twelve years with Joel Steinberg, a
criminal lawyer. It was a place that would later be described by the police and the press as a
cave. And a cave it was—dark, littered, reeking; bloodstains on the bedclothes, the walls.
There was a pet brown-and-white rabbit; there were two tanks of tropical fish, ironically in
excellent condition. The fish swam round and round, warm in their clean water, in the pale
glow of their artificial universes. There was also a witness present, unimplicated in whatever
had occurred the night before—a baby without language, sixteen months old. He was
awake, lying quietly in his playpen on a mat that stank of urine, staring up at the ceiling. Police officer James Botte discovered him there when he walked around the living room to look
for a table lamp—anything that worked. Boxes of old clothes were lying all about. There
seemed to be a lot of dismantled electronic equipment.

There should have been light, a great deal of light. Every bulb in the apartment should
have been burning. In a normal household, there would have been no need for Botte to
grope around like that, looking for a lamp to turn on.

It was 6:45 A.M., Monday, November 2. On a normal Monday, six-year-old Elizabeth
Steinberg would have been waking up soon on the living-room couch, getting herself ready,
without much help from either of her parents, for her father to take her to school. Or maybe
she wouldn't get to school because there was no one to take her. There were more and more
mornings like that lately. In fact, nothing about Elizabeth Steinberg's life had ever really
been normal.

On this particular Monday morning, Elizabeth Steinberg was lying naked on the floor,
her head resting on the edge of the dirty living-room rug, her bare feet protruding into the
little foyer. It was the only uncluttered area the paramedics had been able to find. They were
working on her, trying to get her to breathe, looking for signs of life with their pocket
flashlights.

⚭ ⚭ ⚭

The mother had called 911 around 6:32. She spoke to the operator rather slowly, without
much inflection—sounding calm or numb, however you wanted to interpret it. She seemed
quite collected as she gave the particulars of the family's address. When the operator said,
"And what's going on there?" the woman got mixed up and said, "Um . . . my daughter
doesn't seem to have stopped breathing."

"What is it?" the operator asked sharply.

"My daughter, she was congested and she's stopped breathing. She's six years old."

"Okay, she's having difficulty breathing."

"She's not breathing. We're giving her mouth-to-mouth."

The operator rang an EMS ambulance and recited the address. She told the mother she was sending it through right away. Did the child have asthma or heart problems? she asked the mother. "Does she have a high fever or anything?"

"Uh . . . no."

"Was the eating something? I'm just trying to find out why she would just stop breathing."

The woman hesitated. "Um—I think . . . well . . . I don't really know exactly why." She sounded like a schoolgirl, stumbling over a science question.

"You don't really know? Okay," the operator said.

"Food's coming up," the woman said helpfully. "She's throwing up a lot of food and water."

"Water?"

"And food, yeah."

The operator told her how to give mouth-to-mouth. To tilt the child's head back and pinch off her nose and turn her head to the side if she started vomiting and clean her mouth out. It was important to keep doing that until the ambulance arrived. Dutifully, the woman repeated each instruction aloud.

"Where are they now?" the woman asked.

"They should be there in two minutes."

"They'll be here in two minutes?" She repeated that, too, as if she couldn't believe they'd get there so quickly. She said her husband was doing the mouth-to-mouth.

"You hear me? The ambulance will be there in two minutes. Okay?"

"Yes," said the mother.

"Okay. Thanks."

⚬   ⚬   ⚬

The radio car from the Sixth Precinct, driven by Officer Botte, had arrived at 6:35, followed almost simultaneously by the ambulance from St. Vincent's. Botte and his partner, Vincent DaLuise, rushed into the small downstairs vestibule of 14 West Tenth Street. As Botte later remembered it, they had trouble getting into the building. Apartment 3W didn't answer. They had to ring a number of buzzers before anyone buzzed back. It could have been the Steinbergs, it could have been someone else. It was a delay of only a minute or two, but if there was a child dying up there, every second counted. A neighbor silently pointed to the apartment across the landing—the door with a large, ugly brass eagle on it. The Steinbergs' door shouldn't have been closed; someone should have been standing there to let them in right away. All this was taking another thirty to forty-five seconds. Then a woman opened the door—only a few inches at first. She didn't say a word.

Brian Gearity and John Filangeri, the paramedics from St. Vincent's, heard someone call out, "I've found the apartment!" and ran up the stairs. Gearity, too, remembers the strange slowness with which the door to 3W seemed to open. "All I could see was a face. I couldn't tell how old she was. She looked like an old person in a young body. She looked like the lion in the 'Beauty and the Beast' television show." Gearity asked her "Did you call for an ambulance?" The women's Yes was preceded by silence and was barely audible. "It ran through my mind, when you have a six-year-old in cardiac arrest, it's Let's go!" Gearity recalled in 1988.

"I ran to answer the door," Hedda Nussbaum would say a year later when she was testifying against Joel Steinberg. "I opened the door and let the men in."

The four of them—Botte, Daluise, Filangeri, and Gearity—crowded into the small dark foyer. They would never forget what they saw next. From a room in the rear, a man emerged, tall, bespectacled, wild-haired, his arms stretched out in front of him. He was walking a naked child toward them, walking her backward, holding her up under the armpits like a life-size puppet. Gearity and Filangeri were finding it very hard to see the patient; there was only a little bit of illumination that came in from the outside landing; there seemed to be no way of getting more. Wires were dangling out of switch near the buzzer. The two paramedics were frantically working on the kid and asking Steinberg what had happened.

The man was a rapid talker—rambling sentences poured out of him. Filangeri kept thinking he didn't sound concerned enough—not when you compared him to other parents. Apparently his daughter had just eaten something that had caused her to vomit and then lose consciousness. But why was the child eating at 6 A.M.? Filangeri asked Steinberg. No, no, it was the night before; she had been throwing up since about 8 P.M. and had choked on her vomit about an hour ago and her breathing had stopped. He and his wife hadn't called 911 right away because they thought Lisa would be all right. They had taken her into their bed with them. The child had eaten Chinese vegetables, since the family was vegetarian. The vegetables were fresh, freshly cooked.

Finally Filangeri had to interrupt. Wasn't there any way to get some light? In response, Steinberg asked him an absurdist's question: Was it important?

Filangeri used the resuscitator on the child. Then he tried the Heimlich maneuver. She did bring up a small amount of undigested food.

In the midst of all this, someone came up with a portable fluorescent trouble light. Filangeri had no idea who had provided it; he just saw it when Botte had it in his hand. It was then he noticed the bruises on the child's thin chest, the reddish marks just below her nipples. He asked Steinberg if the child had been beaten. Steinberg said he'd been pounding on his daughter's chest in order to revive her. "I know CPR."

Later, during the trial, one of Steinberg's lawyers said it was Steinberg himself who had produced the fluorescent light, yanked it out of the hall closet, scratching his hand in the process. Botte remembered it as a table lamp he must have managed to find. "Everything was being done very quickly," he said, "in an excited atmosphere." Gearity couldn't remember any light at all.

~ THE PRIVACY OF AMERICAN FAMILIES IS SACROSANCT. IT HAS FAR MORE LEGAL PROtection than the lives of children. With each hour, new infant citizens are born, and there's no way of knowing, of really determining, what fates they're born into. The birth is recorded, the mother and baby leave the hospital; the child drops out of public view, vanishes behind the locked door of the home. As Dr. Richard Krugman, a child-abuse expert, points out, the state doesn't officially hear of the majority of these children again until five or six years later, at the time they start school. Then it becomes possible to track them to a certain extent.

Birth, then, is like a lottery. Babies win, babies lose. In this country, we do not even question this awesome randomness. We accept it as the inescapable order of things. At the same time, we speak loudly about the value of human life, even the life of the fetus. There is far more activism in America on behalf of the unborn than there is on behalf of living children. They have relatively few lobbyists. On the night of January 30, 1989, after the jury delivered its verdict, finding Joel Steinberg guilty of first degree manslaughter in the death of Elizabeth Steinberg, Juror Helen Barthell came to the microphone during the press conference and said she had a special message for Michelle Launders, Lisa Steinberg's natural mother: "Michelle, you did the right thing having that baby. You decided against abortion. That was the right decision." This juror just wanted to make very sure people were reminded that even for the Elizabeth Steinbergs, adoption was preferable to abortion.

In this case, adoption had failed, disastrously and tragically. In fact, neither Elizabeth Steinberg nor her baby brother, Mitchell, had ever been adopted legally. They were big losers in the lottery, born into limbo and mortal peril. It would be more accurate to call them stolen children than adoptees.

The man who had taken them had a profound understanding of the loopholes in the law, an expert's knowledge of how easy it was for children to fall through the cracks in the system, how little their rights counted, compared to his own as an adult. Both Steinberg and Nussbaum apparently understood that their particular chosen life-style made them totally ineligible for a legal adoption. Like many, though, they viewed children as an entitlement; if they were biologically unable to produce their own, they'd just have to get them some other way.

Lisa Steinberg had lived with Joel and Hedda since she was seven days old. Her identity and existence were dependent upon their exercise of will. They told her that she had been "chosen." Children themselves have no such choices.

᚛ᚑ ᚛ᚑ ᚛ᚑ

At the age of six, Lisa Steinberg weighed forty-three pounds. She was a little thinner than most other first-graders. She had big hazel eyes and red hair. If she had ever grown up, people would have called her an Irish beauty. The fine shoulder-length hair hadn't been shampooed for a long time; it was terribly tangled and matted. It hid a large red bruise on the right temple that would be discovered in the emergency room at the hospital, along with two other large fresh bruises on her jaw and the back of her head.

Filangeri had noticed a very ominous sign right after the stretcher was carried into St. Vincent's. Gearity saw it, too: The child's pupils were not equal; the right was larger than the left, an indication of a problem with the brain. The two men looked at each other, and Filangeri shook his head and said in a low voice, "It just happened now."

When the blanket was lifted off the child under the white lights of the pediatric emergency room, the cops and the medics saw all the other bruises. Elizabeth Steinberg's small body was a map of pain. The marks were different colors, different vintages. Red, purple, yellowish-brown. It seemed as if she had been hit just about everywhere—on her arms and the calves of her legs, on her chest, her buttocks. One of the biggest bruises was in the center of her lower back—not a place where a child would be likely to injure herself. There were fresh scratches on her elbows, as if someone had grabbed her there. Her parents had just let her go dirty—her feet and ankles had a crust of black grime. The hair and the feet shocked everyone almost as much as the bruises.

Botte went out to the waiting area to talk to Steinberg, who had accompanied Elizabeth to the hospital. He found him smoking, pacing up and down. But somehow the man didn't seem frantic enough.

"How's my daughter?" Steinberg asked Botte, following this brief inquiry with, "I'm a lawyer. I represent Tommy Morrow and George Mourlot." Botte recognized one of the names, a detective at the Sixth Precinct. Steinberg reached into his jacket for his wallet and pulled out a card to further establish his upper-middle-class credentials. Botte may have looked to him like the kind of young guy he could easily impress. Even after four and a half years as a police officer, Botte still had the slightly diffident manner of a nice kid. He hadn't lost his rosy, cherubic face.

But Botte wasn't so impressed. He had become extremely interested in Steinberg's right hand. There were two small red cuts on the knuckles. When Botte asked Steinberg how he had cut himself, Steinberg said, "I didn't know I had this," and started nervously rubbing his hands together.

In the pediatric emergency room, the little girl with the red hair slept on, unable to move, unable to wake up, unable to tell anyone who had beaten her.

∗ ∗ ∗

Botte left Steinberg and went back to the apartment with Vincent DaLuise to pick up a sample of the food the child was said to have choked on. The woman didn't want to let them in right away. She called out to them to wait—she had to put something on. When she opened the door, she had a bandanna tied around her curly gray hair. Botte had never seen a woman who looked as bad as she did. Hedda Nussbaum resembled a pugilist who had just lost the last of a long series of fights. Two black eyes, a split lip, a nose that no longer had a bridge. "She spoke very slow," Botte remembered in court. "She was kind of withdrawn, very slow responding." When they told her what they'd come for, she limped away from them toward the kitchen, hunched over like an old person. She wasn't crying. Botte had evidently had the sentimental expectation that she would be crying over the little girl. It was like Steinberg all over again: the emotions didn't match up with the situation.

Hedda Nussbaum took a plastic container out of the refrigerator and handed it to Botte. There were soggy vegetables inside. They're rotten, Botte thought to himself. The woman asked DaLuise a weird thing. "Do you have to take all the vegetables?"

Botte went to check out the baby he had seen earlier in the living room. The baby was still in his old, broken-down playpen. In fact, he was tethered to it by a rope that went around his waist. The baby, the mat he was sitting on, the dirty sweatshirt he was wearing, had an awful stench of urine. Even the milk in the bottle the baby was clutching looked curdled to Botte, though he didn't think to take the bottle away to have the contents tested. Maybe there was nothing really the matter with either the vegetables or the milk, it was just that Botte was reacting viscerally and everything he saw seemed rotten, wrong. Nothing about the way these people lived or acted was the way things were supposed to be. He heard the woman say something to the effect that she was just about to change the baby. He wanted to remove him from her and from the premises, but procedurally, all he could do for the moment was fill out a report on suspected abuse and neglect.

He and DaLuise drove back to St. Vincent's with the food sample, then went to the Sixth Precinct, where they notified Special Services for Children and the Sex Crimes Unit. They were both feeling shaken, "a little confused." By the time they returned to St. Vincent's, Steinberg was gone from the waiting room; no one had stopped him. He had just decided to go home.

∗ ∗ ∗

Before the morning of November 2, 1987, it is probable that if you happened to observe Joel Steinberg as he passed you on the street, you would have accepted him as the man he purported to be. A lawyer, therefore a relatively solid citizen—though he wore his black hair too long for the 1980s and his expensive suit may have needed pressing and his dark eyes may have glittered a bit too restlessly behind the thick lenses of his glasses and his loud nasal voice, carried back to you in a fragment of conversation, may have jarred you for a moment. But in a city like New York, you would not have looked at such a man too long, or reflected much upon his strangeness. Encountering him around Greenwich Village, you might have thought "Villagey" or quickly assessed Steinberg as someone who derived his style from the wilder days of the 1970s.

At St. Vincent's, though, the long hair became suspect, the black mustache criminal, the eyes guilty. According to Nancy Dodenhoff, a nurse on duty in the emergency room when Lisa was brought in, the eyes of Steinberg were "glazed. His visual field kept darting back and forth." She observed that he was nervous. "He was wringing his hands. It was not concern for the child." Officer Botte would later testify that Steinberg "looked messy—like a person who had been out all night." Also, his hair was uncombed. "I say they were dirty clothes," Botte said in an accusatory voice. "They weren't well kept." Steinberg's poor grooming would be one more thing to count against him. Yet, in a normal household where a small child had been ill through the night—say, with food poisoning—no one would have thought there was anything suspect about finding a parent with a disheveled appearance.

In less than two hours, however, an image of Joel Steinberg formed in the minds of all those who had dealings with him, even before the battered condition of Hedda Nussbaum was discovered. Shortly this image would be summed up in a word that will probably adhere to Steinberg for the rest of his days. *Monster.* Steinberg had taken on the lurid colors of a dying child's bruises. These bruises that everyone else could very plainly see were bypassed in all of Steinberg's stories about what had happened to his daughter. Even though he was a lawyer, he seemed unaware of his desperate need for a more convincing alibi.

Brian Gearity listened in when a police officer questioned Steinberg in the waiting room. The time frame had been adjusted. Now Steinberg was saying his daughter had trouble breathing only fifteen minutes before the ambulance was summoned, though the vomiting had gone on all through the preceding night. When Gearity heard him say it was his wife who had stayed with the child, he interpolated a question of his own: "Were *you* there?" There was a pause, and a correction was made: "My wife and I took turns with her during the night."

When Steinberg was ushered into the pediatric emergency room, others joined in on the interrogation as Mary Joan Marron, a pediatric specialist, and Patrick Kilhenny, a medical resident, examined Lisa and performed neurological tests. Over half a dozen people fired questions at Steinberg, trying to get as much information as they could. Nurse Dodenhoff called out his answers to the physicians.

Kilhenny had been the first to notice the reddish, right frontal bruise at the hairline. When he examined the child's eyes, the lack of pupillary response indicated there might be brain damage. He found blood in the back of the eyes, gross damage to the retinas. When water was injected into the child's ears, there was no reaction. There was no response to verbal stimuli or to pressure on her sternum. Everything indicated a deep level of coma.

After performing the tests, Kilhenny asked Steinberg whether Lisa had sustained a head injury. Had she fallen or tripped or been in a car accident? Steinberg stuck to his story about the upset stomach, about the vomiting that had begun when Lisa woke up around midnight: "We took her out of bed and she vomited. Later I heard her vomiting in the next room. I let her alone because I thought she was okay."

A child who is vomiting is not okay, Kilhenny thought to himself.

When Steinberg demonstrated how he had performed the Heimlich maneuver on Lisa around 6 A.M., Kilhenny asked him coldly whether that was how she had sustained so many bruises.

"What do you feel about this prognosis?" Steinberg demanded of Kilhenny.

The young doctor's first response was measured, professionally tactful, although he was not trying to spare Steinberg's feelings. Elizabeth would have what he called "neurological deficits."

Steinberg pressed harder. "Will she survive?"

Kilhenny's next answer was much blunter. "Yes, but with permanent damage. The damage will be severe."

"Well, what you're saying is that she's not going to be an Olympic athlete, but she will survive." There seemed to be a smile on the man's face. When Kilhenny testified a year later, he was very sure he had seen that bizarre smile, and he could remember his own "facial expression of disbelief."

Dodenhoff, who had heard Steinberg's remark, had become enraged. She walked up to him and said, brutally, "Your daughter's brain-dead," even though no doctor had yet voiced that opinion. To which he responded, "Is there anything else wrong with her?"

Right in front of him, Dodenhoff made a call to Special Services for Children on the emergency-room telephone, reporting a case of child abuse. She made sure she spoke loud enough for Steinberg to hear every word.

It was shortly after this that Steinberg said he had to be going. A CAT scan was going to be done on Elizabeth, but he evidently didn't want to wait around for the results. He went over to his daughter's bedside for a few moments. Dodenhoff saw him stoop down and kiss her on the forehead, then glance around the room as if to make sure people had observed this fatherly gesture. The kiss was very quick, so quick that Kilhenny didn't remember it. In Dodenhoff's mind, it didn't have a thing to do with affection.

◦ ◦ ◦

It was four blocks from the hospital to the Steinberg apartment. Around 8:30 A.M., David Stiffler, an acquaintance of Steinberg's, was sitting on his stoop on Tenth Street drinking coffee. At this hour, he had often seen Steinberg walking his daughter to P.S. 41. This morning Steinberg was alone, going past him in the wrong direction, carrying what seemed to be an article of Lisa's clothing. Usually Steinberg would call out, "Hey, hey, Dave!" But today he didn't even turn his head. "I didn't observe him crying," Stiffler later told the court.

Barbara Ehrenreich

Nickel-and-Dimed

On (Not) Getting By in America

AT THE BEGINNING OF JUNE 1998 I LEAVE BEHIND EVERYTHING THAT NORMALLY SOOTHES the ego and sustains the body—home, career, companion, reputation, ATM card—for a plunge into the low-wage workforce. There, I become another, occupationally much diminished "Barbara Ehrenreich"—depicted on job-application forms as a divorced homemaker whose sole work experience consists of housekeeping in a few private homes. I am terrified, at the beginning, of being unmasked for what I am: a middle-class journalist setting out to explore the world that welfare mothers are entering, at the rate of approximately 50,000 a month, as welfare reform kicks in. Happily, though, my fears turn out to be entirely unwarranted: during a month of poverty and toil, my name goes unnoticed and for the most part unuttered. In this parallel universe where my father never got out of the mines and I never got through college, I am "baby," "honey," "blondie," and, most commonly, "girl."

My first task is to find a place to live. I figure that if I can earn $7 an hour—which, from the want ads, seems doable—I can afford to spend $500 on rent, or maybe, with severe economies, $600. In the Key West area, where I live, this pretty much confines me to flophouses and trailer homes—like the one, a pleasing fifteen-minute drive from town, that has no air-conditioning, no screens, no fans, no television, and, by way of diversion, only the challenge of evading the landlord's Doberman pinscher. The big problem with this place, though, is the rent, which at $675 a month is well beyond my reach. All right, Key West is expensive. But so is New York City, or the Bay Area, or Jackson Hole, or Telluride, or Boston, or any other place where tourists and the wealthy compete for living space with the people who clean their toilets and fry their hash browns.[1] Still, it is a shock to realize that "trailer trash" has become, for me, a demographic category to aspire to.

So I decide to make the common trade-off between affordability and convenience, and go for a $500-a-month efficiency thirty miles up a two-lane highway from the employment opportunities of Key West, meaning forty-five minutes if there's no road construction and I don't get caught behind some sun-dazed Canadian tourists. I hate the drive, along a roadside studded with white crosses commemorating the more effective head-on collisions, but it's sweet little place—a cabin, more or less, set in the swampy back yard of the converted mobile home where my landlord, an affable TV repairman, lives with his bartender girlfriend. Anthropologically speaking, a bustling trailer park would be preferable, but here I have a gleaming white floor and a firm mattress, and the few resident bugs are easily vanquished.

Besides, I am not doing this for the anthropology. My aim is nothing so mistily subjective as to "experience poverty" or find out how it "really feels" to be a long-term low-wage worker. I've had enough unchosen encounters with poverty and the world of low-wage work to know it's not a place you want to visit for touristic purposes; it just smells too much like fear. And with all my real-life assets—bank account, IRA, health insurance, multiroom home—waiting indulgently in the background, I am, of course, thoroughly insulated from the terrors that afflict the genuinely poor.

No, this is a purely objective, scientific sort of mission. The humanitarian rationale for welfare reform—as opposed to the more punitive and stingy impulses that may actually have motivated it—is that work will lift poor women out of poverty while simultaneously inflating their self-esteem and hence their future value in the labor market. Thus, whatever the hassles involved in finding child care, transportation, etc., the transition from welfare to

---

[1] According to the Department of Housing and Urban Development, the "fair-market rent" for an efficiency is $551 here in Monroe County, Florida. A comparable rent in the five boroughs of New York City is $704; in San Francisco, $713; and in the heart of Silicon Valley, $808. The fair-market rent for an area is defined as the amount that would be needed to pay rent plus utilities for "privately owned, decent, safe, and sanitary rental housing of a modest (non-luxury) nature with suitable amenities."

work will end happily, in greater prosperity for all. Now there are many problems with this comforting prediction, such as the fact that the economy will inevitably undergo a downturn, eliminating many jobs. Even without a downturn, the influx of a million former welfare recipients into the low-wage labor market could depress wages by as much as 11.9 percent, according to the Economic Policy Institute (EPI) in Washington, D.C.

But is it really possible to make a living on the kinds of jobs currently available to unskilled people? Mathematically, the answer is no, as can be shown by taking $6 to $7 an hour, perhaps subtracting a dollar or two an hour for child care, multiplying by 160 hours a month, and comparing the result to the prevailing rents. According to the National Coalition for the Homeless, for example, in 1998 it took, on average nationwide, an hourly wage of $8.89 to afford a one-bedroom apartment, and the Preamble Center for Public Policy estimates that the odds against a typical welfare recipient's landing a job at such a "living wage" are about 97 to 1. If these numbers are right, low-wage work is not a solution to poverty and possibly not even to homelessness.

It may seem excessive to put this proposition to an experimental test. As certain family members keep unhelpfully reminding me, the viability of low-wage work could be tested, after a fashion, without ever leaving my study. I could just pay myself $7 an hour for eight hours a day, charge myself for room and board, and total up the numbers after a month. Why leave the people and work that I love? But I am an experimental scientist by training. In that business, you don't just sit at a desk and theorize; you plunge into the everyday chaos of nature, where surprises lurk in the most mundane measurements. Maybe, when I got into it, I would discover some hidden economies in the world of the low-wage worker. After all, if 30 percent of the workforce toils for less than $8 an hour, according to the EPI, they may have found some tricks as yet unknown to me. Maybe—who knows?—I would even be able to detect in myself the bracing psychological effects of getting out of the house, as promised by the welfare wonks at places like the Heritage Foundation. Or, on the other hand, maybe there would be unexpected costs—physical, mental, or financial—to throw off all my calculations. Ideally, I should do this with two small children in tow, that being the welfare average, but mine are grown and no one is willing to lend me theirs for a month-long vacation in penury. So this is not the perfect experiment, just a test of the best possible case: an unencumbered woman, smart and even strong, attempting to live more or less off the land.

⁕ ⁕ ⁕

On the morning of my first full day of job searching, I take a red pen to the want ads, which are auspiciously numerous. Everyone in Key West's booming "hospitality industry" seems to be looking for someone like me —trainable, flexible, and with suitably humble expectations as to pay. I know I possess certain traits that might be advantageous—I'm white and, I like to think, well-spoken and poised—but I decide on two rules: One, I cannot use any skills derived from my education or usual work—not that there are a lot of want ads for satirical essayists anyway. Two, I have to take the best-paid job that is offered me and of course do my best to hold it; no Marxist rants or sneaking off to read novels in the ladies' room. In addition, I rule out various occupations for one reason or another: Hotel front-desk clerk, for example, which to my surprise is regarded as unskilled and pays around $7 an hour, gets eliminated because it involves standing in one spot for eight hours a day. Waitressing is similarly something I'd like to avoid, because I remember it leaving me bone tired when I was eighteen, and I'm decades of varicosities and back pain beyond that now. Telemarketing, one of the first refuges of the suddenly indigent, can be dismissed on grounds of personality. This leaves certain supermarket jobs, such as deli clerk, or housekeeping in Key West's thousands of hotel and guest rooms. Housekeeping is especially appealing, for reasons both atavistic and practical: it's what my mother did before I came along, and it can't be too different from what I've been doing part-time, in my own home, all my life.

So I put on what I take to be a respectful-looking outfit of ironed Bermuda shorts and scooped-neck T-shirt and set out for a tour of the local hotels and supermarkets. Best Western, Econo Lodge, and HoJo's all let me fill out application forms, and these are, to my relief, interested in little more than whether I am a legal resident of the United States and have committed any felonies. My next stop is Winn-Dixie, the supermarket, which turns out to have a particularly onerous application process, featuring a fifteen-minute "interview" by computer since, apparently, no human on the premises is deemed capable of representing the corporate point of view. I am conducted to a large room decorated with posters illustrating how to look "professional" (it helps to be white and, if female, permed) and warning of the slick promises that union organizers might try to tempt me with. The interview is multiple choice: Do I have anything, such as child-care problems, that might make it hard for me to get to work on time? Do I think safety on the job is the responsibility of management? Then, popping up cunningly out of the blue: How many dollars' worth of stolen goods have I purchased in the last year? Would I turn in a fellow employee if I caught him stealing? Finally, "Are you an honest person?"

Apparently, I ace the interview, because I am told that all I have to do is show up in some doctor's office tomorrow for a urine test. This seems to be a fairly general rule: if you want to stack Cheerio boxes or vacuum hotel rooms in chemically fascist America, you have to be willing to squat down and pee in front of some health worker (who has no doubt had to do the same thing herself). The wages Winn-Dixie is offering—$6 and a couple of dimes to start with—are not enough, I decide, to compensate for this indignity.[2]

I lunch at Wendy's, where $4.99 gets you unlimited refills at the Mexican part of the Superbar, a comforting surfeit of refried beans and "cheese sauce." A teenage employee, seeing me studying the want ads, kindly offers me an application form, which I fill out, though here, too, the pay is just $6 and change an hour. Then it's off for a round of the locally owned inns and guesthouses. At "The Palms," let's call it, a bouncy manager actually takes me around to see the rooms and meet the existing housekeepers, who, I note with satisfaction, look pretty much like me—faded ex-hippie types in shorts with long hair pulled back in braids. Mostly, though, no one speaks to me or even looks at me except to proffer an application form. At my last stop, a palatial B&B, I wait twenty minutes to meet "Max," only to be told that there are no jobs now but there should be one soon, since "nobody lasts more than a couple weeks." (Because none of the people I talked to knew I was a reporter, I have changed their names to protect their privacy and, in some cases perhaps, their jobs.)

Three days go by like this, and, to my chagrin, no one out of the approximately twenty

---

[2] According to the *Monthly Labor Review* (November 1996), 28 percent of work sites surveyed in the service industry conduct drug tests (corporate workplaces have much higher rates), and the incidence of testing has risen markedly since the Eighties. The rate of testing is highest in the South (56 percent of work sites polled), with the Midwest in second place (50 percent). The drug most likely to be detected—marijuana, which can be detected in urine for weeks—is also the most innocuous, while heroin and cocaine are generally undetectable three days after use. Prospective employees sometimes try to cheat the tests by consuming excessive amounts of liquids and taking diuretics and even masking substances available through the Internet.

places I've applied calls me for an interview. I had been vain enough to worry about coming across as too educated for the jobs I sought, but no one even seems interested in finding out how overqualified I am. Only later will I realize that the want ads are not a reliable measure of the actual jobs available at any particular time. They are, as I should have guessed from Max's comment, the employers' insurance policy against the relentless turnover of the low-wage workforce. Most of the big hotels run ads almost continually, just to build a supply of applicants to replace the current workers as they drift away or are fired, so finding a job is just a matter of being at the right place at the right time and flexible enough to take whatever is being offered that day. This finally happens to me at one of the big discount hotel chains, where I go, as usual, for housekeeping and am sent, instead, to try out as a waitress at the attached "family restaurant," a dismal spot with a counter and about thirty tables that looks out on a parking garage and features such tempting fare as "Pollish [sic] sausage and BBQ sauce" on 95-degree days. Phillip, the dapper young West Indian who introduces himself as the manager, interviews me with about as much enthusiasm as if he were a clerk processing me for Medicare, the principal questions being what shifts can I work and when can I start. I mutter something about being woefully out of practice as a waitress, but he's already on to the uniform: I'm to show up tomorrow wearing black slacks and black shoes; he'll provide the rust-colored polo shirt with HEARTHSIDE embroidered on it, though I might want to wear my own shirt to get to work, ha ha. At the word "tomorrow," something between fear and indignation rises in my chest. I want to say, "Thank you for your time, sir, but this is just an experiment, you know, not my actual life."

◦ ◦ ◦

So begins my career at the Hearthside, I shall call it, one small profit center within a global discount hotel chain, where for two weeks I work from 2:00 till 10:00 P.M. for $2.43 an hour plus tips.[3] In some futile bid for gentility, the management has barred employees from using the front door, so my first day I enter through the kitchen, where a red-faced man with shoulder-length blond hair is throwing frozen steaks against the wall and yelling, "Fuck this shit!" "That's just Jack," explains Gail, the wiry middle-aged waitress who is assigned to train me. "He's on the rag again"— a condition occasioned, in this instance, by the fact that the cook on the morning shift had forgotten to thaw out the steaks. For the next eight hours I run after the agile Gail, absorbing bits of instruction along with fragments of personal tragedy. All food must be trayed, and the reason she's so tired today is that she woke up in a cold sweat thinking of her boyfriend, who killed himself recently in an upstate prison. No refills on lemonade. And the reason he was in prison is that a few DUIs caught up with him, that's all, could have happened to anyone. Carry the creamers to the table in a monkey bowl, never in your hand. And after he was gone she spent several months living in her truck, peeing in a plastic pee bottle and reading by candlelight at night, but you can't live in a truck in the summer, since you need to have the windows down, which means anything can get in, from mosquitoes on up.

At least Gail puts to rest any fears I had of appearing overqualified. From the first day

---

[3] According to the Fair Labor Standards Act, employers are not required to pay "tipped employees," such as restaurant servers, more than $2.13 an hour in direct wages. However, if the sum of tips plus $2.13 an hour falls below the minimum wage, or $5.15 an hour, the employer is required to make up the difference. This fact was not mentioned by managers or otherwise publicized at either of the restaurants where I worked.

on, I find that of all the things I have left behind, such as home and identity, what I miss the most is competence. Not that I have ever felt utterly competent in the writing business, in which one day's success augurs nothing at all for the next. But in my writing life, I at least have some notion of procedure: do the research, make the outline, rough out a draft, etc. As a server, though, I am beset by requests like bees: more iced tea here, ketchup over there, a to-go box for table fourteen, and where are the high chairs, anyway? Of the twenty-seven tables, up to six are usually mine at any time, though on slow afternoons or if Gail is off, I sometimes have the whole place to myself. There is the touch-screen computer-ordering system to master, which is, I suppose, meant to minimize server-cook contact, but in practice requires constant verbal fine-tuning: "That's gravy on the mashed, okay? None on the meatloaf," and so forth—while the cook scowls as if I were inventing these refinements just to torment him. Plus, something I had forgotten in the years since I was eighteen: about a third of a server's job is "side work" that's invisible to customers—sweeping, scrubbing, slicing, refilling, and restocking. If it isn't all done, every little bit of it, you're going to face the 6:00 P.M. dinner rush defenseless and probably go down in flames. I screw up dozens of times at the beginning, sustained in my shame entirely by Gail's support—"It's okay, baby, everyone does that sometime"—because, to my total surprise and despite the scientific detachment I am doing my best to maintain, I care.

The whole thing would be a lot easier if I could just skate through it as Lily Tomlin in one of her waitress skits, but I was raised by the absurd Booker T. Washingtonian precept that says: If you're going to do something, do it well. In fact, "well" isn't good enough by half. Do it better than anyone has ever done it before. Or so said my father, who must have known what he was talking about because he managed to pull himself, and us with him, up from the mile-deep copper mines of Butte to the leafy suburbs of the Northeast, ascending from boilermakers to martinis before booze beat out ambition. As in most endeavors I have encountered in my life, doing it "better than anyone" is not a reasonable goal. Still, when I wake up at 4:00 A.M. in my own cold sweat, I am not thinking about the writing deadlines I'm neglecting; I'm thinking about the table whose order I screwed up so that one of the boys didn't get his kiddie meal until the rest of the family had moved on to their Key Lime pies. That's the other powerful motivation I hadn't expected—the customers, or "patients," as I can't help thinking of them on account of the mysterious vulnerability that seems to have left them temporarily unable to feed themselves. After a few days at the Hearthside, I feel the service ethic kick in like a shot of oxytocin, the nurturance hormone. The plurality of my customers are hard-working locals—truck drivers, construction workers, even house-keepers from the attached hotel—and I want them to have the closest to a "fine dining" experience that the grubby circumstances will allow. No "you guys" for me; everyone over twelve is "sir" or "ma'am." I ply them with iced tea and coffee refills; I return, mid-meal, to inquire how everything is; I doll up their salads with chopped raw mushrooms, summer squash slices, or whatever bits of produce I can find that have survived their sojourn in the cold-storage room mold-free.

There is Benny, for example, a short, tight-muscled sewer repairman, who cannot even think of eating until he has absorbed a half hour of air-conditioning and ice water. We chat about hyperthermia and electrolytes until he is ready to order some finicky combination like soup of the day, garden salad, and a side of grits. There are the German tourists who are so touched by my pidgin "Willkommen" and "Ist alles gut?" that they actually tip. (Europeans, spoiled by their trade-union-ridden, high-wage welfare states, generally do not know that they are supposed to tip. Some restaurants, the Hearthside included, allow servers to "grat" their foreign customers, or add a tip to the bill. Since this amount is added before the customers have a chance to tip or not tip, the practice amounts to an automatic penalty for imperfect English.) There are the two dirt-smudged lesbians, just off their construction shift, who are impressed enough by my suave handling of the fly in the piña colada that they take the time to praise me to Stu, the assistant manager. There's Sam, the kindly retired cop, who has to plug up his tracheotomy hole with one finger in order to force the cigarette smoke into his lungs.

Sometimes I play with the fantasy that I am a princess who, in penance for some tiny transgression, has undertaken to feed each of her subjects by hand. But the non-princesses working with me are just as indulgent, even when this means flouting management rules—concerning, for example, the number of croutons that can go on a salad (six). "Put on all you want," Gail whispers, "as long as Stu isn't looking." She dips into her own tip money to buy biscuits and gravy for an out-of-work mechanic who's used up all his money on dental surgery, inspiring me to pick up the tab for his milk and pie. Maybe the same high levels of agape can be found throughout the "hospitality industry." I remember the poster decorating one of the apartments I looked at, which said "If you seek happiness for yourself you will never find it. Only when you seek happiness for others will it come to you," or words to that effect—an odd sentiment, it seemed to me at the time, to find in the dank one-room basement apartment of a bellhop at the Best Western. At the Hearthside, we utilize whatever bits of autonomy we have to ply our customers with the illicit calories that signal our love. It is our job as servers to assemble the salads and desserts, pouring the dressings and squirting the whipped cream. We also control the number of butter patties our customers get and the amount of sour cream on their baked potatoes. So if you wonder why Americans are so obese, consider the fact that waitresses both express their humanity and earn their tips through the covert distribution of fats.

Ten days into it, this is beginning to look like a livable lifestyle. I like Gail, who is "looking at fifty" but moves so fast she can alight in one place and then another without apparently being anywhere between them. I clown around with Lionel, the teenage Haitian busboy, and catch a few fragments of conversation with Joan, the svelte fortyish hostess and militant feminist who is the only one of us who dares to tell Jack to shut the fuck up. I even warm up to Jack when, on a slow night and to make up for a particularly unwarranted attack on my abilities, or so I imagine, he tells me about his glory days as a young man at "coronary school"—or do you say "culinary"?—in Brooklyn, where he dated a knock-out Puerto Rican chick and learned everything there is to know about food. I finish up at 10:00 or 10:30, depending on how much side work I've been able to get done during the shift, and cruise home to the tapes I snatched up at random when I left my real home—Marianne Faithfull, Tracy Chapman, Enigma, King Sunny Ade, the Violent Femmes—just drained enough for the music to set my cranium resonating but hardly dead. Midnight snack is Wheat Thins and Monterey Jack, accompanied by cheap white wine on ice and whatever AMC has to offer. To bed by 1:30 or 2:00, up at 9:00 or 10:00, read for an hour while my uniform whirls around in the landlord's washing machine, and then it's another eight hours spent following Mao's central instruction, as laid out in the Little Red Book, which was: Serve the people.

❖   ❖   ❖

I could drift along like this, in some dreamy proletarian idyll, except for two things. One is management. If I have kept this subject on the margins thus far it is because I still flinch to think that I spent all those weeks under the surveillance of men (and later women) whose job it was to monitor my behavior for signs of sloth, theft, drug abuse, or worse. Not that managers and especially "assistant managers" in low-wage settings like this are exactly the class enemy. In the restaurant business, they are mostly former cooks or servers, still capable of pinch-hitting in the kitchen or on the floor, just as in hotels they are likely to be former clerks, and paid a salary of only about $400 a week. But everyone knows they have crossed over to the other side, which is crudely put, corporate as opposed to human. Cooks want to prepare tasty meals; servers want to serve them graciously; but managers are there for only one reason—to make sure that money is made for some theoretical entity that exists far away in Chicago or New York, if a corporation can be said to have a physical existence at all. Reflecting on her career, Gail tells me ruefully that she had sworn, years ago, never to work for a corporation again. "They don't cut you no slack. You give and you give, and they take."

Managers can sit—for hours at a time if they want—but it's their job to see that no one else ever does, even when there's nothing to do, and this is why, for servers, slow times can be as exhausting as rushes. You start dragging out each little chore, because if the manager on duty catches you in an idle moment, he will give you something far nastier to do. So I wipe, I clean, I consolidate ketchup bottles and recheck the cheesecake supply, even tour the tables to make sure the customer evaluation forms are all standing perkily in their places—wondering all the time how many calories I burn in these strictly theatrical exercises. When, on a particularly dead afternoon, Stu finds me glancing at a *USA Today* a customer has left behind, he assigns me to vacuum the entire floor with the broken vacuum cleaner that has a handle only two feet long, and the only way to do that without incurring orthopedic damage is to proceed from spot to spot on your knees.

On my first Friday at the Hearthside there is a "mandatory meeting for all restaurant employees," which I attend, eager for insight into our overall marketing strategy and the niche (your basic Ohio cuisine with a tropical twist?) we aim to inhabit. But there is no "we" at this meeting. Phillip, our top manager except for an occasional "consultant" sent out by corporate headquarters, opens it with a sneer: "The break room—it's disgusting. Butts in the ashtrays, newspapers lying around, crumbs." This windowless little room, which also houses the time clock for the entire hotel, is where we stash our bags and civilian clothes and take our half-hour meal breaks. But a break room is not a right, he tells us. It can be taken away. We should also know that the lockers in the break room and whatever is in them can be searched at any time. Then comes gossip; there has been gossip; gossip (which seems to mean employees talking among themselves) must stop. Off-duty employees are henceforth barred from eating at the restaurant, because "other servers gather around them and gossip." When Phillip has exhausted his agenda of rebukes, Joan complains about the condition of the ladies' room and I throw in my two bits about the vacuum cleaner. But I don't see any backup coming from my fellow servers, each of whom has subsided into her own personal funk; Gail, my role model, stares sorrowfully at a point six inches from her nose. The meeting ends when Andy, one of the cooks, gets up, muttering about breaking up his day off for this almighty bullshit.

Just four days later we are suddenly summoned into the kitchen at 3:30 P.M., even though there are live tables on the floor. We all—about ten of us—stand around Phillip, who announces grimly that there has been a report of some "drug activity" on the night shift and that, as a result, we are now to be a "drug-free" workplace, meaning that all new hires will be tested, as will possibly current employees on a random basis. I am glad that this part of the kitchen is so dark, because I find myself blushing as hard as if I had been caught toking up in the ladies' room myself: I haven't been treated this way—lined up in the corridor, threatened with locker searches, peppered with carelessly aimed accusations—since junior high school. Back on the floor, Joan cracks, "Next they'll be telling us we can't have sex on the job." When I ask Stu what happened to inspire the crackdown, he just mutters about "management decisions" and takes the opportunity to upbraid Gail and me for being too generous with the rolls. From now on there's to be only one per customer, and it goes out with the dinner, not with the salad. He's also been riding the cooks, prompting Andy to come out of the kitchen and observe—with the serenity of a man whose customary implement is a butcher knife—that "Stu has a death wish today."

Later in the evening, the gossip crystallizes around the theory that Stu is himself the drug culprit, that he uses the restaurant phone to order up marijuana and sends one of the late servers out to fetch it for him. The server was caught, and she may have ratted Stu out or at least said enough to cast some suspicion on him, thus accounting for his pissy behavior. Who knows? Lionel, the busboy, entertains us for the rest of the shift by standing just behind Stu's back and sucking deliriously on an imaginary joint.

The other problem, in addition to the less-than-nurturing management style, is that this job shows no sign of being financially viable. You might imagine, from a comfortable distance, that people who live, year in and year out, on $6 to $10 an hour have discovered some survival stratagems unknown to the middle class. But no. It's not hard to get my co-workers to talk about their living situations, because housing, in almost every case, is the principal source of disruption in their lives, the first thing they fill you in on when they arrive for their shifts. After a week, I have compiled the following survey:

- Gail is sharing a room in a well-known downtown flophouse for which she and a roommate pay about $250 a week. Her roommate, a male friend, has begun hitting on her, driving her nuts, but the rent would be impossible alone.
- Claude, the Haitian cook, is desperate to get out of the two-room apartment he shares with his girlfriend and two other, unrelated, people. As far as I can determine, the other Haitian men (most of whom only speak Creole) live in similarly crowded situations.
- Annette, a twenty-year-old server who is six months pregnant and has been abandoned by her boyfriend, lives with her mother, a postal clerk.
- Marianne and her boyfriend are paying $170 a week for a one-person trailer.
- Jack, who is, at $10 an hour, the wealthiest of us, lives in the trailer he owns, paying only the $400-a-month lot fee.
- The other white cook, Andy, lives on his dry-docked boat, which, as far as I can tell from his loving descriptions, can't be more than twenty feet long. He offers to take me out on it, once it's repaired, but the offer comes with inquiries as to my marital status, so I do not follow up on it.
- Tina and her husband are paying $60 a night for a double room in a Days Inn. This is because they have no car and the Days Inn is within walking distance of the Hearthside. When Marianne, one of the breakfast servers, is tossed out of her trailer for subletting (which is against the trailer-park rules), she leaves her boyfriend and moves in with Tina and her husband.
- Joan, who had fooled me with her numerous and tasteful outfits (hostesses wear their own

clothes), lives in a van she parks behind a shopping center at night and showers in Tina's motel room. The clothes are from thrift shops.[4]

⋅o⋅ ⋅o⋅ ⋅o⋅

It strikes me, in my middle-class solipsism, that there is gross improvidence in some of these arrangements. When Gail and I are wrapping silverware in napkins—the only task for which we are permitted to sit—she tells me she is thinking of escaping from her roommate by moving into the Days Inn herself. I am astounded: How can she even think of paying between $40 and $60 a day? But if I was afraid of sounding like a social worker, I come out just sounding like a fool. She squints at me in disbelief, "And where am I supposed to get a month's rent and a month's deposit for an apartment?" I'd been feeling pretty smug about my $500 efficiency, but of course it was made possible only by the $1,300 I had allotted myself for start-up costs when I began my low-wage life: $1,000 for the first month's rent and deposit, $100 for initial groceries and cash in my pocket, $200 stuffed away for emergencies. In poverty, as in certain propositions in physics, starting conditions are everything.

There are no secret economies that nourish the poor; on the contrary, there are a host of special costs. If you can't put up the two months' rent you need to secure an apartment, you end up paying through the nose for a room by the week. If you have only a room, with a hot plate at best, you can't save by cooking up huge lentil stews that can be frozen for the week ahead. You eat fast food, or the hot dogs and styrofoam cups of soup that can be microwaved in a convenience store. If you have no money for health insurance—and the Hearthside's niggardly plan kicks in only after three months—you go without routine care or prescription drugs and end up paying the price. Gail, for example, was fine until she ran out of money for estrogen pills. She is supposed to be on the company plan by now, but they claim to have lost her application form and need to begin the paperwork all over again. So she spends $9 per migraine pill to control the headaches she wouldn't have, she insists, if her estrogen supplements were covered. Similarly, Marianne's boyfriend lost his job as a roofer because he missed so much time after getting a cut on his foot for which he couldn't afford the prescribed antibiotic.

My own situation, when I sit down to assess it after two weeks of work, would not be much better if this were my actual life. The seductive thing about waitressing is that you don't have to wait for payday to feel a few bills in your pocket, and my tips usually cover meals and gas, plus something left over to stuff into the kitchen drawer I use as a bank. But as the tourist business slows in the summer heat, I sometimes leave work with only $20 in tips (the gross is higher, but servers share about 15 percent of their tips with the bus-boys and bartenders). With wages included, this amounts to about the minimum wage of $5.15 an hour. Although the sum in the drawer is piling up, at the present rate of accumulation it will be more than a hundred dollars short of my rent when the end of the month comes around. Nor can I see any expenses to cut. True, I haven't gone the lentil-stew route yet, but that's because I don't have a large cooking pot, pot holders, or a ladle to stir with (which cost

---

[4] I could find no statistics on the number of employed people living in cars or vans, but according to the National Coalition for the Homeless's 1997 report "Myths and Facts About Homelessness," nearly one in five homeless people (in twenty-nine cities across the nation) is employed in a full- or part-time job.

about $30 at Kmart, less at thrift stores), not to mention onions, carrots, and the indispensable bay leaf. I do make my lunch almost every day—usually some slow-burning, high-protein combo like frozen chicken patties with melted cheese on top and canned pinto beans on the side. Dinner is at the Hearthside, which offers its employees a choice of BLT, fish sandwich, or hamburger for only $2. The burger lasts longest, especially if it's heaped with gut-puckering jalapeños, but by midnight my stomach is growling again.

So unless I want to start using my car as a residence, I have to find a second, or alternative, job. I call all the hotels where I filled out housekeeping applications weeks ago—the Hyatt, Holiday Inn, Econo Lodge, HoJo's, Best Western, plus a half dozen or so locally run guesthouses. Nothing. Then I start making the rounds again, wasting whole mornings waiting for some assistant manager to show up, even dipping into places so creepy that the front-desk clerk greets you from behind bulletproof glass and sells pints of liquor over the counter. But either someone has exposed my real-life housekeeping habits—which are, shall we say, mellow—or I am at the wrong end of some infallible ethnic equation: most, but by no means all, of the working housekeepers I see on my job searches are African Americans, Spanish-speaking, or immigrants from the Central European post-Communist world, whereas servers are almost invariably white and monolingually English-speaking. When I finally get a positive response, I have been identified once again as server material. Jerry's, which is part of a well-known national family restaurant chain and physically attached here to another budget hotel chain, is ready to use me at once. The prospect is both exciting and terrifying, because, with about the same number of tables and counter seats, Jerry's attracts three or four times the volume of customers as the gloomy old Hearthside.

❖   ❖   ❖

Picture a fat person's hell, and I don't mean a place with no food. Instead there is everything you might eat if eating had no bodily consequences—cheese fries, chicken-fried steaks, fudge-laden desserts—only here every bite must be paid for, one way or another, in human discomfort. The kitchen is a cavern, a stomach leading to the lower intestine that is the garbage and dishwashing area, from which issue bizarre smells combining the edible and the offal: creamy carrion, pizza barf, and that unique and enigmatic Jerry's scent—citrus fart. The floor is slick with spills, forcing us to walk through the kitchen with tiny steps, like Susan McDougal in leg irons. Sinks everywhere are clogged with scraps of lettuce, decomposing lemon wedges, waterlogged toast crusts. Put your hand down on any counter and you risk being stuck to it by the film of ancient syrup spills, and this is unfortunate, because hands are utensils here, used for scooping up lettuce onto salad plates, lifting out pie slices, and even moving hash browns from one plate to another. The regulation poster in the single unisex restroom admonishes us to wash our hands thoroughly and even offers instructions for doing so, but there is always some vital substance missing—soap, paper towels, toilet paper—and I never find all three at once. You learn to stuff your pockets with napkins before going in there, and too bad about the customers, who must eat, though they don't realize this, almost literally out of our hands.

The break room typifies the whole situation: there is none, because there are no breaks at Jerry's. For six to eight hours in a row, you never sit except to pee. Actually, there are three folding chairs at a table immediately adjacent to the bathroom, but hardly anyone ever sits here, in the very rectum of the gastro-architectural system. Rather, the function of the peri-toilet area is to house the ashtrays in which servers and dishwashers leave their cigarettes burning at all times, like votive candles, so that they don't have to waste time lighting up again when they dash back for a puff. Almost everyone smokes as if his or her pulmonary well-being depended on it—the multinational mélange of cooks, the Czech dishwashers, the servers, who are all American natives—creating an atmosphere in which oxygen is only an occasional pollutant. My first morning at Jerry's, when the hypoglycemic shakes set in, I complain to one of my fellow servers that I don't understand how she can go so long without food. "Well, I don't understand how you can go so long without a cigarette," she responds in a tone of reproach—because work is what you do for others; smoking is what you do for yourself. I don't know why the antismoking crusaders have never grasped the element of defiant self-nurturance that makes the habit so endearing to its victims—as if, in the American workplace, the only thing people have to call their own is the tumors they are nourishing and the spare moments they devote to feeding them.

Now, the Industrial Revolution is not an easy transition, especially when you have to zip through it in just a couple of days. I have gone from craft work straight into the factory, from the air-conditioned morgue of the Hearthside directly into the flames. Customers arrive in human waves, sometimes disgorged fifty at a time from their tour buses, peckish and whiny. Instead of two "girls" on the floor at once, there can be as many as six of us running around in our brilliant pink-and-orange Hawaiian shirts. Conversations, either with customers or fellow employees, seldom last more than twenty seconds at a time. On my first day, in fact, I am hurt by my sister servers' coldness. My mentor for the day is an emotionally uninflected twenty-three-year-old, and the others, who gossip a little among themselves about the real reason someone is out sick today and the size of the bail bond someone else has had to pay, ignore me completely. On my second day, I find out why. "Well, it's good to see you again," one of them says in greeting. "Hardly anyone comes back after the first day." I feel powerfully vindicated—a survivor—but it would take a long time, probably months, before I could hope to be accepted into this sorority.

I start out with the beautiful, heroic idea of handling the two jobs at once, and for two days I almost do it: the breakfast/lunch shift at Jerry's, which goes till 2:00, arriving at the Hearthside at 2:10, and attempting to hold out until 10:00. In the ten minutes between jobs, I pick up a spicy chicken sandwich at the Wendy's drive-through window, gobble it down in the car, and change from khaki slacks to black, from Hawaiian to rust polo. There is a problem, though. When during the 3:00 to 4:00 P.M. dead time I finally sit down to wrap silver, my flesh seems to bond to the seat. I try to refuel with a purloined cup of soup, as I've seen Gail and Joan do dozens of times, but a manager catches me and hisses "No eating!" though there's not a customer around to be offended by the sight of food making contact with a server's lips. So I tell Gail I'm going to quit, and she hugs me and says she might just follow me to Jerry's herself.

But the chances of this are minuscule. She has left the flophouse and her annoying roommate and is back to living in her beat-up old truck. But guess what? she reports to me excitedly later that evening: Phillip has given her permission to park overnight in the hotel parking lot, as long as she keeps out of sight, and the parking lot should be totally safe, since it's patrolled by a hotel security guard! With the Hearthside offering benefits like that, how could anyone think of leaving?

Gail would have triumphed at Jerry's, I'm sure, but for me it's a crash course in exhaustion management. Years ago, the kindly fry cook who trained me to waitress at a Los Angeles truck stop used to say: Never make an unnecessary trip; if you don't have to walk fast, walk slow; if you don't have to walk, stand. But at Jerry's the effort of distinguishing necessary from unnecessary and urgent from whenever would itself be too much of an energy drain. The only thing to do is to treat each shift as a one-time-only emergency: you've got fifty starving people out there, lying scattered on the battlefield, so get out there and feed them! Forget that you will have to do this again tomorrow, forget that you will have to be alert enough to dodge the drunks on the drive home tonight—just burn, burn, burn! Ideally, at some point you enter what servers call "a rhythm" and psychologists term a "flow state," in which signals pass from the sense organs directly to the muscles, bypassing the cerebral cortex, and a Zen-like emptiness sets in. A male server from the Hearthside's morning shift tells me about the time he "pulled a triple"—three shifts in a row, all the way around the clock—and then got off and had a drink and met this girl, and maybe he shouldn't tell me this, but they had sex right then and there, and it was like, beautiful.

But there's another capacity of the neuromuscular system, which is pain. I start tossing back drugstore-brand ibuprofen pills as if they were vitamin C, four before each shift, because an old mouse-related repetitive-stress injury in my upper back has come back to full-spasm strength, thanks to the tray carrying. In my ordinary life, this level of disability might justify a day of ice packs and stretching. Here I comfort myself with the Aleve commercial in which the cute blue-collar guy asks: If you quit after working four hours, what would your boss say? And the not-so-cute blue-collar guy, who's lugging a metal beam on his back answers: He'd fire me, that's what. But fortunately, the commercial tells us, we workers can exert the same kind of authority over our painkillers that our bosses exert over us. If Tylenol doesn't want to work for more than four hours, you just fire its ass and switch to Aleve.

True, I take occasional breaks from this life, going home now and then to catch up on e-mail and for conjugal visits (though I am careful to "pay" for anything I eat there), seeing *The Truman Show* with friends and letting them buy my ticket. And I still have those what-am-I-doing-here moments at work, when I get so homesick for the printed word that I obsessively reread the six-page menu. But as the days go by, my old life is beginning to look exceedingly strange. The e-mails and phone messages addressed to my former self come from a distant race of people with exotic concerns and far too much time on their hands. The neighborly market I used to cruise for produce now looks forbiddingly like a Manhattan yuppie emporium. And when I sit down one morning in my real home to pay bills from my past life, I am dazzled at the two- and three-figure sums owed to outfits like Club Body Tech and Amazon.com.

❖ ❖ ❖

Management at Jerry's is generally calmer and more "professional" than at the Hearthside, with two exceptions. One is Joy, a plump, blowsy woman in her early thirties, who once kindly devoted several minutes to instructing me in the correct one-handed method of carrying trays but whose moods change disconcertingly from shift to shift and even within one. Then there's B.J., a.k.a. B.J.-the-bitch, whose contribution is to stand by the kitchen counter and yell, "Nita, your order's up, move it!" or, "Barbara, didn't you see you've got another table out there? Come on, girl!" Among other things, she is hated for having replaced the whipped-cream squirt cans with big plastic whipped-cream-filled baggies that have to be squeezed with both hands—because, reportedly, she saw or thought she saw employees trying to inhale the propellant gas from the squirt cans, in the hope that it might be nitrous oxide. On my third night, she pulls me aside abruptly and brings her face so close that it looks as if she's planning to butt me with her forehead. But instead of saying, "You're fired," she says, "You're doing fine." The only trouble is I'm spending time chatting with customers: "That's how they're getting you." Furthermore I am letting them "run me," which means harassment by sequential demands: you bring the ketchup and they decide they want extra Thousand Island; you bring that and they announce they now need a side of fries; and so on into distraction. Finally she tells me not to take her wrong. She tries to say things in a nice way, but you get into a mode, you know, because everything has to move so fast.[5]

I mumble thanks for the advice, feeling like I've just been stripped naked by the crazed enforcer of some ancient sumptuary law: No chatting for you, girl. No fancy service ethic allowed for the serfs. Chatting with customers is for the beautiful young college-educated servers in the downtown carpaccio joints, the kids who can make $70 to $100 a night. What had I been thinking? My job is to move orders from tables to kitchen and then trays from kitchen to tables. Customers are, in fact, the major obstacle to the smooth transformation of information into food and food into money—they are, in short, the enemy. And the painful thing is that I'm beginning to see it this way myself. There are the traditional asshole types—frat boys who down multiple Buds and then make a fuss because the steaks are so emaciated and the fries so sparse—as well as the variously impaired—due to age, diabetes, or literacy issues—who require patient nutritional counseling. The worst, for some reason, are the Visible Christians—like the ten-person table, all jolly and sanctified after Sunday-night service, who run me mercilessly and then leave me $1 on a $92 bill. Or the guy with the crucifixion T-shirt (SOMEONE TO LOOK UP TO) who complains that his baked potato is too hard and his iced tea too icy (I cheerfully fix both) and leaves no tip. As a general rule, people wearing crosses or WWJD? (What Would Jesus Do?) buttons look at us disapprovingly no matter what we do, as if they were confusing waitressing with Mary Magdalene's original profession.

I make friends, over time, with the other "girls" who work my shift: Nita, the tattooed twenty-something who taunts us by going around saying brightly, "Have we started making money yet?" Ellen, whose teenage son cooks on the graveyard shift and who once managed a restaurant in Massachusetts but won't try out for management here because she prefers being a "common worker" and not "ordering people around." Easy-going fiftyish Lucy, with the raucous laugh, who limps toward the end of the shift because of something that has gone wrong with her leg, the exact nature of which cannot be determined without health insurance. We talk about the usual girl things—men, children, and the sinister allure of Jerry's chocolate peanut-butter cream pie—though no one, I notice, ever brings up anything potentially expensive, like shopping or movies. As at the Hearthside, the only recreation ever referred to is partying, which requires little more than some beer, a joint, and a few close friends. Still, no one here is homeless, or cops to it anyway, thanks usually to a working husband or boyfriend. All in all, we form a reliable mutual-support group: If one of us is feeling sick or overwhelmed, another one will "bev" a table or even carry trays for

[5] In *Workers in a Lean World: Unions in the International Economy* (Verso, 1997), Kim Moody cites studies finding an increase in stress-related workplace injuries and illness between the mid-1980s and the early 1990s. He argues that rising stress levels reflect a new system of "management by stress," in which workers in a variety of industries are being squeezed to extract maximum productivity, to the detriment of their health.

her. If one of us is off sneaking a cigarette or a pee,[6] the others will do their best to conceal her absence from the enforcers of corporate rationality.

But my saving human connection—my oxytocin receptor, as it were—is George, the nineteen-year-old, fresh-off-the-boat Czech dishwasher. We get to talking when he asks me, tortuously, how much cigarettes cost at Jerry's. I do my best to explain that they cost over a dollar more here than at a regular store and suggest that he just take one from the half-filled packs that are always lying around on the break table. But that would be unthinkable. Except for the one tiny earring signaling his allegiance to some vaguely alternative point of view, George is a perfect straight arrow—crew-cut, hardworking, and hungry for eye contact. "Czech Republic," I ask, "or Slovakia?" and he seems delighted that I know the difference. "Václav Havel," I try. "Velvet Revolution, Frank Zappa?" "Yes, yes, 1989," he says, and I realize we are talking about history.

My project is to teach George English. "How are you today, George?" I say at the start of each shift. "I am good, and how are you today, Barbara?" I learn that he is not paid by Jerry's but by the "agent" who shipped him over—$5 an hour, with the agent getting the dollar or so difference between that and what Jerry's pays dishwashers. I learn also that he shares an apartment with a crowd of other Czech "dishers," as he calls them, and that he cannot sleep until one of them goes off for his shift, leaving a vacant bed. We are having one of our ESL sessions late one afternoon when B.J. catches us at it and orders "Joseph" to take up the rubber mats on the floor near the dishwashing sinks and mop underneath. "I thought your name was George," I say loud enough for B.J. to hear as she strides off back to the counter. Is she embarrassed? Maybe a little, because she greets me back at the counter with "George, Joseph—there are so many of them!" I say nothing, neither nodding nor smiling, and for this I am punished later when I think I am ready to go and she announces that I need to roll fifty more sets of silverware and isn't it time I mixed up a fresh four-gallon batch of blue-cheese dressing? May you grow old in this place, B.J., is the curse I beam out at her when I am finally permitted to leave. May the syrup spills glue your feet to the floor.

I make the decision to move closer to Key West. First, because of the drive. Second and third, also because of the drive: gas is eating up $4 to $5 a day, and although Jerry's is as high-volume as you can get, the tips average only 10 percent, and not just for a newbie like me. Between the base pay of $2.15 an hour and the obligation to share tips with the busboys and dishwashers, we're averaging only about $7.50 an hour. Then there is the $30 I had to spend on the regulation tan slacks worn by Jerry's servers—a setback it could take weeks to absorb. (I had combed the town's two downscale department stores hoping for something cheaper but decided in the end that these marked-down Dockers, originally $49, were more likely to

---

[6] Until April 1998, there was no federally mandated right to bathroom breaks. According to Marc Linder and Ingrid Nygaard, authors of *Void Where Prohibited: Rest Breaks and the Right to Urinate on Company Time* (Cornell University Press, 1997), "The right to rest and void at work is not high on the list of social or political causes supported by professional or executive employees, who enjoy personal workplace liberties that millions of factory workers can only daydream about. . . . While we were dismayed to discover that workers lacked an acknowledged legal right to void at work, [the workers] were amazed by outsiders' naive belief that their employers would permit them to perform this basic bodily function when necessary. . . . A factory worker, not allowed a break for six-hour stretches, voided into pads worn inside her uniform; and a kindergarten teacher in a school without aides had to take all twenty children with her to the bathroom and line them up outside the stall door when she voided."

survive a daily washing.) Of my fellow servers, everyone who lacks a working husband or boyfriend seems to have a second job: Nita does something at a computer eight hours a day; another welds. Without the forty-five-minute commute, I can picture myself working two jobs and having the time to shower between them.

So I take the $500 deposit I have coming from my landlord, the $400 I have earned toward the next month's rent, plus the $200 reserved for emergencies, and use the $1,100 to pay the rent and deposit on trailer number 46 in the Overseas Trailer Park, a mile from the cluster of budget hotels that constitute Key West's version of an industrial park. Number 46 is about eight feet in width and shaped like a barbell inside, with a narrow region—because of the sink and the stove—separating the bedroom from what might optimistically be called the "living" area, with its two-person table and half-sized couch. The bathroom is so small my knees rub against the shower stall when I sit on the toilet, and you can't just leap out of the bed, you have to climb down to the foot of it in order to find a patch of floor space to stand on. Outside, I am within a few yards of a liquor store, a bar that advertises "free beer tomorrow," a convenience store, and a Burger King—but no supermarket or, alas, laundromat. By reputation, the Overseas park is a nest of crime and crack, and I am hoping at least for some vibrant, multicultural street life. But desolation rules night and day, except for a thin stream of pedestrian traffic heading for their jobs at the Sheraton or 7-Eleven. There are not exactly people here but what amounts to canned labor, being preserved from the heat between shifts.

❧ ❧ ❧

In line with my reduced living conditions, a new form of ugliness arises at Jerry's. First we are confronted—via an announcement on the computers through which we input orders—with the new rule that the hotel bar is henceforth off-limits to restaurant employees. The culprit, I learn through the grapevine, is the ultra-efficient gal who trained me—another trailer-home dweller and a mother of three. Something had set her off one morning, so she slipped out for a nip and returned to the floor impaired. This mostly hurts Ellen, whose habit it is to free her hair from its rubber band and drop by the bar for a couple of Zins before heading home at the end of the shift, but all of us feel the chill. Then the next day, when I go for straws, for the first time I find the dry-storage room locked. Ted, the portly assistant manager who opens it for me, explains that he caught one of the dishwashers attempting to steal something, and, unfortunately, the miscreant will be with us until a replacement can be found—hence the locked door. I neglect to ask what he had been trying to steal, but Ted tells me who he is—the kid with the buzz cut and the earring. You know, he's back there right now.

I wish I could say I rushed back and confronted George to get his side of the story. I wish I could say I stood up to Ted and insisted that George be given a translator and allowed to defend himself, or announced that I'd find a lawyer who'd handle the case pro bono. The mystery to me is that there's not much worth stealing in the dry-storage room, at least not in any fenceable quantity: "Is Gyorgi here, and am having 200—maybe 250—ketchup packets. What do you say?" My guess is that he had taken—if he had taken anything at all—some Saltines or a can of cherry-pie mix, and that the motive for taking it was hunger.

So why didn't I intervene? Certainly not because I was held back by the kind of moral paralysis that can pass as journalistic objectivity. On the contrary, something new—something loathsome and servile—had infected me, along with the kitchen odors that I could still sniff on my bra when I finally undressed at night. In real life I am moderately brave, but plenty of brave people shed their courage in concentration camps, and maybe something similar goes on in the infinitely more congenial milieu of the low-wage American workplace. Maybe, in a month or two more at Jerry's, I might have regained my crusading spirit. Then again, in a month or two I might have turned into a different person altogether—say, the kind of person who would have turned George in.

But this is not something I am slated to find out. When my month-long plunge into poverty is almost over, I finally land my dream job—housekeeping. I do this by walking into the personnel office of the only place I figure I might have some credibility, the hotel attached to Jerry's, and confiding urgently that I have to have a second job if I am to pay my rent and, no, it couldn't be front-desk clerk. "All right," the personnel lady fairly spits, "So it's housekeeping," and she marches me back to meet Maria, the housekeeping manager, a tiny, frenetic Hispanic woman who greets me as "babe" and hands me a pamphlet emphasizing the need for a positive attitude. The hours are nine in the morning till whenever, the pay is $6.10 an hour, and there's one week of vacation a year. I don't have to ask about health insurance once I meet Carlotta, the middle-aged African-American woman who will be training me. Carla, as she tells me to call her, is missing all of her top front teeth.

❦ ❦ ❦

On that first day of housekeeping and last day of my entire project—although I don't yet know it's the last—Carla is in a foul mood. We have been given nineteen rooms to clean, most of them "checkouts," as opposed to "stayovers," that require the whole enchilada of bedstripping, vacuuming, and bathroom-scrubbing. When one of the rooms that had been listed as a stay-over turns out to be a checkout, Carla calls Maria to complain, but of course to no avail. "So make up the motherfucker," Carla orders me, and I do the beds while she sloshes around the bathroom. For four hours without a break I strip and remake beds, taking about four and a half minutes per queen-sized bed, which I could get down to three if there were any reason to. We try to avoid vacuuming by picking up the larger specks by hand, but often there is nothing to do but drag the monstrous vacuum cleaner—it weighs about thirty pounds—off our cart and try to wrestle it around the floor. Sometimes Carla hands me the squirt bottle of "BAM" (an acronym for something that begins, ominously, with "butyric"; the rest has been worn off the label) and lets me do the bathrooms. No service ethic challenges me here to new heights of performance. I just concentrate on removing the pubic hairs from the bathtubs, or at least the dark ones that I can see.

I had looked forward to the breaking-and-entering aspect of cleaning the stay-overs, the chance to examine the secret, physical existence of strangers. But the contents of the rooms are always banal and surprisingly neat—zipped up shaving kits, shoes lined up against the wall (there are no closets), flyers for snorkeling trips, maybe an empty wine bottle or two. It is the TV that keeps us going, from Jerry to Sally to Hawaii Five-O and then on to the soaps. If there's something especially arresting, like "Won't Take No for an Answer" on Jerry, we sit down on the edge of a bed and giggle for a moment as if this were a pajama party instead of a terminally dead-end job. The soaps are the best, and Carla turns the volume up full blast so that she won't miss anything from the bathroom or while the vacuum is on. In room 503, Marcia confronts Jeff about Lauren. In 505, Lauren taunts poor cuckolded Marcia. In 511, Helen offers Amanda $10,000 to stop seeing Eric, prompting Carla to emerge from the bathroom to study Amanda's troubled face. "You take it, girl," she advises. "I would for sure."

The tourists' rooms that we clean and, beyond them, the far more expensively appointed interiors in the soaps, begin after a while to merge. We have entered a better world—a world of comfort where every day is a day off, waiting to be filled up with sexual intrigue. We, however, are only gatecrashers in this fantasy, forced to pay for our presence with backaches and perpetual thirst. The mirrors, and there are far too many of them in hotel rooms, contain the kind of person you would normally find pushing a shopping cart down a city street—bedraggled, dressed in a damp hotel polo shirt two sizes too large, and with sweat dribbling down her chin like drool. I am enormously relieved when Carla announces a half-hour meal break, but my appetite fades when I see that the bag of hot-dog rolls she has been carrying around on our cart is not trash salvaged from a checkout but what she has brought for her lunch.

When I request permission to leave at about 3:30, another housekeeper warns me that no one has so far succeeded in combining housekeeping at the hotel with serving at Jerry's: "Some kid did it once for five days, and you're no kid." With that helpful information in mind, I rush back to number 46, down four Advils (the name brand this time), shower, stooping to fit into the stall, and attempt to compose myself for the oncoming shift. So much for what Marx termed the "reproduction of labor power," meaning the things a worker has to do just so she'll be ready to work again. The only unforeseen obstacle to the smooth transition from job to job is that my tan Jerry's slacks, which had looked reasonably clean by 40-watt bulb last night when I handwashed my Hawaiian shirt, prove by daylight to be mottled with ketchup and ranch-dressing stains. I spend most of my hour-long break between jobs attempting to remove the edible portions with a sponge and then drying the slacks over the hood of my car in the sun.

I can do this two-job thing, is my theory, if I can drink enough caffeine and avoid getting distracted by George's ever more obvious suffering.[7] The first few days after being caught he seemed not to understand the trouble he was in, and our chirpy little conversations had continued. But the last couple of shifts he's been listless and unshaven, and tonight he looks like the ghost we all know him to be, with dark half-moons hanging from his eyes. At one point, when I am briefly immobilized by the task of filling little paper cups with sour cream for baked potatoes, he comes over and looks as if he'd like to explore the limits of our shared vocabulary, but I am called to the floor for a table. I resolve to give him all my tips that night and to hell with the experiment in low-wage money management. At eight, Ellen and I grab a snack together standing at the mephitic end of the kitchen counter, but I can only manage two or three mozzarella sticks and lunch had been a mere handful of McNuggets. I am not tired at all, I assure myself, though it may be that there is simply no more "I" left to do the tiredness monitoring. What I would see, if I were more alert to the situation, is that the forces of destruction are already massing against me. There is only one cook on duty, a young man named Jesus ("Hay-Sue," that is) and he is new to the job. And there is Joy, who shows up to take over in the middle of the shift, wearing high heels and a long, clingy white dress and fuming as if she'd just been stood up in some cocktail bar.

Then it comes, the perfect storm. Four of my tables fill up at once. Four tables is nothing for me now, but only so long as they are obligingly staggered. As I bev table 27, tables 25, 28, and 24 are watching enviously. As I bev 25, 24 glowers because their bevs haven't even been ordered. Twenty-eight is four yuppyish types, meaning everything on the side and ag-

---

[7] In 1996, the number of persons holding two or more jobs averaged 7.8 million, or 6.2 percent of the workforce. It was about the same rate for men and for women (6.1 versus 6.2), though the kinds of jobs differ by gender. About two thirds of multiple jobholders work one job full-time and the other part-time. Only a heroic minority—4 percent of men and 2 percent of women—work two full-time jobs simultaneously. (From John F. Stinson Jr., "New Data on Multiple Jobholding Available from the CPS," in the *Monthly Labor Review*, March 1997.)

onizing instructions as to the chicken Caesars. Twenty-five is a middle-aged black couple, who complain, with some justice, that the iced tea isn't fresh and the tabletop is sticky. But table 24 is the meteorological event of the century: ten British tourists who seem to have made the decision to absorb the American experience entirely by mouth. Here everyone has at least two drinks—iced tea and milk shake, Michelob and water (with lemon slice, please)— and a huge promiscuous orgy of breakfast specials, mozz sticks, chicken strips, quesadillas, burgers with cheese and without, sides of hash browns with cheddar, with onions, with gravy, seasoned fries, plain fries, banana splits. Poor Jesus! Poor me! Because when I arrive with their first tray of food—after three prior trips just to refill bevs—Princess Di refuses to eat her chicken strips with her pancake-and-sausage special, since, as she now reveals, the strips were meant to be an appetizer. Maybe the others would have accepted their meals, but Di, who is deep into her third Michelob, insists that everything else go back while they work on their "starters." Meanwhile, the yuppies are waving me down for more decaf and the black couple looks ready to summon the NAACP.

Much of what happened next is lost in the fog of war. Jesus starts going under. The little printer on the counter in front of him is spewing out orders faster than he can rip them off, much less produce the meals. Even the invincible Ellen is ashen from stress. I bring table 24 their reheated main courses, which they immediately reject as either too cold or fossilized by the microwave. When I return to the kitchen with their trays (three trays in three trips), Joy confronts me with arms akimbo: "What is this?" She means the food—the plates of rejected pancakes, hash browns in assorted flavors, toasts, burgers, sausages, eggs. "Uh, scrambled with cheddar," I try, "and that's . . ." "NO," she screams in my face. "Is it a traditional, a super-scramble, an eye-opener?" I pretend to study my check for a clue, but entropy has been up to its tricks, not only on the plates but in my head, and I have to admit that the original order is beyond reconstruction. "You don't know an eye-opener from a traditional?" she demands in outrage. All I know, in fact, is that my legs have lost interest in the current venture and have announced their intention to fold. I am saved by a yuppie (mercifully not one of mine) who chooses this moment to charge into the kitchen to bellow that his food is twenty-five minutes late. Joy screams at him to get the hell out of her kitchen, please, and then turns on Jesus in a fury, hurling an empty tray across the room for emphasis.

I leave. I don't walk out, I just leave. I don't finish my side work or pick up my credit-card tips, if any, at the cash register or, of course, ask Joy's permission to go. And the surprising thing is that you *can* walk out without permission, that the door opens, that the thick tropical night air parts to let me pass, that my car is still parked where I left it. There is no vindication in this exit, no fuck-you surge of relief, just an overwhelming, dank sense of failure pressing down on me and the entire parking lot. I had gone into this venture in the spirit of science, to test a mathematical proposition, but somewhere along the line, in the tunnel vision imposed by long shifts and relentless concentration, it became a test of myself, and clearly I have failed. Not only had I flamed out as a housekeeper/server, I had even forgotten to give George my tips, and, for reasons perhaps best known to hardworking, generous people like Gail and Ellen, this hurts. I don't cry, but I am in a position to realize, for the first time in many years, that the tear ducts are still there, and still capable of doing their job.

✤   ✤   ✤

When I moved out of the trailer park, I gave the key to number 46 to Gail and arranged for my deposit to be transferred to her. She told me that Joan is still living in her van and that Stu had been fired from the Hearthside. I never found out what happened to George.

In one month, I had earned approximately $1,040 and spent $517 on food, gas, toiletries, laundry, phone, and utilities. If I had remained in my $500 efficiency, I would have been able to pay the rent and have $22 left over (which is $78 less than the cash I had in my pocket at the start of the month). During this time I bought no clothing except for the required slacks and no prescription drugs or medical care (I did finally buy some vitamin B to compensate for the lack of vegetables in my diet). Perhaps I could have saved a little on food if I had gotten to a supermarket more often, instead of convenience stores, but it should be noted that I lost almost four pounds in four weeks, on a diet weighted heavily toward burgers and fries.

How former welfare recipients and single mothers will (and do) survive in the low-wage workforce, I cannot imagine. Maybe they will figure out how to condense their lives—including child-raising, laundry, romance, and meals—into the couple of hours between full-time jobs. Maybe they will take up residence in their vehicles, if they have one. All I know is that I couldn't hold two jobs and I couldn't make enough money to live on with one. And I had advantages unthinkable to many of the long-term poor—health, stamina, a working car, and no children to care for and support. Certainly nothing in my experience contradicts the conclusion of Kathryn Edin and Laura Lein, in their recent book *Making Ends Meet: How Single Mothers Survive Welfare and Low-Wage Work,* that low-wage work actually involves more hardship and deprivation than life at the mercy of the welfare state. In the coming months and years, economic conditions for the working poor are bound to worsen, even without the almost inevitable recession. As mentioned earlier, the influx of former welfare recipients into the low-skilled workforce will have a depressing effect on both wages and the number of jobs available. A general economic downturn will only enhance these effects, and the working poor will of course be facing it without the slight, but nonetheless often saving, protection of welfare as a backup.

The thinking behind welfare reform was that even the humblest jobs are morally uplifting and psychologically buoying. In reality they are likely to be fraught with insult and stress. But I did discover one redeeming feature of the most abject low-wage work—the camaraderie of people who are, in almost all cases, far too smart and funny and caring for the work they do and the wages they're paid. The hope, of course, is that someday these people will come to know what they're worth, and take appropriate action.

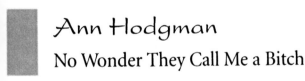

Ann Hodgman
No Wonder They Call Me a Bitch

I'VE ALWAYS WONDERED ABOUT DOG FOOD. IS A GAINES-BURGER REALLY LIKE A HAMburger? Can you fry it? Does dog food "cheese" taste like real cheese? Does Gravy Train actually make gravy in the dog's bowl, or is that brown liquid just dissolved crumbs? And exactly what *are* by-products?

Having spent the better part of a week eating dog food, I'm sorry to say that I now know the answers to these questions. While my dachshund, Shortie, watched in agonies of yearning, I gagged my way through can after can of stinky, white-flecked mush and bag after bag of stinky, fat-drenched nuggets. And now I understand exactly why Shortie's breath is so bad.

Of course, Gaines-burgers are neither mush nor nuggets. They are, rather, a miracle of beauty and packaging—or at least that's what I thought when I was little. I used to beg my mother to get them for our dogs, but she always said they were too expensive. When I finally bought a box of cheese-flavored Gaines-burgers—after twenty years of longing—I felt deliciously wicked.

"Dogs love real beef," the back of the box proclaimed proudly. "That's why Gaines-burgers is the only beef burger for dogs with real beef and no meat by-products!" The copy was accurate: meat by-products did not appear in the list of ingredients. Poultry by-products did, though—right there next to preserved animal fat.

One Purina spokesman told me that poultry by-products consist of necks, intestines, undeveloped eggs and other "carcass remnants," but not feathers, heads, or feet. When I told him I'd been eating dog food, he said, "Oh, you're kidding! Oh, no!" (I came to share his alarm when, weeks later, a second Purina spokesman said that Gaines-burgers *do* contain poultry heads and feet—but *not* undeveloped eggs.)

Up close my Gaines-burger didn't much resemble chopped beef. Rather, it looked—and felt—like a single long, extruded piece of redness that had been chopped into segments and formed into a patty. You could make one at home if you had a Play-Doh Fun Factory.

I turned on the skillet. While I waited for it to heat up I pulled out a shred of cheese-colored material and palpated it. Again, like Play-Doh, it was quite malleable. I made a little cheese bird out of it; then I counted to three and ate the bird.

There was a horrifying rush of cheddar taste, followed immediately by the dull tang of soybean flour—the main ingredient in Gaines-burgers. Next I tried a piece of red extrusion. The main difference between the meat-flavored and cheese-flavored extrusions is one of texture. The "cheese" chews like fresh Play-Doh, whereas the "meat" chews like Play-Doh that's been sitting out on a rug for a couple of hours.

Frying only turned the Gaines-burger black. There was no melting, no sizzling, no warm meat smells. A cherished childhood illusion was gone. I flipped the patty into the sink, where it immediately began leaking rivulets of red dye.

As alarming as the Gaines-burgers were, their soy meal began to seem like an old friend when the time came to try some *canned* dog foods. I decided to try the Cycle foods first. When I opened them, I thought about how rarely I use can openers these days, and I was suddenly visited by a long-forgotten sensation of can-opener distaste. *This* is the kind of unsavory place can openers spend their time when you're not watching! Every time you open a can of, say, Italian plum tomatoes, you infect them with invisible particles of by-product.

I had been expecting to see the usual homogeneous scrapple inside, but each can of Cycle was packed with smooth, round, oily nuggets. As if someone at Gaines had been tipped off that a human would be tasting the stuff, the four Cycles really were different from one another. Cycle-1, for puppies, is wet and soyish. Cycle-2, for adults, glistens nastily with fat, but it's passably edible—a lot like some canned Swedish meatballs I once got in a Care package at college. Cycle-3, the "lite" one, for fatties, had no specific flavor; it just tasted like dog food. But at least it didn't make me fat.

Cycle-4, for senior dogs, had the smallest nuggets. Maybe old dogs can't open their mouths as wide. This kind was far sweeter than the other three Cycles—almost like baked beans. It was also the only one to contain "dried beef digest," a mysterious substance that the Purina spokesman defined as "enzymes" and my dictionary defined as "the products of digestion."

Next on the menu was a can of Kal Kan Pedigree with Chunky Chicken. Chunky *chicken?* There were chunks in the can, certainly—big, purplish-brown chunks. I forked one chunk out (by now I was becoming more callous) and found that while it had no discernible chicken flavor, it wasn't bad except for its texture—like meat loaf with ground-up chicken bones.

In the world of canned dog food, a smooth consistency is a sign of low quality—lots of cereal. A lumpy, frightening, bloody, stringy horror is a sign of high quality—lots of meat. Nowhere in the world of wet dog foods was this demonstrated better than in the fanciest I tried—Kal Kan's Pedigree Select Dinners. These came not in a can but in a tiny foil packet with a picture of an imperious Yorkie. When I pulled open the container, juice spurted all over my hand, and the first chunk I speared was trailing a long gray vein. I shrieked and went instead for a plain chunk, which I was able to swallow only after taking a break to read some suddenly fascinating office equipment catalogues. Once again, though, it tasted no more alarming than, say, canned hash.

Still, how pleasant it was to turn to *dry* dog food! Gravy Train was the first I tried, and I'm happy to report that it really does make a "thick, rich, real beef gravy" when you mix it with water. Thick and rich, anyway. Except for a lingering rancid-fat flavor, the gravy wasn't beefy, but since it tasted primarily like tap water, it wasn't nauseating either.

My poor dachshund just gets plain old Purina Dog Chow, but Purina also makes a dry food called Butcher's Blend that comes in Beef, Bacon & Chicken flavor. Here we see dog food's arcane semiotics at its best: a red triangle with a *T* stamped into it is supposed to suggest beef; a tan curl, chicken; and a brown *S*, a piece of bacon. Only dogs understand these messages. But Butcher's Blend does have an endearing slogan: "Great Meaty Tastes—without bothering the Butcher!" *You know, I wanted to buy some meat, but I just couldn't bring myself to bother the butcher . . .*

Purina O.N.E. ("Optimum Nutritional Effectiveness") is targeted at people who are unlikely ever to worry about bothering a tradesperson. "We chose chicken as a primary ingredient in Purina O.N.E. for several reasonings," the long, long essay on the back of the bag announces. Chief among these reasonings, I'd guess, is the fact that chicken appeals to people who are—you know—*like us*. Although our dogs do nothing but spend eighteen-hour days alone in the apartment, we still want them to be *premium* dogs. We want them to cut down on red meat, too. We also want dog food that comes in a bag with an attractive design, a subtle typeface, and no kitschy pictures of slobbering golden retrievers.

Besides that, we want a list of the Nutritional Benefits of our dog food—and we get it on O.N.E. One thing I especially like about this list is its constant references to a dog's "hair coat," as in "Beef tallow is good for the dog's skin and hair coat." (On the other hand, beef tallow merely provides palatability, while the dried beef digest in Cycle provides palatability *enhancement.*)

I hate to say it, but O.N.E. was pretty palatable. Maybe that's because it has about 100 percent more fat than, say, Butcher's Blend. Or maybe I'd been duped by the packaging; that's been known to happen before.

As with people food, dog snacks taste much better than dog meals. They're better looking too. Take Milk-Bone Flavor Snacks. The loving-hands-at-home prose describing each flavor is colorful; the writers practically choke on their own exuberance. Of bacon they say, "It's so good, your dog will think it's hot off the frying pan." Of liver: "The only taste your dog wants more than liver—is even more liver!" Of poultry: "All those farm fresh flavors deliciously mixed in one biscuit. Your dog will bark with delight!" And of vegetable: "Gardens of taste! Specially blended to give your dog that vegetable flavor he wants—but can rarely get!"

Well, I may be a sucker, but advertising *this* emphatic just doesn't convince me. I lined up all seven flavors of Milk-Bone Flavor Snacks on the floor. Unless my dog's palate is a lot more sensitive than mine—and considering that she steals dirty diapers out of the trash and eats them, I'm loath to think it is—she doesn't detect any more difference in the seven flavors than I did when I tried them.

I much preferred Bonz, the hard-baked, bone-shaped snack stuffed with simulated marrow. I liked the bone part, that is; it tasted almost exactly like the cornmeal it was made of. The mock marrow inside was a bit more problematic: in addition to looking like the sludge that collects in the treads of my running shoes, it was bursting with tiny hairs.

I'm sure you have a few dog food questions of your own. To save us time, I've answered them in advance.

Q: Are those little cans of Mighty Dog actually branded with the sizzling word BEEF, the way they show in the commercials?

A: You should know by now that that kind of thing never happens.

Q: Does chicken-flavored dog food taste like chicken-flavored cat food?

A: To my surprise, chicken cat food was actually a little better—more chickeny. It tasted like inferior canned pâté.

Q: Was there any dog food that you just couldn't bring yourself to try?

A: Alas, it was a can of Mighty Dog called Prime Entree with Bone Marrow. The meat was dark, dark brown, and it was surrounded by gelatin that was almost black. I knew I would die if I tasted it, so I put it outside for the raccoons.

Joan Didion
from Salvador

THE THREE-YEAR-OLD EL SALVADOR INTERNATIONAL AIRPORT IS GLASSY AND WHITE AND splendidly isolated, conceived during the waning of the Molina "National Transformation" as convenient less to the capital (San Salvador is forty miles away, until recently a drive of several hours) than to a central hallucination of the Molina and Romero regimes, the projected beach resorts, the Hyatt, the Pacific Paradise, tennis, golf, water-skiing, condos, *Costa del Sol*; the visionary invention of a tourist industry in yet another republic where the leading natural cause of death is gastrointestinal infection. In the general absence of tourists these hotels have since been abandoned, ghost resorts on the empty Pacific beaches, and to land at this airport built to service them is to plunge directly into a state in which no ground is solid, no depth of field reliable, no perception so definite that it might not dissolve into its reverse.

The only logic is that of acquiescence. Immigration is negotiated in a thicket of automatic weapons, but by whose authority the weapons are brandished (Army or National Guard or National Police or Customs Police or Treasury Police or one of a continuing proliferation of other shadowy and overlapping forces) is a blurred point. Eye contact is avoided. Documents are scrutinized upside down. Once clear of the airport, on the new highway that slices through green hills rendered phosphorescent by the cloud cover of the tropical rainy season, one sees mainly underfed cattle and mongrel dogs and armored vehicles, vans and trucks and Cherokee Chiefs fitted with reinforced steel and bulletproof Plexiglas an inch thick. Such vehicles are a fixed feature of local life, and are popularly associated with disappearance and death. There was the Cherokee Chief seen following the Dutch television crew killed in Chalatenango province in March of 1982. There was the red Toyota three-quarter-ton pickup sighted near the van driven by the four American Catholic workers on the night they were killed in 1980. There were, in the late spring and summer of 1982, the three Toyota panel trucks, one yellow, one blue, and one green, none bearing plates, reported present at each of the mass detentions (a "detention" is another fixed feature of local life, and often precedes a "disappearance") in the Amatepec district of San Salvador. These are the details—the models and colors of armored vehicles, the makes and calibers of weapons, the particular methods of dismemberment and decapitation used in particular instances—on which the visitor to Salvador learns immediately to concentrate, to the exclusion of past or future concerns, as in a prolonged amnesiac fugue.

⚬ ⚬ ⚬

Terror is the given of the place. Black-and-white police cars cruise in pairs, each with the barrel of a rifle extruding from an open window. Roadblocks materialize at random, soldiers fanning out from trucks and taking positions, fingers always on triggers, safeties clicking on and off. Aim is taken as if to pass the time. Every morning *El Diario de Hoy* and *La Prensa Gráfica* carry cautionary stories. "*Una madre y sus dos hijos fueron asesinados con arma cortante (corvo) por ocho sujetos desconocidos el lunes en la noche*": A mother and her two sons hacked to death in their beds by eight *desconocidos,* unknown men. The same morning's paper: the unidentified body of a young man, strangled, found on the shoulder of a road. Same morning, different story: the unidentified bodies of three young men, found on another road, their faces partially destroyed by bayonets, one faced carved to represent a cross.

It is largely from these reports in the newspapers that the United States embassy compiles its body counts, which are transmitted to Washington in a weekly dispatch referred to by embassy people as "the grimgram." These counts are presented in a kind of tortured code that fails to obscure what is taken for granted in El Salvador, that government forces do most of the killing. In a January 15 1982 memo to Washington, for example, the embassy issued a "guarded" breakdown on its count of 6,909 "reported" political murders between September 16 1980 and September 15 1981. Of these 6,909, according to the memo, 922 were "believed committed by security forces," 952 "believed committed by leftist terrorists," 136 "believed committed by rightist terrorists," and 4,889 "committed by unknown assailants," the famous *desconocidos* favored by those San Salvador newspapers still publishing. (The figures actually add up not to 6,909 but to 6,899, leaving ten in a kind of official limbo.) The memo continued:

> The uncertainty involved here can be seen in the fact that responsibility cannot be fixed in the majority of cases. We note, however, that it is generally believed in El Salvador that a large number of the unexplained killings are carried out by the security forces, officially or unofficially. The Embassy is aware of dramatic claims that have been made by one interest group or another in which the security forces figure as the primary agents of murder here. El Salvador's tangled web of attack and vengeance, traditional criminal violence and political mayhem make this an impossible charge to sustain. In saying this, however, we make no attempt to lighten the responsibility for the deaths of many hundreds, and perhaps thousands, which can be attributed to the security forces. . . .

The body count kept by what is generally referred to in San Salvador as "the Human Rights Commission" is higher than the embassy's, and documented periodically by a photographer who goes out looking for bodies. These bodies he photographs are often broken into unnatural positions, and the faces to which the bodies are attached (when they are attached) are equally unnatural, sometimes unrecognizable as human faces, obliterated by acid or beaten to a mash of misplaced ears and teeth or slashed ear to ear and invaded by insects. "*Encontrado en Antiguo Cuscatlán el día 25 de Marzo 1982: camison de dormir celeste,*" the typed caption reads on one photograph: found in Antiguo Cuscatlán March 25 1982 wearing a sky-blue nightshirt. The captions are laconic. Found in Soyapango May 21 1982. Found in Mejicanos June 11 1982. Found at El Playón May 30 1982, white shirt, purple pants, black shoes.

The photograph accompanying that last caption shows a body with no eyes, because the vultures got to it before the photographer did. There is a special kind of practical information that the visitor to El Salvador acquires immediately, the way visitors to other places acquire information about the currency rates, the hours for the museums. In El Salvador one learns that vultures go first for the soft tissue, for the eyes, the exposed genitalia, the open mouth. One learns that an open mouth can be used to make a specific point, can be stuffed with something emblematic; stuffed, say, with a penis, or, if the point has to do with land title, stuffed with some of the dirt in question. One learns that hair deteriorates less rapidly than flesh, and that a skull surrounded by a perfect corona of hair is a not uncommon sight in the body dumps.

All forensic photographs induce in the viewer a certain protective numbness, but dissociation is more difficult here. In the first place these are not, technically, "forensic" photographs, since the evidence they document will never be presented in a court of law. In the second place the disfigurement is too routine. The locations are too near, the dates too recent. There is the presence of the relatives of the disappeared: the women who sit every day in this cramped office on the grounds of the archdiocese, waiting to look at the spiral-bound photo albums in which the photographs are kept. These albums have plastic covers bearing soft-focus color photographs of young Americans in dating situations (strolling through autumn foliage on one album, recumbent in a field of daisies on another), and the women, looking for the bodies of their husbands and brothers and sisters and children, pass them from hand to hand without comment or expression.

One of the more shadowy elements of the violent scene here [is] the death squad. Existence of these groups has long been disputed, but not by many Salvadorans. . . . Who constitutes the death squads is yet another difficult question. We do not believe that these squads exist as permanent formations but rather as ad hoc vigilante groups that coalesce according to perceived need. Membership is also uncertain, but in addition to civilians we believe that both on- and off-duty members of the security forces are participants. This was unofficially confirmed by right-wing spokesman Maj. Roberto D'Aubuisson who stated in an interview in early 1981 that security force members utilize the guise of the death squad when a potentially embarrassing or odious task needs to be performed.

—From the confidential but later declassified January 15, 1982 memo previously cited, drafted for the State Department by the political section at the embassy in San Salvador.

The dead and pieces of the dead turn up in El Salvador everywhere, every day, as taken for granted as in a nightmare, or a horror movie. Vultures of course suggest the presence of a body. A knot of children on the street suggests the presence of a body. Bodies turn up in the brush of vacant lots, in the garbage thrown down ravines in the richest districts, in public rest rooms, in bus stations. Some are dropped in Lake Ilopango, a few miles east of the city, and wash up near the lakeside cottages and clubs frequented by what remains in San Salvador of the sporting bourgeoisie. Some still turn up at El Playón, the lunar lava field of rotting human flesh visible at one time or another on every television screen in America but characterized in June of 1982 in the *El Salvador News Gazette*, an English-language weekly edited by an American named Mario Rosenthal, as an "uncorroborated story . . . dredged up from the files of leftist propaganda." Others turn up at Puerta del Diablo, above Parque Balboa, a national *Turicentro* described as recently as the April–July 1982 issue of *Aboard TACA*, the magazine provided passengers on the national airline of El Salvador, as "offering excellent subjects for color photography."

I drove up to Puerta del Diablo one morning in June of 1982, past the Casa Presidencial and the camouflaged watch towers and heavy concentrations of troops and arms south of town, on up a narrow road narrowed further by landslides and deep crevices in the roadbed, a drive so insistently premonitory that after a while I began to hope that I would pass Puerta del Diablo without knowing it, just miss it, write it off, turn around and go back. There was however no way of missing it. Puerta del Diablo is a "view site" in an older and distinctly literary tradition, nature as lesson, an immense cleft rock through which half of El Salvador seems framed, a site so romantic and "mystical," so theatrically sacrificial in aspect, that it might be a cosmic parody of nineteenth-century landscape painting. The place presents itself as pathetic fallacy: the sky "broods," the stones "weep," a constant seepage of water weighting the ferns and moss. The foliage is thick and slick with moisture. The only sound is a steady buzz, I believe of cicadas.

Body dumps are seen in El Salvador as a kind of visitors' must-do, difficult but worth the detour. "Of course you have seen El Playón," an aide to President Alvaro Magaña said to me one day, and proceeded to discuss the site geologically, as evidence of the country's geothermal resources. He made no mention of the bodies. I was unsure if he was sounding me out or simply found the geothermal aspect of overriding interest. One difference between El Playón and Puerta del Diablo is that most bodies at El Playón appear to have been killed somewhere else, and then dumped; at Puerta del Diablo the executions are believed to occur in place, at the top, and the bodies thrown over. Sometimes reporters will speak of wanting to spend the night at Puerta del Diablo, in order to document the actual execution, but at the time I was in Salvador no one had.

The aftermath, the daylight aspect, is well documented. "Nothing fresh today, I hear," an embassy officer said when I mentioned that I had visited Puerta del Diablo. "Were there any on top?" someone else asked. "There were supposed to have been three on top yesterday." The point about whether or not there had been any on top was that usually it was necessary to go down to see bodies. The way down is hard. Slabs of stone, slippery with moss, are set into the vertiginous cliff, and it is down this cliff that one begins the descent to the bodies, or what is left of the bodies, pecked and maggoty masses of flesh, bone, hair. On some days there have been helicopters circling, tracking those making the descent. Other days there have been militia at the top, in the clearing where the road seems to run out, but on the morning I was there the only people on top were a man and a woman and three small children, who played in the wet grass while the woman started and stopped a Toyota pickup. She appeared to be learning how to drive. She drove forward and then back toward the edge, apparently following the man's signals, over and over again.

We did not speak, and it was only later, down the mountain and back in the land of the provisionally living, that it occurred to me that there was a definite question about why a man and a woman might choose a well-known body dump for a driving lesson. This was one of a number of occasions, during the two weeks my husband and I spent in El Salvador, on which I came to understand, in a way I had not understood before, the exact mechanism of terror.

⚬ ⚬ ⚬

Whenever I had nothing better to do in San Salvador I would walk up in the leafy stillness of the San Benito and Escalón districts, where the hush at midday is broken only by the occasional crackle of a walkie-talkie, the click of metal moving on a weapon. I recall a day in San Benito when I opened my bag to check an address, and heard the clicking of metal on metal all up and down the street. On the whole no one walks up here, and pools of blossoms lie undisturbed on the sidewalks. Most of the houses in San Benito are more recent than those in Escalón, less idiosyncratic and probably smarter, but the most striking architectural features in both districts are not the houses but their walls, walls built upon walls, walls stripped of the usual copa de oro and bougainvillea, walls that reflect successive generations of violence: the original stone, the additional five or six or ten feet of brick, and finally the barbed wire, sometimes concertina, sometimes electrified; walls with watch towers, gun ports, closed-circuit television cameras, walls now reaching twenty and thirty feet.

San Benito and Escalón appear on the embassy security maps as districts of relatively few "incidents," but they remain districts in which a certain oppressive uneasiness prevails. In the first place there are always "incidents"—detentions and deaths and disappearances— in the *barrancas*, the ravines lined with shanties that fall down behind the houses with the walls and the guards and the walkie-talkies; one day in Escalón I was introduced to a woman who kept the lean-to that served as a grocery in a *barranca* just above the Hotel Sheraton. She was sticking prices on bars of Camay and Johnson's baby soap, stopping occasionally to sell a plastic bag or two filled with crushed ice and Coca-Cola, and all the while she talked in a low voice about her fear, about her eighteen-year-old son, about the boys who had been taken out and shot on successive nights recently in a neighboring *barranca*.

In the second place there is, in Escalón, the presence of the Sheraton itself, a hotel that has figured rather too prominently in certain local stories involving the disappearance and death of Americans. The Sheraton always seems brighter and more mildly festive than either the Camino Real or the Presidente, with children in the pool and flowers and pretty women in pastel dresses, but there are usually several bulletproofed Cherokee Chiefs in the parking area, and the men drinking in the lobby often carry the little zippered purses that in San Salvador suggest not passports or credit cards but Browning 9-mm. pistols.

It was at the Sheraton that one of the few American *desaparecidos*, a young free-lance writer named John Sullivan, was last seen, in December of 1980. It was also at the Sheraton, after eleven on the evening of January 3 1981, that the two American advisers on agrarian reform, Michael Hammer and Mark Pearlman, were killed, along with the Salvadoran director of the Institute for Agrarian Transformation, José Rodolfo Viera. The three were drinking coffee in a dining room off the lobby, and whoever killed them used an Ingram MAC-10, without sound suppressor, and then walked out through the lobby, unapprehended. The Sheraton has even turned up in the investigation into the December 1980 deaths of the four American churchwomen, Sisters Ita Ford and Maura Clarke, the two Maryknoll nuns; Sister Dorothy Kazel, the Ursuline nun; and Jean Donovan, the lay volunteer. In *Justice in El Salvador: A Case Study,* prepared and released in July of 1982 in New York by the Lawyers' Committee for International Human Rights, there appears this note:

On December 19, 1980, the [Duarte government's] Special Investigative Commission reported that "a red Toyota 3/4-ton pickup was seen leaving (the crime scene) at about 11:00 P.M. on December 2" and that "a red splotch on the burned van" of the church-women was being checked to determine whether the paint splotch "could be the result of a collision between that van and the red Toyota pickup." By February 1981, the Maryknoll Sisters' Office of Social Concerns, which has been actively monitoring the investigation, received word from a source which it considered reliable that the FBI had matched the red splotch on the burned van with a red Toyota pickup belonging to the Sheraton hotel in San Salvador. . . . Subsequent to the FBI's alleged matching of the paint splotch and a Sheraton truck, the State Department has claimed, in a communication with the families of the churchwomen, that "the FBI could not determine the source of the paint scraping."

There is also mention in this study of a young Salvadoran businessman named Hans Christ (his father was a German who arrived in El Salvador at the end of World War II), a part owner of the Sheraton. Hans Christ lives now in Miami, and that his name should have even come up in the Maryknoll investigation made many people uncomfortable, because it was Hans Christ, along with his brother-in-law, Ricardo Sol Meza, who, in April of 1981, was first charged with the murders of Michael Hammer and Mark Pearlman and José Rodolfo Viera at the Sheraton. These charges were later dropped, and were followed by a series of other charges, arrests, releases, expressions of "dismay" and "incredulity" from the American embassy, and even, in the fall of 1982, confessions to the killings from two former National Guard corporals, who testified that Hans Christ had led them through the lobby and pointed out the victims. Hans Christ and Ricardo Sol Meza have said that the dropped case against them was a government frame-up, and that they were only having drinks at the Sheraton the night of the killings, with a National Guard intelligence officer. It was logical for Hans Christ and Ricardo Sol Meza to have drinks at the Sheraton because they both had interests in the hotel, and Ricardo Sol Meza had just opened a roller disco, since closed, off the lobby into which the killers walked that night. The killers were described by witnesses as well dressed, their faces covered. The room from which they walked was at the time I was in San Salvador no longer a restaurant, but the marks left by the bullets were still visible, on the wall facing the door.

Whenever I had occasion to visit the Sheraton I was apprehensive, and this apprehension came to color the entire Escalón district for me, even its lower reaches, where there were people and movies and restaurants. I recall being struck by it on the canopied porch of a restaurant near the Mexican embassy, on an evening when rain or sabotage or habit had blacked out the city and I became abruptly aware, in the light cast by a passing car, of two human shadows, silhouettes illuminated by the headlights and then invisible again. One shadow sat behind the smoked glass windows of a Cherokee Chief parked at the curb in front of the restaurant; the other crouched between the pumps at the Esso station next door, carrying a rifle. It seemed to me unencouraging that my husband and I were the only people seated on the porch. In the absence of the headlights the candle on our table provided the only light, and I fought the impulse to blow it out. We continued talking, carefully. Nothing came of this, but I did not forget the sensation of having been in a single instant demoralized, undone, humiliated by fear, which is what I meant when I said that I came to understand in El Salvador the mechanism of terror.

3/3/81: Roberto D'Aubuisson, a former Salvadoran army intelligence officer, holds a press conference and says that before the U.S. presidential election he had been in touch with a number of Reagan advisers and those contacts have continued. The armed forces should ask the junta to resign, D'Aubuisson says. He refuses to name a date for the action, but says "March is, I think, a very interesting month." He also calls for the abandonment of the economic reforms. D'Aubuisson had been accused of plotting to overthrow the government on two previous occasions. Observers speculate that since D'Aubuisson is able to hold the news conference and pass freely between Salvador and Guatemala, he must enjoy considerable support among some sections of the army. . . . 3/4/81: In San Salvador, the U.S. embassy is fired upon; no one is injured. Chargé d'Affaires Frederic Chapin says, "This incident has all the hallmarks of a D'Aubuisson operation. Let me state to you that we oppose coups and we have no intention of being intimidated."

> —From the "Chronology of Events Related to Salvadoran Situation" prepared periodically by the United States embassy in San Salvador.

Tom Wolfe
from The Right Stuff

YEAGER

ANYONE WHO TRAVELS VERY MUCH ON AIRLINES IN THE UNITED STATES SOON GETS TO know the voice of *the airline pilot* . . . coming over the intercom . . . with a particular drawl, a particular folksiness, a particular down-home calmness that is so exaggerated it begins to parody itself (nevertheless!—it's reassuring) . . . the voice that tells you, as the airliner is caught in thunderheads and goes bolting up and down a thousand feet at a single gulp, to check your seat belts because "it might get a little choppy" . . . the voice that tells you (on a flight from Phoenix preparing for its final approach into Kennedy Airport, New York, just after dawn): "Now, folks, uh . . . this is the captain . . . ummmm . . . We've got a little ol' red light up here on the control panel that's tryin' to tell us that the *landin'* gears're not . . . uh . . . *lockin'* into position when we lower 'em . . . Now . . . I don't believe that little ol' red light knows what it's *talkin'* about—I believe it's that little ol' red light that iddn' workin' right" . . . faint chuckle, long pause, as if to say, *I'm not even sure all this is really worth going into—still, it may amuse you* . . . "But . . . I guess to play it by the rules, we oughta *humor* that little ol' light . . . so we're gonna take her down to about, oh, two or three hundred feet over the runway at Kennedy, and the folks down there on the ground are gonna see if they caint give us a *visual* inspection of those ol' landin' gears"—with which he is obviously on intimate ol'-buddy terms, as with every other working part of this mighty ship—"and if I'm right . . . they're gonna tell us everything is co-pa*cetic* all the way aroun' an' we'll jes take her on in" . . . and, after a couple of low passes over the field, the voice returns: "Well, folks, those folks down there on the ground—it must be too early for 'em or somethin'—I 'spect they still got the *sleepers* in their eyes . . . 'cause they say they caint tell if those ol' landin' gears are all the way down or not . . . But, you know, up here in the cockpit we're convinced they're all the way down, so we're jes gonna take her on in . . . And oh" . . . (*I almost forgot*) . . . "while we take a little swing out over the ocean an' empty some of that surplus fuel we're not gonna be needin' anymore—that's what you might be seein' comin' out of the wings—our lovely little ladies . . . if they'll be so kind . . . they're gonna go up and down the aisles and show you how we do what we call 'assumin' the position'" . . . another faint chuckle (*We do this so often, and it's so much fun, we even have a funny little name for it*) . . . and the stewardesses, a bit grimmer, by the looks of them, than *that voice*, start telling the passengers to take their glasses off and take the ballpoint pens and other sharp objects out of their pockets, and they show them *the position*, with the head lowered . . . while down on the field at Kennedy the little yellow emergency trucks start roaring across the field—and even though in your pounding heart and your sweating palms and your broiling brainpan you *know* this is a critical moment in your life, you still can't quite bring yourself to be*lieve* it, because if it were . . . how could *the captain*, the man who knows the actual situation most intimately . . . how could he keep on drawlin' and chucklin' and driftin' and lollygaggin' in that particular voice of his—

Well!—who doesn't know that voice! And who can forget it!—even after he is proved right and the emergency is over.

That particular voice may sound vaguely Southern or Southwestern, but it is specifically Appalachian in origin. It originated in the mountains of West Virginia, in the coal country, in Lincoln County, so far up in the hollows that, as the saying went, "they had to pipe in daylight." In the late 1940's and early 1950's this up-hollow voice drifted down from on high, from over the high desert of California, down, down, down, from the upper reaches of the Brotherhood into all phases of American aviation. It was amazing. It was *Pygmalion* in reverse. Military pilots and then, soon, airline pilots, pilots from Maine and Massachusetts and the Dakotas and Oregon and everywhere else, began to talk in that poker-hollow West Virginia drawl, or as close to it as they could bend their native accents. It was the drawl of the most righteous of all the possessors of the right stuff: Chuck Yeager.

Yeager had started out as the equivalent, in the Second World War, of the legendary Frank Luke of the 27th Aero Squadron in the First. Which is to say, he was the boon-docker, the boy from the back country, with only a high-school education, no credentials, no cachet or polish of any sort, who took off the feed-store overalls and put on a uniform and climbed into an airplane and lit up the skies over Europe.

Yeager grew up in Hamlin, West Virginia, a town on the Mud River not far from Nitro, Hurricane Whirlwind, Salt Rock, Mud, Sod, Crum, Leet, Dollie, Ruth, and Alum Creek. His father was a gas driller (drilling for natural gas in the coalfields), his older brother was a gas driller, and he would have been a gas driller had he not enlisted in the Army Air Force in 1941 at the age of eighteen. In 1943, at twenty, he became a flight officer, i.e., a non-com who was allowed to fly, and went to England to fly fighter planes over France and Germany. Even in the tumult of the war Yeager was somewhat puzzling to a lot of other pilots. He was a short, wiry, but muscular little guy with dark curly hair and a tough-looking face that seemed (to strangers) to be saying: "You best not be lookin' me in the eye, you peckerwood, or I'll put four more holes in your nose." But that wasn't what was puzzling. What was puzzling was the way Yeager talked. He seemed to talk with some older forms of English elocution, syntax, and conjugation that had been preserved uphollow in the Appalachians. There were people up there who never said they disapproved of anything, they said: "I don't hold with it." In the present tense they were willing to *help* out, like anyone else; but in the past tense they only *holped*. "H'it weren't nothin' I hold with, but I holped him out with it, anyways."

In his first eight missions, at the age of twenty, Yeager shot down two German fighters. On his ninth he was shot down over German-occupied French territory, suffering flak wounds; he bailed out, was picked up by the French underground, which smuggled him across the Pyrenees into Spain disguised as a peasant. In Spain he was jailed briefly, then released, whereupon he made it back to England and returned to combat during the Allied invasion of France. On October 12, 1944, Yeager took on and shot down five German fighter planes in succession. On November 6, flying a propeller-driven P-51 Mustang, he shot down one of the new jet fighters the Germans had developed, the Messerschmitt-262, and damaged two more, and on November 20 he shot down four FW-190s. It was a true Frank Luke-style display of warrior fury and personal prowess. By the end of the war he had thirteen and a half kills. He was twenty-two years old.

In 1946 and 1947 Yeager was trained as a test pilot at Wright Field in Dayton. He amazed his instructors with his ability at stunt-team flying, not to mention the unofficial business of hassling. That plus his up-hollow drawl had everybody saying, "He's a natural-born stick 'n' rudder man." Nevertheless, there was something extraordinary about it when a man so young, with so little experience in flight test, was selected to go to Muroc Field in California for the XS-1 project.

Muroc was up in the high elevations of the Mojave Desert. It looked like some fossil landscape that had long since been left behind by the rest of terrestrial evolution. It was full of huge dry lake beds, the biggest being Rogers Lake. Other than sagebrush the only vegetation was Joshua trees, twisted freaks of the plant world that looked like a cross between cactus and Japanese bonsai. They had a dark petrified green color and horribly crippled branches. At dusk the Joshua trees stood out in silhouette on the fossil wasteland like some arthritic nightmare. In the summer the temperature went up to 110 degrees as a matter of course, and the dry lake beds were covered in sand, and there would be windstorms and sandstorms right out of a Foreign Legion movie. At night it would drop to near freezing, and in December it would start raining, and the dry lakes would fill up with a few inches of water, and some sort of putrid prehistoric shrimps would work their way up from out of the ooze, and sea gulls would come flying in a hundred miles or more from the ocean, over the mountains, to gobble up these squirming little throwbacks. A person had to see it to believe it: flocks of sea gulls wheeling around in the air out in the middle of the high desert in the dead of winter and grazing on antediluvian crustaceans in the primordial ooze.

When the wind blew the few inches of water back and forth across the lake beds, they became absolutely smooth and level. And when the water evaporated in the spring, and the sun baked the ground hard, the lake beds became the greatest natural landing fields ever discovered, and also the biggest, with miles of room for error. That was highly desirable, given the nature of the enterprise at Muroc.

Besides the wind, sand, tumbleweed, and Joshua trees, there was nothing at Muroc except for two quonset-style hangars, side by side, a couple of gasoline pumps, a single concrete runway, a few tarpaper shacks, and some tents. The officers stayed in the shacks marked "barracks," and lesser souls stayed in the tents and froze all night and fried all day. Every road into the property had a guardhouse on it manned by soldiers. The enterprise the Army had undertaken in this godforsaken place was the development of supersonic jet and rocket planes.

At the end of the war the Army had discovered that the Germans not only had the world's first jet fighter but also a rocket plane that had gone 596 miles an hour in tests. Just after the war a British jet, the Gloster Meteor, jumped the official world speed record from 469 to 606 in a single day. The next great plateau would be Mach 1, the speed of sound, and the Army Air Force considered it crucial to achieve it first.

The speed of sound, Mach 1, was known (thanks to the work of the physicist Ernst Mach) to vary at different altitudes, temperatures, and wind speeds. On a calm 60-degree day at sea level it was about 760 miles an hour, while at 40,000 feet, where the temperature would be at least sixty below, it was about 660 miles an hour. Evil and baffling things happened in the transonic zone, which began at about .7 Mach. Wind tunnels choked out at such velocities. Pilots who approached the speed of sound in dives reported that the controls would lock or "freeze" or even alter their normal functions. Pilots had crashed and died because they couldn't budge the stick. Just last year Geoffrey de Havilland, son of the famous British aircraft designer and builder, had tried to take one of his father's DH 108s to Mach 1. The ship started buffeting and then disintegrated, and he was killed. This led engineers to speculate that the shock waves became so severe and unpredictable at Mach 1, no aircraft could survive them. They started talking about "the sonic wall" and "the sound barrier."

So this was the task that a handful of pilots, engineers, and mechanics had at Muroc. The place was utterly primitive, nothing but bare bones, bleached tarpaulins, and corrugated tin rippling in the heat with caloric waves; and for an ambitious young pilot it was perfect. Muroc seemed like an outpost on the dome of the world, open only to a righteous few, closed off to the rest of humanity, including even the Army Air Force brass of command control, which was at Wright Field. The commanding officer at Muroc was only a colonel, and his superiors at Wright did not relish junkets to the Muroc rat shacks in the first place. But to pilots this prehistoric throwback of an airfield became . . . shrimp heaven! the rat-shack plains of Olympus!

Low Rent Septic Tank Perfection . . . yes; and not excluding those traditional essentials for the blissful hot young pilot: Flying & Drinking and Drinking & Driving.

Just beyond the base, to the southwest, there was a rickety wind-blown 1930's-style establishment called Pancho's Fly Inn, owned, run, and bartended by a woman named Pancho Barnes. Pancho Barnes wore tight white sweaters and tight pants, after the mode of Barbara Stanwyck in *Double Indemnity*. She was only forty-one when Yeager arrived at Muroc, but her face was so weatherbeaten, had so many hard miles on it, that she looked older, especially to the young pilots at the base. She also shocked the pants off them with her vulcanized tongue. Everybody she didn't like was an old bastard or a sonofabitch. People she liked were old bastards and sonsabitches, too. "I tol' 'at ol' bastard to get 'is ass on over here and I'd g'im a drink." But Pancho Barnes was anything but Low Rent. She was the granddaughter of the man who designed the old Mount Lowe cable-car system, Thaddeus S. C. Lowe. Her maiden name was Florence Leontine Lowe. She was brought up in San Marino, which adjoined Pasadena and was one of Los Angeles' wealthiest suburbs, and her first husband—she was married four times—was the pastor of the Pasadena Episcopal Church, the Rev. C. Rankin Barnes. Mrs. Barnes seemed to have few of the conventional community interests of a Pasadena matron. In the late 1920's, by boat and plane, she ran guns for Mexican revolutionaries and picked up the nickname Pancho. In 1930 she broke Amelia Earhart's air-speed record for women. Then she barnstormed around the country as the featured performer of "Pancho Barnes's Mystery Circus of the Air." She always greeted her public in jodhpurs and riding boots, a flight jacket, a white scarf, and a white sweater that showed off her terrific Barbara Stanwyck chest. Pancho's desert Fly Inn had an airstrip, a swimming pool, a dude ranch corral, plenty of acreage for horseback riding, a big old guest house for the lodgers, and a connecting building that was the bar and restaurant. In the barroom the floors, the tables, the chairs, the walls, the beams, the bar were of the sort known as extremely weatherbeaten, and the screen doors kept banging. Nobody putting together such a place for a movie about flying in the old days would ever dare make it as dilapidated and generally go-to-hell as it actually was. Behind the bar were many pictures of airplanes and pilots, lavishly autographed and inscribed, badly framed and crookedly hung. There was an old piano that had been dried out and cracked to the point of hopeless desiccation. On a good night a huddle of drunken aviators could be heard trying to bang, slosh, and navigate their way through old Cole Porter tunes. On average nights the tunes were not that good to start with. When the screen door banged and a man walked through the door into the saloon, every eye in the place checked him out. If he wasn't known as somebody who had something to do with flying at Muroc, he would be eyed like some lame goddamned mouseshit sheepherder from *Shane*.

The plane the Air Force wanted to break the sound barrier with was called the X-I at the outset and later on simply the X-I. The Bell Aircraft Corporation had built it under an Army contract. The core of the ship was a rocket of the type first developed by a young Navy inventor, Robert Truax, during the war. The fuselage was shaped like a 50-caliber bullet—an object that was known to go supersonic smoothly. Military pilots seldom drew major test assignments; they went to highly paid civilians working for the aircraft corporations. The prime pilot for the X-I was a man whom Bell regarded as the best of the breed. This man looked like a movie star. He looked like a pilot from out of *Hell's Angels*. And on top of everything else there was his name: Slick Goodlin.

The idea in testing the X-I was to nurse it carefully into the transonic zone, up to seven-tenths, eight-tenths, nine-tenths the speed of sound (.7 Mach, .8 Mach, .9 Mach) before attempting the speed of sound itself, Mach 1, even though Bell and the Army already knew the X-I had the rocket power to go to Mach 1 and beyond, if there *was* any *beyond*. The consensus of aviators and engineers, after Geoffrey de Havilland's death, was that the speed of sound was an absolute, like the firmness of the earth. The sound barrier was a farm you could buy in the sky. So Slick Goodlin began to probe the transonic zone in the X-I, going up to .8 Mach. Every time he came down he'd have a riveting tale to tell. The buffeting, it was so fierce—and the listeners, their imaginations aflame, could practically see poor Geoffrey de Havilland disintegrating in midair. And the goddamned aerodynamics—and the listeners got a picture of a man in ballroom pumps skidding across a sheet of ice, pursued by bears. A controversy arose over just how much bonus Slick Goodlin should receive for assaulting the dread Mach 1 itself. Bonuses for contract test pilots were not unusual; but the figure of $150,000 was now bruited about. The Army balked, and Yeager got the job. He took it for $283 a month, or $3,396 a year; which is to say, his regular Army captain's pay.

The only trouble they had with Yeager was in holding him back. On his first powered flight in the X-I he immediately executed an unauthorized zero-g roll with a full load of rocket fuel, then stood the ship on its tail and went up to .85 Mach in a vertical climb, also unauthorized. On subsequent flights, at speeds between .85 Mach and .9 Mach, Yeager ran into most known airfoil problems—loss of elevator, aileron, and rudder control, heavy trim pressures, Dutch rolls, pitching and buffeting, the lot—yet was convinced, after edging over .9 Mach, that this would all get better, not worse, as you reached Mach 1. The attempt to push beyond Mach 1—"breaking the sound barrier"—was set for October 14, 1947. Not being an engineer, Yeager didn't believe the "barrier" existed.

October 14 was a Tuesday. On Sunday evening, October 12, Chuck Yeager dropped in at Pancho's along with his wife. She was a brunette named Glennis, whom he had met in California while he was in training, and she was such a number, so striking, he had the inscription "Glamorous Glennis" written on the nose of his P-51 in Europe and, just a few weeks back, on the X-I itself. Yeager didn't go to Pancho's and knock back a few because two days later the big test was coming up. Nor did he knock back a few because it was the weekend. No, he knocked back a few because night had come and he was a pilot at Muroc. In keeping with the military tradition of Flying & Drinking, that was what you did, for no other reason than that the sun had gone down. You went to Pancho's and knocked back a few and listened to the screen doors banging and to other aviators torturing the piano and the nation's repertoire of Familiar Favorites and to lonesome mouse-turd strangers wandering in through the banging doors and to Pancho classifying the whole bunch of them as old bastards and miserable peckerwoods. That was what you did if you were a pilot at Muroc and the sun went down.

So about eleven Yeager got the idea that it would be a hell of a kick if he and Glennis saddled up a couple of Pancho's dude-ranch horses and went for a romp, a little rat race, in the moonlight. This was in keeping with the military tradition of Flying & Drinking and Drinking & Driving, except that this was prehistoric Muroc and you rode horses. So Yeager and his wife set off on a little proficiency run at full gallop through the desert in the moonlight amid the arthritic silhouettes of the Joshua trees. Then they start racing back to the corral, with Yeager in the lead and heading for the gateway. Given the prevailing conditions, it being nighttime, at Pancho's, and his head being filled with a black sandstorm of many badly bawled songs and vulcanized oaths, he sees too late that the gate has been closed. Like many a hard-driving midnight pilot before him, he does not realize that he is not equally gifted in the control of all forms of locomotion. He and the horse hit the gate, and he goes flying off and lands on his right side. His side hurts like hell.

The next day, Monday, his side still hurts like hell. It hurts every time he moves. It hurts every time he breathes deep. It hurts every time he moves his right arm. He knows that if he goes to a doctor at Muroc or says anything to anybody even remotely connected with his superiors, he will be scrubbed from the flight on Tuesday. They might even go so far as to put some other miserable peckerwood in his place. So he gets on his motorcycle, an old junker that Pancho had given him, and rides over to see a doctor in the town of Rosamond, near where he lives. Every time the goddamned motorcycle hits a pebble in the road, his side hurts like a sonofabitch. The doctor in Rosamond informs him he has two broken ribs and he tapes them up and tells him that if he'll just keep his right arm immobilized for a couple of weeks and avoid any physical exertion or sudden movements, he should be all right.

Yeager gets up before daybreak on Tuesday morning—which is supposed to be the day he tries to break the sound barrier—and his ribs still hurt like a sonofabitch. He gets his wife to drive him over to the field, and he has to keep his right arm pinned down to his side to keep his ribs from hurting so much. At dawn, on the day of a flight, you could hear the X-I screaming long before you got there. The fuel for the X-I was alcohol and liquid oxygen, oxygen converted from a gas to a liquid by lowering its temperature to 297 degrees below zero. And when the lox, as it was called, rolled out of the hoses and into the belly of the X-I, it started boiling off and the X-I started steaming and screaming like a teakettle. There's quite a crowd on hand, by Muroc standards . . . perhaps nine or ten souls. They're still fueling the X-I with the lox, and the beast is wailing.

The X-I looked like a fat orange swallow with white markings. But it was really just a length of pipe with four rocket chambers in it. It had a tiny cockpit and a needle nose, two little straight blades (only three and a half inches thick at the thickest part) for wings, and a tail assembly set up high to avoid the "sonic wash" from the wings. Even though his side was throbbing and his right arm felt practically useless, Yeager figured he could grit his teeth and get through the flight—except for one specific move he had to make. In the rocket launches, the X-I, which held only two and a half minutes' worth of fuel, was carried up to twenty-six thousand feet underneath a B-29. At seven thousand feet, Yeager was to climb down a ladder from the bomb bay of the B-29 to the open doorway of the X-I, hook up to the oxygen system and the radio microphone and earphones, and put his crash helmet on and prepare for the launch, which would come at twenty-five thousand feet. This helmet was a home-made number. There had never been any such thing as a crash helmet before, except in stunt flying. Throughout the war pilots had used the old skin-tight leather helmet-and-goggles. But the X-I had a way of throwing the pilot around so violently that there was danger of get-ting knocked out against the walls of the cockpit. So Yeager had bought a big leather foot-ball helmet—there were no plastic ones at the time—and he butchered it with a hunting knife until he carved the right kind of holes in it, so that it would fit down over his regular flying helmet and the earphones and the oxygen rig. Anyway, then his flight engineer, Jack Ridley, would climb down the ladder, out in the breeze, and shove into place the cockpit door, which had to be lowered out of the belly of the B-29 on a chain. Then Yeager had to push a handle to lock the door airtight. Since the X-I's cockpit was minute, you had to push the handle with your right hand. It took quite a shove. There was no way you could move into position to get enough leverage with your left hand.

Out in the hangar Yeager makes a few test shoves on the sly, and the pain is so incred-ible he realizes that there is no way a man with two broken ribs is going to get the door closed. It is time to confide in somebody, and the logical man is Jack Ridley. Ridley is not only the flight engineer but a pilot himself and a good old boy from Oklahoma to boot. He will understand about Flying & Drinking and Drinking & Driving through the goddamned Joshua trees. So Yeager takes Ridley off to the side in the tin hangar and says: Jack, I got me a little ol' problem here. Over at Pancho's the other night I sorta . . . dinged my god-damned ribs. Ridley says, Whattya mean . . . *dinged?* Yeager says, Well, I guess you might say I damned near like to . . . *broke* a coupla the sonsabitches. Whereupon Yeager sketches out the problem he foresees.

Not for nothing is Ridley the engineer on this project. He has an inspiration. He tells a janitor named Sam to cut him about nine inches off a broom handle. When nobody's look-ing, he slips the broomstick into the cockpit of the X-I and gives Yeager a little advice and counsel.

So with that added bit of supersonic flight gear Yeager went aloft.

At seven thousand feet he climbed down the ladder into the X-I's cockpit, clipped on his hoses and lines, and managed to pull the pumpkin football helmet over his head. Then Ridley came down the ladder and lowered the door into place. As Ridley had instructed, Yea-ger now took the nine inches of broomstick and slipped it between the handle and the door. This gave him just enough mechanical advantage to reach over with his left hand and whang the thing shut. So he whanged the door shut with Ridley's broomstick and was ready to fly.

At 26,000 feet the B-29 went into a shallow dive, then pulled up and released Yeager and the X-I as if it were a bomb. Like a bomb it dropped and shot forward (at the speed of the mother ship) at the same time. Yeager had been launched straight into the sun. It seemed to be no more than six feet in front of him, filling up the sky and blinding him. But he man-aged to get his bearings and set off the four rocket chambers one after the other. He then ex-perienced something that became known as the ultimate sensation in flying: "booming and zooming." The surge of the rockets was so tremendous, forced him back into his seat so vi-olently, he could hardly move his hands forward the few inches necessary to reach the con-trols. The X-I seemed to shoot straight up in an absolutely perpendicular trajectory, as if de-termined to snap the hold of gravity via the most direct route possible. In fact, he was only climbing at the 45-degree angle called for in the flight plan. At about .87 Mach the buffet-ing started.

On the ground the engineers could no longer see Yeager. They could only hear . . . that poker-hollow West Virginia drawl.

"Had a mild buffet there . . . jes the usual instability . . ."

Jes the usual instability?

Then the X-I reached the speed of .96 Mach, and that incredible caint-hardlyin' aw-shuckin'drawl said:

"Say, Ridley . . . make a note here, will ya?" (*if you ain't got nothin' better to do*) ". . . elevator effectiveness *re*-gained."

Just as Yeager had predicted, as the X-I approached Mach 1, the stability improved. Yeager had his eyes pinned on the machometer. The needle reached .96, fluctuated, and went off the scale.

And on the ground they heard . . . that voice:

"Say, Ridley . . . make another note, will ya?" (*if you ain't too bored yet*) ". . . there's somethin' wrong with this ol' machometer . . ." (faint chuckle) ". . . it's gone kinda screwy on me . . ."

And in that moment, on the ground, they heard a boom rock over the desert floor— just as the physicist Theodore von Kármán had predicted many years before.

Then they heard Ridley back in the B-29: "If it is, Chuck, we'll fix it. Personally I think you're seeing things."

Then they heard Yeager's poker-hollow drawl again:

"Well, I guess I am, Jack . . . And I'm still goin' upstairs like a bat."

The X-I had gone through "the sonic wall" without so much as a bump. As the speed topped out at Mach 1.05, Yeager had the sensation of shooting straight through the top of the sky. The sky turned a deep purple and all at once the stars and the moon came out—and the sun shone at the same time. He had reached a layer of the upper atmosphere where the air was too thin to contain reflecting dust particles. He was simply looking out into space. As the X-I nosed over at the top of the climb, Yeager now had seven minutes of . . . Pilot Heaven . . . ahead of him. He was going faster than any man in history, and it was almost silent up here, since he had exhausted his rocket fuel, and he was so high in such a vast space that there was no sensation of motion. He was master of the sky. His was a king's solitude, unique and inviolate, above the dome of the world. It would take him seven minutes to glide back down and land at Muroc. He spent the time doing victory rolls and wing-over-wing aerobatics while Rogers Lake and the High Sierras spun around below.

◦ ◦ ◦

On the ground they had understood the code as soon as they heard Yeager's little exchange with Ridley. The project was secret, but the radio exchanges could be picked up by anyone within range. The business of the "screwy machometer" was Yeager's deadpan way of announcing that the X-I's instruments indicated Mach 1. As soon as he landed, they checked out the X-I's automatic recording instruments. Without any doubt the ship had gone supersonic. They immediately called the brass at Wright Field to break the tremendous news. Within two hours Wright Field called back and gave some firm orders. A top security lid was being put on the morning's events. That the press was not to be informed went without saying. But neither was anyone else, anyone at all, to be told. Word of the flight was not to go beyond the flight line. And even among the people directly involved—who were there and knew about it, anyway—there was to be no celebrating. Just what was on the minds of the brass at Wright is hard to say. Much of it, no doubt, was a simple holdover from wartime, when every breakthrough of possible strategic importance was kept under wraps. That was what you did—you shut up about them. Another possibility was that the chief at Wright had never quite known what to make of Muroc. There was some sort of weird ribald aerial tarpaper mad-monk squadron up on the roof of the desert out there . . .

In any case, by mid-afternoon Yeager's tremendous feat had become a piece of thunder with no reverberation. A strange and implausible stillness settled over the event. Well . . . there was not supposed to be any celebration, but come nightfall . . . Yeager and Ridley and some of the others ambled over to Pancho's. After all, it was the end of the day, and they were pilots. So they knocked back a few. And they had to let Pancho in on the secret, because Pancho had said she'd serve a free steak dinner to any pilot who could fly supersonic and walk in here to tell about it, and they had to see the look on *her* face. So Pancho served Yeager a big steak dinner and said they were a buncha miserable peckerwoods all the same, and the desert cooled off and the wind came up and the screen doors banged and they drank some more and bawled some songs over the cackling dry piano and the stars and the moon came out and Pancho screamed oaths no one had ever heard before and Yeager and Ridley roared and the old weatherbeaten bar boomed and the autographed pictures of a hundred dead pilots shook and clattered on the frame wires and the faces of the living fell apart in the reflections, and by and by they all left and stumbled and staggered and yelped and bayed for glory before the arthritic silhouettes of the Joshua trees. Shit!—there was no one to tell except for Pancho and the goddamned Joshua trees!

Jon Krakauer
from Into Thin Air

SUMMIT 1:25 P.M., MAY 10, 1996, 29,028 FEET

[O]ur wreck is certainly due to this sudden advent of severe weather, which does not seem to have any satisfactory cause. I do not think human beings ever came through such a month as we have come through, and we should have got through in spite of the weather but for the sickening of a second companion, Captain Oates, and a shortage of fuel in our depots for which I cannot account, and finally, but for the storm which has fallen on us within 11 miles of the depot at which we hoped to secure our final supplies. Surely misfortune could scarcely have exceeded this last blow. . . . We took risks, we knew we took them; things have come out against us, and therefore we have no cause for complaint, but bow to the will of Providence, determined still to do our best to the last. . . .

Had we lived, I should have had a tale to tell of the hardihood, endurance, and courage of my companions which would have stirred the heart of every Englishman. These rough notes and our dead bodies must tell the tale.

—*Robert Falcon Scott,*
in "Message to the Public,"
penned just prior to his death in
Antarctica on March 29, 1912,
from Scott's Last Expedition

SCOTT FISCHER ASCENDED TO THE SUMMIT AROUND 3:40 ON THE AFTERNOON OF MAY 10 TO find his devoted friend and sirdar, Lopsang Jangbu, waiting for him. The Sherpa pulled his radio from inside his down jacket, made contact with Ingrid Hunt at Base Camp, then handed the walkie-talkie to Fischer. "We all made it," Fischer told Hunt, 11,400 feet below. "God, I'm tired." A few minutes later Makalu Gau arrived with two Sherpas. Rob Hall was there, too, waiting impatiently for Doug Hansen to appear as a rising tide of cloud lapped ominously at the summit ridge.

According to Lopsang, during the fifteen or twenty minutes Fischer spent on the summit, he complained repeatedly that he wasn't feeling well—something the congenitally stoic guide almost never did. "Scott tell to me, 'I am too tired. I am sick, also, need medicine for stomach,'" the Sherpa recalls. "I gave him tea, but he drank just a little bit, just half cup. So I tell to him, 'Scott, please, we go fast down.' So we come down then."

Fischer started down first, about 3:55. Lopsang reports that although Scott had used supplemental oxygen during the entire ascent and his third canister was more than three-quarters full when he left the summit, for some reason he took his mask off and stopped using it.

Shortly after Fischer left the top, Gau and his Sherpas departed as well, and finally Lopsang headed down—leaving Hall alone on the summit awaiting Hansen. A moment after Lopsang started down, about 4:00, Hansen at last appeared, toughing it out, moving painfully slowly over the last bump on the ridge. As soon as he saw Hansen, Hall hurried down to meet him.

Hall's obligatory turn-around time had come and gone a full two hours earlier. Given the guide's conservative, exceedingly methodical nature, many of his colleagues have expressed puzzlement at this uncharacteristic lapse of judgment. Why, they wondered, didn't he turn Hansen around much lower on the mountain, as soon as it became obvious that the American climber was running late?

Exactly one year earlier, Hall had turned Hansen around on the South Summit at 2:30 P.M., and to be denied so close to the top was a crushing disappointment to Hansen. He told me several times that he'd returned to Everest in 1996 largely as a result of Hall's advocacy—he said Rob had called him from New Zealand "a dozen times" urging him to give it another shot—and this time Doug was absolutely determined to bag the top. "I want to get this thing done and out of my life," he'd told me three days earlier at Camp Two. "I don't want to have to come back here. I'm getting too old for this shit."

It doesn't seem far-fetched to speculate that because Hall had talked Hansen into coming back to Everest, it would have been especially hard for him to deny Hansen the summit a second time. "It's very difficult to turn someone around high on the mountain," cautions Guy Cotter, a New Zealand guide who summitted Everest with Hall in 1992 and was guiding the peak for him in 1995 when Hansen made his first attempt. "If a client sees that the summit is close and they're dead-set on getting there, they're going to laugh in your face and keep going up." As the veteran American guide Peter Lev told *Climbing* magazine after the disastrous events on Everest, "We think that people pay us to make good decisions, but what people really pay for is to get to the top."

In any case, Hall did not turn Hansen around at 2:00 P.M.—or, for that matter, at 4:00, when he met his client just below the top. Instead, according to Lopsang, Hall placed Hansen's arm around his neck and assisted the weary client up the final forty feet to the summit. They stayed only a minute or two, then turned to begin the long descent.

When Lopsang saw that Hansen was faltering, he held up his own descent long enough to make sure Doug and Rob made it safely across a dangerously corniced area just below the top. Then, eager to catch Fischer, who was by now more than thirty minutes ahead of him, the Sherpa continued down the ridge, leaving Hansen and Hall at the top of the Hillary Step.

Just after Lopsang disappeared down the Step, Hansen apparently ran out of oxygen and foundered. He'd expended every last bit of his strength to reach the summit—and now there was nothing left in reserve for the descent. "Pretty much the same thing happened to Doug in '95," says Ed Viesturs, who, like Cotter, was guiding the peak for Hall that year. "He was fine during the ascent, but as soon as he started down he lost it mentally and physically; he turned into a zombie, like he'd used everything up."

At 4:30 P.M., and again at 4:41, Hall got on the radio to say that he and Hansen were in trouble high on the summit ridge and urgently needed oxygen. Two full bottles were waiting for them at the South Summit; if Hall had known this he could have retrieved the gas fairly quickly and then climbed back up to give Hansen a fresh tank. But Andy Harris, still at the oxygen cache, in the throes of his hypoxic dementia, overheard these radio calls and broke in to tell Hall—incorrectly, just as he'd told Mike Groom and me—that all the bottles at the South Summit were empty.

Groom heard the conversation between Harris and Hall on his radio as he was descending the Southeast Ridge with Yasuko Namba, just above the Balcony. He tried to call Hall to correct the misinformation and let him know that there were in fact full oxygen canisters waiting for him at the South Summit, but, Groom explains, "my radio was malfunctioning. I was able to receive most calls, but my outgoing calls could rarely be heard by anyone. On the couple of occasions that my calls were being picked up by Rob, and I tried to tell him where the full cylinders were, I was immediately interrupted by Andy, transmitting to say there was no gas at the South Summit."

Unsure whether there was oxygen waiting for him, Hall decided that the best course of action was to remain with Hansen and try to bring the nearly helpless client down without gas. But when they got to the top of the Hillary Step, Hall couldn't get Hansen down the 40-foot vertical drop, and their progress ground to a halt. "I can get myself down," Hall reported over the radio, gasping audibly for breath. "I just don't know how the fuck I can get this man down the Hillary Step without any oxygen."

Shortly before 5:00, Groom finally managed to get through to Hall and communicate that there actually was oxygen at the South Summit. Fifteen minutes later, Lopsang arrived at the South Summit on his way down from the top and encountered Harris.[1] At this point, according to Lopsang, Harris must have finally understood that at least two of the oxygen canisters stashed there were full, because he pleaded with the Sherpa to help him carry the life-sustaining gas up to Hall and Hansen on the Hillary Step. "Andy says he will pay me five hundred dollars to bring oxygen to Rob and Doug," Lopsang recalls. "But I am supposed to take care of just my group. I have to take care of Scott. So I say to Andy, no, I go fast down."

At 5:30, as Lopsang left the South Summit to resume his descent, he turned to see Harris—who must have been severely debilitated, if his condition when I'd seen him on the South Summit two hours earlier was any indication—plodding slowly up the summit ridge to assist Hall and Hansen. It was an act of heroism that would cost Harris his life.

---

[1] It wasn't until I interviewed Lopsang in Seattle on July 25, 1996, that I learned he had seen Harris on the evening of May 10. Although I'd spoken briefly with Lopsang several times previously, I'd never thought to ask whether he'd encountered Harris on the South Summit, because at that point I was still certain I'd seen Harris at the South Col, 3,000 feet below the South Summit, at 6:30 P.M. Moreover, Guy Cotter *had* asked Lopsang if he'd seen Harris, and for some reason—perhaps a simple misunderstanding of the question—on that occasion Lopsang said no.

⚬ ⚬ ⚬

A few hundred feet below, Scott Fischer was struggling down the Southeast Ridge, growing weaker and weaker. Upon reaching the top of the rock steps at 28,400 feet, he was confronted with a series of short but troublesome rappels that angled along the ridge. Too exhausted to cope with the complexities of the rope work, Fischer slid directly down an adjacent snow slope on his butt. This was easier than following the fixed lines, but once he was below the level of the rock steps it meant that he had to make a laborious 330-foot rising traverse through knee-deep snow to regain the route.

Tim Madsen, descending with Beidleman's group, happened to glance up from the Balcony around 5:20 and saw Fischer as he began the traverse. "He looked really tired," Madsen remembers. "He'd take ten steps, then sit and rest, take a couple more steps, rest again. He was moving real slow. But I could see Lopsang above him, coming down the ridge, and I figured, shoot, with Lopsang there to look after him, Scott would be O.K."

According to Lopsang, the Sherpa caught up with Fischer about 6:00 P.M., just above the Balcony: "Scott is not using oxygen, so I put mask on him. He says, 'I am very sick, too sick to go down. I am going to jump.' He is saying many times, acting like crazy man, so I tie him on rope, quickly, otherwise he is jumping down into Tibet."

Securing Fischer with a 75-foot length of rope, Lopsang persuaded his friend not to jump and then got him moving slowly toward the South Col. "The storm is very bad now," Lopsang recalls. "BOOM! BOOM! Two times like sound of gun, there is big thunder. Two times lightning hit very close near me and Scott, very loud, very scared."

Three hundred feet below the Balcony, the gentle snow gully they'd been gingerly descending gave way to outcroppings of loose, steep shale, and Fischer was unable to handle the challenging terrain in his ailing condition. "Scott cannot walk now, I have big problem," says Lopsang. "I try to carry, but I am also very tired. Scott is big body, I am very small; I cannot carry him. He tell to me, 'Lopsang, you go down. You go down.' I tell to him. 'No, I stay together here with you.'"

About 8:00 P.M., Lopsang was huddling with Fischer on a snow-covered ledge when Makalu Gau and his two Sherpas appeared out of the howling blizzard. Gau was nearly as debilitated as Fischer and was likewise unable to descend the difficult bands of shale, so his Sherpas sat the Taiwanese climber beside Lopsang and Fischer and then continued down without him.

"I stay with Scott and Makalu one hour, maybe longer," says Lopsang. "I am very cold, very tired. Scott tell to me, 'You go down, send up Anatoli.' So I say, 'O.K., I go down, I send quick Sherpa up and Anatoli.' Then I make good place for Scott and go down."

Lopsang left Fischer and Gau on a ledge 1,200 feet above the South Col and fought his way down through the storm. Unable to see, he got far off route toward the west, ended up below the level of the Col before he realized his error, and was forced to climb back up the northern margin of the Lhotse Face[2] to locate Camp Four. Around midnight, nevertheless, he made it to safety. "I go to Anatoli tent," reported Lopsang. "I tell to Anatoli, 'Please, you go up, Scott is very sick, he cannot walk. Then I go to my tent, just fall asleep, sleep like dead person."

---

[2] Early the next morning while searching the Col for Andy Harris, I came across Lopsang's faint crampon tracks in the ice leading up from the lip of the Lhotse Face, and mistakenly believed they were Harris's tracks headed *down* the face—which is why I thought Harris had walked off the edge of the Col.

◦ ◦ ◦

Guy Cotter, a longtime friend of both Hall's and Harris's, happened to be a few miles from Everest Base Camp on the afternoon of May 10, where he was guiding an expedition on Pumori, and had been monitoring Hall's radio transmissions throughout the day. At 2:15 P.M. he talked to Hall on the summit, and everything sounded fine. At 4:30, however, Hall called down to say that Doug was out of oxygen and unable to move. "I need a bottle of gas!" Hall pleaded in a desperate, breathless voice to anyone on the mountain who might be listening. "Somebody, please! I'm begging you!"

Cotter grew very alarmed. At 4:53 he got on the radio and strongly urged Hall to descend to the South Summit. "The call was mostly to convince him to come down and get some gas," says Cotter, "because we knew he wasn't going to be able to do anything for Doug without it. Rob said he could get himself down O.K., but not with Doug."

But forty minutes later, Hall was still with Hansen atop the Hillary Step, going nowhere. During radio calls from Hall at 5:36, and again at 5:57, Cotter implored his mate to leave Hansen and come down alone. "I know I sound like the bastard for telling Rob to abandon his client," confessed Cotter, "but by then it was obvious that leaving Doug was his only choice." Hall, however, wouldn't consider going down without Hansen.

There was no further word from Hall until the middle of the night. At 2:46 A.M., Cotter woke up in his tent below Pumori to hear a long, broken transmission, probably unintended: Hall had been wearing a remote microphone clipped to the shoulder strap of his backpack, which was occasionally keyed on by mistake. In this instance, says Cotter, "I suspect Rob didn't even know he was transmitting. I could hear someone yelling—it might have been Rob, but I couldn't be sure because the wind was so loud in the background. But he was saying something like, 'Keep moving! Keep going!' presumably to Doug, urging him on."

If this was indeed the case, it meant that in the wee hours of the morning Hall and Hansen—perhaps accompanied by Harris—were still struggling from the Hillary Step toward the South Summit through the gale. And if so, it also meant that it had taken them more than ten hours to move down a stretch of ridge that was typically covered by descending climbers in less than half an hour.

Of course, this is highly speculative. All that is certain is that Hall called down at 5:57 P.M. At that point, he and Hansen were still on the Step; and at 4:43 on the morning of May 11, when he next spoke to Base Camp, he had descended to the South Summit. And at that point neither Hansen nor Harris was with him.

In a series of transmissions over the next two hours, Rob sounded disturbingly confused and irrational. During the call at 4:43 A.M., he told Caroline Mackenzie, our Base Camp doctor, that his legs no longer worked, and that he was "too clumsy to move." In a ragged, barely audible voice, Rob croaked, "Harold was with me last night, but he doesn't seem to be with me now. He was very weak." Then, obviously befuddled, he asked, "Was Harold with me? Can you tell me that?"[3]

By this point Hall had possession of two full oxygen canisters, but the valves on his mask were so choked with ice that he couldn't get the gas to flow. He indicated, however,

---

[3] I'd already reported with absolute certainty that I'd seen Harris on the South Col at 6:30 P.M., May 10. When Hall said that Harris was with him up on the South Summit—3,000 feet higher than where I said I'd seen him—most people, thanks to my error, wrongly assumed that Hall's statements were merely the incoherent ramblings of an exhausted, severely hypoxic man.

that he was attempting to de-ice the oxygen rig, "which," says Cotter, "made us all feel a little better. It was the first positive thing we'd heard."

At 5:00 A.M., Base Camp patched through a call on the satellite telephone to Jan Arnold, Hall's wife, in Christchurch, New Zealand. She had climbed to the summit of Everest with Hall in 1993, and she entertained no illusions about the gravity of her husband's predicament. "My heart really sank when I heard his voice," she recalls. "He was slurring his words markedly. He sounded like Major Tom or something, like he was just floating away. I'd been up there; I knew what it could be like in bad weather. Rob and I had talked about the impossibility of being rescued from the summit ridge. As he himself had put it, 'You might as well be on the moon.'"

At 5:31, Hall took four milligrams of oral dexamethasone and indicated he was still trying to clear his oxygen mask of ice. Talking to Base Camp, he asked repeatedly about the condition of Makalu Gau, Fischer, Beck Weathers, Yasuko Namba, and his other clients. He seemed most concerned about Andy Harris and kept inquiring about his whereabouts. Cotter says they tried to steer the discussion away from Harris, who in all likelihood was dead, "because we didn't want Rob to have another reason for staying up there. At one point Ed Viesturs jumped on the radio from Camp Two and fibbed, 'Don't worry about Andy; he's down here with us.'"

A little later, Mackenzie asked Rob how Hansen was doing. "Doug," Hall replied, "is gone." That was all he said, and it was the last mention he ever made of Hansen.

On May 23, when David Breashears and Ed Viesturs reached the summit, they would find no sign of Hansen's body; they did, however, find an ice ax planted about fifty vertical feet above the South Summit, along a very exposed section of ridge where the fixed ropes came to an end. It's quite possible that Hall and/or Harris managed to get Hansen down the ropes to this point, only to have him lose his footing and fall 7,000 feet down the sheer Southwest Face, leaving his ice ax jammed into the ridge where he slipped. But this, too, is merely conjecture.

What might have happened to Harris remains even harder to discern. Between Lopsang's testimony, Hall's radio calls, and the fact that another ice ax found on the South Summit was positively identified as Andy's, we can be reasonably sure he was at the South Summit with Hall on the night of May 10. Beyond that, however, virtually nothing is known about how the young guide met his end.

At 6:00 A.M., Cotter asked Hall if the sun had reached him yet. "Almost," Rob replied—which was good, because he'd mentioned a moment earlier that he was shaking uncontrollably in the awful cold. In conjunction with his earlier revelation that he was no longer able to walk, this had been very upsetting news to the people listening down below. Nevertheless, it was remarkable that Hall was even alive after spending a night without shelter or oxygen at 28,700 feet in hurricane-force winds and windchill of one hundred degrees below zero.

During this same radio call, Hall asked after Harris yet again: "Did anyone see Harold last night except myself?" Some three hours later Rob was still obsessing over Andy's whereabouts. At 8:43 A.M. he mused over the radio, "Some of Andy's gear is still here. I thought he must have gone ahead in the nighttime. Listen, can you account for him or not?" Wilton attempted to dodge the question, but Rob persisted in his line of inquiry: "O.K. I mean his ice ax is here and his jacket and things."

"Rob," Viesturs replied from Camp Two, "if you can put the jacket on, just use it. Keep going down and worry only about yourself. Everybody else is taking care of other people. Just get yourself down."

After struggling for four hours to de-ice his mask, Hall finally got it to work, and by 9:00 A.M. he was breathing supplemental oxygen for the first time; by then he'd spent more than sixteen hours above 28,700 feet without gas. Thousands of feet below, his friends stepped up their efforts to cajole him to start down. "Rob, this is Helen at Base Camp," Wilton importuned, sounding as if she was on the brink of tears. "You think about that little baby of yours. You're going to see its face in a couple of months, so keep on going."

Several times Hall announced he was preparing to descend, and at one point we were sure he'd finally left the South Summit. At Camp Four, Lhakpa Chhiri and I shivered in the wind outside the tents, peering up at a tiny speck moving slowly down the upper Southeast Ridge. Convinced that it was Rob, coming down at last, Lhakpa and I slapped each other on the back and cheered him on. But an hour later my optimism was rudely extinguished when I noticed that the speck was still in the same place: it was actually nothing but a rock—just another altitude-induced hallucination. In truth, Rob had never even left the South Summit.

❖   ❖   ❖

Around 9:30 A.M., Ang Dorje and Lhakpa Chhiri left Camp Four and started climbing toward the South Summit with a thermos of hot tea and two extra canisters of oxygen, intending to rescue Hall. They faced an exceedingly formidable task. As astounding and courageous as Boukreev's rescue of Sandy Pittman and Charlotte Fox had been the night before, it paled in comparison to what the two Sherpas were proposing to do now: Pittman and Fox had been a twenty-minute walk from the tents over relatively flat ground; Hall was 3,000 vertical feet above Camp Four—an exhausting eight- or nine-hour climb in the best of circumstances.

And these were surely not the best of circumstances. The wind was blowing in excess of 40 knots. Both Ang Dorje and Lhakpa were cold and wasted from climbing to the summit and back just the day before. If they did somehow manage to reach Hall, moreover, it would be late afternoon before they got there, leaving only one or two hours of daylight in which to begin the even more difficult ordeal of bringing him down. Yet their loyalty to Hall was such that the two men ignored the overwhelming odds and set out toward the South Summit as fast as they could climb.

Shortly thereafter, two Sherpas from the Mountain Madness team—Tashi Tshering and Ngawang Sya Kya (a small, trim man, graying at the temples, who is Lopsang's father)—and one Sherpa from the Taiwanese team headed up to bring down Scott Fischer and Makalu Gau. Twelve hundred feet above the South Col the trio of Sherpas found the incapacitated climbers on the ledge where Lopsang had left them. Although they tried to give Fischer oxygen, he was unresponsive. Scott was still breathing, barely, but his eyes were fixed in their sockets, and his teeth were tightly clenched. Concluding that he was beyond hope, they left him on the ledge and started descending with Gau, who, after receiving hot tea and oxygen, and with considerable assistance from the three Sherpas, was able to move down to the tents on a short-rope under his own power.

The day had started out sunny and clear, but the wind remained fierce, and by late morning the upper mountain was wrapped in thick clouds. Down at Camp Two the IMAX team reported that the wind over the summit sounded like a squadron of 747s, even from 7,000 feet below. Meanwhile, high on the Southeast Ridge, Ang Dorje and Lhakpa Chhiri pressed on resolutely through the intensifying storm toward Hall. At 3:00 P.M., however, still 700 feet below the South Summit, the wind and subzero cold proved to be too much for them, and the Sherpas could go no higher. It was a valiant effort, but it had failed—and as they turned around to descend, Hall's chances for survival all but vanished.

Throughout the day on May 11, his friends and teammates incessantly begged him to make an effort to come down under his own power. Several times Hall announced that he was preparing to descend, only to change his mind and remain immobile at the South Summit. At 3:20 P.M., Cotter—who by now had walked over from his own camp beneath Pumori to the Everest Base Camp—scolded over the radio, "Rob, get moving down the ridge."

Sounding annoyed, Hall fired back, "Look, if I thought I could manage the knots on the fixed ropes with me frostbitten hands, I would have gone down six hours ago, pal. Just send a couple of the boys up with a big thermos of something hot—then I'll be fine."

"Thing is, mate, the lads who went up today encountered some high winds and had to turn around," Cotter replied, trying to convey as delicately as possible that the rescue attempt had been abandoned, "so we think your best shot is to move lower."

"I can last another night here if you send up a couple of boys with some Sherpa tea, first thing in the morning, no later than nine-thirty or ten," Rob answered.

"You're a tough man, Big Guy," said Cotter, his voice quavering. "We'll send some boys up to you in the morning."

At 6:20 P.M., Cotter contacted Hall to tell him that Jan Arnold was on the satellite phone from Christchurch and was waiting to be patched through. "Give me a minute," Rob said. "Me mouth's dry. I want to eat a bit of snow before I talk to her." A little later he came back on and rasped in a slow, horribly distorted voice, "Hi, my sweetheart. I hope you're tucked up in a nice warm bed. How are you doing?"

"I can't tell you how much I'm thinking about you!" Arnold replied. "You sound so much better than I expected. . . . Are you warm, my darling?"

"In the context of the altitude, the setting, I'm reasonably comfortable," Hall answered, doing his best not to alarm her.

"How are your feet?"

"I haven't taken me boots off to check, but I think I may have a bit of frostbite. . . ."

"I'm looking forward to making you completely better when you come home," said Arnold. "I just know you're going to be rescued. Don't feel that you're alone. I'm sending all my positive energy your way!"

Before signing off, Hall told his wife, "I love you. Sleep well, my sweetheart. Please don't worry too much."

These would be the last words anyone would hear him speak. Attempts to make radio contact with Hall later that night and the next day went unanswered. Twelve days later, when Breashears and Viesturs climbed over the South Summit on their way to the top, they found Hall lying on his right side in a shallow ice hollow, his upper body buried beneath a drift of snow.

Sebastian Junger

from The Perfect Storm

THE ZERO-MOMENT POINT

Behold a pale horse, and his name who sat on him was Death, and Hell followed with him.

—*Revelation 6:8*

IN THE 1950S AND 1960S, THE U.S. GOVERNMENT DECIDED TO DETONATE A SERIES OF NU-clear devices in the Pacific Ocean. The thinking was that deep water would absorb the shock-wave and minimize the effect on the environment, while still allowing scientists to gauge the strength of the explosions. But an oceanographer named Bill Van Dorn, associated with the Scripps Institute in La Jolla, California, warned them that a nuclear explosion in the wrong place "could convert the entire continental shelf into a surf zone."

Concerned, the Navy ran a series of wave tank tests to see what kind of stresses their fleet could take. (They'd already lost three destroyers to a typhoon in 1944. Before going down the ships had radioed that they were rolling through arcs of 140 degrees. They down-flooded through their stacks and sank.) The Navy subjected model destroyers and aircraft carriers to various kinds of waves and found that a single nonbreaking wave—no matter how big it was—was incapable of sinking a ship. A single *breaking* wave, though, would flip a ship end-over-end if it was higher than the ship was long. Typically, the ship would climb the wave at an angle of forty-five degrees, fail to gain the top, and then slide back down the face. Her stern would bury itself into the trough, and the crest of the wave would catch her bow and flip her over. This is called pitch-poling; Ernie Hazard was pitch-poled on Georges Bank. It's one of the few motions that can end ship-to-shore communication instantly.

Another is a succession of waves that simply drives the boat under—"founders," as mariners say. The dictionary defines founder as "to cave in, sink, fail utterly, collapse." On a steel boat the windows implode, the hatches fail, and the boat starts to downflood. The crew is prevented from escaping by the sheer force of the water pouring into the cabin—it's like walking into the blast of a fire hose. In that sense, pitch-poling is better than foundering because an overturned boat traps air in the hold and can stay afloat for an hour or more. That might allow members of the crew to swim out a doorway and climb into a life raft. The rafts are designed to inflate automatically and release from the boat when she goes down. In theory the EPIRB floats free as well, and begins signalling to shore. All the crew has to do is stay alive.

By the late hours of October 28th the sea state is easily high enough to either pitch-pole the *Andrea Gail* or drive her under. And if she loses power—a clogged fuel filter, a fouled prop—she could slew to the side and roll. The same rule applies to capsizing as to pitch-poling: the wave must be higher than the boat is wide. The *Andrea Gail* is twenty feet across her beam. But even if the boat doesn't get hit by a non-negotiable wave, the rising sea state allows Billy less and less leeway to maneuver. If he maintains enough speed to steer, he beats the boat to pieces; if he slows down, he looses rudder control. This is the end result of two days of narrowing options; now the only choice left is whether to go upsea or down, and the only outcome is whether they sink or float. There's not much in between.

If the conditions don't subside, the most Billy can realistically hope for is to survive until dawn. Then at least they'll have a chance of being rescued—now it's unthinkable. "In violent storms there is so much water in the air, and so much air in the water, that it becomes impossible to tell where the atmosphere stops and the sea begins," writes Van Dorn. "That may literally make it impossible to distinguish up from down." In such conditions a helicopter pilot could never pluck six people off the deck of a boat. So, for the next eight hours, the crew of the *Andrea Gail* must keep the pumps and engine running and just hope they don't encounter any rogue waves. Seventy-footers are roaming around the sea state like surly giants and there's not much Billy can do but take them head-on and try to get over the top before they break. If his floodlights are out he wouldn't even have that option—he'd just feel a drop into the trough, a lurch, and the boat starting up a slope way too steep to survive.

"Seventy foot seas—I'd be puttin' on my diapers at that point," says Charlie Reed. "I'd be quite nervous. That's higher than the highest point on the *Andrea Gail*. I once came home from the Grand Banks in 35-foot seas. It was a scary fuckin' thought—straight up, straight down, for six days. My guess is that Billy turned side-to and rolled. You come off one of those seas cocked, the next one comes at a different angle, it pushes the boat around and then you roll. If the boat flips over—even with everything dogged down—water's gonna get in. The boat's upside-down, the plywood's buckling, that's the end."

When Ernie Hazard went over on Georges Bank in 1982, the motion wasn't a violent one so much as a huge, slow somersault that laid the boat over on her back. Hazard remembers one wave spinning them around and another lifting them end-over-end. It wasn't like rolling a car at high speeds, it was more like rolling a house. Hazard was 33 at the time; three years earlier he'd answered a newspaper ad and got a job on the *Fair Wind*, a lobster boat out of Newport, Rhode Island. The storm hit on their last trip of the year, late November. The crew were all good friends; they celebrated the end of their season at a steakhouse and then left for Georges Bank late the next morning. The winds were light and the forecast called for several more days of fair weather. By dawn it was blowing a hundred.

> We were driving the boat well. You point the boat into the sea and try to hold your own until it blows out—stay there, take your pounding. You balance the boat, flood the tanks, try to save what you have on deck. There was the typical howling of wind in the wires and there was a lot of foam because of the wind, yellow foam, spindrift. We'd lose power on the waves because they were more foam than water, the propeller just couldn't bite.
>
> It happened quick. We were close to the edge of the continental shelf and the seas were getting large, starting to break. Cresting. I remember looking out the pilothouse and this monster wave came and broke over the bow and forced us backwards. There was nothing to hold us there and we must have dug the stern in and then spun around. Now we're in a full following sea. We never went more than one more wave when we buried our bow in the trough and flipped over. There was the wave breaking and then a sensation of the boat turning, and the next thing I knew we were upside-down. Floating inside the boat.
>
> I happened to surface in a small air pocket and I didn't know if I was upside down or standing on the walls or what. I made a dive into the pilothouse and I could see some light—it could have been a window or a porthole, I don't know—and when I got back up into the wheelhouse there was no more air. It was all gone. I was thinking, "This is it. Just take a mouthful of water and it's over." It was very matter-of-fact. I was at a fork in the road and there was work to do—swim or die. It didn't scare me, I didn't think about my family or anything. It was more business-like. People think you always have to go for life, but you don't. You can quit.

For reasons that he still doesn't understand, Hazard didn't quit. He made a guess and swam. The entire port side of the cabin was welded steel and he knew if he picked that direction, he was finished. He felt himself slide through a narrow opening—the door? a window?—and suddenly he was back in the world. The boat was hull-up, sliding away fast, and the life raft was convulsing at the end of its tether. It was his only hope; he wriggled out of his clothes and started to swim.

Whether the *Andrea Gail* rolls, pitch-poles, or gets driven down, she winds up, one way or another, in a position from which she cannot recover. Among marine architects this is know as the zero-moment point—the point of no return. The transition from crisis to catastrophe is fast, probably under a minute, or someone would've tripped the EPIRB. (In fact the EPIRB doesn't even signal when it hits the water, which means it has somehow malfunctioned. In the vast majority of cases, the Coast Guard knows when men are dying offshore.) There's no time to put on survival suits or grab a life vest; the boat's moving through the most extreme motion of her life and there isn't even time to shout. The refrigerator comes out of the wall and crashes across the galley. Dirty dishes cascade out of the sink. The T.V., the washing machine, the VCR tapes, the men, all go flying. And, seconds later, the water moves in.

When a boat floods, the first thing that happens is that her electrical system shorts out. The lights go off, and for a few moments the only illumination is the frenetic blue of sparks arcing down into the water. It's said that people in extreme situations perceive things in distorted, almost surreal ways, and when the wires start to crackle and burn, perhaps one of the crew thinks of fireworks—of the last Fourth of July, walking around Gloucester with his girlfriend and watching colors blossom over the inner harbor. There'd be tourists shuffling down Rogers Street and fishermen hooting from bars and the smell of gunpowder and fried clams drifting through town. He'd would have his whole life ahead of him, that July evening; he'd have every choice in the world.

And he wound up swordfishing. He wound up, by one route or another, on this trip, in this storm, with this boat filling up with water and one or two minutes left to live. There's no going back now, no rescue helicopter that could possibly save him. All that's left is to hope it's over fast.

When the water first hits the trapped men, it's cold but not paralyzing, around 52 degrees, according to infrared photos taken from satellites. A man can survive up to four hours in that temperature if something holds him up. If the boat rolls or flips over, the men in the wheelhouse are the first to drown. Their experience is exactly like Hazard's except that they don't make it out of the wheelhouse to a life raft; they inhale and that's it. After that the water rises up the companionway, flooding the galley and berths, and then starts up the inverted engine room hatch. It may well be pouring in the aft door and the fish hatch, too, if either failed during the sinking. If the boat is hull-up and there are men in the engine room, they are the last to die. They're in absolute darkness, under a landslide of tools and gear, the water rising up the companionway and the roar of the waves probably very muted through the hull. If the water takes long enough, they might attempt to escape on a lungful of air—down the companionway, along the hall, through the aft door and out from under the boat—but they don't make it. It's too far, they die trying. Or the water comes up so hard and fast that they can't even think. They're up to their waists and then their chests and then their chins and then there's no air at all. Just what's in their lungs, a minute's worth or so.

The instinct not to breathe underwater is so strong that it overcomes the agony of running out of air. No matter how desperate the drowning person is, he doesn't inhale until he's on the verge of losing consciousness. At that point there's so much carbon dioxide in the blood, and so little oxygen, that chemical sensors in the brain trigger an involuntary breath whether he's underwater or not. That is called the "break point"; laboratory experiments have shown the break point to come after 87 seconds. It's a sort of neurological optimism, as if the body were saying, *Holding our breath is killing us, and breathing in might not kill us, so we might as well breathe in.* If the person hyperventilates first—as free divers do, and as a frantic person might—the break point comes as late as 140 seconds. Hyperventilation initially flushes carbon dioxide out of the system, so it takes that much longer to climb back up to critical levels.

Until the break point, a drowning person is said to be undergoing "voluntary apnea," choosing not to breathe. Lack of oxygen to the brain causes a sensation of darkness closing in from all sides, as in a camera aperture stopping down. The panic of a drowning person is mixed with an odd incredulity that this is actually happening. Having never done it before, the body—and the mind—do not know how to die gracefully. The process is filled with desperation and awkwardness. "So *this* is drowning," a drowning person might think. "So *this* is how my life finally ends."

Along with the disbelief is an overwhelming sense of being wrenched from life at the most banal, inopportune moment imaginable. "I can't die, I have tickets to next week's game," is not an impossible thought for someone who is drowning. The drowning person may even feel embarrassed, as if he's squandered a great fortune. He has an image of people shaking their heads over his dying so senselessly. The drowning person may feel as if it's the last, greatest act of stupidity in his life.

These thoughts shriek through the mind during the minute or so that it takes a panicked person to run out of air. When the first involuntary breath occurs most people are still conscious, which is unfortunate, because the only thing more unpleasant than running out of air is breathing in water. At that point the person goes from voluntary to involuntary apnea, and the drowning begins in earnest. A spasmodic breath drags water into the mouth and windpipe, and then one of two things happen. In about ten percent of people, water—anything—touching the vocal cords triggers an immediate contraction in the muscles around the larynx. In effect, the central nervous system judges something in the voice box to be more of a threat than low oxygen levels in the blood, and acts accordingly. This is called a laryngospasm. It's so powerful that it overcomes the breathing reflex and eventually suffocates the person. A person with laryngospasm drowns without any water in his lungs.

In the other ninety percent of people, water floods the lungs and ends any waning transfer of oxygen to the blood. The clock is running down now; half-conscious and enfeebled by oxygen depletion, the person is in no position to fight his way back up to the surface. The very process of drowning makes it harder and harder not to drown, an exponential disaster curve similar to that of a sinking boat. Occasionally someone makes it back from this dark world, though, and it's from these people that we know what drowning feels like. In 1892 a Scottish doctor named James Lowson was on a steamship bound for Colombo, Sri Lanka, when they ran into a typhoon and went down in the dead of night. Most of the 150 people on board sank with the ship, but Lowson managed to fight his way out of the hold and over the side. The ship sank out from under his feet, dragging him down, and the last thing he remembers is losing consciousness underwater. A few minutes later the buoyancy of his life vest shot him to the surface, though, and he washed up on an island and lived to write about his experiences in the *Edinburgh Medical Journal.* He attributed the clarity of his recollection to the "preternatural calm" of people facing death. It's as close as one is going to get to the last moments of the *Andrea Gail:*

All afternoon the hammering of the big seas on the doomed vessel went on, whilst night came only to add darkness to our other horrors. Shortly before ten o'clock three tremendous seas found their way down the stokehole, putting out the fires, and our situation was desperate. The end came shortly before midnight, when there was a heavy crash on the reef, and the vessel was lying at the bottom of the Straits of Formosa in under a minute.

With scarcely time to think I pulled down the life-belts and, throwing two to my companions, tied the third on myself and bolted for the companionway. There was no time to spare for studying humanity at this juncture, but I can never forget the apparent want of initiative in all I passed. All the passengers seemed paralyzed—even my companions, some of them able military men. The stewards of the ship, uttering cries of despair and last farewells, blocked the entrance to the deck, and it was only by sheer force I was able to squeeze past them. Getting out on deck, a perfect mountain of water seemed to come from overhead, as well as from below, and dashed me against the bridge companionway. The ship was going down rapidly, and I was pulled down with her, struggling to extricate myself.

I got clear under water and immediately struck out to reach the surface, only to go farther down. This exertion was a serious waste of breath, and after ten or fifteen seconds the effort of inspiration could no longer be restrained. It seemed as if I was in a vice which was gradually being screwed up tight until it felt as if the sternum and spinal column must break. Many years ago my old teacher used to describe how painless and easy a death by drowning was—"like falling about in a green field in early summer"— and this flashed across my brain at the time. The "gulping" efforts became less frequent, and the pressure seemed unbearable, but gradually the pain seemed to ease up. I appeared to be in a pleasant dream, although I had enough will power to think of friends at home and the sight of the Grampians, familiar to me as a boy, that was brought into my view. Before losing consciousness the chest pain had completely disappeared and the sensation was actually pleasant.

When consciousness returned, I found myself at the surface, and managed to get a dozen good inspirations. Land was about four hundred yards distant, and I used a bale of silk and then a long wooden plank to assist me to shore. On landing, and getting behind a sheltering rock, no effort was required to produce *copius emesis*. After the excitement, sound sleep set in, and this sleep lasted three hours, when a profuse diarrhea came on, evidently brought on by the sea water ingested. Until morning broke all my muscles were in a constant tremor which could not be controlled. (Several weeks later) I was sleeping in a comfortable bed and, late in the evening, a nightmare led to my having a severe struggle with the bedroom furniture, finally taking a "header" out of the bed and coming to grief on the floor.

Lowson guesses that laryngospasm prevented water from entering his lungs when he was unconscious. The crew of the *Andrea Gail* either have laryngospasms or completely inundated lungs. They are suspended, open-eyed and unconscious, in the flooded enclosures of the boat. The darkness is absolute and the boat may already be on her way to the bottom. At this point only a massive amount of oxygen could save these men. They have suffered, at most, a minute or two. Their bodies, having imposed increasingly drastic measures to keep functioning, have finally started to shut down. Water in the lungs washes away a substance called surfactant, which enables the alvioli to leech oxygen out of the air. The alvioli themselves, grape-like clusters of membrane on the lung wall, collapse because blood cannot get through the pulmonary artery. The artery has constricted in an effort to shunt blood to areas of the lungs where there is more oxygen. Unfortunately, those don't exist. The heart labors under critically low levels of oxygen and starts to beat erratically—"like a bag full of worms," as one doctor says. This is called ventricular fibrillation. The more irregularly the heart beats, the less blood it moves and the faster life-functions decline. Children—who have proportionally stronger hearts than adults—can maintain a heartbeat for up to five minutes without air. Adults die faster. The heart beats less and less effectively until, after several minutes, there's no movement at all. Only the brain is alive.

The central nervous system does not know what has happened to the body; all it knows is that not enough oxygen is getting to the brain. Orders are still being issued—*Breathe! Pump! Circulate!*—that the body cannot obey. If the person were defibrillated at that moment, he might possibly survive. He could be given cardiopulmonary resuscitation, put on a respirator, and coaxed back to life. Still, the body is doing everything it can to delay the inevitable. When cold water touches the face, an impulse travels along the trigeminal nerve to the central nervous system and lowers the metabolic rate. The pulse slows down and the blood pools where it's needed most, in the heart and skull. It's a sort of temporary hibernation that drastically reduces the body's need for oxygen. Nurses will splash ice water on the face of a person with a racing heart to trigger the same reaction.

The diving reflex, as this is called, is compounded by the general effect of cold temperature on tissue—it preserves it. All chemical reactions, and metabolic processes, become honey-slow, and the brain can get by on less than half the oxygen it normally requires. There are cases of people spending forty or fifty minutes under lake ice and surviving. The colder the water, the stronger the diving reflex, the slower the metabolic processes, and the longer the survival time. The crew of the *Andrea Gail* do not find themselves in particularly cold water, though; it may add five or ten minutes to their lives. And there is no one around to save them anyway. The electrical activity in their brain gets weaker and weaker until, after fifteen or twenty minutes, it ceases altogether.

The body could be likened to a crew that resorts to increasingly desperate measures to keep their vessel afloat. Eventually the last wire has shorted out, the last bit of decking has settled under the water. Tyne, Pierre, Sullivan, Moran, Murphy, and Shatford are dead.

5
The Art of the Particular: Creative Nonfiction Classified by Subject

U nder the wide umbrella of the term *creative nonfiction* I've placed three main genres of nonfiction writing that aspire to art: memoir, the personal essay, and literary journalism. These are classifications by *form*. Of course it's also possible to divide artful nonfiction in other ways. So in this section I'll classify some more very good examples of creative nonfiction, but this time by particular *content*.

Good writers have always made real art writing about nature, travel, science, culture, sports, gardening, love, biography, religion, food, history, animals, medicine, coming of age, sexuality, family, and many other subjects often grouped in genres, though not all writing about gardening, for example, is creative writing, or meant to be. Humor is certainly an art in itself, and often takes the form of a particular kind of essay, often brought to the level of art. But for the sake of economy, and because they are important and venerable, I'll stick to the first four subject categories I have named above in this paragraph, call them subgenres of creative nonfiction, and provide three examples of each. Why three? Simply to show how a personal essayist, a memoirist, and a literary journalist have handled each of these old categories now happily fitted under a new rubric: creative nonfiction.

Nature Writing

Nature writing deserves your extensive attention in its own right, and to a depth in no way possible here. In American letters, think immediately of Emerson and his acolyte Thoreau. In fact, Thoreau's *Walden* is the blueprint for the tone and scope and concerns of much of traditional American nature writing, and perhaps for the early tendency of nature writing toward maleness, now abating. Love and respect for nature is the first requirement. Preservation and conservation are often themes. Reflection is the mode, and spiritual awakening (sometimes to the point of ecstasy) is often the point. On the other end of the nature writing continuum, and more and more so, is scientific inquiry, problem solving, social criticism, and often pessimism. Nature writing puts authorial powers of description to the test: how to translate the glories, mystery, and meanness of nature for readers?

421

The simplest definition I can come up with is that nature writing is any engagement with nature in prose nonfiction, so long as the prose aspires to art. So a treatise on the wavelengths of gamma rays, while certainly writing about nature, is not necessarily nature writing. All of the excellences that tend other creative nonfiction toward art must apply here.

Twentieth-century concern for the environment and the popularity of movements to protect the earth from its hard use and sometimes abuse by humans may be responsible for the burgeoning interest in nature writing (and probably nature TV shows and movies, for that matter: nature as entertainment). Many of the finest of our essayists consider themselves nature writers. And though most try to avoid nostalgia or sentimentality, all nature writing is a kind of elegy: in an age of high technology, wilderness is no longer possible, and wildness must follow its only home.

Readers interested in further study of nature writing have many fine resources, top among them *The Norton Book of Nature Writing*, edited by Robert Finch and John Elder (both well-regarded nature writers themselves), and the two-volume biographical reference work *American Nature Writers*, edited by Mr. Elder and published by Scribner. *Sisters of the Earth*, edited by Lorraine Anderson, makes a good and necessary effort to include women in the discussion, where in the past they may have been excluded. For a scholarly take on the genre, try *Nature Writing and America: Essays upon a Cultural Type*, edited by Peter A. Fritzell and published by the Iowa State University Press.

Literary Travel

The tradition of travel writing is distinctly British, and nefariously colonial: with feelings of superiority, the wealthy traveler visits some outpost of the British Empire, little noticing in his search for the exotic that the pesky people of the countries he visits have deep lives and rich cultural institutions. American travel writing echoed this mode for many years, but lately on both sides of the Atlantic some very new takes on the old form are emerging. Oh, Englishman Redmond O'Hanlon still takes death-defying and arrogant (but wonderfully observed and often hilarious) trips into the Congo or the Amazon basin, but gentler trips abound, and a more anthropological, respectful tone. Writers seem to be becoming more aware of their own place in their observations, and often take the opportunity of travel to explore the greater issues of humanity.

In travel, awareness is heightened, routines left behind: new insights are possible, including insights into the self and into others. Most of the best travel writing involves one person moving alone in unfamiliar territory, meeting people serially. The stranger provides all the character the writer needs, the strange surroundings all the setting. The chronology of the trip can provide an automatic structure, but it needn't. Food plays a strong role in travel writing, as do all things daily. And it's that microscopic view pressed up against the biggest pictures of all—geography, nationality, ethnicity—that makes the best travel writing literary.

Readers interested in the genre will have no trouble finding critical studies and collections to peruse. A very good start might be the travel writing collected in *In Trouble Again*, which is the Winter 1986 (number 20) issue of *Granta*, the British literary quarterly. A good writer to study might be Paul Theroux, who has made a distinguished (if often controversial) career of literary travel.

The Science Essay

Scientists have long tried to explain their arcane ponderings to the rest of us—and a tradition of essays for the nonspecialist has developed. Most, of course, are meant to transmit plain scientific information, but some are meant to transmit more, to move beyond a mere teaching function to transmit the love of science, for example, or the emotional states of doctors and other scientists as they go about their work, or the tumbling doubt of people who know that even in the hard sciences truth is elusive, or the transcendent beauty and horror that are the constant discovery of scientists, whose job is to look for other things: facts and figures. Science, or a particular moment in science, or a subject or object as viewed by science, becomes metaphorical, and yet another tool for the examination of the human condition.

Readers interested in scientists as writers and writing about science subjects will have a good start with editor Lee Gutkind's special science issues of his quarterly literary magazine, *Creative Nonfiction*. Also of interest will be *The New Science Journalists*, edited by Ted Antin and Rick McCourt, and published by Ballantine.

Creative Cultural Criticism

In calling this section "Creative Cultural Criticism"—by willfully throwing in the word *creative*—I risk being lit on fire and thrown off a cliff by my colleagues who are critics, and whose work is certainly creative, even if it doesn't particularly aspire to art. Nothing is more important to art than criticism, but nothing is more annoying to artists, or then again as gratifying, depending on how clearly the critic sees: the critic affects the artist either way. But listen: nothing is less important to the general culture than cultural criticism, since we all grind on regardless. The art critic may take herself seriously indeed, but the cultural critic had best not.

Creative cultural criticism differs from more traditional criticism in that it puts the critic in the midst of her subject. The critic's fallible life and tastes are as open to dissection as the subject she picks. And the subjects aren't standard. Writers in this broad category have written about the best-seller lists rather than books, the face in art as opposed to artwork, the meanings of illness itself rather than artwork about illness.

And because of the diffuse nature of the beast, the reader interested in reading more creative cultural criticism will have to do her own legwork: *The New Yorker, Harper's, The Atlantic Monthly*, these are perhaps the most reliable sources for such writing (regular, slightly skeptical reading in all three periodicals is a must for any student of creative nonfiction in any case). *The New York Review of Books* is often home to creative critics as well. Good literary magazines like *The Georgia Review, The Threepenny Review*, and *The Sewanee Review* all offer examples of the form in every issue. And writers of creative cultural criticism tend to mention other writers extensively—once one gets going, the path won't end.

NATURE WRITING

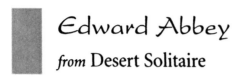

Edward Abbey

from Desert Solitaire

HAVASU

ONE SUMMER I STARTED OFF TO VISIT FOR THE FIRST TIME THE CITY OF LOS ANGELES. I WAS riding with some friends from the University of New Mexico. On the way we stopped off briefly to roll an old tire into the Grand Canyon. While watching the tire bounce over tall pine trees, tear hell out of a mule train and disappear with a final grand leap into the inner gorge, I overheard the park ranger standing nearby say a few words about a place called Havasu, or Havasupai. A branch, it seemed, of the Grand Canyon.

What I heard made me think that I should see Havasu immediately, before something went wrong somewhere. My friends said they would wait. So I went down into Havasu— fourteen miles by trail—and looked things over. When I returned five weeks later I discovered that the others had gone on to Los Angeles without me.

That was fifteen years ago. And still I have not seen the fabulous city on the Pacific shore. Perhaps I never will. There's something in the prospect southwest from Barstow which makes one hesitate. Although recently, driving my own truck, I did succeed in penetrating as close as San Bernardino. But was hurled back by what appeared to be clouds of mustard gas rolling in from the west on a very broad front. Thus failed again. It may be however that Los Angeles will come to me. Will come to all of us, as it must (they say) to all men.

But Havasu. Once down in there it's hard to get out. The trail led across a stream wide, blue and deep, like the pure upper reaches of the River Jordan. Without a bridge. Dripping wet and making muddy tracks I entered the village of the Havasupai Indians where unshod ponies ambled down the only street and the children laughed, not maliciously, at the sight of the wet white man. I stayed the first night in the lodge the people keep for tourists, a rambling old bungalow with high ceilings, a screened verandah and large comfortable rooms. When the sun went down the village went dark except for kerosene lamps here and there, a few open fires, and a number of lightning bugs or fireflies which drifted aimlessly up and down Main Street, looking for trouble.

The next morning I bought a slab of bacon and six cans of beans at the village post office, rented a large comfortable horse and proceeded farther down the canyon past miniature cornfields, green pastures, swimming pools and waterfalls to the ruins of an old mining camp five miles below the village. There I lived, mostly alone except for the ghosts, for the next thirty-five days.

There was nothing wrong with the Indians. The Supai are a charming cheerful completely relaxed and easygoing bunch, all one hundred or so of them. But I had no desire to live *among* them unless clearly invited to do so, and I wasn't. Even if invited I might not have accepted. I'm not sure that I care for the idea of strangers examining my daily habits and folkways, studying my language, inspecting my costume, questioning me about my religion, classifying my artifacts, investigating my sexual rites and evaluating my chances for cultural survival.

So I lived alone.

The first thing I did was take off my pants. Naturally. Next I unloaded the horse, smacked her on the rump and sent her back to the village. I carried my food and gear into the best-preserved of the old cabins and spread my bedroll on a rusty steel cot. After that came a swim in the pool beneath a great waterfall nearby, 120 feet high, which rolled in mist and thunder over caverns and canopies of solidified travertine.

In the evening of that first day below the falls I lay down to sleep in the cabin. A dark night. The door of the cabin, unlatched, creaked slowly open, although there was no perceptible movement of the air. One firefly flickered in and circled my bacon, suspended from the roofbeam on a length of baling wire. Slowly, without visible physical aid, the door groaned shut. And opened again. A bat came through one window and went out another, followed by a second firefly (the first scooped up by the bat) and a host of mosquitoes, which did not leave. I had no netting, of course, and the air was much too humid and hot for sleeping inside a bag.

I got up and wandered around outside for a while, slapping at mosquitoes, and thinking. From the distance came the softened roar of the waterfall, that "white noise" as soothing as hypnosis. I rolled up my sleeping bag and in the filtered light of the stars followed the trail that wound through thickets of cactus and up around ledges to the terrace above the mining camp. The mosquitoes stayed close but in lessening numbers, it seemed, as I climbed over humps of travertine toward the head of the waterfall. Near the brink of it, six feet from the drop-off and the plunge, I found a sandy cove just big enough for my bed. The racing creek as it soared free over the edge created a continuous turbulence in the air sufficient to keep away all flying insects. I slept well that night and the next day carried the cot to the place and made it my permanent bedroom for the rest of July and all of August.

What did I do during those five weeks in Eden? Nothing. I did nothing. Or nearly nothing. I caught a few rainbow trout, which grew big if not numerous in Havasu Creek. About once a week I put on my pants and walked up to the Indian village to buy bacon, canned beans and Argentine beef in the little store. That was all the Indians had in stock. To vary my diet I ordered more exotic foods by telephone from the supermarket in Grand Canyon Village and these were shipped to me by U.S. Mail, delivered twice a week on muleback down the fourteen-mile trail from Topocoba Hilltop. A little later in the season I was able to buy sweet corn, figs and peaches from the Supai. At one time for a period of three days my bowels seemed in danger of falling out, but I recovered. The Indians never came down to my part of the canyon except when guiding occasional tourists to the falls or hunting a stray horse. In late August came the Great Havasupai Sacred Peach Festival and Four-Day Marathon Friendship Dance, to which I was invited and in which I did participate. There I met Reed Watahomagie, a good man, and Chief Sinyala and a fellow named Spoonhead who took me for five dollars in a horse race. Somebody fed my pick a half-bushel of green figs just before the race. I heard later.

The Friendship Dance, which continued day and night to the rhythm of drums made of old inner tube stretched over #10 tomato cans while ancient medicine men chanted in the background, was perhaps marred but definitely not interrupted when a drunken free-for-all exploded between Spoonhead and friends and a group of visiting Hualapai Indians down from the rim. But this, I was told, happened every year. It was a traditional part of the ceremony, sanctified by custom. As Spoonhead told me afterwards, grinning around broken teeth, it's not every day you get a chance to wallop a Hualapai. Or skin a paleface, I reminded him. (Yes, the Supai are an excellent tribe, healthy, joyous and clever. Not only clever but shrewd. Not only shrewd but wise: e.g., the Bureau of Indian Affairs and the Bureau of Public Roads, like most government agencies always meddling, always fretting and itching and sweating for something to do, last year made a joint offer to blast a million-dollar road down into Havasu Canyon at no cost whatsoever to the tribe, thus opening their homeland to the riches of motorized tourism. The people of Supai or at least a majority of them voted to reject the proposal.) And the peach wine flowed freely, like the water of the river of life. When the ball was over I went home to my bunk on the verge of the waterfall and rested for two days.

On my feet again, I explored the abandoned silver mines in the canyon walls, found a few sticks of dynamite but no caps or fuses. Disappointing; but there was nothing in that area anyway that required blowing up. I climbed through the caves that led down to the foot of Mooney Falls, 200 feet high. What did I do? There was nothing that had to be done. I listened to the voices, the many voices, vague, distant but astonishingly human, of Havasu Creek. I heard the doors creak open, the doors creak shut, of the old forgotten cabins where no one with tangible substance or the property of reflecting light ever entered, ever returned. I went native and dreamed away days on the shore of the pool under the waterfall, wandered naked as Adam under the cottonwoods, inspecting my cactus gardens. The days became wild, strange, ambiguous—a sinister element pervaded the flow of time. I lived narcotic hours in which like the Taoist Chuang-tse I worried about butterflies and who was dreaming what. There was a serpent, a red racer, living in the rocks of the spring where I filled my canteens; he was always there, slipping among the stones or pausing to mesmerize me with his suggestive tongue and cloudy haunted primeval eyes. Damn his eyes. We got to know each other rather too well I think. I agonized over the girls I had known and over those I hoped were yet to come. I slipped by degrees into lunacy, me and the moon, and lost to a certain extent the power to distinguish between what was and what was not myself: looking at my hand I would see a leaf trembling on a branch. A *green* leaf. I thought of Debussy, of Keats and Blake and Andrew Marvell. I remembered Tom o'Bedlam. And all those lost and never remembered. Who would return? To be lost again? I went for walks. I went for walks. I went for walks and on one of these, the last I took in Havasu, regained everything that seemed to be ebbing away.

⌘   ⌘   ⌘

Most of my wandering in the desert I've done alone. Not so much from choice as from necessity—I generally prefer to go into places where no one else wants to go. I find that in contemplating the natural world my pleasure is greater if there are not too many others contemplating it with me, at the same time. However, there are special hazards in traveling alone. Your chances of dying, in case of sickness or accident, are much improved, simply because there is no one around to go for help.

Exploring a side canyon off Havasu Canyon one day, I was unable to resist the temptation to climb up out of it onto what corresponds in that region to the Tonto Bench. Late in the afternoon I realized that I would not have enough time to get back to my camp before dark, unless I could find a much shorter route than the one by which I had come. I looked for a shortcut.

Nearby was another little side canyon which appeared to lead down into Havasu Canyon. It was a steep, shadowy, extremely narrow defile with the usual meandering course and overhanging walls; from where I stood, near its head, I could not tell if the route was feasible all the way down to the floor of the main canyon. I had no rope with me—only my walking stick. But I was hungry and thirsty, as always. I started down.

For a while everything went well. The floor of the little canyon began as a bed of dry sand, scattered with rocks. Farther down a few boulders were wedged between the walls; I climbed over and under them. Then the canyon took on the slickrock character—smooth, sheer, slippery sandstone carved by erosion into a series of scoops and potholes which got bigger as I descended. In some of these basins there was a little water left over from the last flood, warm and fetid water under an oily-looking scum, condensed by prolonged evaporation to a sort of broth, rich in dead and dying organisms. My canteen was empty and I was very thirsty but I felt that I could wait.

I came to a lip on the canyon floor which overhung by twelve feet the largest so far of these stagnant pools. On each side rose the canyon walls, roughly perpendicular. There was no way to continue except by dropping into the pool. I hesitated. Beyond this point there could hardly be any returning, yet the main canyon was still not visible below. Obviously the only sensible thing to do was to turn back. I edged over the lip of stone and dropped feet first into the water.

Deeper than I expected. The warm, thick fluid came up and closed over my head as my feet touched the muck at the bottom. I had to swim to the farther side. And here I found myself on the verge of another drop-off, with one more huge bowl of green soup below.

This drop-off was about the same height as the one before, but not overhanging. It resembled a children's playground slide, concave and S-curved, only steeper, wider, with a vertical pitch in the middle. It did not lead directly into the water but ended in a series of step-like ledges above the pool. Beyond the pool lay another edge, another drop-off into an unknown depth. Again I paused, and for a much longer time. But I no longer had the option of turning around and going back. I eased myself into the chute and let go of everything—except my faithful stick.

I hit rock bottom hard, but without any physical injury. I swam the stinking pond dog-paddle style, pushing the heavy scum away from my face, and crawled out on the far side to see what my fate was going to be.

Fatal. Death by starvation, slow and tedious. For I was looking straight down an overhanging cliff to a rubble pile of broken rocks eighty feet below.

⚬ ⚬ ⚬

After the first wave of utter panic had passed I began to try to think. First of all I was not going to die immediately, unless another flash flood came down the gorge; there was the pond of stagnant water on hand to save me from thirst and a man can live, they say, for thirty days or more without food. My sun-bleached bones, dramatically sprawled at the bottom of the chasm, would provide the diversion of the picturesque for future wanderers—if any man ever came this way again.

My second thought was to scream for help, although I knew very well there could be no other human being within miles. I even tried it but the sound of that anxious shout, cut short in the dead air within the canyon walls, was so inhuman, so detached as it seemed from myself, that it terrified me and I didn't attempt it again.

I thought of tearing my clothes into strips and plaiting a rope. But what was I wearing?—boots, socks, a pair of old and ragged blue jeans, a flimsy T-shirt, an ancient and rotten sombrero of straw. Not a chance of weaving such a wardrobe into a rope eighty feet long, or even twenty feet long.

How about a signal fire? There was nothing to burn but my clothes; not a tree, not a shrub, not even a weed grew in this stony cul-de-sac. Even if I burned my clothing the chances of the smoke being seen by some Hualapai Indian high on the south rim were very small; and if he did see the smoke, what then? He'd shrug his shoulders, sigh, and take another pull from his Tokay bottle. Furthermore, without clothes, the sun would soon bake me to death.

There was only one thing I could do. I had a tiny notebook in my hip pocket and a stub of pencil. When these dried out I could at least record my final thoughts. I would have plenty of time to write not only my epitaph but my own elegy.

But not yet.

There were a few loose stones scattered about the edge of the pool. Taking the biggest first, I swam with it back to the foot of the slickrock chute and placed it there. One by one I brought the others and made a shaky little pile about two feet high leaning against the chute. Hopeless, of course, but there was nothing else to do. I stood on the top of the pile and stretched upward, straining my arms to their utmost limit and groped with fingers and fingernails for a hold on something firm. There was nothing. I crept back down. I began to cry. It was easy. All alone, I didn't have to be brave.

Through the tears I noticed my old walking stick lying nearby. I took it and stood it on the most solid stone in the pile, behind the two topmost stones. I took off my boots, tied them together and hung them around my neck, on my back. I got up on the little pile again and lifted one leg and set my big toe on the top of the stick. This could never work. Slowly and painfully, leaning as much of my weight as I could against the sandstone slide, I applied more and more pressure to the stick, pushing my body upward until I was again stretched out full length above it. Again I felt about for a fingerhold. There was none. The chute was smooth as polished marble.

No, not quite that smooth. This was sandstone, soft and porous, not marble, and between it and my wet body and wet clothing a certain friction was created. In addition, the stick had enabled me to reach a higher section of the S-curved chute, where the angle was more favorable. I discovered that I could move upward, inch by inch, through adhesion and with the help of the leveling tendency of the curve. I gave an extra little push with my big toe—the stones collapsed below, the stick clattered down—and crawled rather like a snail or slug, oozing slime, up over the rounded summit of the slide.

The next obstacle, the overhanging spout twelve feet above a deep plunge pool, looked impossible. It *was* impossible, but with the blind faith of despair I slogged into the water and swam underneath the drop-off and floundered around for a while, scrabbling at the slippery rock until my nerves and tiring muscles convinced my numbed brain that *this was not the way.* I swam back to solid ground and lay down to rest and die in comfort.

Far above I could see the sky, an irregular strip of blue between the dark, hard-edged canyon walls that seemed to lean toward each other as they towered above me. Across that narrow opening a small white cloud was passing, so lovely and precious and delicate and forever inaccessible that it broke the heart and made me weep like a woman, like a child. In all my life I had never seen anything so beautiful.

The walls that rose on either side of the drop-off were literally perpendicular. Eroded by weathering, however, and not by the corrasion of rushing floodwater, they had a rough surface, chipped, broken, cracked. Where the walls joined the face of the overhang they formed almost a square corner, with a number of minute crevices and inch-wide shelves on either side. It might, after all, be possible. What did I have to lose?

When I had regained some measure of nerve and steadiness I got up off my back and tried the wall beside the pond, clinging to the rock with bare toes and fingertips and inching my way crabwise toward the corner. The watersoaked, heavy boots dangling from my neck, swinging back and forth with my every movement, threw me off balance and I fell into the pool. I swam out to the bank, unslung the boots and threw them up over the drop-off, out of sight. They'd be there if I ever needed them again. Once more I attached myself to the wall, tenderly, sensitively, like a limpet, and very slowly, very cautiously, worked my way into the corner. Here I was able to climb upward, a few centimeters at a time, by bracing myself against the opposite sides and finding sufficient niches for fingers and toes. As I neared the top and the overhang became noticeable I prepared for a slip, planning to push myself away from the rock so as to fall into the center of the pool where the water was deepest. But it wasn't necessary. Somehow, with a skill and tenacity I could never have found in myself under ordinary circumstances, I managed to creep straight up that gloomy cliff and over the brink of the drop-off and into the flower of safety. My boots were floating under the surface of the little puddle above. As I poured the stinking water out of them and pulled them on and laced them up I discovered myself bawling again for the third time in three hours, the hot delicious tears of victory. And up above the clouds replied—thunder.

I emerged from that treacherous little canyon at sundown, with an enormous fire in the western sky and lightning overhead. Through sweet twilight and the sudden dazzling flare of lightning I hiked back along the Tonto Bench, bellowing the *Ode to Joy*. Long before I reached the place where I could descend safely to the main canyon and my camp, however, darkness set in, the clouds opened their bays and the rain poured down. I took shelter under a ledge in a shallow cave about three feet high—hardly room to sit up in. Others had been here before: the dusty floor of the little hole was littered with the droppings of birds, rats, jackrabbits and coyotes. There were also a few long gray pieces of scat with a curious twist at one tip—cougar? I didn't care. I had some matches with me, sealed in paraffin (the prudent explorer); I scraped together the handiest twigs and animal droppings and built a little fire and waited for the rain to stop.

It didn't stop. The rain came down for hours in alternate waves of storm and drizzle and I very soon had burnt up all the fuel within reach. No matter. I stretched out in the coyote den, pillowed my head on my arm and suffered through the long long night, wet, cold, aching, hungry, wretched, dreaming claustrophobic nightmares. It was one of the happiest nights of my life.

Sue Hubbell

from A Country Year

SPRING

THE RIVER TO THE NORTH OF MY PLACE IS CLAIMED BY THE U.S. PARK SERVICE, AND THE creek to the south is under the protection of the Missouri State Conservation Department, so I am surrounded by government land. The deed to the property says my farm is a hundred and five acres, but it is probably something more like ninety. The land hasn't been surveyed since the mid-1800s and it is hard to know where the boundaries are; a park ranger told me he suspected that the nineteenth-century surveyor had run his lines from a tavern, because the corners seem to have been established by someone in his cups.

The place is so beautiful that it nearly brought tears to my eyes the first time I saw it twelve years ago; I feel the same way today, so I have never much cared about the number of acres, or where the boundary lines run or who, exactly, owns what. But the things that make it so beautiful and desirable to me have also convinced others that this is prime land, too, and belongs to them as well. At the moment, for instance, I am feeling a bit of an outsider, having discovered that I live in the middle of an indigo bunting ghetto. As ghettos go, it is a cheerful one in which to live, but it has forced me to think about property rights.

Indigo buntings are small but emphatic birds. They believe that they own the place, and it is hard to ignore their claim. The male birds—brilliant, shimmering blue—perch on the garden posts or on top of the cedar trees that have taken over the pasture. From there they survey their holdings and belt out their songs, complicated tangles of couplets that waken me first thing in the morning; they keep it up all day, even at noon, after the other birds have quieted. The indigo buntings have several important facts to tell us, especially about who's in charge around here. The dull brown, sparrowlike females and juveniles are more interested in eating; they stay nearer the ground and search the low-growing shrubs and grasses for seeds and an occasional caterpillar, but even they know what's what. One day, walking back along the edge of the field, I came upon a young indigo bunting preoccupied with song practice. He had not yet dared take as visible a perch as his father would have chosen, but there he was, clinging to a bare twig and softly running through his couplets, getting them all wrong and then going back over them so quietly that had I not been within a few feet of him I would not have heard.

Another time I discovered that the back door of the honey house had blown open and the room was filled with a variety of winged creatures. Most were insects, but among them I found a half-grown indigo bunting who had blundered in and was trying to find his way out, beating his small wings against the screened window. Holding him carefully, I stroked the back of his neck to try to soothe him, but discovered that his heart was not beating in terror. Perhaps he was so young that he had not learned fear, but I prefer to think that like the rest of his breed he was simply too pert and too sure of his rights to be afraid. He eyed me crossly and tweaked my giant thumb with his beak to tell me that I was to let him go right this minute. I did so, of course, and watched him fly off to the tall grasses behind the honey house, where I knew that one family of indigo buntings had been nesting.

Well, they think they own the place, and their assurance is only countered by a scrap of paper in my files. But there are other contenders, and perhaps I ought to try to take a census and judge claims before I grant them title. There are other birds who call this place theirs—buzzards, who work the updrafts over the river and creek, goldfinches, wild turkey, phoebes and whippoorwills. But it is a pair of cardinals who have ended up with the prize piece of real estate—the spot with the bird feeder. I have tapes of birdsongs, and when I play them I try to skip the one of the cardinal, because the current resident goes into a frenzy of territorial song when he hears his rival. His otherwise lovely day is ruined.

And what about the coyote? For a while she was confident that this was her farm, especially the chicken part of it. She was so sure of herself that once she sauntered by in daylight and picked up the tough old rooster to take back to her pups. However, the dogs grew wise to her, and the next few times she returned to exercise her rights they chased her off, explaining that this farm belonged to them and that the chicken flock was their responsibility.

When I start thinking about it that way—that those who inhabit the land and use it have a real claim to it in a nonlegal sort of way—the whole question gets complicated.

A long time ago, before I came to live in the Ozarks, I spent a springtime working on a plot of university research land. I was young and in love, and most tasks seemed happy ones, but the project would have captured my fancy anyway. There were three contrasting habitats being studied: upland forest, bottomland and sandy waste. My job was to dig up a cube of earth from each place every week, sift it, count and rough-classify the inhabitants visible to the naked eye, and then plot the population growth. The resulting curve, a joyous, vibrant freshening of life, matched the weather and my own pulse beat.

That particular love has quieted, and I have not excavated cubes of earth on this place, but I know what is going on down there: Millions of little bodies are fiercely metabolizing and using the land. I dare not even think what numbers I would come up with if I added a pocket lens or microscope to my census-taking tools. But there are other residents I *can* count who do have arguable title here. There are twenty hives of bees back by the woodlot in my home beeyard, each hive containing some 60,000 bees. That makes 1,200,000 bee souls flitting about making claim to all the flowers within two miles.

On the other hand, there are the copperheads, who make walking the fields a boot affair, and all their snakish kin. How am I to count them and judge their claims? There are the turtles who eat the strawberries in the garden, the peepers who own the pond. What about raccoon and skunk and deer rights? What about the bobcat who denned in the cliff by the river and considers my place to be the merest sliver of her own?

It begins to make me dizzy even trying to think of taking a census of everybody who lives here; and all of them seem to have certain claims to the place that are every bit as good as and perhaps better than mine.

Up the road there is a human squabble going on over some land less happily situated. Rather than lying between two environmentally benign government stake-outs, that land and all that surrounds it is in private hands. One owner wants to bulldoze and develop, and so the boundary question is becoming a sticky one. There is talk about having an expensive survey made to establish who owns what. As a spinoff, I suppose that corners will be set and lines run, and then I may know whether this farm is a hundred and five acres or ninety or some other definity.

The indigo buntings probably won't care.

꙰ I MET PAUL, THE BOY WHO WAS TO BECOME MY HUSBAND, WHEN HE WAS SIXTEEN AND I was fifteen. We were married some years later, and the legal arrangement that is called marriage worked well enough while we were children and while we had a child. But we grew older, and the son went off to school, and marriage did not serve as a structure for our lives as well as it once had. Still, he was the man in my life for all those years. There was no other. So when the legal arrangement was ended, I had a difficult time sifting through the emotional debris that was left after the framework of an intimate, thirty-year association had broken.

I went through all the usual things: I couldn't sleep or eat, talked feverishly to friends, plunged recklessly into a destructive affair with a man who had more problems than I did but who was convenient, made a series of stupid decisions about my honey business and pretty generally botched up my life for several years running. And for a long, long time, my mind didn't work. I could not listen to the news on the radio with understanding. My attention came unglued when I tried to read anything but the lightest froth. My brain spun in endless, painful loops, and I could neither concentrate nor think with any semblance of order. I had always rather enjoyed having a mind, and I missed mine extravagantly. I was out to lunch for three years.

I mused about structure, framework, schemata, system, classification and order. I discovered a classification Jorge Luis Borges devised, claiming that

A certain Chinese encyclopedia divides animals into:
- a. Belonging to the Emperor
- b. Embalmed
- c. Tame
- d. Sucking pigs
- e. Sirens
- f. Fabulous
- g. Stray dogs
- h. Included in the present classification
- i. Frenzied
- j. Innumerable
- k. Drawn with a very fine camel-hair brush
- l. Et cetera
- m. Having just broken the water pitcher
- n. That from a long way off look like flies.

Friends and I laughed over the list, and we decided that the fact that we did so tells more about us and our European, Western way of thinking than it does about a supposed Oriental world view. We believe we have a more proper concept of how the natural world should be classified, and when Borges rumples that concept it amuses us. That I could join in the laughter made me realize I must have retained some sense of that order, no matter how disorderly my mind seemed to have become.

My father was a botanist. When I was a child he reserved Saturday afternoons for me, and we spent many of them walking in woods and rough places. He would name the plants we came upon by their Latin binomials and tell me how they grew. The names were too hard for me, but I did understand that plants had names that described their relationships one to another and found this elegant and interesting even when I was six years old.

So after reading the Borges list, I turned to Linnaeus. Whatever faults the man may have had as a scientist, he gave us a beautiful tool for thinking about diversity in the world. The first word in his scheme of Latin binomials tells the genus, grouping diverse plants which nevertheless share a commonality; the second word names the species, plants alike enough to regularly interbreed and produce offspring like themselves. It is a framework for understanding, a way to show how pieces of the world fit together.

I have no Latin, but as I began to botanize, to learn to call the plants around me up here on my hill by their Latin names, I was diverted from my lack of wits by the wit of the system.

Commelina virginica, the common dayflower, is a rangy weed bearing blue flowers with unequal sepals, two of them showy and rounded, the third hardly noticeable. After I identified it as that particular *Commelina*, named from a sample taken in Virginia, I read in one of my handbooks, written before it was considered necessary to be dull to be taken seriously:

Delightful Linnaeus, who dearly loved his little joke, himself confesses to have named the day-flowers after three brothers Commelyn, Dutch botanists, because two of them—commemorated in the showy blue petals of the blossom—published their works; the third, lacking application and ambition, amounted to nothing, like the third inconspicuous whitish third petal.

There is a tree growing in the woodland with shiny, oval leaves that turn brilliant red early in the fall, sometimes even at summer's end. It has small clusters of white flowers in June that bees like, and later blue fruits that are eaten by bluebirds and robins. It is one of the tupelos, and people in this part of the country call it black-gum or sour-gum. When I was growing up in Michigan I knew it as pepperidge. Its botanic name is *Nyssa sylvatica*. *Nyssa* groups the tupelos, and is derived from the Nyseides—the Greek nymphs of Mount Nysa who cared for the infant Dionysus. *Sylvatica* means "of the woodlands." *Nyssa sylvatica*, a wild, untamed name. The trees, which are often hollow when old, served as beehives for the first American settlers, who cut sections of them, capped them and dumped in the swarms that they found. To this day some people still call beehives "gums," unknowingly acknowledging the common name of the tree. The hollow logs were also used for making pipes that carried salt water to the salt works in Syracuse in colonial days. The ends of the wooden pipes could be fitted together without using iron bands, which would rust.

This gives me a lot to think about when I come across *Nyssa sylvatica* in the woods.

I botanized obsessively during that difficult time. Every day I learned new plants by their Latin names. I wandered about the woods that winter, good for little else, examining the bark of leafless trees. As wildflowers began to bloom in the spring, I carried my guidebooks with me, and filled a fat notebook as I identified the plants, their habitats, habits and dates of blooming. I had to write them down, for my brain, unaccustomed to exercise, was now on overload.

One spring afternoon, I was walking back down my lane after getting the mail. I had two fine new flowers to look up when I got back to the cabin. Warblers were migrating, and I had been watching them with binoculars; I had identified one I had never before seen. The sun was slanting through new leaves, and the air was fragrant with wild cherry (*Prunus serotina: Prunus*—plum, *serotina*—late blooming) blossoms, which my bees were working eagerly. I stopped to watch them, standing in the sunbeam. The world appeared to have been running along quite nicely without my even noticing it. Quietly, gratefully, I discovered that a part of me that had been off somewhere nursing grief and pain had returned. I had come back from lunch.

One back, I set about doing all the things that one does when one returns from lunch. I cleared the desk and tended to the messages that others had left. I had been gone for a long time, so there was quite a pile to clear away before I could settle down to the work of the afternoon of my life, the work of building a new kind of order, a structure on which a fifty-year-old woman can live her life alone, at peace with herself and the world around her.

⟲ ONE SPRING EVENING A COUPLE OF YEARS AGO, I WAS SITTING IN THE BROWN leather chair in the living room reading the newspaper and minding my own business when I became aware that I was no longer alone.

Looking up, I discovered that the three big windows that run from floor to ceiling were covered with frogs.

There were hundreds of them, inch-long frogs with delicate webbed feet whose finger-like toes ended in round pads that enabled them to cling to the smooth surface of the glass. From their toe structure, size and light-colored bellies, I supposed them to be spring peepers, *Hyla crucifer,* and went outside for a closer look. I had to be careful where I put my feet, for the grass in front of the windows was thick with frogs, waiting in patient ranks to move up to the lighted surface of the glass. Sure enough, each pinkish-brownish frog had a back criss-crossed with the dark markings that give the species its scientific name. I had not known before that they were attracted to light.

I let my newspaper go and spent the evening watching them. They did not move much beyond the top of the windows, but clung to the glass or the moldings, seemingly unable to decide what to do next. The following morning they were gone, and I have never seen them at the windows since. It struck me as curious behavior.

These window climbers were silent; we usually are only aware of spring peepers at winter's end—I first hear their shrill bell-like mating calls in February from the pond up in the field. The males produce the calls by closing their mouths and nasal openings and forcing air from their lungs over the vocal cords into their mouths, and then back over the vocal cords into the lungs again. This sound attracts the females to the pond, and when they enter the water the males embrace them, positioning their vents directly above those of the females. The females then lay their eggs, which the males fertilize with their milt.

It is a clubby thing, this frog mating, and the frogs are so many and their calls so shrill and intense that I like to walk up to the pond in the evenings and listen to the chorus, which, to a human, is both exhilarating and oddly disturbing at close range. One evening I walked there with a friend, and we sat by the edge of the pond for a long time. Conversation was inappropriate, but even if it had not it would have been impossible. The bell-like chorus completely surrounded us, filled us. It seemed to reverberate with the shrill insistence of hysteria, driving focused thought from our heads, forcing us not only to hear sound but to feel it.

Comparing notes as we walked back to my cabin, we were startled to discover that we had both wondered, independently, whether that was what it was like to go mad.

A slightly larger cousin of the spring peeper that belongs to the same genus, the gray tree frog, commonly lives in my beehives during the summer months. These frogs cling under the protective overhang of the hive cover, and as I pry up the lid, they hop calmly to the white inner cover and sit there placidly eying me.

They are a pleasing soft grayish-green, marked with darker moss-colored patches, and look like a bit of lichen-covered bark when they are on a tree. Having evolved this wonderfully successful protective coloration, the safest behavior for a gray tree frog in a tight spot is to stay still and pretend to be a piece of bark. Sitting on the white inner cover of the beehive, the frog's protective coloration serves him not at all, but of course he doesn't know that, and not having learned any value in conspicuously hopping away, he continues to sit there looking at me with what appears to be smug self-satisfaction and righteous spunk.

Last evening I was reading in bed and felt rather than heard a soft plop on the bed next to me. Peering over the top of my glasses, I saw a plump, proud gray tree frog inspecting me. We studied each other for quite a time, the gray tree frog seemingly at ease, until I picked him up, carried him out the back door and put him on the hickory tree there. But even in my cupped hands he moved very little, and after I put him on the tree he sat quietly, blending in beautifully with the bark. A serene frog.

The sills in my bedroom are rotten, so I supposed that he had found a hole to come through and wondered if he'd had friends. I looked under the bed and discovered three more gray tree frogs, possibly each one a frog prince. Nevertheless, I transferred them to the hickory.

There was something in the back of my mind from childhood Sunday-school classes about a plague of frogs, so I took down my Bible and settled back in bed to search for it. I found the story in Exodus. It was one of those plagues that God sent to convince the Pharaoh to let the Jews leave Egypt.

> And the Lord spake unto Moses, Go unto Pharaoh, and say unto him, Thus saith the Lord, Let my people go, that they may serve me.
> And if thou refuse to let them go, behold, I will smite all thy borders with frogs:
> And the river shall bring forth frogs abundantly, which shall go up and come into thine house, and into thy bedchamber, and upon thy bed . . .

This was exciting stuff; my evening had taken on a positively biblical quality. I was having a plague of frogs, and had obviously had another the evening that the spring peepers had crawled up the living-room windows. Actually, I enjoyed both plagues, but Pharaoh didn't. The writer of Exodus tells us that Pharaoh was so distressed by frogs in his bed that he called Moses and said,

> Intreat the Lord, that he may take away the frogs from me, and from my people; and I will let the people go, that they may do sacrifice unto the Lord.

A fussy man, that Pharaoh, and one easily unnerved.

I once knew a pickerel frog, *Rana palustris*, frog of the marshes, who might have changed Pharaoh's mind. The pickerel frog was an appealing creature who lived in my barn one whole summer. He was handsome, grayish with dark, square blotches highlighted with yellow on his legs. I found him in the barn one morning trying to escape the attentions of the cat and the dogs. At some point he had lost the foot from his right front leg, and although the stump was well healed, his hop was awkward and lopsided. I decided that he would be better off taking his chances with wild things, so I carried him out to the pond and left him under the protective bramble thicket that grows there. But the next day he was back in the barn, having hopped the length of a football field to get there. So I let him stay, giving him a dish of water and a few dead flies.

All summer long I kept his water fresh, killed flies for him and kept an eye out for his safety. Pickerel frogs sometimes live in caves, and I wondered if the dim light of the barn and the cool concrete floor made him think he had discovered a cave where the service was particularly good. That part of the barn serves as a passageway to my honey house, and I grew accustomed to seeing him as I went in and out of it. I came to regard him as a tutelary sprite, the guardian of the honey house, the Penate Melissus.

Then one day the health inspector came for his annual tour. Like Pharaoh, the health inspector is a fussy man. Once he gave me a hard time because there were a few stray honeybees in the honey house. Bees, he explained patiently, were insects, and regulations forbade insects in a food-processing plant. I pointed out, perhaps not so patiently, that these insects had made the food, and that until I took it from them, they were in continuous, complete and intimate contact with it. He gave up, but I know he didn't like it. So I wasn't sure how he'd react to the pickerel frog squatting outside the honey-house door with his bowl of water and mason-jar lid full of dead flies. But the health inspector is a brisk man, and he walked briskly by the frog and never saw him. I was thankful.

Years ago, in an introductory biology class, I cut up a frog, carefully laying aside the muscles, tracing the nerves and identifying the organs. I remember that as I discarded the carcass I was quite pleased with myself, for now I knew all about frogs and could go on to learn the remaining one or two things about which I still had some small ignorance. I was just about as smug as a gray tree frog on a white beehive.

In the years after that, and before I moved to the Ozarks, I also lived a brisk life, and although I never had much reason to doubt that I still knew all about frogs, I don't think I ever thought about them, for, like the health inspector, I never saw any.

Today my life has frogs aplenty and this delights me, but I am not so pleased with myself. My life hasn't turned out as I expected it would, for one thing. For another, I no longer know all about anything. I don't even know the first thing about frogs, for instance. There's nothing like having frogs fill up my windows or share my bed or require my protection to convince me of that.

I don't cut up frogs anymore, and I read more poetry than I did when I was twenty. I just read a couplet about the natural world by an anonymous Japanese poet. I copied it out and put it up on the wall above my desk today:

> Unknown to me what resideth here
> Tears flow from a sense of unworthiness and gratitude.

My three hundred hives of bees are scattered across the hills of southern Missouri in outyards on farmers' pastures or at the edge of their woodlots. I give each family who has one of those outyards a gallon of honey a year as rent, but mostly farmers just like having the hives around, for the bees pollinate their fruit and vegetables and the clover in their pastures.

Bees fly two miles or more as they forage for nectar. I once calculated that the eighteen million bees in my hives cover a thousand square miles of the Ozarks in their flights. In the spring I spend most of my time driving to the outyards, taking care of the bees and getting them ready for the major nectar flows from which they will make the honey crop.

I use a big truck to haul the honey to market, but for the work around here I drive a courageous 1954 red Chevy half-ton pickup named "Press on Regardless" because it runs zestfully without many parts that are normally considered to be automotive necessities. That pickup and I have been over some rough spots, through mud and hard times, and I like to take good care of it.

Today was cold and rainy, not good weather for bee work, so I spent the day working on the pickup. I went out to the center part of the barn where I keep it, made a fire in the wood stove and turned the radio on to the public station I can get from the university eighty miles to the north. The radio promised that it would give me Albinoni's Concerto in C for Two Oboes and Strings. I started checking the pickup's vital fluids. The transmission oil was okay, but I had to add half a can of brake fluid to the master cylinder. I let out the crankcase oil, as it was time to change it. While the oil was draining, I jacked up the front of the pickup, rolled under it on my creeper and with bits of caked mud and grease falling into my eyes, greased the front end. My pickup has twenty grease points, and they have to be tended often in a truck that old.

While lying there on the creeper, Albinoni drifting through my brain, I noticed that I had been careless with the right rear shock absorber. Not only was it missing, but the bracket that held it in place had ripped loose. I added five quarts of new oil to the crankcase, reversed the truck, checked the oil level in the rear end, and then jacked it up to grease the rear prings. Afterwards I replaced the starter button above the starter assembly. The foot starter has been balky recently, and Ermon, my neighbor, a mechanic who lives across the hollow, had told me that the button needed replacing and showed me how to do it. The old one came out easily enough, but screwing in the new one with my fingertips backed up against the engine block while I sprawled over the fender was hard and took me past Albinoni, through Mozart, Beethoven and right on up to the Romantics before I was done. I wondered how the mechanic with his bigger fingers could manage it so deftly.

After I was finished, I peeled off my greasy coveralls, pleased and mildly surprised as I always am to find myself clean enough underneath to receive company in a parlor.

Outdoors the weather had still not improved for beework, so I drove into town to do errands. I stopped at the auto-parts store to buy a new set of shock absorbers, and then went over to my favorite salvage yard to buy a spare universal joint. The kind of driving that I do is hard on universal joints, and the last time I sheared one in two my neighbor mechanic had replaced it with the last one he had and told me to find another that I could carry as a spare in my glove box.

The salvage-yard man is a friend of mine, and I knew that buying the universal joint would take some time, just the thing that both he and I would enjoy on a rainy day. When I went into his shop he was cutting a junked Pontiac into usable parts with a welding torch. I leaned up against his tool bench to wait for him to finish a cut. When he stopped, he pushed back his welding helmet and nodded to me. He poured a cup of coffee for me and another for himself. We talked about the weather, discussing the pros and cons of rain past, present and future. Then he wondered what I was a-needing. I mentioned the universal joint for my Chevy. No, no, he seldom got those old rigs in nowadays, and they were always stripped clean of good parts when he did.

I have lived in the Ozarks twelve years now, so I did not say thank you and leave. I knew that so far he had just said howdy. I asked him how he was getting along with the 1934 pickup he had bought and was restoring.

"Not getting along worth a damn," he said. "Seems like folks come in looking for parts and interrupting all the time. Got me as fussed as a fart in a mitten." He looked hard at me. I took his comment for what it was worth and settled back more comfortably against the toolbench.

"Want to get to work on it, too," he said. "It's just like the first pickup that I ever did own. Say, did I tell you about that rig?"

No, he hadn't.

He leaned back against a crumpled fender. "It was a thirty-four Chevy that I'd bought from old Peg-Leg Potter," he said. "It was a pretty thing, and I was proud to drive that pickup home. But the next day I noticed that it was making a knocking noise that just wasn't right at all, so I crawled under that pickup and took the oil pan off. Well, old Peg-Leg Potter, whatever else he was, he wasn't much of a mechanic, because he'd worn out a bearing and just wrapped a piece of bacon rind round the rod to make do. Why, you can't run no pickup on bacon rind! Well, I caught my daddy asleep one day and I cut me a piece of shoe leather right out of the tongue of his shoe, and I took out that bacon rind and put the shoe leather in its place, and then I drove that thirty-four Chevy on down the road and traded it for a 1948 Ford. The old boy that I traded to, he come round to see me the next week complaining about the shoe leather. I says to him, I says, 'Don't talk to me about it. Why, I *improved* that pickup. You go talk to old Peg-Leg Potter. He thinks you can run a pickup on bacon rind.'"

If I had laughed or even smiled I would have ruined the transaction, so I tried to arrange my face in a way that acknowledged that I'd heard a good story but that I still knew a joke from a jaybird and that I still lacked a universal joint. I said that the rain appeared to be letting up some and I guessed I'd get going.

"If you wasn't in such an all-fired hurry, I expect I might find you a U-joint somewheres," he said, and rummaged around on a shelf until he found one.

The only time I have ever wished I were a man was at that moment, for what I should have said next was, "How much would a man have to give for that old U-joint now?" But I'm not and I couldn't and I didn't. And the word "woman" won't work in that question. So instead I asked him how much it was, he told me, I paid him and he returned to his cutting torch.

⌇ ANYONE WHO HAS KEPT BEES IS A PUSHOVER FOR A SWARM OF THEM. WE ALWAYS drop whatever we are doing and go off to pick one up when asked to do so. It doesn't make sense, because from a standpoint of serious beekeeping and honey production a swarm isn't much good. Swarms are headed up by old queens with not much vitality or egg-laying potential left, and so a beekeeper should replace her with a new queen from a queen breeder. He will probably have to feed and coddle the swarm through its first year; it will seldom produce any extra honey the first season. And yet we always hive them.

There is something really odd about swarms, and I notice that beekeepers don't talk about it much, probably because it is the sort of thing we don't feel comfortable about trying to put into words, something the other side of rationality.

The second year I kept bees, I picked up my first swarm. I was in the middle of the spring beework, putting in ten to twelve hours a day, and very attuned to what the bees were doing out there in their hives. That day had begun with a heavy rainstorm, and so rather than working out in the beeyards, I was in the honey house making new equipment. By afternoon the rain had stopped, but the air was warm and heavy, charged and expectant. I began to feel odd, tense and anticipatory, and when the back of my neck began to prickle I decided to take a walk out to the new hives I had started. Near them, hanging pendulously from the branch of an apple tree, was a swarm of bees. Individual bees were still flying in from all directions, adding their numbers to those clinging around their queen.

In the springtime some colonies of bees, for reasons not well understood, obey an impulse to split in two and thus multiply by swarming. The worker bees thoughtfully raise a new queen bee for the parent colony, and then a portion of the bees gather with the old queen, gorge themselves with honey and fly out of the hive, never to return, leaving all memory of their old home behind. They cluster somewhere temporarily, such as on the branch of my apple tree. If a beekeeper doesn't hive them, scout bees fly from the cluster and investigate nearby holes and spaces, and report back to the cluster on the suitability of new quarters.

We know about two forms of honeybee communication. One is chemical: information about food sources and the wellbeing of the queen and colony is exchanged as bees continually feed one another with droplets of nectar which they have begun to process and chemically tag. The other form of communication is tactile: bees tell other bees about good things such as food or the location of a new home by patterned motions. These elaborate movements, which amount to a highly stylized map of landmarks, direction and the sun's position, are called the bee dance.

Different scout bees may find different locations for the swarm and return to dance about their finds. Eventually, sometimes after several days, an agreement is reached, rather like the arrival of the Sense of the Meeting among Quakers, and all the bees in the cluster fly off to their new home.

I watched the bees on my apple tree for a while with delight and pleasure, and then returned to the barn to gather up enough equipment to hive them. As I did so, I glanced up at the sky. It was still dark from the receding thunderstorm, but a perfect and dazzling rainbow arched shimmering against the deep blue sky, its curve making a stunning and pleasing contrast with the sharp inverted V of the barn roof. I returned to the apple tree and shook the bees into the new beehive, noticing that I was singing snatches of one of Handel's coronation anthems. It seemed as appropriate music to hive a swarm by as any I knew.

Since then, I have learned to pay attention in the springtime when the air feels electric and full of excitement. It was just so one day last week. I had been working quietly along the row of twelve hives in an outyard when the hair on the back of my neck began to stand on end. I looked up to see the air thick with bees flying in toward me from the north. The swarm was not from any of my hives, but for some reason bees often cluster near existing hives while they scout a new location. I closed up the hive I was working on and stood back to watch. I was near a slender post oak sapling, and the bees began to light on one of its lower limbs right next to my elbow. They came flying in, swirling as they descended, spiraling around me and the post oak until I was enveloped by the swarm, the air moving gently from the beat of their wings. I am not sure how long I stood there. I lost all sense of time and felt only elation, a kind of human emotional counterpart of the springlike, optimistic, burgeoning, state that the bees were in. I stood quietly; I was nothing more to the bees than an object to be encircled on their way to the spot where they had decided, in a way I could not know, to cluster. In another sense I was not remote from them at all, but was receiving all sorts of meaningful messages in the strongest way imaginable outside of human mental process and language. My skin was tingling as the bees brushed past and I felt almost a part of the swarm.

Eventually the bees settled down in the cluster. Regaining a more suitable sense of my human condition and responsibilities, I went over to my pickup and got the empty hive that I always carry with me during swarming season. I propped it up so that its entrance was just under the swarm. A frame of comb from another hive was inside and the bees in the cluster could smell it, so they began to walk up into the entrance. I watched, looking for the queen, for without her the swarm would die. It took perhaps twenty minutes for all of them to file in, and the queen, a long, elegant bee, was one of the last to enter.

I screened up the entrance and put the hive in the back of the pickup. After I was finished with my work with the other hives in the beeyard, I drove back home with my new swarm.

I should have ordered a new queen bee, killed the old one and replaced her, but in doing that I would have destroyed the identity of the swarm. Every colony of bees takes its essence, character and personality from the queen who is mother to all its members. As a commercial beekeeper, it was certainly my business to kill the old queen and replace her with a vigorous new one so that the colony would become a good honey producer.

But I did not.

~ THE LOCAL VFW HAS A CAMPGROUND ON THE RIVER DIRECTLY BELOW MY FARM. During the warm weather, its members and their families come there to swim, cook out and sometimes camp overnight.

The VFW is an important social organization in town and sponsors civic events as well as fish fries, barbecues and pig roasts at the slightest hint of a patriotic occasion. The members are mostly World War II veterans. Here as elsewhere, many of the veterans of Vietnam are a bitter lot, not interested in socializing in an organization reminding them of war. One of them, who was repairing a tire for me at a gas station in town, asked if I wasn't the Bee Lady who lived up by the VFW campground? I was. Was he a member of the VFW?

"Nah, I can't stand listening to those old guys sitting around telling about how a war should be fought," he said savagely.

None of the VFW members or their wives are close friends of mine, but I know many in the group and they often invite me to join them at their cookouts. The invitations are a friendly gesture, not meant to be accepted, but a politeness that establishes that we are good neighbors. But, like my mother, the VFW seems to believe that I don't eat properly, because every time they cook out down there, one of the veterans drives back up the hill with a box full of barbecued meat, fried potatoes, baked beans, and salad, enough food for days.

"Brought you some groceries," the veteran will say with a grin, and drive back down the hill to his friends.

At the end of the summer, the VFW holds a stag party on a Saturday. There is very little real hell-raising from what I ever hear, but much talk of it beforehand. One member told me that the wife of a new recruit was upset because they had told her that on the night of the stag party a canoe full of naked women always floated down the river at precisely 10 P.M. The man's wife was just a young thing and she believed them and got pretty riled up, the veteran told me, laughing hard, and then added, "Hell, by ten o'clock we're all so drunk we wouldn't know if the Queen of Sheba floated down the river."

One afternoon last summer, Virgil, a VFW member, and his wife, Mary Lou, whom I know well, stopped by my place and said they were roasting a goat down there for a few friends and really would like me to join them. I hadn't seen them for a while and had been working hard, so the prospect of an evening of roasted goat and good-old-boy banter was a welcome one; I thanked them and said I'd come down later. Before I left I searched for something to contribute to the feast. The refrigerator held some scraps of raw vegetables, just enough for the salad I had intended to have for supper, an opened jar of mustard that was evolving into a higher life form, and half a jug of red wine left over from dinner with friends the week before. The cupboard was no better: some stale crackers and half a bottle of teriyaki sauce. Half a jug of wine seemed more festive than half a bottle of teriyaki sauce, so I slung it over my shoulder and walked down the hill to the campground. When I got there, Virgil peered at the level of wine in the jug.

"I knew it was a long walk down the hill, but I didn't know it was *that* long," he said, his face innocent of a smile.

The evening was a pleasant one. The goat, roasted in herbs, was delicious, the company good, and Virgil kept everyone limp with laughter with his straight-faced stories. I was glad I had accepted their invitation.

Last Friday night a tired and troubled veteran shot and killed himself at the campground. I did not hear the shot and did not know the man, but I did know the two veterans who were pounding on my door minutes later.

I was in bed reading when I heard them. I got up, put on a robe, and answered the door. The two men were incoherent and weeping. I knew something was terribly wrong but I couldn't find out what. I brought them into the living room and had them sit down, and gradually made out what had happened. They had been trying for two hours to talk the man out of suicide, but he had gone ahead with it and they were racking themselves for their failure.

They wanted to use my telephone to call the sheriff and the man's family, but the horror still in front of their eyes made it impossible for them to read the telephone book. I looked up the numbers for them, helped them to place their calls and tried to find something to say, but there were no words that could undo what had been done. Then they asked me to call Virgil, a good man in a crisis. They wanted him with them. I said I would, and asked them to stay with me for the half hour that it would take the sheriff to get here. I would make some coffee. I did not think it was good for them to go back and sit alone with that body whose head had been ripped apart with a shotgun blast, but they would not stay, and drove their pickup down to the river, the wheels spinning gravel in the darkness. I made the call to Virgil, and he said he would go to them immediately.

Then my telephone began to ring. Here in the country, listening to the police scanner vies with television as an evening's entertainment. People throughout the neighborhood had heard the sheriff saying he was on his way to investigate a reported death at the VFW campground, and the curious were calling to ask what had happened.

I cannot see the road from my cabin, but soon I heard traffic on it and knew that the sheriff, Virgil and perhaps some of the other veterans were arriving; I felt a little easier about the two men who had been here. Sleep was impossible that night, and I thought with sorrow of the unknown man whose life had become such pain to him that he had to leave it.

The next afternoon, one of the veterans who had knocked on my door the night before came to see me. His eyes were red, his face was creased with fatigue and he was staggeringly drunk. He told me that all the boys had decided the best thing to do was to have a family party at the campground for the rest of the weekend and to camp out there that night, or else no one would ever be able to go there again. It was important that I come down for dinner. It was important. Very. Very. Important. Very important. Very.

I said I would come, and assured him that I understood.

The campground had been taken over by death; it had to be returned to life and parties before it grew a ghost. The two men needed to talk to me at a party there. The night before they had not been just a pair of good old boys, but two men who had seen horror and had brought it into my living room. I had not been the Bee Lady on the hill, but a woman who had put her arms around them when they cried. Now it was time for us to go back to what we had all been before.

When the sun set, I walked down the hill to the campground. We all ate something or other. I sat with the circle of wives and daughters, and we talked of something or other. The men sat by themselves, drinking. After a while I talked with the two men who had come to my cabin. We agreed that what had happened was bad, but that time would help a person to forget. They thanked me for letting them use the telephone, and then I walked back up the hill.

John McPhee

from Annals of the Former World

ACCORDING TO PRESENT THEORY, MANY EXOTIC TERRANES MOVED IN FROM THE WESTERN ocean and collected against North America during a span of about three hundred million years which ended roughly forty million years ago, increasing the continent to something like its present size. Three of these assembled at the latitude of Interstate 80. It was the first of these collisions that crunched and folded the wine-red sandstone near Carlin. The second, in the early Triassic, is what apparently caused the whole Carlin unconformity to revolve quite close to its present position. Sonomia, as the second terrane has been named, included much of what is now western Nevada and eastern California, and is said to have come into the continent with such force—notwithstanding that it was moving an inch or so a year—that it overlapped its predecessor by as much as eighty kilometres before it finally stopped. The evidence of this event is known locally as the Golconda Thrust, and both its upper and lower components are exposed in a big roadcut on the western flank of Golconda Summit, where the interstate, coming up out of Pumpernickel Valley, crosses a spur of the Sonoma Range. Small wonder that Deffeyes pulled over when we came to it and said, "Let's stick our eyeballs on this one."

It was dawn at the summit. We had been awake for hours and had eaten a roadhouse breakfast sitting by a window in which the interior of the room was reflected against the black of the morning outside while a television mounted on a wall behind us resounded with the hoofbeats of the great horse Silver. *The Lone Ranger.* Five A.M. CBS's good morning to Nevada. Waiting for bacon and eggs, I put two nickels in a slot machine and got two nickels back. The result was a certain radiance of mood. Deffeyes, for his part, was thinking today in troy ounces. It would take a whole lot more than two nickels to produce a similar effect on him. Out for silver, he was heading into the hills, but first, in his curiosity, he walked the interstate roadcut, now and again kicking a can. The November air was in frost. He seemed to be smoking his breath. He remarked that the mean distance between beer cans across the United States along I-80 seemed to be about one metre. Westward, tens of hundreds of square miles were etched out by the early light: basins, ranges, and—below us in the deep foreground—Paradise Valley, the village Golconda, sinuous stands of cottonwood at once marking and concealing the Humboldt. The whole country seemed to be steaming, vapors rising from warm ponds and hot springs. The roadcut was long, high, and benched. It was sandstone, for the most part, but at its lower, westernmost end the blasting had exposed a dark shale that had been much deformed and somewhat metamorphosed, the once even bedding now wrinkled and mashed—rock folded up like wet laundry. "You can spend hours doping out one of these shattered places, just milling around trying to find out what's going on," Deffeyes said cautiously, but he was fairly sure he knew what had happened, for the sandstone that lay above contained many volcanic fragments and was full of sharp-edged grains of chert and quartz, highly varied in texture, implying to him a volcanic source and swift deposition into the sea (almost no opportunity for streams to have rounded off the grains), implying, therefore, an island arc standing in deep water on a continental margin—an Aleutian chain, a Bismarck Archipelago, a Lesser Antilles, a New Zealand, a Japan, thrust upon and overlapping the established continent, a piece of which was that mashed-up shale. Deffeyes mused his way along the cut. "There is complexity here because you have not only the upper and lower plates of the Golconda Thrust, which happened in the early

Triassic; you also have basin-range faulting scarcely a hundred yards away—enormously complicating the regional picture. If you look at a geologic map of western Canada and Alaska, you can see the distinct bands of terrane that successively attached themselves to the continent. Here the pattern has been all broken up and obscured by the block faulting of the Basin and Range, not to mention the great outpouring of Oligocene welded tuff. So this place is a handsome mess. If you ever want to study this sort of collision more straightfor-wardly, go to the Alps, where you had a continent-to-continent collision and that was it."

So much for theory. This roadcut contained both extremities of Deffeyes' wide interests in geology, and his attention was now drawn to a large gap in the sandstone, faulted open probably six or seven million years ago and now filled with rock crumbs, as if a bomb had gone off there in the ground. The material was gradated outward from a very obvious core. In a country full of living hot springs, this was a dead one. Sectioned by the road builders, it remembered in its swirls and convolutions the commotion of water raging hot in rock. The dead hot spring had developed cracks, and they had been filled in by a couple of generations of calcite veins. Deffeyes was busy with his hammer, pinging, chipping samples of the calcite. "This stuff is too handsome to leave out here," he said, filling a canvas bag. "There was a lot of thermal action here. Most of this material is not even respectable rock anymore. It's like soil. In 1903, a mining geologist named Waldemar Lindgren found cinnabar in crud like this at Steamboat, near Reno. Cinnabar is mercury sulphide. He also found cinnabar in the fis-sures through which water had come up from deep in the crust. He thought, Aha! Mercury deposits are hot-spring deposits! And he applied that idea to ore deposits generally. He started classifying them according to the temperature of the water from which they were de-posited—warm, hot, hotter, and so on. We know now that not all metal deposits are hy-drothermal in origin, but more than half of them are. As you know, the hot water, circulat-ing deep, picks up whatever is there—gold, silver, molybdenum, mercury, tin, uranium—and brings it up and precipitates it out near the surface. A vein of ore is the filling of a fissure. A map of former hot springs is remarkably close to a map of metal discoveries. Old hot springs like this one brought up the silver of Nevada. It would do my heart good to find silver right here in this roadcut and put it to the local highway engineer."

He took some samples, which eventually proved to be innocent of silver, and we got back into the pickup. We soon left the interstate for a secondary road heading north—up a pastel valley, tan, with a pale-green river course, fields of cattle and hay. It was a valley that had been as special to the Paiutes as the Black Hills were to the Sioux. The Paiutes gave it up slowly, killing whites in desperation to keep it, and thus bringing death on themselves. The first pioneers to settle in this "desert" were farmers—an indication of how lush and beauti-ful the basin must have appeared to them, ten miles wide and seventy miles long, framed in serrated ridges of north-south-trending mountains: range, basin, range. Magpies, looking like scale-model jets, kept rising into flight from the side of the road and gaining altitude over the hood of the pickup. Deffeyes said they were underdeveloped and reminded him of *Archaeopteryx,* the Jurassic bird. We crossed cattle guards that were nothing more than stripes painted on the road, indicating that Nevada cattle may be underdeveloped, too, with I.Q.s in one digit, slightly lower than the national norm.

For eight million years, Deffeyes was saying, as the crustal blocks inexorably pulled apart here and springs boiled up along the faults, silver had been deposited throughout the Basin and Range. The continually growing mountains sometimes fractured their own ore deposits, greatly complicating the sequence of events and confusing the picture for anyone who might come prospecting for ores. There was another phenomenon, however, that had once made prospecting dead simple. Erosion, breaking into hot-spring and vein deposits, concentrated the silver. Rainwater converted silver sulphides to silver chloride, heavy stuff that stayed right where it was and—through thousands of millennia—increased in concentration as more rain fell. These were the deposits, richer than an Aztec dream, that were known to geologists as supergene enrichments. Miners called them surface bonanzas. In the eighteen-sixties, and particularly in the eighteen-seventies, they were discovered in range after range. A big supergene enrichment might be tens of yards wide and a mile long, lying at or near the surface. Instant cities appeared beside them, with false-front saloons and tent ghettos, houses of sod, shanties made of barrels. The records of these communities suggest uneven success in the settling of disputes between partners over claims: "Davison shot Butler through the left elbow, breaking the bone, and in turn had one of his toes cut off with an axe." They were places with names like Hardscrabble, Gouge Eye, Battle Mountain, Treasure Hill. By the eighteen-nineties, the boom was largely over and gone. During those thirty years, there were more communities in Nevada than there are now. "Silver is our most depleted resource, because it gave itself away," said Deffeyes, looking mournful. "You didn't need a Ph.D. in geology to find a supergene enrichment."

All you needed was Silver Jim. Silver Jim was a Paiute, and he, or a facsimile, took you up some valley or range and showed you grayish rock with touches of green that had a dull waxy lustre like the shine on the horn of a cow. Horn silver. It was just lying there, difficult to lift. Silver Jim could show you horn silver worth twenty-seven thousand dollars a ton. Those were eighteen-sixties dollars and an uninflatable ton. You could fill a wheelbarrow and go down the hill with five thousand dollars' worth of silver. Three or four years ago, a miner friend of Deffeyes who lives in Tombstone, Arizona, happened to find on his own property an overlooked fragment of a supergene enrichment, a narrow band no more than a few inches thick, six feet below the cactus. Knocking off some volcanic overburden with a front-end loader, the miner went after this nineteenth-century antique and fondly dug it out by hand. He said to his children, "Pay attention to what I'm doing here. Look closely at the rock. We will never see this stuff again." In a couple of hours of a weekend afternoon, he took twenty thousand dollars from the ground.

We were off on dirt roads now with a cone of dust behind us, which Deffeyes characterized as the local doorbell. He preferred not to ring it. This talkative and generous professor—who ordinarily shares his ideas as rapidly as they come to him, spilling them out in bunches like grapes—was narrow-eyed with secrecy today. He had stopped at a courthouse briefly, and—an antic figure, with his bagging sweater and his Beethoven hair—had revealed three digits to a county clerk in requesting to see a registry of claims. The claims were coded in six digits. Deffeyes kept the fourth, fifth, and sixth to himself like cards face down on a table. He found what he sought in the book of claims. Now, fifty miles up the valley, we had long since left behind us its only town, with its Odd Fellows Hall, its mercantile company, its cottonwoods and Lombardy poplars; and there were no houses, no structures, no cones of dust anywhere around us. The valley was narrowing. It ended where ranges joined. Some thousands of feet up the high face of a distant and treeless mountain we saw an unnaturally level line.

"Is that a road?" I asked him.

"That's where we're going," he said, and I wished he hadn't told me.

Looking up there, I took comfort in the reflection that I would scarcely be the first journalist to crawl out on a ledge in the hope of seeing someone else get rich. In 1869, the editor of the *New York Herald,* looking over his pool of available reporters, must have had no difficulty in choosing Tom Cash to report on supergene enrichments. Cash roved Nevada. He reported from one place that he took out his pocketknife and cut into the wall of a shaft, removing an ore of such obviously high assay that he could roll it in his fingers and it would not crumble. Cash told the mine owner that he feared being accused of exaggeration—"of making false statements, puffing"—with resulting damage to his journalistic reputation. There was a way to avoid this, he confided to the miner. "I would like to take a sample with me of some of the richest portions." The miner handed him a fourteen-pound rock containing about a hundred and fifty troy ounces of silver (seventy-three per cent). In the same year, Albert S. Evans, writing in the San Francisco *Alta California,* described a visit with a couple of bankers and a geologist to a claim in Nevada where he was lowered on a rope into a mine. "The light of our candles disclosed great black sparkling masses of silver on every side. The walls were of silver, the roof over our heads was of silver, and the very dust that filled our lungs and covered our boots and clothing with a gray coating was of fine silver. We were told that in this chamber a million dollars' worth of silver lies exposed to the naked eye and our observations confirm the statement. How much lies back of it, Heaven only knows."

Heaven knew exactly. For while the supergene enrichments—in their prodigal dispersal through the Basin and Range—were some of the richest silver deposits ever discovered in the world, they were also the shallowest. There was just so much lying there, and it was truly bonanzan—to print money would take more time than to pick up this silver—but when it was gone it was gone, and it went quickly. Sometimes—as in the Comstock Lode in Virginia City—there were "true veins" in fissures below, containing silver of considerable value if more modest assay, but more often than not there was nothing below the enrichment. Mining and milling towns developed and died in less than a decade.

We were on our way to a nineteenth-century mine, and were now turning switchbacks and climbing the high mountainside. Deffeyes, in order to consult maps, had turned over the wheel to me. He said his interest in the secondary recovery of silver had been one result of certain computer models that had been given wide circulation in the early nineteen-seventies, using differential equations to link such things as world population, pollution, resources, and food, and allow them to swim forward through time, with a resulting prediction that the world was more or less going to come to an end by the year 2000, because it would run out of resources. "We have found all obvious deposits, and, true enough, we've got to pay the price," he said. "But they did not take into account reserves or future discoveries or picking over once again what the old-timers left behind." Seeking commissions from, for example, the Department of Energy, he began doing studies of expectable discoveries of petroleum and uranium. He sort of slid inadvertently from uranium into silver after a syndicate of New York businessmen came to him to ask for his help in their quest for gold. The group was called Eocene and was interested in scavenging old mines. Deffeyes pointed out to them that while new gold strikes were still occurring in the world and new gold mines were still being developed, no major silver mine had been discovered since 1915. The pressure for silver was immense. Dentistry and photography used two-thirds of what there was, and there were no commercial substitutes. "We've been wiped out. We've gone through it, just as we have gone through magnesium and bromine. You can raise the price of silver all you want to but you won't have a new mine." He predicted that as prices went up silver would probably outperform gold. The potentialities in the secondary recovery of silver appeared to him to be a lot more alluring than working through tailings for gold. Eocene engaged him as a consultant, to help them scavenge silver.

Now far above the basin, we were on the thin line we had seen from below, a track no wider than the truck itself, crossing the face of the mountain. It curved into reentrants and out around noses and back into reentrants and out to more noses. I was on the inboard side, and every once in a while as we went around a nose I looked across the hood and saw nothing but sky—sky and the summits of a distant range. We could see sixty, seventy miles down the valley and three thousand feet down the mountain. The declivity was by no means sheer, just steep—a steepness, I judged, that would have caused the vehicle, had it slipped off the road, to go end over end enveloped in flame at a hundred yards a bounce. My hands slid on the wheel. They were filmed in their own grease.

The equanimous Deffeyes seemed to be enjoying the view. He said, "Where did you learn to drive a truck?"

"Not that it's so god-damned difficult," I told him, "but this is about the first time."

Before 1900, the method used in this country to extract silver from most ores was to stamp the rock to powder in small stamp mills, then stir the powder into hot salt water and mercury, and, after the mercury had attracted the silver, distill the mercury. In 1887, a more thorough extraction process had been developed in England whereby silver ores were dissolved in cyanide. The method moved quickly to South Africa and eventually to the United States. An obvious application was to run cyanide through old tailings piles to see what others had missed, and a fair amount of such work was done, in particular during the Depression. There had been so many nineteenth-century mines in Nevada, however, that Deffeyes was sure that some had been ignored. He meant to look for them, and the first basin he prospected was the C Floor of Firestone Library, up the hill from his office in Princeton. There he ran through books and journals and began compiling a catalogue of mines and mills in the Basin and Range that had produced more than a certain number of dollars' worth of silver between 1860 and 1900. He prefers not to bandy the number. He found them in many places, from barrel-cactus country near the Colorado River to ranges near the Oregon line, from the Oquirrh Mountains of Utah to the eastern rampart of the Sierra Nevada. In all, he listed twenty-five. The larger ones, like the Comstock, had been worked and reworked and cyanided to death, and "tourists were all over them like ants." A scavenger had best consider lesser mines, out-of-the-way mines—the quick-shot enrichments, the small-fissure lodes, where towns grew and died in six years. He figured that any mine worth, say, a million dollars a hundred years ago would still be worth a million dollars, because the old mills at best extracted ninety per cent of the silver in the ores, and the ten per cent remaining would be worth about what the ninety per cent had been worth then. Pulling more books and journals off the shelves, he sought to learn if and where attention had been paid to various old mines in the nineteen-thirties, and wherever he discovered activity at that time he crossed off those mines.

His next move was to buy aerial photographs from the United States Geological Survey. The pictures were in overlapping pairs, and each pair covered sixteen square miles. "You look at them with stereo equipment and you are a giant with eyeballs a mile apart and forty thousand feet in the air. God, do you have stereovision! Things jump off the earth. You look for tailings. You look for dumps. You look for the faint scars of roads. The environmentalists are right. A scar in this climate will last. It takes a long time for the terrain to erase a road. You try to reason like a miner. If this was a mine, now where would I go for water? If this was a mill here, by this stream, then where is the mine? I was looking for mines that were not marked on maps. I could see dumps in some places. They stood out light gray. The old miners made dumps of rock that either contained no silver at all or did not contain enough silver to be worth their while at the time. I tried to guess roughly the volume of the dumps.

Mill tailings made unnatural light-gray smudges on the pictures. Some of the tailings and dumps I found in these mountains appear on no maps I've seen."

He flew to Nevada, chartered a light plane, and went over the country a thousand feet above the ground, taking fresh private pictures with a telephoto lens. When he flew over places where other scavengers looked up and waved, he crossed those places off his list. He went in on the ground then, to a number of sites, and collected samples. He had machines at home that could deal with the samples in ways unheard of just a few years before, let alone in the nineteenth century. Kicking at old timbers, he looked at the nails. Wire nails came into use in 1900 and are convenient index fossils of the Age of Cyanide. He hoped for square nails.

Deffeyes was on his own now. His relationship with Eocene had faded out after they had chosen, on various points, to follow counsel other than his, and they transferred their scrutiny to Arizona, preferring not to cope with winter. One day in Princeton, his wife, Nancy Deffeyes, was looking through a stack of hundred-year-old *Engineering & Mining Journals* when she found a two-line reference to certain mining efforts in the eighteen-seventies that eventually assumed prominence on her husband's list, and that was what had brought him here and why we were crawling like a Japanese beetle across the face of this mountain.

We turned a last corner, with our inner wheels resting firmly on the road and the two others supported by Deffeyes' expectations. Now we were moving along one wall of a big V-shaped canyon that eventually became a gulch, a draw, a crease in the country, under cottonwoods. In the upper canyon, some hundreds of acres of very steep mountainside were filled with holes and shafts, hand-forged ore buckets, and old dry timbers. There were square nails in the timbers. An ore bucket was filled with square nails. "Good litter," Deffeyes said, and we walked uphill past the mine and along a small stream into the cottonwoods. The stream was nearly dry. Under the cottonwoods were the outlines of cabins almost a century gone. Here at seven thousand feet in this narrow mountain draw had lived a hundred people, who had held their last election a hundred years earlier. They had a restaurant, a brewery, a bookstore. They had seven saloons. And now there was not so much as one dilapidated structure. There were only the old unhappy cottonwoods, looking alien and discontented over the moist bed of the creek. Sixteen stood there, twisted, surviving—most of them over four feet thick. "Those cottonwoods try an environmentalist's soul," Deffeyes said. "They transpire water like running fountains. If you were to cut them down, the creek would run. Cottonwoods drink the Humboldt. Some of the tension in this country is that miners need water. Getting rid of trees would preserve water. By the old brine-and-mercury method, it took three tons of water to mill one ton of ore. There was nothing like that in this creek. They had to take the ore from here to a big enough stream, and that, as it happens, was a twelve-mile journey using mules. They would have gone out of here with only the very best ore. There was probably a supergene enrichment here over a pretty good set of veins. They took what they took and were gone in six years."

We walked back down to the mine, below which the stream—in flash flood once or twice a century over several million years—had cut the deep sharp V of its remarkably plunging valley. A number of acres of one side had been used as a dump, and Deffeyes began to sample this unused ore. "They must have depended on what they could see in the rock," he said. "If it was easy to see, they got it all. If it was complicated and gradational, they couldn't differentiate as well, and I think they threw it here." The material was crumbly, loose, weathered, unstable underfoot, a pyramid side of decomposing shards. Filling small canvas bags at intervals of six feet, he worked his way across it. With each step, he sank in above his ankles. He was about two hundred feet above the stream. Given the steepness of the ground and the proximity of all the loose material to the critical angle of repose, I had no trouble imagining that he was about to avalanche, and that he would end up in an algal pool of the trickling stream below us, buried under megatons of unextracted silver. The little stream was a jumble of boulders, testimony of the floods, with phreatophytes around the boulders like implanted spears. Deffeyes obviously was happy and without a fear in the world. When a swift-rising wind blew dust in his face, he mooed. Working in cold sunshine with his orange-and-black conical cap on his head, he appeared to be the Gnome of Princeton, with evident ambition to escalate to Zurich.

To make a recovery operation worthwhile, he said, he would have to get five ounces of silver per ton. The figures would turn out to be better than that. Before long, he would have a little plastic-lined pond of weak cyanide, looked after by a couple of technicians, down where the ore from this mine had been milled. A blue streak in the tailings there would come in at fifty-eight ounces a ton—richer than any tailings he had ever found in Nevada. "You put cyanide on that ore, the silver leaps out of it," he would say. "I have enough cyanide there to kill Cincinnati. People have a love-hate relationship with cyanide. Abelson showed that lightning acts on carbon dioxide and other atmospheric components to make hydrogen cyanide, and hydrogen cyanide polymerizes and later reacts with water to form amino acids, which are the components of proteins—and that may be how life began. Phil Abelson is an editor at *Science*. He's a geochemist, and he worked on the Manhattan Project. To get the silver out of here at an acceptable price, you need small-scale technology. You need miniaturized equipment, simple techniques. In the nineteenth century, they made sagebrush fires to heat the brine to dissolve the silver chloride. When mercury picked up the silver, they knew they had 'the real stuff' from the squeak. A mercury-and-silver mixture is what the dentist uses, and when he mashes it into your tooth it makes the same squeak."

Deffeyes' methodology would depend on more than sagebrush and sound. In time, he would have a portable laboratory there, size of a two-hole privy, and in it would be, among other things, a silver single-ion electrode and an atomic-absorption spectrophotometer. He could turn on a flame, close two switches, and see at once the amount of silver in a sample. For a short while, he would have a five-pound ingot of raw silver on the floor, propping open the door. When he was finished with his pond, he would withdraw the cyanide and turn it into a marketable compound known as Prussian blue. He would cover his pond with dirt and sow it with crested wheat.

And now, finishing up his sampling at the mine in the mountains, he filled a large burlap bag with ore he would take home to improve his technique of extraction. The smaller samples he had taken were for assays of silver in various parts of the slope. "I'm nothing but a ragpicker," he said. "A scavenger armed with a forty-thousand-dollar X-ray machine." The wind picked up another cloud of dust off the dump and blew it into his face. He mooed. "That may feel like dirt to you, but it feels like money to me," he said.

"How much money would you say that felt like?" I asked him.

He took out a Magic Marker and began to do metric conversions, geometry, and arithmetic on the side of a new canvas bag. "Well, this section of the dump is at least fifteen thousand cubic metres," he said. "That is the most conservative figure. At two hundred dollars a ton, that works out to about three million dollars, left here in the side of the hill."

"What are those red stakes up there?"

"Somebody seems to think they're finding new ore. I'm interested in the old stuff, down here."

"If you've got good silver in those bags, what about Eocene? What if they decide they still own you? What if they go to the sheriff?"

"Eocene doesn't own me, and Eocene doesn't own the contents of my head. The law has long since decided that. But if anybody comes after me I want you to go to jail cheerfully rather than surrender your notes."

As we wound down the mountain at the end of the day, we stopped to regard the silent valley—the seventy miles of basin under a rouge sky, the circumvallate mountains, and, the better part of a hundred miles away, Sonoma Peak, of the Sonoma Range. Deffeyes said, "If you reduced the earth to the size of a baseball, you couldn't feel that mountain. With a tele-photo lens, you could convince someone it was Everest." Even at this altitude, the air was scented powerfully with sage. There was coyote scat at our feet. In the dark, we drove back the way we had come, over the painted cattle guards and past jackrabbits dancing in the road, pitch-dark, and suddenly a Black Angus was there, standing broadside, middle of the road. With a scream of brakes, we stopped. The animal stood still, thinking, its eyes un-moving—a wall of beef. We moved slowly after that, and even more slowly when a white sphere materialized on our right in the moonless sky. It expanded some, like a cloud. Its light became so bright that we stopped finally and got out and looked up in awe. A smaller ob-ject, also spherical, moved out from within the large one, possibly from behind it. There was a Saturn-like ring around the smaller sphere. It moved here and there beside the large one for a few minutes and then went back inside. The story would be all over the papers the fol-lowing day. The *Nevada State Journal* would describe a "Mysterious Ball of Light" that had been reported by various people at least a hundred miles in every direction from the place where we had been. "By this time we decided to get the hell out of there," a couple of hunters reported, "and hopped in our pickup and took off. As we looked back at it, we saw a smaller craft come out of the right lower corner. This smaller craft had a dome in the middle of it and two wings on either side, but the whole thing was oval-shaped." Someone else had said, "I thought it was an optical illusion at first, but it just kept coming closer and closer so that I could see it wasn't an illusion. Then something started coming out of the side of it. It looked like a star, and then a ring formed around it. A kind of ring like you'd see around Sat-urn. It didn't make any noises, and then it vanished."

"Now we're both believers," said one of the hunters. "And I don't ever want to see an-other one. We're pretty good-sized men and ain't scared of nothing except for snakes and now flying saucers."

After the small sphere disappeared the large one rapidly faded and also disappeared. Deffeyes and I were left on the roadside among the starlighted eyes of dark and motionless cattle. "Copernicus took the world out of the center of the universe," he said. "Hutton took us out of a special place somewhere near the beginning of things and left us awash in the middle of the immensity of time. An extraterrestrial civilization could show us where we are with regard to the creation of life."

Gretel Ehrlich

from Questions of Heaven

Why climb a mountain?

Look! a mountain there.

I don't climb mountain.
Mountain climbs me.
Mountain is myself.
I climb on myself.

There is no mountain
nor myself.
Something
moves up and down
in the air.

—*Nanao Sakaki*

LIJIANG

IN THE MORNING OUR TRAIN ARRIVED IN THE SOUTHWESTERN CITY OF KUNMING AND WE met our new driver, Feng. Small and stoop shouldered, he jammed us and our camping gear into his VW with a nervous sweetness. We were going to the once isolated town of Lijiang on the border between Han China and Tibet, to Peter Goullart's *Forgotten Kingdom,* to Joseph Rock's Nancho Kingdom, to the World War II Flying Tigers' airbase, to Shangri-la, the town on which James Hilton based his lost paradise.

All roads to paradise first pass through purgatory. But before leaving Kunming, we stopped to eat. In the street markets between the usual pens of live snakes, chickens, turtles, eels, and fish, we bought fresh bananas, oranges, and Asian pears and went to a small corner restaurant to fill up on a Kunming specialty: noodles in red pepper broth so hot (in both ways) it cooked the slivers of meat and fish dropped into it.

Kunming's gracious, semitropical, tree-lined avenues were chockablock with small shops, all selling cheap American-style clothes and Japanese toys. One storefront turned out to be a miniature hospital. Open to the street were four beds, three of them occupied by patients, with a doctor and nurse administering IVs as pedestrians, bicycles, motorbikes, taxis and trucks roared by.

The trip to Lijiang from Kunming would take seventeen hours by car and we had already been twenty-four hours on the train. During World War II, Kunming had been General Stilwell's base, the jump-off place for moving supplies over the hump in Burma. The first leg of our trip from Kunming to Dali would follow that historic road.

I watched Feng's soft, twitching, apologetic face in the rear-view mirror as we headed out of the city. He had rolled his pant legs shin-high before slipping into the cramped driver's seat as if in preparation for the wild ride to come. And wild it was. Feng drove maniacally, impatiently, honking his horn every few seconds, alternately jerking forward and slamming on his brakes as we threaded our way through Chinese gridlock. I closed my eyes and prayed for the cool, streetwise Mr. Tong to reappear at the wheel, but he did not. The oranges and apples I had bought rolled like billiard balls, hitting the back of my head. Zhang put on his earphones and closed his eyes.

I had been reading *Forgotten Kingdom*, a memoir about Lijiang written by Peter Goullart, an ebullient Russian who escaped with his mother during the Revolution and landed in Shanghai. When his mother died in 1924, Peter was already fluent in Chinese, had spent time in a Taoist monastery, and landed a much needed job with the Chinese government setting up local crafts cooperatives in remote parts of China. His work eventually led him to the isolated mountain town of Lijiang.

He wrote: "The prospect of travelling on the Burma Road filled me with dread. This great highway, although marvelously constructed, well kept and extremely picturesque, has been a notorious killer. It climbs several mountain ranges of about 10,000 feet by a series of hairpin turns and runs along the edge of giddy precipices . . . I can never forget the sight of countless heavy trucks lying at the bottom of deep ravines, smashed beyond salvage."

Narrow and unshouldered, the road to Lijiang was an unruly ribbon that pulled over the accordioned landscape, mountain pass after mountain pass, some as high as 13,000 feet. The turns were sharp and the way was vertiginous, and every switchback was the scene of an accident: a whole wheel spun off the axle of one logging truck, while another lost its load in the center of the road. Yet another truck had tumbled over a verge just before we passed by. Not much had changed since Peter Goullart had passed through fifty years before.

To distract myself, I studied a map. The Yunnan plateau is a series of steps descending from the Himalayas. Long ropes of northwest-southeast ranges curve down, with deep river valleys between. At the lower elevations the mountains are dry with red soil and scrub pines, their streams bordered by bamboo. At times the vegetation looked like California's: eucalyptus and sycamore trees gave shade to hard-used humans and animals, and bougainvillea crawled up the adobe walls of the Yi houses.

The literature of travel in ancient China represents a spatial progression through a string of spheres linked by a single road: we sped across range after range, valley after valley. Time was demarked in ancient travelogues by what is called the "hoary stems" system: each year, month, and day was denoted using two characters—one heavenly, the other, earthly—with the cycle repeating after sixty combinations, linear sequences within recurring cycles describing the permutations of heaven and hell.

The road we took that morning, the Burma Road, began to feel like such a cyclical path: time swirled as the alpine glories of each mountain range were defiled by terror. In my library at home I had looked at a Lijiang shaman's scenes of hell. Called the *Dongba's Road Map*, it showed scenes of dread, the lower and middle realms full of "demons, torturers, civil magistrates, and humans."

The car swerved and straightened and I thought about other scenes of literary purgatory: the sixth book of Virgil's *Aeneid*, the circumambulations in Seamus Heaney's *Station Island*, the cold *bardos* of the *Tibetan Book of the Dead*. To get to paradise, or to enlightenment, one must first go through the initiatory rites; one must become dead before waking. As we drove I thought of Virgil's lines in the *Aeneid*: "Souls for whom a second body is in store: their drink is the water of Lethe, and it frees from care in long forgetfulness."

❖   ❖   ❖

How many mountains had we crossed and how many rivers? I longed to be freed from care and would have welcomed a bottle of tequila. Villages merged one into another as we sped through, always too fast, Feng's hand always on the horn. Five slaughtered pigs lay in a row by the side of the road—for sale, Feng told me. Around another mountain peasants threw sheaves of grain onto the asphalt, letting our rolling tires thresh it for them. After we passed, the peasants quickly swept up the loosened grain with bamboo brooms. Everywhere animals were tied up except for the gangs of goats on the side of the highway. They ate anything green that had not already been eaten by humans. Men, women, and children planted rice seedlings in straight lines marked by strings stretched across the field which were moved each time a row was completed. The foothills and mountains had been clear-cut and the standing windbreaks of eucalyptus trees were sheared of their arms. Insecticide sprayed from backpacks glistened on the dull frosting of night soil, and women bent down into the mud of the paddy, their hoes slick with water and earth.

Some of the women coming from the fields had black eyes and bandaged legs. "What happened to them?" I asked Zhang. "They've been beaten by the men who hired them," Zhang said, then turned his head away. "The women who need work go to the city's labor pools where these men bring them back to the country, rape and beat them, and make them work the fields."

Zhang slept again, Feng smoked, and I opened the windows to keep from getting carsick. I thought of the prostitutes I had seen on the planes and in the hotel lobbies. Mao had insisted that men stop beating their wives. He admired women, reminding the men that women "hold up half the sky." Bride prices, female slavery, binding of feet, prostitution, child marriages, and female infanticide were all prohibited. But since the 1980s, equality for women seems to be a thing of the past. No women hold important political or business offices. Their feet are not bound, but the poor and uneducated are often traded and used in any way desired. In 1993 a group of men who traded in women, were caught by police; they had already abducted 1,800 women from the Beijing labor market and sold them in a distant province. In some villages retarded women are bought for cash or in exchange for a horse or pig. They are prized because they obey, bear children, and work hard in the fields. The killing of female babies, with its long history in China, is also on the rise again. It's reported that since 1990, a million baby girls go missing each year.

We drove through high mountain villages where women held up long skeins of garlic. After a long silence, Feng woke Zhang to translate for him so he could tell me the story of his life. He had been born in Kunming but during the Great Leap Forward he was sent to a labor reform camp near what was then the Burmese border and stayed for eighteen years. The famine had just begun and he went hungry along with millions of others. He hated country life and was often beaten. In 1976 he was allowed to return to his hometown. There was no work and his wife left him. Their child was raised by her grandmother. "It's not the work that was hard, it was to be hungry," he said, sipping from his ever present jar of green tea.

We passed an overloaded truck that had tipped into a ditch and had come to rest against a tree. The drivers, apparently expecting no help for a while, were making beds under a gray tarp beneath the back of the overhanging load. Moving uphill towards a blind hairpin turn, Feng suddenly accelerated. It took me a moment to understand what he was doing: he was trying to pass the truck in front of us as a logging truck on the other side was coming downhill toward us. I screamed into his ear: "NO!" He was so shocked his foot went for the brake and we were saved. Then he complained to Zhang that I shouldn't disrupt his driving.

On the next pass he tried it again and I yelled at Zhang that I wanted to stop, get out, and walk to Lijiang. Both men laughed at me and Feng continued at breakneck speed through the middle of villages, honking down horse carts and women burdened with baskets of vegetables. Surely this would be over soon. I was nauseous and asked again to stop. Finally Feng pulled up to a roadside restaurant. While he was outside at the communal bathroom, Zhang explained to me that Feng was fragile, that he had a drinking problem, that he had been suicidal—Zhang's way of consoling me. What made me feel even sicker was the thought of having to return to Kunming from Lijiang on this same road.

Feng emerged from the kitchen, having ordered for us since he was familiar with Yunnan cuisine. He had a sweet, fussy way of inspecting the food and insisted that we finish everything on our plates—advice from a man who had known starvation. Before the food came, he sat on the floor at a low table and ordered a water pipe, a hookah, which he lit and inhaled deeply. "Is that opium?" I asked Zhang. (Not an outrageous question since opium has become popular again.) He assured me it was tobacco, which the Yi people grow in these mountains as a crop and store in square towers along the road. Feng was a low altitude man, a driver used to the benign indolence of Kunming and the countryside south which borders Vietnam. "He's tired and doesn't want to go to sleep at the wheel," Zhang explained.

The food was green soybeans, broth with chopped up animal parts whose shapes resembled something out of the Burgess Shale, slivers of bacon, and onions swimming in rancid rapeseed oil. A cop car flashed by, then an ambulance with a battered front fender and a smoking radiator as if carrying victims from its own accident. We had already been driving seven hours and when I asked how much longer we had to go, the sky lowered down with a soft drizzle and Feng looked up and shrugged. All I could think of was how slippery the roads would be in the rain.

❖   ❖   ❖

Looking around, I wondered where the heaven was located to which one addressed such questions. Instead, I thought of the questions I'd asked an environmental consultant to the World Bank. We'd met at a hotel while feasting on rabbit burgers and beer. He had an all-American face and build and sandy hair, but having been educated at the London School of Economics, he spoke with the deadpan wit of the Brits. When I told him I'd just climbed Emei Shan, he looked out the window at a twenty-story high-rise: the Communist Party's new building. "That's the new Emei Shan," he said.

He had been working on water quality issues with the Chinese. For example, Kunming is a city of 1.8 million people and has no sewer system. Raw sewage along with heavy metals and phosphates from numerous factories upstream are dumped into the river and the reservoir used for the city's domestic water supply. There were no water treatment plants and if the Chinese did not purify the city's water, the algae in the reservoir would become so dense the water would be absorbed in their sponge. The city of Kunming would be waterless by the year 2000. In response, the Chinese had done nothing.

〜 STILL DRIVING. DARKNESS INFILTRATED POLLUTED SKIES AND THE ROAD GLISTENED. I'd had face-offs with death more than once and knew I didn't want to die on a remote road in a police state at the hands of a man whose mind had been shattered by hardships and famine. Any place but here, I whispered to myself, then tried to make a stupid pact with Feng: if he would slow down, I would buy him whatever he wanted in Lijiang. He shook his head modestly but his foot was less heavy as we climbed into ever higher mountains during the night.

It was eleven P.M. when we arrived in Dali. Because I had been moving for thirty-four hours, the inertia of my hotel bed constituted another kind of oscillation, a pitch and roll of gratitude that I had survived the ordeal of the road.

Dali marked the end of the Burma Road. The next day was the Butterfly Festival, which we missed because no one would tell us when it began or ended. But there had been traditional dances by one of the minority groups who lived in Dali, the Dai, whose everyday dress and headdress were even more elaborate and colorful than those of the Yi; we saw them swarming home on foot and in horse-drawn carts with bells on the harnesses all morning.

Apart from the festivities, Dali looked like a drug smuggler's haven, full of European and American rebels-without-a-cause who spoke Chinese. I hated the place despite its beguiling pagodas and a cerulean lake spreading out before the town in a wide valley. We moved on.

⋅◊⋅　⋅◊⋅　⋅◊⋅

Again I begged Zhang to tell Feng to drive more slowly, which Zhang refused to do, since, he said, it would make Feng lose face in front of me. I was going to say that losing face was better than being dead, but realized the remark would fall on the deaf ears of a man contemplating suicide.

During lunch I had asked Feng why he hadn't run away from his labor reform camp and crossed the border into Myanmar, what was then Burma. He said Burma was worse. No food at all, and anyway, the villagers would have turned him in to the authorities. I looked heavenward and asked this question: Where does one find sanctuary in such a place? Then my question was answered.

⋅◊⋅　⋅◊⋅　⋅◊⋅

We descended through a roof of clouds illuminated by moonlight. "The air was like champagne . . ." Peter Goullart exclaimed when he topped out on the ridge overlooking the valley surrounding Lijiang. Jade Snow Mountain loomed silver and snow banners flew from its 18,000-foot peak. Lijiang was embraced by mountains: everywhere white peaks rose up like picket fences, small villages and monasteries dotted the foothills, with the coil of a river wound through. Everywhere there were orchards of peach and almond trees and inside were flowers: peonies and roses climbing broken adobe walls.

The Valley of Horses, as Lijiang was sometimes called, is home to a small minority group of 200,000 people called the Naxi (pronounced "Nashi"). Descended from a Tibetan group, the Qiang (whom I'd seen cultivating their fields in Wolong), they are jolly, vivacious, and ruddy faced. Traditionally, the Naxi women run the markets, do all the business, herd the horses, and tend the fields, while the men care for babies, play music, and write poems.

Lijiang's ancient center, called Dayan, is a tight-knit village of tile roofs, cobblestone paths, and wandering canals lined with stone houses and stores. Blessedly off limits to automobiles, the small shops sell food, clothes, hardware, medicine, local carvings and paintings, cigarettes, sweets, and liquor. All walkways eventually give onto a small, stone-paved square where Tibetans set up stands to sell food and goods. "The Chinese wanted to take all this down and build high-rises," a resident painter told me. "But we Naxi said no. And they left it. Now they are glad because they have seen that what is a national treasure to us is a tourist attraction to others. They can have their fancy Western hotels."

The name *Lijiang* means "Beautiful River," and the river is the Yangtze, whose source was only recently found high on the Tibetan plateau by a French archeologist. Now the exquisite old town is surrounded by post-Communist urban sprawl which quickly becomes horse pastures and hay fields again.

Tibetans once ruled western China. During the Tang Dynasty they broke through the borders of Han China and raided the ancient capital of Chang'an. The Naxi came from the northeastern highlands of Tibet and took over the rich farming valleys where the indigenous P'ouy had always lived, forcing them up into the gorges and mountains above the Yangtze River and its tributaries, and keeping the well-watered and fertile plain for themselves. When the Tibetans lost the ground they had gained in China, they, too, retreated to the high plateaus.

In 1253 Khublai Khan invaded the western edge of what is now Yunnan Province, which had not been considered a part of the Middle Kingdom of China. The great Khan took over the Kingdom of Muli to the north but bypassed Lijiang because the Naxi king had paid homage to him in advance, knowing that the Khan's armies invaded only those who resisted him. That's been the hallmark of the Naxi people from the beginning: by being savvy and wise, cheerful and accommodating, they have kept their forgotten kingdom out of the fray.

Until 1949, when the Communist Party took over, Lijiang was a place where life was lived exuberantly. It was a favorite destination of Tibetans, a trading and arts center, the last major town on the caravan route to Lhasa, a place of tolerance and gaiety. The Naxi, numbering around fifty thousand and growing, are dark skinned with broad faces and easy smiles. They speak their own language, as well as Mandarin and Tibetan, and the small temples that dot the mountains just below snowline are painted gold and red—Tibetan in architecture and religious practice.

This valley was so isolated from the rest of the world that the lifeways of the people were never properly collected. Copious notes about Naxi rituals and the Dongba religion were made by Joseph Rock, an Austrian-American botanist and explorer who lived in Lijiang for almost thirty years. But they failed to include a sense of how ceremony and daily life merged. Only Peter Goullart's exuberant memoir of his ten years in Lijiang gives us a taste of how life was lived, of Tibetan merchants and lamas coming and going on the much traveled caravan route to Lhasa; of the ease and timelessness of village life; of Dongba shaman exorcisms and lovers' suicides; of tea shops and music concerts and parties.

⋅❖⋅ ⋅❖⋅ ⋅❖⋅

I had been told to look up a musician and ethnomusicologist in Lijiang named Xuan Ke. Thinking it would be difficult to find him I prepared myself for the usual rounds of questions and suspicions encountered elsewhere. Instead, the first person we asked said sweetly, "He lives just around the corner. In fact, there he is!"

A small-framed, handsome man approached. He had a square-cut face and sensuous lips and when I introduced myself, he smiled, holding out both hands in greeting. He spoke fluent English and didn't care that I was a friend of a friend of his: he simply welcomed me. All I knew about him was this: once a student of piano and conducting at the conservatory in Kunming, Xuan Ke spent twenty years in jail, from 1958 to 1978, and the scars on his wrists from the torture he endured there still showed.

"Now I have been a free man almost as many years as I was jailed," he said, as if astonished at his own realization. "If a man has a hard life at first, then the future is good. Now at sixty-six, I even have a ten-year-old daughter!" he said as we walked. He stopped to turn into a house. "Please come hear our music tonight. Seven o'clock." Then he was gone.

〜 IN THE AFTERNOON WE PICKED UP OUR NAXI TRANSLATOR, SI WENFENG, A YOUNG woman born in Lijiang who wanted to be a tourist guide. On our way to a mountain monastery where she knew the lama, she told me that her name means "wisdom peaks." We drove through foothill villages where wild rose bloomed and wide fields were crowded with mares and newborn foals. Looking out the back window of the car, I could see the central knot of Lijiang: its angled roofs made a design like the Tibetan knot of eternity. Ahead of us, to the north, were the white winding mountains after which Si Wenfeng had been named.

High up in the foothills, at 10,000 feet, Feng decided his small car could go no further, so we walked the red clay road the rest of the way. Ahead we could see a triangular peak with a dark fold down the middle like the central rib of a leaf. "Under that mountain is where the monastery lives," Si Wenfeng said. At a bend in the road we helped a farmer pull a horse-drawn cart out of a bog and in thanks he gave us a ride.

"Under construction" might have been a better name for China. Even this obscure temple was being rebuilt. Young Naxi men were cutting boards and poles with handsaws and inside the temple monks were cutting up pieces of paper on which sutras had been printed. These were rolled, tied with red string, and placed inside pottery statues of bodhisattvas, newly made. "We put the sutras inside the heart, forever to stay there," a doe-eyed young man said.

Another monk who spoke only Tibetan sat on the floor next to the statues and, with his fingers, made a series of graceful gestures called *mudras*—the Dharmachakra *mudra* and the Vitarka *mudra*—which signify the turning of the wheel of the Dharma. These gestures are practiced in order to link the physical with the spiritual, the body and the mind, with no discursive thought between. "I want to make sure the hands of these statues are right," he said. "That's why I am practicing hard."

The head lama of the monastery entered. For a long time he watched the young monk practicing *mudras*. His face was leathery and he had the sharp, clear eyes of a wily animal. When Si Wenfeng greeted him it was obvious that they were old friends. Her family came often to this temple. When we were introduced he said that many people from America had visited him and they were all Buddhists. "You too?" he asked, and I nodded. "Meiguo. Fojiao," I said. ("American. Buddhist.") He laughed at my two words of Chinese and his eyes twinkled. He flirted with the lovely Si Wenfang, then offered Zhang a pinch of snuff from a jade vessel hung around his neck on a gold chain. "From Madras, India," he said proudly, though he confessed he had never been there.

We went down to the monastery shop where the lama coveted an old pocket watch. When I offered to buy it for him, the young salesman said it wasn't for sale. Laughing, the lama pocketed it anyway. Back up in the meditation hall we watched the lama and his monks roll sutras and place them inside the statues. I asked if there were any monks living in the mountains nearby, hermits in the tradition of Milarepa (a Tibetan saint who lived alone in icy Himalayan caves practicing *tummo*, the ability to generate inner heat). The old lama's eyes brightened. "Yes," he said, then paused. "Five hundred years ago there was such a hermit. He lived above this monastery, just two hours walk from here. The hut he lived in was very small. He slept sitting up and didn't eat. Only nettles, just like Milarepa."

Five hundred years. He'd talked about the hermit as if he were still alive and showed me one of the statues in the hermit's likeness. I asked the lama if he had been to the hermit's hut. He said no, but that a visiting Rinpoche had walked to the spot not long ago. When I inquired about how I might find the path, he asked one of the young monks. The monk shook his head. He wasn't sure but gave vague directions which made me wonder if there might not be a hermit living there now. I gave the requisite donation, did three prostrations, and said good-bye.

Walking off the mountain late that day, we were joined by a herd of mares and foals. Two Naxi women in long blue dresses walked behind the animals, idling on their way home. This was the Valley of Horses: as I looked out across the basin below I saw pastures full of mares, geldings, foals, and mule colts everywhere. Watching the two Naxi women amble down a steep path into their village, Si Wenfeng said: "The Naxi are a matriarchal society. The women are in charge of things except that when we marry, we go to live at our husband's parents' house, not the other way around. Naxi men are lazy. Naxi women do all the work, and make all the decisions. Without us they would have nothing; they would starve."

๏   ๏   ๏

Feng waited for us at the bottom of the hill in his slick-soled city shoes and cardigan sweater. Driving back to Lijiang he honked his horn incessantly as villagers shot dirty looks at us. They were bringing in the last of the unplanted seedlings and harvesting enough food for the evening meal. Some women led mares toward home with young foals following. The colts gamboled down into an irrigation ditch, then shot across the road and down into another. Feng lay on his horn and when one of the young horses didn't move, he hit him in the hock with the car. I screamed in protest, to no avail. He only laughed at me. But the horse, a good-sized stud-colt, kicked back, deeply denting the car door. I gave a loud cheer.

๏   ๏   ๏

Fifty years ago pigs ran loose in Lijiang streets and the diet was decidedly Tibetan. Caravans brought yak butter tea, roast mutton, *tsampa* (barley), and *chang* (barley beer), and in social and sexual matters, a Tibetan-style joie de vivre reigned.

At the Din Din Cafe, Zhang talked to the owner's daughter who tantalized him with her tight blue jeans, black boots, and American cigarettes. While dinner was being cooked, she set up shots of Johnny Walker Red at the stand-up Western-style bar, while Feng made the rounds of the shops to buy a local brand of booze, which turned out to be pure grain alcohol. The first good meal I'd had in China was in that cafe. The only hazard was the pet turkey who roamed loose and cleaned your plate if you weren't vigilant.

The food was pan-fried soft noodles with vegetables, a plate stacked with pork chops, fresh steamed vegetables and rice, and the last course, which in China is always soup. My traveler's mirth was enhanced by the discovery of Dynasty wine, a dry red from a northwestern province. At seven o'clock, we went to hear Xuan Ke and his orchestra of Naxi musicians.

We reached the hall where the orchestra performed through a gate in a crumbling stone wall. It looked like a bombed-out school house, its dark recesses lit by candles. Metal folding chairs had been set up and soon enough they were filled with travelers—Germans, Australians, Brits, Canadians, and a few Chinese. The cost of admission was only ten yuan and concerts were given every other night all spring and summer. The musicians ambled in with cigarettes hanging from their lips. Coughing and spitting, they slowly tuned their ancient instruments.

Peter Goullart wrote: "When I was in Lijiang sacred concerts were usually held at some rich man's house. At intervals food and drinks were served to both the participants and the guests. The musical sessions were long and arduous but everybody was happy and attentive.

The instruments were carefully arranged in a long room, sometimes in the enclosed veranda, and the atmosphere was reverent and definitely religious, with the scent of incense burning in great brass burners . . . The old musicians, all formally dressed in long gowns and makwas, took their seats unhurriedly, caressing their long white beards."

Now there was no rich man's house, no food and drink at intermissions, no costumes. The orchestra was made up of peasants and middle-class Chinese, twenty or thirty of them, dressed in American-style clothes or blue Mao suits. One elderly musician's frail frame was bent almost double and another was tall and gaunt with a white beard that reached to the middle of his chest.

When all the candles were lit, Xuan Ke stood and spoke to the audience in a carefully modulated voice, soft but powerful: "Music is medicine. It can bring life or death. Both players and listeners must always be careful!"

As night came on, the room dimmed and candlelight was obscured by swirling cigarette smoke. Xuan Ke described the instruments of Dong Jin, or Taoist music in the ensemble: the *dizi* and *bobo*, flutes; the *pipa* and *sugudu*, pipes; the *sanxian* and the *guzheng*, strings; the *huqin*, a bowed string instrument; drums, cymbals, and clappers, *tishou*; *muyu*, a globular wooden fish; and the beautiful cloud gongs, *yunluo*.

Next, Xuan Ke introduced the players starting with the oldest and most venerated: Sun Ziming, tiny, wizened, born in 1913, had begun studying music at age fourteen and was skilled at most of the instruments in the orchestra. By trade a traditional paper cutter, he now played the cloud gongs. Zhou Yin Xian, 81, tall and lean with a white beard that reached his waist. Once a caravan driver on the southern Silk Road between Chengdu and Lhasa, a round-trip that took seven months. Along the way, he learned Tibetan songs and later became interested in playing music. He Linghan, born in 1930, potbellied and world weary, played in the local opera company as a teenager, and worked as an accountant. He Hongzhang, 1930, was accomplished on all the plucked and bowed string instruments and had been a member of the orchestra since the 1940s. Chen Qiuyuan, 1937, played the drums, cymbals, and some string instruments. Yang Zenglie, 1939, handsome and gentle, was a professional musician, as well as being a published scholar on ancient music, and played all the instruments in the orchestra. Wang Chaoxin, 1954, a happy-go-lucky pig farmer who played flutes, strings, and the *bili* (a Naxi flute) for local dances; Niu Shiguang, 1964, learned the plucked lute from his father who also had been a member of the orchestra; and Huang Limei, the youngest, born in 1974, and the only woman, played the *guzheng*, a zither. "We call her our escapee from karaoke," Xuan Ke said. "She's not like other young people. She believes in real Chinese music. She's very serious." Then he introduced himself, Xuan Ke, 1930, next to the oldest, plays bowed string instruments and tries to bring Dong Jin music to the world.

Sometimes funny, sometimes serious, Xuan Ke asked us to close our eyes: "It is important to quiet your mind and let the music enter you. Do not think of other things, please." After a long silence, he asked us to watch as he pointed to places on his body where the music might enter: between the eyebrows, in the palms of the hands, the solar plexus, behind the knees, on the bottom of the feet. "If the music is allowed to enter you, you will become healed. Look at us! We are never sick in Lijiang!" Xuan Ke exclaimed, laughing, as the musicians behind him coughed. "Now you will hear our music from South of the Clouds."

He hit a large gong and silence fell over the crowd. Picking up his tiny two-stringed instrument, Xuan Ke quietly motioned for the playing to start. In a tremulous voice the old paper cutter chanted the title of the first song: "wu hu oo ii." The song was called "Eight Trigrams," with words taken from the *I Ching*. A sound rose up: an insistent, plangent wall of human voices, cymbals, gongs, drums, and string instruments, some plucked, others bowed, all gyrating together in a slow, sonorous, squeaking, groaning, pots-and-pans surge, punctuated by a deep-cadenced drum and the sudden slurry of cymbals, like heavy-limbed horses walking. The texture of the music was heterophonic, all melodies followed the same tune, with each strand embellished slightly differently so that a repetitive complexity emerged. Then sharp, high, wavering voices came in—the singing was shrill—until hand cymbals and the fish-shaped drum sounded, and the gong rang, then the handheld temple bell, bringing the piece to an end.

After "Eight Trigrams," we heard "Waves Washing the Sand," "Ten Offerings to the Gods," and "The Song of the Water Dragon." Each piece had a distinct orchestration yet there was a sameness throughout, the music having emerged from a place and time more homogeneous than ours. The heavy-footed rhythm moved forward, punctuated with bells and percussion, aerated by high cheeping flutes, and I was brought back to earth again by the rich resonance of the Chinese zither.

My eyes were closed and sounds entered me in elliptical sequences like Chinese narrative, recurring cycles and spheres oscillating within more spheres. When Peter Goullart heard these same tunes sixty years before, played by the parents and grandparents of some of these musicians, he wrote: "It was majestic and inspiring and proceeded in falling and rising cadences. Then, as a climax, the great gong was struck. I have never heard in China such a deep and sonorous gong . . . It was a recital of cosmic life as it was unfolding . . ."

What I was listening to was a living tradition of folk and ceremonial music from eighth- and ninth-century China, a tradition that had been squelched and revived several times, once when Confucius's books of music were burned, and again during the last siege of the Cultural Revolution when traditional music was completely disallowed. Now this ancient art was being revived in a remote corner of a wide mountainous land, and for the first time during my stay in China, I knew I was seeing a fragment of culture, like a very sick patient, being brought back to life.

"Someday the world will know a tribe called the Naxi. After so many years of no freedom, I am hurrying to preserve our culture." Xuan Ke said. "So much ruined, so much lost. I hope I am not too late. This kind of music brings all listeners and all players into harmony with nature, eliminating noise and war while promoting peace. It is music that comes from an expression inside the heart, which is what makes it truly religious."

ᗌ THE NEXT DAY I VISITED XUAN KE AT HIS HOUSE. HIS YOUNG DAUGHTER SANG IN the courtyard. Up stairs so steep and narrow a fat person might not have fit, I found myself in Xuan Ke's tiny book-lined study. He lay Bruce Chatwin's book of essays, *What Am I Doing Here*, on my lap, and opened it to the pages written about Lijiang. Then he showed me other books friends had sent in German, English, French, and Chinese. Xuan Ke's taste was eclectic: he read poetry, musicology, novels, essays, his tape deck piled high with classical music both Western and Eastern—the very music, he said, that had kept him alive during his twenty years in prison. "Every day I hummed that music to myself inside my head. It kept the demons away. But let's not talk about that now," he said pensively.

The phone rang. It was a woman from the Asian Music Society in England. She had asked the orchestra to tour Britain in October with performances in London, Hull, Oxford, Manchester, and Birmingham. "You must come and hear us there," Xuan Ke said. I agreed I would.

While making tea, he talked about his family. His grandfather had been a traditional doctor who traveled by donkey from village to village with medicinal herbs. "He cured many people and also set broken bones," Xuan Ke said. Once his grandfather set the broken hand of a young boy and stayed on for a month at the boy's house to make sure it healed properly. Moved by the doctor's devotion, the boy's father gave his daughter to the doctor for a bride. Xuan Ke's grandfather accepted, and after the wedding the couple traveled together into Tibetan, Yi, Miao, and Pumi villages in the foothills of the Himalayas.

"During the Feast of the Full Moon in a Miao village, my father was born," Xuan Ke said. But when his father was twelve years old, he was abducted by a local leader and kept as a slave for ten years. When the slaveowner was taken ill, the boy called on his grandfather for help. The grandfather came and healed the slaveowner who, in return, gave the boy back to his parents.

By then Xuan Ke's father was twenty-two. While panning for gold near Tiger Leaping Gorge, where the Yangtze River sluices down a steep canyon a few miles north of Lijiang, he heard a woman singing. Her voice was so beautiful that he came back every day to listen. Finally, he convinced her to come to Lijiang with him. They traveled at night by horse and mule and carried a bag of gold dust. "When they arrived in Lijiang, he rented a house with the gold. This is the very house and this is where I was born," Xuan Ke said.

He stood up, a startled look on his face because we were coming to the part of the conversation he dreaded: his life in prison. Xuan Ke looked young and vigorous for his age, especially for a man who had lived through solitary confinement, repeated torture, and starvation, and who had been worked as hard as a draft horse during his healthy years.

It had begun to rain and the smell of mountain air slipped into the room as Xuan Ke put on a tape of Handel's *Water Music*. "Much of what I am has to do with Dr. Joseph Rock and the other foreigners who lived in Lijiang. They liked it here—the Dutch and Germans, Russians, and Americans. My father was hired to work for Joseph Rock in 1922 as a servant and guide, while Rock collected plants, studied the languages of the minorities, took notes on the Naxi religion and the *dongbas*—the shamans. Dr. Rock was very difficult, very bad tempered. He was famous for that, but he worked very hard."

After one year with Dr. Rock, Xuan Ke's father worked for the foreign missionaries in Lijiang. He cooked Western-style food and helped them in many ways since he spoke Tibetan, Yi, Mandarin, Naxi, and soon learned English, German, and some Dutch. He was the first Naxi to be sent to missionary school. The other villagers called him the "foreign slave." "Later they called me the foreign slave's son," Xuan Ke said, smiling.

In 1929 Xuan Ke's father guided an expedition to the Yunnan-Burma border. The dore Roosevelt and his brother Kermit were in the hunting party and they shot a panther on the trip, the same expedition on which they killed a panda. The Roosevelts tipped Xuan Ke's father so well that he was considered a rich man. "That's when he built the second story on the house, the room where we are sitting. At the time it was the only two-story house in Lijiang."

Xuan Ke was christened and sent to missionary school where he was the only Naxi child. By age eleven, his English was so good he was enrolled in boarding school in Kunming. "There were ten pianos there," he remembered. "And many kinds of instruments. I had a good voice like my mother and the teachers told me I should become a musician. I studied piano, voice, then conducting. What I learned was mostly Western music. Later, I learned the ceremonial music of the Han Chinese which is what we now play." He looked out the window and smiled. "Come back and hear us again tonight. You may learn something more."

~ A HATCH OF FLIES BROKE OUT ALL OVER LIJIANG THE AFTERNOON WE TRIED TO FIND Puji Monastery. Feng drove us through villages and wide fields where mares and foals grazed between women planting vegetables. The red clay roads, barely wide enough for one vehicle, were wet. We bumped up and up until the road became too narrow and treacherous, then walked the rest of the way. Si Wenfeng wasn't sure exactly where the monastery was. We climbed up dry canyons and crossed terraced fields past mule colts and the uneven, hand-made adobe farmhouses whose roofs did not quite touch the tops of the walls.

In one village a row of trees curved around a house, making a garden wall of exposed roots. Another wall was made of brush threaded with wild rose. Baby chicks scattered every-where at our feet and, at midday, cocks were crowing. The air was sultry—winter becoming spring becoming summer—and it drizzled warm rain. As we scrambled up a slope I mis-took the repetitive cuckoo bird's call for a factory whistle. A band of horses grazed between village gardens and the beginning of steep foothills, and for the first time since arriving in China, I could breathe and feel and smell and hear.

From a thicket of shrubs we came on a high terraced field where two young men were working and asked the way to the monastery. "Up through there," they said, pointing to a forest of spindly trees. A pine wind blew all the flies away. In a clearing, an ancient wall con-tained a family graveyard, and the stones looked like small trees in the forest, growing slowly and silently for hundreds of years. Then we came to the outer wall of the temple.

The rain had turned frigid. The wall enclosed a tile-roofed temple complex dug into the side of a mountain. We followed it through trees, up hills, down the other side, but couldn't find a gate. Once, after I had fallen behind, I saw Zhang and Si embrace shyly but when I caught up, they were all business again. Finally we came on the entrance to the monastery: two red gates badly in need of paint creaked open. A sign over the entrance read *Daofu*— "good luck." The interior courtyard looked abandoned. Perhaps they meant to say, "Aban-don hope all ye who enter here," as had been written at the entrance to the Tibetan monastery I'd once attended. In the corners of the covered entryway dried pea vines were piled to the ceiling, and beyond, two gnarled cherry trees graced the open courtyard flanked by pots of bonsai peach, pine, and palm. I looked up at a row of second-story windows but saw no faces; Zhang called out, but no one appeared.

Then rain came hard, splashing across each step to the temple. The outer ochre columns gave way to ones that were blood red, and blue and white knots of eternity deco-rated the corbels and rafters. I ran up the stairs and entered the meditation hall. One candle was burning, the flame convulsing sideways as rain on thin roof tiles shattered all other sound. Still no one appeared.

A wall of wooden doors, folded back on either side of the entrance, was painted with scenes of Buddhist stories and had been badly scratched. Inside, *tankas* (paintings) of great teachers and bodhisattvas hung from crumbling walls. I walked by empty incense braziers and faced the main altar, bent down and performed the requisite three prostrations, then turned on my heel. A wall of rain in the courtyard hid the old trees for a moment; their twisted arms showed through slowly as if to tell me with some weird botanic gesture how emptiness is formed, how silence is made, how formlessness is chiseled from form.

Two old caretakers appeared. "We have been sleeping," they reported quietly, because in the country it is normal for the Chinese to take a nap after the noon meal. From a narrow corridor the old lama appeared, barely five feet tall. He carried a toy-sized shovelful of em-bers and ashes and, nodding hello as he passed, proceeded to the incense burner, a rectan-gular bucket on three iron legs. In the residual ash he flattened an indentation that looked like a miniature caldera. Into this he dropped new embers, shaping them into the form of a mountain with the back of his tiny shovel, sprinkling green powder on top, as if to represent trees. In a moment, the peak began smoldering.

When the rain began to let up we looked in toward the courtyard and saw the sky brighten. The lama said he cared for all the plants and trees, that the large trees, the *sakura* (cherry trees), were three hundred years old. From behind dripping eaves a curtain of gray storm clouds pulled apart to reveal the snowcapped mountains that separated Han China from Tibet.

When the lama was a young man, not yet twenty years old, he had walked alone to Lhasa in order to study the Dharma and said it had taken him three months to get there. Bandits stopped him all along the way but when they found he had nothing, owned nothing, they let him pass. He had come from a poor family and had to beg along the caravan trail. Sometimes when he was lonely and sad to have left his parents behind, he cheered himself with the knowledge that he would soon be in Lhasa, studying with a real Rinpoche, and that nothing else mattered.

He was now eighty-six years old and had come to this temple from Wenfeng Monastery fourteen years earlier because the resident lama there had died. "Now I will die here," he said. As he spoke the rain started again but more softly this time. He looked surprised when I told him I had studied with a Rinpoche and had spent a day with the sixteenth Karmapa (an important incarnate lama) when he visited the United States. The lama wasn't sure whether to believe me at first (the translation from Tibetan to Naxi to Chinese to English didn't help) but when I talked about the Karmapa's love of birds and his big aviary in India, the old lama started laughing, "Yes, yes . . . that is him, that is the same Karmapa."

He told me that he'd had visitors from Europe and the United States who had studied Buddhism and even spoke and wrote Tibetan, though he couldn't imagine how the Dharma had gotten all the way over the ocean. I told him it went there the same way it got to China from India: by people on caravan routes who brought not just things, but ideas.

Before leaving, when I thought no one was looking, I did another three prostrations, then three more, and three more. Westerners find the idea of bowing down abhorrent, yet it's not bowing down at all, but rather exerting oneself physically to remove the mundane conditioning of consciousness and ego. I could have and should have continued all day.

The rain let up and when I stood I saw that the lama had been watching me. It was late afternoon and the shadow of the mountain behind the temple had swung over the monastery like a great cape or a carapace which I hoped might protect this place from future political ills. The lama said that during the Cultural Revolution, no one lived in the temple and they practiced at home very quietly. When I asked him what the scenes on the folding doors were, he said, scenes of Shambhala, the future Buddhist Shangri-la. The caretaker, who had once been a lama but had gotten married so that now he only worked there, began preparing for evening meditation. Reluctantly I turned to leave.

The storm had blown over but the darkness of late afternoon spread into the sky. We thanked them all and the caretakers closed the doors behind us. But when I looked back, the old lama was standing in the gate bowing over and over and I turned and bowed to him, walking backwards until I was in the pines, sliding downhill on fallen needles.

~ THE NEXT MORNING I RAN INTO XUAN KE IN LIJAING'S NARROW LANES. IT SEEMED impossible not to run into him; like a politician, he knew everyone and everyone knew him, but he wasn't running for office, only trying to resurrect a five-thousand-year-old culture in a very remote place. "Come to my house," he said, and I followed him up the creaking stairs to his study.

He closed the door, looked at me, then leaned very close, whispering: "Use soft words, please, when you write this. It is very important. Do you understand what I mean? My life could be in danger. Also, say that I thank Deng Xiaoping who gave me my freedom. I would not be alive today if it were not for him."

There was a silence, then he began: "I was in prison for twenty years. It began in 1948 when I was part of a student resistance group against the Kuomintang, fighting for more democracy. But I was so stupid. I could not lie. I stated openly that I was a member and there were spies among the students, so quite soon I was caught and sent to prison for three months. I was seventeen years old and when my father found out where I was, he got someone from the church to write a letter saying: 'Please let him go. He is so young and naive.' I got out. The missionaries from the conservatory begged me not to join again. They offered to send me to California to become a great conductor. But I joined again, this time one of the groups operating in the mountains, called the forest army. I was caught again.

"When Mao took over I was released and went back to Kunming. I became the conductor of an orchestra. We had to play revolutionary music but I always added Western music and rewrote Chinese music with Western harmonies. I became known and began writing articles and music reviews. Always honest. And so, my reputation grew. But high trees catch a lot of wind, the old proverb goes.

"Some things happened and I needed money, so I asked my sister who lived in Calcutta, her husband was Tibetan and was an aide to the Dalai Lama. This was now 1958. A cousin in Hong Kong sent me cash via the Bank of China. I did not know this was the bank that funneled money to the Kuomintang spies. The police came around and forced me to give addresses of my relatives. I refused. So they put me in prison and gave me nothing to eat. Days went by. They did not believe my story about the money. Finally I gave them some addresses, but that was not enough. They wanted names of other people. I was very scared. After I gave them some names, they set me free, but I was not allowed to leave Kunming and my reviews were no longer published. Everything Western—music, songs, and opinions— was prohibited. Mao went around asking all the artists and intellectuals to criticize his government, to help him make it better. We thought he was the second coming of Christ and so we did as we were told. But he betrayed us. Those of us who spoke our minds were punished. It was his clever way of purging the country of enemies so that he could do anything he wanted without dissent. At a meeting of artists I spoke out and said: 'Do you want to see a wall? Go out into the street and even in daylight take a lamp with you, because there is darkness at noon.' After that, I was labeled a rightist.

"Soon after, I was put in prison again. I'd had a love affair with a singer. She wasn't very good but she was ambitious, and she denounced me to the authorities. I went to prison for seven years, this time on the Vietnamese border in a tin mine. My father was also in prison because of his contacts with the Western missionaries. He died in prison in 1959. I never saw him all those years.

"One day a guard asked me if I could paint. I couldn't, but I said yes. I was told to paint eleven communist leaders—Marx, Mao, Engels, Chou En-lai. I got a better room and was allowed to go to town for supplies. Everyone was happy for me. They put up their thumbs. When I was finished with the paintings one of the prisoners who was a spy asked me which one was the hardest to paint and I said, Marx, because of his hair and beard.

"Three days later all three thousand prisoners were ordered to stand outside. Guards in six watchtowers were armed with machine guns. There were police dogs, then the commander asked the spy who had talked to me about the painting to repeat what I, a bad man, had said about the greatest leader on earth, Marx. He told the story.

"'Is it true?' they asked me. I said yes. They came behind me and held my arms so tight I thought they had been dislocated. They said I hated Marx, asked me to admit it. I screamed, 'No, that's not what I meant. I was just talking about a technical problem.' But the prisoners started screaming, 'Beat him! Xuan Ke is a wicked man!'

"When the guards produced a rope, someone said it wasn't good enough, that they must use the wire rope, which they brought out, and they hung me by the wrists. The skin burst. Blood came out. My hands blackened. I do not know how long I hung there in the sun because I lost consciousness after a while. When I came round I was lying on a plank bed. Flies covered my hands and I had no power to chase them off. After, I could never use my right arm properly again.

"I lay in bed for a year. No strength to work. A doctor told me to practice piano in the air with my hands to make them strong, but it didn't work. The next year I had to work in a coal mine. I had a gas lamp on my head because it was dark and dangerous. There were many casualties, many deaths down there. I had good musical ears and when I heard something wrong in the mines I warned everyone, and by this I saved many.

"The next year the political climate improved a little. I was told that if anything was wrong I should report it. I said I had been unfairly accused of contacting the Dalai Lama. But I was not allowed to say that they were wrong and I was right, so I got an extra three years.

"One night I talked in my sleep, in English. In the morning I was accused of practicing English during the night, implying that I wanted to escape. For this I was taken away and beaten. They locked me in an isolation cell for seven months. There were forty-two little ventilation holes in the cement under the wall. The cell was 1.2 square meters. At night, water dripped on my head. I begged the guards to do something but they just laughed. 'That is your own sweat,' they said. Some prisoners went blind in those cells. That is why I rubbed my eyes with the water.

"All those days I practiced breathing slowly. I prayed and meditated and hummed music to myself. Also I sang a Naxi song, 'Wo Tzu,' to scare away the demons. Sometimes the sun glimmered through the holes and I could see the mountains. I counted the trees. I believed that if all the trees remained standing I had nothing to fear, but if one of them should fall over things would turn out badly for me. I received only vegetables and rice once a day. After the meal I thought about the future. I wanted to return to Lijiang, get married, write. I thought about music, about the sacred music that had helped keep me alive.

"When those seven months were over I had to work in a factory where we washed tin. In 1975 an order came from Beijing. Mao said that prisoners were not to be beaten any longer and we had to be paid. We would now be rehabilitated into proper workers. Everybody was happy. The factory was no longer guarded although our freedom of movement was limited. I had met a young woman from the village nearby and wanted to get married. Some of her relatives were also in prison and they thought I was too old—I was 45 and she was 19. But finally we were given a leave to get married.

"In 1977, when the Gang of Four was disbanded most of us were set free. But freedom didn't come to much in those days. I had already lost twenty-one years of freedom. I got a job in a nearby sawmill but still had to report to the authorities regularly. In the evenings I taught English, which was a great success, and later I got a teaching certificate. My wife and

I moved back to Lijiang. At first I rented a house, just like my father, and spent all my time in the library, studying Taoist and Dongba scriptures and thinking about the purpose of sacred music.

"During those seven months in solitary confinement I realized that all singing and music arose from fear, the fear of death. In the Stone Age people believed that spirits devoured the body after death—also real wild animals devoured the living—so these had to be chased away. Ksj, ksj, ksj! Go, go! That's what the songs say, and with them, wild gesticulations. From these arose songs and dance.

"Now I spend my life of freedom thinking about these things, studying the early music of China, Tibet, and of the Naxi. This early music still has the form and content of the first songs. There are sounds in this music to chase away demons, to chase away tigers. In the Naxi language, the word for fear sounds almost like the word for spirit. I think they are the same."

⚭   ⚭   ⚭

Xuan Ke suddenly looked at his watch. "Oh, I have forgotten. The ten of us who are going to London on tour have to go to the hospital for medical exams. Could you give me a ride?"

We wound through the tangled streets of Lijiang and entered the courtyard of the hospital. Inside, the orchestra members were lined up in chairs, all smiling. Xuan Ke introduced me. "She is going to come to London." They all nodded and smiled: Hao, hao . . . yes, yes. "On October 8th. . . ." Then a nurse whisked him away.

Naomi Shihab Nye
One Village

It is fifteen years since I have seen my grandmother. I feel some guilt about this, but her face, when we meet in the village, betrays no slant of blame. She is glad to see me. She blesses me with whispered phrases, Mohammed this, Mohammed that, encircling my head with her silver ring. Later she will ask, "Why didn't you ever write a letter?" and the guilt will return, unabsolved by fact: *She can't read. Who would have thought she'd want a letter?* I had forgotten she is so small, barely reaching my shoulder as I hug her tightly, kissing both cheeks. I am stunned with luckiness; so much can happen in fifteen years.

The village smells familiar—a potent soup of smoke, sheep wool, water on stone. Again it is the nose retrieving memory as much as eyes or ears—I poke into courtyards, filled suddenly with lentil broth, orange blossom, olive oil soap. Whole scenes unfold like recent landscapes; a donkey who once entered the room where we were eating, a dusty boy weeping after a wayward kickball knocked him on the head. I was a teenager when last here, blind in the way of many teenagers: I wanted the world to be like me. Now there is nothing I would like less. I enter the world hoping for a journey out of self as much as in. I come back to this village remembering, but it is more like I have never been here before. This time I am awake.

"What do you do every day?" I ask my grandmother. She replies in Arabic, *cod.* Every day I sit. What else would you want me to do?

But I will find this is not quite true. Each morning she prays, rising at 4:30 to the first muezzin's call. It seems strange that the sun also rises this early. The days stretch out like gauze—we are pulled up from sleep by too much brightness.

Each morning my grandmother walks across the road to *the cow*, singular, to carry home a teakettle of fresh warm milk. Take me with you, I say. And she will take me, laughing because I like this black and white cow enough to touch it on the head and thank it, *Shookrun, haleeb*. She speaks to cows, my grandmother will say later, pointing at me. This is a girl who speaks to cows.

Every day she lights the oven, fat stone mound heated by the dung of sheep and goats, *taboon* for bread cooked on the black rocks. She enters barefooted, her headdress drifting about her. "Could be dangerous," says my father, "I don't think she should light it anymore," but it is one of the ways she remains a vital part of her corner of the village, one of the things she does better than anyone else.

Her face is deeply mapped, her back slightly bent. Three years ago she made a pilgrimage to Mecca, became a *Hajji*. For a year afterward, she wore only white. Today she alters this slightly, wearing a long white dress embroidered with green over black-and-white pajamas. It is cool here in the West Bank in late May; people think of the whole Middle East as a great hot desert, but here in this high, perched village the days feel light and breezy, the land a music of terraced hills.

Feelings crowd in on me; maybe this is what it means to be in your genetic home. That you will feel on fifty levels at once, the immediate as well as the level of blood, the level of uncles, of weeping in the pillow at night, weddings and graves, the babies who didn't make it, level of the secret and unseen. Maybe this is heritage, that deep well that gives us more than we deserve. Each time I write or walk or think, I drop a bucket in. Staring at my grandmother, *my Sitti*, as she sits on the low bed, rocking back and forth in time with conversation, tapping her fingertips on her knees, I think, this is the nectar off which I will feed.

⤙ ⤙ ⤙

"Does he beat you?" she asks of my husband, back home in Texas. "No? Ah, good. Then he is a good man." It is simple to define things here. If God wills it, it happens. A bird poops on my head in the courtyard. "That means you will soon have a boy." Looking up, Sitti says, "It's an impolite mother who didn't put underpants on her baby." Conversation stops. My uncle slaps his head and laughs. "She's always saying things like that."

It's amazing what facts we have about each other. She knows I "write." What does that mean to someone who never did? I know her husband had three simultaneous wives, but my Sitti was in some way "favored." Her husband, my grandfather, died when I was five. We were living in St. Louis; my father lay in silence across his bed for a whole day. "Be kind to him," my mother whispered. My grandmother had a daughter, Naomi, *Naimeh* in Arabic, then five or more babies who died, followed by two sons, of which my father was the last. Naimeh had two children, then died suddenly. My grandmother was having my father at the same time Naimeh birthed her second boy. My grandmother suckled her son and grandson together, one at each breast. I know these things, I grew up on them. But this trip I want to find out more: the large bird-like tattoo on her right hand, for example, from where?

"Many years ago, a gypsy passed through. She was hungry and offered to tattoo someone in exchange for food. She poked pins in me and the blood poured out like water from a spring. Later the skin came off five times and I was left with this. Beautiful, no?" She turns her hand over and over, staring at it. It is beautiful. It is a hand preparing to fly away. I want to hold on to it.

Across the valley, a new Jewish settlement sits, white building blocks shearing off the graceful green hill. At night the lights make a bright outline. No people are visible from here—just buildings, and lights. "What do you feel when you look at that?" I ask my grandmother. "Do you feel like those are your enemies?" In 1948 she lost her home in the Old City of Jerusalem to Israeli occupiers. She moved with her family back to this village. I've always heard that my father's best friend was killed in his presence. My grandmother is a refugee who never went to a camp. My father was a refugee who moved to the United States and married an American. What does Sitti think about all this now, in a region the Arabs will only refer to as the West Bank *via* Israel? Does she feel furious or scared?

She waves at the ugly cats lurking in every corner of the courtyard. Most have terrible fur and bitten-off ears. She pitches a loquat pit at a cat with one eye, and it runs. "See those cats? One night last year an Israeli jeep drove into this village and let them all out. Everyone saw it. What could we do? I think about that. And I think about the good ghosts we used to have in the big room, who floated in the corners up by the ceiling and sang songs late at night after we were asleep. I used to wake up and hear them. Happy friendly ghosts, with warm honey voices, the ghosts of the ones under the ground who used to live here, you know? I tell you, they had parties every night. They were a soft yellow light that glowed. Then the Jews built that settlement across the valley and the ghosts were scared. They all went away. Now you wake up, you hear no singing. And I miss them."

⭑   ⭑   ⭑

My uncle, a stately Arab in a white headdress, functions as *mukhtar,* or mayor, of the village. He is proud of his new yellow-tiled bathroom. It has a toilet, sink, bathtub, and shower, as well as the traditional hole in the floor—for my grandmother. He is planning a new kitchen under the stairs.

His wife, a good-humored woman with square, manly eyeglasses, bore twenty children; eleven survived. Her dresses are a rich swirl of Palestinian embroidery—blue birds and twining leaves, up one side and down the other. Her two daughters remaining at home, Janan and Hanan, are the ones who can sew. Of herself, she says, "I never learned how."

Sitti lives with this family, our family, in one of the oldest homes in the village. My father estimates it at more than two hundred years. Stone walls and high arched ceilings grace the main room, where most of the visiting and eating take place. Sitti sleeps in her own smaller room off the court-yard. The rest of the family sleeps communally, parents on mattresses on the floor, guests on the beds. Everyone gets covered with weighty calico comforters stuffed with sheep's wool. I swear I have come back to something essential here, the immediate life, the life without refrigerated food.

"How did this rice pudding get so cool?" I ask dumbly one morning, and Hanan leads me to the stone cupboard where food is kept. It is sleek and dark, like the inside of a cave. She places my hand against the face of stone and smiles. Goat cheese floats in olive oil in a huge glass jar. A honeydew melon tastes almost icy.

One afternoon a breathless red-faced woman appears in the doorway with a stack of freshly-picked grape leaves. She trades them with my aunt for a sack of *marimea* leaves, good for stomach ailments, brewed in tea. I can see by their easy joking this is something they do often. The woman motions to me that I am to walk home with her, but I'm not sure why. Her Arabic is too jazzy for my slow ear.

Down alleyways, between houses where children spin tops on the flattest stones—as children our father taught us to pare the tops off acorns to make quick spinners—up ancient stairs, past a mosque with its prayer rugs and mats spread out, waiting. Where is this woman taking me?

I stand in the courtyard of her home. Pigeons are nesting in rusted olive oil tins nailed to the wall. Their soft songs curl on the air. The woman comes back with her hands full of square cakes of olive oil soap. She presses it upon me, saying, "Take this to America. You need this in America." She says other things I can't understand. Then she reaches into a nest and pulls out a small bird. She makes the motion of chopping off its head and I protest, "Oh, no! Please! I am not hungry." She wants me to eat this teenaged pigeon today or tomorrow. I tell her I can't eat it tomorrow either. She looks sad. It was a big gift she was offering. "I will take the soap to America," I say. We kiss and stare at one another shyly. A line of children crouches on the next roof, watching us; they giggle behind their hands.

⊷ ⊷ ⊷

What is this need to give? It embarrasses me. I feel I have never learned how to be generous. In a Palestinian refugee camp in Jordan last week, I was overwhelmed by offers of coffee and Pepsi showered on me as I passed. Would I ever do that in the United States? Invite a stranger in off the street, simply because she passed my house?

Here in the village, the gifts I have brought seem foolish when I unpack them. Pantyhose in rainbow colors, two long seersucker nightgowns for the older women, potholders, perfume. What else could I have brought that would better fit this occasion? A lawn of grass? A kitchen table, swoop of formica, so the girls might pare their potatoes sitting up at something, rather than crouched on the floor? Bicycles with sizzling thin wheels, so we might coast together down past the shepherd's field, past the trees of unripe plums? But I unpack a tube of Ben-Gay for Sitti (someone told me she needed this), a plastic bottle of Ecotrin, and give her instructions, like a doctor. I want to make it very clear she should never take more than two pills at once. She nods gravely. She tucks these prizes into her bodice, the front panel of her dress left open at one side like a giant pocket.

"Is there anything else?" she asks. And I run back to my suitcase, unfold a gauzy white scarf bordered with yellow flowers—someone gave me this in Pakistan—I carry it toward her like a child carries a weed-flower tentatively home to mother.

Now she smiles broadly, rocks back on her heels. This strange slash of cloth is a pleaser. She and my aunt unfold one another's presents, touching them and murmuring. This is the worst moment of all. I didn't bring enough, I think. I gaze nervously toward my father, who is smiling shyly. He unpacked his own presents for everyone the day before I arrived. "It's fine," he whispers to me. "We'll go buy them chocolates too. They like chocolates."

In the corner of the room sits a large old wooden trunk painted green. It wears a padlock—this is where Sitti stores her gifts, opening the lock with a key from between her breasts. She places her small pile carefully on top of whatever else is in there, and pats it all down. Janan teases her, "Can we see your treasures?" Sitti protests, locking the trunk hurriedly. "Not now," she says. "Not this minute." I think of the burglar alarms in America, the homes of old silver, furniture, shiny appliances, and remember the way I complain when somebody steals my trash can at night. And it seems very right that a Palestinian would have a trunk in the corner of the room, and lock it, and look at it often, just to make sure it is there.

⊷ ⊷ ⊷

In this village, which used to be famous for grapes, most of the grapes have died. A scourge came ten years ago, they say, and withered the crop. It has never recovered. Now the vines produce only leaves, if people are lucky. A few fields show traces of the old days: arbors where grapes once flourished, small rock shelters built so the people who gathered the grapes could rest in the shade. I want an agricultural expert like the ones we have in Texas to come analyze this soil. I want a farming miracle, right now, to give this village back its favorite food.

The loquats in my uncle's patio hang yellow-ripe and ready. Sitti won't leave the house alone, for fear someone will steal them. One day we almost get her to go to the Turkish baths in Nablus, but she remembers the tree. "I can't leave a ripe tree," she insists. We peel the loquats with tiny knives; their slick seeds collect in an ashtray.

We go for luncheon at the home of Abu Mahmoud, an elderly man known for his militant rhetoric. "I'm bored with him," confides my uncle. But when we arrive, Abu Mahmoud is only interested in talking about gardening. He leads me inch by inch around his property, introducing me to eggplants, peppers, apricot trees, squash. The apple tree will produce for the first time this year. He stuffs my pockets with unripe fruit—I beg him to stop. He crushes herbs between his fingers and holds them under my nose. Then he stands me on his balcony with binoculars, so I can stare at the Jewish settlement across the valley.

"No people live there," he tells me. "Just buildings. Maybe there are guns in the buildings. I'm sure there are guns."

"Are you scared?"

"I'm tired of fighting," he says. "All my life, we've been fighting. I just want to be sure of one thing—that when I wake up in the morning, my fig trees will still be *my* fig trees. That's all."

This sounds reasonable enough.

Another day I'm walking with my father and two old men to Abu Mahmoud's house, to deliver some sweets as a thank-you gift, when an Israeli tank pulls up and trains its gun on us. "Why are you doing this?" I shout in English at the tank. And a soldier rises out of the top and stares at me curiously. I wave my fist as my father tries to quiet me. "What *right* do you have?"

Several years before the official beginning of the Intifada, I know firsthand why little boys throw stones.

◦ ◦ ◦

The wedding picture of my parents hangs high on my uncle's wall. It's slightly crooked; I keep scouting for a ladder, to straighten it. One day I realize how long it has been hanging there. "Did you put that up in 1951?" I ask my grandmother, a woman unsure even of her own age. She says, "I put it up when I got it." My father looks serious in the picture, thin, darkly intense, in a white linen jacket hanging nearly to his knees. My mother, fair and hopeful at his side, already learning about pine nuts and tabooleh. In how many houses have they lived? And suddenly I want to leave the picture crooked, because it may be the single icon of our lives that has stayed in one place.

◦ ◦ ◦

My father and I hike to the tomb of Sheikh Omar, high on a hill. We must overstep the lentil fields to get there. My father stoops to pluck a handful of fresh green lentils, saying, "Once you eat them raw, you never forget the taste." Sometimes I feel this way about my whole life. Who was Omar, when did he live? My father says he was a disciple of Mohammed. He lived a long time ago. The villagers know this is his tomb, so they have built a rugged mound of a mosque to honor him.

Inside, faded prayer rugs cover the floors. A ring of half-burnt candles stands in one corner. We take off our shoes and kneel. I don't really know how to pray like a Muslim, but I know there is something very affecting about people putting down shovels and brooms five times a day to do this. I like how life continues in the rooms where someone is praying. No one stops talking or stares; it is a part of life, the denominator. Everything else is a dancing away.

◦ ◦ ◦

My father wants to show me his land. He bought it in the 1960s, before we came to Jerusalem to live for a year. Now he doesn't know what to do with it. Who can build here, knowing what shakiness sleeps in the ground? Yet people do. They do it every day. In recent years the Israelis have taken to surrounding villages with wire, calling them military zones, and ousting the villagers. The village of Latroun, near the monastery famous for wine, is flattened and gone. I remember it fifteen years ago as a bustling place. Its complete disappearance strikes me as horrendous and bizarre. This is only one erasure of many; in which camp or town do those villagers now reside?

My father's land is steep and terraced, planted with olive trees—five big ones, five small. When my aunt notices a broken branch, she stoops to stroke it, asking, "Why? Why?" She tries to tie it up again with a stalk of wheat.

"I could make a good house here," my father says wistfully "It would make my mother very happy. It would make *your* mother very unhappy. Do you know, my mother's one great hope is that her American son will build a house and come back here to live? How could I ever do that?" I feel a sadness in my father which this land brings out, lays clean before us.

He asks why he is obsessed with property. In Dallas he scouts for condominiums, buys a block of duplexes, renovates it for resale. "Lots of people are that way these days," I tell him. "It's not just you."

"But you don't feel like that?"

My husband and I own our home and a swatch of Texas hillside. The only land that's ever really interested me is the rolling piece of blank paper on my desk. Then again, I'm not a refugee. We've been robbed five, six times, and came the closest to imagining what a refugee might feel. But we had insurance. A refugee has no insurance. A refugee feels violated in a way he might try the rest of his life to understand.

I tell my father I like his land.

◦ ◦ ◦

We walk to a place called the Museum of Curiosity to see a woman who sells "souvenirs." She's big and ruddy, a recent widow, and welcomes us with all kinds of exclamations and flourishes. Her shop offers a jumble of Bedouin coffeepots and amber beads.

I am intrigued by the massive clay pots lining her porch. At my grandmother's house, two of these stand in the courtyard, holding water. I know they were made in this village, which was once a well-known center for pottery. Why not today? My grandmother told me, "The clay went away."

I ask the lady if she sells her graceful pots or keeps them.

She throws up her hands. "Oh, the Israelis love to buy these. Just today a man came and will return later with a truck to pick up a hundred. Maybe they use them for flowers, I don't know."

"Show me the hundred," I say.

She leads me up the hill to another small house and motions me in.

A whole congregation of giant hundred-year-old pots sits gathered, some natural pink clay color, some marked with a blurred zigzag border or iron oxide lines, propped against one another, holding one another up. Their fat-lipped mouths are all wide open. I want to fall down into their darkness, hide there until I learn some secret perpetually eluding me. I want to belong to a quieter time, when these pots stayed living with the hands that made them. I am very sad these pots are going away.

She'll get more, she tells my father. She'll go to smaller villages and buy them up. It's hard times, she says, and people will sell what they have to keep going.

⋅◦⋅ ⋅◦⋅ ⋅◦⋅

We eat dinner with Abu Akram, my first cousin, age fifty-five. This trip I have tried to clarify relationships. For the first time I met a beautiful olive-skinned second cousin named *Sabah,* morning, and we teased each other like sisters.

Abu Akram is at the moment a subject of controversy. He is building a three-story house that will be the tallest one in the village. No one likes it; they claim it blocks the sky. But he wants his whole family to live under one roof, and this is the only way they can have enough room. His sons went away to the Virgin Islands to make some money, but decided to come back. One tells me how lonely he was for his village. "If my sons and daughters do not know their *own real place,* what difference does money make?"

We eat stuffed grape leaves, *hummos,* and *frikke* soup, a delicate broth thickened with wheat. We peel oranges for dessert.

Over the table hangs a hand-tinted portrait of a young man. I ask if this is another cousin.

Abu Akram says no, this is a boy who was in school while he was still the principal. The boy was shot down last year by an Israeli soldier, near the post-office, after someone threw a stone at the tires of the soldier's jeep.

Someone threw a stone? Did this boy throw the stone?

Abu Akram shrugs. "It was never clear. He used to be very good in math. I put the picture up because we all liked him."

⋅◦⋅ ⋅◦⋅ ⋅◦⋅

I ask my grandmother why things happen as they do, and she says God wants them to. I think of a poem by a Vietnamese refugee girl which ends, "God cannot be mean to me forever." I ask my grandmother if God can be mean. She looks at me for a long time and her eyes seem to grow paler. I don't think she ever answers.

⋅◦⋅ ⋅◦⋅ ⋅◦⋅

I ask my grandmother if I may see her hair and she shakes with laughter. "It is only as long as a finger," she says, holding up a finger.

"I don't care. I want to see it." She keeps it so well-hidden under her scarves, it is hard to imagine.

"Then get up tomorrow morning at four o'clock before prayers," she says. "My hair will be visible at four in the morning."

I set my clock.

At four she is still asleep, on top of her covers. I poke her shoulder. "Where hair?" I ask. At 4 A.M. I have no verbs.

She bounds up laughing. "Here, here, here." She unpins her white overscarf and the satiny green and yellow one underneath. She unknots a quilted maroon cap that lives under the scarves and shakes out long strands of multicolored hair, gray, white, henna-red. I touch its waves. "Nice hair," I say. It is much longer than she said it was, rolling over her shoulders. And then she goes to pray.

Small things irritate me—why the Hebrew is larger than the Arabic on road signs, even in the West Bank. My cousin Mary refuses to eat packaged yogurt because the label is in Hebrew. We go to Ramallah one afternoon to find the daughters of a Palestinian writer famous early in this century. We knock on doors to find their house. My father is carrying a message to them from someone he met on the plane.

Gentle, intelligent women, they offer us fresh lemonade and an album of old photographs to look at. Neither has ever married. They have always lived together. What irritates them? They cannot have their telephones listed. If you are an Arab in the West Bank, you don't have directory privileges. "So how many people have we missed who might have visited us? You, you took the time to look. We are occupied people, but we do not wish to be invisible as well."

My father offers to take me to the Sea of Galilee, to Nazareth. He's described Galilee's crisp little fish to me since I was a child. Surely I must want to go taste them. But I don't want to go, not now. For now I want to soak up my grandmother's gravelly voice, her inflections; it's the way I make my own tattoo.

In the mornings Hanan and Janan wash clothes in a big pan in the courtyard. Piece by piece. We hang them on the roof like flags. Our breakfast is fried white cheese, flat bread, rich yellow eggs. My grandmother wants everyone to eat cucumbers, which she peels slowly with a knife.

After lunch, I read and nap. I walk up and down the road. I follow the hillside path to the abandoned home of my Uncle Mohammed and stand on his porch, realizing how the poem I once wrote about him accurately imagined his view into the valley. It's strange to live lines you have already written. I could stay here. There are even shelves, for books. Uncle Mohammed went to Mecca on pilgrimage and was struck down, hit-and-run, by a passing car. It took a month for the news to reach this village.

In the afternoons I prepare dinner with my cousins. We stuff squash, snip mint. One evening I show them how to make mashed potatoes, which inspire my grandmother to say, "Stay here, we'll let you cook all the time."

In the evenings we sit, visit. A generator comes on for three hours and pumps the houses full of light. A television emerges from hiding. All day it had a cloth over its face. We are watching an Egyptian soap opera in which each character does nothing but cry. By the third evening, I call this a comedy. My father switches the channel; there is *Dallas*, big and clear. He says the Arabic subtitles don't fit the actual dialogue at all. When J. R. says, "What a bitch," the Arabic says, "I am displeased at this moment."

Do they like this show? They shrug. Television doesn't seem to interest them much. Maybe they liked it last year, when it was new. The point is, what does it have to do with this life?

⊷   ⊷   ⊷

I try sleeping upstairs for one night, so I can leave a light on late to read. This newest room of the house has its own set of steep stairs down to the outside. At 2 A.M. comes a wild knocking on the door. It takes a while for it to filter through my dreams and rouse me.

Men's voices are shouting, "Open up!" in Arabic. I think, fire? Trouble in the streets? I peek out a side window to see a group of Israeli soldiers, perhaps thirty, with machine guns. I'll be damned if I'm going to open this door.

Suddenly a story returns: my young father in Jerusalem awakened by a similar knocking and the sound of gunfire.

"What shall we do?" wailed his terrified mother.

He said, "Just cover my head."

Tonight I do exactly that, cover my head, and the knocking goes on. I am grateful for these huge iron locks.

Then I hear the soldiers jogging around to try the main entrance. My uncle is roused and steps out, groggy, in his white nightshirt. They want him to come direct them to somebody's house. Reluctantly, he pulls his suitcoat over his pajamas. As *mukhtar,* he is obliged to act as counselor, mediator, guide.

We're all nerves now, everyone awake huddling together in the downstairs big room. Janan serves tea like a sleep-walker. I wonder how many times a day she makes coffee and tea. For every guest, for every meal, between meals, before bed, upon rising, and now, in the middle of the night. I worry about my uncle. When do you know which stories to believe?

Sitti starts humming to me. My father says it's a marriage song.

"But I've been married a long time!" I tease her.

"I know. But I missed the wedding." We talk about my husband. He'll come next year. We'll walk around the whole village, do all this again.

My uncle returns after an hour. He pointed out the house, the soldiers woke the family within, searched the rooms, dumped out every drawer, and smashed the toilet, then arrested the twenty-year-old son. He's been in Syria recently. Bad luck for him.

My uncle feels very upset. He hates giving directions.

"Why the toilet?" I ask.

"They like to smash toilets. Sinks and bathtubs too. It's one of their favorite things to do."

We will not hear of this arrested boy again before we leave. He's been sucked up by silence. For the rest of our stay, I sleep downstairs.

⊸ ⊸ ⊸

One day my father and I catch a bus into Jerusalem. He is going to show me the house his family lost in 1948. He saw it once from the rooftop of my school in the Old City in 1967, and he wept. I'm a little worried about trying to see it face-to-face today, especially after my father stops to uncork a nitroglycerin tablet from his pocket and pop it down without water. He says he hasn't taken a heart pill in two years, but today he's "having pain."

The Old City's hodgepodge self is a comfort, though punctuated by Israeli teenagers with artillery. An Israeli Jewish friend wrote me a letter describing the first time she ever walked through the Souk after the Six-Day War. "At first I felt victorious," she said, "but that feeling dissipated quickly, as I looked into the faces of the old Arab men in front of their shops. By the time I left through another gate, I felt like a trespasser." I buy one short broom for fifty cents from a toothless old man who sits weaving them, straw over straw. My father swears he's been there since his own childhood.

We pass a bright bouquet of T-shirts: Jewish schoolchildren with canteens and lunch pails, listening to their teacher. My father says he walked this road as a schoolboy too. We circle between massive stone walls and vendors with towers of sesame bread.

Once we cut through someone's private garden. "It didn't used to be here," he says. "This used to be a street." We pull back wires and step between.

In front of us, a flight of iron stairs ascends. "I cannot tell you," whispers my father, hand on the railing, "how many times I traveled up and down these stairs."

We seem to be standing in the middle of someone's construction. A pile of stones. A box of nails and tools.

I stare at the house where my father grew up, realizing it is not as I have pictured it. It is much larger, taller, with a view. An old-world, stone, connected-to-other-houses house. I never pictured it connected.

A young Jew in a yarmulke approaches us.

"May I help you?" He picks up a hammer.

"We're just looking," whispers my father. "We just wanted to see something."

The man speaks cheerily. "We're renovating here. This will be one of the new dorms for rabbinical students. Ha—'new'—but can you believe it? This building is seven hundred years old."

He talks so Brooklynish I have to ask, "Are you from New York?"

"I am. But I've decided to be an Israeli." He speaks proudly, with emphasis. "I'm what's called a New Immigrant, under the new plan; have you heard of it? I'm working for the rabbi here; do you know him? It's really fantastic being a settler—now I know how the pilgrims felt."

He's so enthusiastic, I can't help liking him. Anyone would. He's staring at my father, who's still staring at the house. "If you know the rabbi," he repeats, "he might let you see inside."

Now my father looks at him. The refugee and the settler. "I've already seen inside," he says. "I grew up on the inside. I'm an Arab. I used to live here. This used to be our house."

The man looks puzzled. "You mean, you sold it to the rabbi?"

My father shakes his head. "We didn't sell it. We never sold it."

A silence in which the settler half opens his mouth and closes it again and the Arab takes his daughter's arm and steps quietly back.

"I'm sorry," the young man blurts. He looks shaken. He puts out his hand, which my father takes. "I'm really sorry."

And I really think he is.

❧   ❧   ❧

Back in the village, my father reports, "We saw the house," and my grandmother sits up, interested.

"What did it look like?"

"It looked—nice."

❧   ❧   ❧

Once my father arrived from America to find my grandmother in a funeral procession, weeping and wailing for the deceased. He asked, "Who died?"

"I'm not sure," she confided, real tears on her face. "I just wanted to help them out."

❧   ❧   ❧

No one will build a house west of the cemetery. It's bad luck, though the land appears particularly luxuriant there. My grandmother advises us that we are to give thirty pounds to the poor right before she dies and thirty pounds immediately afterwards. We tease her. "But how will we know? If you're not dead yet, how will we know you're going to die?" She is famous for her sudden revivals of health. We're to bury her with a pocket of air above her in the ground, so she'll be ready to sit up when the angels come to visit. She doesn't like to talk to people lying down. If someone reports the birth of a girl baby, she shakes her fist. I ask, "Why are you happier over boy babies?"

"It's obvious," she says. "A girl goes away with her husband and belongs to someone else. A boy sends money home and continues to belong to his own family."

"What about belonging to yourself?" I ask. "I'm married, I work, I'd give my family money if they needed it. What about belonging to the *world?*"

She tilts her head. "You're odd."

⚬ ⚬ ⚬

Three days before we leave, my grandmother starts mooning around the courtyard. She plucks endless bits of invisible lint from her dress. She mumbles to the lemon tree. I ask, "What's wrong? Are you tired?"

Her face trembles and falls into tears. "I'm only going to be tired after you go. Then I'm going to be very, very tired."

When she cries, I cry.

Two days before we leave, the gifts start showering down. My aunt gives me a red velvet prayer rug from Saudi Arabia. My uncle hands over worry beads. "From *me!*" he says in English. He worked in Texas once, in a produce house where everyone spoke Spanish. The souvenir woman delivers a necklace of orange stones. Janan is stitching me a small purse the size of my passport. Her face as she sews is weighty, morose. Hanan produces a shiny-threaded scarf and takes to her bed, claiming stomach trouble. "It's a ritual," says my father. "I refuse to get caught up in this melancholy farewell ritual."

And Sitti, dear Sitti, comes to me with three trinkets from her treasure trunk in hand. A fat yellow bead, a heart-shaped locket carrying the image of the holy mosque at Mecca, and a basketball medal. Two players with outstretched arms are pitching the ball through the hoop. The incongruity of these items makes me want to laugh. "Where did you get these?"

She swears the basketball medal came from Mecca along with the locket.

"But do you know what this is?" my father points to the players. "Do you know what these men are doing?"

She says, "Reaching for God?"

She tells us the yellow bead will guarantee a happy marriage. It's very old, she says. I notice it has a seam, as plastic things do, but I don't mention it. My aunt brings a thread and attaches the trinkets to my prayer beads. When will I ever see these people again? I wonder, stricken with how far apart our lives have planted us. I think, maybe never. I think, I will always be seeing them.

⚬ ⚬ ⚬

A circle of kids across the street chants at me whenever I pass them. "How are you?"—rolling the *r*, speaking the words as one word, musically. They learned it in school. They call out when they see me on the roof.

"I am fine!" I shout. "And how are you?"

Now they chirp, flutter, fly away from me. They are poor, shy kids, dressed in dust and forty colors. They have this new red Arab hair, springing out in curls, and what do they play with? Stones! Sticks! The can that peas come in! And they are happy!

My favorite, a striking girl named Hendia, wears a yellow headband and a dazzling grin. "Hendia!" I shout. "*Shu bitsewee?* What are you doing?" She leaps like a chicken being startled from behind. Yikes! I'm being spoken to! She runs and hides.

My uncle gets mad at the racket. He steps out and waves the kids away.

On this last day I look for Hendia. I have gum for her and candies for all the kids. She is gone, says her sister, to Ramallah to have her picture taken. "Tell her to find me when she gets back."

Later I hear her piping voice. "Naimeh! Howareyou?"

I run to the upper landing and drop her surprises down. She swoops upon them, looking at me curiously.

In Arabic I tell her, "Tomorrow—good-bye."

She says it in English. "Good-bye."

She hides her face.

⁌ ⁌ ⁌

All the relatives file through the house to pay their respects. Sitti sits on the bed with her great-great grandson in her arms. I ask her if she knows the names of all her grandchildren. "Why should I?" she says. "I say, come here, little one—and they come."

I step out into the night, pulling on my sweater, to get one last sense of what we are leaving. One village, in a terribly troubled country full of cousins who should have been able to figure this out by now. What do we really know? And a shadow leaps on me, startling. It is Hendia. She has been waiting in the shadow of the loquat tree for me to emerge. No telling how long she has been here; it is the first time I've seen her enter the courtyard.

Into my hand she presses a packet of peanuts. "Good-bye!" she says again. And runs away so fast I have nothing to thank but the moon.

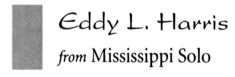

Eddy L. Harris

from Mississippi Solo

16

THE RIVER. BIG HEARTED LIKE YOUR GRANDMOTHER. STERN LIKE THOSE STORIES OF YOUR best friend's father. Double edged like a broadsword and sharp as a razor carving its way through the terrain even as it snakes its way into my being, creating a deep rift and immediately filling in the void as it goes. A strange kind of cleft, one that strangely unites instead of dividing. A river that unifies north and south the same as it connects east and west—rather than creating an impasse—even though this linking bridge is two thousand miles long and a great distance across.

The river has changed many times since Itasca, and will change a lot more before the end. Passing between Minnesota and Wisconsin the river is a monster. Because of the dams, the river backs up in places and spreads out more than two miles across. What probably once was a narrow channel in the old days is now a massive lake that has swallowed up acres and acres of land. The Mississippi River proper has been confined to the navigable channel while the waters surrounding it go by various other names: Sturgeon Lake, Lake Pepin—twenty miles long and so wide you can't see to the other side—Robinson Lake, Big Lake, Spring Lake. And in the middle float those scattered islands that were once rises of high ground. Now that the lowlands have been flooded, ridge tops become islands. None of this would have been created without the dams blocking the flow of the river. The dams have fragmented the Mississippi, altering its character in places, slowing it down, widening it, turning the upper river into a long string of lakes, but no matter what they do to it, no matter how many faces the river puts on, the Mississippi remains only one river. Different phases in an old man's life which, because it touches the lives of so many others along the way, actually connects those lives. A great-grandfather, a church elder, an old man sitting day after day on the same bench in a small town. You might never have paid much attention to him. But he has his effect.

The river can't help but connect, like the old man touching lives however subtly. Or like a national purpose. Like a favorite baseball team. Like poverty. Something shared. A common understanding. Different in intensity and meaning perhaps to each who share it, but a common language that holds together like a delicate infrastructure. No nails, no glue, just some sort of mysteriously strong bond. Like baptism.

The river flows through towns as different from one another as Minneapolis and Portage des Sioux. In some places it runs wild, in some places it is wide and standing still. For some the river means industry, for others beauty, or leisure boating, or duck hunting. But it's all the same river, all things to all men.

I've watched this river forever. It is as familiar to me as a relative. But now all of a sudden I see beyond the surface and river becomes friend. The river shows me more of what it truly is. It allows me an understanding that I could never have gotten without the risk of intimacy. As I strip the varnish off my own exterior and expose hidden layers, the river reciprocates and reveals to me what I otherwise would not have known.

That, then, is what I must be after, seeking an understanding of the river and through the mirror of friendship, an understanding of myself, and through the special unity offered by the river, a better way to see.

17

The river laps lazily at the sides of my canoe, gently slapping a greeting and rocking me as I drift with the flow of the water and coast for a few moments. The waves are meek and comforting today.

I promised myself early on that I would not make race an issue out here. I would try to live my life on the river as I so far have lived my real life; I would not make my being black a part of my success or failure or too great a factor in how I perceive things. After all, I have never considered being black my most significant feature; when I think of myself, black is not the first descriptive term that comes to mind. And yet, how could race not mean a little something extra out here? As my old friend Robert had told me, and he was true so far, here I was traveling from the high north where blacks are pretty scarce and slicing into the deep south where feelings toward blacks are often none too sweet—historically at least. And people will see that I'm black only moments after they see that my canoe is green. Maybe even before.

It's not, I hope, what they'll remember later, and long after I'm gone, maybe they'll talk about a black man in a canoe, but perhaps they won't. Perhaps they will pick up on some other aspect of me and will choose to remember what I'm doing out here, what a sweet smile and happy soul I have, and how I let them treat me kindly. People in this country only need a chance and an excuse to be kind, and they respond.

Not too long ago a girlfriend tried to enlighten me. She told me I was the dumbest, most naive simpleton she had ever run across, a danger to myself and a step in the wrong direction. I had told her that I had not experienced much bigotry, and she blew a gasket. She violently told me that yes I had and that unless I recognized it I would never be able to do anything about it. And in a way she was right. And I may indeed have been blind to it or too stupid to see, but "if a tree falls in the forest. . . ." If you don't perceive a thing, no matter how real or concrete the occurrence, if it doesn't enter your consciousness or affect your awareness, how real could it be? (The converse is true as well.) Or better, what difference does it make?

I told her I didn't allow people to deal with me on the basis of my race. I am more than black and my attitude says so. My *attitude!* I think that plays a big and greatly unappreciated role in how we are treated, and in how we face our world and our selves.

When as a writer I am rejected, my first reaction questions the stupidity of the editor, my second question concerns the writing itself and the realization that maybe it wasn't what the editor was looking for, or maybe—perish the thought—simply not good enough. Never had the rejection been racially motivated. When I was accepted to the university, it was because I was qualified, not because I was black.

When a man downright doesn't like me, I'm sure he has his reasons; I'm not always so likable. But when he doesn't give me a chance, I find a way to force him to. Certain things, no matter how small, you cannot allow. Idiots screaming bravely from passing cars excepted, people should not get away with stupidity without challenge.

Racism—sure it exists, I know that. But its effect and effectiveness depend as much on the reaction as on the action.

I stopped for breakfast one morning early in La Crescent, a dinky little town parked at one end of the bridge that reaches over to La Crosse, Wisconsin. The town isn't much for size but it offered a choice of spots to eat, including a place for pizza. I opted for the one that had the most character, a plain looking diner removed from the center of town. A little place, frequented mostly by locals. The lady tripling as waitress and busboy and cashier seemed to know everyone who walked in, and she greeted each one with a different remark, some personal little tidbit that marked the customer like a brand. Early morning laughter to get the body stirring until the coffee comes.

The breakfast nook was two rooms worth of booths and a counter up front, and three shallow rows of tables in the rear. Everybody in there looked like a farmer or at least somebody who worked hard for a living, laboring with hands and arms and back, and maybe I didn't look too out of place among them walking in with dirty jeans and smelling like a herring. The looks they tossed my way were the recognitions of a stranger. No one stared for very long and if the waitress took a bit longer to get to me and take my order and return with my breakfast, I understood. She was too busy chatting with the regulars to be bothered with a stranger. And when she came to me she somehow had mislaid her friendly face and became a woman with a job to do.

While I waited for my breakfast of chicken livers and scrambled eggs and fried potatoes, a group of three insurance salesmen came in. I don't know if they really sold insurance. They wore ties and jackets and possibly sold farm equipment or maybe held office jobs over in La Crosse, but they reminded me of insurance salesmen. I've yet to see one dressed in a suit that fits well and is not wrinkled, a suit that looks good and is in style and shoes that are more than comfortable. A woman was with them and she wore the female equivalent. They sat in the rear.

At the counter an old man was treating his wife to breakfast out but they sat and ate without saying a word to each other, although both spoke happily to the waitress when she came their way. I guess they had lived together so long they had nothing new to say to one another, or else they just knew. The wife passed the salt and ketchup when the husband needed it. He didn't have to ask for it.

My food arrived and I asked for a clean fork and for mayonnaise for my potatoes. I said please and the waitress smiled. I noticed after that that no one else used the word. She hurried with the fork, but the mayonnaise took forever. The waitress had stopped to talk to three sturdily built women in the booth nearest the register. They were loud and laughing and wore jackets that said River Rat across the back. I was a river rat by then and I wished for a jacket like that.

No one in the place paid any undue attention to my existence or my eating or my being different.

I ate quickly and comfortably and paid. A middle aged man with a puffy face came up to pay as well. I hadn't noticed him with them, but he looked like a part of the group of men wearing those badly fitting suits. It turned out that I was right. This man, at least, *was* an insurance broker, and while we waited for the waitress to finish talking to whomever, he brought up the weather and asked me where I was from. I told him and said what I was doing and he laughed, pointing out the women in their jackets, and he said:

"You should have a jacket like that. Instead of River Rat it should say River Nigger."

He thought it was just the funniest thing and he laughed so loud that everyone looked in our direction. I didn't know if they had heard what he had said and wanted to see my reaction, but they were definitely watching and I felt I could not ignore this man and let him slide by unchallenged, even if he had meant no harm by it. It might, after all, have been a real attempt at friendly though misshapen humor. So why scream and shout?

I put on my toothiest grin and my best African accent and I said rapidly, "I'm from Nigeria. You mean River Niger. Aha-aha-aha!"

I let him struggle to grasp that one and I paid. His face went blank for a second and then knotted into a frown. By the time I got outside he must have figured out what I was really saying: your little joke upsets me and is not funny. And saying it in a way that does not threaten him, that does not attack him and so he cannot defend with anger and arrogance against it.

He hurried out to get me, grabbing me by the arm and saying, "Hey! I didn't mean nothing by it. It was just a joke."

I put my lips together and squeezed them tight and nodded once, but he wouldn't let it drop that easily.

"You're not from Nigeria, are you?"

He wore the most quizzical expression and he was so sincere that I had to laugh.

"I told you where I'm from."

I could almost hear the gears grinding in his head.

"Why'd you say you were from Nigeria? Did what I said bother you that much that you'd rather be from there than here?"

I hadn't meant that, but if it works. . . .

"I know I shouldn't have said it but you know how it is. You hear things and you repeat them and you get used to it. You don't even stop to think." Then he stopped to think. "Unless," he said and his head hung a little lower, "you're the one who's offended. Then it's a different story, isn't it?"

He went on to tell me about the final two games of the World Series which I had missed because of the journey and which had eroded into a fiasco. Grown men throwing tantrums on the ball field and behaving like children, little cry-babies because things weren't going their way.

"And you could see them, right there on camera, saying F-you this and F-you that and I didn't appreciate it. It was uncalled for and I didn't like it one bit. And I'm not a prude, mind you. I was in the Navy, you know."

Twenty years as an insurance broker had done little for him but cause his hair to fall out and make him drink too much. Those little capillaries in his nose and cheeks inflamed his face and gave him the appearance of constant sunburn. Business wasn't too good. Premiums too high. A lot of businesses just can't afford insurance anymore. It's cheaper for them to go out of business, he said, but what can you do, he wanted to know, except close down the law schools for six years. Too many lawyers with nothing to do so they sue sue sue.

But twenty years ago, back when he was in the Navy pulling submarine duty and rearranging the Vietnamese coastline, life was leaner and not so cluttered up.

"Maybe it was Vietnam," he muses. "Maybe that's what did it to us. We could have won that war, you know, and Korea too."

"I guess you miss those Navy days." I'm beginning to feel compassion for this man when only moments before I was feeling contempt. It saddened me that I had made him feel so rotten over a harmless little joke.

"Those were the happiest times of my life."

And now he's back where he started. He's wound around full circle and he gets to the point of this conversation. He tells me about the stint he served in Puerto Rico. A simple story really about a beautiful heiress from Philadelphia who had come to San Juan to get over her grief. The two had met and spent all of their free time together. They slept together in the same room, in the same bed even, but never once did they make love.

"It wasn't that kind of relationship."

Instead, they would tell each other secrets, things they would dare tell no one else. And only once in a while if ever in your life does there appear a soul you truly trust with your own soul. And most likely she's a stranger you'll never see again. And since those days in Puerto Rico, he's not seen the woman ever again and had only received one letter from her, the one that said, "We shouldn't see each other again because we would only try to force something to happen that will only warp the memories." He sent her flowers after that, and that was the last they corresponded.

But in San Juan on hot days when the slightest breeze from the sea felt like a miracle, they would walk and sip rum drinks and talk forever and she told him of the man she was there to forget. The man she loved but whom she could never have because of her family. The only man with whom she had ever. . . .

The story stops while he clears his throat and swallows.

"The only man that she ever, you know," he whispers now, "climaxed with." His eyebrows lift. The whisper disappears. "His name was Raoul and he was a black man and she told me she loved him very very much and she cried and cried and I said to her, 'There's no reason why you shouldn't love him.' And I meant it."

I reckon he did at that. And, I suppose, every man out here who has waved at me so far and wished me luck would get to carving at the core of American racism that lies inside if given the chance. The chance to be helpful. The chance to be friendly. The chance to know that we're not so very different, none of us from the others. I hoped so, anyway. I was traveling south, and because the South still doesn't get very good press, in the back of my mind gnawed a little apprehensive wondering.

Working on that core of American racism is certainly an easier task man-to-man, but on a grand scale chipping at it is as laborious as carving granite. Or so it seems, and I struggle with the confusion the same as I struggle with this river.

If only the racism could be tamed as easily. I should call in the Corps of Engineers for the task.

I waved goodbye to my friend the insurance broker and hoped he would find better days ahead.

⌁   ⌁   ⌁

Cruising steadily southward I moved into the stretch of river that divides Iowa and Wisconsin, and then Iowa and Illinois. The landscape changes and there are high bluffs all around blocking the wind. Trees overhanging still wear their autumn colors but the fire has gone out of them and subdued hues of amber and gold linger in afterglow. From high atop one of the bluffs I look down on the blue water winding and coiling like a giant anaconda. What a sight to behold! And what a heady thought knowing that I'm out there in a boat the size of a peanut.

⌁   ⌁   ⌁

It's peculiar. The littlest things make the biggest impressions. I zipped through Iowa in a hurry, like a man on a mission. Only a few memories surface:

Cheese and crackers and smoked carp purchased from a gasoline station that also functioned as the town's grocery. I had never had carp before and heard only horrible things about it. It's a scavenger fish and will eat anything, but so is a catfish and I love catfish. The man working the station promised I would like the fish, and I really did. I was ready for a beer.

The beer that quenched my thirst didn't come for another fifty miles or so, but I was glad I waited.

I pulled into Dubuque and half expected it to be a reprise of La Crosse, Wisconsin, another river town with old buildings fighting to stay alive in the shadow of new offices and hotels. La Crosse had felt old and sleepy and deserted to me, but I had cruised that place in the early morning. The town was just awakening and what few souls were out were the grumpies with another working day on their minds.

I arrived in Dubuque in the middle of the day. The streets weren't bustling but at least they were alive. It was almost lunchtime.

I gave the city a quick inspection. It sits on a bluff and many of the residential sections of town are steeply hilly. Main Street however is flat as a tabletop and just as straight. I stepped into a dim little saloon on Main Street between 9th and 10th Streets and I had my beer.

Seated there drinking a draft beer and munching barbeque-flavored potato chips was a wiry fellow who probably should have been out working somewhere. He was the only customer and he and the little woman who ran the place were watching soap operas on the TV. She was a dwarf who reminded me of the type of feisty woman you find running saloons in movies about the old West. She didn't talk much, just served up the beers and minded her own business and kept her eyes on the television while I'm sure her ears caught everything that was ever said in here. Finally, after enough questions and her very brief answers and after enough comments about the soap opera, she loosened up and started talking about this saloon. I think what opened her up at last was the request for another Budweiser. She was all out.

"The Budweiser man," she said, "was due here on Tuesday, but he never showed up. He doesn't like coming around here because the orders aren't big enough. Only a case or so at a time. It's not worth the effort for him."

Being from St. Louis I couldn't imagine a place being out of Budweiser, unless of course the bar couldn't keep up with demand.

"No. Lite Beer from Miller," she told me, "is the best seller here, followed by Pabst. That's all they ask for."

So I asked for one too. A Pabst. I don't drink light beers. Too thin.

"Bottle or draft?"

I took mine in a bottle because, it had been pointed out to me, bottled beer comes colder than draft beers. To disprove that, she poured out a glass of draft Pabst and gave it to me free and it seemed just as cold as the beer in the bottle. Unless there had been a remarkable difference, I probably wouldn't have been able to tell anyway, just as I probably only *think* I can tell the difference between light beer and real beer. But I was happy she thought I could, happy for the free beer, and happier still that she cared enough what I thought about the beer in her kegs. And she knew I would not be a regular customer. I had already told her I was just passing through in my canoe.

The man next to me perked up suddenly. There was a commercial on the TV screen and he took a break from the soaps. He was excited about the trip and wanted to know everything.

"What's your ETA?" he wanted to know and then he explained it for me. "Estimated time to arrive."

"Whatever it takes," I said and that seemed to impress him all the more.

"How about them locks?" he asked. "Bet them damn things take a lot of time. You probably spend as much time stuck in them as you do paddling."

I laughed and invited him to tell me about himself.

"Me? Nothing much. I'm just making it."

The soaps came back on.

"How about you?" I asked the bartender. "You making it okay?"

"I do the best I can. Nothing fancy. I try to attract a little business, put in a little live entertainment, but if it's any good it's too expensive, and if it's bad it's just not worth it. The people around here don't notice much anyway."

She sounded like a woman biding her time, saving her money and just waiting for a chance to clear out of here. I had a feeling that she might be here a long time.

Back out on the street I spotted a Chinese restaurant. I crossed over and went down to it and when I got inside the decor struck me as odd. Red everywhere and Chinese lanterns hanging, the restaurant looked like practically every other Chinese restaurant in the western world. I don't know why I expected anything different but it still struck me as odd. And then I knew why. There wasn't an Oriental face in the place. Actually, there was one but he was a customer. He was all dressed in white and looked like a yachtsman, and when I, trying to make friendly conversation, asked him if he had been sailing today, he jumped back startled that a stranger would speak to him and snapped his no with an expression that told me to leave him alone.

A pretty woman dressed in black satiny fake oriental clothing came out to show me to my seat. She carried a menu under her arm but she wasn't smiling like most restaurant hostesses. I should have known better.

I said, "You don't look Chinese." I was trying to be funny, but she failed to see the humor. If she had been a lioness, I would now be headless.

Whew! Dubuque, Iowa.

I got a couple of egg rolls to go and left.

There is a part of town not far from city hall that is closed to automobile traffic. It's lined with shops and has a little clock tower in the center. People hang out here at lunchtime and I stopped to sit in the sun for a minute. A black man passed. He waved exuberantly at me, too much so to be just a friendly wave. He was actually happy to see me, the way Americans get after weeks in a foreign land when they finally hear English spoken. The man waved and kept going. I said to myself again, *Dubuque, Iowa.* It felt really strange.

I next came to Davenport and the sunset that awaited me there. Stripes of blue and swirls of pink and purple, all coming from out of the black of night that sat directly overhead, and fading into an orange glow sitting on the horizon. And I thought, *Some things make everything else worthwhile.* Like those beans and weenies of the first night. Like Robinovich and Emily. Like this sunset streaked with fire and magenta and awash with blue and violet. So simple, yet so spectacular.

◦ ◦ ◦

In Muscatine, Riverside Park sits right on the river. If you slide into town late and pack up early, you could camp there and no one would ever know. Or you could cross the park, cross the road and sleep comfortably in the Hotel Muscatine. An old hotel, nothing fancy, this dark squat box made of bricks sits on the corner and watches the river run. It probably once was a grand hotel but now you can only tell it's a hotel by the sign out front. It houses a travel agency as well as a coffee shop, and I went inside to eat breakfast.

The specialty of the house at dinner time: French cuisine. On the walls hung reproductions of French fine art, Toulouse-Lautrec and the like. And still the place looked like a simple coffee shop. Grey carpeting, booths and wobbly tables. I sat at a wobbly table.

An old lady was running about with the energy of an Iowa tornado taking orders and serving food and working the register and having quick conversations. She even acted as bouncer: loitering in the lobby of the hotel was a scuzzy character who looked about as bad as I must have and maybe even smelled as bad. He had parked his bicycle outside and had come in to use the men's room and to sit. He sat in one of the telephone stalls outside the coffee shop and smoked a cigarette. When he had finished that he got up and just stood around. Maybe he was harmless, maybe he was a bit wacky, but the old lady kept an eye on him and when he became too much for her to bear, she left the coffee shop and threw the fellow out.

I said to her after I had eaten my omelette, potatoes and toast, "That guy looked almost as raggedy as I do."

She winked and smiled and said, "Yeah, but you're paying."

I sat and listened to a grey-haired man in a grey sport coat and brown pants. He was talking about purchasing farm equipment to a curly-haired fat man, probably his son, who wore glasses and a blue polo shirt and blue jeans. The son seemed like a successful rural car dealer. He fidgeted a lot, but it was the old man who said he had things to do.

"So much to do," he said. "I can't keep it all straight. Already in the last five minutes my head is clearing and I can't remember what I'm supposed to do."

I know I should have felt sad for this old man, growing old and losing his memory and talking to his son who didn't particularly want to hear what he was saying. But instead of compassion, a wave of jealousy rushed over me. I knew that when this old man, when all the people in this place recalled this day, they would remember the old lady and the hobo she had thrown out. They wouldn't remember me.

I wanted to be as much a part of their lives as they would forever be of mine. I didn't want to waltz in for a moment and then out again without leaving an impression, but that's what I was doing. I didn't know how to do otherwise, not without intruding and waving a banner and shouting: Hey, look at me. I'm canoeing down the river.

What I was out here was alone and would be until the end. Maybe this was the journey I had in mind. A selfish one, a journey that would have its effects totally on me. A journey of one-way rewards.

All of a sudden I wanted to share something with somebody and by the time I shoved off in Fort Madison I was feeling so alone as to feel frightened and fed up and wanting to go home. That old dread had returned.

Clouds grey and heavy hung on the sky. I put on my yellow suit when it started to rain. The wind began to blow and the canoe to pitch. But I wasn't thinking about that. I couldn't stop worrying about being so alone, and being alone had never disturbed me before. I actually like it and always have, but now suddenly being alone had turned into loneliness. I tried singing, but that only made the rain come down harder.

Not far ahead I see smoke coming from the trees of an island. My map tells me it's Devil's Island but it's supposed to be uninhabited. *What could the smoke be from?* People of course and I drift closer to the shore of the island and hope somebody will see me. A wave, a hello shouted from the bank, anything. I just want to wave and smile.

They did me one better. As I passed they were calling out all sorts of things, but I couldn't hear any of it. The wind was whistling too loud under my rain hood. Finally they gestured at me. There were two of them and they both came right to edge of the river and beckoned for me to come ashore. It was all the invitation I needed and I turned in and paddled hard to reach them.

The river doesn't seem to be moving so fast when you're on it. Paddling makes the canoe go faster than the river itself, and as slowly as the trees slide by beside you, you think you're not going very fast at all. But as soon as you turn and head to shore you find that you should have started your turn an hour ago. By the time you decide to aim for a point directly beside you, you've already passed it and have to work like mad to get back upstream to it. When you're facing upstream you can feel how swiftly the river is moving under you.

I put everything I had into swinging the canoe and digging in the water to get back to them. But I couldn't do it and when I reached the shore I had missed them by quite a ways and had to climb over fallen trees and through the brush to get back to the clearing where they stood by the fire. I ripped my rainsuit.

"We saw you coming from way off up there. We saw that yellow suit."

"But we didn't know you were in a canoe though."

They were standing by the fire getting warm. They were father and son and they were commercial fishers who stretched nets out into the river overnight and came back the next day to check their catch. They lived up in Fort Madison and I asked them right away what their names were.

"I'm Rod and this is my father Vernon."

They asked me mine and I told them.

"What are you doing out here?"

"Going down to New Orleans."

They hardly reacted.

"Wish we'd brought out some hot dogs like we usually do. But we aren't going to be out here long today. Just cleaning these nets and going to get them back out there and go home."

The fire sputtered and threatened to go out. Vernon searched for more wood. I watched how he got the fire started again even though everything was wet.

He laid leaves on the big smoking log to dry and when they had dried they caught on fire. The twigs and sticks he'd placed around the leaves caught fire too once they had dried and the draft from the breeze fed the flames with air. In no time the fire was a blaze again and I stood over it to keep warm.

They went back to clearing their nets of leaves and sticks and debris, stretching them and laying them down neatly so they wouldn't be so tangled up when they went to set them out in the river.

"What kind of work do you do?"

"I'm a writer."

"You going to write a book about this trip?"

"I hope so."

"You going to put us in it?"

"You bet."

They looked at each other and grinned.

I stepped over closer to them to watch what they were doing. The nets were about a hundred yards long each and to clean them in time to get them back out into the river they had to move fast. Their hands were tough and skilled and only Vernon's age slowed them down a little.

Eventually they went off in their flatboat to set the nets. They drop them in the water and secure them in place with long poles. They mark the nets with empty plastic milk jugs and from then on when I saw those milk containers floating in the water I knew they were more than rubbish trashing the river.

They had told me to keep the fire going.

When they came back and we were all standing by the fire again, Rod told me he had been to New Orleans. He hadn't always lived in Fort Madison, but for some reason he had always come back to it.

"You can't stay away from the river too long," he said.

They laughed at the rip in my rain suit.

"Looks like you could stand a new rain suit."

Vernon showed me his. It was ripped as badly as mine.

"They don't last too good, do they?" he said.

"I've seen some," Vernon said, "that are made of thick tough stuff. They last a little longer but they rip up too. But they're better than these cheap ones like he's got."

Next they criticized my shoes.

"What's that on your feet? Tennis shoes?"

"Something like that."

"You ought to get you some boots like these. Then your feet wouldn't get wet."

"I didn't know they were going to get wet, but you know every time I cross the paddle from one side of the canoe to the other, a few drops at a time fall into the canoe. Those few drops turn into quite a puddle after about ten thousand times."

"I can imagine."

"And when it's cold my feet turn to ice."

"What you been doing at night? Camping and building fires?"

"Yeah."

"Well you ought to stay here tonight. This fire's already going and all you have to do is keep her going. And this ain't such a bad spot for camping."

I looked all around and he was right. The clearing was sheltered on all sides by trees to keep the wind out and the branches arching overhead would shield me from the rain. And it was going to rain.

"Going to be a big storm tonight," Vernon said. "Rod is right. You might as well stay right here."

"I think I might."

And I did.

"Well we got to be going. But we're going leave you with this radio so you can have a little music tonight if you want to." He searched his other pockets. "Where'd that extra battery get to?" He found it and handed it to me. "And when you leave in the morning. . . ."

"If you do," Vernon said.

". . . . leave the radio right here." And he showed me a place in the fork of a tree branch where I could stand the radio up.

I watched them go off across the river, one man sitting in the johnboat, the other standing. They were really river rats, their boat hitting those high waves and the bow being lifted high out of the water and crashing down. They didn't slow up at all.

Too quickly they vanished from my sight and I was again all by myself. But this time I had a physical piece of someone else to comfort me in the night. I turned on the radio and dialed in the strongest country music station I could find. It came in from Keokuk, fifteen miles away. Their weather and mine would be the same.

I climbed back through the brush and over the trees and paddled my canoe up to the little cove. I dragged it up on shore, took out my necessities for the night, and left the remainder safe under the overturned canoe. I saw that the wind and the rain were coming out of the northeast and angled the canoe to keep my gear dry. Then I pitched the tent and collected a mountain of firewood for the night. I wanted to keep the fire going as long as I could and on until morning if possible so I would have a way to warm myself and boil the water for my breakfast cereal.

It hadn't been very late in the afternoon when I landed here, but after a while, talking to Vernon and Rod, and a while longer bringing the canoe around and fetching firewood and making camp, it was nigh unto darkness by the time I ate and settled in the tent ready for bed. I turned on the radio.

Country music and reports of rain on the way, which I already knew, and the story of Hurricane Juan beating up the Gulf of Mexico and sending wind and rain up the Mississippi Valley. I knew about the wind and the rain but both seemed to be coming out of the north and east. Very quickly, as if he heard my doubts, the weatherman explained that the wind and the rain were coming out of the south and west. And very quickly after that, the rains came.

Weathermen and birds are the first to know. And if you're an attentive listener, you can detect the rain's advance as well. Listen for the birds. They twitter and chirp so pleasantly that a storm is the last thing on your mind. But two by two the birds fly off and hide. A genetic memory from the days of Noah, perhaps, but they feel the storm in the air and take cover. I wonder where they go. They disappear so thoroughly, only a few lollygaggers stay to make music. Diehard musicians hate to go home.

And then the wind swooshes up and swishes in the trees. The rain is never far behind. But if you still doubt and need further warning, lightning flashes silently and as the storm draws nearer, thunder comes up to join the lightning flashes, closer and closer to each successive flash until at last they happen nearly at the same time. The storm is here.

This storm was more than a storm and I wondered if the tent could take it. Each wave of the storm brought with it more rain, more wind, and when the storm had finally gone by, water still fell from the branches swaying overhead.

Luckily I had parked in the trees. If not, the wind may have been too much and I would have gotten even more soaked than I did. And soaked I was. The vinyl groundsheet that was supposed to keep water out, didn't. And neither did the nylon fly hanging taut across the top of the tent. I was up all night, catching sleep in short spurts, moving about the tent trying to find a new dry spot. I didn't catch much sleep but I did manage to keep the fire going. Every so often I unzipped the tent and tossed on another log. By keeping the fire alive during the night, the wet wood I tossed on it would dry and eventually burn.

When the rain stopped at last and the batteries in the radio had gone completely dead, I fell asleep. In the morning the fire had gone out, but there was just enough smouldering of the last big log to put to use what I had learned from watching Vernon.

I crawled from the tent stiff and wet. I stretched. There was still water dripping from the trees above and enough of it that I thought it might still be raining and I considered getting back inside for a little longer. But the river was still and calm and I could see that it was not raining. When the wind stopped blowing, the branches stopped swaying and the water from above stopped falling. I knew it was time to get up and get going. In fact I could have gotten started hours ago.

I scooped up wet leaves and scattered them around the smouldering piece of wood. I blew on them hard until finally the coals glowed red and little flames leapt out. The leaves smoked and finally caught fire and I piled on the wood. Soon I had a very decent fire and I felt very proud of myself.

I made breakfast, checked the sky for more bad weather and took camp apart. I would have felt better if there had been sun or even a little blue in the sky, but there was none and I still felt fine. I set the radio where I was supposed to and took off. I wanted to leave a note but it would have gotten too wet to be legible or would have blown away.

The morning was beautiful and so was the river. I passed a few floating milk jugs and knew what they were. I steered clear making sure not to disturb the nets below. As I got out of range of the island it occurred to me that once again I had been the receiver of kindness, but at least this time I had made an impression, if only by creating anticipation of a book. But how would it last? The anticipation, until there *was* a book. The impression on them, I didn't know, but not as long as the impression made on me. That would last a lifetime and I wondered, is it always the receiver who is impressed the most? Is it because he benefits most from the contact, because he is most affected?

I had no time to dwell on that then. The wind galed up ferociously and knocked me about. The rains returned and the river told me to get out.

I angled for the town of Montrose and for the briefest of moments actually considered going on all the way down to Keokuk, ten miles down river.

If I hadn't stopped for the night on Devil's Island the storm last night might have caught me in a less sheltered spot. There certainly would have been no fire already built and with every piece of wood wet, getting a fire of my own started would have been an awful task.

And this morning when I awoke, if I had gotten started even a half hour sooner, I would already have passed Montrose and would have had to wait out the coming rains huddled up in a little ball on the bank somewhere.

As it turned out, I got to wait out the rain in Hoenig's River-view Tap, a bar facing the river and the only place available for longterm loitering except the laundromat. The town is only seven blocks deep and eight blocks wide—and that's stretching it.

I poked my head in. A lady with a mop turned.

"Are you open yet?"

She nodded and brought the beer I asked for. I started to undress, first taking off the torn rain suit and then the wet hooded sweatshirt I wore underneath.

I sat on the stool at the end of the bar closest to the door and just hung around watching soap operas on TV when the game shows had disappeared. I had seen more soap operas since I started this trip than ever in my life. But today I didn't mind. Anything to take my mind off my plight. The rain was not letting up. The beer chilled me so I switched to coffee to warm me and drank coffee after coffee after coffee until I was sick of coffee. Then I had a bowl of chili. Local workers came in for lunch and still I sat there. I was there when they came in, I was there when they left. I caught a few queer glances, but no one said a harsh word about my hanging around.

When I felt I'd had enough, and when the rain had stopped and the river looked calmer, I dressed again in my somewhat drier clothes and headed back down to the river and the canoe. I even put the canoe back in the water and thought I could get underway again. But on closer inspection I realized I'd be a fool to try it—expert though I was.

A young couple came down to park and neck in front of the river; they watched me instead. It took a while but I finally realized I'd be going nowhere today. The river had said no. Don't go. And I didn't.

What I did was to search for a place to spend the night. Failing that, because there are no hotels in Montrose, I searched for somewhere to stash canoe and gear while I hitchhiked somewhere that *did* have a hotel.

A fellow in the lumberyard told me I could leave my junk with him and he'd lock it up for the night while I went back up to Fort Madison. That was the closest town with a hotel. Or Keokuk down river. It would have to be Keokuk. I couldn't go backwards.

And then, in my boldest move ever, I asked him, "You don't know anybody with a pick-up truck, do you?"

I could see he was thinking and wondering what I had in mind.

"I got a pick-up."

"You do?" What luck! "Are you going down to Keokuk by any chance? We could put the canoe on the truck and drive it there."

I crossed fingers and toes, and he said, "Yeah, we could do that." He spoke so slowly. "If you don't mind waiting a little bit."

Of course I didn't. Especially when he said I could wait in the lumberyard office. It was warm inside.

He was a thin man with a drooping mustache and long hair. He told me his name was

Elton or Elden (you can ask a man his name and you can ask him to repeat it, but you cannot ask him to spell it) and I think he was related to the man he worked for—son-in-law, or something. They were inside talking and then Elton went to do his work.

I stepped into the warmth and shivered from relief from the cold and wet. I said, "It's freezing out there."

He said, "Ain't too bad if the wind don't blow."

"It's nice and warm in here. Feels good."

"Yep." Then the phone rang.

Elton came back around and said politely, "You ready?" as if he had changed his schedule to accommodate mine and wouldn't go anywhere until I was warm and ready and said so. And maybe he had urgent business in Keokuk, but I rather think he pushed up his trip to the city to keep me from having to wait around long. He did tell me that he would have to get back to the lumberyard and then turn around later and go again to Keokuk where he lived.

We drove down into Keokuk with the windows rolled up and the heater on full blast and Elton told me how hard it is to find work around there. Rural economies were hurting because of the bad situation the farmers were in, but you do the best you can and keep hanging on.

He told me about Keokuk once being the cocaine capital of the U.S. I found it hard to believe, but he said that all the cocaine coming into the country used to come through here.

"Keokuk used to be a wild place," he said, and I am sure he meant about a hundred years ago. We passed a low shopping mall. "Used to be a big time hotel right here, biggest whorehouse around."

Then as we searched for a cheap hotel for me, he told me about the bar scene in town.

"I used to go out all the time till it got so dangerous. Not worth it anymore. People start a fight over just nothing, getting stabbed and shot. I stay home."

He pointed out the lesbian bar and the gay bar and the cowboy bar and the redneck bar and then he told me the wildest story about his days on the road when he and a buddy of his were driving to California, somehow came across a pile of cash (gambling in Las Vegas, I think) and how the buddy swiped the money. I'm not sure if I got the story straight, but somehow the buddy ended up broke and hitchhiking and Elton ran across him in the desert. Elton just kept going and never looked back.

He told me straight-faced and without a ripple in his voice about the agony of hell he and his wife went through when their little child lingered through some horrible illness and finally died.

I didn't know what to say so I just shut up, but my heart hurt. Is it that only kind souls get stepped on or just the contrast between their goodness and their pain that makes it so ironic? This man going out of his way to find me a cheap enough hotel—and we stopped at a few—driving me around and showing me the town, taking me down to the Coast Guard station, this man surely deserved only good fortune. Why did his baby die? Why was it hard finding a really good job?

At the Coast Guard station I asked and received permission to leave my canoe and some of my gear on the Coast Guard dock. I took some things with me and Elton dropped me off at my hotel, a pretty fair walk from the center of town. Then he waved goodbye and he was gone, his head tilted back as he drove and his chin stuck out.

I wanted to go home with Elton, meet his wife, share a meal. Instead I was left wondering if I would ever cross his mind again.

In the bathtub I washed the leaves and sand off my tent and pitched it in the hotel room to dry. I hung up wet clothes all around and my sleeping bag too. I took a sit-down bath and then a shower and scrubbed and scrubbed until I was nearly clean. I lay down on the bed and tried to sleep, but the emptiness inside would not let me sleep. It nagged at me until I cried, sobbing from the sudden yearning to have children. I don't know why: to teach them, to tell them tales. To share with them the parts of me that are important so that whenever I'm away and even long after I'm dead they will think of me and carry me with them and I will forever be a part of their lives.

I must have fallen asleep for a few minutes. When I awoke the longings had yielded to hunger. I dressed in clean clothes and cowboy boots and set out to find—naturally—catfish for dinner.

I would have thought that since this was a river town and a Mississippi River town at that, catfish would be the easiest thing in the world to find. It wasn't. I walked all the way into town searching for a restaurant that served catfish. I asked everyone I passed, but I was just out of luck.

The man in the shoe store told me to try the Holiday Inn. They used to have catfish there, he said.

The bookseller at Copperfield & Co. recommended the Blizzard or the Buzzard or something like that. "The new place that just opened across the street," she said as if she thought I lived here in town. "I haven't eaten there yet, but they say the food is good."

While I was in the bookstore I bought a present for Robinovich, a book which later on got soaked. I sheepishly hesitated to give it to her and lied that I'd had it a long time.

When I crossed the street, there was no catfish. But just to make sure, the waitress said, "Wait and I'll go ask and find out." And she came back with the bad news. She hunched her shoulders and threw open her hands. "Sorry."

"Me too," I replied.

I stopped one more fellow and asked by mistake for good fried chicken and he recommended the Colonel. I suppose he would have sent me to Mc's if I'd wanted a good burger.

So I walked on down to Main and 7th, to a place called the Chuck Wagon. I had given up and was hungry enough now to eat anything.

The motif was cowboy: paintings on the wall of cowboy scenes, deer antlers and Texas longhorns, a big harness hanging with a mirror where the head of the animal goes, and another harness with fake flowers instead of the mirror. All the tables were red and all the booths were wooden, and each booth with its own hatrack on the end. In the other room was a large picture of the power plant dam crossing the river here.

The restaurant was packed, just like a good restaurant ought to be.

"May I help you?"

"Can I get something to eat?"

"Certainly."

"May I check the menu first?"

She gave me one and then she left because if I was looking at the prices and couldn't afford them, she didn't want to embarrass me. That was very kind, but I wasn't checking the prices; I was looking for catfish and when I found it, I released a big sigh.

"Would you like a table?"

I wondered if she was always this sweet and polite.

She led me to my booth and I sat down, giving her back the menu. "I know what I want." And the waitress came and I ordered. "A huge piece of catfish."

"The catfish steak or the whole fish?"

"The whole thing. Deep fried." And I added, "Please."

It came with french fries and slaw, pickles and tomato and lettuce, a roll and butter, and cottage cheese with pineapple mixed in. I don't even like cottage cheese, but I ate it and it was delightful. The entire meal. Even the butter. And a Pepsi full of stinging bubbles to top it all off. I couldn't have asked for anything better.

Maybe they would have ruined a steak or botched linguini with clam sauce, but they did catfish to perfection and I walked out of there a happy man.

I slept well and set out in the morning feeling fine. I even got a ride from the hotel down to the river from two teenagers who had been up all night cleaning and stocking shelves in a grocery store. They were driving around having their morning beer before going home to sleep. They were looking for some excitement before going home because once they went to sleep it would too quickly be another night of work for them as soon as they got up in the evening.

They dropped me off and I set the canoe in the water. I collected my gear from the Coast Guard office and chatted for a minute or two. I asked about the weather and the river level after all the rain. It wouldn't have mattered, of course, even if they told me of floods and high water everywhere. I loaded up and took off.

The few uniformed men standing outside waved after me and before long I was out of sight.

What an abrupt change from yesterday! Today it was breezy but not violent. The water was calm. And I was feeling superb. The sun was shining and the air around me was very warm. I paddled long graceful strokes and moved swiftly out to the center of the river, catching the current and gliding smoothly downstream. Men working at the river's edge stopped to watch me and to wave. The whole world seemed to be waving and smiling and I was once more a very happy man.

THE SCIENCE ESSAY

Elizabeth Marshall Thomas

from The Hidden Life of Dogs

I BEGAN OBSERVING DOGS BY ACCIDENT. WHILE FRIENDS SPENT SIX MONTHS IN EUROPE, I took care of their husky, Misha. An agreeable two-year-old Siberian with long, thin legs and short, thick hair, Misha could jump most fences and travel freely. He jumped our fence the day I took him in. A law requiring that dogs be leashed was in effect in our home city of

Cambridge, Massachusetts, and also in most of the surrounding communities. As Misha violated the law I would receive complaints about him, and with the help of these complaints, some from more than six miles distant, I soon was able to establish that he had developed a home range of approximately 130 square miles. This proved to be merely a preliminary home range, which later he expanded considerably, but interestingly enough, even young Misha's first range was much larger than the ranges of homeless dogs reported in Baltimore by the behavioral scientist Alan Beck. Beck's urban strays had established tiny ranges of but 0.1 to 0.06 square mile. In contrast, Misha's range more closely resembled the 200- to 500-square-mile territories roamed by wolves, most notably the wolves reported by Adolph Murie in "The Wolves of Mount McKinley" and by L. David Mech in "The Wolves of Isle Royale." What was Misha doing?

Obviously, something unusual. Here was a dog who, despite his youth, could navigate flawlessly, finding his way to and from all corners of the city by day and by night. Here was a dog who could evade dangerous traffic and escape the dog officers and the dognappers who at the time supplied the flourishing laboratories of Cambridge with experimental animals. Here was a dog who never fell through the ice on the Charles River, a dog who never touched the poison baits set out by certain citizens for raccoons and other trash-marauders, a dog who never was mauled by other dogs. Misha always came back from his journeys feeling fine, ready for a light meal and a rest before going out again. How did he do it?

For a while I looked for the answer in journals and books, availing myself of the fine libraries at Harvard and reading everything I could about dogs to see if somewhere the light of science had penetrated this corner of dark. But I found nothing. Despite a vast array of publications on dogs, virtually nobody, neither scientist nor layman, had ever bothered to ask what dogs do when left to themselves. The few studies of free-ranging dogs concerned feral dogs, abandoned or homeless dogs. Alone in hostile settings, these forsaken creatures were surely under terrible stress. After all, they were not living under conditions that were natural to them, any more than are wild animals in captivity, imprisoned in laboratories and zoos. How might dogs conduct themselves if left undisturbed in normal circumstances? No one, apparently, had ever asked.

At first, that science had ignored the question seemed amazing. But was it really? We tend to study animals for what they can teach us about ourselves or for facts that we can turn to our advantage. Most of us have little interest in the aspects of their lives that do not involve us. But dogs? Dogs do involve us. They have shared our lives for twenty thousand years. How then had we managed to learn so little about dogs that we could not answer the simplest question: what do they want?

Our ignorance becomes more blameworthy when we consider that no animal could be easier to study. Unlike wild animals, dogs are not afraid of us. To study them we need not invade their habitat or imprison them in ours—our world *is* their natural habitat and always was. Furthermore, because their wild ancestors were not dogs at all but wolves, dogs have never even existed as a wild species. As a result we have had the opportunity to observe dogs since dogs began, an opportunity that for the most part we have chosen to ignore. Hence, curled on the sofa beside me of an evening was a creature of mystery: an agreeable dog with a life of his own, a life that he had no wish to conceal and that he was managing with all the competence of a wild animal, not with any help from human beings but in spite of them.

One evening he got up and stretched, preparatory to voyaging. First he braced his hind legs and stretched backward, head bowed, rump high, to pull tight the muscles of his shoulders. Then he raised his head and dropped his hips to stretch his spine and hind legs, even clenching his hind feet into fists so that the stretch went into his toes. Ready at last, he moved calmly toward the door so that, as usual, I could open it for him. And then, as our eyes met, I had an inspiration. Misha himself would answer my questions. Right in front of me, a long-neglected gate to the animal kingdom seemed waiting to be opened. Misha held the key.

Who could resist the appeal of this notion? No money, no travel, no training, no special instruments were necessary to probe the mystery—one needed only a dog, a notebook, and a pencil. I didn't even regret my total lack of formal training to begin such a project. In fact, because no biologists had ever hinted that they knew or even wondered what ordinary dogs want, my ignorance seemed almost a qualification. Anyway, I didn't feel I'd be ignorant for long. Turning out the lights so that the neighbors wouldn't see me flout the dog laws, at least not in this instance, I opened the door a crack. Out slipped Misha, with me right behind him, and thus our project began.

Again and again we did this, at least two or three nights a week for almost two years, not stopping even after Misha's owners came home to claim him, because by then Misha liked the work we were doing together and wanted to keep at it. Coming to collect me was not difficult for him—his community did not then have a leash law, so of an evening, after his owners let him out, he'd jump their fence and make his way across two cities to find me. Usually he would arrive after dark. By the light on our front porch I'd see him standing in the street, looking up at our windows like a captain looking for a sailor. I would turn out the porch light and crack the door, and Misha would slip inside for a brief visit with my family and also with his, for by then he had married my daughter's husky, the beautiful Maria, and was teaching some of his skills to the four children he had fathered on her. But eventually he would stand poised to go out again, looking back over his shoulder to see which of us would travel with him. Maria always volunteered, and if I wasn't going myself I'd sometimes let her. It was her or me, though, never both of us; if Maria and Misha were together, they traveled fast and wouldn't wait for me. Sometimes I took Maria on a leash, which kept us all together, but mostly I simply went alone with Misha. One by one, dog secrets were revealed through a series of adventures, some of them dangerous, all of them interesting. Misha was Odysseus, and Cambridge was the wine-dark sea.

᷎ THE FIRST QUESTION, PERHAPS THE MOST IMPORTANT, PERHAPS EVEN THE MOST INteresting, I was never able to answer. This was the question of Misha's navigational skills. To be sure, he had been traveling the streets of Cambridge long before I thought to go with him, and had probably memorized some landmarks. But sometimes he seemed to travel without the aid of landmarks, or at least not with the landmarks he had used to get where he was going, since once he had arrived at his destination, he might easily take another route home. Did he use the stars or the position of the sun? Did he see polarized light? Did he, like a carrier pigeon, hear the infrasound made by the Atlantic Ocean, so that he always knew which way was east? Did he use odors floating in the air, as fish use the taste of currents in seawater? I didn't know, and could learn nothing by watching his sure trot, his confident demeanor. To probe more deeply would have required an experiment—blindfolding him, say, and taking him to some distant release point. But that wasn't the nature of our relationship.

I did learn two things, though, about Misha's navigational ability. The first was that his skills were probably not innate, or not entirely so. If they had been, other huskies should have shared them. But I knew other Siberian huskies who could not navigate. One was Misha's wife, Maria. When they were together, Misha established the route for both of them, and not easily, because she, young and enthusiastic, would go bounding ahead of him, often in the wrong direction, requiring him to overtake her. Then, by jumping at her, he would literally have to knock her in the shoulder to try to make her turn. If after all his efforts she still wouldn't go where he wanted, he would resign himself to following her.

Many another dog would have obeyed her leader, but Maria had been a little spoiled by Misha, who encouraged her to do whatever she wanted, even when he knew that what she wanted was wrong. Of the two, he was unquestionably the stronger and could very easily have been dominant, but he was crazy about her. He let her do as she pleased, which seemed to delight her. As a result, though, Maria never learned to find her own way.

In this the dogs were like two people in a car, with the driver learning the route better and more easily than the passenger. And in later years, when Misha was no longer there to show the way, Maria invariably got lost when voyaging. Even when she went out with her adopted daughter, a dingo-spaniel cross named Fatima, who was an excellent navigator, they would get lost. Why? Because in the hierarchy of their group, Maria was at the very top, while Fatima, a generation below, was next to the bottom, and when Fatima traveled with Maria, Maria insisted on leading. Dominant but misinformed, Maria often bungled the job. But she wasn't stupid, even if she couldn't navigate. As soon as she realized she was lost, rather than turning to Fatima for a suggestion, she would simply sit down on someone's doorstep. Fatima would obediently sit down beside her, and eventually I would appear in a car to drive them home. Of course, the people whose house Maria had chosen would have read her identification tag and phoned me, but the particulars of my arrival didn't concern Maria. With her faithful daughter at her heels, she would clamber into the car like a tired shopper getting into a taxi, always to the puzzlement of her benefactors, who, assuming that a lost dog is a frightened dog, would be expecting her to rejoice profusely at the sight of me.

The second thing I learned about Misha's ability to navigate was that although he made his way faultlessly through the city, his technique didn't necessarily apply in the country, especially if he hadn't reached the starting point on his own. From my house in Cambridge, he and Maria sometimes traveled on their own as far as Concord, about twenty miles away, and would successfully find their way home a few days later, sometimes with deer hair in their stools. But if I took these dogs with me when I went to visit relatives in New Hampshire or on Nantucket, and if then the dogs went voyaging, Misha wasn't always able to lead Maria back to my relatives' home. Perhaps he felt less sure of himself in unfamiliar surroundings, and would surrender to her inept leadership. Whatever the reason, if both got lost in the country, they would use Maria's technique for getting home and wait on someone's doorstep for me to show up in the car.

~ ANOTHER VERY IMPORTANT SKILL OF MISHA'S WAS HIS MANAGEMENT OF TRAFFIC. Cambridge suffers from some of the worst drivers in the nation, but no car as much as touched Misha, who, like a civil engineer, had divided the streets and their traffic into four categories and had developed different strategies to deal with each. The worst and most dangerous areas were congestions of multidirectional traffic, such as are found in Central, Porter, or Harvard Square. These areas Misha completely avoided. If he needed to be on the far side of one of them, he simply went around it. The second category was composed of a few limited-access highways, such as Alewife Parkway and Memorial Drive, where the heavy traffic of speeding cars was especially dangerous to dogs, not only because no legal or moral responsibility is attached to killing a dog, but also because dogs are down low, where motorists can't see them. Misha couldn't avoid the highways and still go where he wanted, so, adopting a humble attitude, he approached the cars with diplomacy and tact in an attempt to appease them.

Perhaps not surprisingly, many dogs treat cars as if they were animate. Dogs who chase cars evidently see them as large, unruly ungulates badly in need of discipline and shepherding, and can't help trying to control them. But Misha didn't chase cars. Being a husky and wearing very lightly the long domestication of his species, he felt no compulsion to assist mankind. However, he well understood that cars could be tremendously dangerous, especially when they seemed to be acting angrily and willfully, as they did on the limited-access highways. So he offered them respect. At the edge of the highway Misha would stand humbly, his head and tail low, his eyes half shut, his ears politely folded. If the cars could have seen him, they would have realized that he didn't challenge their authority.

But the moment the cars became few, Misha's humility would vanish. His ears would rise, his tail too, and he would bound fearlessly among them, the very picture of confidence. Over the highway he would skip, and go happily on his way. Never while I was observing him did I hear a scream of tires. Sometimes, though, he would lose me beside a limited-access highway. I lacked his courage, also his speed and skill, and I usually had to wait much longer than he did before the traffic conditions met my requirements for crossing. If traffic separated us, Misha would wait for a while on the far side, but sooner or later he would assume that I had lost interest and would travel on. Calling him back was out of the question for me—I couldn't have asked him to risk the traffic again on my behalf. Rather, if we became separated, I would simply go home. There he would find me waiting whenever his voyaging abated for a time.

Misha's third category of traffic included the main city streets. Cambridge's famous Brattle Street offers a perfect example, especially because Misha often used this street as a thoroughfare. Or rather, he used the sidewalk of Brattle Street as he traveled from one neighborhood to another, just as a human pedestrian would do. When crossing an intersecting street, however, Misha used a better and more intelligent method than his human counterparts. Unlike us, he didn't cross at the corner. Instead, he would turn up the intersecting street and go about twenty feet from the corner, cross there, and return on the sidewalk to Brattle Street's sidewalk, where he would continue his journey. At first I couldn't understand this maneuver, although Misha invariably used it. Then I saw its merits, and copied him thereafter. Why is Misha's method safer? Because at any point along the block, traffic comes from only two directions instead of from four directions, as it does at the intersection. By crossing at midblock, one reduces one's chances of being hit by a turning car. Since learning the midblock technique from Misha, I have noticed that almost all free-ranging dogs do likewise, as do people who need extra time to cross or who depend on their hearing for safety. Certain blind people, for instance, use the same technique.

Safety, however, was not Misha's only consideration. Usually, a tree or lamppost or mailbox or fire hydrant stands just behind the building line at the place where a traveling dog likes to cross the street. For dogs, the object serves the same function as a wayside inn at the ford of a river, a place that most travelers would visit of necessity, and therefore a good place to leave a message or a sign. Misha would visit these fixed objects, and after careful investigation would turn around and lift his leg. This is a very familiar sight to most dog owners. Virtually all male dogs mark permanent items (or what they believe to be permanent items) as they progress along a street. Sometimes Misha would mark repeatedly, passing a little urine, investigating his stain, and passing urine again, sometimes repeating the procedure as many as five or six times before he seemed satisfied and ready to carry on. Sometimes he rotated his body until his belly tilted upward, meanwhile standing on tiptoe to place his mark almost three feet above the ground. But even these very high stains did not always please him. If they weren't to his satisfaction, he would turn around and stretch even more, so that when he investigated, he would find his mark at his own eye level or higher.

What did it mean? Surely more than emptying the bladder. If Misha wanted merely to empty his bladder, he wouldn't bother to lift his leg at all but would bend his knees slightly, so as not to wet his hind feet, and release his urine, puppy-style, on the ground. Was Misha's leg-lifting an attempt to mark territory? That certainly was the popular explanation, an explanation that I had accepted as fact before my observation began. So I kept track of all the places Misha stained in order to learn what he felt he owned. Soon, though, I had an unwieldy sprawl of data that showed his alleged territory to be virtually everywhere he went. Was this possible? Wouldn't a dog as savvy as Misha want to discriminate to some degree between his home ground and distant places? Wouldn't he act one way in the place where he lived and another way in a distant area which he might visit only once? In fact, Misha's leg-lifting was about the same however far from home he happened to be.

In the residential streets, Misha's demeanor changed. Here he took no precaution about cars and never used a sidewalk, but instead moved daringly and purposefully up the middle of the street, eyes front, head and ears forward, tail up, the very picture of intent confidence. Even when he crossed an intersection, he did not alter his demeanor but kept scanning the street ahead. The trouble was that he couldn't see the cars speeding toward him on the cross street. Yet, amazingly, he always escaped them. How did he manage that?

I might never have learned if both his ears had been like the ears of most other huskies, stiff and upright. But they weren't. His left ear was soft at the tip, and when Misha was trotting along in a relaxed manner, the soft left tip bounced. When he was alert and tense, however, or when he noticed or thought of something important, the tip of his left ear would shoot up and stand stiff like the tip of his right ear. One day, while following Misha down a side street on the bike I had taken to using for my dogological studies, I saw his left ear stiffen as he approached an intersection. As was his custom, his eyes never left the street ahead, but the nearer he got to the intersection, the more his two ears stiffened and rotated outward, pointing sideways, so that by the time he was ready to cross, which he always did without changing his speed or shifting his gaze, the cups of his ears were pointing up and down the cross street. If a car was coming, he heard it. What was more, his hearing gave the speed of the car as well as its location, so that all Misha needed to do to avoid being hit was to pick up his pace or slow down, either to beat the car to the intersection or else to let it go across ahead of him. Scanning the street along which he was proceeding, never shifting his gaze to confirm what he heard coming from the sides, Misha would trot across the intersection smoothly, radiating coolness and self-confidence.

Why didn't he look at the cars? Because he was using his eyes to monitor the scene on the far side of the intersection. There, sensing Misha's approach, all the loose dogs of the neighborhood would leave their yards and porches and run out into the street. And Misha wanted to be ready for them. He wanted to see them before they saw him, so he could prepare himself mentally for the meeting. Inevitably, the nearest dog would approach Misha with its tail and ears raised. When the approaching dog was about thirty feet away, Misha would slow his pace and advance more stiffly, his attention closely focused on the other dog, and gradually the two would come together.

Then Misha's neck would arch and his tail would rise. The other dog would stand still to meet him. Misha would approach stiffly and rapidly, and the two would stand slightly past each other, their heads by each other's necks. Misha usually averted his head to look sideways into the eye of the other dog, who usually looked directly but inquiringly at Misha and then averted his head slightly. Holding his tail high during these meetings, Misha kept his ears forward and the hair of his mantle slightly raised. If the other dog tried to investigate his groin or anus, Misha would leap sideways with his rear legs to avoid the investigation. Finally he would make his conclusive gesture: he would face the other dog's side with his neck highly arched and his nose pointing down almost into the other dog's hackles. Only after this would he sometimes switch his stance again and let the other dog investigate him.

Everyone has watched such a meeting. Sometimes just as the tension seems to be relaxing, one dog knocks the other with his hips. Sometimes the second dog does not react visibly and the circling goes on, but sometimes the second dog staggers slightly, then folds his ears and lowers his tail a bit. No person knows exactly what the hip test tells the participants, but probably the dogs have felt each other's mass. At any rate, the test seems to help them reach an agreement. They usually separate soon afterward, each going his own way. Very inconspicuously, Misha would administer the hip test to every dog who cared to encounter him, and invariably emerged from the encounter with his tail high, a sign of his transcendence over the other dog, who emerged with his tail low. Then Misha might invite or be invited by the other dog to play, and the two might frisk briefly. Misha might invite the other dog to follow him, which he did by trotting onward, looking back at the other dog meanwhile.

Always pragmatic, Misha never bothered to circle tiny dogs, but just swept by them or stepped over them, and he never tried to circle huge dogs, whom he pretended to ignore. Anyone would know that he was superior to the tiny dogs, and evidently he didn't want anyone to notice that the huge dogs could have been physically superior to him. Instead, he concentrated on dogs within ten or fifteen pounds of his own size (a size range that probably included more than 90 percent of the dogs he encountered) and circled to establish his superiority to them. He spent more time circling the male dogs than the female dogs, who tended to be less forthcoming, often circling Misha only long enough to learn his sex and attitude before backing off. Whatever the sex of his challenger, though, the moment the encounter ended, Misha, with his supremacy intact, would continue up the street to repeat exactly the same behavior with every dog who didn't retreat from him. On and on he traveled, in long straight lines about the city, concluding his business in one residential neighborhood only to penetrate another, where once again, radiating coolness, he would circle all comers.

⋅❧⋅ ⋅❧⋅ ⋅❧⋅

At first I saw these dog encounters as yet another obstacle to Misha's travels, something like the problems of navigation and of traffic, problems to solve in order to reach his goal. So I followed him patiently from neighborhood to neighborhood, growing increasingly puzzled that he never seemed to find what he sought. I had already decided that he wasn't looking for companionship—he never spent more than a minute with a local dog, and anyway, he had his own group at our house, his loyal wife and children and two other dogs, both pugs, who, because of their small size, had from the start been his subordinates and would heel to him when we all went walking together. (To do this I had only to keep Misha's wife, Maria, on a leash so that she and he couldn't run away together.) I also felt sure that Misha's voyaging wasn't a search for sex, mainly because few if any estrous females were available. Stray dogs stigmatize a neighborhood, and the Cantabridgians, exquisitely sensitive to status, didn't tolerate stigmata well, especially not the jovial crowds of male dogs that inevitably gather to mill outside the house of a female in season, relentlessly marking with urine all the bushes and buildings and mounting people's legs. Occasionally in my travels with Misha I would see a crowd of milling males, but the female who had lured them was never in evidence. Realistic Misha seldom joined the crowd, or not for long. And never while I was traveling with him did he encounter a female he could, as it were, put his leg over.

Finally, having ruled out companionship and sex as Misha's motives for voyaging, I also ruled out food and hunting. At home I offered him plenty to eat, yet he always ate sparingly, and other people's food didn't tempt him. Nor did he overturn garbage cans or care about their contents. Rather, he investigated only the outer surfaces of garbage cans, probably because they had been marked by other dogs. Odoriferous, food-related trash such as fast-food wrappers held little interest for him. And he all but ignored the live suburban prey species, such as cats and small wild mammals. Even squirrels, which most dogs seem unable to resist chasing, Misha coursed very lightly. No sooner had he gotten a squirrel started up a tree than he would abandon it to return to his voyaging, penetrating ever more Cambridge neighborhoods and circling ever more dogs. At last I reached the inescapable conclusion that to circle other dogs was not merely a byproduct of Misha's questing. To circle other dogs was his purpose.

~ THE CONCLUSION WAS DISAPPOINTING. MY LENGTHY AND PAINSTAKING OBSERVA-tions of someone else's husky, an animal whose free-ranging behavior had made my name known in police stations throughout the Greater Boston area, seemed suddenly like peeling an onion. Evidently my efforts were gaining me nothing more than I could have seen by glancing out a window. No hunts? No joining wild packs? "Is this all?" I asked Misha one night with some irritation as my bicycle wobbled behind his pale hindquarters down yet another darkened residential street. Misha heard me. Deviating from his normal eyes-front demeanor, he looked back pleasantly over his shoulder to give me a glance, quick and frank.

So I continued to follow him through the autumn and winter, until a big storm buried Cambridge in snow, so that the trees were plastered in white and the snowbanks rose higher than people's heads. Then I could see what before had been invisible, the footprints and the urine stains of other dogs. Apparently Misha was not the only one who used the midblock method for crossing big streets. The tracks of other dogs revealed that those who were not under the physical control of a person used the midblock method too, whether or not a scent-marked object such as a tree or a fire hydrant was present to lure them. If such a marking post was present, the dogs predictably went to it. Not so predictable was what they actually did there, which was not merely to leave their own stains—an end in itself if the goal was simply to claim territory—but to investigate and overmark the stains of others. And then I noticed that when Misha marked the same place a second or third time, he did so because a particle of another dog's stain remained uncovered. Only when the underlying stain seemed completely obliterated did Misha appear satisfied and ready to move on.

But why? One day, while watching Misha nearly invert himself to place an extremely high stain on a snowbank near our door, I found myself idly thinking that any dog who could make such a stain by a normal tilt of his leg would have to be a giant. And suddenly it hit me. Perhaps that was the point! Perhaps Misha wanted to give the impression that he who had made the stain was a giant. The more I thought about this explanation, the better it seemed. In fact, making the right impression seemed to be Misha's entire strategy.

Just how serious Misha was about his image was brought home to me one afternoon on a main street, after he had managed to pass through the rush-hour traffic on a limited-access highway but I had not. I had turned back and was leaving the area when I noticed a Saint Bernard. This huge dog was well known to the neighborhood for ferociously defending what he assumed was his master's property. The dog became suspicious as we passed his yard, and when I unexpectedly turned back, he came out into the street. There he barked a challenge, making me wonder how I would get by him, since he commanded the entire street and both sidewalks. Meanwhile, Misha had noticed my absence and had once again breasted the river of highway traffic to return to me. As he reappeared from the torrent of cars, the Saint Bernard saw him and began barking furiously. How could Misha go by him without changing course, or scurrying, or bolting, or otherwise seeming to come off second best and thus losing face? He couldn't turn back, because the Saint Bernard might decide to chase him, forcing him into the dangerous traffic. Nor could he keep trotting down the street into the Saint Bernard's space, where, when attacked, he would have to break into an undignified run, not at all cool but hurried and scampering.

For a few seconds things looked bad for Misha. But then he solved the problem brilliantly. Head up, tail loosely high like a banner of self-confidence, he broke into a canter and bounded straight for the Saint Bernard, but without looking at him. Before anyone realized what had happened, Misha was soaring by, his eyes on something far away, as if he didn't realize the Saint Bernard was there. If the monster at that point had decided to attack, Misha would have been already in motion, and as he was much faster than the giant, he could have sped away without seeming to flee. But apparently everything happened so fast that the Saint Bernard felt bewildered. His barking became louder and faster after Misha was past, as if he thought he had failed to get Misha's attention in the first place.

Much has been written about demeanor, especially the demeanor of prey animals when confronted by predators. For instance, an observer in Canada described the behavior of five bison, three healthy and two sick, who were resting in the open when some wolves appeared. At the approach of the wolves, the two sick bison, knowing they were vulnerable, hastily got to their feet, while the three healthy bison, feeling confident, stayed put. The implication of such behavior was not lost on the wolves, who promptly chose one of the sick bison and killed her. Thus, the importance of demeanor cannot be overemphasized, and is widely understood.

I remember the demeanor of a yearling wolf I saw on Baffin Island, where, in the company of four Canadian biologists sent to survey the caribou, I went to visit the wolves. The part of Baffin we visited was not mapped in much detail. We walked to the study area from a DEW Line station, about seventy-five miles over the tundra. Since no human beings have ever lived inland on Baffin, most of the animals didn't know what we were. The wolf in question was startled to see us when, rounding the edge of a hill, he and his mother came upon us resting by a trail. Both wolves seemed surprised by the sight, and the mother streaked off toward the horizon. The youngster, however, was more naive, and not knowing how to behave in such unexpected circumstances, he acted more traditionally. Rather than risk stimulating our predatory instincts by running from us, he chose to appear normal and cool, and he continued trotting as though he knew of nothing wrong. Soon, though, he trotted into the territory of a nesting jaeger, who took to the air and began to dive fiercely at his head. I actually heard the blows her sharp beak gave him. But the youngster was so committed to his display of calm that he couldn't respond. Without as much as a whimper, he jogged determinedly onward while the bird dove repeatedly upon him, biting him so hard that his skin and fur flew. Only when he thought himself far enough away from us that sudden movement on his part wouldn't bring one of us dashing after him did he feel able to deal with the jaeger. But then, changing instantly from a milquetoast to a demon, he hurled himself into the air and almost caught her. Astonished, she flapped and squawked, lost a feather, then gained altitude and flew back to her nest while the young wolf ran after his mother.

Misha understood the importance of a cool demeanor and so did the young wolf, but Misha's adversary, the big Saint Bernard, did not. His passion and intensity on behalf of his owners eventually proved too much for them, and they took him to the local humane society. Supposedly, he was offered for adoption. But most people don't want a huge dog with very strong feelings. No one took him. That humane society was also a dog hospital, where a dog's emergency later took me, and there, to my surprise, I recognized the Saint Bernard, who was standing helplessly in a little wire cage. Our eyes met. His face brightened, because, I think, he recognized me. I saw that he very much hoped I would help him, but alas, I could not. Scheduled for execution, he was waiting to be drained of blood to provide transfusions for dogs more fortunate than he, dogs who were wanted by their owners.

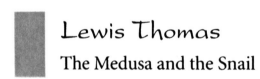

Lewis Thomas
The Medusa and the Snail

WE'VE NEVER BEEN SO SELF-CONSCIOUS ABOUT OUR SELVES AS WE SEEM TO BE THESE DAYS. The popular magazines are filled with advice on things to do with a self: how to find it, identify it, nurture it, protect it, even, for special occasions, weekends, how to lose it transiently. There are instructive books, best sellers on self-realization, self-help, self-development. Groups of self-respecting people pay large fees for three-day sessions together, learning self-awareness. Self-enlightenment can be taught in college electives.

You'd think, to read about it, that we'd only just now discovered selves. Having long suspected that there was *something* alive in there, running the place, separate from everything else, absolutely individual and independent, we've celebrated by giving it a real name. My self.

It is an interesting word, formed long ago in much more social ambiguity than you'd expect. The original root was *se* or *seu,* simply the pronoun of the third person, and most of the descendant words, except "self" itself, were constructed to allude to other, somehow connected people; "sibs" and "gossips," relatives and close acquaintances, came from *seu. Se* was also used to indicate something outside or apart, hence words like "separate," "secret," and "segregate." From an extended root *swedh* it moved into Greek as *ethnos,* meaning people of one's own sort, and *ethos,* meaning the customs of such people. "Ethics" means the behavior of people like one's self, one's own ethics.

We tend to think of our selves as the only wholly unique creations in nature, but it is not so. Uniqueness is so commonplace a property of living things that there is really nothing at all unique about it. A phenomenon can't be unique and universal at the same time. Even individual, free-swimming bacteria can be viewed as unique entities, distinguishable from each other even when they are the progeny of a single clone. Spudich and Koshland have recently reported that motile microorganisms of the same species are like solitary eccentrics in their swimming behavior. When they are searching for food, some tumble in one direction for precisely so many seconds before quitting, while others tumble differently and for different, but characteristic, periods of time. If you watch them closely, tethered by their flagellae to the surface of an antibody-coated slide, you can tell them from each other by the way they twirl, as accurately as though they had different names.

Beans carry self-labels, and are marked by these as distinctly as a mouse by his special smell. The labels are glycoproteins, the lectins, and may have something to do with negotiating the intimate and essential attachment between the bean and the nitrogen-fixing bacteria which live as part of the plant's flesh, embedded in root nodules. The lectin from one line of legume has a special affinity for the surfaces of the particular bacteria which colonize that line, but not for bacteria from other types of bean. The system seems designed for the maintenance of exclusive partnerships. Nature is pieced together by little snobberies like this.

Coral polyps are biologically self-conscious. If you place polyps of the same genetic line together, touching each other, they will fuse and become a single polyp, but if the lines are different, one will reject the other.

Fish can tell each other apart as individuals, by the smell of self. So can mice, and here the olfactory discrimination is governed by the same H_2 locus which contains the genes for immunologic self-marking.

The only living units that seem to have no sense of privacy at all are the nucleated cells that have been detached from the parent organism and isolated in a laboratory dish. Given the opportunity, under the right conditions, two cells from wildly different sources, a yeast cell, say, and a chicken erythrocyte, will touch, fuse, and the two nuclei will then fuse as well, and the new hybrid cell will now divide into monstrous progeny. Naked cells, lacking self-respect, do not seem to have any sense of self.

The markers of self, and the sensing mechanisms responsible for detecting such markers, are conventionally regarded as mechanisms for maintaining individuality for its own sake, enabling one kind of creature to defend and protect itself against all the rest. Selfness, seen thus, is for self-preservation.

In real life, though, it doesn't seem to work this way. The self-marking of invertebrate animals in the sea, who must have perfected the business long before evolution got around to us, was set up in order to permit creatures of one kind to locate others, not for predation but to set up symbiotic households. The anemones who live on the shells of crabs are precisely finicky; so are the crabs. Only a single species of anemone will find its way to only a single species of crab. They sense each other exquisitely, and live together as though made for each other.

Sometimes there is such a mix-up about selfness that two creatures, each attracted by the molecular configuration of the other, incorporate the two selves to make a single organism. The best story I've ever heard about this is the tale told of the nudibranch and medusa living in the Bay of Naples. When first observed, the nudibranch, a common sea slug, was found to have a tiny vestigial parasite, in the form of a jellyfish, permanently affixed to the ventral surface near the mouth. In curiosity to learn how the medusa got there, some marine biologists began searching the local waters for earlier developmental forms, and discovered something amazing. The attached parasite, although apparently so specialized as to have given up living for itself, can still produce offspring, for they are found in abundance at certain seasons of the year. They drift through the upper waters, grow up nicely and astonishingly, and finally become full-grown, handsome, normal jellyfish. Meanwhile, the snail produces snail larvae, and these too begin to grow normally, but not for long. While still extremely small, they become entrapped in the tentacles of the medusa and then engulfed within the umbrella-shaped body. At first glance, you'd believe the medusae are now the predators, paying back for earlier humiliations, and the snails the prey. But no. Soon the snails, undigested and insatiable, begin to eat, browsing away first at the radial canals, then the borders of the rim, finally the tentacles, until the jellyfish becomes reduced in substance by being eaten while the snail grows correspondingly in size. At the end, the arrangement is back to the first scene, with a full-grown nudibranch basking, and nothing left of the jellyfish except the round, successfully edited parasite, safely affixed to the skin near the mouth.

It is confusing tale to sort out, and even more confusing to think about. Both creatures are designed for this encounter, marked as selves so that they can find each other in the waters of the Bay of Naples. The collaboration, if you want to call it that, is entirely specific; it is only this species of medusa and only this kind of nudibranch that can come together and live this way. And, more surprising, they cannot live in any other way; they depend for their survival on each other. They are not really selves, they are specific *others*.

The thought of these creatures gives me an odd feeling. They do not remind me of anything, really. I've never heard of such a cycle before. They are bizarre, that's it, unique. And at the same time, like a vaguely remembered dream, they remind me of the whole earth at once. I cannot get my mind to stay still and think it through.

Atul Gawande
When Doctors Make Mistakes

1—Crash Victim

AT 2 A.M. ON A CRISP FRIDAY IN WINTER, I WAS IN STERILE GLOVES AND GOWN, PULLING A teenage knifing victim's abdomen open, when my pager sounded. "Code Trauma, three minutes," the operating-room nurse said, reading aloud from my pager display. This meant that an ambulance would be bringing another trauma patient to the hospital momentarily, and, as the surgical resident on duty for emergencies, I would have to be present for the patient's arrival. I stepped back from the table and took off my gown. Two other surgeons were working on the knifing victim: Michael Ball, the attending (the staff surgeon in charge of the case), and David Hernandez, the chief resident (a general surgeon in his last of five years of training). Ordinarily, these two would have come later to help with the trauma, but they were stuck here. Ball, a dry, imperturbable forty-two-year-old Texan, looked over to me as I headed for the door. "If you run into any trouble, you call, and one of us will peel away," he said.

I did run into trouble. In telling this story, I have had to change significant details about what happened (including the names of the participants and aspects of my role), but I have tried to stay as close to the actual events as I could while protecting the patient, myself, and the rest of the staff. The way that things go wrong in medicine is normally unseen and, consequently, often misunderstood. Mistakes do happen. We think of them as aberrant; they are anything but.

The emergency room was one floor up, and, taking the stairs two at a time, I arrived just as the emergency medical technicians wheeled in a woman who appeared to be in her thirties and to weigh more than two hundred pounds. She lay motionless on a hard orange plastic spinal board—eyes closed, skin pale, blood running out of her nose. A nurse directed the crew into Trauma Bay 1, an examination room outfitted like an O.R., with green tiles on the wall, monitoring devices, and space for portable X-ray equipment. We lifted her onto the bed and then went to work. One nurse began cutting off the woman's clothes. Another took vital signs. A third inserted a large-bore intravenous line into her right arm. A surgical intern put a Foley catheter into her bladder. The emergency-medicine attending was Samuel Johns, a gaunt, Ichabod Crane-like man in his fifties. He was standing to one side with his arms crossed, observing, which was a sign that I could go ahead and take charge.

If you're in a hospital, most of the "moment to moment" doctoring you get is from residents—physicians receiving specialty training and a small income in exchange for their labor. Our responsibilities depend on our level of training, but we're never entirely on our own: there's always an attending, who oversees our decisions. That night, since Johns was the attending and was responsible for the patient's immediate management, I took my lead from him. But he wasn't a surgeon, and so he relied on me for surgical expertise.

"What's the story?" I asked.

An E.M.T. rattled off the details: "Unidentified white female unrestrained driver in high-speed rollover. Ejected from the car. Found unresponsive to pain. Pulse a hundred, B.P. a hundred over sixty, breathing at thirty on her own . . ."

As he spoke, I began examining her. The first step in caring for a trauma patient is always the same. It doesn't matter if a person has been shot eleven times or crushed by a truck or burned in a kitchen fire. The first thing you do is make sure that the patient can breathe without difficulty. This woman's breaths were shallow and rapid. An oximeter, by means of a sensor placed on her finger, measured the oxygen saturation of her blood. The "O_2 sat" is normally more than ninety-five per cent for a patient breathing room air. The woman was wearing a face mask with oxygen turned up full blast, and her sat was only ninety per cent.

"She's not oxygenating well," I announced in the flattened-out, wake-me-up-when-something-interesting-happens tone that all surgeons have acquired by about three months into residency. With my fingers, I verified that there wasn't any object in her mouth that would obstruct her airway; with a stethoscope, I confirmed that neither lung had collapsed. I got hold of a bag mask, pressed its clear facepiece over her nose and mouth, and squeezed the bellows, a kind of balloon with a one-way valve, shooting a litre of air into her with each compression. After a minute or so, her oxygen came up to a comfortable ninety-eight per cent. She obviously needed our help with breathing. "Let's tube her," I said. That meant putting a tube down through her vocal cords and into her trachea, which would insure a clear airway and allow for mechanical ventilation.

Johns, the attending, wanted to do the intubation. He picked up a Mac 3 laryngoscope, a standard but fairly primitive-looking L-shaped metal instrument for prying open the mouth and throat, and slipped the shoehornlike blade deep into her mouth and down to her larynx. Then he yanked the handle up toward the ceiling to pull her tongue out of the way, open her mouth and throat, and reveal the vocal cords, which sit like fleshy tent flaps at the entrance to the trachea. The patient didn't wince or gag: she was still out cold.

"Suction!" he called. "I can't see a thing."

He sucked out about a cup of blood and clot. Then he picked up the endotracheal tube—a clear rubber pipe about the diameter of an index finger and three times as long—and tried to guide it between her cords. After a minute, her sat started to fall.

"You're down to seventy per cent," a nurse announced.

Johns kept struggling with the tube, trying to push it in, but it banged vainly against the cords. The patient's lips began to turn blue.

"Sixty per cent," the nurse said.

Johns pulled everything out of the patient's mouth and fitted the bag mask back on. The oximeter's luminescent-green readout hovered at sixty for a moment and then rose steadily, to ninety-seven per cent. After a few minutes, he took the mask off and again tried to get the tube in. There was more blood, and there may have been some swelling, too: all the poking down the throat was probably not helping. The sat fell to sixty per cent. He pulled out and bagged her until she returned to ninety-five per cent.

When you're having trouble getting the tube in, the next step is to get specialized expertise. "Let's call anesthesia," I said, and Johns agreed. In the meantime, I continued to follow the standard trauma protocol: completing the examination and ordering fluids, lab tests, and X-rays. Maybe five minutes passed as I worked.

The patient's sats drifted down to ninety-two per cent—not a dramatic change but definitely not normal for a patient who is being manually ventilated. I checked to see if the sensor had slipped off her finger. It hadn't. "Is the oxygen up full blast?" I asked a nurse.

"It's up all the way," she said.

I listened again to the patient's lungs—no collapse. "We've got to get her tubed," Johns said. He took off the oxygen mask and tried again.

Somewhere in my mind, I must have been aware of the possibility that her airway was shutting down because of vocalcord swelling or blood. If it was, and we were unable to get a tube in, then the only chance she'd have to survive would be an emergency tracheostomy: cutting a hole in her neck and inserting a breathing tube into her trachea. Another attempt to intubate her might even trigger a spasm of the cords and a sudden closure of the airway—which is exactly what did happen.

If I had actually thought this far along, I would have recognized how ill-prepared I was to do an emergency "trache." Of the people in the room, it's true, I had the most experience doing tracheostomies, but that wasn't saying much. I had been the assistant surgeon in only about half a dozen, and all but one of them had been non-emergency cases, employing techniques that were not designed for speed. The exception was a practice emergency trache I had done on a goat. I should have immediately called Dr. Ball for backup. I should have got the trache equipment out—lighting, suction, sterile instruments—just in case. Instead of hurrying the effort to get the patient intubated because of a mild drop in saturation, I should have asked Johns to wait until I had help nearby. I might even have recognized that she was already losing her airway. Then I could have grabbed a knife and started cutting her a tracheostomy while things were still relatively stable and I had time to proceed slowly. But for whatever reasons—hubris, inattention, wishful thinking, hesitation, or the uncertainty of the moment—I let the opportunity pass.

Johns hunched over the patient, intently trying to insert the tube through her vocal cords. When her sat once again dropped into the sixties, he stopped and put the mask back on. We stared at the monitor. The numbers weren't coming up. Her lips were still blue. Johns squeezed the bellows harder to blow more oxygen in.

"I'm getting resistance," he said.

The realization crept over me: this was a disaster. "Damn it, we've lost her airway," I said. "Trache kit! Light! Somebody call down to O.R. 25 and get Ball up here!"

People were suddenly scurrying everywhere. I tried to proceed deliberately, and not let panic take hold. I told the surgical intern to get a sterile gown and gloves on. I took a bactericidal solution off a shelf and dumped a whole bottle of yellow-brown liquid on the patient's neck. A nurse unwrapped the tracheostomy kit—sterilized set of drapes and instruments. I pulled on a gown and a new pair of gloves while trying to think through the steps. This is simple, really, I tried to tell myself. At the base of the thyroid cartilage, the Adam's apple, is a little gap in which you find a thin, fibrous covering called the cricothyroid membrane. Cut through that and—voilà! You're in the trachea. You slip through the hole a four-inch plastic tube shaped like a plumber's elbow joint, hook it up to oxygen and a ventilator, and she's all set. Anyway, that was the theory.

I threw some drapes over her body, leaving the neck exposed. It looked as thick as a tree. I felt for the bony prominence of the thyroid cartilage. But I couldn't feel anything through the rolls of fat. I was beset by uncertainty—where should I cut? should I make a horizontal or a vertical incision?—and I hated myself for it. Surgeons never dithered, and I was dithering.

"I need better light," I said.

Someone was sent out to look for one.

"Did anyone get Ball?" I asked. It wasn't exactly an inspiring question.

"He's on his way," a nurse said.

There wasn't time to wait. Four minutes without oxygen would lead to permanent brain damage, if not death. Finally, I took the scalpel and cut. I just cut. I made a three-inch left-to-right swipe across the middle of the neck, following the procedure I'd learned for elective cases. I figured that if I worked through the fat I might be able to find the membrane in the wound. Dissecting down with scissors while the intern held the wound open with retractors, I hit a vein. It didn't let loose a lot of blood, but there was enough to fill the wound: I couldn't see anything. The intern put a finger on the bleeder. I called for suction. But the suction wasn't working; the tube was clogged with the clot from the intubation efforts.

"Somebody get some new tubing," I said. "And where's the light?"

Finally, an orderly wheeled in a tall overhead light, plugged it in, and flipped on the switch. It was still too dim; I could have done better with a flashlight.

I wiped up the blood with gauze, then felt around in the wound with my fingertips. This time, I thought I could feel the hard ridges of the thyroid cartilage and, below it, the slight gap of the cricothyroid membrane, though I couldn't be sure. I held my place with my left hand.

James O'Connor, a silver-haired, seen-it-all anesthesiologist, came into the room. Johns gave him a quick rundown on the patient and let him take over bagging her.

Holding the scalpel in my right hand like a pen, I stuck the blade down into the wound at the spot where I thought the thyroid cartilage was. With small, sharp strokes—working blindly, because of the blood and the poor light—I cut down through the overlying fat and tissue until I felt the blade scrape against the almost bony cartilage. I searched with the tip of the knife, walking it along until I felt it reach a gap. I hoped it was the cricothyroid membrane, and pressed down firmly. Then I felt the tissue suddenly give, and I cut an inch-long opening.

When I put my index finger into it, it felt as if I were prying open the jaws of a stiff clothespin. Inside, I thought I felt open space. But where were the sounds of moving air that I expected? Was this deep enough? Was I even in the right place?

"I think I'm in," I said, to reassure myself as much as anyone else.

"I hope so," O'Connor said. "She doesn't have much longer."

I took the tracheostomy tube and tried to fit it in, but something seemed to be blocking it. I twisted it and turned it, and finally jammed it in. Just then, Ball, the surgical attending, arrived. He rushed up to the bed and leaned over for a look. "Did you get it?" he asked. I said that I thought so. The bag mask was plugged onto the open end of the trache tube. But when the bellows were compressed the air just gurgled out of the wound. Ball quickly put on gloves and a gown.

"How long has she been without an airway?" he asked.

"I don't know. Three minutes."

Ball's face hardened as he registered that he had about a minute in which to turn things around. He took my place and summarily pulled out the trache tube. "God, what a mess," he said. "I can't see a thing in this wound. I don't even know if you're in the right place. Can we get better light and suction?" New suction tubing was found and handed to him. He quickly cleaned up the wound and went to work.

The patient's sat had dropped so low that the oximeter couldn't detect it anymore. Her heart rate began slowing down—first to the sixties and then to the forties. Then she lost her pulse entirely. I put my hands together on her chest, locked my elbows, leaned over her, and started doing chest compressions.

Ball looked up from the patient and turned to O'Connor. "I'm not going to get her an airway in time," he said. "You're going to have to try from above." Essentially, he was admitting my failure. Trying an oral intubation again was pointless—just something to do instead of watching her die. I was stricken, and concentrated on doing chest compressions, not looking at anyone. It was over, I thought.

And then, amazingly, O'Connor: "I'm in." He had managed to slip a pediatric-size endotracheal tube through the vocal cords. In thirty seconds, with oxygen being manually ventilated through the tube, her heart was back, racing at a hundred and twenty beats a minute. Her sat registered at sixty and then climbed. Another thirty seconds and it was at ninety-seven per cent. All the people in the room exhaled, as if they, too, had been denied their breath. Ball and I said little except to confer about the next steps for her. Then he went back downstairs to finish working on the stab-wound patient still in the O.R.

We eventually identified the woman, whom I'll call Louise Williams; she was thirty-four years old and lived alone in a nearby suburb. Her alcohol level on arrival had been three times the legal limit, and had probably contributed to her unconsciousness. She had a concussion, several lacerations, and significant soft-tissue damage. But X-rays and scans revealed no other injuries from the crash. That night, Ball and Hernandez brought her to the O.R. to fit her with a proper tracheostomy. When Ball came out and talked to family members, he told them of the dire condition she was in when she arrived, the difficulties "we" had had getting access to her airway, the disturbingly long period of time that she had gone without oxygen, and thus his uncertainty about how much brain function she still possessed. They listened without protest; there was nothing for them to do but wait.

2—The Banality of Error

To much of the public—and certainly to lawyers and the media—medical error is a problem of bad physicians. Consider some other surgical mishaps. In one, a general surgeon left a large metal instrument in a patient's abdomen, where it tore through the bowel and the wall of the bladder. In another, a cancer surgeon biopsied the wrong part of a woman's breast and thereby delayed her diagnosis of cancer for months. A cardiac surgeon skipped a small but key step during a heart-valve operation, thereby killing the patient. A surgeon saw a man racked with abdominal pain in the emergency room and, without taking a C.T. scan, assumed that the man had a kidney stone; eighteen hours later, a scan showed a rupturing abdominal aortic aneurysm, and the patient died not long afterward.

How could anyone who makes a mistake of that magnitude be allowed to practice medicine? We call such doctors "incompetent," "unethical," and "negligent." We want to see them punished. And so we've wound up with the public system we have for dealing with error: malpractice lawsuits, media scandal, suspensions, firings.

There is, however, a central truth in medicine that complicates this tidy vision of misdeeds and misdoers: *all* doctors make terrible mistakes. Consider the cases I've just described. I gathered them simply by asking respected surgeons I know—surgeons at top medical schools—to tell me about mistakes they had made just in the past year. Every one of them had a story to tell.

In 1991, *The New England Journal of Medicine* published a series of landmark papers from a project known as the Harvard Medical Practice Study—a review of more than thirty thousand hospital admissions in New York State. The study found that nearly four per cent of hospital patients suffered complications from treatment which prolonged their hospital stay or resulted in disability or death, and that two-thirds of such complications were due to errors in care. One in four, or one per cent of admissions, involved actual negligence. It was estimated that, nationwide, a hundred and twenty thousand patients die each year at least partly as a result of errors in care. And subsequent investigations around the country have confirmed the ubiquity of error. In one small study of how clinicians perform when patients have a sudden cardiac arrest, twenty-seven of thirty clinicians made an error in using the defibrillator; they may have charged it incorrectly or lost valuable time trying to figure out how to work a particular model. According to a 1995 study, mistakes in administering drugs—giving the wrong drug or the wrong dose, say—occur, on the average, about once for every hospital admission, mostly without ill effects, but one per cent of the time with serious consequences.

If error were due to a subset of dangerous doctors, you might expect malpractice cases to be concentrated among a small group, but in fact they follow a uniform, bell-shaped distribution. Most surgeons are sued at least once in the course of their careers. Studies of specific types of error, too, have found that repeat offenders are not the problem. The fact is that virtually everyone who cares for hospital patients will make serious mistakes, and even commit acts of negligence, every year. For this reason, doctors are seldom outraged when the press reports yet another medical horror story. They usually have a different reaction: *That could be me.* The important question isn't how to keep bad physicians from harming patients; it's how to keep good physicians from harming patients.

Medical-malpractice suits are a remarkably ineffective remedy. Troyen Brennan, a Harvard professor of law and public health, points out that research has consistently failed to find evidence that litigation reduces medical-error rates. In part, this may be because the weapon is so imprecise. Brennan led several studies following up on the patients in the Harvard Medical Practice Study. He found that fewer than two per cent of the patients who had received substandard care ever filed suit. Conversely, only a small minority among the patients who did sue had in fact been the victims of negligent care. And a patient's likelihood of winning a suit depended primarily on how poor his or her outcome was, regardless of whether that outcome was caused by disease or unavoidable risks of care.

The deeper problem with medical-malpractice suits, however, is that by demonizing errors they prevent doctors from acknowledging and discussing them publicly. The tort system makes adversaries of patient and physician, and pushes each to offer a heavily slanted version of events. When things go wrong, it's almost impossible for a physician to talk to a patient honestly about mistakes. Hospital lawyers warn doctors that, although they must, of course, tell patients about complications that occur, they are never to intimate that they were at fault, lest the "confession" wind up in court as damning evidence in a black-and-white morality tale. At most, a doctor might say, "I'm sorry that things didn't go as well as we had hoped."

There is one place, however, where doctors can talk candidly about their mistakes, if not with patients, then at least with one another. It is called the Morbidity and Mortality Conference—or, more simply, M. & M.—and it takes place, usually once a week, at nearly every academic hospital in the country. This institution survives because laws protecting its proceedings from legal discovery have stayed on the books in most states, despite frequent challenges. Surgeons, in particular, take the M. & M. seriously. Here they can gather behind closed doors to review the mistakes, complications, and deaths that occurred on their watch, determine responsibility, and figure out what to do differently next time.

3—Show and Tell

At my hospital, we convene every Tuesday at five o'clock in a steep, plush amphitheatre lined with oil portraits of the great doctors whose achievements we're meant to live up to. All surgeons are expected to attend, from the interns to the chairman of surgery; we're also joined by medical students doing their surgery "rotation." An M. & M. can include almost a hundred people. We file in, pick up a photocopied list of cases to be discussed, and take our seats. The front row is occupied by the most senior surgeons: terse, serious men, now out of their scrubs and in dark suits, lined up like a panel of senators at a hearing. The chairman is a leonine presence in the seat closest to the plain wooden podium from which each case is presented. In the next few rows are the remaining surgical attendings; these tend to be younger, and several of them are women. The chief residents have put on long white coats and usually sit in the side rows. I join the mass of other residents, all of us in short white coats and green scrub pants, occupying the back rows.

For each case, the chief resident from the relevant service—cardiac, vascular trauma, and so on—gathers the information, takes the podium, and tells the story. Here's a partial list of cases from a typical week (with a few changes to protect confidentiality): a sixty-eight-year-old man who bled to death after heart valve surgery; a forty-seven-year-old woman who had to have a reoperation because of infection following an arteria bypass done in her left leg; a forty-four-year-old woman who had to have bile drained from her abdomen after gall bladder surgery; three patients who had to have reoperations for bleeding following surgery; a sixty-three-year-old man who had a cardiac arrest following heart-bypass surgery; a sixty-six-year-old woman whose sutures suddenly gave way in an abdominal wound and nearly allowed her intestines to spill out. Ms. Williams's case, my failed tracheostomy, was just one case on a list like this. David Hernandez, the chief trauma resident, had subsequently reviewed the records and spoken to me and others involved. When the time came, it was he who stood up front and described what had happened.

Hernandez is a tall, rollicking, good old boy who can tell a yarn, but M. & M. presentations are bloodless and compact. He said something like: "This was a thirty-four-year-old female unrestrained driver in a high-speed rollover. The patient apparently had stable vitals at the scene but was unresponsive, and brought in by ambulance unintubated. She was G.C.S. 7 on arrival." G.C.S. stands for the Glasgow Coma Scale, which rates the severity of head injuries, from three to fifteen. G.C.S. 7 is in the comatose range. "Attempts to intubate were made without success in the E.R. and may have contributed to airway closure. A cricothyroidotomy was attempted without success."

These presentations can be awkward. The chief residents, not the attendings, determine which cases to report. That keeps the attendings honest—no one can cover up mistakes— but it puts the chief residents, who are, after all, underlings, in a delicate position. The successful M. & M. presentation inevitably involves a certain elision of detail and a lot of passive verbs. No one screws up a cricothyroidotomy. Instead, "a cricothyroidotomy was attempted without success." The message, however, was not lost on anyone.

Hernandez continued, "The patient arrested and required cardiac compressions. Anesthesia was then able to place a pediatric E.T. tube and the patient recovered stable vitals. The tracheostomy was then completed in the O.R."

So Louise Williams had been deprived of oxygen long enough to go into cardiac arrest, and everyone knew that meant she could easily have suffered a disabling stroke or been left a vegetable. Hernandez concluded with the fortunate aftermath: "Her workup was negative for permanent cerebral damage or other major injuries. The tracheostomy was removed on Day 2. She was discharged to home in good condition on Day 3." To the family's great relief, and mine, she had woken up in the morning a bit woozy but hungry, alert, and mentally intact. In a few weeks, the episode would heal to a scar.

But not before someone was called to account. A front-row voice immediately thundered, "What do you mean, 'A cricothyroidotomy was attempted without success?'" I sank into my seat, my face hot.

"This was my case," Dr. Ball volunteered from the front row. It is how every attending begins, and that little phrase contains a world of surgical culture. For all the talk in business schools and in corporate America about the virtues of "flat organizations," surgeons maintain an old-fashioned sense of hierarchy. When things go wrong, the attending is expected to take full responsibility. It makes no difference whether it was the resident's hand that slipped and lacerated an aorta; it doesn't matter whether the attending was at home in bed when a nurse gave a wrong dose of medication. At the M. & M., the burden of responsibility falls on the attending.

Ball went on to describe the emergency attending's failure to intubate Williams and his own failure to be at her bedside when things got out of control. He described the bad lighting and her extremely thick neck, and was careful to make those sound not like excuses but merely like complicating factors. Some attending shook their heads in sympathy. A couple of them asked questions to clarify certain details. Throughout, Ball's tone was objective, detached. He had the air of a CNN newscaster describing unrest in Kuala Lumpur.

As always, the chairman, responsible for the over-all quality of our surgery service, asked the final question. What, he wanted to know, would Ball have done differently? Well,

Ball replied, it didn't take long to get the stab-wound patient under control in the O.R., so he probably should have sent Hernandez up to the E.R. at that point or let Hernandez close the abdomen while he himself came up. People nodded. Lesson learned. Next case.

At no point during the M. & M. did anyone question why I had not called for help sooner or why I had not had the skill and knowledge that Williams needed. This is not to say that my actions were seen as acceptable. Rather, in the hierarchy, addressing my errors was Ball's role. The day after the disaster, Ball had caught me in the hall and taken me aside. His voice was more wounded than angry as he went through my specific failures. First, he explained, in an emergency tracheostomy it might have been better to do a vertical neck incision; that would have kept me out of the blood vessels, which run up and down—something I should have known at least from my reading. I might have had a much easier time getting her an airway then, he said. Second, and worse to him than mere ignorance, he didn't understand why I hadn't called him when there were clear signs of airway trouble developing. I offered no excuses. I promised to be better prepared for such cases and to be quicker to ask for help.

Even after Ball had gone down the fluorescent-lit hallway, I felt a sense of shame like a burning ulcer. This was not guilt: guilt is what you feel when you have done something wrong. What I felt was shame: *I* was what was wrong. And yet I also knew that a surgeon can take such feelings too far. It is one thing to be aware of one's limitations. It is another to be plagued by self-doubt. One surgeon with a national reputation told me about an abdominal operation in which he had lost control of bleeding while he was removing what turned out to be a benign tumor and the patient had died. "It was a clean kill," he said. Afterward, he could barely bring himself to operate. When he did operate, he became tentative and indecisive. The case affected his performance for months.

Even worse than losing self-confidence, though, is reacting defensively. There are surgeons who will see faults everywhere except in themselves. They have no questions and no fears about their abilities. As a result, they learn nothing from their mistakes and know nothing of their limitations. As one surgeon told me, it is a rare but alarming thing to meet a surgeon without fear. "If you're not a little afraid when you operate," he said, "you're bound to do a patient a grave disservice."

The atmosphere at the M. & M. is meant to discourage both attitudes—self-doubt and denial—for the M. & M. is a cultural ritual that inculcates in surgeons a "correct" view of mistakes. "What would you do differently?" a chairman asks concerning cases of avoidable complications. "Nothing" is seldom an acceptable answer.

In its way, the M. & M. is an impressively sophisticated and human institution. Unlike the courts or the media, it recognizes that human error is generally not something that can be deterred by punishment. The M. & M. sees avoiding error as largely a matter of will—of staying sufficiently informed and alert to anticipate the myriad ways that things can go wrong and then trying to head off each potential problem before it happens. Why do things go wrong? Because, doctors say, making them go right is hard stuff. It isn't damnable that an error occurs, but there is some shame to it. In fact, the M. & M.'s ethos can seem paradoxical. On the one hand, it reinforces the very American idea that error is intolerable. On the other hand, the very existence of the M. & M., its place on the weekly schedule, amounts to an acknowledgment that mistakes are an inevitable part of medicine.

꘎   ꘎   ꘎

But why do they happen so often? Lucian Leape, medicine's leading expert on error, points out that many other industries—whether the task is manufacturing semiconductors or serving customers at the Ritz-Carlton—simply wouldn't countenance error rates like those in hospitals. The aviation industry has reduced the frequency of operational errors to one in a hundred thousand flights, and most of those errors have no harmful consequences. The buzzword at General Electric these days is "Six Sigma," meaning that its goal is to make product defects so rare that in statistical terms they are more than six standard deviations away from being a matter of chance—almost a one-in-a-million occurrence.

Of course, patients are far more complicated and idiosyncratic than airplanes, and medicine isn't a matter of delivering a fixed product or even a catalogue of products; it may well be more complex than just about any other field of human endeavor. Yet everything we've learned in the past two decades—from cognitive psychology, from "human factors" engineering, from studies of disasters like Three Mile Island and Bhopal—has yielded the same insights: not only do all human beings err but they err frequently and in predictable, patterned ways. And systems that do not adjust for these realities can end up exacerbating rather than eliminating error.

The British psychologist James Reason argues, in his book "Human Error," that our propensity for certain types of error is the price we pay for the brain's remarkable ability to think and act intuitively—to sift quickly through the sensory information that constantly bombards us without wasting time trying to work through every situation anew. Thus systems that rely on human perfection present what Reason calls "latent errors"—errors waiting to happen. Medicine teems with examples. Take writing out a prescription, a rote procedure that relies on memory and attention, which we know are unreliable. Inevitably, a physician will sometimes specify the wrong dose or the wrong drug. Even when the prescription is written correctly, there's a risk that it will be misread. (Computerized ordering systems can almost eliminate errors of this kind, but only a small minority of hospitals have adopted them.) Medical equipment, which manufacturers often build without human operators in mind, is another area rife with latent errors: one reason physicians are bound to have problems when they use cardiac defibrillators is that the devices have no standard design. You can also make the case that onerous workloads, chaotic environments, and inadequate team communication all represent latent errors in the system.

James Reason makes another important observation: disasters do not simply occur; they evolve. In complex systems, a single failure rarely leads to harm. Human beings are impressively good at adjusting when an error becomes apparent, and systems often have built-in defenses. For example, pharmacists and nurses routinely check and counter-check physicians' orders. But errors do not always become apparent, and backup systems themselves often fail as a result of latent errors. A pharmacist forgets to check one of a thousand prescriptions. A machine's alarm bell malfunctions. The one attending trauma surgeon available gets stuck in the operating room. When things go wrong, it is usually because a series of failures conspire to produce disaster.

The M. & M. takes none of this into account. For that reason, many experts see it as a rather shabby approach to analyzing error and improving performance in medicine. It isn't enough to ask what a clinician could or should have done differently so that he and others may learn for next time. The doctor is often only the final actor in a chain of events that set him or her up to fail. Error experts, therefore, believe that it's the process, not the individuals in it, which requires closer examination and correction. In a sense, they want to industrialize medicine. And they can already claim one success story: the specialty of anesthesiology, which has adopted their precepts and seen extraordinary results.

4—Nearly Perfect

At the center of the emblem of the American Society of Anesthesiologists is a single word: "Vigilance." When you put a patient to sleep under general anesthesia, you assume almost complete control of the patient's body. The body is paralyzed, the brain rendered unconscious, and machines are hooked up to control breathing, heart rate, blood pressure—all the vital functions. Given the complexity of the machinery and of the human body, there are a seemingly infinite number of ways in which things can go wrong, even in minor surgery. And yet anesthesiologists have found that if problems are detected they can usually be solved. In the nineteen-forties, there was only one death resulting from anesthesia in every twenty-five hundred operations, and between the nineteen-sixties and the nineteen-eighties the rate had stabilized at one or two in every ten thousand operations.

But Ellison (Jeep) Pierce had always regarded even that rate as unconscionable. From the time he began practicing, in 1960, as a young anesthesiologist out of North Carolina and the University of Pennsylvania, he had maintained a case file of details from all the deadly anesthetic accidents he had come across or participated in. But it was one case in particular that galvanized him. Friends of his had taken their eighteen-year-old daughter to the hospital to have her wisdom teeth pulled, under general anesthesia. The anesthesiologist inserted the breathing tube into her esophagus instead of her trachea, which is a relatively common mishap, and then failed to spot the error, which is not. Deprived of oxygen, she died within minutes. Pierce knew that a one-in-ten-thousand death rate, given that anesthesia was administered in the United States an estimated thirty-five million times each year, meant thirty-five hundred avoidable deaths like that one.

In 1982, Pierce was elected vice-president of the American Society of Anesthesiologists and got an opportunity to do something about the death rate. The same year, ABC's "20/20" aired an exposé that caused a considerable stir in his profession. The segment began, "If you are going to go into anesthesia, you are going on a long trip, and you should not do it if you can avoid it in any way. General anesthesia [is] safe most of the time, but there are dangers from human error, carelessness, and a critical shortage of anesthesiologists. This year, six thousand patients will die or suffer brain damage." The program presented several terrifying cases from around the country. Between the small crisis that the show created and the sharp increases in physicians' malpractice-insurance premiums at that time, Pierce was able to mobilize the Society of Anesthesiologists around the problem of error.

He turned for ideas not to a physician but to an engineer named Jeffrey Cooper, the lead author of a ground-breaking 1978 paper entitled "Preventable Anesthesia Mishaps: A Study of Human Factors." An unassuming, fastidious man, Cooper had been hired in 1972, when he was twenty-six years old, by the Massachusetts General Hospital bioengineering unit, to work on developing machines for anesthesiology researchers. He gravitated toward the operating room, however, and spent hours there observing the anesthesiologists, and one of the first things he noticed was how poorly the anesthesia machines were designed. For example, a clockwise turn of a dial decreased the concentration of potent anesthetics in about half the machines but increased the concentration in the other half. He decided to borrow a technique called "critical incident analysis"—which had been used since the nineteen-fifties to analyze mishaps in aviation—in an effort to learn how equipment might be contributing to errors in anesthesia. The technique is built around carefully conducted interviews, designed to capture as much detail as possible about dangerous incidents: how specific accidents evolved and what factors contributed to them. This information is then used to look for patterns among different cases.

Getting open, honest reporting is crucial. The Federal Aviation Administration has a formalized system for analyzing and reporting dangerous aviation incidents, and its enormous success in improving airline safety rests on two cornerstones. Pilots who report an incident within ten days have automatic immunity from punishment, and the reports go to a neutral, outside agency, NASA, which has no interest in using the information against individual pilots. For Jeffrey Cooper, it was probably an advantage that he was an engineer, and not a physician, so that anesthesiologists regarded him as a discreet, unthreatening interviewer.

The result was the first in-depth, scientific look at errors in medicine. His detailed analysis of three hundred and fifty-nine errors provided a view of the profession unlike anything that had been seen before. Contrary to the prevailing assumption that the start of anesthesia ("takeoff") was the most dangerous part, anesthesiologists learned that incidents tended to occur in the middle of anesthesia, when vigilance waned. The most common kind of incident involved errors in maintaining the patient's breathing, and these were usually the result of an undetected disconnection or misconnection of the breathing tubing, mistakes in managing the airway, or mistakes in using the anesthesia machine. Just as important, Cooper enumerated a list of contributory factors, including inadequate experience, inadequate familiarity with equipment, poor communication among team members, haste, inattention, and fatigue.

The study provoked widespread debate among anesthesiologists, but there was no concerted effort to solve the problems until Jeep Pierce came along. Through the anesthesiology society at first, and then through a foundation that he started, Pierce directed funding into research on how to reduce the problems Cooper had identified, sponsored an international conference to gather ideas from around the world, and brought anesthesia-machine designers into safety discussions.

It all worked. Hours for anesthesiology residents were shortened. Manufacturers began redesigning their machines with fallible human beings in mind. Dials were standardized to turn in a uniform direction; locks were put in to prevent accidental administration of more than one anesthetic gas; controls were changed so that oxygen delivery could not be turned down to zero.

Where errors could not be eliminated directly, anesthesiologists began looking for reliable means of detecting them earlier. For example, because the trachea and the esophagus are so close together, it is almost inevitable that an anesthesiologist will sometimes put the breathing tube down the wrong pipe. Anesthesiologists had always checked for this by listening with a stethoscope for breath sounds over both lungs. But Cooper had turned up a surprising number of mishaps—like the one that befell the daughter of Pierce's friends—involving undetected esophageal intubations. Something more effective was needed. In fact, monitors that could detect this kind of error had been available for years, but, in part because of their expense, relatively few anesthesiologists used them. One type of monitor could verify that the tube was in the trachea by detecting carbon dioxide being exhaled from the lungs. Another type, the pulse oximeter, tracked blood-oxygen levels, thereby providing an early warning that something was wrong with the patient's breathing system. Prodded by Pierce and others, the anesthesiology society made the use of both types of monitor for every patient receiving general anesthesia an official standard. Today, anesthesia deaths from misconnecting the breathing system or intubating the esophagus rather than the trachea are virtually unknown. In a decade, the over-all death rate dropped to just one in more than two hundred thousand cases—less than a twentieth of what it had been.

And the reformers have not stopped there. David Gaba, a professor of anesthesiology at Stanford, has focussed on improving human performance. In aviation, he points out, pilot experience is recognized to be invaluable but insufficient: pilots seldom have direct experience with serious plane malfunction anymore. They are therefore required to undergo yearly training in crisis simulators. Why not doctors, too?

Gaba, a physician with training in engineering, led in the design of an anesthesia-simulation system known as the Eagle Patient Simulator. It is a life-size, computer-driven mannequin that is capable of amazingly realistic behavior. It has a circulation, a heartbeat, and lungs that take in oxygen and expire carbon dioxide. If you inject drugs into it or administer inhaled anesthetics, it will detect the type and amount, and its heart rate, its blood pressure, and its oxygen levels will respond appropriately. The "patient" can be made to develop airway swelling, bleeding, and heart disturbances. The mannequin is laid on an operating table in a simulation room equipped exactly like the real thing. Here both residents and experienced attending physicians learn to perform effectively in all kinds of dangerous, and sometimes freak, scenarios: an anesthesia-machine malfunction, a power outage, a patient who goes into cardiac arrest during surgery, and even a cesarean-section patient whose airway shuts down and who requires an emergency tracheostomy.

Though anesthesiology has unquestionably taken the lead in analyzing and trying to remedy "systems" failures, there are signs of change in other quarters. The American Medical Association, for example, set up its National Patient Safety Foundation in 1997 and asked Cooper and Pierce to serve on the board of directors. The foundation is funding research, sponsoring conferences, and attempting to develop new standards for hospital drug-ordering systems that could substantially reduce medication mistakes—the single most common type of medical error.

Even in surgery there have been some encouraging developments. For instance, operating on the wrong knee or foot or other body part of a patient has been a recurrent, if rare, mistake. A typical response has been to fire the surgeon. Recently, however, hospitals and surgeons have begun to recognize that the body's bilateral symmetry makes these errors predictable. Last year, the American Academy of Orthopedic Surgeons endorsed a simple way of preventing them: make it standard practice for surgeons to initial, with a marker, the body part to be cut before the patient comes to surgery.

The Northern New England Cardiovascular Disease Study Group, based at Dartmouth, is another success story. Though the group doesn't conduct the sort of in-depth investigation of mishaps that Jeffrey Cooper pioneered, it has shown what can be done simply through statistical monitoring. Six hospitals belong to this consortium, which tracks deaths and complications (such as wound infections, uncontrolled bleeding, and stroke) arising from heart surgery and tries to identify various risk factors. Its researchers found, for example, that there were relatively high death rates among patients who developed anemia after bypass surgery, and that anemia developed most often in small patients. The fluid used to "prime" the heart-lung machine caused the anemia, because it diluted a patient's blood, so the smaller the patient (and his or her blood supply) the greater the effect. Members of the consortium now have several promising solutions to the problem. Another study found that a group at one hospital had made mistakes in "handoffs"—say, in passing preoperative lab results to the people in the operating room. The study group solved the problem by developing a pilot's checklist for all patients coming to the O.R. These efforts have introduced a greater degree of standardization, and so reduced the death rate in those six hospitals from four per cent to three per cent between 1991 and 1996. That meant two hundred and ninety-three fewer deaths. But the Northern New England cardiac group, even with its narrow focus and techniques, remains an exception; hard information about how things go wrong is still scarce. There is a hodgepodge of evidence that latent errors and systemic factors may contribute to surgical errors: the lack of standardized protocols, the surgeon's inexperience, the hospital's inexperience, inadequately designed technology and techniques, thin staffing, poor teamwork, time of day, the effects of managed care and corporate medicine, and so on and so on. But which are the major risk factors? We still don't know. Surgery, like most of medicine, awaits its Jeff Cooper.

5—Getting It Right

It was a routine gallbladder operation, on a routine day: on the operating table was a mother in her forties, her body covered by blue paper drapes except for her round, antiseptic-coated belly. The gallbladder is a floppy, finger-length sac of bile like a deflated olive-green balloon tucked under the liver, and when gallstones form, as this patient had learned, they can cause excruciating bouts of pain. Once we removed her gallbladder, the pain would stop.

There are risks to this surgery, but they used to be much greater. Just a decade ago, surgeons had to make a six-inch abdominal incision that left patients in the hospital for the better part of a week just recovering from the wound. Today, we've learned to take out gallbladders with a minute camera and instruments that we manipulate through tiny incisions. The operation, often done as day surgery, is known as laparoscopic cholecystectomy, or "lap chole." Half a million Americans a year now have their gallbladders removed this way; at my hospital alone, we do several hundred lap choles annually.

When the attending gave me the go-ahead, I cut a discreet inch-long semicircle in the wink of skin just above the belly button. I dissected through fat and fascia until I was inside the abdomen, and dropped into place a "port," a half-inch-wide sheath for slipping instruments in and out. We hooked gas tubing up to a side vent on the port, and carbon dioxide poured in, inflating the abdomen until it was distended like a tire. I inserted the miniature camera. On a video monitor a few feet away, the woman's intestines blinked into view. With the abdomen inflated, I had room to move the camera, and I swung it around to look at the liver. The gallbladder could be seen poking out from under the edge.

We put in three more ports through even tinier incisions, spaced apart to complete the four corners of a square. Through the ports on his side, the attending put in two long "graspers," like small-scale versions of the device that a department-store clerk might use to get a hat off the top shelf. Watching the screen as he maneuvered them, he reached under the edge of the liver, clamped onto the gallbladder, and pulled it up into view. We were set to proceed.

Removing the gallbladder is fairly straightforward. You sever it from its stalk and from its blood supply, and pull the rubbery sac out of the abdomen through the incision near the belly button. You let the carbon dioxide out of the belly, pull out the ports, put a few stitches in the tiny incisions, slap some Band-Aids on top, and you're done. There's one looming danger, though: the stalk of the gallbladder is a branch off the liver's only conduit for sending bile to the intestines for the digestion of fats. And if you accidentally injure this main bile duct, the bile backs up and starts to destroy the liver. Between ten and twenty per cent of the patients to whom this happens will die. Those who survive often have permanent liver damage and can go on to require liver transplantation. According to a standard textbook, "injuries to the main bile duct are nearly always the result of misadventure during operation and are therefore a serious reproach to the surgical profession." It is a true surgical error, and, like any surgical team doing a lap chole, we were intent on avoiding this mistake.

Using a dissecting instrument, I carefully stripped off the fibrous white tissue and yellow fat overlying and concealing the base of the gallbladder. Now we could see its broad neck and the short stretch where it narrowed down to a duct—a tube no thicker than a strand of spaghetti peeking out from the surrounding tissue, but magnified on the screen to the size of major plumbing. Then, just to be absolutely sure we were looking at the gallbladder duct and not the main bile duct, I stripped away some more of the surrounding tissue. The attending and I stopped at this point, as we always do, and discussed the anatomy. The neck of the gallbladder led straight into the tube we were eying. So it had to be the right duct. We had exposed a good length of it without a sign of the main bile duct. Everything looked perfect, we agreed. "Go for it," the attending said.

I slipped in the clip applier, an instrument that squeezes V-shaped metal clips onto whatever you put in its jaws. I got the jaws around the duct and was about to fire when my eye caught, on the screen, a little globule of fat lying on top of the duct. That wasn't necessarily anything unusual, but somehow it didn't look right. With the tip of the clip applier, I tried to flick it aside, but, instead of a little globule, a whole layer of thin unseen tissue came up, and, underneath, we saw that the duct had a fork in it. My stomach dropped. If not for that little extra fastidiousness, I would have clipped off the main bile duct.

Here was the paradox of error in medicine. With meticulous technique and assiduous effort to insure that they have correctly identified the anatomy, surgeons need never cut the main bile duct. It is a paradigm of an avoidable error. At the same time, studies show that even highly experienced surgeons inflict this terrible injury about once in every two hundred lap choles. To put it another way, I may have averted disaster this time, but a statistician would say that, no matter how hard I tried. I was almost certain to make this error at least once in the course of my career.

But the story doesn't have to end here, as the cognitive psychologists and industrial-error experts have demonstrated. Given the results they've achieved in anesthesiology, it's clear that we can make dramatic improvements by going after the process, not the people. But there are distinct limitations to the industrial cure, however necessary its emphasis on systems and structures. It would be deadly for us, the individual actors, to give up our belief in human perfectibility. The statistics may say that someday I will sever someone's main bile duct, but each time I go into a gallbladder operation I believe that with enough will and effort I can beat the odds. This isn't just professional vanity. It's a necessary part of good medicine, even in superbly "optimized" systems. Operations like that lap chole have taught me how easily error can occur, but they've also showed me something else: effort does matter; diligence and attention to the minutest details can save you.

This may explain why many doctors take exception to talk of "systems problems," "continuous quality improvement," and "process reëngineering." It is the dry language of structures, not people. I'm no exception: something in me, too, demands an acknowledgment of my autonomy, which is also to say my ultimate culpability. Go back to that Friday night in the E.R., to the moment when I stood, knife in hand, over Louise Williams, her lips blue, her throat a swollen, bloody, and suddenly closed passage. A systems engineer might have proposed some useful changes. Perhaps a backup suction device should always be at hand, and better light more easily available. Perhaps the institution could have trained me better for such crises, could have required me to have operated on a few more goats. Perhaps emergency tracheostomies are so difficult under any circumstances that an automated device could have been designed to do a better job. But the could-haves are infinite, aren't they? Maybe Williams could have worn her seat belt, or had one less beer that night. We could call any or all of these factors latent errors, accidents waiting to happen.

But although they put the odds against me, it wasn't as if I had no chance of succeeding. Good doctoring is all about making the most of the hand you're dealt, and I failed to do so. The indisputable fact was that I hadn't called for help when I could have, and when I plunged the knife into her neck and made my horizontal slash my best was not good enough. It was just luck, hers and mine, that Dr. O'Connor somehow got a breathing tube into her in time.

There are all sorts of reasons that it would be wrong to take my license away or to take me to court. These reasons do not absolve me. Whatever the limits of the M. & M., its fierce ethic of personal responsibility for errors is a formidable virtue. No matter what measures are taken, medicine will sometimes falter, and it isn't reasonable to ask that it achieve perfection. What's reasonable is to ask that medicine never cease to aim for it.

CREATIVE CULTURAL CRITICISM

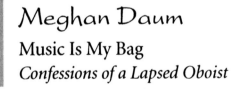

Meghan Daum
Music Is My Bag
Confessions of a Lapsed Oboist

PICTURE A FIFTEEN-YEAR-OLD BOY WITH THE EARLY TRACES OF A MUSTACHE WHO HANGS out in the band room after school playing the opening bars of a Billy Joel song on the piano, and who, in an unsuccessful attempt at a personal style, wears a fedora hat and a scarf decorated with a black-and-white design of a piano keyboard. He is the boy who, in addition to having taught himself some tunes from the *Songs in the Attic* sheet music he bought at the local Sam Ash, probably plays the trombone in the marching band, and also no doubt experienced a seminal moment one afternoon as he vaguely flirted with a not-yet-kissed clarinet-playing girl, a girl who is none too popular but whose propensity for leaning on the piano as he plays the opening chords of "Captain Jack" clued him in to the hitherto unimagined social possibilities of the marching band.

If the clarinet-playing girl is an average student musician, she carries her plastic Selmer in the standard-issue black plastic case. If she has demonstrated any kind of proficiency, she carries her Selmer in a tote bag that reads MUSIC IS MY BAG. The boy in the piano-key scarf definitely has music as his bag. He may not yet have the tote bag, but the hat, the Billy Joel, and the euphoria brought on by a sexual awakening centered entirely around band is all he needs to be delivered into the unmistakable world of Music Is My Bag.

I grew up in that world. The walls of my parents' house were covered with framed art posters from musical events: the San Francisco Symphony's 1982 production of *St. Matthew Passion*, the Metropolitan Opera's 1976 production of *Aida*, the original Broadway production of *Sweeney Todd*. Ninety percent of the books on the shelves were about music, if not actual musical scores. Childhood ceramics projects made by my brother and me were painted with eighth notes and treble clef signs. We owned a deck of cards with portraits of the great composers on the back. A baby grand piano overtook the room that would have been the dining room if my parents hadn't forgone a table and renamed it "the music room." This room also contained an imposing hi-fi system and a $300 wooden music stand. Music played at all times: Brahms, Mendelssohn, cast recordings of Sondheim musicals, a cappella Christmas albums. When my father sat down with a book he read musical scores, humming quietly and tapping his foot. When I was ten my mother decided we needed to implement a before-dinner ritual akin to saying grace, so she composed a short song, asking us all to contribute a lyric, and we held hands and sang it before eating. My lyric was, "There's a smile on our face and it seems to say all the wonderful things we've all done today." My mother insisted on harmonizing at the end. She also did this when singing "Happy Birthday."

Harmonizing on songs like "Happy Birthday" is a clear indication of the Music Is My Bag personality. If one does not have an actual bag that reads MUSIC IS MY BAG—as did the violist in the chamber music trio my mother set up with some women from the Unitarian Church—a $300 music stand will more than suffice. To avoid confusion, let me also say that there are many different Bags in life. Some friends of my parents have a $300 dictionary stand, a collection of silver bookmarks, and once threw a dinner party wherein the guests had to dress up as members of the Bloomsbury group. These people are Literature Is My Bag. I also know people who belong to Movies Are My Bag; they are easily detectable by key chains shaped like projectors, outdated copies of *Halliwell's Film Guide*, and one too many T-shirts from obscure venues like the San Jose Film Festival. Cats Are My Bag people are too well-known to require explanation, and the gaudiness of their paraphernalia—the figurines, coffee-table books, and refrigerator magnets—tends to give the category dominance over the slightly more subtle Dogs Are My Bag. Perhaps the most annoying Bag is Where I Went to College Is My Bag: Yale running shorts, plastic Yale tumblers, Yale Platinum Visa cards, and, yes, even Yale screen savers—all in someone pushing forty, the perennial contributor to the class notes.

Having a Bag connotes the state of being overly interested in something yet, in a certain way, not interested enough. It has a hobbyish quality to it, a sense that the enthusiasm developed at a time when the person was lacking in some significant area of social or intellectual life. Music Is My Bag is the mother of all Bags, not just because in the early 1980s some consumer force of the public-radio-fund-drive variety distributed a line of tote bags displaying that slogan but because its adherents—or "music lovers," as they tend to call themselves—give off an aura that distinguishes them from the rest of the population. It's an aura that has to do with a sort of benign cluelessness, a condition that even in middle age smacks of that phase between prepubescence and real adolescence.

Music Is My Bag people have a sexlessness to them, a pastiness. They can never seem to find a good pair of jeans. You can easily spot them on the street: the female French horn player in concert dress hailing a cab to Lincoln Center at around seven in the evening, her earrings too big, her hairstyle unchanged since 1986. The fifty-something recording engineer with the running shoes and the shoulder bag. The Indiana marching band kids in town for the Macy's Thanksgiving Day Parade, snapping photos of one another in front of the Hard Rock Cafe, having sung their parts from the band arrangement of *Hello, Dolly!* the whole way on the bus, thinking, *knowing*, that it won't get any better than this. Like all Music Is My Bag people, they are too much in love with trappings and memorabilia, saving the certificates of participation from regional festivals, the composer-a-month calendars, the Mostly Mozart posters. Their sincerity trumps all attempts at snideness. The boys' sarcasm falls short of irony; the girls will never be great seducers. They will all grow up to look like high school band directors no matter what profession they choose, with pets named Wolfgang and Gershwin and hemlines that are never quite right.

◆   ◆   ◆

I played the oboe, which is not an instrument to be taken lightly. The oboist runs a high risk of veering deeply into Music Is My Bag, mostly because getting beyond the entry level requires an absorption with technique that can render a person vulnerable to certain vagaries of the wind ensemble subculture, which inevitably concerns itself with the sociopolitical superstructure of the woodwind section. Within this subtype, the oboist faces the twin temptations of narcissism, in contemplating the disproportionate number of solo passages written for the oboe, and pride, because it is she who sounds the A that tunes the orchestra.

The oboe is a difficult instrument, beautiful when played well, horrible when played poorly. Yet even when it produces a lovely sound, it is not an instrument for the vain. The embouchure puckers the face into an unnatural grimace, an expression well documented in the countless photographs from my childhood that suggest some sort of facial deformity: the lipless girl. Then there is the question of moisture. Oboe playing revolves almost entirely around saliva. Spit gets caught in the keys and the joints and must be blown out using cigarette rolling paper as a blotter (a scandalous drugstore purchase for a twelve-year-old girl). Spit accumulates on the floor if you play for too long. Spit must be constantly sucked out from both sides of the reed. Fragile and temperamental, the reed is the oboe player's chronic medical condition. It must be tended to constantly. It must be wet but never too wet, hard enough to emit a decent sound but soft enough to blow air through. The oboist must never stray far from liquid; the reed is forever in her mouth or in a paper cup of water that teeters on the music stand or being doused at a drinking fountain in Parsippany High School at the North Jersey Regional Band and Orchestra audition. After a certain age, the student oboist must learn to make her own reeds, building them from bamboo using knives and shavers—a seemingly eighteenth-century exercise that ought to require an apprenticeship. But oboists, occupying a firm, albeit wet, patch of ground under the tattered umbrella of Music Is My Bag, never quite live in the same era as everyone else.

Although I did, at one point, hold the title of second-best high school player in the state of New Jersey, I was a mediocre oboist. My discipline was lacking, my enthusiasm virtually nil, and my comprehension of rhythm (in keeping with a lifelong math phobia) held me back considerably. But being without an aptitude for music was, in my family, tantamount to being a Kennedy who knows nothing of politics. Aptitude was something, perhaps even the only thing, I possessed. As indifferent to the oboe as I was—and I once began an orchestra rehearsal without noticing that I had neglected to screw the bell, the entire bottom portion, onto the rest of my instrument—I managed to be good enough to play in the New Jersey All-State High School Orchestra as well as in a local adult symphony. I even gained acceptance to a music conservatory. These aren't staggering accomplishments unless you consider the fact that I rarely practiced. If I had practiced with any regularity and determination I could have been, as my parents would have liked me to be, one of those kids who was schlepped to Juilliard on Saturdays. If I had practiced slightly more than that I could have gone to Juilliard for college. If I had practiced a lot I could have ended up in the New York Philharmonic.

And yet I didn't practice. I haven't picked up the oboe since my junior year in college, where, incidentally, I sat first chair in the orchestra even though I did not practice once the entire time.

I never practiced and yet I always practiced. My memory is of always being unprepared, yet I was forced to sit in the chair for so many hours that I suspect something else must have been at work, a lack of consciousness, a failure of concentration, an inability to practice on my own. "Practice" was among the top five words spoken in our family, the other four being Meghan, Mom, Dad, and Evan. Today, almost ten years since I last practiced, the word has finally lost the resonance of our usage. I now think of practice in terms of law or medicine. There is a television show called *The Practice*, and it seems odd to me that I never associate the word sprawled across the screen with the word that was woven relentlessly through our family discourse. For my entire childhood and adolescence, practicing was both a given and a punishment. When we were bad, we practiced. When we were idle, we practiced. Before dinner and TV and friends coming over and bedtime and a thousand other things that beckoned with possibility, we practiced. "You have practicing and homework," my mother said every day. In that order. My father said the same thing without the part about homework.

Much of the reason I could never quite get with the oboe-playing program was that I developed, at a very young age, a deep contempt for the Music Is My Bag world. Instead of religion, my family had music, and it was the church against which I rebelled. I had clergy for parents: my father was a professional composer and arranger, a keyboard player and trombonist, who scored the Gulf War for ABC; my mother was a pianist and music educator of the high-school-production-of-*Carousel* genre. My own brother was a reluctant Christ figure. A typically restless second child in youth (he quit piano lessons but later discovered he could play entirely by ear), my brother recently completed the final mix of a demo CD of songs he wrote and performed in the style of mid-Eighties pop, late Doobie Brothers groove. His Los Angeles house is littered with Billy Joel and Bruce Hornsby sheet music, back issues of *Stereo Review*, the liner notes to the digital remastering of John Williams's score for *Star Wars*. Music is the bag.

✧ ✧ ✧

I compose songs in my sleep. I can't do it awake. I'll dream of songwriters singing onstage. I'll hear them perform new songs, songs I've never heard, songs I therefore must have written. In childhood I never put one thought toward composing a song. It would have been like composing air, creating more of something of which there was already quite enough. Wind players such as flutists and saxophonists need as much air as they can get. Oboists are always trying to get rid of air. They calibrate what they need to get the reed to vibrate, end up using even less, and dispense with the rest out of the corners of their mouths. It's all about exhaling. On an eighth rest, they're as likely to blow air out as they are to steal a breath. There's always too much of everything for oboists: too much air, too many bars when they're not playing and too many bars when there's hardly anyone playing but them, too many percussion players dropping triangles on the floor, too many violinists playing "Eleanor Rigby" before the rehearsal starts.

Most orchestras have only two oboists, first chair and second chair, pilot and copilot. The second oboist is the perpetual back-up system, the one on call, the one who jumps in and saves the other when his reed dries up in the middle of a solo, when he misses his cue, when he freezes in panic before trying to hit a high D. I've been first oboist and I've been second oboist, and first is better, though not by much. It's still the oboe. Unlike the gregarious violinist or the congenial cellist, the oboist is a lone wolf. To play the oboe in an orchestra is to complete an obstacle course of solos and duets with the first flutist, who if she is hardcore Music Is My Bag will refer to herself as a "flautist." Oboe solos dot the great symphonies like land mines, the pizzicati that precede them are drum rolls, the conductor's pointing finger is an arrow for the whole audience to see: here comes the oboe, two bars until the oboe, now, *now.* It's got to be nailed, one flubbed arpeggio, one flat half note, one misplaced pinky in the middle of a run of sixteenth notes, and *everyone* will hear. Everyone.

My parents' presence at a high school orchestra concert turned what should have been a routine event into something akin to the finals of the Olympic women's figure skating competition. Even from the blinding, floodlit stage I could practically see them in the audience, clucking at every error, grimacing at anything even slightly out of tune. Afterward, when the other parents—musically illiterate chumps—were patting their kids on the head and loading the tuba into the station wagon, I would receive my critique. "You were hesitating in the second part of the Haydn Variations." "You overanticipated in the Berceuse section of the Stravinsky." "Your tone was excellent in the first movement, but then your chops ran out." My brother, who was forced for a number of years to play the French horn, once was reduced to a screaming fight with our father in the school parking lot, the kind of fight possible only between fathers and sons. He'd bumbled too many notes, played out of tune, committed some treasonous infraction against the family reputation. My father gave him the business on the way to the car, eliciting the alto curses of a fourteen-year-old, pages of music everywhere, an instrument case slammed on the pavement.

This sort of rebellion was not my style. I cried instead. I cried in the seventh grade when the letter telling me I'd been accepted to the North Jersey Regional Band and Orchestra arrived three days late. I cried in the tenth grade when I ended up in the All-State Band instead of the orchestra. I cried when I thought I'd given a poor recital (never mind that the audience thought I was brilliant—all morons), cried before lessons (underprepared), cried after lessons (sentenced to a week of reviewing the loathsome F sharp étude). Mostly, though, I cried during practice drills supervised by my father. These were torture sessions wherein some innocent tooting would send my father racing downstairs from his attic study, screaming, "Count, count, you're not counting! Jesus Christ!" Out would come a pencil, if not an actual conductor's baton, and he would begin hitting the music stand, forcing me to repeat the tricky fingerings again and again, speeding up the tempo so that I'd be sure to hit each note when we took it back down to real time. These sessions would last for hours, my mouth muscles shaking, tears welling up from fatigue and exasperation. If we had a copy of the piano part, my mother would play the accompaniment, and together my parents would bark commands: "Articulate the eighth notes more. More staccato on the tonguing. Don't tap your foot, tap your toe inside your shoe." The postman heard a lot of this. The neighbors heard all of it. After practicing we'd eat dinner, but not before that song: "There's a smile on our face, and it seems to say all the wonderful things . . ." "Good practice session today," my mother would say, dishing out the casserole, WQXR's *Symphony Hall* playing over the kitchen speakers. "Yup, sounding pretty good," my father would say. "How about one more go at it before bed?"

⬦ ⬦ ⬦

My mother called my oboe a "horn." This infuriated me. "Do you have your horn?" she'd ask every single morning. "Do you need your horn for school today?" She maintained that this terminology was technically correct, that among musicians a "horn" was anything into which air was blown. My oboe was a $4,000 instrument, high-grade black granadilla with sterling silver keys. It was no horn. But such semantics are a staple of Music Is My Bag, the overfamiliar stance that reveals a desperate need for subcultural affiliation, the musical equivalent of people in the magazine business who refer to publications like *Glamour* and *Forbes* as "books." As is indicated by the use of "horn," there's a subtly macho quality to Music Is My Bag. The persistent insecurity of musicians, especially classical musicians, fosters a kind of jargon that would be better confined to the military or major league baseball. Cellists talk about rock stops and rosin as though they were comparing canteen belts or brands of glove grease. They have their in-jokes and aphorisms: "The Rock Stops Here," "Eliminate Violins in Our Schools."

I grew up surrounded by phrases like "rattle off that solo," "nail that lick," and "build up your chops." "Chops" is a word that should be invoked only by rock-and-roll guitarists but is more often uttered with the flailing, badly timed anti-authority of the high school clarinet player. Like the violinist who plays "Eleanor Rigby" before rehearsal, the clarinet player's relationship to rock and roll maintains its distance. Rock music is about sex. It is something unloved by parents and therefore unloved by Music Is My Bag people, who make a vocation of pleasing their parents, of studying trig and volunteering at the hospital and making a run for the student government even though they're well aware they have no chance of winning. Rock and roll is careless and unstudied. It might possibly involve drinking. It most certainly involves dancing. It flies in the face of the central identity of Music Is My Baggers, who chose as their role models those painfully introverted characters from young adult novels: the klutz, the bookworm, the late bloomer. When given a classroom assignment to write about someone who inspires her. Music Is My Bag will write about her grandfather or perhaps Jean-Pierre Rampal. If the bad-attitude kid in the back row writes about AC/DC's Angus Young, Music Is My Bag will believe in her heart that he should receive a failing grade. Rock and roll, as her parents would say when the junior high drama club puts on a production of *Grease*, "is not appropriate for this age group." Even in the throws of adolescence, Music Is My Bag will deny adolescence. Even at age sixteen, she will hold her ears when the rock music gets loud, saying it ruins her sense of overtones, saying she has sensitive ears. Like a retiree, she will classify the whole genre as nothing but a bunch of noise, though it is likely that she is a fan of Yes.

During the years when I was a member of the New Jersey All-State Orchestra, I would carpool to rehearsals with the four or so other kids from my town who made All-State every year. This involved spending as much as two hours each way in station wagons driven by people's parents, and, inevitably, the issue of music would arise: what music would be played in the car? Among the most talented musicians in school was a girl named Elizabeth Ostling, who was eventually hired as the second flutist for the Boston Symphony Orchestra at age twenty-one, and at the age of fifteen was unaccountably possessed by an enthusiasm for the Christian singer Amy Grant. Next to Prokofiev and the Hindemith Flute Sonata, Amy Grant occupied the number-one spot in her studious, late-blooming heart. Since Elizabeth's mother, like many parents of Baggers, was devoted solely to her daughter's musical and academic career, she did most of the driving to such boony spots as Chatham High School, Monmouth Regional, and Long Branch Middle School. Mile after New Jersey Turnpike mile, we were serenaded by the wholesome synthesizers of songs like "Saved By Love" and "Wait for the Healing," only to spill out of the car and take no small relief in the sound of twenty-five of New Jersey's best student violinists playing "Eleanor Rigby" before the six-hour rehearsal.

To participate in a six-hour rehearsal of the New Jersey All-State Orchestra is to see the accessories of Bagdom tumble from purses, knapsacks, and totes; here more than anyplace are the real McCoys, actual Music Is My Bag bags, canvas satchels filled with stereo Walkmans and A.P. math homework and Trapper Keeper notebooks featuring the piano-playing Schroeder from the *Peanuts* comic strip. When we paused for dinner I would embark on oboe maintenance, putting the reed in water, swabbing the instrument dry, removing the wads of wax that, during my orthodontic years, I placed over my front teeth to keep the inside of my mouth from bleeding. Just as I had hated the entropy of recess back in grade school, I loathed the dinner breaks at All-State rehearsals. To maximize rehearsal time, the wind section often ate separately from the strings, which left me alone with the band types, the horn players and percussionists who wore shirts with slogans like "Make Time for Half-time." They'd wolf down their sandwiches and commence with their jam session, a cacophonous white noise of scales, finger exercises, and memorized excerpts from their hometown marching numbers. During these dinner breaks, I'd generally hang with the other oboist. For some reason, this was almost always a tall girl who wore sneakers with corduroy pants and a turtleneck with nothing over it. This is fairly typical Music Is My Bag garb, though oboists have a particular spin on it, a spin characterized more than anything by lack of spin. Given the absence in most classical musicians of a style gene, this is probably a good thing. Oboists don't accessorize. They don't wear buttons on their jackets that say "Oboe Power" or "Who Are You Going to Tune To?"

There's high-end Bagdom and low-end Bagdom, with a lot of room in between. Despite my parents' paramilitary practice regimens, I have to give them credit for being fairly high-end Baggers. There were no piano-key scarves in our house, no "World's Greatest Trombonist" figurines, no plastic tumblers left over from my father's days as assistant director of the Stanford University Marching Band. Such accessories are the mandate of the lowest tier of Music Is My Bag, a stratum whose mascot is PDQ Bach, whose theme song is "Piano Man," and whose regional representative is the kid in high school who plays not only the trumpet but the piano, saxophone, flute, string bass, accordion, and wood block. This kid, considered a wunderkind by his parents and the rest of the band community, plays none of these instruments well, but the fact that he knows so many different sets of fingerings, the fact that he has the potential to earn some college money by performing as a one-man band at the annual state teachers' conference, makes him a hometown hero. He may not be a football player. He may not even gain access to the Ivy League. But in the realm of Music Is My Bag, the kid who plays every instrument, particularly when he can play Billy Joel songs on every instrument, is the alpha male.

The flip side of the one-man band are those Music Is My Baggers who are not musicians at all. These are the kids who twirl flags or rifles in the marching band, the ones who blast music in their rooms and play not air guitar but air keyboards, their hands fluttering out in front of them, the hand positions not nearly as important as the attendant head motions. This is the essence of Bagdom, which is to take greater pleasure in the reverb than the melody, to love the lunch break more than the rehearsal, the rehearsal more than the performance, the clarinet case more than the clarinet. It is to think nothing of sending away for the deluxe packet of limited-edition memorabilia that is being sold for the low, low price of one's entire personality. It is to let the trinkets do the talking.

◦ ◦ ◦

I was twenty-one when I stopped playing the oboe. I wish I could come up with a big, dramatic reason why. I wish I could say that I sustained some kind of injury that prevented me from playing (it's hard to imagine what kind of injury could sideline an oboist—lip strain? carpal tunnel syndrome?), or that I was forced to sell my oboe in order to help a family member in crisis, or, better yet, that I suffered a violent attack in which my oboe was used as a weapon against me before being stolen and melted down for artillery. But the truth has more to do with what in college I considered to be an exceptionally long walk from my dormitory to the music building. Without the prodding of my parents or the structure of a state-run music education program, my oboe career had to run on self-motivation alone, and when my senior year started I neither registered for private lessons nor signed up for the orchestra, dodging countless calls from the director imploring me to reassume my chair.

Since then I haven't set foot in a rehearsal room, put together a folding music stand, fussed with a reed, marked up music, practiced scales, tuned an orchestra, or performed any of the countless activities that previously had dominated my existence. There are moments every now and then when I'll hear an oboe-dominated section of the Bach Mass in B Minor or the Berceuse section of Stravinsky's *Firebird Suite* and long to find a workable reed and pick the instrument up again. But then I imagine how terrible I'll sound after eight dormant years, and I just put the whole idea out of my mind before I start to feel sad about it. I can still smell the musty odor of my oboe case, the old-ladyish whiff of the velvet lining and the tubes of cork grease and the damp fabric of the key pads. Unlike the computer on which I now work, my oboe had the sense of being an ancient thing. Brittle and creaky, it was vulnerable when handled by strangers. It needed to be packed up tight, dried out in just the right places, kept away from the heat and the cold and from anyone too stupid to distinguish it from a clarinet.

What I really miss about the oboe is having my hands on it. I could come at that instrument from any angle and know every indentation on every key, every spot that leaked air, every nick on every square inch of wood. I knew precisely how its weight was distributed between my right thumb and left wrist, and I knew, above all, that the weight would feel the same way every time, every day, for every year that I played. But I put my oboe down, and I never picked it back up. I could have been a pretty good oboist if I had practiced, if I had ignored the set design and just played the instrument. But I didn't and I wasn't. When I look back I hardly recognize myself, that person who could play a Mozart sonata by memory, whose fingers could move three times faster than I now type—a person who was given a gift, but who walked away from it because of piano-key scarves and fedora hats and all those secondary melodies that eventually became the only thing I could hear.

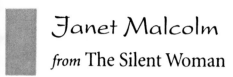

Janet Malcolm

from The Silent Woman

III

ON MARCH 18, 1991, A MONTH AFTER MY RETURN TO NEW YORK FROM ENGLAND, I WROTE A letter to Jacqueline Rose:

Dear Jacqueline:

There was a moment during our talk in February that was like one of those moments during an analytic session when the air is suddenly charged with electricity, and what has ignited the spark is some small, casual, unconsidered action by one of the inter-locutors. When you produced the passage from Ted Hughes's letter about literary crit-icism and the living and the dead, and I remarked on the sentence that I had not seen in Olwyn's copy of it, there was (and I will be interested to know if this description con-forms with your experience) an almost palpable thickening of the emotional atmos-phere. Your realization that you had unwittingly shown me something you felt you should not have shown me affected us both strongly. As I thought about the moment later in Freudian terms, it seemed to me that issues of secrets and forbidden knowledge, as well as of sibling rivalry (the image of two women fighting over something—over a man?), had been stirred up. In addition, the moment raised for me the question of the place of morality in post-structuralist discourse. You value doubt and accept the anxi-ety of uncertainty—but you also have very definite notions of what is right and wrong. You immediately felt it wrong to "give" me what Ted Hughes had "given" you. When you asked me not to quote the sentence I should not have seen, you used the word "ethically." Doesn't the very idea of ethics imply a standard, a norm, a canon of accept-able behavior? And isn't there some discontinuity between your position as a post-structuralist literary theorist and your attentiveness to the requirements of living in the world as a morally scrupulous person? Finally (and more directly to the point of our respective Plathian enterprises), doesn't this tiny incident of suppression in a sense re-produce the larger suppressions of the Hugheses? Now that I have seen the sentence, can I "un-see" it?

I never received a reply to this letter—or expected one—since I never sent it. After reading it over, I marked it "Letter not sent" and put it away in a folder.

The genre of the unsent letter might reward study. We have all contributed to it, and the literary archives are full of specimens. In the Plath archive at the Lilly Library, for example, there are several of Aurelia Plath's unsent letters to Hughes—letters in which she permitted herself to say what she finally decided she couldn't permit herself to say. But she carefully preserved the letters, and included them in the material she turned over to the archive. The preservation of the unsent letter is its arresting feature. Neither the writing nor the not send-ing is remarkable (we often make drafts of letters and discard them), but the gesture of keep-ing the message we have no intention of sending is. By saving the letter, we are in some sense "sending" it after all. We are not relinquishing our idea or dismissing it as foolish or un-worthy (as we do when we tear up a letter); on the contrary, we are giving it an extra vote of confidence. We are, in effect, saying that our idea is too precious to be entrusted to the gaze of the actual addressee, who may not grasp its worth, so we "send" it to his equivalent in fan-tasy, on whom we can absolutely count for an understanding and appreciative reading. Like

Anne Stevenson with Olwyn, I had been tempted by the idea of collaboration with Jacqueline Rose on the rendering of the moment between us over Ted Hughes's letter. But I feared that she would not read the scene as I had read it, that she would tell me that her own experience of the moment had been entirely different and that I had my nerve attributing motives and feelings to her that she did not have. So I tore up the airmail envelope I had addressed to her. But I did not tear up the letter itself, and as I now pluck it from its place of hibernation the thought floats into my mind that some of the early English novels were novels-in-letters.

The moment with Jacqueline Rose that had affected me so strongly and moved me to write my own epistolary fiction took place in the middle of a conversation I had with her at her very handsome flat, in West Hampstead, a few days after my return to London from Devon and Somerset. I was greeted by a small, attractive woman in her early forties, wearing a short and close-fitting skirt and a sweater, whose face was framed by a great deal of artfully unruly blond hair, and whose whole person was surrounded by a kind of nimbus of self-possession. That she was an adept of a theory of criticism whose highest values are uncertainty, anxiety, and ambiguity was a curious but somehow unameliorating facet of her formidable clarity, confidence, and certainty. During our meeting, her manner was engaging—neither too friendly nor too distant—and on a scale of how people should conduct themselves with journalists I would give her a score of 99. She understood the nature of the transaction—that it was a transaction—and had carefully worked out for herself exactly how much she had to give in order to receive the benefit of the interview. In most interviews, both subject and interviewer give more than is necessary. They are always being seduced and distracted by the encounter's outward resemblance to an ordinary friendly meeting. The meal that is often thrown around it like a cloth, to soften the edges; the habits of chat and banter; the conversational reflexes, whereby questions are obediently answered and silences too quickly filled—all these inexorably pull the interlocutors away from their respective desires and goals. However, Rose never—or almost never—forgot, or let me forget, that we were not two women having a friendly conversation over a cup of tea and a box of biscuits but participants in a special, artificial exercise of subtle influence and counterinfluence, with an implicit antagonistic tendency.

Rose teaches English literature at the University of London, and now, as if addressing a class, she gave a crisp, succinct account of the events that had led her to make public her dealings with the Plath estate. "I took careful legal advice on questions of citations and permissions," she said. "I had followed the business with Linda Wagner-Martin and Anne Stevenson, and I knew this was a potentially difficult area. After I finished a rough draft of my book, in early 1990, I wrote to Olwyn Hughes asking permission for the four poems I quote in full, and Olwyn gave it to me in a very friendly letter." But when Rose, following further legal advice, sent her manuscript to the Hugheses, all smiles ceased. Although Rose is a critic of distinction and originality, in the eyes of the Hugheses she was just another member of the pack of Ted Hughes's tormentors and pursuers, and they fought the publication of *The Haunting of Sylvia Plath* with their usual clumsy fierceness. First, they attempted to revoke the permissions for the four poems, and then, when that failed ("Legally, once you've given permission, then that is a contract, and I had paid," Rose told me), they attempted to persuade Rose to make changes in her text. What stuck in the Hugheses' craw (as Rose had expected it would) was a chapter called "The Archive," which she describes in the book as "a reading—of necessity speculative—of the editing of Plath's work," and which studies the omissions from the letters and journals with a very critical eye. It also takes some savage pokes at *Bitter Fame:* Rose characterizes the book as "something of a 'cause célèbre' in the genre of abusive biography," and she joins Alvarez in protesting the book's sternness with Plath and indulgence of Hughes. In accordance with post-structuralist theory, Rose argues for suspension of all certainty about what happened, and thus of judgment and blame. "I'm not *ever* interested in what happened between Plath and Hughes," she told me. "My position is that you're left with a tangle of competing viewpoints, and if you try to make sense of it you'll go wrong one way or another. You have to live with the anxiety that such uncertainty generates. It's not helpful to resolve it too fast." In her book Rose says of *Bitter Fame*, "One of the strangest effects of reading this book, especially if you have read the unedited letters and journals, is that it precisely becomes impossible to know whom to believe." (In fact, it is *only* if you have read the letters and journals—or have been in other ways alerted to the controversial character of the Plath-Hughes narrative—that *Bitter Fame* seems strange. The lay reader, who knows only what the biographer tells him, reads it, as he reads every other biography, in a state of bovine equanimity.) Rose continues her argument:

> Like the child caught up in a hideous divorce case between its parents, the writing of the life of Sylvia Plath, both by herself and by those who knew her, forces you—and makes it impossible for you—to take sides. Whom to believe, how to know, what is the truth of the case? Behind the self-interest of the protagonists lies a drama about the limits and failure of knowledge and self-knowing. We can settle it, like indeed the proceedings of a divorce case, but only by entering into the false and damaging forms of certainty for which those settlements are so renowned.

What Rose leaves out of account (and what her colleagues in the academy left out of account in their anxious and contorted writings about another hideous divorce case, that of Paul de Man and his wartime journalism) is the psychological impossibility of a writer's not taking sides. "Forces you," yes. But "makes it impossible for you," no. Without some "false and damaging" certainty, no writing on any subject is humanly possible. The writer, like the murderer, needs a motive. Rose's book is fuelled by a bracing hostility toward Ted and Olwyn Hughes. It derives its verve and forward thrust from the cool certainty with which (in the name of "uncertainty" and "anxiety") she presents her case against the Hugheses. In the "Archive" chapter, her accusations against Hughes for his "editing, controlling, and censoring" reach an apogee of harshness. If it had truly been impossible for Rose to take a side, her book would not have been written; it would not have been worth taking the trouble to write. Writing cannot be done in a state of desirelessness. The pose of fair-mindedness, the charade of evenhandedness, the striking of an attitude of detachment can never be more than rhetorical ruses; if they were genuine, if the writer *actually* didn't care one way or the other how things came out, he would not bestir himself to represent them.

Rose is the libber in whom the Hugheses finally met their match, who could not be contemptuously dismissed, who was a serious and worthy opponent. In *The Haunting of Sylvia Plath* she speaks for the dead poet and against Hughes in a way no other writer has done. She objects not only to Hughes's suppressions in the journals and letters but to his presentation of Plath as a high-art poet and of *Ariel* as the tiny nugget of gold extracted from the ore of a painfully misdirected writing life. Rose rejects the distinction between high and low art, good and bad writing, "true" and "false" selves on which the Hughes view is posited. To Rose, the stories written for the "slicks" (as Plath described them to her mother) are no less worthy of examination than the *Ariel* poems. For Rose, there are no "waste products." All Plath's writings are precious to her; all the genres she wrote in, all the voices she assumed—

and all the voices buzzing around her since her death—are welcomed into Rose's bazaar of postmodernist consciousness.

The Haunting of Sylvia Plath is a brilliant achievement. The framework of deconstructive, psychoanalytic, and feminist ideology on which Rose has mounted her polemic against the Hugheses gives the work a high intellectual shimmer. There are close to eight hundred footnotes. One is dazzled, excited, somewhat intimidated. The Hugheses, however, were upset and angered; they could hear only Rose's reproachful aria. They could catch only the note of hostility that Rose herself was evidently unaware of—that perhaps only they, as the subjects of her criticism, could fully hear. In a letter to Anne Stevenson, Olwyn wrote of what it felt like to be attacked in Rose's book: "I wonder if you have the slightest idea how enormously unpleasant it is to open such a manuscript as Rose's and meet that malevolent surge—from a person one has never heard of before."

As the reader knows, I, too, have taken a side—that of the Hugheses and Anne Stevenson—and I, too, draw on my sympathies and antipathies and experiences to support it. My narrative of Rose has an edge; my silver-plated scissors are ever at the ready to take snips at her. In another context—if, that is, I had read *The Haunting of Sylvia Plath* as a book on a subject in which I had no investment—I would have felt nothing but admiration for it, since I tend to support the new literary theorists in their debate with the traditionalists. But in the Plath-Hughes debate my sympathies are with the Hugheses, and thus, like a lawyer defending a case he knows to be weak and yet obscurely feels is just, I steel myself against the attractions of the opposition's most powerful and plausible witness.

In her apartment, having finished her account of the hard time the Hugheses had given her over the "Archive" chapter, Jacqueline Rose poured tea and went on to speak of "another area of trouble with the estate," which she said she found "at least as interesting." This area was a chapter of Rose's book called "No Fantasy Without Protest," whose centerpiece is a reading of Plath's poem "The Rabbit Catcher." Ted Hughes had taken violent exception to this reading and had asked Rose to remove it. Rose had not expected Hughes to be happy with her "Archive" chapter, but she was utterly unprepared for his objections to the "Rabbit Catcher" reading, which said nothing critical of him, and, in fact, took issue with the conventional feminist reading of the poem as a parable of the domination of men over women—the snares the narrator encounters on a walk in the country being seen as the trap that conventional marriage is for women—and as a direct commentary on Plath's own marriage. Rose offers an alternative reading, which finds in the poem's arresting, enigmatic imagery a fantasy of androgyny. Although no commentator had ever found this fantasy before—it is doubtful whether Plath herself would have been aware of it—Rose's reading does not seem very remarkable in today's climate of acceptance of both enacted and imagined homosexuality; the bisexual component of human sexuality is a commonplace of post-Freudian thought. But for Hughes—perhaps for the whole pre-Freudian English nation—the idea of unstable sexual identity was unacceptable, and Rose's suggestion that Plath even thought about such things as lesbian sex (never mind doing them) struck Hughes as abhorrent beyond imagination. I speak for Hughes so confidently because he made his views public in a letter written in response to a letter by Rose and published in the *TLS* on April 10, 1992. In his letter Hughes movingly, if bafflingly, told of his concern about the injurious effect that Rose's reading of "The Rabbit Catcher" would have on his children (now in their thirties). "Professor Rose distorts, reinvents etc Sylvia Plath's 'sexual identity' with an abandon I could hardly believe—presenting her in a role that I vividly felt to be humiliating to Sylvia Plath's children," he wrote, and he went on:

I tried to jolt Ms Rose into imagining their feelings, seeing her book (as I have seen it) in a friend's house and assuming instantly that their friend now thinks about their mother the thoughts Professor Rose has taught. . . .

Having thought it through for her in that way, I did not see how Ms Rose could fail to have full and instant knowledge of the peculiar kind of suffering such a moment induces—the little dull blow of something like despair, the helpless rage and shame for their mother, the little poisoning of life, the bitter but quite useless fury against the person who shot this barbed arrow into them just to amuse herself. And the unending accumulation of such moments, since Rose's book is now in the college libraries for good, her idea percolating into all subsequent books about their mother.

Hughes makes what Rose wrote sound so unspeakable and unprintable that I had better hasten to quote the offensive or inoffensive passage (as the case may be), so that the reader can decide for himself. It concerns the first two stanzas of "The Rabbit Catcher," which read:

> It was a place of force—
> The wind gagging my mouth with my own blown hair,
> Tearing off my voice, and the sea
> Blinding me with its lights, the lives of the dead
> Unreeling in it, spreading like oil.
>
> I tasted the malignity of the gorse,
> Its black spikes,
> The extreme unction of its yellow candle-flowers.
> They had an efficiency, a great beauty,
> And were extravagant, like torture.

In her "No Fantasy Without Protest" chapter Rose writes of this opening:

For the sexuality that it writes cannot be held to a single place—it spreads, blinds, unreels like the oil in the sea. Most crudely, that wind blowing, that gagging, calls up the image of oral sex and then immediately turns it around, gagging the speaker with her own blown hair, her hair in her mouth, her tasting the gorse (Whose body—male or female—is this? Who—man or woman—is tasting whom?), even while "black spikes" and "candles" work to hold the more obvious distribution of gender roles in their place. For Freud, such fantasies, such points of uncertainty, are the regular unconscious subtexts—for all of us—of the more straightforward reading, the more obvious narratives of stable sexual identity which we write.

At her tea table, Rose continued her cogent account of her struggle with Ted Hughes over her reading of "The Rabbit Catcher." She said, "In my communications to Hughes I said—and I say this over and over again in my book—'Look, I'm in no sense speaking of Plath's lived sexual identity in the world, about which I know nothing. I'm only discussing fantasy.' But he says that the distinction is not viable, because the fantasy concerns very intimate aspects of their life. It's true, it is intimate and it is private. But if you cannot talk about fantasy in a discussion of the literary writings of Sylvia Plath, then you cannot talk about Sylvia Plath. Because that's what she writes about. About the psyche and about inner images. Wonderful inner images of difficulty and pain—images which implicate us all, I think. I don't accept the reading that says they demonstrate her pathology. I'm not interested in the question of whether she was pathological or not. I don't think one knows, and I think you can only make statements like 'She was pathological' if you are absolutely sure of your own sanity, which I consider a morally unacceptable position."

I asked Rose if Ted Hughes had been appreciative of other parts of her book. "No," she said. She added, allowing a note of bitterness to get into her voice, "Hughes wrote an article in which he was very critical of Ronald Hayman's reading of a poem in *The Colossus*. He said that in the classroom this kind of literal interpretation would be a joke. Therefore I thought—as it turned out, foolishly—that there might be some appreciation for my more complex readings of the poems. But I've not had one positive statement from Ted Hughes or from Olwyn Hughes."

I mentioned that I had met Olwyn a few days earlier, and Rose asked, "What did she say to you about my book?" I told her what she already knew—that Olwyn had been displeased—and when Rose pressed for details I cited the passage in the Hughes letter that Olwyn had handed me in the Indian restaurant.

Rose looked at me with surprise. "The passage about what literary critics do to the living and the dead?" she asked.

"Yes."

Rose sat still for a moment, looking thoughtful. Then she abruptly left the room, saying over her shoulder, "I want to see if it's the same passage." She returned with a sheet of paper and handed it to me. I glanced at it and said, "Yes, that's it. It's an interesting perspective, isn't it?"

"Well, it's an argument against the right to do criticism," Rose said. "This line about how critics reinvent the living—'They extend over the living that licence to say whatever they please, to ransack their psyches and reinvent them however they please.' It implies two things. First, that I am saying I have *the* truth about the Hugheses' lives—which I never say I do—and, second, that they themselves possess it, and any interpretation beyond theirs is a violation of that singular truth."

"May I look at this again?" I said, reaching for the sheet, the better to follow Rose's discussion.

"Yes, of course. I mean, in the end he leaves no room for literary criticism. Which may be what Ted Hughes wants to say. Which is a very interesting thing to say. But it also means there's no room for reading, rereading, interpretation, and discussion of meanings in our culture. The implications of this are really quite extraordinary."

"Here's a sentence I hadn't seen. It's striking," I said, looking up from the paper in my hand. "It wasn't in the passage Olwyn showed me: 'Miss Rose thought she was writing a book about a writer dead thirty years and seems to have overlooked, as I say, the plain fact that she has ended up writing a book largely about me.'"

Rose said very quickly, "I don't think you can quote that without asking Ted Hughes. I think that would be a problem legally." (Later, I did ask for and receive permission to quote the line.) "And, in fact, I wouldn't have shown you that if I wasn't wanting to check the passage Olwyn quoted to you." In her discomposure, Rose had slipped into a more colloquial syntax: "wasn't wanting to check" was unusual in her impressive, lecturer's speech.

I began to say something further about the significance of the extra sentence—how it affected the meaning of the rest of the passage—and Rose, again uncharacteristically, interrupted. "Well, I know," she said. "But this is awkward. I don't feel I should give you communications I've received from Ted and Olwyn Hughes. They were directed to me. They were not meant for public circulation. I only showed you this because Olwyn Hughes showed you a passage from a communication to me, right? And it just so happens that you have therefore seen an additional sentence. I think this is an awkward area, ethically. And I would ask you not to quote that sentence." She thought briefly and then added, "Yes, I think I have to say that."

This, then, was the charged "moment" of my unsent letter. I render it with the help of a tape recording, which preserved the words that passed between Rose and me but did not catch any of the language of face and body by which we all speak to one another and sometimes say what we dare not put into words. Deconstructive writers use the word "aporia" to refer to a place in a text of unexpected difficulty or impasse, a passage that does not yield to the reader's usual quick, logical, frontal approaches to understanding. Rose and I had reached an aporia in our encounter—something unexpected and complicated had occurred. I remember feeling that she and I were struggling over something—were having a fight about some central, unacceptable thing—but today, two years later, much of what was going on between us has left no objective trace of itself, and I no longer have the conviction I once had that Jacqueline Rose and I were fighting over Ted Hughes. Like a biographer, I have only the evidence of texts—in this case, the "fictional" text of my unsent letter and the "factual" text of my tape recording—to guide me in my narrative. They are not guides that feel very reliable to me.

᠊ᢀ ᢀ ᢀ

In her memoir of Plath at Cambridge, Jane Baltzell Kopp (the girl who made fun of Plath's Samsonite luggage) reported an incident that falls rather short of its intended effect. Kopp writes of being astonished by Plath's white fury on discovering that five books she had lent Kopp had been returned to her with Kopp's pencilled marks added to Plath's inked underlinings. Kopp seems oblivious of the offense she committed in writing in a borrowed book; she quotes Plath's "Jane, how *could* you?" as if it were a peculiar reaction. Plath, on the other hand, thought Kopp's act outrageous enough to mention in a letter to her mother and in a subsequent journal entry: "I was furious, feeling my children had been raped, or beaten, by an alien." Biography can be likened to a book that has been scribbled in by an alien. After we die, our story passes into the hands of strangers. The biographer feels himself to be not a borrower but a new owner, who can mark and underline as he pleases. Kopp makes the point that it was Plath's own dark underlinings that "emboldened" her to make her "few pencil marks." (In Plath's version, Kopp wrote "all over" the five books.) Writers on Plath have felt (consciously or unconsciously) something of the same sense of permission, as if they had been given the right to act boldly, even wildly, where ordinarily they would be cautious and tread delicately. In Plath's "cathartic blowup" (as she described it in her journal), she brought Kopp to her knees, shaming her into cleaning up the pencil marks. Hughes's distress over the mess the various new owners have made of the book that he once jointly owned with Plath—but which her death and fame, and his own fame, have ruthlessly taken from him—is understandable, but his efforts to get them to clean up their marks have brought him only grief; he is no longer in possession, he has no say in the matter. His attempt to meddle with Linda Wagner-Martin's biography gave her bland book a status and an interest it would not have otherwise had; his attempt to meddle with Jacqueline Rose's study gave this more substantial work a similar réclame. As Wagner-Martin had punished and triumphed over Hughes (and Olwyn) with the account in her preface of their hard dealings with her, so Rose, in *her* preface, with the composed air appropriate to such occasions, calmly laid out, one by one, the four aces the Hugheses had dealt her:

In correspondence with the Hugheses, this book was called "evil." Its publisher was told it would not appear. At one point an attempt was made to revoke previously granted permissions to quote from Plath's work. I was asked to remove my reading of "The Rabbit Catcher," and when I refused, I was told by Ted Hughes that my analysis would be damaging for Plath's (now adult) children, and that speculation of the kind I was seen as engaging in about Sylvia Plath's sexual identity would in some countries be "grounds for homicide."

Rose's book came out in England in June, 1991, to almost universal acclaim. It received substantial, largely admiring reviews in the *TLS* and the *London Review of Books*, from Joyce Carol Oates and Elaine Showalter, respectively. In the daily English press, it was reviewed together with Ronald Hayman's *The Death and Life of Sylvia Plath*, which (happily for Rose) had been published at the same time; the shallowness of Hayman's book provided a foil for Rose's scholarly seriousness, and several reviewers were quick to structure their reviews around the disparity. The Hugheses' difficulty with this distinction may be imagined. I felt for them, even as I knew the distinction to be just, beyond any argument.

After my return to New York, in February, Olwyn, in correspondence and telephone conversations, continued to voice her vexation over the Rose book. "The book is a determination to show Ted as a monster," she said to me on one occasion. "Rose reads dark Machiavellian thoughts into everything—thoughts that I assure you nobody ever had. There isn't one interesting or intelligent thing in the book. She's a structuralist, she's a feminist, she's a God knows what. Did you actually meet her?"

I said I did.

"What is she like? Does she have four eyes?"

"She's a very attractive woman, very precise and confident."

"Is she English or American?"

"She's English."

There was a long pause; Olwyn had obviously wanted Rose to be American. She resumed: "The way she goes on about Sylvia's sexual life—it's incredible, it's libellous."

"You can't libel the dead," I said.

"But, in a way, that passage libels everybody, doesn't it? It libels Ted, it libels Carol, it libels any woman he ever had anything to do with."

"This is getting very complicated," I said.

"It's appalling. It's so intended. It's so nasty. And they talk about *my* wickedness, denying permission to these angels to quote. What can one do? Should one just let them quote and let the myths get wilder and wilder—or should one try to correct them, as I have done?"

Olwyn's attempt to correct Rose—which consisted of sending her a document of twenty single-spaced typewritten pages, entitled "Notes Re J. Rose's Mss—'The Haunting of Sylvia Plath'"—only provided further grist for Rose's deconstructive mill. She coolly added the "Notes" to the hundreds of texts she cites in her footnotes and quotes from in her own text. Rose's method of citation reminds me of those prison scenes in historical movies where aristocrats and beggars, virtuous women and prostitutes, righteous men and thieves have all been thrown into one cell and are being treated by the guard with elaborate democratic sameness. In *The Haunting of Sylvia Plath*, the writings of Freud, James, Ronald Hayman, and a friend of Aurelia Plath's are all accorded the same grave attention; and Olwyn's "Notes" and Ted's letters to Rose are treated simply as interesting late-in-the-day contributions to the book, rather than as angry attacks on it. ("I found their comments helpful, meaningful, and informative, as they repeatedly fed into and contributed to the overall argument of the book," Rose writes.) In August, 1991—her fur sleek and a few feathers still around her mouth—Rose wrote me a long letter replying to some questions I had put to her (in a sent letter) after reading the final version of her book:

> On the question of why we sent the Hugheses the manuscript. We (i.e., myself and Virago) were legally advised to do so. We knew that publishing on Plath was a difficult process, and both Virago's lawyer and counsel considered that sending the manuscript was in fact the way to secure the book's final publication. We would know the reaction, the likelihood of legal action, and how or whether to respond to the possibility in advance.

I had also asked Rose to explain an odd term, "textual entities," she uses in her introduction. ("In this book, in the analysis of [Plath's] writings, I am never talking of real people, but of textual entities (Y and X), whose more than real reality, I will be arguing, goes beyond them to encircle us all.") She replied that here, again, a legal consideration had guided her. Lawyers had advised her to use the term to make it impossible for Hughes to sue her, she wrote, and she gave an illustration: "Although violence is one of the repeated themes of Plath's writing, I at no point deduce from that writing that any violence necessarily passed between them. To do so would have been legally defamatory, and the book could not have appeared." She added, "More important, however, I have no desire to make such a suggestion, as it seems to me that I have absolutely no way of knowing this, and firmly believe that writing is as much a place to explore what did not happen but is—say—most feared or desired as what did."

Perhaps no greater tribute could have been paid to Rose's position, and to the poststructuralist vision of writing as a kind of dream, which no one (including the dreamer-writer) ever gets to the bottom of, than the tribute Ted Hughes paid in his April 24, 1992, letter to the *TLS*, where he wrote of his shock and dismay on learning that Rose had interpreted his remark about homicide as a threat. In her own letter to the *TLS* Rose had indignantly quoted the remark: "I was told . . . that to speculate on a mother's sexual identity would in some countries be 'grounds for homicide.' If this is not illegitimate pressure (it did not—I of course checked with Virago's lawyer—legally constitute a threat), then I would like to know what is." Hughes wrote that his intention had been to arouse her "common (even maternal) sensibility":

> I cast about for some historical example, a situation in which what is perceived as a fanciful, verbalized, public injury to a mother's "sexual identity" strikes into her children with a pain that is not only violently real, but is also well recorded, documentary, believed by Professor Rose. I lit on the obvious case, and asked her to imagine how it would be, to interpret some local mother's "sexual identity," publicly (even publishing it to the world), as she had interpreted Sylvia Plath's—in one of those pride and honour societies of the Mediterranean.
>
> I was so strenuously locked into beating at her door, as I have described, simply to wake her up—it never dawned on me that all she could feel was *threatened*. . . .
>
> I was trying, rather desperately and with a sense of futility, to get her to look into her heart, but the only effect I had, as she now tells, was that she consulted her lawyer.

David Foster Wallace

Shipping Out
On the (Nearly Lethal) Comforts of a Luxury Cruise

The Four-Color Brochure, Part 1

I have now seen sucrose beaches and water a very bright blue. I have seen an all-red leisure suit with flared lapels. I have smelled suntan lotion spread over 2,100 pounds of hot flesh. I have been addressed as "Mon" in three different nations. I have seen 500 upscale. Americans dance the Electric Slide. I have seen sunsets that looked computer-enhanced. I have (very briefly) joined a conga line.

I have seen a lot of really big white ships. I have seen schools of little fish with fins that glow. I have seen and smelled all 145 cats inside the Ernest Hemingway residence in Key West, Florida. I now know the difference between straight bingo and Prize-O. I have seen fluorescent luggage and fluorescent sunglasses and fluorescent pince-nez and over twenty different makes of rubber thong. I have heard steel drums and eaten conch fritters and watched a woman in silver lamé projectile-vomit inside a glass elevator. I have pointed rhythmically at the ceiling to the two-four beat of the same disco music I hated pointing at the ceiling to in 1977.

I have learned that there are actually intensities of blue beyond *very bright* blue. I have eaten more and classier food than I've ever eaten, and done this during a week when I've also learned the difference between "rolling" in heavy seas and "pitching" in heavy seas. I have heard a professional cruise-ship comedian tell folks, without irony, "But seriously." I have seen fuchsia pantsuits and pink sport coats and maroon-and-purple warm-ups and white loafers worn without socks. I have seen professional blackjack dealers so lovely they make you want to clutch your chest. I have heard upscale adult U.S. citizens ask the ship's Guest Relations Desk whether snorkeling necessitates getting wet, whether the trapshooting will be held outside, whether the crew sleeps on board, and what time the Midnight Buffet is. I now know the precise mixocological difference between a Slippery Nipple and a Fuzzy Navel. I have, in one week, been the object of over 1,500 professional smiles. I have burned and peeled twice. I have met Cruise Staff with the monikers "Mojo Mike," "Cocopuff," and "Dave the Bingo Boy."

I have felt the full clothy weight of a subtropical sky. I have jumped a dozen times at the shattering, flatulence-of-the-gods-like sound of a cruise ship's horn. I have absorbed the basics of mah-jongg and learned how to secure a life jacket over a tuxedo. I have dickered over trinkets with malnourished children. I have learned what it is to become afraid of one's own cabin toilet. I have now heard—and am powerless to describe—reggae elevator music.

I now know the maximum cruising speed of a cruise ship in knots (though I never did get clear on just what a knot is). I have heard people in deck chairs say in all earnestness that it's the humidity rather than the heat. I have seen every type of erythema, pre-melanomic lesion, liver spot, eczema, wart, papular cyst, pot belly, femoral cellulite, varicosity, collagen and silicone enhancement, bad tint, hair transplants that have not taken—i.e., I have seen nearly naked a lot of people I would prefer not to have seen nearly naked. I have acquired and nurtured a potentially lifelong grudge against the ship's hotel manager (whose name was Mr. Dermatis and whom I now and henceforth christen Mr. Dermatitis[1]), an almost reverent respect for my table's waiter, and a searing crush on my cabin steward, Petra, she of the dimples and broad candid brow, who always wore a nurse's starched and rustling whites and smelled of the cedary Norwegian disinfectant she swabbed bathrooms down with, and who cleaned my cabin within a centimeter of its life at least ten times a day but could never be caught in the actual act of cleaning—a figure of magical and abiding charm, and well worth a postcard all her own.

I now know every conceivable rationale for somebody spending more than $3,000 to go on a Caribbean cruise. To be specific: voluntarily and for pay, I underwent a 7-Night Caribbean (7NC) Cruise on board the m.v. *Zenith* (which no wag could resist immediately rechristening the m.v. *Nadir*), a 47,255-ton ship owned by Celebrity Cruises, Inc., one of the twenty-odd cruise lines that operate out of south Florida and specialize in "Megaships," the floating wedding cakes with occupancies in four figures and engines the size of branch banks.[2] The vessel and facilities were, from what I now understand of the industry's standards, absolutely top-hole. The food was beyond belief, the service unimpeachable, the shore excursions and shipboard activities organized for maximal stimulation down to the tiniest detail. The ship was so clean and white it looked boiled. The western Caribbean's blue varied between baby-blanket and fluorescent; likewise the sky. Temperatures were uterine. The very sun itself seemed preset for our comfort. The crew-to-passenger ratio was 1.2 to 2. It was a Luxury Cruise.

All of the Megalines offer the same basic product—not a service or a set of services but more like a feeling: a blend of relaxation and stimulation, stressless indulgence and frantic tourism, that special mix of servility and condescension that's marketed under configurations of the verb "to pamper." This verb positively studs the Megalines' various brochures: ". . . as you've never been pampered before," ". . . to pamper yourself in our Jacuzzis and saunas," "Let us pamper you," "Pamper yourself in the warm zephyrs of the Bahamas." The fact that adult Americans tend to associate the word "pamper" with a certain *other* consumer product is not an accident, I think, and the connotation is not lost on the mass-market Megalines and their advertisers.

---

[1] Somewhere he'd gotten the impression that I was an investigative journalist and wouldn't let me see the galley, bridge, or staff decks, or interview any of the crew in an on-the-record way, and he wore sunglasses indoors, and epaulets, and kept talking on the phone for long stretches of time in Greek when I was in his office after I'd skipped the karaoke semifinals in the Rendez-Vous Lounge to make a special appointment to see him, and I wish him ill.

[2] Of the Megalines out of south Florida there's also Commodore, Costa, Majesty, Regal, Dolphin, Princess, Royal Caribbean, Renaissance, Royal Cruise Line, Holland America, Cunard, Norwegian Cruise Line, Crystal, and Regency Cruises. Plus the Wal-Mart of the cruise industry, Carnival, which the other lines refer to sometimes as "Carnivore." The present market's various niches—Singles, Old People, Theme, Special Interest, Corporate, Party, Family, Mass-Market, Luxury, Absurd Luxury, Grotesque Luxury—have all pretty much been carved and staked out and are now competed for viciously. The 7NC Megaship cruiser is a genre of ship all its own, like the destroyer. The ships tend to be designed in America, built in Germany, registered out of Liberia and both captained and owned, for the most part, by Scandinavians and Greeks, which is kind of interesting since these are the same peoples who have dominated sea travel pretty much forever. Celebrity Cruises is owned by the Chandris Group; the **X** on their three ships smokestacks isn't an **X** but a Greek chi, for Chandris a Greek shipping family so ancient and powerful they apparently regarded Onassis as a punk.

Pampered to Death, Part 1

Some weeks before I underwent my own Luxury Cruise, a sixteen-year-old male did a half gainer off the upper deck of a Megaship. The news version of the suicide was that it had been an unhappy adolescent love thing, a shipboard romance gone bad. But I think part of it was something no news story could cover. There's something about a mass-market Luxury Cruise that's unbearably sad. Like most unbearably sad things, it seems incredibly elusive and complex in its causes yet simple in its effect: on board the *Nadir* (especially at night, when all the ship's structured fun and reassurances and gaiety ceased) I felt despair. The word "despair" is overused and banalized now, but it's a serious word, and I'm using it seriously. It's close to what people call dread or angst, but it's not these things, quite. It's more like wanting to die in order to escape the unbearable sadness of knowing I'm small and weak and selfish and going, without doubt, to die. It's wanting to jump overboard.

I, who had never before this cruise actually been on the ocean, have for some reason always associated the ocean with dread and death. As a little kid I used to memorize shark-fatality data. Not just attacks. Fatalities. The Albert Kogler fatality off Baker's Beach, California, in 1963 (great white); the USS *Indianapolis* smorgasbord off Tinian in 1945 (many varieties, authorities think mostly makos and blacktip);[3] the most-fatalities-attributed-to-a-single-shark series of incidents around Matawan/Spring Lake, New Jersey, in 1926 (great white again; this time they netted the fish in Raritan Bay and found human parts *in gastro*—I know which parts, and whose). In school I ended up writing three different papers on "The Castaway" section of *Moby-Dick,* the chapter in which a cabin boy falls overboard and is driven mad by the empty immensity of what he finds himself floating in. And when I teach school now I always teach Stephen Crane's horrific "The Open Boat," and I get bent out of shape when the kids think the story's dull or just a jaunty adventure: I want them to suffer the same marrow-level dread of the oceanic I've always felt, the intuition of the sea as primordial nada, bottomless depths inhabited by tooth-studded things rising angelically toward you. This fixation came back with a long-repressed vengeance on my Luxury Cruise,[4] and I made such a fuss about the one (possible) dorsal fin I saw off starboard that my dinner companions at Table 64 finally had to tell me, with all possible tact, to shut up about the fin already.

I don't think it's an accident that 7NC Luxury Cruises appeal mostly to older people. I don't mean decrepitly old, but like fiftyish people for whom their own mortality is something more than an abstraction. Most of the exposed bodies to be seen all over the daytime *Nadir* were in various stages of disintegration. And the ocean itself turns out to be one enormous engine of decay. Seawater corrodes vessels with amazing speed—rusts them, exfoli-

---

[3] Robert Shaw as Quint reprised the whole incident in 1975's *Jaws,* a film, as you can imagine, that was like fetish-porn to me at age thirteen.

[4] I'll admit that on the very first night of the 7NC I asked the staff of the *Nadir*'s Five-Star Caravelle Restaurant whether I could maybe have a spare bucket of au jus drippings from supper so that I could try chumming for sharks off the back rail of the top deck, and that this request struck everybody from the maître d' on down as disturbing and maybe even disturbed, and that it turned out to be a serious journalistic faux pas, because I'm almost positive the maître d' passed this disturbing tidbit on to Mr. Dermatitis and that it was a big reason why I was denied access to places like the ship's galley, thereby impoverishing the sensuous scope of this article. It also revealed how little I understood the *Nadir*'s sheer size: twelve decks up is 150 feet, and the *au jus* drippings would have dispersed into a vague red cologne by the time they hit the water, with concentrations of blood inadequate to attract or excite a serious shark, whose fin would have probably looked like a pushpin from that height anyway.

ates paint, strips varnish, dulls shine, coats ships' hulls with barnacles and kelp and a vague and ubiquitous nautical snot that seems like death incarnate. We saw some real horrors in port, local boats that looked as if they had been dipped in a mixture of acid and shit, scabbed with rust and goo, ravaged by what they float in.

Not so the Megalines' ships. It's no accident they're so white and clean, for they're clearly meant to represent the Calvinist triumph of capital and industry over the primal decay-action of the sea. The *Nadir* seemed to have a whole battalion of wiry little Third World guys who went around the ship in navy-blue jumpsuits scanning for decay to overcome. Writer Frank Conroy, who has an odd little essay-mercial in the front of Celebrity Cruises' 7NC brochure, talks about how "it became a private challenge for me to try to find a piece of dull bright-work, a chipped rail, a stain in the deck, a slack cable, or anything that wasn't perfectly shipshape. Eventually, toward the end of the trip, I found a capstan [a type of nautical hoist, like a pulley on steroids] with a half-dollar-sized patch of rust on the side facing the sea. My delight in this tiny flaw was interrupted by the arrival, even as I stood there, of a crewman with a roller and a bucket of white paint. I watched as he gave the entire capstan a fresh coat and walked away with a nod."

Here's the thing: A vacation is a respite from unpleasantness, and since consciousness of death and decay are unpleasant, it may seem weird that the ultimate American fantasy vacation involves being plunked down in an enormous primordial stew of death and decay. But on a 7NC Luxury Cruise, we are skillfully enabled in the construction of various fantasies of triumph over just this death and decay. One way to "triumph" is via the rigors of self-improvement (diet, exercise, cosmetic surgery; Franklin Quest time-management seminars), to which the crew's amphetaminic upkeep of the *Nadir* is an unsubtle analogue. But there's another way out, too: not titivation but titillation; not hard work but hard play. See in this regard the 7NC's constant activities, festivities, gaiety, song; the adrenaline, the stimulation. It makes you feel vibrant, alive. It makes your existence seem non-contingent.[5] The hard-play option promises not a transcendence of death-dread so much as just drowning it out: "Sharing a laugh with your friends[6] in the lounge after dinner, you glance at your watch and mention that it's almost showtime. . . . When the curtain comes down after a standing ovation, the talk among your companions turns to, 'What next?' Perhaps a visit to the casino or a little dancing in the disco? Maybe a quiet drink in the piano bar or a starlit stroll around the deck? After discussing all your options, everyone agrees: 'Let's do it all!'"

Dante this isn't, but Celebrity Cruises' brochure is an extremely powerful and ingenious piece of advertising. Luxury Megalines' brochures are always magazine-size, heavy and glossy, beautifully laid out, their text offset by art-quality photos of upscale couples[7] tanned

---

[5] The Nadir's got literally hundreds of cross-sectional maps of the ship on every deck, at every elevation and junction, each with a red dot and a YOU ARE HERE. It doesn't take long to figure out that these are less for orientation than for reassurance.

[6] Constant references to "friends" in the brochure's text, part of this promise of escape from dread is that no cruiser is ever alone.

[7] Always couples, and even in group shots it's always groups of couples. I never did get hold of a brochure for an actual Singles Cruise, but the mind reels. There was a "Singles Get Together" (sic) on the *Nadir* that first Saturday night, held in Deck 8's Scorpio Disco, which after an hour of self-hypnosis and controlled breathing I steeled myself to go to, but even the Get Together was three-fourths established couples, and the few of us Singles under like seventy all looked grim and self-hypnotized, and the whole affair seemed like a true wrist-slitter, and I beat a retreat after half an hour because *Jurassic Park* was scheduled to run on the TV that night, and I hadn't yet looked at the whole schedule and seen that *Jurassic Park* would play several dozen times over the coming week.

faces in a kind of rictus of pleasure. Celebrity's brochure, in particular, is a real two-napkin drooler. It has little hypertextish offsets boxed in gold, with bites like INDULGENCE BECOMES EASY and RELAXATION BECOMES SECOND NATURE and (my favorite) STRESS BECOMES A FAINT MEMORY. The text itself is positively Prozacian: "Just standing at the ship's rail looking out to sea has a profoundly soothing effect. As you drift along like a cloud on water, the weight of everyday life is magically lifted away, and you seem to be floating on a sea of smiles. Not just among your fellow guests but on the faces of the ship's staff as well. As a steward cheerfully delivers your drinks, you mention all of the smiles among the crew. He explains that every Celebrity staff member takes pleasure in making your cruise a completely carefree experience and treating you as an honored guest.[8] Besides, he adds, there's no place else they'd rather be. Looking back out to sea, you couldn't agree more."

This is advertising (i.e., fantasy-enablement), but with a queerly authoritarian twist. Note the imperative use of the second person and a specificity out of detail that extends even to what you will say (you *will* say "I couldn't agree more" and "*Let's do it all!*"). You are, here, excused from even the work of constructing the fantasy, because the ads do it for you. And this near-parental type of advertising makes a very special promise, a diabolically seductive promise that's actually kind of honest, because it's a promise that the Luxury Cruise itself is all about honoring. The promise is not that you *can* experience great pleasure but that you *will*. They'll make certain of it. They'll micromanage every iota of every pleasure-option so that not even the dreadful corrosive action of your adult consciousness and agency and dread can fuck up your fun. Your troublesome capacities for choice, error, regret, dissatisfaction, and despair will be removed from the equation. You will be able—finally, for once—to relax, the ads promise, because you will have no choice. Your pleasure will, for 7 nights and 6.5 days, be wisely and efficiently managed. Aboard the *Nadir*, as is ringingly foretold in the brochure, you will get to do "something you haven't done in a long, long time: *Absolutely Nothing.*"

How long has it been since you did Absolutely Nothing? I know exactly how long it's been for me. I know how long it's been since I had every need met choicelessly from someplace outside me, without my having to ask. And that time I was floating, too, and the fluid was warm and salty, and if I was in any way conscious I'm sure I was dreadless, and was having a really good time, and would have sent postcards to everyone wishing they were here.

Boarding

A 7NC's pampering is maybe a little uneven at first, but it starts right at the airport, where you don't have to go to Baggage Claim, because people from the Megaline get your suitcases

---

[8] The press liaison for Celebrity's P.R. firm (the charming and Debra Winger–voiced Ms. Wiessen) had this bold explanation for the cheery service: "The people on board—the staff—are really part of one big family. You probably noticed this when you were on the ship. They really love what they're doing and love serving people and they pay attention to what everybody wants and needs." This was not what I observed. What I observed was that the *Nadir* was one very tight ship, run by an elite cadre of very hard-assed Greek officers and supervisors, that the staff lived in mortal terror of these bosses, who watched them with enormous beadiness at all times, and that the crew worked almost Dickensianly hard, too hard to feel truly cheery about it. My sense was that Cheeriness was up there with Celerity and Servility on the clipboarded evaluation sheets the Greek bosses were constantly filling out on the crew. My sense was that a crewman could get fired for a pretty small lapse, and that getting fired by these Greek officers might well involve a spotlessly shined shoe in the ass and then a really long swim.

for you and take them straight to the ship. A bunch of other Megalines besides Celebrity Cruises operate out of Fort Lauderdale, and the flight down from O'Hare is full of festive-looking people dressed for cruising. It turns out that the retired couple sitting next to me on the plane is booked on the *Nadir*. This is their fourth Luxury Cruise in as many years. It is they who tell me about the news reports of the kid jumping overboard. The husband wears a fishing cap with a very long bill and a T-shirt that says BIG DADDY.

7NC Luxury Cruises always start and finish on a Saturday. Imagine the day after the Berlin Wall came down if everybody in East Germany was plump and comfortable-looking and dressed in Caribbean pastels, and you'll have a pretty good idea what the Fort Lauderdale airport terminal looks like today. Near the back wall, a number of brisk-looking older ladies in vaguely naval outfits hold up printed signs—HIND, CELEB, CUND CRN. You're supposed to find your particular Megaline's brisk lady and coalesce around her as she herds a growing ectoplasm of *Nadir*ites out to buses that will ferry you to the piers and what you quixotically believe will be immediate and hassle-free boarding. Apparently the airport is just your average sleepy midsize airport six days a week and then every Saturday resembles the fall of Saigon.

Now we're riding to the piers in a column of eight chartered Greyhounds. Our convoy's rate of speed and the odd deference shown by other traffic give the whole procession a vaguely funereal quality. For Lauderdale proper looks like one extremely large golf course, but the Megalines' piers are in something called Port Everglades, an industrial area zoned for blight, with warehouses and transformer parks and stacked boxcars and vacant lots. We pass a huge field of those hammer-shaped automatic oil derricks all bobbing fellatially, and on the horizon past them is a fingernail clipping of shiny sea. Whenever we go over bumps or train tracks, there's a huge mass clicking sound from all the cameras around everybody's neck. I haven't brought any sort of camera and feel a perverse pride about this.

The *Nadir*'s traditional berth is Pier 21. "Pier," although it conjures for me images of wharfs and cleats and lapping water, turns out here to denote something like what "airport" denotes; viz., a zone and not a thing. There is no real view of the ocean, no docks, no briny smell to the air, but as we enter the pier zone there are a lot of really big white ships that blot out most of the sky.

From inside, Pier 21 seems kind of like a blimpless blimp hangar, high-ceilinged and echoey. It has walls of unclean windows on three sides, at least 2,500 orange chairs in rows of twenty-five, a kind of desultory snack bar, and rest rooms with very long lines. The acoustics are brutal and it's tremendously loud. Some of the people in the rows of chairs appear to have been here for days: they have the glazed encamped look of people at airports in blizzards. It's now 11:32 A.M., and boarding will not commence one second before 2:00 P.M.; a P.A. announcement politely but firmly declares Celebrity's seriousness about this. The P.A. lady's voice is what you imagine a British supermodel would sound like. Everyone clutches a numbered card like identity papers at Checkpoint Charlie. Pier 21's pre-boarding blimp hangar is not as bad as, say, New York City's Port Authority bus terminal at 5:00 P.M. on Friday, but it bears little resemblance to any of the stressless pamper-venues detailed in the Celebrity brochure, which I am not the only person in here thumbing through and looking at wistfully. A lot of people are also now staring with subwayish blankness at other people. A kid whose T-shirt says SANDY DUNCAN'S EYE[9] is carving something in the plastic of his

---

[9] Journalistic follow-up has revealed that this is the name of a band that I feel confident betting is: Punk.

chair. There are quite a few semi-old people traveling with really desperately old people who are clearly their parents. Men after a certain age simply should not wear shorts, I've decided; the skin seems denuded and practically crying out for hair, particularly on the calves. It's just about the only body area where you actually want *more* hair on older men. A couple of these glabrous-calved guys are field-stripping their camcorders with military expertise. There's also a fair number of couples in their twenties and thirties, with a honeymoonish aspect to the way their heads rest on each other's shoulders.

Somewhere past the big gray doors behind the rest rooms' roiling lines is a kind of umbilical passage leading to what I assume is the actual *Nadir*, which outside the hangar's windows presents as a tall wall of total white metal. The Chicago lady and BIG DADDY are playing Uno with another couple, who turn out to be friends they'd made on a Princess Alaska cruise in '93. By this time I'm down to slacks and T-shirt and tie, and the tie looks like it's been washed and hand-wrung. Perspiring has lost its novelty. Celebrity Cruises seems to be reminding us that the real world we're leaving behind includes crowded public waiting areas with no A.C. and indifferent ventilation. Now it's 12:55 P.M. Although the brochure says the *Nadir* sails at 4:30 and that you can board anytime from 2:00 P.M. until then, it looks as it all 1,374 *Nadir* passengers are already here, plus a fair number of relatives and well-wishers.

Every so often I sort of orbit the blimp hangar, eavesdropping, making small talk. The universal topic of discussion is "Why Are You Here?" Nobody uses the word "pamper" or "luxury." The word that gets used over and over is "relax." Everybody characterizes the upcoming week as either a long-put-off reward or a last-ditch effort to salvage sanity and self from some inconceivable crockpot of pressure, or both. A lot of the explanatory narratives are long and involved and some are sort of lurid—including a couple of people who have finally buried a terminal, hideously lingering relative they'd been nursing at home for months.

Finally we are called for boarding and moved in a columnar herd toward the Passport Check and Deck 3 gangway beyond. We are greeted (each of us) and escorted to our cabins by not one but two Aryan-looking hostesses from the Hospitality Staff. We are led over plush plum carpet to the interior or what one presumes is the actual *Nadir*, washed now in high-oxygen A.C. that seems subtly balsam-scented, pausing, if we wish, to have our pre-cruise photo taken by the ship's photographer, apparently for some Before and After souvenir ensemble Celebrity Cruises will try to sell us at the end of the week. My hostesses are Inga and Geli, and they carry my book bag and suit coat, respectively. I start seeing the first of more WATCH YOUR STEP signs than anyone could count—it turns out that a Megaship's flooring is totally uneven, and everywhere there are sudden little steplets up and down. It's an endless walk—up, fore, aft, serpentine through bulkheads and steel-railed corridors, with mollified jazz coming out of little round speakers in a beige enamel ceiling. At intervals on every wall are the previously mentioned cross-sectioned maps and diagrams.[10]

---

[10] Like all Megaships, the *Nadir* has given each deck some 7NC-related name rather than a number, and already I am forgetting whether the Fantasy Deck is Deck 7 or 8. Deck 12 is called the Sun Deck; 11 is the Marina Deck and has the pool and café; 10 I forget; 9 is the Bahamas Deck; 8 is Fantasy and 7 is Galaxy (or vice versa), and they contain all the venues for serious eating and dancing and casinoing and Headline Entertainment; 6 I never did get straight; 5 is the Europa Deck and comprises the Nadir's corporate nerve center—a huge high-ceilinged bank-looking lobby with everything done in lemon and salmon and brass plating around the Guest Relations Desk and the Purser's Desk and the Hotel Manager's Desk, with water running down massive pillars with a sound that all but drives you to the nearest urinal; 4 is cabins; everything below is all business and off-limits.

The elevator is made of glass and is noiseless, and Inga and Geli smile slightly and gaze at nothing as together we ascend, and it's a very close race as to which of the two smells better in the enclosed chill. Soon we are passing little teak-lined shipboard shops with Gucci, Waterford, Wedgwood, Rolex, and there's a crackle in the jazz and an announcement in three languages about Welcome and *Willkommen* and how there will be a compulsory Lifeboat Drill an hour after sailing.

By 3:15 P.M. I am installed in *Nadir* Cabin 1009 and immediately eat almost a whole basket of free fruit and lie on a really nice bed and drum my fingers on my swollen tummy.

Under Sail

Our horn is genuinely planet-shattering. Departure at 4:30 turns out to be a not untasteful affair of crepe and horns. Each deck has walkways outside, with railings made of really good wood. It's now overcast, and the ocean way below is dull and frothy. Docking and undocking are the two times the Megacruiser's captain actually steers the ship; Captain G. Panagiotakis has now wheeled us around and pointed our snout at the open sea, and we—large and white and clean—are under sail.

The whole first two days and nights are bad weather, with high-pitched winds, heaving seas, spume lashing the portholes' glass. For forty-plus hours it's more like a North Sea Cruise, and the Celebrity staff goes around looking regretful but not apologetic, and in all fairness it's hard to find a way to blame Celebrity Cruises, Inc. for the weather. The staff keeps urging us to enjoy the view from the railings on the lee side of the *Nadir*. The one other guy who joins me in trying out the non-lee side has his glasses blown off by the gale. I keep waiting to see somebody from the crew wearing the traditional yellow slicker, but no luck. The railing I do most of my contemplative gazing from is on Deck 10, so the sea is way below, slopping and heaving around, so it's a little like looking down into a briskly flushing toilet. No fins in view.

In heavy seas, hypochondriacs are kept busy taking their gastric pulse every couple of seconds and wondering whether what they're feeling is maybe the onset of seasickness. Seasickness-wise, though, it turns out that bad weather is sort of like battle: there's no way to know ahead of time how you'll react. A test of the deep and involuntary stuff of a man. I myself turn out not to get seasick. For the whole first rough-sea day, I puzzle over the fact that every other passenger on the m.v. *Nadir* looks to have received identical little weird shaving-cuts below his or her left ear—which in the case of female passengers seems especially strange—until I learn that these little round Band-Aidish things on everybody's neck are special new super-powered transdermal motion-sickness patches, which apparently nobody with any kind of clue about 7NC Luxury Cruising now leaves home without. A lot of the passengers get seasick anyway, these first two howling days. It turns out that a seasick person really does look green, though it's an odd and ghostly green, pasty and toadish, and more than a little corpselike when the seasick person is dressed in formal dinner wear.

For the first two nights, who's feeling seasick and who's not and who's not now but was a little while ago or isn't feeling it yet but thinks it's maybe coming on, etc., is a big topic of conversation at Table 64 in the Five-Star Caravelle Restaurant.[11] Discussing nausea and vomiting while eating intricately prepared gourmet foods doesn't seem to bother anybody.

---

[11] This is on Deck 7, the serious dining room, and it's never called just "the Caravelle Restaurant" (and never just "the Restaurant")—it's always "the Five-Star Caravelle Restaurant."

Common suffering and fear of suffering turn out to be a terrific ice-breaker, and ice-breaking is pretty important, because on a 7NC you eat at the same designated table with the same companions all week.

There are seven other people with me at good old Table 64, all from south Florida. Four know one another in private landlocked life and have requested to be at the same table. The other three people are an old couple and their granddaughter, whose name is Mona. I am the only first-time Luxury Cruiser at Table 64. With the conspicuous exception of Mona, I like all my tablemates a lot, and I want to get a description of supper out of the way fast and avoid saying much about them for fear of hurting their feelings by noting any character defects or eccentricities that might seem potentially mean. Besides me, there are five women and two men, and both men are completely silent except on the subjects of golf, business, transdermal motion-sickness prophylaxis, and the legalities of getting stuff through customs. The women carry Table 64's conversational ball. One of the reasons I like all these women (except Mona) so much is that they laugh really hard at my jokes, even lame or very obscure jokes, although they all have this curious way of laughing where they sort of *scream* before they laugh, so that for one excruciating second you can't tell whether they're getting ready to laugh or whether they're seeing something hideous and screamworthy over your shoulder.

My favorite tablemate is Trudy, whose husband is back home managing some sudden crisis at the couple's cellular-phone business and has given his ticket to Alice, their heavy and extremely well-dressed daughter, who is on spring break from Miami U. and who is for some reason very anxious to communicate to me that she has a Serious Boyfriend, whose name is apparently Patrick. Alice's continual assertion of her relationship-status may be a defensive tactic against Trudy, who keeps pulling professionally retouched 4 × 5 glossies of Alice out of her purse and showing them to me with Alice sitting right there, and who, every time Alice mentions Patrick, suffers some sort of weird facial tic or grimace where the canine tooth on one side of her face shows but the other side's doesn't. Trudy is fifty-six and looks—and I mean this in the nicest possible way—rather like Jackie Gleason in drag, and has a particularly loud pre-laugh scream that is a real arrhythmia-producer, and is the one who coerces me into Wednesday night's conga line, and gets me strung out on Snowball Jackpot Bingo. Trudy is also an incredible lay authority on 7NC Luxury Cruises, this being her sixth in a decade; she and her best friend, Esther (thin-faced, subtly ravaged-looking, the distaff part of the couple from Miami), have tales to tell about Carnival, Princess, Crystal, and Canard too fraught with libel potential to reproduce here.

By midweek it starts to strike me that I have never before been party to such a minute and exacting analysis of the food and service of a meal I am just at that moment eating. Nothing escapes the attention of T and E: the symmetry of the parsley sprigs atop the boiled baby carrots, the consistency of the bread, the flavor and mastication-friendliness of various cuts of meat, the celerity and flambé technique of the various pastry guys in tall white hats who appear tableside when items have to be set on fire (a major percentage of the desserts in the Five-Star Caravelle Restaurant have to be set on fire), and so on. The waiter and busboy keep circling the table, going "Finish? Finish?" while Esther and Trudy have exchanges like:

"Honey you don't look happy with the potatoes. What's the problem."

"I'm fine. It's fine. Everything's fine."

"Don't lie. Honey with that face who could lie? Frank am I right? This is a person with a face incapable of lying."

"There's nothing wrong Esther darling, I swear it."

"You're not happy with the conch."

"All right. I've got a problem with the conch."

"Did I tell you? Frank, did I tell her? [Frank silently probes his ear with pinkie.] Was I right? Trudy I could tell just by looking you weren't happy."

"I'm fine with the potatoes. It's the conch."

"Did I tell you about seasonal fish on ships? What did I tell you?"

"The potatoes are good."

Mona is eighteen. Her grandparents have been taking her on a Luxury Cruise every spring since she was five. Mona always sleeps through both breakfast and lunch and spends all night at the Scorpio Disco and in the Mayfair Casino playing the slots. She is six two if she's an inch. She's going to attend Penn State next fall, because the agreement is that she'll receive a four-wheel-drive vehicle if she goes someplace where there might be snow. She is unabashed in recounting this college-selection criterion. She is an incredibly demanding passenger and diner, but her complaints about slight aesthetic and gustatory imperfections at table lack Trudy and Esther's discernment and come off as simply churlish. Mona is also kind of strange-looking: a body like Brigitte Nielsen or some centerfold on steroids, and above it, framed in resplendent blond hair, the tiny unhappy face of a kind of corrupt doll. Her grandparents, who retire every night right after supper, always make a small ceremony after dessert of handing Mona $100 to "go have some fun" with. This $100 bill is always in one of those little ceremonial bank envelopes that has Franklin's face staring out of a porthole-like window in the front, and written on the envelope in red Magic Marker is always "We Love You, Honey." Mona never once says thank you. She also rolls her eyes at just about everything her grandparents say, a habit that very quickly drives me up the wall.

Mona's special customary gig on 7NC Luxury Cruises is to lie to the waiter and maître d' and say that Thursday is her birthday, so that at the Formal supper on Thursday she gets bunting and a heart-shaped helium balloon tied to her chair, and her own cake, and pretty much the whole restaurant staff comes out and forms a circle around her and sings to her. Her real birthday, she informs me on Monday, is July 29, and when I quietly observe that July 29 is also the birthday of Benito Mussolini, Mona's grandmother shoots me kind of a death-look, although Mona herself is excited at the coincidence, apparently confusing the names Mussolini and Maserati.

The weather in no way compromised the refinement of meals at Table 64. Even in heavy seas, 7NC Megaships don't yaw or throw you around or send bowls of soup sliding across tables. Only a certain slight unreality to your footing lets you know you're not on land. At sea, a room's floor feels somehow 3-D, and your footing demands a slight attention that good old static land never needs. You don't ever quite hear the ship's big engines, but when your feet are planted you can feel them—a kind of spinal throb, oddly soothing.

Walking is a little dreamy also. There are constant slight shifts in torque from the waves action. When heavy waves come straight at a Megaship's snout, the ship goes up and down along its long axis—this is called "pitching." It produces the disorienting sensation that you're walking on a very slight downhill grade and then level and then on a very slight uphill grade. Some evolutionarily retrograde reptile-brain part of the central nervous system is apparently reawakened, though, and manages all this so automatically that it requires a good deal of attention to notice anything more than that walking feels a little dreamy.

"Rolling," on the other hand, is when waves hit the ship from the side and make it go up and down along its crosswise axis. When the *Nadir* rolls, what you feel is a very slight increase in the demands placed on the muscles of your left leg, then a strange absence of all demand, then extra demands on the right leg.

We never pitch badly, but every once in a while some really big, *Poseidon Adventure*-grade wave must have come and hit the *Nadir's* side, because the asymmetric leg-demands sometimes won't stop or reverse and you keep having to put more and more weight on one leg until you're exquisitely close to tipping over. The cruise's first night, steaming southeast for Jamaica, features some really big waves from starboard, and in the casino after supper it's hard to tell who's had too much of the '71 Richebourg and who's just doing a roll-related stagger. Add in the fact that most of the women are wearing high heels, and you can imagine some of the vertiginous staggering-flailing-clutching that goes on. Almost everyone on the *Nadir* has come in couples, and when they walk during heavy seas they tend to hang on each other like freshman steadies. You can tell they like it: the women have this trick of sort of folding themselves into the men and snuggling as they walk, and the men's postures improve and their faces firm up and they seem to feel unusually solid and protective. It's easy to see why older couples like to cruise.

Heavy seas are also great for sleep, it turns out. The first two mornings there's hardly anybody at Early Seating Breakfast. Everybody sleeps in. People with insomnia of years' standing report uninterrupted sleep of nine, ten, even eleven hours. Their eyes are childlike and wide with wonder as they report this. Everyone looks younger when they've had a lot of sleep. There's rampant daytime napping too. By the end of the week, when we've had all manner of weather, I finally see what it is about heavy seas and marvelous rest: in heavy seas you feel rocked to sleep, the windows' spume a gentle shushing, engines' throb a mother's pulse.

The Four-Color Brochure, Part 2

Did I mention that famous writer and Iowa Writers' Workshop Chairperson Frank Conroy has his own experiential essay about cruising right there in Celebrity's 7NC brochure? Well he does, and the thing starts out on the Pier 21 gangway that first Saturday with his family:[12]

> With that single, easy step, we entered a new world, a sort of alternate reality to the one on shore. Smiles, handshakes; and we were whisked away to our cabin by a friendly young woman from Guest Relations.

Then they're outside along the rail for the *Nadir's* sailing:

> . . . We became aware that the ship was pulling away. We had felt no warning, no trembling of the deck, throbbing of the engines or the like. It was as if the land were magically receding, like some ever-so-slow reverse zoom in the movies.

This is pretty much what Conroy's whole "My Celebrity Cruise or 'All This and a Tan, Too'" is like. Its full implications don't hit me until I reread it supine on Deck 12 the first

---

[12] Conroy took the same Celebrity cruise as I, the Seven-Night Western Caribbean on the good old *Nadir*, in May 1994. He and his family cruised for free. I know details like this because Conroy talked to me on the phone, and answered nosy questions, and was frank and forthcoming and in general just totally decent about the whole thing.

sunny day. Conroy's essay is graceful and lapidary and persuasive. I submit that it is also completely insidious and bad. Its badness does not consist so much in its constant and mesmeric references to fantasy and alternate realities and the palliative powers of professional pampering—

> I'd come on board after two months of intense and moderately stressful work, but now it seemed a distant memory. . . . I realized it had been a week since I'd washed a dish, cooked a meal, gone to the market, done an errand or, in fact, anything at all requiring a minimum of thought and effort. My toughest decisions had been whether to catch the afternoon showing of *Mrs. Doubtfire* or play bingo.

—nor in the surfeit of happy adjectives and the tone of breathless approval throughout—

> Bright sun, warm still air, the brilliant blue-green of the Caribbean under the vast lapis lazuli dome of the sky . . . For all of us, our fantasies and expectations were to be exceeded, to say the least. . . . When it comes to service, Celebrity Cruises seems ready and able to deal with anything.

Rather, part of the essay's real badness can be found in the way it reveals once again the Megaline's sale-to-sail agenda of micro-managing not only one's perceptions of a 7NC but even one's own interpretation and articulation of those perceptions. In other words, Celebrity's P.R. people go and get a respected writer to pre-articulate and endorse the 7NC experience, and to do it with a professional eloquence and authority that few lay perceivers and articulators could hope to equal.[13] But the really major badness is that the project and placement of "My Celebrity Cruise . . ." are sneaky and duplicitous and well beyond whatever eroded pales still exist in terms of literary ethics. Conroy's "essay" appears as an inset, on skinnier pages and with different margins than the rest of the brochure, creating the impression that it has been excerpted from some large and objective thing Conroy wrote. But it hasn't been. The truth is that Celebrity Cruises paid Frank Conroy up-front to write it,[14] even though nowhere in or around the essay is there anything acknowledging that it's a paid endorsement, not even one of the little "So-and-so has been compensated for his services" that flashes at your TV screen's lower right during celebrity-hosted infomercials. Instead, inset on this weird essaymercial's first page is a photo of Conroy brooding in a black turtleneck, and below the photo an author bio with a list of Conroy's books that includes the 1967

[13] E.g., after reading Conroy's essay on board, whenever I'd look up at the sky, it wouldn't be the sky I was seeing, it was the *vast lapis lazuli dome of the sky.*

[14] Phone inquiries about the origins of Professor Conroy's essaymerical yielded two separate explanations: (1) From Celebrity Cruises' P.R. liaison Ms. Wiessen (after a two-day silence that I've come to understand as the P.R. equivalent of covering the microphone with your hand and learning over to confer with counsel): "Celebrity saw an article he wrote in *Travel and Leisure* magazine, and they were really impressed with how he could create these mental postcards, so they went to ask him to write about his cruise experience for people who'd never been on a cruise before, and they did pay him to write the article, and they really took a gamble, really, because they had to pay him whether he liked it or not, and whether they liked the article or not but . . . [dry little chuckle] obviously they liked the article, and he did a good job, so that's the Mr. Conroy story, and those are his perspectives on his experience." (2) From Frank Conroy (with the small sigh that precedes a certain kind of weary candor): "I prostituted myself."

classic *Stop-Time*, which is arguably the best literary memoir of the twentieth century and is one of the books that first made poor old humble yours truly want to try to be a writer.

In the case of Frank Conroy's "essay," Celebrity Cruises is trying to position an ad in such a way that we come to it with the lowered guard and leading chin we reserve for coming to an essay, for something that is art (or that is at least trying to be art). An ad that pretends to be art is—at absolute best—like somebody who smiles at you only because he wants something from you. This is dishonest, but what's insidious is the cumulative effect that such dishonesty has on us: since it offers a perfect simulacrum of goodwill without goodwill's real substance, it messes with our heads and eventually starts upping our defenses even in cases of genuine smiles and real art and true goodwill. It makes us feel confused and lonely and impotent and angry and scared. It causes despair.[15]

But for this particular 7NC consumer, Conroy's ad-as-essay ends up having a truthfulness about it that I'm sure is unintentional. As my week on the *Nadir* wears on, I begin to see this essaymercial as a perfectly ironic reflection of the mass-market cruise experience itself. The essay is polished, powerful, impressive, clearly the best that money can buy. It presents itself as being for my benefit. It manages my experiences and my interpretation of those experiences and takes care of them for me in advance. It seems to care about me. But it doesn't, not really, because first and foremost it wants something from me. So does the cruise itself. The pretty setting and glittering ship and sedulous staff and solicitous fun-managers all want something from me, and it's not just the price of my ticket—they've already got that. Just what it is that they want is hard to pin down, but by early in the week I can feel it building: it circles the ship like a fin.

Pampered to Death, Part 2

Celebrity's brochure does not lie or exaggerate, however, in the luxury department, and I now confront the journalistic problem of not being sure how many examples I need to list in order to communicate the atmosphere of sybaritic and nearly insanity-producing pampering on board the m.v. *Nadir*. Take, as one example, the moment right after sailing when I want to go out to Deck 10's port rail for some introductory vista-gazing and thus decide I need some zinc oxide for my peel-prone nose. My zinc oxide's still in my big duffel bag, which at that point is piled with all of Deck 10's other luggage in the little area between the 10-Fore elevator and the 10-Fore staircase while little guys in cadet-blue Celebrity jumpsuits, porters (entirely Lebanese, it seems), are cross-checking the luggage tags with the *Nadir's* passenger list and lugging everything to people's cabins.

---

[15] This is related to the phenomenon of the Professional Smile, a pandemic in the service industry, and no place in my experience have I been on the receiving end of as many Professional Smiles as I was on the *Nadir*: maître d's, chief stewards, hotel managers' minions, cruise director—their P.S.'s all come on like switches at my approach. But also back on land: at banks, restaurants, airline ticket counters, and on and on. You know this smile—the one that doesn't quite reach the smiler's eyes and signifies nothing more than a calculated attempt to advance the smiler's own interests by pretending to like the smilee. Why do employers and supervisors force professional service people to broadcast the Professional Smile? Am I the only person who's sure that the growing number of cases in which normal-looking people open up with automatic weapons in shopping malls and insurance offices and medical complexes is somehow causally related to the fact that these venues are well-known dissemination-loci of the Professional Smile?

So I come out and spot my duffel among the luggage, and I start to grab and haul it out of the towering pile of leather and nylon, thinking I'll just whisk the bag back to Cabin 1009 myself and root through it and find my zinc oxide. One of the porters sees me starting to grab the bag, though, and he dumps all four of the massive pieces of luggage he's staggering with and leaps to intercept me. At first I'm afraid he thinks I'm some kind of baggage thief and wants to see my claim check or something. But it turns out that what he wants is my duffel: he wants to carry it to 1009 for me. And I, who am about half again this poor little herniated guy's size (as is the duffel bag itself), protest politely, trying to be considerate, saying Don't Fret, Not a Big Deal, Just Need My Good Old Zinc Oxide, I'll Just Get the Big Old Heavy Weather-Stained Sucker Out of Here Myself.

And now a very strange argument ensues, me versus the Lebanese porter, because, I now understand, I am putting this guy, who barely speaks English, in a terrible kind of sedulous-service double bind, a paradox of pampering: The Passenger's Always Right versus Never Let a Passenger Carry His Own Bag. Clueless at the time about what this poor man is going through, I wave off both his high-pitched protests and his agonized expression as mere servile courtesy, and I extract the duffel and lug it up the hall to 1009 and slather the old beak with zinc oxide and go outside to watch Florida recede cinematically à la F. Conroy.

Only later do I understand what I've done. Only later do I learn that that little Lebanese Deck-10 porter had his head just about chewed off by the (also Lebanese) Deck-10 Head Porter, who had his own head chewed off by the Austrian Chief Steward, who received confirmed reports that a passenger had been seen carrying his own bag up the port hallway of Deck 10 and now demanded a rolling Lebanese head for this clear indication of porterly dereliction, and the Austrian Chief Steward had reported the incident to a ship's officer in the Guest Relations Department, a Greek guy with Revo shades and a walkie-talkie and epaulets so complex I never did figure out what his rank was; and this high-ranking Greek guy actually came around to 1009 after Saturday's supper to apologize on behalf of practically the entire Chandris shipping line and to assure me that ragged-necked Lebanese heads were even at that moment rolling down various corridors in piacular recompense for my having had to carry my own bag. And even though this Greek officer's English was in lots of ways better than mine, it took me no less than ten minutes to detail the double bind I'd put the porter in—brandishing at relevant moments the actual tube of zinc oxide that had caused the whole snafu—ten or more minutes before I could get enough of a promise from the Greek officer that various chewed-off heads would be reattached and employee records unbesmirched to feel comfortable enough to allow the officer to leave[16]; and the whole incident was incredibly frazzling and despair-fraught, and filled almost half a spiral notebook, and is here recounted in only its barest psychoskeletal outline.

This grim determination to indulge the passenger in ways that go far beyond any halfway-sane passenger's own expectations is everywhere on the *Nadir*. Some wholly random examples: My cabin bathroom has plenty of thick fluffy towels, but when I go up to lie in the sun I don't have to take any of my cabin's towels, because the two upper decks' sun areas have big carts loaded with even thicker and fluffier towels. These carts are stationed at

---

[16] In further retrospect, I think the only thing I really persuaded this Greek officer of was that I was very weird, and possibly unstable, which impression I'm sure was shared with Mr. Dermatitis and combined with that same first night's *au-jus*-as-shark-bait request to destroy my credibility with Dermatitis before I even got in to see him.

convenient intervals along endless rows of gymnastically adjustable deck chairs that are themselves phenomenally fine deck chairs, sturdy enough for even the portliest sunbather but also narcoleptically comfortable, with heavy-alloy frames over which is stretched some mysterious material that combines canvas's quick-drying durability with cotton's absorbency and comfort—certainly a welcome step up from public pools' deck-chair material of Kmartish plastic that sticks to your skin and produces farty suction-noises whenever you shift your sweaty weight on it. And each of the sun decks is manned by a special squad of full-time Towel Guys, so that when you're well-done on both sides and ready to quit and you spring easily out of the deck chair you don't have to pick up your towel and take it with you or even bus it into the cart's Used Towel slot, because a Towel Guy materializes the minute your fanny leaves the chair and removes your towel for you and deposits it in the slot. (Actually, the Towel Guys are such overachievers that even if you get up for just a second to reapply zinc oxide or gaze contemplatively out over the railing at the sea, when you turn back around your towel's often gone and your deck chair has been refolded to its uniform 45-degree at-rest angle, and you have to readjust your chair all over again and go to the cart to get a fresh fluffy towel, of which there is admittedly not a short supply.)

Down in the Five-Star Caravelle Restaurant, the waiter[17] will not only bring you a lobster—as well as a second and even a third lobster[18]—with methamphetaminic speed but will also incline over you with gleaming claw-cracker and surgical fork and dismantle it for you, sparing you the green goopy work that's the only remotely rigorous thing about lobster. And at the Windsurf Café, up on Deck 11 by the pools, where there's always an informal buffet lunch, there's never that bovine line that makes most cafeterias such a downer, and there are about seventy-three varieties of entrée alone, and the sort of coffee you marry somebody for being able to make; and if you have too many things on your tray, a waiter will materialize as you peel away from the buffet and will carry your tray (even though it's a cafeteria, there are all these waiters standing around with Nehru jackets and white towels draped over left arms watching you, not quite making eye contact but scanning for any little way to be of service, plus plum-jacketed sommeliers walking around to see if you need a non-buffet libation, plus a whole other crew of maître d's and supervisors watching the waiters and sommeliers and tall-hatted buffet servers to make sure you don't do something for yourself that could be done for you).

Every public surface on the m.v. *Nadir* that isn't stainless steel or glass or varnished parquet or dense and good-smelling sauna-type wood is plush blue carpet that never has a chance to accumulate even one flecklet of lint because jumpsuited Third World guys are always at it with Siemens A.G.® vacuums. The elevators are Euroglass and yellow steel and stainless steel and a kind of wood-grain material that looks too shiny to be real wood but makes a sound when you thump it that's an awful lot like real wood.[19] The elevators and stairways between decks seem to be the particular objects of the anal retention of a whole special Elevator and Staircase custodial crew. During the first two days of rough seas, when

---

[17] Table 64's waiter is Tibor, a Hungarian and a truly exceptional person, about whom if there's any editorial justice you will learn a lot more someplace below.

[18] Not until Tuesday's Lobster Night at the 5☆ C.R. did I really empathetically understand the Roman phenomenon of the vomitorium.

[19] The many things on the *Nadir* that were wood-grain but not real wood were such wonderful and painstaking imitations of wood that a lot of times it seemed like it would have been simpler and less expensive simply to have used real wood.

people vomited a lot (especially after supper and apparently *extra*-especially on the elevators and stairways), these puddles of vomit inspired a veritable feeding-frenzy of wet/dry
vacs and spot remover and all-trace-of-odor-eradicator chemicals applied by this elite Special Forces-type crew.

And don't let me forget room service, which on a 7NC Luxury Cruise is called "cabin
service." Cabin service is in addition to the eleven scheduled daily opportunities for public
eating, and it's available twenty-four hours a day and is free: all you have to do is hit × 72 on
the bedside phone, and ten or fifteen minutes later a guy who wouldn't even *dream* of hitting you up for a gratuity appears with: "Thinly Sliced Ham and Swiss Cheese on White
Bread with Dijon Mustard" or "The Combo: Cajun Chicken with Pasta Salad, and Spicy
Salsa," or a whole page of other sandwiches and platters from the Services Directory— and
the stuff deserves to be capitalized, believe me. As a kind of semi-agoraphobe who spends
massive amounts of time in my cabin, I come to have a really complex dependency/shame
relationship with cabin service. Since finally finding out about it Monday, I've ended up
availing myself of cabin service every night—more like twice a night, to be honest—even
though I find it extremely embarrassing to be calling up × 72 asking to have even *more* rich
food brought to me when there have already been eleven gourmet eating-ops that day.[20]
Usually what I do is spread my notebooks and *Fielding's Guide to Worldwide Cruises 1995*
and pens and various materials out all over the bed so that when the cabin service guy appears at the door he'll see all this belletristic material and figure I'm working really hard on
something belletristic right here in the cabin and have doubtless been too busy to have hit
all the public meals and thus am legitimately entitled to the indulgence of even more rich
food.

My experience with the cabin cleaning, though, is perhaps the ultimate example of
pampering stress. The fact of the matter is that I rarely even see 1009's Cabin Steward, Petra,
which is why, on the occasions when I do see her, I practically hold her prisoner and yam-
mer at her like an idiot. But I have good reason to believe she sees me, because every time I
leave 1009 for more than like half an hour, when I get back it's cleaned and dusted again and
the towels replaced and the bathroom agleam. Don't get me wrong: in a way it's great. I'm
in Cabin 1009 a lot, and I also come and go a lot, and when I'm in here I sit in bed and write
in bed while eating fruit and generally mess up the bed. But whenever I dart out and then
come back, the bed is freshly made up and hospital cornered and there's another mint-
centered chocolate on the pillow.

I grant that mysterious invisible room cleaning is every slob's fantasy, like having a
mom without the guilt. But there is also a creeping uneasiness about it that presents—at
least in my own case—as a kind of paranoia. Because after a couple days of this fabulous invisible room cleaning, I start to wonder how exactly Petra knows when I'm in 1009 and

---

[20] This is counting the Midnight Buffet, which tends to be a kind of lamely lavish costume-partyish
thing with theme-related foods—Oriental, Caribbean, Tex-Mex—and which I plan to mostly skip
except to say that Tex-Mex Night out by the pools featured what must have been a seven-foot-high
ice sculpture of Pancho Villa that spent the whole party dripping steadily onto the mammoth sombrero of Tibor, whose waiter's contract forces him on Tex-Mex Night to wear a serape and a straw
sombrero with a 17-inch radius (he let me measure it when the reptilian maître d' wasn't looking)
and to dispense four-alarm chili from a steam table placed right underneath an ice sculpture, and
whose face on occasions like this expresses a combination of mortification and dignity that seems
somehow to sum up the whole plight of postwar Eastern Europe.

when I'm not. It's now that it occurs to me that I hardly ever see her. For a while I try experiments, like all of a sudden darting out into the 10-Port hallway to see if I can catch Petra hunched somewhere keeping track of who is decabining, and I scour the whole hallway-and-ceiling area for evidence of some kind of camera monitoring movements outside the cabin doors. Zilch on both fronts. But then I see that the mystery's even more complex and unsettling than I'd first thought, because my cabin gets cleaned always and only during intervals when I'm gone for more than half an hour. When I go out, how can Petra or her supervisors possibly know how long I'm going to be gone? I try leaving 1009 a couple of times and then dashing back after ten or fifteen minutes to see whether I can catch Petra *in delicti,* but she's never there. I try making an ungodly mess, then leaving and hiding somewhere on a lower deck, then dashing back after exactly twenty-nine minutes—again when I come bursting through the door there's no Petra and no cleaning. Then I leave the cabin with exactly the same expression and appurtenances as before and this time stay hidden for *thirty-one* minutes and then haul ass back—again no sighting of Petra, but now 1009 is sterilized and gleaming, and there's a mint on the pillow's new case. I scrutinize every inch of every surface I pass as I circle the deck during these little experiments: no cameras or motion-sensors or anything in evidence anywhere that would explain how They know.[21] So for a while I theorize that somehow a special crewman is assigned to each passenger and follows that passenger at all times, using extremely sophisticated personal-surveillance techniques and reporting back to Steward HQ my movements and activities and projected time of cabin-return. For about a day I try taking evasive actions—whirling to check behind me, popping around corners, darting in and out of gift shops via different doors, etc.—but I never see one flaming sign of anybody engaged in surveillance. By the time I quit trying, I'm feeling half-crazed, and my countersurveillance measures are drawing frightened looks and even some temple-tapping from 10-Port's other guests.

My Cabin

I who am not a true agoraphobe but am what might be called a "borderline agoraphobe" or "semi-agoraphobe," come therefore understandably to love very deeply "Cabin 1009/Exterior Port."[22] It is made of a fawn-colored enamelish polymer and its walls are extremely thick and solid: I can drum annoyingly on the wall above my bed for up to five minutes before my aft neighbors pound (very faintly) back. My cabin is thirteen size-eleven Keds long by twelve Keds wide. The cabin door has three separate locking technologies and trilingual lifeboat and -jacket instructions bolted to its wall and a whole deck of multilingual Do not disturb cards hanging from the inside knob. Right by the door is the Wondercloset, a complicated honeycomb of shelves and drawers and hangers and cubbyholes and a Personal

---

[21] The answer to why I don't just ask Petra how she does it is that Petra's English is extremely limited and primitive, and in sad fact I'm afraid my whole deep feeling of attraction to Petra the Slavonian Steward has been erected on the flimsy foundation of the only two English clauses she seems to know, one or the other of which she uses in response to every question, joke, or protestation of undying love: "Is no problem" and "You are a funny thing."

[22] "1009" indicates that it's the ninth cabin on Deck 10. "Port" refers to the side of the ship it's on, and "Exterior" means that I have a window. There are also "Interior" cabin off the inner sides of the decks' halls, but I hereby advise any prospective 7NC passenger with claustrophobic tendencies to make sure and specify "Exterior" when making cabin reservations.

Fireproof Safe. The Wondercloset is so intricate in its utilization of every available cubic centimeter that all I can say is it must have been designed by a very organized person indeed. Inside are extra chamois blankets and hypoallergenic pillows and plastic Celebrity Cruises bags of all different sizes and configurations for your laundry, optional dry cleaning, etc.

The cabin's porthole is indeed round, but it is not small, and in terms of its importance to the room's mood and *raison* it resembles a cathedral's rose window. It's made of that kind of very thick glass that tellers at drive-up banks stand behind. You can thump the glass with your fist and it won't even vibrate. Every morning at exactly 8:34 A.M. a Filipino guy in a blue jumpsuit stands on one of the lifeboats that hang in rows between Decks 9 and 10 and sprays my porthole with a hose, to get the salt off, which is always fun to watch.

Cabin 1009's dimensions are just barely on the good side of the line between very snug and cramped. Packed into its near-square are a big good bed and two bedside tables with lamps and an 18-inch TV with five At-Sea Cable® options. There's also a white enamel desk that doubles as a vanity, and a round glass table on which sits a basker that's alternately filled with fresh fruit and husks and rinds of same. Every time I leave the cabin for more than the requisite half-hour I come back to find a new basket of fruit, covered in snug blue-tinted plastic wrap, on the glass table. It's good fresh fruit and it's always there. I've never eaten so much fruit in my life.

My Bathroom

Cabin 1009's bathroom deserves extravagant praise. I've seen more than my share of bathrooms, and this is one bitchingly nice bathroom. It is five and a half Keds to the edge of the shower's step up and sign to WATCH YOUR STEP. The room is done in white enamel and gleaming stylized brushed and stainless steel. Its overhead lighting is some kind of blue-intensive Eurofluorescence that's run through a diffusion filter so that it's diagnostically acute without being brutal. Next to the light switch is an Alisco Scirocco® hair dryer that's brazed right onto the wall and comes on automatically when you take it out of the mount; the Scirocco's HIGH setting just about takes your head off. The sink is huge, and its bowl is deep without seeming precipitous or ungentle of grade. Good plate mirror covers the whole wall over the sink. The steel soap dish is straited to let sog-water out and minimize that annoying underside-of-the-bar slime. The ingenious consideration of the anti-slime soap dish is particularly affecting. Keep in mind that 1009 is a mid-price single cabin. The mind positively reels at what a luxury penthouse-type cabin's bathroom must be like.

Merely enter 1009's bathroom and hit the overhead lights and on comes an automatic exhaust fan whose force and aerodynamism give steam or offensive odors just no quarter at all.[23] The fan's suction is such that if you stand right underneath its louvered vent it makes your hair stand straight up on your head, which together with the abundantly rippling action of the Scirocco hair dryer makes for hours of fun in the lavishly lit mirror.

The shower itself overachieves in a very big way. The HOT setting's water is exfoliatingly hot, but it takes only one preset manipulation of the shower knob to get perfect 98.6-degree water. My own personal home should have such water pressure: the shower-head's force

---

[23] 1009's bathroom always smells of a strange but not unnice Norwegian disinfectant. The cabin itself, on the other hand, after it's been cleaned, has no odor. None. Not in the carpets, the bedding, the insides of the desk drawers, the wood of the Wondercloset's doors: nothing. This, too, eventually starts giving me the creeps.

pins you helplessly to the stall's opposite wall, and the head's MASSAGE setting makes your eyes roll up and your sphincter just about give.[24] The showerhead and its flexible steel line are also detachable, so you can hold the head and direct its punishing stream just at your particularly dirty right knee or something.

But all this is still small potatoes compared with 1009's fascinating and potentially malevolent toilet. A harmonious concordance of elegant form and vigorous function, flanked by rolls of tissue so soft as to be without perforates for tearing, my toilet has above it this sign:

> THIS TOILET IS CONNECTED TO A VACUUM
> SEWAGE SYSTEM. PLEASE DO NOT THROW INTO
> THE TOILET ANYTHING [SIC] THAN ORDINARY
> TOILET WASTE AND TOILET PAPER

The toilet's flush produces a brief but traumatizing sound, a kind of held high-B gargle, as of some gastric disturbance on a cosmic scale. Along with this sound comes a suction so awesomely powerful that it's both scary and strangely comforting: your waste seems less removed than *hurled* from you, and with a velocity that lets you feel as though the waste is going to end up someplace so far away that it will have become an abstraction, a kind of existential sewage-treatment system.[25]

---

[24] This detachable and concussive showerhead can allegedly also be employed for non-hygienic and even prurient purposes. I overheard guys from a small University of Texas vacation contingent (the only college-age group on the whole *Nadir*) regale one another with tales of their ingenuity with the showerhead. One guy in particular was fixated on the idea that somehow the shower's technology could be rigged to administer fellatio if he could just get access to a "metric ratchet set." Your guess here is as good as mine.

[25] The *Nadir*'s Vacuum Sewage System begins after a while to hold such a fascination for me that I end up going hat in hand back to Hotel Manager Dermatitis to ask once again for access to the ship's nether parts. But once again I pull a boner with Dermatitis: I innocently mention my specific fascination with the ship's Vacuum Sewage System—which boner is consequent to another and prior boner by which I'd failed to discover in my pre-boarding research that there'd been, just a few months before this, a tremendous scandal in which a Megaship had been discovered dumping waste over the side in mid-voyage, in violation of numerous national and maritime codes, and had been videotaped doing this by a couple of passengers who subsequently apparently sold the videotape to some network newsmagazine, and so the whole Megacruise industry was in a state of almost Nixonian paranoia about unscrupulous journalists trying to manufacture scandals about Megaships' handling of waste. Even behind his mirrored sunglasses I can tell that Mr. Dermatitis is severely upset about my interest in sewage, and he denies my request to eyeball the V.S.S. with a complex defensiveness that I can't even begin to chart out here. It is only later that night at supper, at good old Table 64 in the 5☆ C.R., that my cruise-savvy tablemates fill me in on the waste scandal, and they scream with mirth at the clay-footed naïveté with which I'd gone to Dermatitis with what was in fact an innocent if puerile fascination with hermetically evacuated waste; and such is my own embarrassment and hatred of Mr. Dermatitis by this time that I begin to feel that if the Hotel Manager really does think I'm some kind of investigative journalist with a hard-on for shark dangers and sewage scandals, then he might think it would be worth the risk to have me harmed in some way. And, through a set of neurotic connections I won't even try to defend, I, for about a day and a half, begin to fear that the *Nadir*'s Greek episcopate will somehow contrive to use the incredibly potent and forceful 1009 toilet itself for the assassination—that they'll, I don't know, like somehow lubricate the bowl and up the suction to where not just my waste but I myself will be sucked down through the seat's opening and hurled into some kind of abstract septic exile.

The Ocean

Traveling at sea for the first time is a chance to realize that the ocean is not one ocean. The water changes. The Atlantic that seethes off the eastern United States is glaucous and light-less and looks mean. Around Jamaica, though, it's more like a milky aquamarine. Off the Cayman Islands it's an electric blue, and off Cozumel it's almost purple. Same deal with the beaches. You can tell right away that south Florida's sand comes from rocks: it hurts your bare feet and has that sort of mineralish glitter to it. But Ocho Rios's beach is more like dirty sugar, and Cozumel's is like clean sugar, and at places along the coast of Grand Cayman the sand's texture is more like flour, silicate, its white as dreamy and vaporous as clouds' white. The only real constant to the nautical topography of the *Nadir*'s Caribbean is its unreal and almost retouched-looking prettiness. It's impossible to describe right; the closest I can come is to say that it all looks: expensive.

Table 64's Waiter

Our waiter's name is, as previously mentioned, Tibor. Mentally I refer to him as "the Tib-ster," but never out loud. Tibor has dismantled my artichokes and my lobsters and taught me that extra-well-done is not the only way meat can be palatable. We have sort of bonded, I feel. He is thirty-five and about five four and plump, and his movements have the birdlike economy characteristic of small plump graceful men. His face is at once round and pointy, and rosy. His tux never wrinkles. His hands are soft and pink. Menu-wise, Tibor advises and recommends, but without the hauteur that has always made me hate the gastropedantic waiters in classy restaurants. He is omnipresent without being unctuous or oppressive; he is kind and warm and fun. He is the Head Waiter for Tables 64–67 at all three meals. He can carry three trays without precariousness and never looks harried or on the edge the way most multitable waiters look. He seems like he cares.

Tibor's cuteness has been compared by the women at Table 64 to that of a button. But I have learned not to let his cuteness fool me. Tibor is a pro. His commitment to personally instantiating the *Nadir*'s fanatical commitment to excellence is the one thing about which he shows no sense of humor. If you fuck with him in this area he will feel pain and will make no effort to conceal it. On the second night at supper, for example, Tibor was circling the table and asking each of us how our entrée was, and we all regarded this as just one of those perfunctory waiter-questions and perfunctorily smiled back and said Fine, Fine—and Tibor finally stopped and looked down at us all with a pained expression and changed his timbre slightly so that it was clear he was addressing the whole table: "Please. I ask each: is excel-lent? Please. If excellent, you say, and I am happy. If not excellent, please: do not say excel-lent. Let me fix. Please." There was no hauteur or pedantry or even anger as he addressed us. He just meant what he said. His expression was babe-naked, and we heard him, and noth-ing was perfunctory again.

Mornings, the Tibster wears a red bow tie and smells faintly of sandalwood. Early Seat-ing Breakfast is the best time to be with Tibor, because he's not very busy and can be initi-ated into chitchat without looking pained at neglecting his duties. He doesn't know I'm on the *Nadir* as a pseudojournalist. I'm not sure why I haven't told him—somehow I think it might make things hard for him. During E.S.B. chitchat I never ask him anything about the *Nadir* (except for precise descriptions of whatever dorsal fins he's seen), not out of defer-ence to Mr. Dermatitis's injunctions but because I'd just about die if Tibor got into any trouble on my account.

Tibor's ambition is someday to return to his native Budapest for good and with his *Nadir*-savings open a sort of newspaper-and-beret-type sidewalk café that specializes in something called cherry soup. With this in mind, two days from now in Fort Lauderdale I'm going to tip the Tibster way more than the suggested $3 U.S. per diem, balancing out my total expenses by radically undertipping both our liplessly sinister maître d' and our sommelier, an unctuously creepy Ceylonese guy the whole table has christened the Velvet Vulture.

Port Call

Mornings in port are a special time for the semi-agoraphobe, because just about everybody else gets off the ship and goes ashore for Organized Shore Excursions or for unstructured peripatetic tourist stuff, and the m.v. *Nadir*'s upper decks have the eerily delicious deserted quality of your folks' house when you're home sick as a kid and everybody else is gone. We're docked off Cozumel, Mexico. I'm on Deck 12. A couple of guys in software-company T-shirts jog fragrantly by every couple of minutes, but other than that it's just me and the zinc oxide and hat and about a thousand empty and identically folded deck chairs. The 12-Aft Towel Guy has almost nobody to exercise his zeal on, and by 10:00 A.M. I'm on my fifth new towel.

Here the semi-agoraphobe can stand alone at the ship's highest port rail and look pensively out to sea, which off Cozumel is a kind of watery indigo through which you can see the powdery white of the bottom. In the middle distance, underwater coral formations are big cloud-shapes of deeper purple. Out past the coral, the water gets progressively darker in orderly stripes, a phenomenon that I think has to do with perspective. It's all extremely pretty and peaceful. Besides me and the Towel Guy and the orbiting joggers, there's only a supine older lady reading *Codependent No More* and a man standing way up at the fore part of the starboard rail videotaping the sea. This sad and cadaverous guy, who by the second day I'd christened Captain Video, has tall hard gray hair and Birkenstocks and very thin hairless calves, and he's one of the cruise's more prominent eccentrics.[26] Pretty much everybody on the *Nadir* qualifies as camera-crazy, but Captain Video camcords absolutely everything, including meals, empty hallways, endless games of geriatric bridge—even leaping onto Deck 11's raised stage during Tuesday's Pool Party to get the crowd from the musicians' angle. He is the only passenger besides me who I know for a fact is cruising without a relative or companion, and certain additional similarities between him and me tend to make me uncomfortable, and I try to avoid him.

From Deck 12's starboard rail you can look down at the army of *Nadir* passengers being disgorged by the Deck 3 gangway. They keep pouring out of the door and down the narrow gangway. As each person's sandal hits the pier a sociolinguistic transformation from Cruiser to Tourist is effected. A serpentine line of 1,300-plus upscale tourists with currency to unload and experiences to experience stretches all the way down the Cozumel pier, which leads to a kind of megaquonset structure where Organized Shore Excursions and T-shirts and

---

[26] Other eccentrics include: the bloated and dead-eyed guy who sits in the same chair at the same 21 table in the casino every day from noon to 3:00 A.M., drinking Long Island iced tea and playing 21 at a narcotized underwater pace; the hairy-stomached guy of maybe fifty who sleeps by the pool every minute, even in the rain, a copy of *Megatrends* open on his chest; and the two old couples who sit in upright chairs just inside the clear plastic walls that enclose Deck 11, never moving, watching the ocean and ports like they're something on TV.

cabs or mopeds into San Miguel are available. The word around good old Table 64 last night was that in primitive and incredibly poor Cozumel the U.S. dollar is treated like a U.F.O.: "They worship it when it lands."

Locals along the Cozumel pier are offering *Nadir*ites a chance to have their picture taken holding a very large iguana. Yesterday, on the Grand Cayman pier, locals had offered them the chance to have their picture taken with a guy wearing a peg leg and hook, while off the *Nadir*'s port bow a fake pirate ship plowed back and forth across the bay all morning, firing blank broadsides and getting on everybody's nerves.

Off to the southeast, now, another Megacruiser is moving in to dock. It moves like a force of nature and resists the idea that so much mass is being steered by anything like a hand on a tiller. I can't imagine what trying to maneuver one of these puppies into the pier is like. Parallel parking a semi into a spot the same size as the semi with a blindfold on and four tabs of LSD in you might come close. Our docking this morning at sunrise involved an antlike frenzy of crewmen and shore personnel and an anchor that spilled from the ship's navel and upward of a dozen ropes, which the crew insists on calling "lines," even though each one is at least the same diameter as a tourist's head.

I cannot convey to you the sheer and surreal scale of everything: the towering ship, the ropes, the anchor, the pier, the *vast lapis lazuli dome of the sky*. Looking down from a great height at your countrymen waddling into poverty-stricken ports in expensive sandals is not one of the funner moments of a 7NC Luxury Cruise, however. There is something inescapably *bovine* about a herd of American tourists in motion, a certain greedy placidity. I feel guilty by perceived association. I've barely been out of the U.S.A. before, and never as part of a high-income herd, and in port—even up here above it all on Deck 12, watching—I'm newly and unpleasantly conscious of being an American, the same way I'm always suddenly conscious of being white every time I'm around a lot of non-white people. I cannot help imagining us as we appear to them, the bored Jamaicans and Mexicans, or especially to the non-Aryan and hard-driven crew of the *Nadir*. All week I've found myself doing everything I can to distance myself in the crew's eyes from the bovine herd I'm part of: I eschew cameras and sunglasses and pastel Caribbeanwear; I make a big deal of carrying my own luggage and my own cafeteria tray and am effusive in my thanks for the slightest service. Since so many of my shipmates shout, I make it a point of special pride to speak extra-quietly to crewmen whose English is poor. But, of course, part of the overall despair of this Luxury Cruise is that whatever I do I cannot escape my own essential and newly unpleasant Americanness. Whether up here or down there, I am an American tourist, and am thus *ex officio* large, fleshy, red, loud, coarse, condescending, self-absorbed, spoiled, appearance-conscious, greedy, ashamed, and despairing.

Up on 12-Aft, Captain Video isn't filming now but is looking at the harbor through a square he's made of his hands. He's the type where you can tell without even looking closely that he's talking to himself. This other white cruise ship is docking right next to us, a procedure that apparently demands a lot of coded blasts on its world-ending horn. But maybe the single best visual in the harbor is the group of *Nadir*ites learning to snorkel in the lagoon-ish waters just offshore; off the port bow I can see a good 150 solid citizens floating face-down, motionless, looking like the massed and bloated victims of some hideous mishap—from this height it's a macabre and riveting sight. I have given up looking for dorsal fins in port. It turns out that sharks are never seen in pretty Caribbean ports, though a couple of Jamaicans had lurid if dubious stories of barracudas that could take off a limb in one surgical drive-by.

Now right up alongside the *Nadir*, on the other side of the pier, is finally docked and se-cured the m.v. *Dreamward*, with the peach-on-white color scheme that I think means it's owned by Norwegian Cruise Line.[27] Its Deck 3 gangway now protrudes and almost touches our Deck 3 gangway—sort of obscenely—and the *Dreamward*'s passengers, identical in all important respects to the *Nadir*'s passengers, are now streaming down the gangway and massing and moving down the pier in a kind of canyon of shadow made by the tall walls of our two ships' hulls. A lot of the *Dreamward*'s passengers turn and crane to marvel at the size of what's just disgorged them. Captain Video, inclined now way over the starboard rail so that only the toes of his sandals are still touching deck, is filming them as they look up at us; and more than a few of the *Dreamward*ites way below lift their own camcorders and point them up our way in a kind of retaliatory gesture, and for just a moment they and Cap-tain Video compose a tableau that looks almost classically postmodern.

Because the *Dreamward* is lined up right next to us, almost porthole to porthole, with its Deck 12's port rail right up flush against our Deck 12's starboard rail, the *Dreamward*'s shore-shunners and I can stand at the rails and check each other out like muscle cars lined up at a stoplight. I can see the *Dreamward*'s rail-leaners looking the *Nadir* up and down, their faces shiny with high-SPF sunblock. The *Dreamward* is blindingly white, white to a de-gree that seems somehow aggressive and makes the *Nadir*'s white look more like buff or cream. Its snout is a little more tapered and aerodynamic-looking than our snout, and its trim is a kind of fluorescent peach, and the beach umbrellas around its Deck 11 pools are also peach, whereas our beach umbrellas are salmon, which has always seemed odd, given the white-and-navy motif of the *Nadir*, and now seems to me ad hoc and shabby. The *Dreamward* has more pools on Deck 11 than we do, and what looks like a whole other ad-ditional pool behind clear glass on Deck 6; and its pools' blue is that distinctive chlorine-blue, whereas the *Nadir*'s two small pools are both seawater and kind of icky.

On all its decks, all the way down, the *Dreamward*'s cabins have little white balconies for private open-air sea gazing. Its Deck 12 has a full-court basketball setup with peach-colored nets and backboards as white as Communion wafers. I notice that each of the little towel carts on the *Dreamward*'s Deck 12 is manned by its very own Towel Guy, and that their Towel Guys are ruddily Nordic and wear neither sunglasses nor a look of Dickensian oppression.

The point is that, standing here next to Captain Video, looking, I start to feel an almost prurient envy of the *Dreamward*. I imagine its interior to be cleaner than ours, larger, more lavishly appointed. I imagine the *Dreamward*'s food being even more varied and punctil-iously prepared, its casino less depressing, its stage entertainment less cheesy, its toilets less menacing, its pillow mints bigger. The little private balconies outside the *Dreamward*'s cab-ins, in particular, seem far superior to a porthole of bank-teller glass, which now seems sud-denly chintzy and sad.

I am suffering here from a delusion, and I know it's a delusion, this envy of another ship, but still it's painful. It's also representative of a psychological syndrome that I notice has gotten steadily worse as my Luxury Cruise wears on, a mental list of dissatisfactions that started off picayune but has quickly become despair-grade. I know that the syndrome's cause is not simply the contempt bred of a week's familiarity with the poor old *Nadir*, and

---

[27] The *Nadir* itself is navy trim on a white field. All the Megalines have their own trademark color schemes—lime green on white, aqua on white, robin's egg on white, barn red on white, white being an invariable constant.

that the source of all the dissatisfactions isn't the *Nadir* at all but rather that ur-American part of me that craves pampering and passive pleasure: the dissatisfied-infant part of me, the part that always and indiscriminately WANTS. Hence this syndrome by which, for example, just four days ago I experienced such embarrassment over the perceived self-indulgence of ordering even more gratis food from cabin service that I littered the bed with fake evidence of hard work and missed meals, whereas by last night I find myself looking at my watch in real annoyance after fifteen minutes and wondering where the fuck is that cabin service guy with the tray already. And by now I notice how the tray's sandwiches are kind of small, and how the wedge of dill pickle always soaks into the starboard crust of the bread, and how the port hallway is too narrow to really let me put the used cabin service tray outside 1009's door at night when I'm done eating, so that the tray sits in the cabin all night and in the morning adulterates the olfactory sterility of 1009 with a smell of rancid horseradish, and how this seems, by the Luxury Cruise's fifth day, deeply dissatisfying.

Death and Conroy notwithstanding, we're maybe now in a position to appreciate the falsehood at the dark heart of Celebrity's brochure. For this—the promise to state the part of me that always and only WANTS—is the central fantasy the brochure is selling. The thing to notice is that the real fantasy here isn't that this promise will be kept but that such a promise is keepable at all. This is a big one, this lie.[28] And of course I want to believe it; I want to believe that maybe this ultimate fantasy vacation will be *enough* pampering, that this time the luxury and pleasure will be so completely and faultlessly administered that my infantile part will be sated at last. But the infantile part of me is, by its very nature and essence, insatiable. In fact, its whole *raison* consists of its insatiability. In response to any environment of extraordinary gratification and pampering, the insatiable-infant part of me will simply adjust its desires upward until it once again levels out at its homeostasis of terrible dissatisfaction. And sure enough, after a few days of delight and then adjustment on the *Nadir*, the Pamper-swaddled part of me that WANTS is now back, and with a vengeance. By Wednesday, I'm acutely conscious of the fact that the A.C. vent in my cabin hisses (loudly), and that although I can turn off the reggae Muzak coming out of the speaker in the cabin I cannot turn off the even louder ceiling-speaker out in the 10-Port hall. Now I notice that when Table 64's towering busboy uses his crumb-scoop to clear off the tablecloth between courses he never seems to get quite *all* the crumbs. When Petra makes my bed, not all the hospital corners are at exactly the same angle. Most of the nightly stage entertainment in the Celebrity Show Lounge is so bad it's embarrassing, and the ice sculptures at the Midnight Buffet often look hurriedly carved, and the vegetable that comes with my entrée is continually overcooked, and it's impossible to get really *numbingly* cold water out of 1009's bathroom tap.

I'm standing here on Deck 12 looking at the *Dreamward*, which I bet has cold water that'd turn your knuckles blue, and, like Frank Conroy, part of me realizes that I haven't washed a dish or tapped my foot in line behind somebody with multiple coupons at a supermarket checkout in a week; and yet instead of feeling refreshed and renewed I'm anticipating how totally stressful and demanding and unpleasurable a return to regular landlocked adult life is going to be now that even just the premature removal of a towel by a sepulchral crewman seems like an assault on my basic rights, and the sluggishness of the Aft elevator is an outrage. And as I'm getting ready to go down to lunch I'm mentally drafting a really mordant footnote on my single biggest peeve about the *Nadir:* they don't even have Mr. Pibb; they foist Dr. Pepper on you with a maddeningly unapologetic shrug when any

---

[28] It might well be The Big One, come to think of it.

fool knows that Dr. Pepper is no substitute for Mr. Pibb, and it's an absolute goddamned travesty, or—at best—extremely dissatisfying indeed.

Some Organized Fun

Every night, Cabin Steward Petra, when she turns down the bed, leaves on your pillow— along with the day's last mint and Celebrity's printed card wishing you sweet dreams in six languages—the next day's *Nadir Daily*, a little four-page ersatz newspaper printed on white in a royal-blue font. The *ND* has historical nuggets on upcoming ports, pitches for Organized Shore Excursions and specials in the Gift Shop, and stern stuff in boxes with malaprop headlines like QUARANTINES ON TRANSIT OF FOOD and MISUSE OF DRUG ACTS 1972.

We've rounded the final turn and are steaming on our return vector from Cozumel toward Key West, and today is one of the week's two "At-Sea" days, when shipboard activities are at their densest and most organized. This is the day I've picked to use the *ND* as a Baedeker as I leave Cabin 1009 for a period well in excess of half an hour and plunge headfirst into the experiential fray and keep a precise and detailed log of some really representative activities:

10:00 A.M.: Three simultaneous venues of Managed Fun, all aft on Deck 9: *Darts Tournament, take aim and hit the bull's eye! Shuffleboard Shuffle, join your fellow guests for a morning game. Ping-Pong Tournament, meet the Cruise Staff at the tables, Prizes to the Winners!* Organized shuffleboard has always filled me with dread. Everything about it suggests infirm senescence and death: it's a game played on the skin of a void, and the rasp of the sliding puck is the sound of that skin getting abraded away bit by bit. I also have a morbid but wholly justified fear of darts stemming from a childhood trauma too hair-raising to discuss here. I play Ping-Pong for an hour.

11:00 A.M.: *Navigation Lecture. Join Captain Nico and learn about the ship's Engine Room, the Bridge, and the basic "nuts and bolts" of the ship's operation.* I am there. The m.v. *Nadir* can carry 460,000 gallons of nautical-grade diesel fuel. It burns between 40 and 70 tons of this fuel a day, depending on how hard it's traveling. The ship has two turbine engines on each side, one big "Papa" and one (comparatively) little "Son." Each engine has a propeller that is 17 feet in diameter and is adjustable through a lateral rotation of 23.5 degrees for maximum torque. It takes the *Nadir* .9 nautical miles to come to a complete stop from a speed of 18 knots. The *Nadir* can go slightly faster in certain kinds of rough seas than it can go in calm seas (this is for technical reasons that won't fit on the napkin I'm taking notes on). Captain Nico's English is not going to win any elocution ribbons, but he is a veritable blowhole of hard data. He's about my age and height and is just ridiculously good-looking.[29] Captain Nico wears Ray-Bans, but without a touristic fluorescent cord. This is also the day my paranoia about Mr. Dermatitis contriving somehow to jettison me from the *Nadir* via Cabin 1009's Vacuum-Suction Toilet is at its emotional zenith, and I've decided in advance to keep a real low journalistic profile at this event. I ask a total of one little innocuous question, right at the start, and Captain Nico responds with a witticism—"How we start

---

[29] Something else I've learned on this Luxury Cruise is that no man can ever look any better than he looks in the white full-dress uniform of a naval officer. Women of all ages and estrogen levels swooned, sighed, wobbled, lash-hatted, growled, and hubba'd when one of these navally resplendent Greek officers went by, a phenomenon that I don't imagine helped the Greeks' humility one

engines? Not with the key of ignition, I can tell you!"—that gets a large and rather unkind laugh from the crowd.

It turns out that the long-mysterious "m.v." in "m.v. *Nadir*" stands for "motorized vessel." The m.v. *Nadir* cost $250,310,000 U.S. to build. It was christened in Papenburg, West Germany, in 1992 with a bottle of ouzo instead of champagne. The *Nadir*'s three onboard generators produce 9 megawatts of power. The ship's bridge turns out to be what lies behind the very intriguing triple-locked bulkhead near the aft Towel Cart on Deck 10. The bridge is "where the equipments are—radars, indication of weathers and all these things." Two years of postgraduate study is required of officer wannabes just to get a handle on the navigational math involved; "also there is much learning for the computers." Captain Nico explains that the *Nadir* subscribes to something called GPS: "This Global Positioning System is using the satellites above to know the position at all times, which gives this data to the computer." It emerges that when we're not negotiating ports and piers, a kind of computerized Autocaptain pilots the ship.[30]

The all-male audience here consists of bald solid thick-wristed fiftyish men who all look like the kind of guy who rises to CEO a company out of its engineering department instead of some MBA program. A number of them are clearly Navy veterans or yachtsmen or something. They compose a very knowledgeable audience and ask involved questions about the "bore" and "stroke" of the engines, the management of "multi-radial torque," and the hydrodynamics of "midship stabilizers." They're all the kinds of men who look like they're smoking cigars even when they're not. Everybody's complexion is hectic from sun and salt spray and a surfeit of Slippery Nipples. A 7NC Megaship's maximum possible cruising speed is 21.4 knots. No way I'm going to raise my hand in this kind of crowd and ask what a knot is.

12:40 P.M.: I seem to be out on 9-Aft hitting golf balls off an Astroturf square into a densemesh nylon net that balloons impressively out toward the sea when a golf ball hits it. Thanatopic shuffleboard continues over to starboard; ominous little holes in the deck, bulkhead, railing, and even my little Astroturf square testify to my wisdom in having steered clear of the A.M. Darts Tourney.

2:00 P.M.: Now I'm in Deck 12's Olympic Health Club, in the back area, in the part that's owned by Steiner of London®, a kind of floating spa, and I'm asking to be allowed to watch one of the "Phytomer/Ionithermie Combination Treatment De-Toxifying Inch Loss Treatments" that some of the heftier ladies onboard have been raving about, and I am being told that it's not really a spectator-type thing, that there's nakedness involved, and that if I want to see it I'm going to have to be the subject of one. Between the quoted price of the treatment and some pretty troubling references in the Steiner of London brochure to "electrodes using faradism and galvanism." I opt to forfeit this bit of managed pampering. If you back off from something really big, the creamy-faced staffers then try to sell you on a facial, which they say "a number" of male *Nadir*ites have pampered themselves with this week, but I decline this as well, figuring that at this point in the week the procedure would consist mostly in exfoliating half-peeled skin.

2:30 P.M.: Now I'm down in Deck 8's Rainbow Room for *"Behind the Scenes." Meet your*

---

[30] This helps explain why *Nadir* Captain G. Panagiotakis usually seems so phenomenally unbusy, why his real job seems to be to stand in various parts of the *Nadir* and try to look vaguely presidential, which he would except for his habit of wearing sunglasses inside, which makes him look more like a Third World strongman.

Cruise Director Scott Peterson and find out what it's really like to work on a cruise ship! Scott Peterson is a tan guy with tall rigid hair, a highwatt smile, an escargot mustache, and a gleaming Rolex—basically the sort of guy who looks entirely at home in sockless white loafers and a mint-green golf shirt—and is one of my very least favorite Celebrity Cruises employees, though with Scott Peterson it's a case of mildly enjoyable annoyance rather than the terrified loathing I feel for Mr. Dermatitis. The very best way to describe Scott Peterson's demeanor is that it looks like he's constantly posing for a photograph nobody is taking. He mounts the Rainbow Room's low brass dais, reverses his chair, sits like a cabaret singer, and holds forth. There are maybe fifty people attending, and I have to admit that some of them seem to like Scott Peterson a lot, and to enjoy his talk, a talk that, not surprisingly, turns out to be more about what it's like to be Scott Peterson than about what it's like to work on the good old *Nadir.* Topics covered include where and under what circumstances Scott Peterson grew up, how Scott Peterson got interested in cruise ships, how Scott Peterson and his college roommate got their first jobs together on a cruise ship, some hilarious booboos in Scott Peterson's first months on the job, every celebrity Scott Peterson has personally met and shaken the hand of, how much Scott Peterson loves the people he gets to meet working on a cruise ship, how much Scott Peterson loves just working on a cruise ship in general, how Scott Peterson met the future Mrs. Scott Peterson working on a cruise ship, and how Mrs. Scott Peterson now works on a different cruise ship and how challenging it is to sustain an intimate relationship as warm and in all respects wonderful as that of Mr. and Mrs. Scott Peterson when you work on different cruise ships and lay eyes on each other only about every sixth week, except that now Scott Peterson's grateful to be able to announce that Mrs. Scott Peterson happens to be on a well-earned vacation and is as a rare treat here this week cruising on the m.v. *Nadir* with him and is, as a matter of fact, right here with us in the audience today, and wouldn't Mrs. S. P. like to stand up and take a bow.

3:05 P.M.: I've darted for a minute into Deck 7's Celebrity Show Lounge to catch some of the rehearsals for tomorrow night's climactic Passenger Talent Show. Two crew-cut and badly burned U. Texas guys are doing a minimally choreographed dance number to a recording of "Shake Your Groove Thing." Assistant Cruise Director Dave the Bingo Boy is coordinating activities from a canvas director's chair at stage left. A septuagenarian from Halifax, Virginia, tells six jokes and sings "One Day at a Time (Sweet Jesus)." A retired Century 21 realtor from Idaho does a long drum solo to "Caravan." The climactic Passenger Talent Show is apparently a 7NC tradition, as was Tuesday's Special Costume Party. Some of the *Nadir*ites are deeply into this stuff and have brought their own costumes and props. A lithe Canadian couple does a tango complete with pointy black shoes and a rose in teeth. The finale is apparently going to be four consecutive stand-up comedy routines delivered by very old men. These men totter on one after the other. One has a three-footed cane, another a necktie that looks uncannily like a Denver omelette, another an excruciating stutter. What follow are four successive interchangeable routines where the manner and humor are like exhumed time capsules of the 1950s: jokes about how impossible it is to understand women, about how very much men want to play golf and how their wives try to keep them from playing golf, etc. The routines have the same kind of flamboyant unhipness that makes my own grandparents objects of my pity, awe, and embarrassment all at the same time. One of the senescent quartet refers to his appearance tomorrow night as a "gig."

3:20 P.M.: The *ND* neglects to mention that the trapshooting is a *competitive* Organized Activity. The charge is $1 a shot, but you have to purchase your shots in sets of ten, and there's a large and vaguely gun-shaped plaque for the best score. I arrive at 8-Aft late; a male

*Nadir*ite is already shooting, and several other males have formed a line and are waiting to shoot. The *Nadir*'s wake is a big fizzy **V** way below the aft rail. Two sullen Greek NCOs in earmuffs run the show. I am seventh and last in line. The other guys refer to the targets as "pigeons," but what they really look like is little discuses painted the Day-Glo orange of expensive hunting wear. The orange, I posit, is for ease of visual tracking, and the color must really help, because the trim bearded guy in aviator glasses currently shooting is wreaking absolute devastation in the air over the stern.

I assume you already know the basic trapshooting conventions from movies or TV: the lackey at the weird little catapultish device, the bracing and pointing and order to "Pull," the combination thud and *kertwang* of the catapult, the brisk crack of the weapon, and the midair disintegration of the luckless pigeon. Everybody in line with me is male, though there are a number of females in the crowd that's watching the competition from the 9 Aft balcony above and behind us.

From the line, watching, three things are striking: (a) what on TV is a brisk crack is here a whooming roar that apparently is what a shotgun really sounds like; (b) trapshooting looks comparatively easy, because now the stocky older guy who's replaced the trim bearded guy at the rail is also blowing these little fluorescent plates away one after the other, so that a steady rain of lumpy orange crud is falling into the *Nadir*'s wake; (c) a clay pigeon, when shot, undergoes a frighteningly familiar-looking midflight peripeteia—erupting material, changing vector, and plummeting seaward in a corkscrewy way that all eerily recalls footage of the 1986 *Challenger* disaster.

All the shooters who precede me seem to fire with a kind of casual scorn, and all get eight out of ten or above. But it turns out that, of these six guys, three have military-combat backgrounds, another two are L. L. Bean–model-type brothers who spend weeks every year hunting various fast-flying species with their "Papa" in southern Canada, and the last has got not only his own earmuffs, plus his own shotgun in a special crushed-velvet-lined case, but also his own trapshooting range in his backyard[31] in North Carolina. When it's finally my turn, the earmuffs they give me have somebody else's ear-oil on them and don't fit my head very well. The gun itself is shockingly heavy and stinks of what I'm told is cordite, small public spirals of which are still exiting the barrel from the Korea-vet who preceded me and is tied for first with 10/10. The two brothers are the only entrants even near my age; both got scores of 9/10 and are now appraising me coolly from identical prep-school-slouch positions against the starboard rail. The Greek NCOs seem extremely bored. I am handed the heavy gun and told to "be bracing a hip" against the aft rail and then to place the stock of the weapon against, no, *not* the shoulder of my hold-the-gun arm but the shoulder of my pull-the-trigger arm. (My initial error in this latter regard results in a severely distorted aim that makes the Greek by the catapult do a rather neat drop-and-roll.)

Let's not spend a lot of time drawing this whole incident out. Let me simply say that, yes, my own trapshooting score was noticeably lower than the other entrants' scores, then simply make a few disinterested observations for the benefit of any novice contemplating trapshooting from a 7NC Megaship, and then we'll move on: (1) A certain level of displayed ineptitude with a firearm will cause everyone who knows anything about firearms to converge on you all at the same time with cautions and advice and handy tips. (2) A lot of the advice in (1) boils down to exhortations to "lead" the launched pigeon, but nobody explains whether this means that the gun's barrel should move across the sky with the pigeon or should instead sort of lie in static ambush along some point in the pigeon's projected path. (3) Whatever a "hair trigger" is, a shotgun does not have one. (4) If you've never fired a gun before, the urge to close your eyes at the precise moment of concussion is, for all practical purposes, irresistible. (5) The well-known "kick" of a fired shotgun is no misnomer; it knocks you back several steps with your arms pinwheeling wildly for balance, which when you're holding a still-loaded gun results in mass screaming and ducking and then on the next shot a conspicuous thinning of the crowd in the 9-Aft gallery above. Finally, (6), know that an unshot discus's movement against the *vast lapis lazuli dome* of the open ocean's sky is sun-like—i.e., orange and parabolic and right-to-left—and that its disappearance into the sea is edge-first and splashless and sad.

The Headline Entertainment

Other Celebrity Showtime headline entertainments this week have included a Vietnamese comedian who juggles chain saws, a husband-and-wife team that specializes in Broadway love medleys, and, most notably, a singing impressionist named Paul Tanner, who made simply an enormous impression on Table 64's Trudy and Esther, and whose impressions of Engelbert Humperdinck, Tom Jones, and particularly Perry Como were apparently so stirring that a special Popular Demand Encore Performance by Paul Tanner has been hastily scheduled to follow tomorrow night's climactic Passenger Talent Show. For tonight, though, the *Nadir Daily* announces: CELEBRITY SHOWTIME *Celebrity Cruises Proudly Presents* HYPNOTIST NIGEL ELLERY.

Hypnotist Nigel Ellery is British and looks uncannily like a 1950s B-movie villain. Introducing him, Cruise Director Scott Peterson informs us that Nigel Ellery "has had the honor of hypnotizing both Queen Elizabeth II and the Dalai Lama."[32] Nigel Ellery's act combines hypnotic hijinks with rather standard Borscht Belt patter and audience abuse. And it ends up being such an absurdly suitable microcosm of the week's whole 7NC Luxury Cruise experience that it's almost like a setup, some weird form of pseudojournalistic pampering.

First off, we learn that not everyone is susceptible to serious hypnosis: Nigel Ellery puts the Celebrity Show Lounge's whole 300-plus crowd through some simple in-your-seat tests to determine who is suggestibly "gifted" enough to "participate" in the "fun" to come.[33] Second, when the six most suitable subjects—all still locked in their complex contortions from the in-your-seat tests—are assembled onstage, Nigel Ellery spends a very long time reassuring them and us that absolutely nothing will happen that they do not wish to have happen. He then persuades a young lady from Akron that a loud Hispanic voice is issuing from the left cup of her brassiere. Another lady is induced to smell something ghastly coming off the man in the chair next to her, a man who himself believes that the seat of his chair periodically heats to 100 degrees Celsius. The other three subjects, respectively, flamenco, believe they are not just nude but woefully ill-endowed, and are made to shout "Mommy, I wanna wee-wee!" when Nigel Ellery tells them good night. The audience laughs very hard at all the right times. And there is something genuinely funny (not to mention symbolic) about watching these well-dressed U.S. adult cruisers behave strangely for no reason they under-

---

[32] Not, one would presume, at the same time.

[33] I, who know from hard experience that I am hypnotizable, think about sports statistics and deliberately flunk a couple of the tests to avoid getting up there.

stand; it is as if the hypnosis enables them to construct fantasies so vivid that the subjects do not even know they are fantasies, which is of course funny.

Maybe the single most strikingly comprehensive 7NC symbol, though, is Nigel Ellery himself. The hypnotist's boredom and hostility are not only undisguised but incorporated kind of ingeniously into the entertainment itself: Ellery's boredom gives him the same air of weary expertise that makes us trust doctors and policemen, and his hostile stage-persona is what gets the biggest roars of approval and laughter from the crowd. He does unkind imitations of people's U.S. accents. He ridicules questions from the subjects and audience. He makes his eyes burn Rasputinishly and tells people they're going to wet the bed at exactly 3:00 A.M. Each moment of naked ill-will is followed by a palms-out assurance that he's just kidding and that he loves us and that we are a simply marvelous audience. The spectators— mostly middle-aged, it looks like—rock back and forth with mirth and slap their knees and dab at their eyes with hankies.

For me, at the end of a full day of Managed Fun, Nigel Ellery's act is not particularly astounding or side-splitting or entertaining. What it is is weird. There's something crucially key about Luxury Cruises in evidence here: being entertained by someone who clearly dislikes you, and feeling that you deserve that dislike at the same time you resent it. The show's climax has the six subjects all lined up doing syncopated Rockette kicks. Because my own dangerous mesmeric susceptibility makes it important that I not follow Ellery's hypnotic suggestions too closely or get too deeply involved, I find myself, in my plush seat, going farther and farther away, sort of creatively visualizing an epiphanic Frank Conroy–type moment of my own, trying to see the hypnotist and subjects and audience and ship itself with the eyes of someone not aboard. Imaging the m.v. *Nadir* right at this moment, all lit up and steaming north, in the dark, at night, with a strong west wind pulling the moon backward through a skein of clouds—the *Nadir* a constellation, complexly aglow, angelically white, festive, imperial. Yes, this: it would look like a floating palace to any poor soul out here on the ocean at night, alone in a dinghy, or not even in a dinghy but simply and terribly floating, treading water, out of sight of land. This deep disassociative trance—Nigel Ellery's true unconscious gift to me—lasted all through the next day and night. This period I spent entirely in Cabin 1009, in bed, mostly looking out the spotless porthole, with trays and rinds all around me, feeling a little bit dulled but mostly good—good to be on the *Nadir* and good to know that soon I would get off the ship, that I had survived (in a way) being pampered to death (in a way)—and so I stayed in bed. And even though the trance made me miss the final night's Talent Show and Midnight Farewell Buffet and Saturday's docking (at which there was apparently even more crepe and waving and explosive goodwill) and a chance to have my After-photo taken with Captain G. Panagiotakis, reentry into the stresses and demands of quotidian landlocked real-world life wasn't nearly as bad as a week of absolutely nothing had led me to fear.

LaVergne, TN USA
28 May 2010
184244LV00002B/1/P